Public International l
in the
Modern World

David H Ott
BA, MA, JD, LLM
Lecturer in Public Law at Aberdeen University

PITMAN
150
YEARS

Pitman Publishing
128 Long Acre, London WC2E 9AN

© David H. Ott 1987

First published in Great Britain 1987

British Library Cataloguing in Publication Data
Ott, David H.
   Public international law in the modern world.
   1. International law
   I. Title
   341   JX3091

ISBN 0 273 02815 4

Printed and bound in Great Britain at The Bath Press, Avon

Contents

Acknowledgements **vi**
Preface **vii**
List of Abbreviations **ix**
Table of Cases **xi**
Table of Treaties **xvii**
Table of Legislation **xxi**

1 The nature of international law 1
Introduction · The state system · The natural law response · The doctrine of
positivism · The 'sociological' alternative

2 The sources of international law 12
Custom · Treaties · General principles of law · Judicial decisions and the writings
of publicists · Codification and progressive development

3 The relationship between international and municipal law 32
The relationship of the two systems : monist or dualist? · National law in the
international system · International law in the municipal system

4 International legal personality 47
States as international legal persons · States with limited sovereignty · Semi-states :
countries not recognised to have full statehood : 'Proto-states' : colonies and peoples
entitled to self-determination · Public international organisations · Semi-public
intergovernmental organisations · Private international organisations · Individuals

5 Recognition 85
Recognition of governments : the traditional search for criteria · Avoiding the
problem : the Estrada doctrine · Effect in international law of non-recognition of
de facto governments · Recognition and municipal law · Governments-in-exile ·
Effect of non-recognition of a *de facto* state · Effect of withdrawal of recognition

6 Acquisition of territory 105
The traditional view : 'modes of acquisition' · Principles of the modern approach :
peaceful acquisition · Principles of the modern approach : the problem of conquest
· Cases on peaceful acquisition · Cases on acquisition by force · Special situations

7 Rights in foreign territory 129
Servitudes · International rivers · Interoceanic canals

8   State jurisdiction   135

Introduction to jurisdiction · Traditional bases of jurisdiction · Effect of means used to acquire jurisdiction · Jurisdiction arising from treaties · The future of jurisdiction

9   Immunity from jurisdiction   150

Absolute sovereign immunity · Restrictive theory of sovereign immunity · The 'act of state' doctrine · Diplomatic immunity · Other international immunities

10   State responsibility   166

General principles of state responsibility · Aliens: introduction · Aliens: whose claim is it? · Aliens: what basic legal principles govern claims? · Aliens: procedural questions · Aliens: substantive bases for protection

11   The law of treaties   190

General questions · Treaty making · Entry into force of a treaty · Observance of treaties · Application of treaties · Treaty interpretation · Third states · Amendment of a treaty · General provisions on invalidity, termination and suspension of treaties · Specific provisions on invalidity · Terminating, suspending or withdrawing from a treaty · Effects of invalidity, termination and suspension · Dispute settlement · State succession to treaties

12   The law of the sea   206

Development of the law of the sea · Internal waters · Territorial sea · The contiguous zone · International straits · Continental shelf · Exclusive fisheries zone : exclusive economic zone · The high seas · The deep sea-bed

13   International human rights   238

Introduction · Development of human rights · Obligations *erga omnes* · The United Nations human rights regime · Civil and politial rights under the UN regime · Economic, social and cultural rights under the UN regime · Rights of brotherhood and solidarity under the UN regime · Regional regimes

14   Human rights in Europe   260

The European Convention on Human Rights · Activating the European Convention's mechanism · Implementing rights · Right to life · Maltreatment · Slavery · Liberty, arrest and detention · The right to a hearing · Retrospective laws · Privacy · Belief · Free speech · Joining with others · Forming a family · Remedies · Equal treatment · The First Protocol · The Fourth Protocol · The Convention in British law · The Helsinki Final Act

15   Environmental law   289

Introduction · General norms · Pollution · Conservation · Co-ordinated environmental protection · Future environmental problems

16   War and peace   306

The use of force · The law of war · Disarmament

17   Peaceful settlement of disputes   332

Methods and disputes · Non-adjudicatory procedures · Adjudicatory methods: arbitration · Adjudicatory methods: the World Court

18 International institutions 349

Introduction · Classification of international institutions · Origins of international institutions in the search for world order · The League of Nations · The United Nations · Regional international organisations · General legal problems of international institutions · The future of international institutions in the search for world order

Appendices
1 General bibliography 380
2 Passing your examination 381

Index 385

Acknowledgements

When thinking of those who contributed to making this book possible, I must first record my gratitude for the support I have received from my wife, Philippa, who has throughout offered both encouragement and good advice. I dedicate this Handbook to her as a token of appreciation for all she has done to help bring my work to fruition.

John Rankin, my colleague in the teaching of international law at Aberdeen University, also made a significant contribution by giving constructive comments on certain sections of the text and by very kindly relieving me of many chores connected with the running of our classes.

I should also like to thank Emlyn Williams LLB for his careful reading and editing of my typescript.

A word of thanks should go to those of my students whose lively interest in international law stimulated my own thoughts on the subject and so contributed, directly or indirectly, to this book. I think particularly of Roderick Paisley, Arlene Donaghy, and members of Aberdeen University's teams in the Jessup International Law Moot Court Competition: Mary Scanlon, Gary Ling, Fiona Boyd, Helen Regan, Andrew Webster, Sheila Mann, and James Barbour-Smith.

Finally, I wish to acknowledge the help given by the Aberdeen Law Faculty's secretarial staff: Eileen Carr, Susan Kilpatrick, Maureen Mercer, and Amanda Nicholls.

David H. Ott

Preface

This book is meant to help the student of international law achieve a thorough understanding of the subject's main topics without having to read a 1,500-page text weighed down with footnotes. But, at the same time, every effort has been made to avoid the danger of producing an outline so spare that no-one could read it with any real interest or excitement.

For the chief attraction of international law is that it is not a pinched and bloodless academic discipline but rather ranges over a spectrum of issues that are generally recognised as critical in the latter part of the twentieth century: war and peace, environmental protection, human rights, state power and many others. The bare bones of the law on these questions, although intriguing to the scholar, are hardly enough to give the non-specialist a sense of having eaten a proper meal.

And the non-specialist is right to suspect that history and international relations, jurisprudence and economics, religion and morality all affect international law in the widest sense and must at least be noted by anyone trying to understand what the subject is all about.

On the other hand, for the student facing an examination there is no substitute for the nitty-gritty detail out of which successful answer papers must be produced. And there is plenty of that in this book as well, with review questions at the end of each chapter to help highlight the critical points. An Appendix on examination technique illustrates how a student can assemble it all on the day in a way that does justice to his or her knowledge and effort.

Most students will have been taking an organised course with lectures and set readings, and for them this book should be seen as an aid to pulling their course material together and fixing the key concepts. It will give them a framework for revision and will fill in any gaps in their study.

For those who are studying international law entirely on their own the initial value of this book will be to guide the student through the jungle of cases, treaties and commentaries so as to reach the end of the path without having fallen into any of the bogs and pitfalls that lie along the way. But once having reached that goal, the student can use the book as a map of where he or she has been so as to develop a good framework for revision. In this regard the book can profitably be used in conjunction with Prof. D. J. Harris' excellent *Cases and Materials on International Law* or with *International Law: Cases and Materials* edited by Louis Henkin, Richard Pugh, Oscar Schachter and Hans Smit. It will also prove interesting to students reading Weston, Falk, and D'Amato's thought-provoking *International Law and World Order*.

For non-law students, and particularly those doing international relations, a particular advantage of this book is that it does not require from the student any prior knowledge of the law or of legal thinking. Even someone who has never studied law should be able, provided he or she is prepared to accept the subject on its own terms, to understand from this book what international law is.

But it is hoped also that those who approach international law simply out of curiosity or in search of the answer to a particular question will find the book worth consulting and even reading further.

And, having for several years past written articles on international legal problems for *The Scotsman* newspaper in Edinburgh, the author is more than usually aware of the extent to which international law is as much at home in the (better) daily papers as in the classroom. That awareness also is reflected here, with the expectation that journalists and others who want a 'quick read' on some current topic will find what they are looking for without unnecessary fuss or bother.

A final word to the student: international law is very much a subject that has developed its own particular structure and rules and that fact must be accepted. It is therefore no good skipping over the first two chapters on the mistaken assumption that one knows all about the nature and sources of international law from having studied conveyancing, family law or international relations. Chapter 2 is probably the single most important one in the book and mastering it will make the rest of your study much easier.

David H. Ott
1987

NOTE
The cross references in the tables of Cases, Treaties and Legislation and the text of this book consist of the relevant chapter number followed by the section number in bold type.

List of Abbreviations

AD	*Annual Digest of Public International Law Cases*
AJIL	*American Journal of International Law*
CMLR	*Common Market Law Reports*
CTS	*Consolidated Treaty Series*
DRECHR	*Decisions and Reports of the European Commission of Human Rights*
E. Com. HR	European Commission of Human Rights
E. Ct. HR	European Court of Human Rights
ICJ	International Court of Justice
ILC	International Law Commission
ILM	*International Legal Materials*
ILR	*International Law Reports*
Int. Arb.	Moore, *International Arbitrations*
Int. Leg.	Hudson, *International Legislation*
Malloy	Malloy, *Treaties, Conventions, Acts, Protocols and Agreements Between the United States of America and other Powers*
L. Ed.	*Lawyers Edition* of United States Supreme Court reports
LNOJ	League of Nations Official Journal
LNTS	League of Nations Treaty Series
Peaslee Const.	Peaslee, *Constitutions of Nations*
PCIJ	Permanent Court of International Justice
RIAA	United Nations *Reports of International Arbitration Awards*
UKTS	United Kingdom Treaty Series
UNTS	United Nations Treaty Series
UST	United States Treaties
USTS	United States Treaty Series
YBECHR	Yearbook of the European Convention on Human Rights

Table of Cases

Aaland Islands Case, LNOJ Special Supp. No.3 p. 3 7:3

Abdulaziz, Cabales and Balkandali Cases, E. Ct. H.R., Ser. A, No. 94 14:**56, 61**

Abu Dhabi Arbitration, 18 ILR 144 2:**47, 54**

Airey Case, E. Ct. H.R., Ser. A, No. 32 14:**41**

Alabama Claims Arbitration, 1 Moore Int. Arb. 485 17:**11**

Alcom Ltd. v. Republic of Colombia, [1984] 2 All E.R. 6 9:**17**

Alfred Dunhill of London Inc. v. Republic of Cuba, 48 L. Ed. 2d 301 9:**19**

Amekrane Case, E. Com. H.R. Report 19 July 1974 8:**31, 26**

Anglo-Iranian Oil Company Case (Interim Measures), [1951] ICJ Rep 89 17:**25**

Anglo-Iranian Oil Co. Case, [1952] ICJ Rep 93 and [1952] ICJ Pleadings 10:**32,37**

Anglo-Iranian Oil Co. Ltd. v. Jaffrate, 20 ILR 316 9:**20**

Anglo-Norwegian Fisheries Case, [1951] ICJ Rep 116 2:**13, 52**; 6:**12**; 12:**15, 18**

Appeal Relating to the Jurisdiction of the ICAO Council, [1972] ICJ Rep 46 11:**34**

Arantzazu Mendi, [1939] AC 256 5:**33, 35**

Arrowsmith v. United Kingdom, E. Com. H.R. Report 12 Oct 1978 14:**46**

Artico Case, E. Ct. H.R., Ser. A, No. 37 14:**38**

Asylum Case, [1950] ICJ Rep 266 2:**10, 19**

Attorney-General v. Solomon Toledano, 40 ILR 40 5:**40**

Atty.-Gen. for Canada v. Atty.-Gen. for Ontario, [1937] AC 326 3:**18**

Attorney-General of Israel v. Eichmann, 36 ILR 5 8:**13, 18**

Attorney General of New Zealand v. Ortiz, 1982 3 WLR 570 8:**2**

Austria v. Italy, 4 YBECHR 116 14:**2**

Austro-German Customs Union Case (Customs Regime between Germany and Austria Case), PCIJ Rep., Ser. A/B, No. 41 4:**10,14**

Banco Nacional de Cuba v. Farr, Whitlock & Co., 383 F. 2d 166 9:**19**

Banco Nacional de Cuba v. Sabbatino, 376 US 398 5:**42**; 9:**19, 20**

Barcelona Traction Case, [1970] ICJ Rep 3 15:**7**; 10:**10, 24**; 13:**20**

Barthold v. Fed. Rep. of Germany, E. Ct. H.R., Ser. A, No. 90 14:**52**

Belgian Linguistic Case, E. Ct. H.R., Ser. A, No. 6 14:**58**

Belgian Police Case, E. Ct. H. R., Ser. A, No. 19 14:**54, 59**

Benthem Case, E. Ct. H.R., Ser. A, No. 97 14:**31**

Bernstein v. Van Heyghen Freres, 163 F. 2d 246 9:**19**

Blackmer v. United States, 284 US 421 8:**10**

Bolivar Railway Company Claim, 9 RIAA 445 10:**8**

Bönisch Case, E. Ct. H.R., Ser. A, No. 92 14:**34**

Bramelid and Malmstrom v. Sweden, E. Com. H.R., Report 12 Dec 83 14:**35**

BP v. Libya, 53 ILR 297 10:**13, 36**

British Nylon Spinners Ltd. v. ICI, [1952] All E.R. 780 8:**5**

Brüggemann and Scheuten Case, E. Com. H.R. Report 12 Jul 1977 14:**41**

Buchholz Case, E. Ct. H.R., Ser. A, No. 42 14:**36**

Berkina Faso v. Mali, ICJ Judgment 22 Dec 1986 6:**14**

Buttes Gas & Oil Co. v. Hammer, 1981 3 All E.R. 616 9:**20**

Caire Claim, 5 RIAA 516 10:**3**

Campbell and Cosans Case, E. Ct. H.R., Ser. A, No. 48 14:**18, 63**

Campbell and Fell Case, E.Ct. H.R., Ser. A, No. 80 14:**32**

Can Case, E. Com. H.R. Report 12 Jul 1984 14:**38**

Capps Case (United States v. Guy W. Capps, Inc.), 204 F. 2d 655 3:**24**

Carl Zeiss Stiftung v. Rayner and Keeler Ltd (No. 2) [1967] 1 AC 853 5:**22, 40**

Caroline Case, 2 Moore Digest of Int. Law 412 16:**9**

Certain Expenses of the UN Case, [1962] ICJ Rep 151 16:**7**

Chamizal Arbitration, 5 AJIL 782 6:**35**

Chattin Claim, 4 RIAA 282   10:27
Chorzow Factory Case, PCIJ Ser. A, No. 17
   10:13, 14, 34, 38
Chow Hung Ching v. R., 77 CLR 449   3:29
Chung Chi Cheung v. R., [1939] AC 160
   12:13
Civil Air Transport Inc. v. Central Air
   Transport Corp., [1953] AC 70   4:18, 21
Claim against the Empire of Iran Case, 45
   ILR 57   9:7
Clark v. Allen, 331 US 503   11:38
Clipperton Island Case, 2 RIAA 1105   6:28
Commission v. Council, 10 CMLR 335   4:53
Commonwealth of Australia v. State of
   Tasmania, 57 ALJR 450   3:29
Conditions for Admission to the UN Case,
   [1948] ICJ Rep   17:28
I Congreso del Partido, 1981 3 WLR 329
   9:8,12
Continental Ore Co. v. Union Carbide &
   Carbon Corp., 8 L. Ed 2d 777   8:7
Continental Shelf (Libya v. Malta) Case, 24
   ILM 1189   12:42
Continental Shelf (Tunisia v. Libya) Case,
   [1982] ICJ Rep 18   12:40, 46
Cooper v. Stuart, 14 AC 286 (1889)   6:2
Corfu Channel Case, [1949] ICJ Rep 4   10:3;
   12:25, 29
Costa v. ENEL, 3 CMLR 425   3:26
Creole Case, 4 Moore Int. Arb. 4349–4378
   12:12
Cyprus v. Turkey (1975), 2 DRECHR 125
   14:12

Danish Sex Education Case, E. Ct. H.R., Ser.
   A, No. 23   14:63
De Cubber Case, E. Ct. H.R., Ser. A, No. 86
   14:35
De Geillustreerde Pers NV v. The
   Netherlands, E. Com. H.R. Report 16 Sep
   1976   14:48
De Jong, Baljet, van den Brink Cases, E. Ct.
   H.R., Judgment of 22 May, 1984   14:24
Delcourt Case, E. Ct. H.R., Ser. A, No. 11
   14:34
Deutsche Continental Gas-Gesellschaft v.
   Polish State, 5 AD 11   4:3
De Weer Case, E. Ct. H.R., Ser. A, No. 35
   14:33
Dickson Car Wheel Company Case, 4 RIAA
   669   10:23
Diggs v. Shultz, 470 F.2d 461   3:22
Diversion of Water from the Meuse Case, PCIJ
   Ser. A/B, No. 70   2:50
Donnelly v. United Kingdom, 16 YBECHR
   212   10:22; 14:3
Dralle v. Republic of Czechoslovakia, [1950]
   ILR 155   9:5

Draper Case, E. Com. H.R. Report of 10 Jul
   1980   14:55
Dudgeon Case, E. Ct. H.R. Ser. A, No. 45
   14:41

East Africa Asians Cases, 13 YBECHR 928
   14:19
Eastern Carelia Case, PCIJ Ser. B, No. 5
   17:29
Edye v. Robertson (Head Money Cases), 28 L.
   Ed. 798   3:22
Elon Moreh Case, 19 ILM 148   3:28
Engel Case, E. Ct. H.R., Ser. A, No. 22
   14:21, 32
English Channel Arbitration, 18 ILM 397
   2:54; 12:39, 41

Filartiga v. Pena-Irala, 19 ILM 966   2:31, 32;
   3:19; 13:12, 52
Fisheries Jurisdiction Case (Interim
   Protection), [1972] ICJ Rep 12   17:25
Fisheries Jurisdiction Case (Merits), [1974]
   ICJ Rep 3   2:50; 6:13; 11:36; 12:45
First National City Bank v. Banco Nacional
   de Cuba, 32 L.Ed. 2d 466   9:19
Free Zones of Upper Savoy and the District of
   Gex Case, PCIJ Ser. A/B, No. 46   11:23

Gdynia Ameryka Linie Zeglugowe Spolka
   Akcyjna v. Boguslawski, 1953 AC 11   5:20
Gelbtrunk Claim, 1902 US For. Rel. 876
   10:8
Golder v. United Kingdom, E. Ct. H.R., Ser.
   A, No. 18   14:33, 44
Granital Case, see S.p.A Granital
Greek Case, 12 YBECHR 194   10:22
Guaranty Trust Co. of New York v. United
   States, 82 L.Ed. 1224   5:31
Guincho Case, E. Ct. H.R., Ser. A, No. 81
   14:36
Gulf of Maine Case, 23 ILM 1197   2:52;
   12:41, 42
Guzzardi Case, E. Ct. H.R., Ser. A, No. 39
   14:21, 24, 25

Haile Selassie v. Cable and Wireless Ltd. (No.
   2), [1939] 1 Ch 182   5:19
Hamer Case, E. Com. H.R. Report 13 Dec
   1979   14:55
Handelswerkerij G.J. Bier and Stichting
   Reinwater v. Mines de Potasse d'Alsace
   S.A., 19 CMLR 284   8:7
Handyside Case, E. Ct. H.R., Ser. A, No. 24
   14:49
Harman v. United Kingdom, E. Com. H.R.,
   Admiss. Decn. 10 May 1984   14:51
Hesperides Hotels v. Aegean Holidays Ltd.,
   [1978] Q.B. 205 (C.A.)   5:23

Home Missionary Society Claim, 6 RIAA 42
  10:3

I'm Alone Case, 3 RIAA 1609   12:59
In re Jolis, [1933–1934] AD No. 77   8:18
Interhandel Case, [1959] ICJ Rep 6   10:22;
  17:22, 23
Internationale Handelsgesellschaft m.b. H. *v.*
  Einfuhr und Vorratstelle fur Getreide und
  Futtermittel, 11 CMLR 255   3:25
International Registration of Trade Mark
  (Germany) Case, 28 ILR 82   4:15
Interpretation of the Agreement of 25 March
  1951 between the WHO and Egypt Case,
  [1980] ICJ Rep 73   2:56
Interpretation of Peace Treaties Case, [1950]
  ICJ Rep 65   11:16; 17:29
Iran Hostages Case (US Diplomatic and
  Consular Staff in Tehran Case) (Interim
  Measures) [1979] ICJ Rep 7   17:25
Iran Hostages Case, [1980] ICJ Rep 3   9:23;
  10:13; 16:15; 17:20
I.R.C. *v.* Collco Dealings Ltd., [1962] AC 1
  3:17
Ireland *v.* United Kingdom, E. Ct. H.R., Ser.
  A, Judgment of 18 Jan 1978   14:3, 10, 13,
  17, 60
Island of Palmas Case, 2 RIAA 829   4:5, 13,
  36; 6:2, 23–6; 17:13

Jalapa Railroad and Power Co. Claim, 8
  Whiteman 908   10:30
James *v.* United Kingdom, E. Ct. H.R., Ser.
  A, No. 98   14:62
Janes Claim, 4 RIAA 82   10:27
Joyce *v.* Director of Public Prosecutions,
  [1946] AC 347   8:9, 11
Jurisdiction of the Courts of Danzig (Danzig
  Railway Officials) Case, PCIJ, Ser. B, No.
  15   4:60; 13:8

Kaplan Case, E. Com. H.R. Report 17 Jul
  1980   14:31
Klass Case, E. Ct. H.R., Ser. A, No. 28   14:31,
  43
König Case, E. Ct. H.R., Ser. A, No. 27
  14:31, 36
Koowarta *v.* Bjelke-Petersen, 56 ALJR 625
  3:29

Lake Lanoux Case, 24 ILR 101   7:10; 15:12
Lawless Case, E. Ct. H.R. Ser. A, No.3   10:22;
  14:24
Leander *v.* Sweden, E. Com. H.R. Report 17
  May 1985   14:42
Legal Consequences Case, [1971] ICJ Rep 16
  4:31, 35, 45
Legal Status of Eastern Greenland Case, PCIJ
  Ser. A/B, No. 53   6:30; 11:4

Letelier *v.* Republic of Chile, 488 F. Supp 665
  9:7, 15
LIAMCO Case, 20 ILM 1   10:36, 37
Lotus Case, PCIJ Ser. A, No. 10   2:10, 15–18;
  8:7
Luedicke, Belkacem and Koç Case. E. Ct.
  H.R., Ser. A, No. 28   14:38
Luther *v.* Sagor, [1921] 3 K.B. 532   5:17, 18

Mackeson's Case (R. *v.* Bow Street
  Magistrates, ex p. Mackeson), 75 Cr. App.R.
  24   8:18
Mallen Case, 4 RIAA 173   10:29
Malone *v.* Metropolitan Police Commissioner
  (No. 2), [1979] Ch 344   3:17
Malone *v.* United Kingdom, E. Ct. H.R., Ser.
  A, No. 82   3:17; 14:43
Marckx Case, E. Ct. H.R., Ser. A, No. 31
  14:41, 59
Matznetter Case, E. Ct. H.R. Ser. A, No. 10
  14:24
Mauritian Women Case, 1981 Rep. Hum. R.
  Committee, 36 GAOR Supp 40,
  p166   13:27
Mavrommatis Palestine Concessions
  (Jurisdiction) Case, PCIJ Ser. A, No. 2
  4:60. 10:18; 11:22; 17:4
Military and Paramilitary Activities in and
  against Nicaragua Case, *see* Nicaragua *v.*
  United States
Minquiers and Ecrehos Case, [1953] ICJ Rep
  47   6:14, 31
Missouri *v.* Holland, 64 L. Ed. 641   3:24
Molvan *v.* Attorney-General for Palestine,
  [1948] AC 351 (P.C.)   8:13; 12:54
Monnell and Morris *v.* United Kingdom, E.
  Ct. H.R., Judgment 2 March, 1987   14:22
Mortensen *v.* Peters, [1906] 8 F.(J.) 93   3:4, 14

Nationality Decrees in Tunis and Morocco
  Case, PCIJ Ser. B, No. 4   4:24; 8:11
Naulilaa Case, 2 RIAA 1012   16:11
Neer Claim, 4 RIAA 60   10:19
Neumeister Case, E. Ct. H.R. Ser. A, No. 5
  14:24, 37
Nicaragua *v.* United States (Jurisdiction)
  (1984), 24 ILM 59   17:18, 24, 30
Nicaragua *v.* United States (Merits) (1986), 25
  ILM 1023   16:10, 23; 17:30
North American Dredging Co. Case, 4 RIAA
  26   10:21
North Atlantic Fisheries Arbitration, 11 RIAA
  167   7:3
Northern Cameroons Case, [1963] ICJ Rep 15
  17:26
North Sea Continental Shelf Cases, [1969] ICJ
  Rep 3   2:10, 11, 22–8, 52, 56; 12:7, 36, 38,
  41; 16: 37

Norwegian Loans Case, [1957] ICJ Rep 9
  17:23
Nottebohm Case, [1955] ICJ Rep 4   4:8; 8:11;
  10:23–4; 12:53
Noyes Claim, 6 RIAA 308   10:29
Nuclear Test Cases (Interim Measures) (1973),
  [1973] ICJ Rep 99   17:20, 25
Nuclear Test Cases (1974), [1974] ICJ Rep
  253   11:4; 12:51; 15:17

Officier van Justitie v. Kramer, 18 CMLR
  440   4:51
Oyama v. California, 92 L. Ed. 249   13:22
Oztürk Case, E. Ct. H.R., Ser. A, No. 73
  14:38

Palmas Case, see Island of Palmas Case
Paquete Habana, 44 L. Ed. 320   3:19
Parlement Belge Case, 4 PD 129   3:16
Pataki and Dunshirn v. Austria   14:34
Petrogradsky Mejdunarodny Kommerchesky
  Bank v. National City Bank, 253 NY 23
  15:28
Piersack Case, E. Ct. H.R., Ser. A, No. 53
  14:35
Polish Upper Silesia Case, PCIJ Ser. A, No. 7
  10:6
Polites v. Commonwealth, 70 CLR 60   3:29

Quintanilla Claim, 4 RIAA 101   10:27

R. v. Burgess, ex p. Henry, 55 CLR 608   3:29
R. v. Chief Immigration Officer, ex p. Bibi,
  [1976] 3 All ER 843   3:17
R. v. Keyn, 2 Ex D 63   3:9
R. v. Plymouth Justices ex p. Driver, The
  Times, 19 April, 1985   8:18
Rasmussen v. Denmark, E. Ct. H.R., Ser. A,
  No. 87   14:61
Re Al-Fin Corporation's Patent, [1970] Ch 160
  5:24
Re Drummond Wren, [1945] 4 OR 778   13:22
Regan v. Wald, 23 ILM 792   13:34
Reparation for Injuries Suffered in the Service
  of the United Nations Case, [1949] ICJ Rep
  174   2:40; 4:51, 54; 11:16, 23
Republic of Mexico v. Hoffman, 324 US 30
  9:10
Republic of Vietnam v. Pfizer, 556 F. 2d 892
  5:43
Reservations to the Convention on Genocide
  Case, [1951] ICJ Rep 15   11:7
Right of Passage Case (Preliminary
  Objections) (1957), [1957] ICJ Rep 125
  17:22
Right of Passage Case (Merits), [1960] ICJ Rep
  6   7:5
Rights of Minorities in Polish Upper Silesia
  Case, PCIJ Ser. A, No. 15   17:20

Rights of Nationals of the United States in
  Morocco Case, [1952] ICJ Rep 176   4:24
Ringeisen Case, E. Ct. H.R., Ser. A, No. 13
  14:31
River Oder Case (Jurisdiction of the
  International Commission of the River
  Oder), PCIJ Ser. A, No. 23   7:8; 15:12
Roberts Claim, 4 RIAA 77   10:27
RSFSR v. Cibrario, 235 NY 255   5:35
Russian Reinsurance Co. v. Stoddard, 240 NY
  149   5:27
Rustomjee v. the Queen, [1876] 1 QBD 487
  10:18

Salimoff & Co. v. Standard Oil of New York,
  262 NY 220   5:26
Sapphire-NIOC Arbitration, 13 ICLQ 987
  10:32
Schmidt and Dahlström, E. Ct. H.R., Ser. A,
  No. 21   14:54
Schooner Exchange v. McFaddon, 3 L. Ed.
  287   9:2, 19
Sei Fujii v. California, 38 Cal(2d) 718   3:21;
  13:22
Shimoda Case, 32 ILR 626   16:37
Skiriotes v. Florida, 85 L. Ed. 1193   8:10
Silver Case, E. Ct. H.R., Ser. A, Judgment of
  25 Mar 1983   14:33
Socony Vacuum Oil Co. Case, 21 ILR 55
  5:12
South-West Africa Cases, 1966 ICJ Rep 6
  1:22; 2:31, 32, 41, 48; 3:2; 4:29, 30; 13:1, 19
S.p.A. Granital v. Amministrazione
  Finanziaria, 21 Com. Mkt. L. Review 756
  3:26
Spanish Government v. Felipe Campuzano,
  33 AJIL 609   5:33
Sramek Case, E. Ct. H.R., Ser. A, No. 84
  14:35
State of the Netherlands v. Federal Reserve
  Bank of New York, 201 F (2d) 455   5:38
Status of South-West Africa Case, [1950] ICJ
  Rep 146   4:28, 32
Stewart Case, E. Com. H.R. Decn. on
  inadmissibility 10 Jul 1984   14:15
Stögmuller Case, E. Ct. H.R. Ser. A, No. 9
  14:24
Sunday Times Case, E. Ct. H.R., Ser. A, No.
  30   14:11, 50
Sutter Case, E. Ct. H.R. Ser. A, No. 74   14:34
Swedish Engine Drivers Union Case, E. Ct.
  H.R. Ser. A, No. 20   14:54

Techt v. Hughes, 229 NY 222   11:38
Tel-Oren v. Libyan Arab Republic, 726 F. 2d
  774   4:46
Temple of Preah Vihear Case, [1962] ICJ Rep
  6   2:44; 6:34
Texaco v. Libya, 17 ILM 1   2:33; 10:13, 32, 38

Thai-Europe Tapioca Service Ltd. *v.* Govt. of
Pakistan, [1975] 3 All ER 961   **3:12**
Thakrar, R. *v.* Immigration Officer ex parte,
[1974] QB 684   **3:11**
Tinoco Claims Arbitration, 1 RIAA 369   **5:11**
Trail Smelter Case (1941) 3 RIAA 1905   **15:5,
7, 9, 10, 11, 19**; **17:13**
Trendtex Trading Corp. *v.* Central Bank of
Nigeria, [1977] QB 529   **3:12, 29**; **9:11**
Triquet *v.* Bath, 3 Burr 1478   **3:7,8**
Tsemel *v.* Minister of Defence, 1 Pal. Yrbk.
Int. Law 164   **3:28**
Tyrer Case, E. Ct. H.R. Ser. A, No. 26   **14:18**

Underhill *v.* Hernandez, 168 US 250   **9:19**
Union Bridge Company Claim, 6 RIAA 138
10:7
United States *v.* Archer, 51 F. Supp. 708   **8:13**
United States *v.* Belmont, 81 L. Ed.
1134   **3:23**
United States *v.* Imperial Chemical Industries,
105 F. Supp 215   **8:5**
United States *v.* Pink, 86 L. Ed. 796   **3:23**
United States *v.* the Insurance Companies, 89
US 99   **5:25, 40**
US Diplomatic and Consular Staff in Tehran
Case, *see* Iran Hostages Case
Upright *v.* Mercury Business Machines Co.,
213 NYS 2d 417   **5:27**

Vagrancy Cases, E. Ct. H.R. Ser. A. No. 12
14:25
Van Oosterwijck Case, E. Com. H.R. Report 1
Mar 1979, E. Ct. H.R. Ser. A, No. 40   **14:41**
Verlinden BV *v.* Central Bank of Nigeria, 103
S.Ct. 1962   **9:16**
Victory Transport Inc. *v.* Comisaria General
de Abastecimientos y Transportes, 336 F. 2d
354   **9:6, 9, 10**

Weeks *v.* United Kingdom, E. Ct. H.R.
Judgment of 2 March, 1987   **14:28**
Weinberger Case, 1981 Rep. Hum. R.
Committee, 36 GAOR, Supp 40, p 114
13:33
Wemhoff Case, E. Ct. H.R., Ser. A, No. 7
11:22; **14:24, 36**
Western Sahara Case [1975] ICJ Rep.
12   **4:45**; **6:11, 14, 25, 32–3**; **17:28, 29**
West Rand Central Gold Mining Co. *v.* R,
[1905] 2KB 391   **3:10**
Whitney *v.* Robertson, 124 US 190   **3:22**
Wildenhus' Case, 120 US 1   **12:10**
Wimbledon Case, PCIJ Ser. A, No. 1   **4:10,
11**; **7:14**
Winterwerp *v.* Netherlands, E. Com. H.R.
Report 15 Dec 1977, E. Ct. H.R. Ser. A, No.
33   **14:25, 31**
Wulfsohn *v.* R. S. F. S. R., 234 NY 372   **5:34**

X *v.* Fed. Rep. of Germany, No. 6357/73, E.
Com. H.R. Decn. Admiss. 8 Oct 1974
14:41
X *v.* United Kingdom, E. Com. H.R. Report
12 Oct 1978   **14:41**
X *v.* United Kingdom (1981), E. Ct. H.R. Ser.
A, No. 46   **14:25, 28**

Youmans Claim, 4 RIAA 110   **10:7**
Young, James and Webster Cases, E. Ct. H.R.
Ser. A, No. 44   **14:54, 56**

Zafiro Claim, 6 RIAA 160   **10:7**
Zamir *v.* United Kingdom, ECHR Committee
of Min. Decn. 25 Jan 1985, Res DH (85)3
14:26

Table of Treaties

Treaty of Union (1707) Halsbury's Statutes, vol. 6, 501 **4:49**

Treaty of Utrecht (1713) 28 CTS 295 **6:27**

Jay Treaty (1794) 1 Malloy 590 **17:11**

St Petersburg Declaration (1868) 1 AJIL Supp. 95 16:**35**

Constantinople Convention (1888) 3 AJIL Supp 123 **17:12; 11:23**

Hague Convention on the Pacific Settlement of Disputes (1899) 187 CTS 410 **17:5,11**

Hague Conventions on the Pacific Settlement of Disputes (1907) 205 CTS 233 **17:5,11**

Hague Convention with respect to the Laws and Customs of War by Land (1899) 187 CTS 429 **16:25**

Hay – Pauncefote Treaty (1901) 32 Stat. 1903 **7:13**

Hay – Bunau-Varilla Treaty (1903) USTS No. 431 **7:13**

Fourth Hague Convention on the Laws and Customs of War on Land (1907) UKTS 9(1910) Cd. 5030 **6:20**; 16:**25, 26, 27**

Hague Regulations 1907 UKTS 9(1910) Cd. 5030 **3:28**; 6:**20, 21**; 8:**16**; 13:**11**; 16:**25-37**

Treaty of Versailles (1919) 225 CTS 188 4:**10**; 7:**14**; 11:**23**

Covenant of the League of Nations 225 CTS 195 4:**18, 26-32**; 6:**17**; 13:**9**; 16:**2, 38**; 17:**14**; 18:**8-10**

Spitsbergen Treaty (1920) Hudson I Int. Leg. 436 **6:42**

Barcelona Convention and Statute on the Regime of Navigable Waterways of International Rivers (1921) UKTS 28 (1923) Cmd. 1193 **7:8-9**

Lausanne Convention (1923) Hudson, I Int. Leg. 1028 **12:29**

Geneva Protocol for Prohibition of Use in War of Asphyxiating, Poisonous or other Gases and of Bacteriological Methods of Warfare (1925) UKTS 24(1930) Cmd. 3604 **16:35**

Geneva General Act for Pacific Settlement of Disputes (1928) UKTS 32(1931) Cmd. 3930 **16:2; 17:20**

Treaty Providing for the Renunciation of War as an Instrument of National Policy (1928) UKTS 29(1929) Cmd. 3410 **6:17; 16:2**

Lateran Treaty (1929) Peaslee 3 Const. Pt 2 (3rd ed.) 1187 **4:21**

Montevideo Convention on the Rights and Duties of States (1933) USTS 881 **4:3, 11-13, 15, 17, 42; 5:24**

London Convention (1933) 172 LNTS 241 **15:20**

Montreux Convention (1936) UKTS 30(1937) Cmd 5551 **12:29**

Washington Convention (1940) 36 AJIL Supp. 193 **15:20**

Chicago Convention on International Civil Aviation (1944) UKTS 8 (1953) Cmd. 8742 **6:49; 8:29; 18:28**

United Nations Charter (1945) 1 UNTS xvi 2:**21, 26, 28, 30-32, 39, 40, 56**; 3:**21**; 4:**15, 28, 32-3, 35, 38, 39, 41-3, 45, 48, 51**; 5:**4, 51**; 6:**17-20, 39**; 9:**26**; 10:**10-11, 21**; 11:**13, 16, 18, 23, 31, 38, 40**; 12:**50**; 13:**15, 21-5, 52**; 15:**4, 28**; 16:**3-23, 39**; 17:**1, 3, 4, 9, 14-15, 20, 27**; 18:**12-27, 29-32**

Statute of International Court of Justice (1945) 1 UNTS xvi 2:**2, 10, 33, 34, 42, 43, 48, 51-52, 56**; 4:**18**; 10:**32**; 12:**37, 46**; 17:**14-25, 27, 28, 30**; 18:**1**

Convention on the Privileges and Immunitites of the United Nations (1946) 1 UNTS 15 **9:26**

International Whaling Convention (1946) UKTS 5 (1949) Cmd. 7604 **15:7**

Charter of the Organisation of American States (Bogotá Pact) (1948) 46 AJIL Supp. 43 **18:40-41**

Convention on the Prevention and Punishment of the Crime of Genocide (1948) 78 UNTS 277 **4:61; 11:7-8**

Geneva Conventions (1949) 75 UNTS 31 ff. **16:31**

Third Geneva Convention (1949) 75 UNTS 135 **16:29-30**

Fourth Geneva Convention for the Protection of Civilian Persons in Time of War (1949) 75 UNTS 287 3:**28**; 4:**60-61**; 6:**20-21**; 8:**16**; 11:**34, 36**; 13:**11**; 16:**25, 33, 34**

European Convention on Human Rights
(1950) UKTS 71 (1953) Cmd. 8969   3:**17–18**;
4:**60**; 8:**31**; 10:2, **22**; **11:11, 22**; 13:3, 13, 53;
14:**1–71**

European Convention on Human Rights
Protocols
Protocol I UKTS 46 (1954) Cmd. 9221
14:18, **62, 64**
Protocol IV UK Misc. 6 (1964) Cmnd. 2309
14:**65–7**
Protocol VI 22 ILM 538   14:14

N.A.T.O. Status of Forces Agreement (1951)
UKTS 3 (1955) Cmd. 9363   8:**22**

E.C.S.C. Treaty (1951) 261 UNTS 140   4:**53**

International Convention for the Protection
of Plants and Plant Products 150 UNTS
67 15:**23**

Convention Relating to Status of Refugees
(1951) 189 UNTS 150   13:**36**

Convention Relating to Status of Stateless
Persons (1954) 360 UNTS 117   10:**23**

European Cultural Convention (1954) 218
UNTS 139   18:**38**

European Convention on Extradition (1957)
359 UNTS 276   8:**25**

Convention on Protection and Integration of
Indigenous and Other Tribal and Semi-
Tribal Populations in Independent
Countries (1957) 328 UNTS 247   13:**43**

Treaty of Rome (1957) UKTS 15 (1979)
Cmnd. 7480   2:**39**; 3:**25**; 4:**52**

Euratom Treaty (2nd Treaty of Rome) (1957)
UKTS 15 (1979) Cmnd. 7480   4:**53**

Geneva Convention on the High Seas (1958)
450 UNTS 82   7:**6**; 8:**29**; 12:**7, 48–9, 52,
56–9, 76**; 15:**15**

Geneva Convention on the Continental Shelf
(1958) 499 UNTS 311   2:**22, 24, 28**; 12:**7,
34–9, 41, 43**; 15:**15**

Geneva Convention on the Territorial Sea
and Contiguous Zone (1958) 516 UNTS
205   6:**12**; 12:**7, 14–22, 24, 26, 28, 29, 43**

Geneva Convention on Fishing and
Conservation of the Living Resources of the
High Seas (1958) 559 UNTS 285   12:**7**

Treaty of Guarantee (Britain, Greece, Turkey)
(1959) Cmnd. 1093   4:**20**

Antarctic Treaty (1959) 402 UNTS 71   6:**44–7**;
15:**10**; 16:**43**

Vienna Convention on Diplomatic Relations
(1961) 500 UNTS 95 9:**22–3**; 17:**20**

European Social Charter (1961) UKTS 38
(1965) Cmnd. 2643   13:**13**

Convention on Reduction of Statelessness
(1961) UKTS 158(1975) Cmnd. 6364   13:**37**

Tokyo Convention on Offences on Board
Aircraft (1963) 704 UNTS 219   8:**29**

Treaty Banning Nuclear Weapon Tests in the
Atmosphere, in Outer Space and Under

Water (1963) 480 UNTS 43   12:**51**; 15:**17,
19**; 16:**41**

Vienna Convention on Consular Relations
(1963) 596 UNTS 261   17:**20**

Employment Policy Convention (1964) 569
UNTS 65   13:**47**

Convention for the Settlement of Investment
Disputes Between States and the Nationals
of Other States (1965) 575 UNTS 159   17:**11**

International Covenant on Economic Social
and Cultural Rights (1966) 6 ILM 360
13:**13, 25, 45, 46–51**

International Covenant on Civil and Political
Rights (1966) 6 ILM 368   1:**11**; 4:**27**; 10:**26**;
13:**3, 13, 23, 25, 27–45**; 14:14

International Convention on the Elimination
of all Forms of Racial Discrimination
(1966) 5 ILM 352   13:**27**

Treaty for the Prohibition of Nuclear
Weapons in Latin America (1967) 6 ILM
521   12:**51**; 16:**42**

Outer Space Treaty (1967) 6 ILM 386   6:**49**;
16:**43**

African Convention on the Conservation of
Natural Resources (1968)   18:**45**

European Convention on Jurisdiction and
Enforcement of Judgements (1968) 8 ILM
229   8:**7**

Treaty on the Non-Proliferation of Nuclear
Weapons (1968) 7 ILM 809   16:**40, 41**

International Convention Relating to
intervention on the High Seas in Cases of
Oil Pollution Casualties (1969) 9 ILM
25   15:**16**

International Convention on Civil Liability
for Oil Pollution (1969) 9 ILM 45   15:**16**

Vienna Convention on Law of Treaties
(1969)   8 ILM 679   2:**3, 20, 31, 35, 40, 41**;
6:**20**; 11:**1–41**; 18:**48, 52, 55**

American Convention on Human Rights
(1969) 9 ILM 673   4:**60**; 13:**3, 54**; 18:**42**

Hague Convention for Suppression on
Unlawful Seizure of Aircraft (1970) 10 ILM
133   8:**29**

Sea-Bed Treaty (1971) UKTS 13(1973) Cmnd.
5266   16:**43**

Montreal Convention for Suppression of
Unlawful Acts Against The Safety of Civil
Aviation (1971) 10 ILM 1151   8:**29**

Convention on Wetlands of International
Importance especially Waterfowl Habitat
(1971) UKTS 34 (1976) Cmnd. 6465   15:**23**

International Convention on the
Establishment of an International Fund For
Compensation for Oil Pollution Damage
(1971) UKTS 95 (1978) Cmnd. 7383   15:**16**

Convention Relating to Civil Liability in the
Field of Maritime Carriage of Nuclear
Material (1971) UK Misc. 39 (1972) Cmnd.

5094   15:17

Convention on International Liability for Damages caused by Space Objects (1972) UKTS 16 (1974) Cmnd. 5551   10:4

European Convention on State Immunity (1972) UKTS 74 (1979) Cmnd. 7742   9:17

Salt I (1972)

  Agreement on Limitation of Strategic Weapons 11 ILM 791   16:44

  Treaty on Limitation of Anti-Ballistic Missile Systems (ABM Treaty) 11 ILM 784   16:44

Convention for Protection of the World Cultural and Natural Heritage (1972) 11 ILM 1358   3:29; 15:23

Convention on the Prohibition of the Development, Production and Stockpiling of Bacteriological (Biological) and Toxin Weapons (1972) UKTS 11 (1976) Cmnd. 6397   16:35, 45

Convention for Prevention of Marine Pollution by Dumping of Wastes and Other Matter (1972) 11 ILM 1294   15:17, 18

Convention on the Prevention and Punishment of Crimes Against Internationally Protected Persons Including Diplomatic Agents (1973) 13 ILM 41   9:25; 10:29

International Convention for Prevention of Pollution From Ships (1973) 12 ILM 1319   11:18; 15:16

International Convention on the Suppression and Punishment of the Crime of Apartheid (1973) 13 ILM 50   8:17

International Convention on International Trade in Endangered Species of Wild Fauna and Flora (1973) 12 ILM 1085   15:23

Convention for Prevention of Marine Pollution From Land Based Sources (1974) 13 ILM 352   15:17

Treaty on the Limitation of Underground Nuclear Weapon Tests (1974) 13 ILM 906   16:41

Helsinki Convention on Protection of Baltic Sea Area (1974) 13 ILM 546   15:15

Convention on the Prohibition of Military or Any Other Hostile Use of Environmental Modification Techniques (1976) 16 ILM 88   15:23

Barcelona Convention for Protection of Mediterranean Against Pollution (1976) 15 ILM 290   15:15

Panama Canal Treaty (1977) 16 ILM 1022   7:13

European Convention on Suppression of Terrorism (1977) UKTS 93 (1978) Cmnd. 7390   8:27

Neutrality Treaty (US – Panama) (1977) 16 ILM 1040   7:13

Protocol I to the Geneva Conventions of 1949 UK Misc. 19 (1977) Cmnd. 6927   15:28; 16:26, 29–30, 32, 35, 36

Protocol II, same as Protocol I   16:31

Vienna Convention on Succession of States in Respect of Treaties (1978) 17 ILM 1488   11:41

Kuwait Convention (1978) 17 ILM 511   15:15

Convention on the Elimination of Discrimination Against Women (1979) 19 ILM 33   13:27

Moon Treaty (1979) 18 ILM 1434   6:50; 16:43

Salt II (1979) 18 ILM 1112   16:44

Lomé Convention (1979) 19 ILM 327   4:53

Convention on the Conservation of European Wildlife and Natural Habitats (1979) UKTS 56 (1982) Cmnd. 8738   15:23

Convention on Long-Range Transboundary Air Pollution (1979) 18 ILM 1442   15:19
  Protocol (1984) 24 ILM 484   15:19

International Convention Against the Taking of Hostages (1979) 18 ILM 1456   8:30

Convention on the Conservation of Antarctic Marines Living Resources (1980) 19 ILM 841   6:46; 15:23

African Charter on Human and Peoples' Rights (1981) 21 ILM 58   18:45

Algiers Accords (1981) 20 ILM 223   17:12

Convention on Prohibitions or Restrictions on Use of Certain Conventional Weapons Which May be Deemed to be Excessively Injurious or to Have Indiscriminate Effects (1981) 19 ILM 1523   16:35

Abidjan Convention (1981) 20 ILM 746   15:15

Law of the Sea Convention (1982) 21 ILM 1261   7:6; 12:7, 14–15, 18–22, 24, 26–30, 36, 37, 41–4, 46–52, 55–9, 62–7, 71, 74–6; 15:15; 18:54

Agreement Concerning Interim Arrangements Relating to Polymetallic Nodules of the Deep Sea Bed (1982) 21 ILM 950   12:77

Agreement to amend the 1929 Lateran Concord (1984) 24 ILM 1589   4:21

Treaty of Peace and Friendship (Chile and Argentina) (1984) 24 ILM 11   6:43

Lomé Convention (1984) 24 ILM 588   4:53

U.N. Convention Against Torture and Other Cruel, Inhuman, or Degrading Treatment or Punishment (1984) 23 ILM 1027   13:30

Provisional Understanding Regarding Deep Seabed Matters (1984) 23 ILM 1354   12:77

Anglo-Irish Agreement (1985) 24 ILM 1579   3:16

Convention for the Protection of the Ozone Layer (1985), see 80 AJIL 157   15:23

South Pacific Nuclear Free Zone Treaty (1985) 24 ILM 1442   12:51; 16:42

Cartagena Protocol (1985) 25 ILM 529   18:43

Vienna Convention on Law of Treaties
Between States and International
Organisations or Between International
Organisations (1986) 25 ILM 543   11:3
Single European Act (1986) 25 ILM 506
4:54; 18:33

Other International Documents

Universal Declaration of Human Rights
(1948), UN General Assembly Res.
217A(III)   2:31; 13:4, **13, 16, 25–52**
Stockholm Declaration on the Human
Environment (1972) 11 ILM 1416   14:**4–7,
10–11, 22, 24**
Helsinki Final Act (1975), 14 ILM
1292   4:**48–9**; 14:**70–71**

Table of Legislation

United Kingdom   Continental Shelf Act 1964, 1964 Statutes c. 29   12:**43**
Diplomatic Privileges Act 1964, 1964 Statutes c.81   9:**22**
State Immunity Act 1978, 1978 Statutes c.33   9:**17**
Protection of Trading Interests Act 1980, 21 ILM 834   8:**7**
Deep Sea Mining (Temporary Provisions) Act 1981, 20 ILM 1217   12:**68–76**
Prevention of Terrorism (Temporary Provisions) Act 1984, 54(1) Statutes 271   13:**34**

United States   United State Constitution, XVII Blaustein   2:**41**; 3:**19–24**; 4:**59**; 11:**27**
Foreign Sovereign Immunities Act (1976), 90 Stat. 2891   9:**14–16**
Taiwan Relations Act (1979), 18 ILM 873   5:**44**
Deep Seabed Hard Mineral Resources Act (1980), 19 ILM 1003   12:**68–77**

Soviet Union   Constitution of the USSR (1977), XVII Blaustein   9:**4**
Statute on Trade Representations of the USSR Abroad, *see* Butler, *Soviet Law* 334–335   9:**4**

Federal Republic of Germany   Grundgesetz (Basic Law) (1949), VI Blaustein   3:**25**
Act on Interim Regulation of Deep Seabed Mining (1980) 19 ILM 1330   12:**68–77**

France   Constitution (1958), V Blaustein   3:**27**

Australia   Constitution, I Blaustein   3:**29**

Note: *Blaustein* above refers to the volumes of Blaustein & Flanz, *Constitutions of the Countries of the World* (Oceana, Dobbs Ferry, N.Y.), where documents are arranged alphabetically in loose-leaf fascicles.

1 The nature of international law

Introduction

1. Why is it important to understand the nature of international law? Unlike national legal systems, with clearly defined constitutional, legislative, and judicial arrangements for determining and applying the law, international law depends for its development and application on the varying interplay of a wide range of influences. To understand what that law is and how it is made to work (or why it fails to work), therefore, one must look beyond the 'black-letter law' to the historical, jurisprudential, social and political factors that are intimately connected with what international law is today.

To take a recent example that illustrates the point very well: during the campaign against the installation in Britain of United States cruise missiles in 1983, some persons brought before magistrates on such charges as obstructing the highway argued in their defence that the construction, installation or use of such weapons would be illegal under international law. The defendants said, therefore, that far from being legitimately punishable under the national law of the United Kingdom, they should have been regarded as carrying out their duty to uphold international law.

To evaluate this defence one must not only understand the particular rules of international law on the points at issue but also appreciate where international law comes from, why states are bound by it and to what extent, whether and when it may legitimately be taken to reflect more than the will of states, what role it assigns to the rights, duties and interests of the individual, and how it interacts with national legal systems.

Furthermore, the relative lack of detailed statements of international law on many points that arise in day to day practice means that the international lawyer has to develop the ability to unearth the fundamental principles at work in international law and then reason from them to a solution in the case at hand. But to do that one must first be ready to identify such principles and place them within their proper context in the overall structure of international law.

2. A definition of public international law. As its name suggests, international law is (or was initially) the law operating 'among nations' or states. Thus, in traditional international law states were at the centre of the whole system and even today states and their activities remain the main focus of international law.

In recent decades, however, other entities besides states have come to play a role in the international legal arena, with a significant impact on the nature and purposes of international law, but the legal implications of this development are still hotly debated and will be considered further in Chap. 4. Suffice it to say here that those entities which are international legal persons are considered the 'subjects' of international law, directly obligated under it and capable of directly acting on the international level to maintain their rights. Entities which do not have international legal personality are considered to be merely the 'objects' of international law, affected by that law only indirectly through its working in states.

The state system

3. Introduction. There is no obvious reason why a universal law governing the whole world should concentrate solely or primarily on states as its subjects and one must consider why that is in fact how international law developed.

A hint of the explanation may be found in the name itself: Law 'among states' is thought by some to signify that the law operates horizontally on the same level as the states and is generated by them, rather than being law which comes from above the states. International law is therefore often said to arise only from the will of 'sovereign' (i.e. autonomous) states and so to be capable of existing only within a state system and only to the extent desired by states. But history and jurisprudence suggest one should not rule out alternative possibilities.

4. Non-state alternatives. In the Middle Ages the Papacy and the Holy Roman Empire offered Europe (the birthlace of modern international law) alternatives to the state system. Against a background of feudalism in which political and ecclesiastical relationships transcended 'frontiers', each in its different way suggested a possibility of universal order.

On the political level, the Holy Roman Empire, while not strictly speaking supra-national, did exercise a wide enough dominion in west-central Europe to retard the formation of national states for several centuries. The Empire's legacy to European political thought was a certain sense that Europe's problems could never really be solved without a legal and political order that brought Europeans together rather than perpetuated their divisions.

During the High Middle Ages (up to about 1300), the Papacy claimed a universal jurisdiction over the whole of Christendom and thereby implicitly maintained that, at least on some matters, local rulers (and even the Holy Roman Emperor) were subject to a higher authority. The Papacy's claim was accepted by many people who believed that there was a divine law which stood above the world and governed everything in it. The Church was considered uniquely qualified to interpret and apply this law not just in religious matters but in human affairs generally.

5. Decline of the universal system. The political dominance of the Empire and the supreme authority of the Papacy were eventually challenged by two developments that were critically influential in the creation of modern Europe and its international law.

The first was the rise of new territorial states, such as England and France, whose rulers did not wish to be subject to any authority outside their own realms, whether of the Emperor or the Pope. There were many low political motives for this development, but the effect was gradually to undermine the basis for any papal or imperial claim of supra-national jurisdiction in Christendom.

The papal claim was in any case coming under attack in the second great upheaval in early modern Europe, the Protestant revolt against the religious authority and doctrine of the Papacy. In some cases, notably England under Henry VIII, the creation of the nation-state and the rise of Protestantism combined to raise the autonomy of states and their rulers to unprecedented heights.

The result was that these new states now seemed free from any higher authority. Many thinking men were gravely concerned at this turn of events. Sir Thomas More, for example, opposed the policies of Henry VIII at least in part out of a fear that the destruction of the Church's universal authority would lead to anarchy and war. He believed that papal authority provided a necessary theoretical basis for the relations of european states even though – as More himself admitted – the Papacy of his time did not live up to its responsibilities.

But despite these and similar objections the European state system, and the divisions within Christendom, continued to solidify until the Peace of Westphalia, ending the Thirty Years' War in 1648, confirmed the new basis of European relations.

The natural law response

6. **General.** Many legal thinkers besides More were profoundly troubled by this new situation and they tried to devise some doctrine of international law that would reimpose some sort of order on Europe. To do this some went back to the idea of universal law reflected in nature, natural law as it came to be called.

7. **Origins of natural law.** The idea of natural law originated in the Roman concept of *jus naturale*, 'natural law' in the sense that it was based on principles which were thought to arise from the nature of man as a rational and social being. This concept was combined with that of *jus gentium*, the 'law of peoples' or 'nations', by which the Romans meant the law which governed their relations with non-Romans. *Jus gentium* was said to be universally applicable because it reflected simple and reasonable principles that could apply to all.

Thus, in these two concepts a strong emphasis was placed on the role of reason in developing the law, and that emphasis was continued by medieval Christian theologians. They developed the view that it was possible to understand divine law because it was reflected in nature itself: nature was the result of divine law in operation and could therefore be taken as a guide to that law. St Thomas Aquinas in particular argued that the divine law which nature reflected could be discovered by human reason.

8. **Natural law in the new state system.** The founders of modern international law adopted the idea of natural law with varying degrees of enthusiasm, perhaps the most complete expression of its role coming in the work of the Spanish scholar Francisco Suarez (1548–1617). 'The human race,' he wrote 'though divided ... still has a certain unity, not only as a species but ... politically and morally as is indicated by the precept of mutual love and charity which extends to all.' Consequently, 'though each ... state ... is in itself a perfect community ... nevertheless each ... inasmuch as it is related to the human race, is in a sense also a member of this universal society.' Each state needed a law to govern its relations with other states in that universal society, and this was to a great extent discoverable by 'natural reason', though, as we shall see below, state practice also played a role. (Quoted in Nussbaum, *A Concise History of the Law of Nations*, 87–88.)

9. **The Enlightenment.** Hugo Grotius (1583–1645), the 'father of international law', is generally (but not universally) held to have modernised natural law by basing it on secular rationalism, thereby paving the way for its acceptance in the

European Enlightenment. The emphasis of the Enlightenment on the importance of reason in understanding the world chimed in well with the natural law idea that reason could be used to discover and apply international law. The example of Newton's universal laws of motion in the physical sciences also encouraged people to assume that there must be universal legal norms as well which arose out of the way man and the world are created. The success of newtonian science made it easier to suppose that there was an order and logic in nature which the human intellect could comprehend.

10. Natural law and natural rights. Natural law, and its derivative idea of natural rights (i.e. rights which men had inherently and irrevocably simply by virtue of being human beings), were particularly favoured in England and in English-speaking North America. Sir Wiliam Blackstone (1723–80), in his *Commentaries on the Laws of England,* even suggested that the law of nature was superior to all others and was 'binding all over the globe in all countries and at all times.' 'No human laws,' he went on, 'are of any validity, if contrary to this.' (Quoted in Brierly, *The Law of Nations,* 22.)

This was a very radical doctrine and, not surprisingly, was taken up by the revolutionary movements in America and France.

The American *Declaration of Independence* (1776) emphasises that all men are created equal (i.e. are equal by nature and not because of any human laws) and consequently are 'endowed by their Creator with certain unalienable Rights' (i.e. rights which could not be given up or be taken away by any human action).

The French *Declaration of the Rights of Man and of the Citizen* (1789) speaks similarly of 'natural, inalienable rights' and states that 'Men are born ... free and equal in rights'.

11. Decline and revival. Although natural law remained a main theme in international law into the nineteenth century, it was gradually superseded by the doctrine of positivism, which continued as the dominant idea in law into this century.

But if natural law plays such a necessary role, why did it decline in the nineteenth century? Part of the explanation may be that in application natural law may have seemed too much dependent on the subjective personal opinions or views of the people who were attempting as it were to read the natural law from what they thought to be the nature of man and society.

Jean Jacques Rousseau (1712–78), for example, looked out at the world and thought he saw it as a place where 'Man was born free, but everywhere he is in chains'. Edmund Burke (1729–97), on the other hand, though he was a clear exponent of natural law ('the law of humanity, justice, equity – the law of nature, and of nations', he once wrote), concluded that nature was above all orderly and declared that 'Good order is the foundation of all good things'. Thus, while Rousseau's ideas of natural law inclined towards breaking the chains that bound men, regardless of the resulting disorder, Burke came to believe that the natural law was opposed to revolution, or at least to the French Revolution.

This problem of interpreting the natural order correctly so as to know what natural law required was particularly a problem in international law where it was very difficult to know what international society was like and what its nature required.

Writers on international law therefore looked for a test to know what the natural law in the international sphere was. As there had been, even in the time of Suarez, some willingness to derive some rules of international law from the actual practice of states, legal writers began to suggest that one could look at what states did (their state practice) over a period of time and assume that this probably reflected the law which nature and reason dictated.

The point was made by the great English judge Lord Mansfield (1705–93), who said: 'The Law of Nations is founded on justice, equity, convenience, and the reason of the thing and *confirmed* by long usage'. (Quoted in Brierly, *The Law of Nations*, 68.)

But of course it is one thing to say that state practice *confirms* the law and quite another to say that such practice *creates* the law. This became a critical distinction in the eighteenth century as the doctrine of positivism gained increasing numbers of adherents.

Positivism in turn declined in the twentieth century as disenchantment with the excesses of positivist law in Nazi Germany and Soviet Russia, and the increasing concern with human rights, turned some people again towards natural law.

Thus one finds the United Nations-inspired International Covenant on Civil and Political Rights (1966) reviving in its preamble the idea of the 'inalienable rights of all members of the human family' which are said to derive 'from the inherent dignity of the human person'.

12. Usefulness of natural law. Even if one does not go so far as these words imply in accepting the idea of natural law, Brierly has argued that the basic concept of natural law is a necessary part of international law for two reasons. First, natural law reaffirms that there is a purpose in law lying behind the mere 'black-letter' rules and thereby encourages attempts to apply the law, not mechanically, but rather so as to further that underlying purpose.

Secondly, Brierly notes that natural law's appeal to reason permits the law to be applied flexibly and be adapted to changing circumstances. Thus, where the existing law may seem inadequate, natural law permits a reasonable solution to be sought beyond the rules already formulated.

The doctrine of positivism

13. General. Positivism meant essentially the view that law, and particularly international law, did not arise from an authority above or beyond the state but was in fact merely the product of the consent of states expressed either in treaties or in state practice. The resulting law was said to be 'positive' in the sense that states had 'put it in place' (from the Latin *pono, ponere, positum* to put, place). According to the strict doctrine of positivism, states are not bound by any 'law' to which they have not consented.

Positivism, therefore, often serves in practice to reinforce the inclination of a state to do what suits its particular goals at any one time. Consequently, the development of positivism has in fact tended to parallel the development of individualistic political theories. Although this is perhaps not in principle a necessary consequence of the theory, its actual relevance to the history of positivism cannot be ignored.

14. Origins of positivism. The beginnings of positivism in international law go back to the period of the renaissance and reformation when the new sovereign nation-states were coming into being around the year 1500 and the spirit of humanistic individualism created an atmosphere of 'unbridled subjectivity', as the historian Burckhardt commented in *The Civilization of the Renaissance in Italy*. In the legal sphere, the very idea of 'sovereignty' implied that the ruler and his state were free of all authority imposed from outside.

The theory's political basis was laid in the works of Niccolo Machiavelli (1469-1527), the Florentine official and writer who is sometimes regarded as the father of political science. In his book *The Prince* he made clear that the ruler was free to disregard any outside constraint that conflicted with his state's self-interest. 'A prince', he wrote, 'in order to maintain the state ... is often obliged to act against his promise, against charity, against humanity, and against religion.' Or again in a similar vein: 'there are two means of fighting: one according to the laws, the other with force; the first way is proper to man, the second to beasts; but because the first in many cases is not sufficient, it becomes necessary to resort to the second.'

15. Development of positivism. In the seventeenth century, the Dutch writer Hugo Grotius (see **9**), although accepting natural law, nevertheless gave some encouragement to positivism insofar as he was willing to allow rules of international law to be inferred from state practice on the ground that practice was a reliable indication of states' consent to be bound by those rules.

The situation in which Grotius' country found itself at that time prompted him to defend Dutch claims on statehood, freedom of the seas, and the wartime capture of enemy ships. By the early 1600s Holland had won *de facto* independence from Spain and was interested in wedging its way into the international community in which it had previously played no role and whose laws had been developed without reference to it. Holland had at one and the same time to uphold the idea of a general international law which obligated all states (and particularly those that were still hostile to the new state) and to avoid being bound by previously established rules of law that worked to its disadvantage. A combination of natural law with a positivist reliance on consent as reflected in state practice would have served both these purposes.

This interesting example of the influence of political circumstances on the philosophy of international law is parallelled today in the attitude of many third world and developing countries who adopt a very positivistic attitude towards rules of law that might work to their disadvantage but a natural law attitude towards law that imposes obligations on other states, particularly the developed industrial countries of Europe and North America.

16. The Enlightenment. In the eighteenth century positivism paradoxically benefitted from the same scientific rationalism that encouraged natural law thinking – an example of how dominant intellectual themes in a particular epoch can be applied to produce contradictory conclusions depending on the general philosophical or political viewpoint of the writer.

In this instance, philosophers and legal thinkers tried to examine international society scientifically but what they seemed to find differed from what they thought natural law would require. The Swiss jurist Emerich de Vattel (1714-69) attempted to reconcile theory and perceived reality by paying lip-service to natural law while in fact expanding on the positivist elements in previous thinking.

According to de Vattel, international law operated on two levels. The fundamentals were determined by natural law, but his conception of these fundamentals was limited to a few truisms such as that all states, if they were independent, were equally soveriegn. De Vattel did not believe that such natural law principles were enforceable against states but were in effect simply the background against which the second level of international law operated.

The law on this second level was enforceable because it was positivistic, voluntary law which states had accepted. This concept, often called *voluntarism*, effectively removed natural law from an important role in creating international law.

The scientific bent of the eighteenth century also worked against natural law by discounting assumptions that could not be proved by empirical scientific observations. Jeremy Bentham (1748-1832), for example, thought that laws should be determined according to a measurable 'utilitarian calculus' of observable benefits and disadvantages rather than according to any general philosophical or religious belief. Such ideas were so common towards the end of the eighteenth century that Edmund Burke complained that he lived in an age of 'sophisters, economists and calculators'.

17. Positivism and nationalism. At the beginning of the nineteenth century, positivism, because it emphasised the freedom of each state to choose what laws it would be governed by, became mixed up with ideas of nationalism that were then developing. In this conception each nation was a unique cultural and political entity which was not suited by laws imposed from an external international system that could not possibly share the uniqueness of the nation's history and experience. This attitude was encouraged by romantic ideas about the need to give autonomy and freedom to what the followers of the German legal philosopher von Savigny called the *Volksgeist*, the 'national spirit', of each country in order that each should develop to its full potential.

18. Positivism and 'science'. The new evolutionary ideas of Charles Darwin (1809-82) began in the middle of the nineteenth century to affect international relations and hence, to some extent, international law as well. Darwinism emphasised the idea of the struggle for survival of the fittest in the animal world, and some statesmen began to act as if states also were engaged in a competition in which only the 'fittest' (whatever that meant) were entitled to survive. This view was particularly evident in the relations between european countries and the colonial territories they were acquiring in Asia and Africa.

The result was that natural law was replaced by extreme positivism (for europeans) whereby strong states, because of their 'fitness', were entitled to force their own views about international law on weaker nations (who were not allowed to claim positivist rights for themselves).

Another problem arising out of Darwinism was that it seemed to indicate that change and adaptation were at the heart of existence, whereas natural law implied that there were at least some unchanging inherent principles that should be reflected in the application of international law.

19. Positivism and communism. The next important advance in the position of positivism in international law came in the 1920s when the communist government was established in the Soviet Union. The new communist regime had a number of problems with the conservative and non-communist states of Europe and America, who were thought in Moscow to be trying to impose an essentially non-communist system of international law on the Soviet state. The new regime then adopted officially the view that the Soviet Union was bound only by those parts of international law to which it had specifically agreed.

This practical policy was reinforced in theory by the argument (made, e.g., by the Soviet expert on international law, G. I. Tunkin) that natural law is to be repudiated because it leads to, and indeed requires, religion and belief in a superhuman authority.

Western writers and governments have rejected this Soviet view, or at least its implications, although some by their actions have occasionally seemed not too far from sharing it in practice.

20. Positivism and the new states. In more recent years a strong element of positivism has run through the attitude of newly-independent third world countries who do not wish to be bound by some of the previous international law on economic questions and who therefore argue that states are bound only by law which they have specifically accepted. On the other hand natural law ideas seem to permeate the views of these countries on such questions as the inalienable right of a people to self-determination.

21. Objections to positivism. Although positivism has thus become more widely accepted over the past 200 years, this popularity has not allayed the doubts of some writers.

There are, to begin with, the practical difficulties of maintaining a legal system based solely on consent. Real law implies a continuing relationship of rights and duties, which in turn requires that consent, once given, cannot arbitrarily be withdrawn. But in practice states often act as if mere withdrawal of consent can at any time terminate obligations. This appears to make positive law rest on state discretion.

To get round this weakness in positivism its advocates have offered various ingenious but awkward arguments to reconcile absolute state sovereignty and the need for state consent with the maintenance of legal obligations even if a state attempts to withdraw its consent. It must be said that these arguments do not seem to have had a decisive influence on state practice, and that, after all, is the central point on which positivism is based.

But the objectors to positivism point out in addition that in fact express consent by states to particular rules of international law is often impossible to find and yet those rules are operative and binding in international law. To meet this objection positivists are driven to arguing for some mechanism of implied consent but this is theoretically a dubious proposition.

On the jurisprudential level, positivists sometimes have sought to explain the legal role of consent by anchoring it in some underlying principle which could be the ultimate norm for international law. The Italian scholar and former President of the Permanent Court of International Justice, Dionisio Anzilotti (1867–1950), suggested that consent created law by virtue of the fundamental principle *pacta sunt servanda* ('agreements must be observed') since this meant that consent had binding effect and so could create legal rights and duties. But the justification for relying on this principle is essentially the natural law view that such a principle is inherent in the international system as at present constituted (because international relations would be impossible if states failed to honour their word). Positivism would then be based on natural law.

Apart from these conceptual weaknesses of positivism, there is the practical problem that, as a matter of fact, general international law has traditionally been considered applicable to states merely by virtue of their being members of the international community. New states, for example, are said to be bound by the law as it exists when they enter that community, whether they expressly consent to be bound or not. British and American international lawyers have been particularly emphatic in advocating this view.

22. The interrelation of natural law and positivism. The correct conclusion seems therefore to be that positivism presupposes some natural law basis for the importance of consent in forming law. One must then attempt to determine how the two concepts may work together in answering a particular legal problem.

In general, it seems correct to say that it is more convenient to look first for positive law to which the parties to any dispute have explicitly committed themselves, as this may solve the problem without further difficulty.

In cases where positive law is lacking, recourse may be had to natural law. As Brierly points out this option is particularly useful in allowing a court to avoid a *non liquet*, that is, a situation where the tribunal may refuse to decide a case because it believes there is no law applicable to the issues of the dispute.

The really difficult case, however, is when positive law and natural law may be thought to diverge. This is particularly likely to occur in the area of human rights where positive law has tended to emphasise the right of a sovereign state to do what it likes within its own territory while natural law may give paramount importance to the rights of the individual. In such a situation the international lawyer may be forced at the end of the day to choose whether he favours positivism or natural law. Without such a choice, made after the most careful consideration of the jurisprudential basis of international law, it may be impossible to decide some cases.

A notable example of this sort of situation was the *South-West Africa Cases* (1966) in which the views of a number of judges on the International Court of Justice clearly distinguished them as positivists or advocates of natural law when faced with the problem of calling South Africa to account for its administration of South-West Africa (Namibia). While the majority opinion, for example, emphasised that legal rights had to be given 'juridical expression and be clothed in legal form' by such things as the treaties and agreements of states, Judge Kotaro Tanaka, dissenting, argued that human rights derive from the 'concept of man as a person and his relationship with society which cannot be separated from universal human nature'. In Tanaka's view, therefore, 'the existence of human rights does not depend on the will of a state; neither internally on its law or any other legislative measure, nor internationally on treaty or custom, in which the express or tacit will of a state constitutes the essential element'. Indeed, 'States are not capable of creating human rights by law or by convention; they can only confirm their existence and give them protection. The role of the state is no more than declaratory.' (See 2:**48**.)

23. Positivism, natural law and the sources of international law. The actual mechanics of determining what the law is in a particular case may thus be affected by one's view of these two philosophies of law.

Positivists, who believe, as, for example, soviet international lawyers generally seem to, that states are bound only by what they clearly consent to, will tend to confine their search for the law to sources of law that demonstrate such consent. The most obvious of these is treaties. Positivism thus tends to limit the sources from which law can be derived and in so doing also restricts the means for changing the law to those same sources.

Advocates of natural law, on the other hand, will look beyond sources that demonstrate consent and will be more willing to take account of broad legal principles and the application of logic and reason to legal problems. This may tend to promote the progressive development of the law.

The result is that one's conclusions in a particular international legal case may depend to a greater or lesser extent on one's general jurisprudential view about the nature of international law and the sources of its rules and principles.

The 'sociological' alternative

24. General. Although the natural law/positivism clash has remained at the heart of the debate over international law, in the twentieth century what may broadly be called sociological approaches have also been attempted as a way of relating international law to the observed realities of the world community.

25. America. This tendency has been particularly pronounced in the United States, where the legal realist movement associated with Karl Llewellyn and the sociological jurisprudence of Roscoe Pound each in its own way sought to derive law from the social circumstances of individuals and groups. In the sphere of international legal studies Myres McDougal has emphasised that international law should not be seen as a body of doctrine and rules divorced from power and social processes but as the result of the interacting responses to problems by decision-makers who are attempting to deal with concrete questions in a setting where many political and other variables must be taken into account. This interaction of decisions by leaders and officials in many countries produces international law by building up a repertoire of actions and claims which the majority of decision-makers assert for their own countries and allow to others in what McDougal calls a 'process of reciprocal tolerance of unilateral claim'.

26. Alvarez. Another version of the sociological approach is reflected in several opinions of Judge Alvarez in cases before the International Court of Justice. He saw modern international law as arising from what might be thought of as the sociological foundations of international society – the awakening 'juridical conscience of peoples' and the 'social interdependence' that has replaced individualism in the modern world and has required the law to seek 'international social justice'.

The debate continues.

Progress test 1

1. Discuss whether international law may be considered simply as a system of 'black-letter rules'.   **(1)**
2. Must international law be based on the state system?   **(3, 4)**
3. Define international law.   **(2)**
4. What is positivism?   **(13)**
5. Why did natural law develop?   **(6–8)**

6. How did natural law influence thinking on human rights?   (**10**)

7. Discuss the difficulties in giving effect to natural law.   (**11**)

8. Is positivism more suited to the state system than natural law?   (**8, 12, 14, 16–17, 21**)

9. Can positivism and natural law be reconciled in practice?   (**22, 23**)

10. Are there any persuasive alternatives to the natural law and positivist positions?   (**24–26**)

Bibliography

Encyclopedia of International Law, Vol. 7, article on 'The History of the Law of Nations'. (Elsevier, Amsterdam, 1984)

Brierly, *The Law of Nations*, 6th ed. (Oxford, 1963)

Dumbauld, *The Life and Writings of Hugo Grotius* (Univ. of Oklahoma Press, Norman, 1969).

Edwards, *Hugo Grotius The Miracle of Holland* (Nelson-Hall, Chicago, 1981).

McConica, *Thomas More* (H.M.S.O., London, 1977)

McDougal, 'The Hydrogen Bomb Tests and the International Law of the Sea', 49 Am. J. Intl. Law 356.

Nussbaum, *A Concise History of the Law of Nations*, 2nd ed. (Macmillan, New York, 1954)

Tunkin, *Theory of International Law* (trans. W. E. Butler) (Allen & Unwin, London, 1974).

Whiteman, ed., *Digest of International Law*, Vol. 1 (Department of State, Washington, 1963)

2 The sources of international law

1. Definition of a legal 'source'. 'Sources' of law are, generally speaking, the authoritative and necessary inputs into the process of determining what the law is. In most legal systems there are two types of source:

(a) the *formal* source, which establishes (usually by means of a constitutional document) who has the power to make the laws, parliamentary supremacy being, for example, a formal source of law in Britain; and

(b) the *material* sources, which are those documents (such as statutes and court decisions) that provide evidence of what the law is and may be reliably consulted as such.

In international law, the failure definitively to resolve the dispute over positivism and natural law has meant that there is no universal agreement over what are the formal sources of international law. In practice, this has meant that everyone simply assumes in light of his own particular philosophical or jurisprudential orientation that there are formal sources and then proceeds to look for the material sources that may provide indications of the law which is relevant to solving the problem at hand. Although this is theoretically unsatisfactory, it does not seem to have greatly hindered the development of international law except in some specific areas such as human rights.

2. The material sources of international law. A generally accepted statement indicating what are the material sources of international law is contained in the Statute (or constitution) of the International Court of Justice, the principal judicial organ of the United Nations (and often referred to as the 'World Court'). Article 38 of the ICJ Statute says (in part):

1. The Court, whose function is to decide in accordance with international law such disputes as are submitted to it, shall apply:

(a) international conventions, whether general or particular, establishing rules expressly recognised by the contesting states;

(b) international custom, as evidence of a general practice accepted as law;

(c) the general principles of law recognised by civilised nations;

(d) subject to the provisions of Article 59, judicial decisions and the teachings of the most highly qualified publicists of the various nations, as subsidiary means for the determination of rules of law.

(Article 59 indicates that the court's own decisions do not create binding precedents for later cases.)

3. Priority. The four categories referred to in (a) – (d) above are considered by most international lawyers to be the 'sources' of international law, but there is some disagreement about whether they are listed in order of their substantive legal authoritativeness or whether the sources are in that regard on a par with each other.

It is probably correct to consider that the listing provides only a handy checklist of sources in the order a court may follow to find the applicable law in the most convenient manner. An international convention (that is, a treaty) between the parties to a dispute may contain their specific agreement to apply a certain rule of law to the problem at issue, and if that is so, the ICJ need not, in general, look any further. By relying on the specific undertakings of the parties in this way, the court avoids arguments over the nature and extent of the broader law reflected in international custom or general principles of law.

Thus, the listing in Article 38 is simply a hierarchy of convenience and not one based on the relative legal authority or weight of the sources. It may be possible therefore that in certain circumstances a source lower down the list would prevail over one higher up. According to the Vienna Convention on the Law of Treaties (1969), Article 53, a treaty, for example, is void if it conflicts with a peremptory norm of general international law (*see* **20**). It is doubtful, however, that the sources in category (*d*) would have this effect since they are specifically stated to be subsidiary.

4. Significance of priority. These conclusions about the order of Article 38's listing may be significant in the positivist-natural law dispute, as it is often argued that sources (*a*) and (*b*) (conventions and custom) are basically positive law sources, while categories (*c*) and (*d*) are, potentially at least, natural law sources. These conclusions would have the effect of allowing some natural law sources a potentially equal standing with positive law sources in the application of international law. This argument has been put with particular force by Brierly in *The Basis of Obligation in International Law.*

5. Importance of custom. Furthermore, from a historical perspective, custom has until fairly recent times been a more important source of international law than treaties, and this suggests another reason for treating the listing in Article 38 as not reflecting some fundamental hierarchy of international law. Indeed, it is argued that conceptually custom must be fundamental to treaty law, since it is the pre-existing customary law principle *pacta sunt servanda* (agreements must be observed) that gives treaties their binding effect in law.

Custom may therefore reasonably be the first source to be examined here in detail.

Custom

6. The process of forming customary law. The essence of the formation of customary international law is the gradually combining effect of the practice of a number of states with regard to a particular type of legal problem or situation. At the beginning of this process a rule of customary law does not exist; at the end it does. The question then is: at what point in between did the rule come into existence?

To help in this determination international law has developed tests to be applied in evaluating instances of observed state action. One must examine the evidence for the nature, extent and significance of state practice and determine whether that practice establishes that the required elements of custom are present and have in fact combined to generate a rule of law.

It is usual to distinguish customary law that is found in this way from mere *usage*, that is, a habitual state activity that is not required by international law but is observed as a matter of goodwill at the discretion of the particular state.

7. The problem of evaluating the evidence for state practice. In general, the examination of state activities is concerned with what states actually do when faced with a particular problem. The difficulty is that states may act out of some momentary interest which leads them away from what a more considered judgment might suggest international law requires.

Thus state actions are often inconsistent and it is difficult to weigh conflicting actions to determine which constitute real evidence of state practice reflecting a state's general views on international law.

The problem of military intervention in the internal affairs of other states displays this problem of inconsistency at its worst. In 1968, soviet and other Warsaw Pact armies invaded Czechoslovakia to put down a movement towards liberalisation within the country. The soviet justification (which has become known as the 'Brezhnev doctrine' or the doctrine of limited sovereignty) was that the USSR and its allies were entitled to intervene in cases where the 'socialist' system in a communist country had been threatened. The United States denounced intervention to maintain or restore a government or political system favoured by the interveners. Such intervention, according to the American representative at the UN, was a violation of the right of self-determination and an act of aggression under the UN Charter.

In 1983, United States military forces intervened in Grenada in what seemed to many observers an attempt to re-establish a government there which would be inclined towards the United States. The Soviet Union denounced intervention in the internal affairs of sovereign states as a violation of international law.

What are the views of the Soviet Union and the United States on the limitations imposed by international law on intervention? It is difficult to say from an examination of these instances of state action; the observer is left wondering whether either country, in view of the inconsistencies in the position of each, can claim to have contributed anything to the formation of customary law.

In examining state actions, then, the international lawyer must be very careful not to attach undue weight to any particular act of state self-interest.

8. The evidence of state practice. With that caveat in mind, however, the lawyer may consider as evidence of state practice a wide variety of things, some of more value than others.

There are first the documents generated by states in their conduct of foreign relations. Diplomatic correspondence, policy statements, press releases, and opinions of official legal advisers may all come within this category.

Then one may find more general expressions of a state's views on international law in such things as official manuals on legal questions. Both the United States and the United Kingdom publish manuals on the law of war which may be taken as expressions of each state's views on the conduct of military activities.

The actual decisions of governments on questions with some international legal relevance are often good indications of state practice. Similarly, legislation and judicial decisions of the state's higher courts may reflect that state's practice on the international legal issues raised.

On the international level, the comments by a state on draft treaties produced by the UN International Law Commission, or the voting of that state in international bodies (particularly the UN General Assembly), may offer good indications of a state's practice – may indeed even in some sense be state practice.

More generally, the language used in the treaties a state signs may reflect its practice, as may also a pattern of treaties in which a state has fairly consistently agreed to a certain view of the relevant international law in agreements with its treaty partners.

It is within the framework of such evidences of state practice that the international lawyer must decide whether the elements of customary law are present.

9. The elements of custom. Once it has been determined what is the real practice of states with regard to some legal point, that practice must next be examined to see whether it reflects what are generally recognised to be the indispensable elements whose presence transforms practice into customary law. These elements are discussed below (*see* **10–13**).

10. Element 1: opinio juris. This is the belief that a certain practice is obligatory as a matter of law. Thus Article 38(1)b of the ICJ Statute speaks of a 'general practice *accepted as law*'. If a practice is not so accepted, but is regarded as simply a discretionary act performed out of political or other non-legal motives, then it is an example of a usage which may merely reflect international friendliness or diplomatic tact – what international law calls comity.

In the *Asylum Case* (1950) the World Court emphasised the importance of a practice being the expression of a right belonging to one party and a duty lying on the other party. Without that nexus of legal obligation, and the *opinio juris* which recognises it, there is no custom.

Unfortunately, although this requirement of *opinio juris* makes practical sense as a means of distinguishing custom from comity, it is illogical insofar as it requires new rules of customary law to be generated by a process which must assume a belief that those rules are *already* legally binding.

Nevertheless, the World Court has insisted on this and the main question in several cases has been how to decide whether a practice is motivated by *opinio juris* or not. In the *Lotus Case* (PCIJ 1927), the court indicated that one could not infer *opinio juris* from a particular practice unless the state involved was 'conscious of having a duty' in that regard. This has been criticised as requiring the judges and others to determine the psychological viewpoint of a state as if it were a real person. Several respected writers have suggested that the better position is to infer *opinio juris* from practice which reasonably bears that inference unless there are clear indications from the state to the contrary. But in the *North Sea Continental Shelf Cases* (1969) the court reiterated the *Lotus* view although a slight shift occurred in *Nicaragua* v. *US* (1986).

11. Element 2: duration. This has to do with the length of time a practice has been followed. Long duration may be helpful in establishing a custom, but the ICJ indicated in the *North Sea Continental Shelf Cases* that even a short duration might suffice when state practice has been extensive and virtually uniform. In other words, a short duration may be offset to some extent by a strong showing with regard to the remaining elements of custom (*see* 12:46).

12. Element 3: uniformity and consistency. Uniformity means that the practice of states should not vary greatly from state to state. Consistency implies that there should not be contradictions or discrepancies in the practice of states between one relevant instance and another.

13. Element 4: generality. This relates to whether a practice is fairly widespread among a majority of states: a practice common in only one area of the world or observed by only a minority of states would not generate international customary law for all. However, all states may be bound by custom arising from generally followed practice without the need for universality.

It may be possible, nevertheless, for a state which objects to a particular general practice to avoid in certain circumstances being obligated as a matter of customary law. The *Anglo-Norwegian Fisheries Case* (1951) is generally understood to recognise the possibility of a state's being a *persistent objector* and thus not bound by a particular custom on account of having objected to the relevant practice right from the beginning of its transformation into a rule of customary international law. On the other hand, a *subsequent objector*, which remained silent while the custom was in process of formation and spoke out only after it had become law, would not be able to escape being obligated unless other affected states acquiesced in the subsequent objector's attempt to avoid being bound.

These observations about the position of states that object to a rule of customary law are important for a corollary that is implicit in them, namely, that if a state makes neither a persistent objection nor a subsequent objection to a particular rule, then that state is bound by the rule, even without an explicit acceptance.

14. Case law on custom. General statements about the nature of state practice and the elements of custom must be translated into reality in actual cases to see what their significance and effect are. Previous decisions, particularly of the World Court, are good models of how this can be done.

15. The Lotus Case (1927) and the nature of customary law. In August 1926 on the high seas a collision occurred between the French steamer *Lotus* and a Turkish ship, the *Boz Kourt*, which was sunk. The *Lotus* steamed into Turkish waters and docked in Istanbul. The Turkish authorities promptly brought criminal charges under Turkish law against the officer in charge of the *Lotus* at the time of the collision. France objected that this was contrary to international law on the argument that jurisdiction over individuals on vessels on the high seas belongs solely to the state whose flag the ship was flying ('exclusive flag-state jurisdiction').

16. The nature of international law. The French began by arguing that if international law had not specifically granted Turkey the right to exercise its jurisdiction, Turkey was barred from doing so. This implies that what international law does not specifically permit, it prohibits. Permission could be shown by state practice or other evidence that states had accepted non-flag-state jurisdiction. The implication that Turkey would otherwise have been bound, even against its will, to forego the exercise of jurisdiction indicates elements of natural law thinking in the French position.

Turkey argued that there could not be restrictions on state action without positive law accepted by states and embodying those restrictions.

The PCIJ was in effect faced at the outset with a question about the nature of international law: was a state's freedom of action limited without its consent or was positive law supreme, so that a state could do as it pleased unless it had explicitly or implicitly agreed to a limitation?

The court decided on this issue that rules of law binding on states emanate from their own free will as expressed in treaties or custom. Therefore unless it could be proved that Turkey had accepted a limitation on its jurisdiction there could be no presumption of such a limitation.

17. Use of a pattern of treaties to prove a general rule. France then attempted to prove that there was a rule of customary international law giving exclusive flag-state jurisdiction in all cases.

As part of its examination of this aspect of the case, the court considered various treaties as evidence of state practice. It noted that there were treaties between various countries recognising exclusive flag-state jurisdiction, but in the court's view this did not necessarily prove that the parties to those treaties believed such jurisdiction to be required by a rule of customary international law. The very fact that those states thought they had to sign treaties on the subject suggested that they might not have the *opinio juris* required for the formation of a rule of customary law: treaties may indeed indicate the belief of the parties that no customary rule exists on the point, so that a treaty is needed to fill the gap.

On this basis the court determined that there was no rule of customary law giving exclusive flag-state jurisdiction in all cases, and France suggested as an alternative that there was at least exclusive jurisdiction in criminal cases arising out of collisions.

18. State practice to prove a specific rule: need for opinio juris. France argued that state practice could be inferred from an examination of judicial proceedings after such collisions. Such an examination would reveal, France said, that criminal charges by the non-flag state were rarely brought. This, so the argument went, showed the tacit consent of non-flag states to exclusive flag-state jurisdiction.

The court decided, however, that abstention from prosecution would be evidence of a binding custom only if the abstaining state were 'conscious of having a duty to abstain'. In other words, as mentioned earlier (*see* 10), practice without a clear indication of *opinio juris* could not be assumed to generate customary law.

The court went further and stated that when non-flag states had instituted proceedings, the flag states had generally not objected. The court seemed to believe that this failure to object indicated that the flag states thought non-flag state jurisdiction was permissible under international law.

The French case therefore failed, largely because of the court's view as to the nature of international law and the process whereby customary law is formed.

19. The Asylum Case (1950) and regional custom. This case between Colombia and Peru revolved around the question of the status of diplomatic asylum as a rule of customary law. Colombia had given diplomatic asylum in its embassy in Peru to a Peruvian rebel leader. The Peruvians said this man was a criminal, in which case he would not have been entitled to diplomatic asylum. Colombia argued, however, that Latin America had developed a particular rule of its own in regard to diplomatic asylum that allowed the state granting asylum to make its own judgement on whether the individual concerned was a criminal or not. Colombia had therefore to show, among other things, that there could be *regional customary law* that differed from general international customary law.

The decision of the ICJ was that regional customary law was indeed possible, so long as the requisite elements of customary law were present, with the required general practice being understood to refer to generality within the particular regional grouping of states involved. (The court did not, however, find that the practice argued for by Colombia was indeed a general one within Latin America.)

20. Regional custom and jus cogens. But does this mean that states are completely free to establish whatever customary law they like within their own regions? In the past, when positivism was the dominant view and the UN Charter and other fundamental elements of international law were not in place, the answer would probably have been 'Yes'. But there is a strong argument to be made today that what is called *jus cogens* has altered the position.

The Vienna Convention on the Law of Treaties (1969) in Article 53, defines *jus cogens* as a 'peremptory norm' ('peremptory' here meaning admitting no refusal or denial) which is 'a norm accepted and recognised by the international community of states as a whole as a norm from which no derogation is permitted and which can be modified only by a subsequent norm of general international law having the same character'. Thus it would not be permissible for a regional grouping to depart from an established rule of *jus cogens* since such a departure could be legitimate only if the international community as a whole solemnly abandoned the rule in question.

21. General implications of jus cogens. Some legal writers suggest an almost natural law basis for rules of *jus cogens*, namely that they are inherent in the international legal order and fundamental to the existence of the international community. An example of such a *jus cogens* rule would be the prohibition of genocide, since it must be fundamental to the existence of the international community that its component elements (national or other distinct groups) cannot legally be destroyed. The prohibition of aggressive war may also be a rule of *jus cogens* in light of the UN Charter's restriction of the use of force in Articles 2(4) and 51.

This point is relevant in evaluating the legal validity of what has come to be called the 'Brezhnev doctrine' under which the Soviet Union purported to be entitled to intervene militarily in the affairs of states in the 'socialist' bloc on the ground that 'socialist international law' permitted this. The implication was that a kind of regional law had been developed among the 'socialist' states that allowed departure from general international law on this point. Such intervention would normally be considered the waging of aggressive war, a view implicitly adopted by the Soviet Union when it signed the UN Charter.

The existence and effect of *jus cogens* rules in such a situation are obviously of critical importance, and are not surprisingly hotly debated among international lawyers.

22. North Sea Continental Shelf Cases (1969): customary law for treaties. In these consolidated cases in which Denmark and the Netherlands opposed West Germany the central issue was whether customary international law could be generated by a multilateral treaty. The treaty in question was the 1958 Geneva Convention on the Continental Shelf, to which West Germany was not a party while Denmark and The Netherlands were. The latter two states argued that West Germany was nevertheless bound by the rules enunciated in the convention on the ground that this treaty had in some way caused the formation of general customary international law.

23. Custom from norm-creating provisions. The ICJ indicated that this could happen with regard to provisions in the treaty that were 'norm-creating', i.e. that were intended to embody fundamental legal rules rather than merely secondary obligations. Such norm-creating provisions, when implemented by relevant state practice accompanied by *opinio juris* and the other elements of custom as appropriate, could be the foundation upon which customary law was built.

Examining the particular provision at issue in the case, the court decided that it was in fact a secondary one and one which furthermore allowed a wide and ill-defined set of special circumstances to affect its implementation. These factors militated against its being intended by the drafters of the treaty to be a plainly fundamental rule of general application. Moreover, the provision in question could under the treaty have reservations made to it; i.e. a state upon becoming a party to the treaty could indicate that it would not accept being bound by the provision. In the court's view the fact that the drafters permitted reservations to the provision indicated that they did not consider the rule stated in it to be so fundamentally important that all parties would have to accept it. Taken together, then, the indications in the convention itself were that the provision in question was not intended to be norm-creating.

24. Custom from state practice. Nevertheless, it was conceivable that even a provision that was not meant to be norm-creating might be taken by states as a basis for practice and *opinio juris* and so generate a rule of customary law anyway. The court therefore considered whether the elements of custom were present.

Regarding duration, the court was faced with the fact that only eleven years had intervened between the signing of the conventioin in 1958 and the court case in 1969. This relatively short period did not preclude the formation of custom provided that 'within the period in question, short though it might be, state practice, including that of states whose interests are specially affected, should have been both extensive and virtually uniform'.

25. Duration and specially affected states. By emphasising the position of specially affected states, the court sought to avoid a situation in which a group of states might attempt to hurry the formation of a rule of customary law in order to impose obligations on specially affected states without their having had time to make their attitude known and register their objections.

26. General implications of concern with specially affected states. This concern may have implications beyond those originally envisaged by the court. It is argued, for example, that the handful of states possessing nuclear weapons have by their actions since 1945 established a rule of customary law to the effect that use of such weapons would be legal, despite customary and other legal prohibitions on warfare that fails to discriminate in its effects between combatants and non-combatants. In this situation, which are the specially affected states whose practice must be taken into account? Only those that possess nuclear weapons, or those that would be devastated by their use? The point could be significant in view, for example, of the possible state practice represented by UN General Assembly Resolution 1653 of 24 November 1961 (only sixteen years after the first use of nuclear weapons) in which 55 out of the 101 states present in the Assembly voted for the proposition that the use of nuclear weapons would violate the UN Charter and be contrary to the rules of international law.

27. Court's conclusions. In the *North Sea Continental Shelf Cases* the court, considering the evidence of state practice, concluded that there was not sufficient practice exhibiting clear *opinio juris* to generate a new customary rule. This was because many states followed the provision in question as an application of the convention as such rather than as the basis for a rule of customary law, while other states did not give that clear indication of *opinio juris* which the court held to be necessary, given that inferring of *opinio juris* was impermissible.

Consequently, the provision in question did not form the basis of a rule of customary international law binding West Germany.

28. Judge Sorensen's dissent: a new 'source' of law? In a strong dissent, the Danish member of the court, Judge Sorensen, argued that the position of the Geneva Convention on the Continental Shelf was different from that of an ordinary multilateral treaty in that it had originally been drafted by the UN General Assembly's International Law Commission and approved in the Assembly. Having in mind that the Commission was composed of legal experts representing the main forms of civilisation and the principal legal systems of the world and that the Assembly's membership was almost universal, production of a treaty by these two bodies, in keeping with their functions under the UN Charter to codify and progressively develop international law, went beyond traditional notions of custom. Such a treaty 'may well constitute, or come to constitute, the decisive evidence of generally accepted new rules of international law'. This sounds almost like a claim that such a treaty would amount to binding legislation, an intriguing but so far not generally accepted proposition.

Judge Sorensen was closer to the usual view, however, when he went on to suggest that a treaty of this kind 'may serve as an authoritative guide for the practice of states ... and its provisions thus become the nucleus around which a new set of generally recognised legal rules may crystallise'.(*See* also 12:41–2.)

29. A note on General Assembly resolutions. Judge Sorensen's emphasis on the importance of United Nations action in generating law for which, as he wrote, 'the word "custom" ... may not even be an adequate expression' raises the problem of the effect of General Assembly resolutions in the creation of new law. There are basically four possibilities:

(*a*) that such resolutions have no legal effect;

(*b*) that they are authoritative interpretations of the pre-existing law in the UN Charter;

(*c*) that they help create customary law;

(*d*) that they have an almost legislative effect.

30. Possibility (a): no legal effect. This argument depends on the statement in the UN Charter, Article 10, that the General Assembly may only 'discuss' matters within the scope of the Charter and 'make recommendations'. By definition these are not orders and cannot have the binding effect necessary to create legal obligations and duties. It is sometimes also suggested that the act of voting for a mere recommendation cannot be state practice contributing to the growth of customary law since, it is said, the knowledge that the recommendation is not binding prevents the requisite *opinio juris*. Even if a state indicated that it felt obliged to vote for a certain recommendation, the obligation (and hence the rule of customary law) would exist independently and not in the resolution itself.

As a strict and literal interpretation of the regime established in 1945 under the UN Charter, this argument persuades many, but the view of *opinio juris* upon which it partly relies seems to take no account of the illogicality mentioned above whereby all new customary law is supposedly the result of the belief of states that the new rules are already part of the law. To emphasise this paradox only in the case of General Assembly resolutions seems unjustifiably selective and not in keeping with the flexibility international law implicitly accepts in allowing the notion of customary law in spite of the illogicality embedded in its process of creation.

31. Possibility (b): authoritative interpretations. This view is less troubled by the limitations imposed by restriction of the Assembly to discussion and recommendation. International law recognises (as in Article 31(3) of the 1969 Vienna Convention on the Law of Treaties) that the interpretation of a treaty may be affected by the subsequent practice of the parties to it. It is not too far from this to say that voting in the Assembly in favour of certain interpretations of the Charter (e.g. on the content of human rights law) amounts to practice that may clarify and develop the relevant Charter provisions.

This understanding is particularly apt when applied to resolutions that take the form of declarations of principle on legal questions, most notably the Universal Declaration of Human Rights of 1948. Thus, in the *Filartiga* v. *Pena-Irala* case a United States federal court in 1980 said, on the question of whether torture was prohibited under international law, that 'UN declarations are significant because they specify with great precision the obligations of member nations under the Charter'.

A somewhat similar view of the role of General Assembly resolutions was put forward by Judge Jessup in his dissenting opinion in the *South West Africa Cases* (1966). The judicial task of the court was, he said, to interpret constitutional documents like those in that case (and like the UN Charter) by applying contemporary international community standards for which statements in General Assembly resolutions provided proof.

32. Possibility (c): creation of customary law. This could arguably happen in one of three ways:

(*a*) A state's vote in favour of a resolution might be state practice with *opinio juris* because the state regards the resolution as in itself legally binding. But this notion is open to the objection that under the UN Charter most General Assembly resolutions are only recommendatory and therefore cannot be binding.

(*b*) A state's vote for a resolution could be state practice with *opinio juris* because the vote is an acknowledgement by the state that the content of the resolution accords with the requirements of international law and cannot legitimately be rejected. From this possibility some writers have gone a step further to speak of a process of 'parliamentary diplomacy' whereby the will of the international community can be quickly and accurately reflected in resolutions, with the accumulation of such authoritative pronouncements producing new international law. Judge Tanaka, dissenting in the *South West Africa Cases* (1966), described this process as 'the middle way between legislation by convention and the traditional process of custom making'. The court in the *Filartiga Case* mentioned in **31** implicitly endorsed this view with regard to resolutions on human rights. (*See* **13:12**.)

(*c*) The resolution may enunciate principles or rules which later state practice (with *opinio juris*) adopts as customary law. This role for General Assembly resolutions is widely accepted, but one should remember that in this situation the subsequent practice, and not the resolution *per se*, is what is generating the new law.

33. Possibility (d): quasi-legislative effect. After the General Assembly in December 1963 adopted unanimously the 'Declaration of Legal Principles Governing the Activities of States in the Exploration and Use of Outer Space' (Resolution 1962), the United States representative said that a resolution of that kind, approved unanimously, 'represented the law as generally accepted in the international community'. This was understood to mean that one resolution of that kind could create law where none had existed previously, in effect could legislate new international law. This view was contested at the time and remains debatable.

The key to the American claim was the unanimity with which the resolution was adopted. If a resolution purporting to set out new 'law' were adopted only by a majority, the situation would be different. In the *Texaco* v. *Libya* arbitration of 1977, the arbitrator held that such a resolution, if not simply reaffirming previously existing law (*lex lata*), would be merely *de lege ferenda*, that is, a suggestion of what the law ought to be rather than a statement of what it presently is. Although many international lawyers would accept this opinion in principle, considerable room for disagreement remains in trying to determine which resolutions it applies to.

If General Assembly resolutions did have quasi-legislative effect, and were thus a source of law distinct from both treaties and custom, the list of sources in Article 38 of the ICJ Statute would have to be considered incomplete and out-of-date. Since its original version was produced nearly seventy years ago, this would not be surprising.

Treaties

34. Introduction. Article 38(1)(a) of the ICJ Statute indicates as a source of law 'international conventions, whether general or particular, establishing rules expressly recognised by the contesting states'. 'Conventions' in this usage means essentially 'treaties' and should not be confused with the notion of convention in British constitutional law.

35. Definition of a treaty. The Vienna Convention on the Law of Treaties (1969), which was an attempt to codify and develop the law on the subject and which is often referred to in the examination of treaty problems, defines a treaty in Article 2 as an international agreement between states in written form and governed by international law. Customary international law would also recognise as treaties agreements which are not in writing provided their existence can be satisfactorily proved.

36. Types of treaties. Treaties may be either *bilateral* (between only two parties) or *multilateral* (between more than two parties).

37. Nature of treaties. A treaty may serve in effect as an international contract between two states, or it may be what will be called here a 'law-making' treaty, or it may very rarely have a legislative effect.

38. Contractual treaties. Some writers (e.g. Sir Gerald Fitzmaurice) have suggested that treaties are strictly speaking sources of obligation rather than sources of law. That is, treaties of the kind intended do not establish a regime of legal principles and rules against which the conduct of the parties can be measured, but rather simply state the mutual obligations which the parties have undertaken to perform. Treaties which have this character may properly be called 'contractual' by analogy to contracts in private law.

39. 'Law-making' treaties. 'Law-making' treaties are concerned with establishing general norms or overall legal regimes in accordance with which the parties to such a treaty agree to order their conduct and relations with each other.

Whereas the operative effect of a contractual agreement may come to an end when the parties have done (or failed to do) certain specified things, a law-making treaty may involve an open-ended commitment to a certain legal regime without regard to the parties' performance of reciprocal obligations.

The Treaty of Rome which established the European Economic Community in 1957 is in this sense a law-making treaty insofar as it operates as a kind of constitutional document from which is derived law which binds the Community's members *vis-à-vis* the Community as a whole rather than simply in terms of reciprocal obligations between the member states.

The UN Charter, as regards the members of the organisation, also functions as a constitutional and law-making treaty whereby, for example, the members have general obligations to the international community not to disrupt international peace and security as well as bilateral obligations to each other in that regard.

40. 'Legislative' treaties. Although there is no reason in principle why states should not establish law-making treaties for themselves, there is an objection in principle to what we are calling here 'legislative' treaties, i.e. treaties concluded by some states which purport to determine the law and obligations incumbent upon other states that are not parties.

Customary international law and Article 34 of the Vienna Convention adopt the position that in general a treaty does not create obligations or rights for a third state without its consent. The effect of this would be that there are no legislative treaties in the sense described, but occasionally suggestions are nevertheless made that certain treaties are in fact legislative.

Lord McNair, for example, argued that there could be 'dispositive' treaties creating or affecting territorial rights and effectively imposing legal consequences on third parties, and 'constitutive or semi-legislative' treaties establishing international legal regimes of one kind or another.

In 1920 a commission of jurists appointed by the League of Nations to consider the legal position regarding the Aaland Islands, lying at the mouth of the Gulf of Bothnia between Sweden and Finland, concluded that a treaty of 1856 created a special international status for the islands such that every interested state (whether party to the 1856 treaty or not) had the right to insist upon compliance with the treaty provisions.

In the *Reparation for Injuries Suffered in the Service of the United Nations Case* (1949) the World Court held that the UN Charter created the UN as an entity possessing 'objective international personality' such that Israel, though not a member of the UN at the relevant time, was obliged to acknowledge the UN's existence and pay it damages for the assassination of the UN's representative in Jerusalem by Jewish terrorists.

Professor Hans Kelsen has gone further and suggested that the Charter imposes general obligations on non-members by virtue of Article 2(6), which requires the UN to 'ensure that states which are not members of the United Nations act in accordance with' the organisation's principles. Professor Kelsen himself calls this a 'revolutionary' application of the Charter, and precisely for that reason it has been strongly contested by many writers.

41. A note on the derivation of law from law-making treaties. While questions of interpretation of contractual treaties generally are settled by considering either the intent of the parties at the time they drafted the treaty or the objective ordinary meaning of the words (the latter approach is preferred in Article 31 of the Vienna Convention), law-making or quasi-constitutional treaties are often subjected to a teleological interpretation, i.e. one aiming to give effect to the treaties' purposes or aims and objects. This involves not only examining the language of the treaty and the circumstances of its drafting but also, in the words of Sir Gerald Fitzmaurice, 'the place it has come to have in international life'.

Judge Jessup, dissenting in the *South West Africa Cases* (1966), emphasised the importance of interpreting constitutional treaties so as to carry out their purposes as they are now understood in the light of contemporary standards and not simply according to the standards that applied at the time the treaty was signed. This in effect regards such an international convention as, in the famous words of United States Chief Justice John Marshall on the American Constitution, a 'living document'.

The application of a teleological approach to law-making treaties thus opens up a potentially broad area for legal development at the hands of an adventurous court.

General principles of law

42. Introduction. The precise meaning and application of Article 38(1)c of the ICJ Statute, which speaks of 'the general principles of law recognized by civilized nations', has been the subject of more fundamental disagreement than any other provision in that article.

First of all, the concept of 'civilised nations' is dubious. The idea appeared at a time when the European powers were representing themselves as the most civilised in the world, but what 'civilisation' meant in that context was always questionable. When seen from outside, European civilisation's chief attribute seemed to be mastery of the techniques of war. It is indicative that a leading Japanese figure at the end of the Russo-Japanese War (1905) felt able to claim that Japan had finally proved she was a 'civilised nation' by destroying the Russian fleet in the Far East, and it is perhaps even more significant that the European powers themselves accepted that victory as an indication that Japan should be admitted to the club of leading states. With these origins, the test of 'civilisation' is, not surprisingly, no longer much emphasised.

As to the idea of general principles, there are basically three divergent understandings of this source:

(a) that it allows the court to adopt specific rules of procedure or maxims of law which are generally applied in national courts;

(b) that it permits the court to treat the principles of national law as a reservoir of principles from which general concepts of law can be derived and applied on the international level;

(c) that it enables the court to discover and use the fundamental principles which underlie the legal organisation of the international community, in other words, to apply natural law.

43. Rules of procedure and maxims of law. Lord Walter Phillimore, considered by some one of the great international lawyers of his generation and the co-author of Article 38 (along with Elihu Root, an American lawyer and Secretary of State), indicated that he intended general principles to mean rules of procedure, basic principles of legal conduct, such as good faith, and principles like *res judicata*. This category could also cover, in his view, maxims of law (such as that 'no man should be judge in his own case', *nemo judex in causa sua*).

The advantage of limiting Article 38(1)c this strictly is that it confines the court to 'principles' which are almost unarguable and incontrovertible, as well as being necessarily almost universal in widely differing legal systems. It is clear, for example, that no genuinely legal system could resolve disputes by allowing one party to judge his own case, and that no legal system could keep functioning if there were not some device like *res judicata* for preventing repetitive litigation by the same parties with the same subject matter in dispute.

44. Difficulties with the 'rules and maxims' view. The difficulty with such a limitation is that it is barren from the point of view of promoting the development of international law, since it depends absolutely on the most traditional elements in national legal systems, and it runs the risk of letting a court simply label the situation before it in a particular case with a tag that does not correspond to the human and political realities at stake.

In the *Temple of Preah Vihear Case* (1962) the ICJ was faced with a territorial dispute between Thailand and Cambodia in which Cambodia relied on the failure of Thailand to protest when French colonial maps of the disputed area were drawn in the early 1900s in such a way as to show the area in Cambodia and not in Thailand. As part of its rationale the court stated simply: *qui tacet consentire videtur si loqui debuisset ac potuisset,* 'he who is silent appears to consent if he should, and could, have spoken'. This was presented with little explanation of how it applied to the facts of the case, and Sir Percy Spender, a dissenting judge, criticised the result as reducing the law to the 'formless content of a maxim', that is, a legal truism that is so general that one cannot anchor the law of the case to the particular facts of the case. He considered this objectionable because such reliance on a maxim risks concealing a court's sloppy thinking or poor reasoning.

The view that general principles are essentially rules of procedure or maxims also overlooks the possibility (suggested by Sir Gerald Fitzmaurice) that principles should be understood to answer the question 'why?' whereas rules answer the question 'how?'. Principles must in this view be able to offer explanations about the applicable law and not simply instructions about what to do.

Another dissenting judge in the *Temple of Preah Vihear Case*, Judge Alfaro, seemed to adopt this view when he suggested that the usefulness of national law was in providing the means for analysing particular rules in national legal systems so as to extract the motivating reason that lies behind them for application by the court on the international level.

Thus the tendency of modern thinking seems to be away from Phillimore's narrow concept of general principles.

45. The 'reservoir of principles'. The idea of the reservoir of principles (a phrase popularised by Sir Humphrey Waldock) may more easily accommodate this newer tendency than the idea of maxims could, although even this concept has the limitation that it tends to exclude substantive principles (about which there may be disagreement) and to concentrate on the rules which drive the national legal systems through their work. The reservoir idea focusses on technical points like the principles of liability, reparations, and the administration of justice.

This emphasis on legal technicalities and procedures may, however, suit lawyers, especially in those countries where the legal profession sees its role to be oiling the machinery of power instead of improving the situation of individuals through law.

46. Natural law. The narrowness of the two preceding views of general principles has led some lawyers to seek ways of expanding the scope of this concept in order to bring into consideration factors that otherwise may be overlooked by a tribunal, in particular natural law.

47. General principles in 'internationalised' contracts. Reason and common sense, which have traditionally been important in the English legal system (as witness Lord Mansfield's view quoted in 1:11), may, for example, enter international law through this source. In the *Abu Dhabi Arbitration* (1951), a case between the sheikhdom of Abu Dhabi and an oil development company, the arbitrator, Lord Asquith, spoke of national law rules 'so firmly grounded in reason' as to be part of the 'principles rooted in the good sense and common practice of the generality of civilised nations – a sort of – "modern law of nature"'.

In arbitrations of this kind, involving so-called 'internationalised contracts' (*see* 10:32) between a sovereign and a private company, general principles of law are often prescribed as the law of the case. This is because the parties usually cannot agree to apply one particular national law, while at the same time, since one party is not a state, the dispute may arguably be outside the scope of those parts of public international law that are generated by custom and treaties. This application of general principles is unique therefore in fitting neither into public nor private law and consequently not deriving its jurisprudential validity from any positivist sources like legislation or consent. Lord Asquith's classification of this application as resort to a 'modern law of nature' therefore seems apt.

48. General principles and human rights. But it has been urged that natural law must play a role also in determining questions that would on the face of it appear purely questions of public law, most notably with regard to human rights. In the *South West Africa Cases* (1966) Judge Tanaka, dissenting, argued that Article 38(1)c incorporated natural law into international law, in as much as the text of that article was a compromise between the positivism of Root and Phillimore and the views of some continental jurists who saw it as allowing reference to '*la conscience juridique des peuples civilisés*', the juridical consciousness and morality of civilised peoples (not, one notes, simply of civilised states). This argument is an interesting reminder that one cannot always rely on the interpretation of a provision offered by its drafter when others may have approved the text with quite different ideas and understandings in mind (*see* also 1:22).

Equity as an element of general principles

49. Equity in national law. In Anglo-American legal systems 'equity' is usually distinguished from 'law' insofar as equity allows the flexible disposition of cases according to ideas of fairness rather than according to the strict application of rules of law which could, in the circumstances of the case, produce unfair or unjust results. This view of equity originally implied the judge's (and particularly the Lord Chancellor's) discretionary power to determine a case in light of the general principles of justice, although in recent centuries even equity has been considerably narrowed and regulated by the development of rules of equity – a somewhat paradoxical turn of events.

50. Equity in international law: in the reservoir of principles or autonomous? In international law the position of equity is less restricted, though there are theoretical problems regarding where it fits into the scheme of Article 38. When the *Diversion of Water from the Meuse Case* (1937) was before the Permanent Court of International Justice, Judge Hudson, concurring, supported the view that equity was a part of international law and meant essentially 'general principles of justice' derivable from the principles observable in national legal systems. Thus, equity would appear in this view to be a part of that reservoir of principles which was discussed above.

In more recent years, however, the ICJ has appeared to conceive of equity's being implicit in the rules of international law in a more general way than Judge Hudson did. In the *North Sea Continental Shelf Cases*, the court indicated that just and equitable decisions find their 'objective justification in considerations lying not outside but within the rules'. In the *Fisheries Jurisdiction (Merits) Case* (1974) it saw the main problem as 'not a matter of finding simply an equitable solution, but an equitable solution derived from the applicable law'.

In the *Continental Shelf (Tunisia* v. *Libya)* Case (1982) the World Court continued the process of making equity an autonomous feature of international law. It said in part:

> Equity as a legal concept is a direct emanation of the idea of justice. The court whose task is by definition to administer justice is bound to apply it. In the course of the history of legal systems the term 'equity' has been used to define various legal concepts. It was often contrasted with the rigid rules of positive law, the severity of which had to be mitigated in order to do justice. In general, this contrast has no parallel in the development of international law; the legal concept of equity is a general principle directly applicable as law. Moreover, when applying positive international law, a court may choose among several interpretations of the law the one which appears, in the light of the circumstances of the case, to be closest to the requirements of justice ... [The court] is bound to apply equitable principles as part of international law, and to balance up the various considerations which it regards as relevant in order to produce an equitable result. While it is clear that no rigid rules exist as to the exact weight to be attached to each element in the case, this is very far from being an exercise of discretion or conciliation; nor is it an operation of distributive justice.

This view of equity implies a conception that has moved some distance from the reservoir of principles idea insofar as it sees equity arising from the nature of international law as a system seeking to achieve justice rather than from the specific principles of national legal systems.

51. Ex aequo et bono. Article 38(2) of the ICJ Statute gives the court power to decide a case *ex aequo et bono*, i.e. according to what is fair and appropriate, if the parties to the case agree. This is not the same thing as applying equity within the established system of law. *Ex aequo et bono* implies deciding according to what suits the facts of the case, regardless of the law. This is often said to be in effect a licence for the court to legislate in the sense of creating new law for the parties, and is rarely resorted to because hardly ever authorised by the parties in cases before the court.

Judicial decisions and the writings of publicists

52. Judicial decisions. Whereas the items listed in Article 38(1)a–c may be thought of as in themselves 'sources' of law, Article 38(1)d refers to judicial decisions as 'subsidiary means for the determination' of law. This is taken by many authorities to indicate that judicial decisions of national or international tribunals should be consulted only as a convenient device for discovering what the law, created elsewhere and by other processes, actually is.

This understanding is reinforced by the statement in Article 59 of the Statute that a decision of the ICJ itself is binding only on the parties in the particular case, that is, it is not binding on the court or parties in later cases: so there is no doctrine of *stare decisis* or binding precedent under the Statute. Even less therefore would the court be bound to apply the decisions of lesser courts or tribunals.

Although this view of the role of courts as 'law-determining' agencies rather than law-creating ones is thus impeccably logical, it may in fact overlook the inevitable creative impact of judicial decisions which seem to mark a watershed between one legal regime and another. The *Anglo-Norwegian Fisheries Case* (1951), for example, is generally regarded as having powerfully encouraged the development of a new method for measuring the territorial sea of states, and, while the ICJ did not create the new law, its decision played a more creative role than simply that of determining the law.

In the *Gulf of Maine Case* (1984) the court went so far as to say that its decision in the *North Sea Continental Shelf Cases* (1969) had exercised a formative influence on the development of the relevant law of the sea.

This is really not surprising given the importance in international law of reason in shaping the law's development. A well-reasoned decision is bound to influence the course of the law's development and will indeed be looked to precisely for that purpose. The effect of judicial decisions thus is rather more subtle than a strict reading of Article 38 might suggest.

53. Factors affecting the usefulness of court decisions. As Professor Georg Schwarzenberger has suggested, the critical factors in deciding whether to refer to, or rely on, judicial decisions are in the end less related to their theoretically subordinate status than to their intrinsic merit. That merit is affected by two considerations: the intellectual and legal reputation of the particular court and the degree to which the decision in question is itself cogently and reasonably argued.

The reputation of a court in terms of its reliability on issues of international law depends on such things as its ability to arrive at decisions free of extraneous political influence or pressure, its international orientation and the degree to which it is inclined to respect international law, and the general legal standards it maintains in its hearing and decision of cases.

Professor Schwarzenberger, applying this test to the ICJ itself, gives it high marks, although he feels that occasionally the need to accommodate a sufficient number of disparate views among the judges to produce a majority decision leads to opinions that simply are not persuasive presentations of the law. In contrast, the dissenting opinions of individual judges are often better argued because such judges can present a single view coherently and without fudging in order to attract the support of colleagues.

The ICJ is not by any means the only international tribunal. The Court of Justice of the European Communities and the European Court of Human Rights are both judicial bodies of acknowledged standing, although the fact they are charged specifically with interpreting certain treaties means that their decisions are not always generally relevant to international law at large.

54. Arbitral decisions. Another important body of judicial decisions springs from international arbitration proceedings, either of the state-private party variety, such as the *Abu Dhabi Arbitration* mentioned earlier (*see* 47), or the state-state kind, like the *UK-France Delimitation of the Continental Shelf Arbitration* (1977-78) (often referred to as the *English Channel Arbitration*). The first type is usually resorted to under a private contract or because the parties are not subject to a common international or national legal regime. State-state arbitrations are sometimes preferred to submission of the case to the ICJ because arbitration provides more flexibility than reference to a court: the parties to an arbitration proceeding can jointly appoint the arbitrator or panel of arbitrators and they can restrict by agreement the questions which the tribunal is allowed to consider and the law it is to apply in reaching a decision.

While these factors encourage arbitration they do raise questions about the general usefulness and applicability of the resulting decisions. To the extent that an arbitrator might be chosen for reasons of politics rather than because of his legal erudition, and to the extent that the law which the parties prescribe is unduly restricted, so that relevant legal issues are not raised or determined, an arbitral decision may be of limited value to the student of international law who is attempting to determine what the general law is on some point. Such decisions must therefore be handled cautiously.

55. Teachings of publicists. 'Publicists' in this connotation means primarily scholars and legal experts writing studies of international law and its application.

In the early development of international law writings of this kind by such men as Suarez, Grotius and de Vattel were fundamentally important in influencing that law's development. The growth of custom, the emphasis on state practice, and more recently the generation of law on a large scale by international conventions have all tended to reduce the current role played by the writings of publicists. Nevertheless, courts, and particularly national courts, occasionally do rely on such writings as coherent and well-reasoned statements of the law, particularly with regard to questions of customary law or ones relating to specialised areas of expertise.

The difficulty with relying too heavily on the writings of publicists is that even the best lawyer and scholar may give inadequate attention to certain aspects of a problem when he is simply writing to please himself rather than, say, writing an arbitral award or acting as an international judge. The writer does not have the stimulation of engaging in or hearing careful arguments in a courtroom that aim to explore every relevant question, and inevitably his writing may suffer from that lack.

The persuasive value of the very best legal writing nevertheless remains a significant input into the development of international law.

56. Codification and the progressive development of international law. As indicated above (*see* **22**), Article 13(1)a of the UN Charter charges the General Assembly with responsibility for 'encouraging the progressive development of international law and its codification'. To help it in this activity the Assembly created the International Law Commission, a body of legal experts chosen to reflect the positions of the major legal systems of the world. The ILC prepares drafts of conventions on subjects for which the development of binding treaty law seems desirable. Such treaties, once signed and in force, of course, fall into the category of international conventions under Article 38(1)a of the ICJ Statute.

But do the drafts of these treaties, along with the usually detailed commentaries which the ILC prepares with them, have themselves any standing as 'sources'?

Sir Hirsch Lauterpacht argued that such texts, in view of the expertise of the ILC members who draft them, at least can be regarded as writings of the 'most highly qualified publicists' under Article 38(1)d of the Statute.

As noted earlier, Judge Sorensen, dissenting in the *North Sea Continental Shelf Cases*, suggested that the process of producing the text of a treaty in the ILC and the General Assembly could almost have a kind of legislative effect. He also went on to note that the

> very act of formulating or restating an existing customary rule may have the effect of defining its contents more precisely and removing such doubts as may have existed as to its exact scope or the modalities of its application. The opportunity may also be taken of adapting the rule to contemporary conditions, whether factual or legal in the international community.

Thus the process of setting down existing law ('codification') may merge with the process of promoting new law ('progressive development'). A draft treaty may be consulted as a persuasive restatement of current law but the elements of new law in it may be taken up at the same time.

The ICJ, as in the *Interpretation of the Agreement of 25 March 1951 between the WHO and Egypt Case* (1980), has been prepared to take note of ILC drafts in attempting to determine the applicable law.

The precise weight to be accorded such drafts would appear to depend on the relative balance in them between progressive development and mere codification and the persuasiveness and reasonableness of the rules they set out.

Progress test 2

1. What are the 'sources' of international law? **(2)**
2. What is the distinction between custom and usage? **(6)**
3. List ten evidences of state practice. **(8)**
4. What are the elements of customary international law? **(9–13)**
5. Define *opinio juris*. **(10)**
6. May *opinio juris* be inferred from state practice alone? **(10)**
7. How long a duration is required for the formation of a rule of customary law? **(11)**
8. What are the legal consequences of the difference between a persistent objector and a subsequent objector? **(13)**
9. Is regional customary law possible? **(19)**
10. How does *jus cogens* affect your answer to Question 9? **(20)**
11. May a treaty generate customary law? **(23)**
12. May United Nations resolutions generate customary law? **(29–33)**
13. Are there such things as 'legislative' treaties? **(40)**
14. Explain the teleological approach to treaty interpretation. **(41)**
15. Does Article 38(1)c of the ICJ Statute refer to natural law? **(46–48)**
16. Is equity part of international law? **(49–50)**
17. Is there really no precedent in the case law of the ICJ? **(50)**

Bibliography

Fitzmaurice, 'The General Principles of International Law Considered from the Standpoint of the Rule of Law', 92 Hague Recueil at 7.

Fitzmaurice, 'The Law and Procedure of the International Court of Justice: Treaty Interpretation and certain other Treaty Points', *British Yearbook of International Law*, vol 28 (1951).

Kelsen, *The Law of the United Nations*, pp 106–110, 5th imp. (N.Y., 1966).

McNair, *The Law of Treaties*, Chap. XIV, 2nd ed. (Oxford, 1961).

Nish, *The Origins of the Russo-Japanese War*, Introduction (Longman, London, 1985)

Schwarzenberger, *International Law*, vol. I, pp. 30 ff, 3rd ed. (1957).

Waldock, 'General Course on Public International Law', 106 *Hague Recueil* at 54.

3 The relationship between international and municipal law

1. Introduction. The relationship of international law and national law ('municipal' or 'domestic' law in international legal parlance) has two aspects:

(*a*) the jurisprudential question of the relation between the two systems of law; and

(*b*) the practical problem of the effect of each system's law within the other system.

For example, how, if at all, should international treaties or custom operate within a national legal system? What should be the effect on the international level of national legislation?

The relationship of the two sytems: monist or dualist?

2. Monism. *Monism* is the view that international law and municipal law are interrelated parts of one overarching legal system.

Some writers take this to imply that the two parts must operate so that municipal law is consistent with international law, thereby in effect subordinating municipal to international.

For others, particularly advocates of natural law, monism implies that each part must be in accord with the values and rules of the overarching system. Thus, Judge Tanaka, dissenting in the *South West Africa Cases* (1966) discussed earlier (*see* 1:22), presupposes a monist position in which human rights are the same, and apply equally, in the two branches of law.

There are even monists who argue that municipal law derives its effectiveness from international law which, by recognising a state's exclusive sovereignty in its own territory, establishes the necessary precondition for that state to claim unchallenged observance of its municipal law.

Some positivists (notably Prof. Hans Kelsen) also take a monist view, apparently on the basis that the will of states provides a common factor in the generation of both municipal and international law.

3. Dualism. *Dualism*, on the other hand, holds that international law and municipal law are quite separate systems and do not stand in any relationship of superiority or subordination to each other. Thus each may purport to govern the same matters without either one taking account of the other. This position is often advocated by positivists, who see in it the opportunity for a state to apply municipal law on the national level without any obligation to make it conform to international law.

4. Avoiding the problem. In an attempt to avoid the problem of some hierarchy of importance between municipal and international law, Sir Gerald Fitzmaurice has suggested that the controversy is in fact misconceived, since the two systems operate in quite distinct fields and one therefore cannot really govern matters entirely within the other's sphere. This does not altogether settle the question, however, at least as regards areas of law that are shared between the two systems, human rights being the prime example. It also may tend to limit the ability of the individual at the national level to enforce his internationally recognised rights, since it allows the offending state to argue that it has no obligation on the national level to observe such rights but merely an obligation on the international level *vis-à-vis* other states. Given that internationally recognised rights (or rights arising from natural law) can only be made effective on the national level (since almost everybody lives in, or is the citizen of, some state), this is a serious drawback.

In practice, however, it appears that the monist/dualist controversy has less influence on the interaction between the two systems than does the fact that the problem usually arises within one system or the other, with the persons responsible for resolving the problem feeling bound to operate completely within the rules of their particular system. Thus the Lord Justice-General, Lord Dunedin, in the Scottish case of *Mortensen* v. *Peters* (1906) declared that his was not 'a tribunal sitting to decide whether an Act of the Legislature is *ultra vires* as in contravention of generally acknowledged principles of international law'. This statement appears less a denial of the supremacy of international law than simply a reference to the obvious fact that a Scottish court is constituted and empowered to act entirely by virtue of, and in accordance with, the law of Scotland. But this leaves open the important question of whether, and to what extent, international law should be regarded as part of the law of Scotland, or, indeed, of any other country.

National law in the international system

5. General rule. Generally, national law has no effect on the duties or obligations of states on the international level. Thus, a state may not plead its own municipal law as an excuse or justification for violating international law.

International law in the municipal system

6. Introduction. In general, customary law and treaty law are the two areas of international law whose relationship to municipal law is most often at issue. The 'general principles of law recognised by civilised nations' are presumably less significant because the narrow traditional view of their originating in national law allows any reference to international law to be short-circuited by simply turning from the beginning to the principles of the particular municipal system in which the case has arisen. This view is less helpful if one looks to general principles for the clarification of human rights or equity in the international sense.

Because it is usually national courts that must resolve questions about the application of international law, differences in approach have developed from country to country. The following sections look at the position of states whose law will be of most interest to students in the major English-language legal systems.

Customary international law in the United Kingdom

7. Incorporation versus transformation. A long debate has raged in British, and particularly English, courts about the position of customary international law in British law and about how that position is achieved. In *Triquet* v. *Bath* (1764) Lord Chief Justice Mansfield affirmed that the law of nations 'in its full extent' was 'part of the law of England'. But precisely what this meant and how it came about continued to be the subject of some debate.

Lord Mansfield himself, as noted earlier (*see* 1:11), was a believer in natural law and apparently adopted the monist view that the international and municipal legal systems were interrelated in such a way that rules of customary international law were, where relevant, automatically part of English law without any action by courts, Crown or Parliament. This automatic inclusion of international law is known as *incorporation.*

The opposing doctrine, called *transformation*, maintains on the other hand that international customary law does not become applicable in the English legal system unless and until its rules are transformed into rules of English law in some appropriate way (e.g. by judicial decision or Act of Parliament).

In practice, the two doctrines may often produce the same result. But in theory they are quite different in as much as transformation, by not recognising the direct applicability of customary international law, tends to a dualist and positivist conclusion and may limit the freedom of municipal judges to apply that law.

The leading cases in this area are often thought to demonstrate a movement away from Lord Mansfield's eighteenth-century monism towards dualism in the nineteenth and twentieth centuries, although in fact a careful reading of the decisions reveals that the *ratio decidendi* did not always reach the monist/dualist controversy.

British cases on customary international law and British law

8. Triquet *v.* **Bath** (1764). The problem for Lord Mansfield in this case was whether an Act of Parliament dealing with some aspects of what we would now call diplomatic immunity was the only law English courts could apply on that subject, or whether they could look to what we now call customary international law as well. Lord Mansfield upheld the view that such international law in its full extent was part of the law of England. The Act of Parliament itself, insofar as it dealt with the question at issue, had to be understood as merely declaratory of international law and had not been thought a necessary precondition for English courts to apply the international rules: these rules could thus be applied without an Act of Parliament. In effect, therefore, English courts could apply customary international law where English law was silent on the point at issue.

9. R. *v.* **Keyn (1876).** The precise meaning and scope of the judgment given on behalf of a bare majority of the Court for Crown Cases Reserved by Lord Chief Justice Cockburn has been much debated. Many of the problems argued over by later commentators may be resolved, however, by a strict analysis of the decision based squarely on the precise *ratio decidendi* which Lord Cockburn established by the way he formulated the main issue in the case.

The facts were that Keyn, the German captain of a German merchant ship, was charged under English law before an English court with manslaughter after a collision between his ship and a British ship in the English Channel at a point within three miles of the English coast.

The issue was therefore whether an English court could exercise criminal jurisdiction over a foreigner with regard to a crime allegedly committed on a foreign ship at sea within three miles of the English coast, having in mind that international law was said to recognise the right of the coastal state to claim as part of its territory (and hence exercise jurisdiction over) the area of sea up to three miles from its coastline (the so-called 'three-mile limit of the territorial sea'). Lord Cockburn held that the English court could not exercise jurisdiction.

The *ratio decidendi* was as follows. Under customary international law, English jurisdiction over a foreigner on board a foreign ship could be exercised if, at the relevant times, that foreigner was subject to English law by reason of his ship's being in English territorial waters. But the extent of English territorial waters was in doubt. International law on the width of the territorial sea was in fact debated; even if that were clear, had England chosen to claim the rights accorded her under international law so as to make the relevant area of the sea subject to the jurisdiction of English courts?

Such a claim would be necessary since international law merely *allowed* jurisdiction over a three-mile territorial sea to those states wishing to claim it but did not automatically confer it on them. To make such a claim a state had to offer 'some outward manifestation of the national will, in the shape of open practice or municipal legislation, so as to amount, at least constructively, to an occupation of that which was before unappropriated.'

As regards the present case, there had been no such manifestation of the national will by, for example, an Act of Parliament, and therefore no claim had been made to English jurisdiction over those areas of the sea where international law might have allowed that jurisdiction. Without such a claim, English courts could not act as if their jurisdiction had been extended to the sea areas in question.

Read in this way *R.* v. *Keyn* does *not* stand for the general proposition that international law can only be applied by English courts if first transformed into English law by Act of Parliament. Thus, when Parliament, by the Territorial Waters Jurisdiction Act 1878, responded to the decision by adopting the three-mile limit, it was merely making that claim which Lord Cockburn had found lacking and was *not* transforming the rule of international law into English law.

10. West Rand Central Gold Mining Co. *v.* **R. (1905).** The basic issue here was whether under international law Britain, as conqueror of South Africa in the Boer War (1899–1902), was liable for the financial obligations of its South African predecessor government towards the plaintiff company. The King's Bench Division held that international law imposed no such liability. Thus the court did not have to reach the incorporation question but merely had to consider how to find what the international law on the matter was. A failure by later judges and commentators to appreciate this key point about the decision has led to considerable confusion on the problem in British legal thinking.

Lord Chief Justice Alverstone began his judgment by reaffirming that international customary law would be acknowledged and applied by English courts when appropriate, but he went on to indicate that this raised the question of how the existence of a rule of customary international law could be established to the satisfaction of an English court. In answer, he said that 'the international law sought to be applied must ... be proved by satisfactory evidence, which must show either that the particular proposition put forward has been recognised and acted upon by our own country, or that it is of such a nature, and has been so widely and generally accepted, that it can hardly be supposed that any civilised state would repudiate it.'

This statement accords with the traditional view on the formation of customary law and is quite in keeping with the position that such law would be regarded by English courts as applicable through incorporation.

Using language rather loosely, but still addressing himself to the problem of proving the existence of a customary law rule, Lord Alverstone went on to observe, however, that Lord Mansfield's remarks on incorporation 'ought not to be construed so as to include as part of the law of England opinions of text-writers' on matters for which no ⎿ pporting British state practice could be found. Still less would courts regard as incorporated writings which were contrary to English law.

This, again, is not at variance with the doctrine of incorporation, since that doctrine is concerned with custom as a source of law and not with the writings of publicists as a source.

But by introducing the problem of proving the existence of a rule of customary law by satisfactory evidence, Lord Alverstone has been mistakenly supposed by some to have implied that such a rule can be considered by a British court only as a matter of 'fact' rather than a rule of law binding as such. If this were correct, it would raise serious doubts about whether customary international law, as law, could ever be incorporated into the law of England, since judicially noticed 'facts' merely help to determine how the law is applied rather than determine what the content of the law is.

If customary international law is regarded only as a 'fact' (which of itself has no binding character), then it would seem that the transformation doctrine would necessarily be the only correct one: that the international legal 'fact' becomes binding in a British court only after being changed into 'law' by some mechanism of the British legal system. On that basis the rule of customary law would be operative in the British legal system *only* as a rule of British law. But this does not seem to be what Lord Alverstone actually meant, since his remarks were in the context of proving the existence of a customary rule, not of applying it in a British court.

11. Later cases. Nevertheless, later judges have had a good deal of difficulty on this point, and have, in addition, provided much scope for confusing the student of international law (and each other) by using the language of incorporation while in fact seeming to think in terms of transformation.

In *Chung Chi Cheung* v. *R.* (1939), for example, Lord Atkin, delivering the opinion of the Privy Council, said that 'so far, at any rate, as the courts of this country are concerned, international law has no validity save in so far as its principles are accepted and adopted by our own domestic law'. In *Ex p. Thakrar* (1974) Lord Denning rightly took this to bear the meaning that transformation was necessary for an international rule to '*become* part of our law' (emphasis supplied), clearly indicating thereby that such a rule could not be automatically part of English law merely by virtue of being part of international law. Yet Lord Atkin went on to say that English courts 'acknowledge the existence of a body of rules which nations accept amongst themselves' and would 'seek to ascertain what the relevant rule is, and having found it, they will treat it as incorporated into the domestic law.'

The two parts of Lord Atkin's speech taken together seem to mean in effect that transformation is the operative rule of law which determines the position of customary international law in the British municipal system, while incorporation is simply the rule of judicial procedure that explains how transformation is made to work in practice. In effect, then, British courts will 'incorporate' into their legal analysis rules of international custom that have been 'transformed' into British law.

12. Precedent. This is an inherently unsatisfactory situation, particularly in regard to the problem of precedent. Lord Scarman pointed out in *Thai-Europe Tapioca Service Ltd* v. *Govt of Pakistan* (1975) that 'a rule of international law, once incorporated (*sic*) into our law by decisions of a competent court, is not an inference of fact but a rule of law. It therefore becomes part of our municipal law and the doctrine of *stare decisis* applies as much to that as to a rule of law with a strictly municipal provenance.'

To his credit, Lord Denning later came to accept that this result was ridiculous insofar as it threatened to make British law more and more out of step with international developments as time went by. In *Trendtex Trading Corp.* v. *Central Bank of Nigeria* (1977) he faced the issue squarely and produced, it is submitted, the correct answer:

> Under the doctrine of incorporation, when the rules of international law change, our English law changes with them. But, under the doctrine of transformation, the English law does not change. It is bound by precedent.
> ... As between these two schools of thought, I now believe that the doctrine of incorporation is correct. Otherwise I do not see that our courts could ever recognise a change in the rules of international law.
> ... the rules of international law, *as existing from time to time*, do form part of our English law. (emphasis supplied)

The words 'from time to time' are particularly important in that they imply English law's continuing relationship with international law, which the courts simply recognise and rely upon as necessary in particular cases. This effectively represents a return to the true doctrine of incorporation as approved by Lord Mansfield.

13. Conclusions from the English cases. Thus the proper view would appear to be that a rule of customary international law binding internationally upon Britain at the time relevant to a particular case is directly enforceable in British courts as part of the law which those courts are empowered to apply and should no more be regarded merely as a matter of 'fact' than are Acts of Parliament or decisions of the Court of Appeal.

The logic of this monist view of incorporation is not, however, maintained in the almost unanimously held opinion of nineteenth and twentieth century judges that rules of customary international law which are contrary to British statute or case law are not incorporated into British law. Lord Denning, by treating newly developed customary international law as automatically incorporated into English law even to the detriment of prior precedent, went some way to uphold this logic. But the supremacy of Parliament and its statutes remains unchallenged.

14. A Scottish case. In *Mortensen* v. *Peters* (1906) the Scottish Court of Justiciary was faced with an appeal by the Danish captain of a Norwegian-registered fishing boat against his conviction of having violated a statutory prohibition of fishing in the Moray Firth at a point beyond the three-mile limit. Mortensen argued that the statute could not apply to a foreigner outside the territorial jurisdiction of the British Crown and that a point beyond three miles from the coast was outside that jurisdiction according to international law. In interpreting the statute it could not be presumed, he argued, that Parliament meant either to exceed its jurisdiction or to violate the established rules of international law. According to international law a state's jurisdiction extended only to three miles from the coast except in the case of bays *inter fauces terrae* ('within the enclosure of the land'); the Moray Firth, however, was not, according to international legal writers, such a bay.

As noted earlier (*see* 4), Lord Dunedin declined to consider any questions relating to the compatibility of the statute with international law. He considered the issue entirely one of the construction to be put on the statute, a question that involved interpreting it according to the law which the court could apply, including such international law as had 'been adopted and made part of the law of Scotland'. He seized upon the defendant's agreement that under international law jurisdiction could be exercised over a bay *inter fauces terrae* and examined whether it would be conceivable that Parliament had intended to justify British jurisdiction by treating the Moray Firth as such a bay. Scottish legal writings, the similar categorising of other bays by statute, and cases allowing a state to legislate for such a bay all indicated that Parliament could conceivably have intended to class the Moray Firth in that way. The appeal therefore failed.

At the end of the day, then, the strict *ratio decidendi* of this opinion did not require the court to uphold an Act of Parliament that was in violation of international law, nor did it require the court to apply or refuse to apply customary international law. The court was merely applying an Act of Parliament whose interpretation depended in part on rules of international law which the court could take into account as part of the law of Scotland. It is true, nevertheless, that such rules would be part of that law by adoption, in other words, by a process of transformation. 'There is no such thing', Lord Dunedin said, 'as a standard of international law extraneous to the domestic law of a kingdom, to which appeal may be made.'

Treaty law in United Kingdom law

15. General note. The relationship of international treaty law to British municipal law is strongly affected by the allocation of treaty-making authority in the British constitutional system to the Crown, i.e. to the executive, and not to Parliament. If Parliament is the supreme law-maker within Britain, can a treaty operate as law internally without Parliament's having legislated its contents in statutes?

In theory, international law recognises the possibility that a treaty might operate on the national level without an act of Parliament, in which case the treaty would be regarded as 'self-executing'. A treaty which would not operate unless enacted by the legislature as national law is termed a 'non-self-executing' treaty.

In practice, however, this distinction is not very relevant to British law, since only treaties relating to the conduct of war or the transfer of territory are considered to form part of British law without legislation. The cases insist on the necessity of acts of Parliament in all other situations regardless of the nature or purpose of the treaty.

British cases on treaties and British law

16. The Parlement Belge case. *The Parlement Belge* (1879) is the leading case in this area, and was decided by Sir Robert Phillimore, the outstanding English international lawyer of the time, as a matter of fundamental constitutional principle. The facts were that the United Kingdom, by treaty entered into with Belgium, gave Belgian postal ships the status of public ships of war, thereby under international law effectively exempting such ships from the civil jurisdiction of British courts. One of these ships, *The Parlement Belge*, collided with, and damaged, a British vessel, whose owners then sued the Belgian ship in the Admiralty Division claiming compensation. The defence offered by counsel for *The Parlement Belge* was that the ship had been excluded from British admiralty jurisdiction by the treaty and that the plaintiffs therefore could not have their case heard. In effect, according to this argument, the British owners of the damaged vessel had had their common law right to sue in this situation taken away from them by treaty.

Phillimore held that a treaty could not remove private rights in this way without an Act of Parliament. Such a use of the treaty-making prerogative of the Crown would 'be without precedent, and in principle contrary to the laws of the constitution'. Although this result might create problems for Belgian postal ships, 'the remedy ... is not to be found in depriving the British subject without his consent, direct or implied, of his right of action'.

This decision on its terms is constitutionally correct and an important protection of the rights of the citizen. The relevance of the *Parlement Belge* principle was highlighted when Britain and Ireland in 1985 signed the Anglo-Irish Agreement on Northern Island. Mr Enoch Powell MP, representing northern Protestants opposed to the agreement, argued that it had no legal effect within the United Kingdom because its provisions had not been enacted into law by Parliament.

The *Parlement Belge* precedent has, however, been applied in cases since 1879 more or less indiscriminately to all types of treaties, regardless of their character or purpose, with occasionally bizarre consequences.

17. Later misapplications and the problem of human rights. Thus one finds Lord Denning MR in *R* v. *Chief Immigration Officer, ex p. Bibi* (1976) applying the rule Phillimore intended to be a protection of private rights in such a way as to prevent an English court from enforcing the European Convention on Human Rights (to which Britain is a party) as English law. 'Treaties', he said, 'do not become part of our law until they are made law by Parliament'.

The resulting problem of the British government's being obliged, and the citizen's being entitled, to have the Convention respected in Britain while the courts cannot apply it, has provoked some judges to ingenious attempts to give that treaty some weight short of direct applicability. They emphasise its character as a statement of guiding principles or an aid to interpretation of British statutes, which are presumed not to be in conflict with the Convention.

It seems clear, however, from *IRC* v. *Collco Dealings Ltd* (1962), that where the words of a subsequent statute are unambiguously clear, they will prevail over a prior treaty. Although the words of Lord Simonds in this case might be construed to envisage a possible exception where 'broad considerations of justice or expediency' are involved, it is unlikely that any British court would refuse to apply a clearly formulated statute because it conflicted with a treaty, even one as crucially important as the European Convention on Human Rights. In consequence, persons in Britain whose rights under that Convention have been violated are compelled to raise their cases before the European Human Rights Commission, in the process expending a great deal of time and money and embarrassing the United Kingdom before European public opinion.

In *Malone* v. *Metropolitan Police Commissioner (No. 2)* (1979), for example, the Vice–Chancellor declined to apply Article 8 of the Convention (which protects the individual's privacy of correspondence) to the tapping of Mr Malone's telephone. The case was then taken to the Human Rights Commission and Court in Strasbourg, the Court ruling (in *Malone* v. *United Kingdom* on 2 August 1984) that British procedures on tapping violated the Convention's requirements for proper safeguards on interception of communications.

It must be noted, however, that the European Community Treaties are in contrast directly applicable in British courts by virtue of s. 2(1) of the European Communities Act 1972, which so provides.

18. International consequences of not applying a treaty internally. The failure to give legal effect in Britain to obligations contained in an international treaty may, as with the European Convention on Human Rights, put Britain in violation of international law, but British courts will not for that reason apply the treaty as law binding on them. In *Attorney-General for Canada* v. *Attorney-General for Ontario* (1937), Lord Atkin, delivering the opinion of the Privy Council, indicated that, while a treaty may bind the state as against the other contracting parties, Parliament may simply refuse to perform it and thus leave the state in default. The remedy for that default must then be obtained on the international level.

On that level the inadequacy of the state's municipal law system would not offer a valid defence, since, according to the International Law Commission and many case decisions, a state 'may not invoke provisions in its constitution or laws as an excuse for failure to perform' its international legal duties (1949 Declaration of the Rights and Duties of States, Article 13).

Customary international law in the United States

19. General note. In *The Paquete Habana* (1900), the United States Supreme Court stated:

> International law is part of our law, and must be ascertained and administered by the courts of justice ... For this purpose, where there is no treaty and no controlling executive or legislative act or judicial decision, resort must be had

to the customs and usages of civilized nations.

American courts frequently apply customary international law, an interesting recent example being *Filartiga* v. *Pena-Irala* (1980) which gave effect to international law against torture. (*See* also 2:31; 13:12.)

A problem arises, however, from the two-tier American legal system, with state and federal courts. State courts were for long assumed to be applying that law as part of their own common law inherited from England, with the result that each state was entitled to make its own determination of international law, apart from any conclusions the federal courts might reach on the same questions. Recently, however, certain constitutional experts have suggested that issues of international law are the concern of the national government and that therefore the opinions of federal courts on these questions should be decisive, with appeals running from contrary state court judgements to the Supreme Court itself.

The American Constitution does not help matters, as it is silent on the question of customary international law, except for an implicit reference which is contained in Article I, s. 8: 'The Congress shall have Power ... To define and punish Piracies and Felonies committed on the high Seas, and Offences against the Law of Nations.'

As in Britain, courts in the United States apply customary law without the necessity of enactment by statute. If there is relevant domestic legislation but it is contrary to customary law, the courts will normally apply the legislation, although they will interpret general or ambiguous language in a statute in a manner consistent with international law.

American courts adopt the view that neither Congress nor the President is forbidden by the Constitution to violate customary international law, although such a violation might expose the United States to legitimate international liability.

Treaty law in United States law

20. General rule. Article VI of the Constitution defines the position of treaty law in significant language:

'This Constitution, and the Laws of the United States ...; and all Treaties made ... under the Authority of the United States, shall be the supreme Law of the Land; and the Judges in every State shall be bound thereby, anything in the Constitution or Laws of any State to the Contrary notwithstanding.'

Thus treaties override state law and are appropriately subject to adjudication not only in the state courts but also in the federal system, with the Supreme Court empowered to overrule state court judgments.

21. Self-executing treaties. Because treaties are, along with Acts of Congress, the supreme law of the land, it is theoretically easier in the United States than in Britain for an appropriately drafted treaty to be 'self-executing'. The courts will look to see whether the treaty in question is 'full and complete' in and of itself, without need of implementing legislation, and capable of being applied as it stands to govern individual rights and duties. If so, it will be regarded as self-executing.

But in *Sei Fujii* v. *California* (1952), the California Supreme Court held that the treaty in question (the UN Charter) did not in the relevant parts meet this test. The plaintiff's case was that the Charter's human rights provisions forbade California to enact a statute discriminating against aliens. The court held that the 'fundamental provisions in the charter pledging cooperation in promoting observance of fundamental freedoms lack the mandatory quality and definiteness which would indicate an intent to create justiciable rights in private persons immediately upon ratification. Instead they are framed as a promise of future action by the member nations.'

22. Legislative violation of treaties. The constitutional provision making legislation and treaties equally the law of the land means in effect that treaties are not superior to federal statutes and so may, like statutes, be affected by subsequent enactments. Valid treaties still in force for the United States on the international level may therefore be inoperative in municipal law by virtue of having been superseded by a later Act of Congress, as the US Supreme Court made clear in *Edye* v. *Robertson* (*The Head Money Cases*) (1884). Thus, in *Diggs* v. *Schultz* (1972) a federal appeal court held that federal legislation aiming to evade UN Security Council sanctions against Rhodesia that were mandatory according to America's obligations under the UN Charter overrode those obligations for the purposes of American municipal law. But the plaintiff individuals and religious groups did have standing to sue the federal government on the ground that they had been directly injured by American failure to abide by the UN sanctions.

However, the Supreme Court stated in *Whitney* v. *Robertson* (1888) that when a treaty and a federal statute 'relate to the same subject, the courts will always endeavor to construe them so as to give effect to both, if that can be done without violating the language of either.'

23. 'Treaties' and 'executive agreements'. A curious feature of American law in this area is that the Constitutional definition of a treaty is different from that applied in international law. In order to be a 'treaty' under Article II, s. 2, of the Constitution, an agreement made by the President must also be approved by a two-thirds majority vote in the Senate. A treaty approved in this way then becomes 'the supreme law of the land' as discussed above.

International law would also recognise as treaties some accords reached by the President without such Senate approval, so-called 'executive agreements'. Although not provided for in the Constitution, executive agreements are often dealt with as though they were 'treaties'. This can come about because the Congress has approved of the agreement by a joint resolution of both Houses (thus giving some legislative backing while avoiding the problem of the large majority required by the Constitution in a Senate vote) or because the agreement was made pursuant to the President's power to conduct foreign relations. Executive agreements are regularly used for trade and postal accords and also in order to maintain confidentiality, which might be lost if the matter were debated in the Senate.

In *United States* v. *Belmont* (1937) the Supreme Court held that an executive agreement made in conjunction with the President's exercise of his power to recognise foreign governments overrode conflicting state laws. The court also accepted that such an agreement could be valid without Senate approval. The effect of this decision, and of *United States* v. *Pink* (1942), was (as the Supreme Court said in the latter case) to give executive agreements associated with recognition a 'similar dignity' to that of treaties as 'the law of the land'.

Unfortunately, neither the courts nor the legal writers have been able to decide the limits of the President's power to influence municipal law in this way, and there is argument particularly whether an executive agreement could, as a treaty would, override prior federal legislation. Such an effect would be very doubtful.

24. The permissible scope of treaties. Is there any limitation on the matters which executive agreements and treaties can cover while purporting to have effect as the law of the land? Although in *Missouri* v. *Holland* (1920) the Supreme Court allowed a treaty *not otherwise prohibited by the Constitution* to bring into the federal sphere a matter of concern that would without a treaty have been left by the Constitution to the states, the correct answer in general is that neither the President nor Congress may act in this regard in such a way as to violate the Constitution itself, since it is the Constitution which establishes and circumscribes the powers of both.

In the *Capps Case* (1953), Chief Judge Parker, giving judgment for a federal Court of Appeal, attempted to extend this reasoning to cover also executive agreements dealing with matters which the Constitution expressly vested in the Congress and not in the President. The effect would be that such an agreement would have no force as the law of the land on matters which the Constitution states are exclusively within the powers of Congress. This would appear a perfectly reasonable interpretation of the constitutional law at issue.

Charles Evans Hughes, speaking on the eve of taking up his appointment as Chief Justice of the United States Supreme Court in 1929, argued that the fundamental limitation on the making of treaties and agreements was that they could only 'pertain to our external relations'. Others have suggested that such accords must be limited to matters of 'international concern'. While these suggestions are at first glance quite reasonable, there is the danger that, applied too strictly, they might prevent the conclusion of treaties on such questions as human rights, where a major goal would be precisely to affect the municipal legal system.

Professor Louis Henkin, in his *Foreign Affairs and the Constitution*, has attempted to get round the problem by suggesting that human rights accords are intended to accomplish the foreign policy aim of promoting rights in other countries by reciprocal arrangements in which the United States also agrees to respect those rights. This is a good lawyer's argument.

Custom and treaties in the law of other states

25. West Germany. Article 25 of the Basic Law (Constitution) of the Federal Republic of Germany provides that 'The general rules of international law shall form part of federal law. They shall take precedence over the laws and create rights and duties directly for the inhabitants of the federal territory.' The phrase 'general rules of international law' is understood to encompass customary international law, but the Federal Constitutional Court has made clear that treaties are not covered by Article 25. The effect of this interpretation is to give customary international law precedence even over legislation, while treaties are at best merely on an equal level with statutes.

Clashes between constitutional provisions on fundamental rights and the law of the European Economic Community deriving its authority from the Treaty of Rome have caused particular difficulty. The West German Constitutional Court has taken the position that Community law cannot override such provisions, while the European Court of Justice, in *Internationale Handelsgesellschaft mbH* v. *Einfuhr and Vorratstelle fur Getreide und Futtermittel* (1970), held that the validity and effect of Community law in a member state of the EEC 'cannot be affected by allegations that it strikes at either the fundamental rights as formulated in that state's constitution or the principles of a national constitutional structure'. The European Court noted, however, that fundamental rights were part of the general principles of law which the Court was empowered to uphold.

26. Italy. For many years Italy had similar problems with the place of European law in the Italian municipal system, but in *S.p.A. Granital* v. *Amministrazione finanziaria* (1984) the Italian Constitutional Court decided that Community law should be treated as an autonomous legal system under which Italy was bound, regardless of whether it was originally treaty or customary law. This effectively reverses the long-standing and famous Italian court decision in *Costa* v. *ENEL* (1964).

27. France. The French constitutional position, by contrast, gives greater scope to treaty law. Article 55 of the Constitution of 1958 states that properly ratified treaties or agreements 'have an authority superior to that of laws' (i.e. of statutes).

28. Israel. In general, the Israeli municipal law system adopts the British attitude towards the inclusion of international customary law and the exclusion of treaty law unless there is appropriate enacting legislation by the Knesset (parliament). Interesting legal questions have arisen since 1967, however, about the application of international law by the Israeli High Court of Justice in cases arising from events outside the territory of Israel but within the territories occupied and administered by Israeli military forces. In the *Elon Moreh Case* (1979) the High Court held the establishment of an Israeli settlement in the occupied West Bank illegal under international customary law (of which the Hague Regulations of 1907 were said to be declaratory) but refused to apply relevant provisions of the Fourth Geneva Convention of 1949 on the ground that there had been no legislation transforming the Convention's provisions into the municipal law by which the Israeli courts were governed.

Without any intervening legislation, however, the High Court found it possible, in *Tsemel* v. *The Minister of Defence* (May 1983), to apply Article 78 of the Fourth Geneva Convention to the detention of persons in the areas of Lebanon occupied by Israel in 1982. This decision is the better of the two on this point, since it is clear that international law (both customary and treaty law) governs the actions of the Israeli occupation authorities in territories outside Israel, and not Israeli municipal law. As the court indicated in *Tsemel*, the actions of the executive are subject to the control of the court, whether taking place within the areas where the law of the state of Israel applies or outside them.

Clearly, when the court is sitting in judgment on executive acts outside the scope of Israeli law, the law to be applied may well be international custom and treaties, making the situation one of choice-of-law rather than of international law in municipal law.

29. Australia. Australia also has traditionally followed the British view on incorporation of customary international law into Australian Common Law and on the non-self-executing nature of most treaty law. In *Chow Hung Ching* v. *R.* (1948), however, two judges of the Australian High Court somewhat confused matters by rejecting the view of Blackstone and Mansfield that international customary law in its full extent was part of the Common Law. Rather, they believed, custom was merely a 'source' which, by implication, Australian judges could draw from or not, as they chose. But this leads to results inconsistent with the automatic application of international customary law by Australian courts and raises problems about precedent and the continuing applicability of custom similar to those Lord Denning had to deal with in *Trendtex* (*see* **12**).

Where international custom and municipal statute diverge, however, 'legislation otherwise within the power of the Commonwealth Parliament does not become invalid because it conflicts with a rule of international law' (*Polites* v. *The Commonwealth*, High Court of Australia (1945)).

An interesting feature of the Australian federal system is that the conclusion of an international agreement on some topic gives the central Commonwealth government additional legislative authority *vis-à-vis* the states. The Canberra government may enact federal legislation binding on the states in order to fulfil treaty commitments undertaken in pursuance of the Commonwealth's powers to handle 'external affairs' under s. 51 of the Commonwealth Constitution (*R* v. *Burgess, ex p. Henry* (1936). In *Koowarta* v. *Bjelke-Petersen* (1982) a divided High Court held that Australia's adherence to the International Convention on the Elimination of all Forms of Racial Discrimination was an 'external affair' entitling the Commonwealth to pass the Racial Discrimination Act (1975) which made unlawful in the states discriminatory acts based on race and related characteristics. Similarly, in *Commonwealth of Australia* v. *State of Tasmania* (1983) the High Court held that the federal government could legitimately legislate for, and regulate, a Tasmanian hydro-electric project in order to implement the Convention for the Protection of the World Cultural and Natural Heritage.

Thus treaty-making may have a direct effect on Australian municipal law insofar as it alters the division of legislative powers between state and federal governments.

In both of these recent decisions, moreover, there were separate concurring opinions from judges who believed that the Commonwealth's law-making powers under s. 51 were not limited to the implementation of treaty obligations but could extend to any matter which is a topic of international debate or concern.

Progress test 3

1. Relate the debate on monism v. dualism to the problem of human rights. (4)

2. May a state plead its municipal law as an excuse for violating international law? (5)

3. What is incorporation? **(7)**

4. What is transformation? **(7)**

5. Is the decision in *R.* v. *Keyn* consistent with that in *Triquet* v. *Bath*? **(8, 9)**

6. Did Lord Alverstone's opinion in *West Rand Central Gold Mining Co.* v. *R.* reject the doctrine of incorporation? **(10)**

7. Did Lord Atkin in *Chung Chi Cheung* v. *R.* adopt the transformation doctrine? **(11)**

8. Why did the problem of precedent bring the incorporation/transformation dispute to a head in English law? **(12)**

9. What was the judgment in *The Parlement Belge*? **(16)**

10. Does the European Convention on Human Rights operate as law in British courts without having been enacted as legislation by Parliament? **(17)**

11. What are self-executing treaties? **(15)**

12. In American law is the UN Charter a self-executing treaty? **(21)**

Bibliography

Fitzmaurice, 'The General Principles of International Law considered from the Standpoint of the Rule of Law', 92 *Hague Recueil* at 70–80.

Palestine Yearbook of International Law, vol. 1, pp. 164–174. for a translation of *Tsemel* v. *Minister of Defence*.

4 International legal personality

1. Introduction. The key issue here is: who or what has direct rights and duties under international law? An entity in that position is said to have *international legal personality*, that is, a legally recognised identity as a primary actor in the international legal system. Such an entity is then an international legal person and a *subject* of international law.

Entities which lack this direct and primary relationship are said to be merely the *objects* of international law, affected by it but not acting on its level and therefore without international legal personality.

It was natural in the period of classical international law, after independent countries had come to dominate the world scene, within the state system where they were the only actors, that only states were thought to have international legal personality. In the age of the United Nations, self-determination and human rights, however, a key development in international law has been the broadening of the category of international legal person to include non-state entities. But one may begin with states as the central legal persons in international law.

States as international legal persons

2. A simple rule. The traditional view that only states had international legal personality had at least the merit of simplicity. There was only one class of legal persons and their rights and duties were those of states. One had therefore simply to determine whether the entity under consideration was a state in order to discover if it had international legal personality.

3. Criteria for statehood. International lawyers have turned for guidance on this to the *Montevideo Convention on the Rights and Duties of States* (1933) which attempted to set out the criteria for statehood that were generally recognised in customary international law. Article I of the Convention says:

> The State as a person of international law should possess the following qualifications: (*a*) a permanent population; (*b*) a defined territory; (*c*) government; (*d*) capacity to enter into relations with other states.

Some of these criteria pose more significant problems in the determination of statehood than others. Population and territory, for example, are generally not particularly difficult aspects to deal with since even a few thousand people living permanently in a tiny area have been found sufficient to generate statehood, as in the case of Nauru.

'A defined territory' does not require fixed frontiers, at least according to American representatives arguing for the admission of Israel to the United Nations in 1948. 'Many states', it was said, including the United States, 'have begun their existence with their frontiers unsettled', and the reason for a requirement of defined territory was simply that 'one cannot contemplate a state as a kind of disembodied spirit'. The arbitral tribunal in *Deutsche Continental Gas-Gesellschaft* v. *Polish State* (1929) indicated that the issue is primarily whether the state's territory has 'a sufficient consistency'.

But the criteria of 'government' and 'capacity to enter into relations with other states' are more of a problem.

They can best be understood if viewed in the perspective of the fundamental concept that underlies and links them: sovereignty, and, along with it, its derivative concept of state independence.

4. Sovereignty. Since the beginning of the modern state system the idea of a state's absolute and exclusive authority and control over its own territory has been an essential feature of international law. That idea is summed up in the word 'sovereignty'. Statehood in general implied absolute sovereignty over a particular territory (in contrast to feudal hierarchies of lord and vassal in which authority was divided) so that no external power could claim any say in what went on there.

Independence is really the international aspect of sovereignty. On the international level, the state, if it is fully sovereign, is not under the dictatorial control or authority of any other state.

These ideas of internal and external sovereignty, which all fully sovereign states in theory possessed to the same extent, gave rise to the principle of *the sovereign equality of states*.

Thus international law has always been keenly interested in the question of who controls territory and the resolution of many important disputes has turned on the answer. Sovereignty is important not only theoretically but practically as well.

5. The Island of Palmas Case and the practical significance of sovereignty. The central role of sovereignty in traditional international law was set out in a leading arbitration decision in 1928. In the *Island of Palmas Case*, which concerned a dispute over colonial territory between the United States and The Netherlands, the arbitrator, Max Huber, linked sovereignty with the fulfilment of international law by states:

> Territorial sovereignty ... has as a corollary a duty: the obligation to protect within the territory the rights of other states, in particular their right to integrity and inviolability in peace and war, together with the rights each state may claim for its nationals in foreign territory. Without manifesting its territorial sovereignty in a manner corresponding to circumstances, the state cannot fulfil this duty.

He went on to indicate why in these circumstances the actual exercise of authority was so important in determining questions of sovereignty and, as will be seen in a later chapter, of territory:

> International law, the structure of which is not based on any super-state organisation, cannot be presumed to reduce a right such as territorial sovereignty, with which almost all international relations are bound up, to the category of an abstract right, without concrete manifestations.

One of the critical issues in present-day international law is whether the traditional picture painted by Huber is still correct in relation to such questions as human rights, self-determination, and the illegal use of military force, where rights are often necessarily abstract just when they matter most – when they are being denied.

Nevertheless, with the state system remaining at the centre of international law, Huber's analysis still seems generally valid, at least in regard to most disputes over statehood and title to territory. Consequently, international law continues generally to emphasise sovereignty and the actual exercise of authority and control as a critical factor in such disputes. This is evident in the application of the criteria of 'government' and 'capacity to enter into relations with other states' in the determination of statehood.

6. Government. This third criterion of statehood implies that there should be some organised authority capable of asserting its control throughout at least a large part of the claimed territory of the state. That authority need not be a government in the usual sense, with ministers, departments and a bureaucracy; a military or other controlling apparatus may suffice.

But this factual issue of control is often evaluated in light of the political context in which the question of statehood arises. The position may appear different depending on whether or not the previous sovereign of the territory recognises the new state.

Thus, in the case of the Belgian Congo in 1960, the country's statehood was generally acknowledged once the colonial power had left, despite the immediate eruption of civil war and the descent of the Congo into anarchy.

On the other hand, the attempt of Finland to break free of Russia after the 1917 Revolution, with results similar to those in the Congo, was not considered to have immediately created the conditions necessary for statehood. A commission of jurists appointed by the League of Nations to examine the dispute between Sweden and Finland over the Aaland Islands concluded that disorganisation of social and political life, ineffectual 'authorities', civil war, divisions in the army and the police, and foreign intervention on the side of the various contending parties, all made it very difficult to say that Finland had attained statehood at the beginning of its attempt to assert independence. 'A definitely constituted sovereign state' did not come into existence 'until a stable political organisation had been created, and until the public authorities had become strong enough to assert themselves throughout the territories of the state without the assistance of foreign troops.'

Overt foreign intervention in these situations, as the commission's statement suggests, is sometimes a critical factor in deciding on statehood, such intervention being taken to raise the possibility that the local authorities may not in fact be a 'government' but merely agents of the intervening power.

7. Independence and the problem of internal armed conflict. Thus, an unstated but vital condition for genuine government in this context is independence of foreign control. International law is particularly concerned with this factor when the new entity which is claiming statehood is being carved out of the territory of an existing state, since the law respects the right of such a state not to have its territorial integrity disrupted by foreign intervention, although secession or dismemberment of an existing state from within by indigenous forces is not prohibited by international law (even if illegal under municipal law).

This emphasis on independence creates many complicated political and legal problems in situations of internal armed conflict, since on the one hand intervention by foreign powers is at least initially forbidden, while on the other hand the aims of the people claiming to establish a new state may be not merely politically attractive but in accord with national or individual rights such as self-determination.

International law's attempt to take account of these opposing interests has focussed primarily on developing different categories of internal conflict and attaching to them varying consequences depending largely on the degree to which a particular conflict may approximate full-scale war.

This is an inherently unsatisfactory approach to the problem, not only because evaluation of the actual situation on the ground is often difficult and subject to disagreement, but also, and perhaps more importantly, because it puts a premium on raising the level of violence in order to reach the threshold beyond which the law will allow legitimate international interest and involvement.

Thus traditional international law has attempted to place internal conflict along a spectrum ranging from riots, to rebellion, to insurgency, to belligerency. *Riots* and *rebellions* are considered to be merely sporadic attacks on the existing order which at least in theory the state's forces of law and order will be able to put down. Foreign intervention in a rebellion, as by recognising rebel-held areas as a state, is illegal. It is sometimes suggested that foreign states, faced with a situation of rebellion, are entitled to help only the existing government, although many writers argue that this also would amount to forbidden intervention (*see 16:23*).

Insurgency is further along the spectrum towards full-scale war and is effectively a category designed to be as vague as possible in order to allow foreign states a certain freedom of manoeuvre in dealing with an internal war, that is, the ability to determine their relations with the conflicting parties without regard to the legal restraints that operate at the next higher level.

That level, *belligerency*, comes about when the anti-government forces have established a 'government' of some sort and a military organisation which controls a substantial area of the original state's territory and is capable of raising the level of warfare to that which may exist between states. At this point the anti-government forces qualify to be regarded as a *belligerent community* which can claim the right to be treated as a state engaged in war. This entails the right to demand neutrality from all states that are not participants in the conflict. The status of belligerent community also imposes duties on the insurgents to respect the laws of war and the persons and property of neutral foreigners.

Thus, although a belligerent community is not entitled to exchange diplomatic representatives with foreign states or to demand membership in international organisations, it does have rights and duties under international law and would appear therefore to have some measure of international legal personality.

At this stage foreign intervention in favour of the insurgents loses its illegal character, presumably on the argument that the belligerent community has already established a considerable measure of independence without foreign help, intervention then being more or less equivalent to co-belligerency on the part of allied states in an international war.

The difficulty is that these categories of internal armed conflict, which may have important implications for the question of statehood, are both elastic and vague, leaving plenty of room for error, misjudgment and bad faith in the determination of a new entity's independence of foreign control.

8. Absence of independence in newly created entity. When, following a war or other separatist movement, an entity is established which did not exist before, the question of independence is still relevant, as can be seen in the Manchukuo case. In 1931 Japan invaded the Chinese province of Manchuria and in 1932 supported the proclamation there of a new 'state', Manchukuo. Under international law, if a genuinely independent state had come into existence in Manchuria, the territory would no longer have been part of China.

A League of Nations Commission examined the matter and found that, although the Prime Minister and his cabinet were Chinese Manchurians, the heads of departments actually in control of affairs were Japanese. Japanese military occupation of the country, and the dependence of the Manchukuo government on Japanese troops to maintain the administration's authority, along with related factors, all suggested that Japan was in a position to exercise 'irresistible pressure' on the Manchukuo government. The new entity was therefore not in fact independent, and the territory of Manchukuo remained part of China.

International law has also had to deal with the situation of Transkei and other African 'homelands' (or 'Bantustans') declared independent by South Africa as a means of hiving off large numbers of black citizens in the hope of improving the white minority's demographic position and hence strengthening apartheid in the country. No state other than South Africa has recognised the independence of these homelands and it seems clear that they are economically subservient to that country and in a weak position to resist its will. The UN General Assembly has held the declarations of independence for these entities invalid and regards them as still integral parts of South Africa.

9. Loss of an existing state's governmental authority or independence. Interestingly, international law, when dealing with the question of loss of statehood, puts much less emphasis on maintenance of government control or independence.

Statehood continues even when, as in the case of the Spanish civil war in the 1930s or the chaos in Lebanon in the 1980s, the original central government loses control over some, or even all, of the national territory. There appears to be an unspoken initial presumption that in such situations it is primarily a question who is the government rather than whether the state continues to exist.

But a state clearly may voluntarily cease to exist by deliberately alienating so much of its sovereignty as no longer to be able to play an independent role in the international community, as Scotland and England both did in 1707 when uniting to form Great Britain by the Treaty of Union.

10. Cases on partial abandonment of sovereignty. Can a state lose its statehood, however, by some act short of such a complete abandonment of sovereignty?

This was the question raised in the *Austro-German Customs Union Case*, decided by the Permanent Court of International Justice in 1931. By the Treaty of St Germain in 1919 and a Protocol to that treaty in 1922, Austria had committed itself not to alienate its independence, political or economic, without the consent of the League of Nations Council. In 1931 Germany and Austria signed an agreement aimed at allowing them to 'assimilate' their tariff and economic policies. The independence of both states was reaffirmed in the agreement and each was allowed to conclude with third parties treaties that did not conflict with the Austro-German understanding.

The agreement caused an international crisis because certain countries claimed to see it as a preliminary to German annexation of Austria, and the case was referred to the World Court. A majority of the court's judges held that the customs union did violate Austria's previous undertakings not to alienate its independence, but they indicated that independence for Austria under the earlier treaty had been specially defined so as to cover such a situation as had arisen with the customs union.

The judges who did not vote for this majority opinion appear, however, to have analysed the law more correctly when they held that loss of independence would come about only through surrendering the state's sovereign authority within its own territory and thereby creating a position of subordination to another state. Restrictions that fell short of that could be accepted without loss of independence according to agreements made in exercise of the state's sovereign power to undertake international legal obligations. According to the dissenting judges, 'every treaty entered into between independent States restricts to some extent the exercise of the power incidental to sovereignty. Complete and absolute sovereignty unrestricted by any obligations imposed by treaties is impossible.'

The PCIJ had already adopted essentially this reasoning in an earlier dispute also involving Germany, *The Wimbledon Case* (1923). Under Article 380 of the Treaty of Versailles, Germany had been forced to accept that the Kiel Canal, an artificial waterway entirely within German territory and linking the country's Baltic and North Sea coasts, 'shall be maintained free and open to the vessels of commerce and of war of all nations at peace with Germany on terms of entire equality'. In 1921 Poland, with the support of France, was waging war against Soviet Russia, and a French company wished to send military supplies to Poland on the British ship *S.S. Wimbledon*, travelling to the port of Danzig via the Kiel Canal. Germany had declared its neutrality in this war and claimed, correctly in regard to the law of war, that the passage through German territory of a ship carrying military material to one of the belligerents would violate that neutrality. The German government argued, again correctly, that, as a sovereign state, Germany had a positive duty under international law to uphold its neutral status against all infringements.

When France then invoked Article 380 of the Versailles Treaty, Germany argued that this provision could not legitimately be interpreted as imposing on Germany the obligation of permitting violations of its neutrality, as that would in effect have taken away its sovereign right to keep aloof from foreign wars if it wished.

The court held that Germany's right to declare and maintain its neutrality was limited by the conditions laid down in Article 380 but declined to accept that this implied the destruction of German sovereignty:

No doubt any convention creating an obligatioin of this kind places a restriction upon the exercise of the sovereign rights of the state, in the sense that it requires them to be exercised in a certain way. But the right of entering into international engagements is an attribute of state sovereignty.

11. **Independence and the capacity for foreign relations.** This extract from the *Wimbledon Case* indicates that independence and the sovereign power to enter into international agreements, and hence the capacity to establish relations with other states, are all bound together. Indeed, the Montevideo Convention's fourth criterion for statehood is often thought synonymous with independence. As is evident from the language of a separate opinion by Judge Anzillotti in the *Austro-German Customs Union Case*, independence means that 'the state has over it no other authority than that of international law' and therefore it is free to conduct its foreign relations with whomever it wishes without having to consult any superior authority.

Therefore much of the preceding discussion on independence and government applies with equal force to this fourth criterion. Nevertheless, the two criteria are properly to be distinguished. The existence or absence of genuine and independent national 'government' is largely a matter of internal sovereignty that carries international legal consequences. But capacity for foreign relations seems to involve the international legal relationship of the new entity with other states.

This may raise considerable problems, since it has to do with the attitude of other states towards the new entity and, in particular, with the question of recognition: Do other states recognise the new entity and what are the implications if they do, or if they do not?

12. **An example of the problem of recognition and statehood.** The case of Southern Rhodesia illustrates the main difficulty here. Prior to 1965 Southern Rhodesia had been a 'self-governing' British colony whose situation certainly fulfilled the first three criteria of statehood (population, territory, government). In that year the country's white minority administration declared 'independence' and announced it was ready to establish relations with other states, evidently intending thereby to meet the Montevideo Convention's remaining criterion. Nevertheless, the United Nations Security Council categorised the new entity as an 'illegal racist minority régime' and called upon United Nations members not to have dealings with it. Officially at least none did, save South Africa. The general opinion among international legal experts is that Southern Rhodesia was not a state.

This episode appears to suggest that the capacity to enter into foreign relations with other states cannot be attained without their agreement. Crudely, one might say (as many international lawyers and statesmen once thought) that membership of the international community (i.e. statehood) is like belonging to an exclusive club: no one gets in without the prior approval of the current members. Or, to use the terminology of international law, in order to be a state the new entity would have to be recognised by other members of the international community. This analysis helps to explain how it was that Southern Rhodesia could in 1980 suddenly become a state merely by changing its government, but it is not altogether satisfactory, since it leaves unresolved a number of problems relating to recognition and statehood which seem to call for a more sophisticated explanation.

13. Recognition and statehood: constitutive and declaratory views. The idea that recognition is necessary to constitute the new entity a state is called the *constitutive view of recognition* and was once widely held. It is criticised, however, for being simplistic in that it reduces statehood to a matter of the arbitrary decisions of other states and it fails to deal adequately with the problem of how the law gets implemented, that is, how the international legal system is made to work.

If one accepts the view of Arbitrator Huber in the *Palmas Case,* for that law to operate effectively the authorities within each territory must be able and willing to abide by it and enforce it in the areas over which they exercise control. If a new entity were not recognised and thus could claim not to be a state in the international legal system, that entity would be in a position to argue that it had no obligation to carry out international law in its territory.

When the Spanish colonies in South America attained *de facto* independence from Spain after 1808, Britain eventually recognised them as independent states (in spite of Spanish objections) and offered a justification which took this factor into account. The British Foreign Secretary, George Canning, wrote:

> ...all political communities are responsible to other political communities for their conduct ... [Without recognition of the new states there would be only two other alternatives:] the total irresponsibility of unrecognised States [which would be] absurd ... [or] the treatment of their Inhabitants as ... Outlaws [which would be] monstrous ... [In these circumstances] no other choice remained for Gt. Britain ... but to recognise ... their political existence as States, and thus to bring them within the pale of those rights and duties, which civilised Nations are bound mutually to respect, and are entitled reciprocally to claim from each other.

In the same paper, Canning wrote of the former Spanish colonies being 'countries, whose independent existence was *in fact* established, but to whom the acknowledgement of that independence was denied' (emphasis supplied). He evidently did not believe that British recognition had the constitutive effect of creating the statehood of these countries.

Canning's position seems closer to what is called the *declaratory view of recognition*, that recognition is, as he wrote, an 'acknowledgement' of an already existing fact. Its purpose would be simply to demonstrate that the recognising state considered that legal relationships existed between it and the recognised state and that it regarded this state as a member of the international community.

This declaratory view seems the more correct one. Under it recognition would not create the statehood of the new entity but would simply be a necessary step for giving effect to the consequences of that statehood in the context of relations with other states.

The Montevideo Convention (*see* 3) adopts the declaratory view emphatically in Article 3: 'The political existence of the state is independent of recognition by the other states.' That Article goes on:

> Even before recognition the state has the right to defend its integrity and independence ... and to organise itself as it sees fit.
>
> The exercise of these rights has no other limitation than the exercise of the

rights of other states according to international law.

Article 6 of the Convention draws the obvious corollary of this: 'The recognition of a state merely signifies that the state which recognises it accepts the personality of the other, with all the rights and duties determined by international law.'

14. Reconciling the declaratory view and the Southern Rhodesia case. The declaratory view seems the better one but does not on the face of it explain what happened in the Southern Rhodesia case. Yet these may be reconciled if one returns to the concept of independence.

The definition of independence offered by Judge Anzilotti in the *Austro-German Customs Union Case* was that 'the state has over it no other authority than that of international law itself'. This means that any international entity always remains subject to international law, which is therefore necessarily decisive on the question of the entity's status or character within the international legal system.

One of the consequences of this is that the requirements of international law with respect to the establishment of a state cannot be evaded by any entity that wishes to have internationally effective statehood. When international law itself forbids the very basis on which the new entity has been set up, even the state's independence is insufficient to produce a statehood which is validated and made effective within the international legal system.

In the case of Southern Rhodesia it has been suggested that, at least with regard to the independence of former colonial territories, self-determination of a country's whole population is a requirement of international law without which any claim to statehood is invalid.

The refusal of the United Nations to recognise Southern Rhodesia would then not be a question of non-recognition preventing statehood, but rather a matter of the United Nations determining that Southern Rhodesia had not fulfilled all the requirements of international law. Thus, Rhodesian statehood would have come about in 1980 because the transition from one government to another would have in fact represented the passage from denial of self-determination to fulfilment of it.

A difficulty with this line of argument is, of course, that it may be taken to open the door to imposing a variety of conditions on a country before its independence becomes operative as statehood in international law. This objection, however, is more apparent than real, since imposing a requirement of self-determination goes to the very heart of the state's relationship to its territory and population: can that relationship be valid and legally effective when most of the people who live in the territory are unconnected with the state and indeed hostile to it?

By contrast, most other requirements that have from time to time been suggested (following certain economic policies, ending human rights violations, ceasing other contraventions of international law), although they are important, do not have this same direct relationship to the very bases of statehood.

15. A duty to recognise? The remaining problem with recognition is whether, if a new state meets all the requirements of international law, existing states have a duty to recognise it.

The argument that there is such a duty has long been controversial, in spite of the reasons in favour of it. The United States, for example, has maintained that, far from being a duty, recognition is a 'high political act', as with American recognition of Israel in 1948, not subject to a calculus of legal rights and obligations. Other general objections centre on the undeniable fact that a state cannot against its will be legitimately forced to establish those full relations with another state or entity which recognition implies. States are free to deal with, or not deal with, whomever they choose.

The politicization of recognition which these views may lead to is itself objectionable. On the one hand, a state which genuinely exists may not be recognised for political reasons; on the other hand an entity which is not a state may be given recognition to which it is not entitled or be recognised before it truly fulfils the conditions of statehood. This leads to what is called *premature recognition*. Such recognition before the facts warrant it may well serve to undermine the rights of an existing state or other interested party when international law would otherwise protect them.

In any case, as a practical matter a state may in certain circumstances have to act as if another state existed as a matter of law, even without recognition. For example, mere non-recognition would not in general excuse unprovoked aggression against the unrecognised state, because that state would be entitled to the basic legal protections arising from its actual existence regardless of whether the aggressor state recognised it, as Article 3 of the Montevideo Convention (*see* 13) made clear.

Thus, recognition may be divisible for the purposes of international law into two distinct categories: formal diplomatic recognition entailing normalisation of relations; and tacit recognition involving merely abstention from violating the new state's fundamental rights. The first type of recognition would be discretionary, the second obligatory.

This conclusion would appear to be particularly apt in view of the fact that almost every state in the world is a member of the United Nations and is consequently bound to observe the provisions of the Charter towards all other members, regardless of non-recognition.

This view of recognition also helps to clarify incidents that would otherwise be difficult to explain. Thus, for example, Britain did not immediately recognise Israel as a state in 1948; but when Israeli aircraft operating illegally over Egypt shot down two RAF planes in January 1949 Britain at once contacted the Israeli government to lay the basis for a claim of compensation. Clearly, Britain believed that Israel existed as a state even without recognition.

Even decisions which on their face adopt a constitutive approach seem to accept the reality of an unrecognised state's existence. Thus, in the *International Registration of Trade-mark (Germany) Case*, decided by the West German Federal Supreme Court in 1959, with regard to the East German state the court held that 'any entity which exists *in fact* requires, in addition, the *recognition* of its existence' in order for its existence to have any legal effect *vis-à-vis* another state. An unrecognised state cannot confer 'upon itself the status of a subject of international law in relation to states which do not recognise it' by acceding to a multilateral treaty to which the non-recognising states are also parties. The meaning of this appears to be that statehood as an objective fact exists without recognition, but some of the political and legal consequences of statehood depend for their realisation on recognition.

16. Recognition of governments. Unfortunately, the law on recognition of states is often made needlessly more confusing by discussing it along with the separate question of the recognition of governments. The two should be distinguished for reasons which will be evident from Chap. 5.

At this point it is sufficient to indicate that the recognition of statehood arises when an entity which hitherto has not had international legal personality claims to be a member of the international community, whereas the recognition of a government involves most often a hitherto existing state in which a revolution or other extra-constitutional event has produced a new regime that wishes to be acknowledged as the legitimate administration. Where the questions of statehood and government coincide, as when a new entity might qualify as a state but the identity of its government is in doubt, the recognition of a government will in the first instance be an aspect of the recognition of the state itself and should be treated as such.

States with limited sovereignty

17. Introduction. Apart from states that are recognised to be full members of the international community in every respect, there are a few states that fulfil the Montevideo criteria for statehood but are nevertheless held to be distinguishable on the basis of limitations on their sovereignty unique to themselves.

18. Liechtenstein. On the question of the admission of Liechtenstein to the League of Nations, for example, a committee of the organisation determined in 1920 that, because she had 'chosen to depute to others some of the attributes of sovereignty' (such as customs and postal administration and diplomatic representation in foreign countries) and also had no army, Liechtenstein 'could not discharge all the international obligations' which membership in the League of Nations might entail.

Thus, the decisive factor in this case was not Liechtenstein's general inadequacy as a state but rather the specific nature of the limitations on its exercise of sovereignty when viewed from the perspective of the system established in the Covenant of the League. For other purposes, therefore, it remained possible for Liechtenstein to act, and be treated, as a state in the fullest sense. In 1949, for example, it became a party to the Statute of the ICJ (which, under Articles 34 and 35, is limited to 'states'), and was the plaintiff in the *Nottebohm Case* (*Liechtenstein* v. *Guatemala*) in 1955.

19. Western Samoa. Western Samoa became independent in 1962, but in a Treaty of Friendship with New Zealand in the same year agreed that the latter would help Western Samoa in its foreign relations, in such a manner, however as to 'in no way impair' the new state's rights 'to formulate its own foreign policies'. In 1970 Western Somoa was admitted to membership in the Commonwealth and in 1976 it entered the United Nations.

20. Cyprus. Cyprus attained independent statehood in 1960 by agreement between Britain, Greece and Turkey, and has been a member of the UN since then, in spite of the limitations on its sovereignty contained in the 1959 Treaty of Guarantee between the three countries mentioned. Under Article 4 of that pact, each guarantor power was given the right to intervene in Cyprus's internal affairs in order to maintain the status quo established between the Greek Cypriot and Turkish Cypriot communities on the island at the time of independence. Cyprus's international personality is generally held to have continued even after Turkey exercised its rights in 1974 by invading the island following a coup d'état organised by the Greek military dictatorship against Cyprus's legitimate government.

From a legal point of view it would appear impossible for Turkish military intervention to deprive the Cypriot state of its existence, given that such intervention could only be legitimate if it fell within the provisions of the Treaty of Guarantee, whose sole aim and justification is to preserve the independence of Cyprus. The treaty therefore could not serve as the pretext for any subsequent Turkish attempt to partition the island or set up an independent Turkish Cypriot state. When the Turkish Cypriot administration on the island declared the independence of the 'Turkish Republic of Northern Cyprus' in November 1983, the entity was recognised only by Turkey and was condemned by the UN Security Council.

21. The Vatican City and the Holy See: in a class by themselves? The State of the Vatican City, an enclave in Rome, is an international legal person whose head of state is the Pope. This status is not affected by its having a minuscule territory, tiny population, or very close practical ties to Italy. The Vatican City as such has been a party to some international treaties (as on telecommunications) that have a specifically territorial application. But when relations with Italy were first regularised by the Lateran Treaty of 1929, Italy recognised 'the sovereignty of the Holy See in the international domain as an attribute inherent in its nature, in accordance ... with the requirements of its mission in the world' and 'the sovereignty and jurisdiction of the Holy See over the City of the Vatican'. This implies that the Holy See (understood perhaps as the equivalent of the Catholic Church as a world-wide institution under the Papacy) is a separate international legal person. In fact, the Holy See as such has been admitted to full membership in UN specialised agencies such as the International Labour Office and the World Health Organisation, and has become a party to many treaties that are open only to states. The relations of both entities with Italy are now governed by a new agreement signed in February 1984.

'Semi-states': countries not recognised to have full statehood

22. Introduction. When the international legal system was still largely the creature of the West, the problem arose of classifying entities that were geographically and demographically separate countries but whose full political independence Western imperial powers did not wish to recognise. Two categories were developed to accommodate this situation: protected states, and mandated and trust territories.

Protected states

23. The general system. The system of protected states, affecting countries as far apart as Tunis in North Africa, Bukhara and Khiva in Central Asia, and Tonkin in Indo-China, was the product of nineteenth-century European imperialism's desire to subject some previously independent countries to colonial control of their foreign policy while leaving a measure of internal authority to the native rulers. Third World countries which thereby lost their international independence to the imperial powers were said to be 'protectorates', each country being 'protected' by its imperial master from the attentions of rival European empires.

In Africa the system of protectorates was also applied to countries which had been superimposed on existing tribal structures during the European division of the continent into what the General Act of the Berlin Conference of 1885 called (for the first time in international affairs) 'spheres of influence'. The African protectorates were generally acknowledged to be little more than colonies.

Although in the period following World War II most of these protected countries attained independence, individually or as part of larger states, those in Central Asia have been firmly incorporated into the Soviet Union.

24. Problems of the relationship of protectorates to third states. While protectorates were still a feature of the international legal scene, the chief problem they created was that of their relationship to third states. The PCIJ, in its advisory opinion in the *Nationality Decrees in Tunis and Morocco Case* (1923), indicated that the precise status of every protected state depended on the provisions of the treaty or agreement between the imperial power and the indigenous authorities setting up the protectorate and also on the 'conditions under which the Protectorate has been recognised by third Powers as against whom there is an intention to rely on the provisions of these treaties'.

In the *Rights of Nationals of the United States in Morocco Case* (1952), the ICJ held that the Treaty of Fez, signed in 1912 between the French Government and Morocco following German attempts to assert influence there during the Agadir Crisis of 1911, was a contractual arrangement whereby France was empowered to conclude treaties with third states on Morocco's behalf. Such a treaty would bind Morocco to the same extent as if made by her directly.

25. Need for intention to create a protectorate. In the light of the discussion above on states with limited sovereignty which nevertheless retain full international legal personality (though not necessarily enjoying membership of international organisations), it would appear that, in order for the loss of independence which a protectorate implies to occur, the specific intention to create a protectorate must exist when the relevant treaty is signed. In the absence of such an intention, it is doubtful that a protectorate could now be inferred in law, whatever the actual political relationships involved.

The situation of Bhutan, a Himalayan country between India and China, is worth noting in this connection. In the 1949 Treaty of Friendship between India and Bhutan, India undertook not to interfere in Bhutan's internal affairs, while Bhutan agreed 'to be guided by the advice of the Government of India with regard to its external relations'. On the face of it, this is a classic agreement to establish a protectorate. But one notes that Bhutan was admitted to the United Nations in 1971 and in the 1980s, without modification of the Friendship Treaty, Bhutan began to implement a policy of expanding its direct relations with foreign states, particularly China and Nepal. It seems doubtful that Bhutan can any longer be considered an Indian protectorate, in spite of the 1949 agreement's continuing in effect.

Mandated and trust territories

26. The mandate system in general. While the category of protectorate was introduced into international law to provide the imperial powers with a device to exercise whatever degree of control over the protected territory they could impose, without regard to the legal position of the indigenous inhabitants, the system of mandated territories set imperial control in the context of the embryonic national rights of those people.

The concept of mandates arose at the end of World War I, when the victorious powers wished to place colonies formerly belonging to the defeated German and Turkish empires under allied control. President Wilson of the United States, however, had insisted, in his Fourteen Points statement of American war aims, that freedom for subject peoples was one of the principles the allies were fighting for. To reconcile these potentially conflicting positions the mandate system was established under the auspices of the League of Nations.

The League Covenant's Article 22, which applied to conquered territories 'inhabited by peoples not yet able to stand by themselves under the strenuous conditions of the modern world', enunciated the principle that 'the well-being and development of such peoples form a sacred trust of civilization'.

This trust was to be performed by giving a mandate for 'the tutelage of such peoples' to 'advanced nations' acting 'as Mandatories on behalf of the League'.

Article 22 then went on to categorise the mandated territories. The highest category, the Class A mandates, were communities that had been under Turkish rule and were adjudged at the time (1919) to 'have reached a stage of development where their existence as independent nations can be provisionally recognised' subject to 'advice and assistance' from the mandatory power. 'The wishes of these communities', the provision continued, 'must be a principal consideration in the selection of the Mandatory'. The countries assigned to this most advanced category were the Arab nations of Palestine, Jordan, Syria and Iraq.

The Class B mandates, particularly in Central Africa, were considered to require greater control by the mandatory to guarantee such things as freedom of conscience and religion, prohibition of the slave trade, and 'equal opportunities for the trade and commerce of other Members of the League'.

Class C mandates, and specifically South-West Africa and certain south Pacific islands, were considered so far from being fit for independence that they could 'best be administered under the laws of the Mandatory as integral portions of its territory'.

The mandates would be assigned individually by the League to the mandatory power with specific indications of the latter's degree of authority or control, and each mandatory was required to submit an annual report to the League of Nations permanent commission for mandated territories.

Apart from the League's failure to take account of the wishes of the inhabitants in the Class A mandates (who favoured either immediate independence or American, rather than British or French, mandates in their countries), two significant legal issues in Article 22 have continued to generate disagreement. They are:

(*a*) Who were entitled to be its beneficiaries and what rights could they claim, and against whom?

(*b*) Who possessed sovereignty over the mandated territories?

Although most mandates resulted in independence for the nations concerned without requiring these questions to be answered, two persistent problems – Britain's mandate in Palestine and South Africa's in South-West Africa (now Namibia) – hinged on them.

27. Palestine. When the League of Nations drew up the mandate for Palestine, it incorporated the British government's previously announced policy of facilitating the establishment there of a Jewish national home, which would involve Jewish immigration from Europe and elsewhere into the territory. Fearing that this would lead inevitably to the creation of a Jewish state there, the Arab majority objected that the mandate unconstitutionally violated the Covenant by frustrating the national independence which Article 22 had provisionally recognised for those who were Palestine's indigenous inhabitants as of 1919.

But the British view of the Palestine mandate did not put such emphasis on the legal role of Article 22 or indeed of the League of Nations in general. The Covenant could not be relied upon by the Palestinians to establish their rights in opposition to the policy of the mandatory power, as Lord Balfour, who had been British Foreign Secretary at the end of the war, made clear in a speech to the League's Council:

> Remember that a mandate is a self-imposed limitation by the conquerors on the sovereignty which they obtained over conquered territories ... the Allied Powers ... have asked the League of Nations to assist them ... But the League of Nations is not the author of the policy, but its instrument.

He concluded that the 'mandates are neither made by the League, nor can they, in substance, be altered by the League.'

This statement must be read also to constitute a rejection of the Palestinian argument that sovereignty over Palestine, resting no longer in the former Turkish rulers nor in the League of Nations or the Mandatory power, must rightfully have belonged as of 1919 to the Arab inhabitants. But Lord Balfour's was not the last word on the sovereignty issue or on the question of the Covenant's constitutional and legal role, which were both revived in relation to South-West Africa.

In 1947, the Arab League proposed referring the Palestine case to the ICJ for consideration of these and related points, but the UN General Assembly declined to do so, deciding instead (in an act beyond its powers under the UN Charter) to partition the country into a Jewish and an Arab state. Whether that UN approval for a Palestinian state within the territory of the mandate as it was in 1947 still constitutes a legal basis for Palestinian statehood there at present is hotly disputed.

28. Namibia: the first phase. The problem of South-West Africa (or, as it has been called since 1968, Namibia) arose in its current form at the end of World War II.

In connection with the dissolution of the League of Nations in April 1946 and the transfer of its duties to the United Nations, the Charter of the new organisation, in Articles 75 to 91, set up the trusteeship system for administering certain non-self-governing territories, among them such of those held as mandates 'as may be placed thereunder by means of trusteeship agreements'.

The new arrangements were intended to emphasise the individual and group rights of the indigenous peoples of these territories to a greater extent than the mandate system had, in particular the right of self-determination, whose promotion was declared in Article 1 of the Charter to be a fundamental purpose of the United Nations.

South Africa declined to place South-West Africa under the trusteeship system on the ground that, since the territory had been administered in accordance with the League Covenant as an integral portion of South Africa, the area should now be internationally recognised as subject to South African annexation. This was strongly opposed in the UN General Assembly, which recommended in 1946 that South Africa conclude an agreement with the United Nations making South-West Africa a trust territory. South Africa refused.

In 1949 the General Assembly asked the ICJ for an advisory opinion on the situation. In the *Status of South-West Africa Case* (1950) the court held that the creation of the mandate 'did not involve any cession of territory or transfer of sovereignty to the Union of South Africa'. In a separate opinion, Lord McNair said that sovereignty over a mandated territory was 'in abeyance' until independence and that consequently the mandatory's powers were limited to those necessary for carrying out the mandate.

According to the court the rules regulating the mandate had given the territory an 'international status' recognised by all the members of the League of Nations, including South Africa. That status had not been affected by the demise of the League as that organisation's functions had been transferred to the United Nations. Since the United Nations was in effect the successor in interest to the League, the contractual relationship which the mandate agreement had created now existed between South Africa and the UN.

Therefore in the court's view South Africa continued to be bound by the obligations of Article 22 of the Covenant as well as by the subsidiary duties to transmit petitions from the territory's inhabitants to the United Nations, to submit annual reports to the UN in connection with its supervisory functions over the mandate, and to accept the substitution of the ICJ for the Permanent Court of International Justice in questions arising under the mandate.

The court, however, did not hold that South Africa was under an obligation to conclude a trusteeship agreement with the United Nations, as the UN could not unilaterally force a party with which its predecessor had entered into contractual relations to alter the terms of that contract. By the same token, South Africa could not unilaterally modify the status of South-West Africa, any change requiring the consent of the United Nations.

29. Namibia: the South-West Africa Cases (1966). The consequence of these conclusions was to make the meaning and effect of Article 22 of the Covenant the key issue in later discussions of the problem, notably the *South-West Africa Cases* (1962 and 1966).

In the 1950s and 1960s the problem came to centre on South Africa's insistence on implementing the apartheid system of racial segregation in South-West Africa as if it were part of South Africa itself. Two African states that had been members of the League of Nations, Ethiopia and Liberia, raised cases against South Africa in the ICJ.

In preliminary hearings in 1962, South Africa challenged both the ICJ's jurisdiction and the standing of the petitioning states to sue. The court held that it had jurisdiction and that Article 7 of the Mandate for South-West Africa indicated that members of the League did have legal rights and interests in seeing that the mandatory power observed its obligations towards the territory's inhabitants to promote their welfare.

The cases raised by each petitioner then went on to hearings on their merits. In the *South-West Africa Cases* (1966), the court rendered its final judgment. Astonishingly, this was that South Africa's preliminary objections had after all been correct insofar as the petitioners' standing to sue (their *locus standi*) was limited to questions in which their own interests were directly involved. On matters like the mandatory's treatment of the territory's inhabitants, South Africa's obligations ran only to the League of Nations as an institution and not to its members individually, so that only the League (which had been defunct for twenty years) could enforce them. The court indicated quite clearly (in para. 57 of the judgment) that if this meant that no one was now entitled to claim due performance of the mandate, then so be it.

This decision came about because of changes in the court's composition which put judges who had been in the minority in 1962 in a bare majority in 1966. It was attacked both on procedural grounds (the issue of the petitioners' standing had not been re-argued following what everyone had assumed was the 1962 decision's definitive ruling on the question) and on grounds of law and legal philosophy, with major dissenting opinions from Judges Jessup and Tanaka.

30. Namibia: the consequences of the South-West Africa Cases judgment. The dissenting opinions of Judges Jessup and Tanaka served not only to suggest a vigorous alternative to the view of the law which the ICJ had adopted but also to expose the weaknesses of the court's approach to carrying out its judicial duties. But while the dissents helped preserve something of the ICJ's intellectual and legal reputation, the majority decision itelf provoked a major backlash in the United Nations.

On 27 October 1966, the UN General Assembly, by a vote of 114 in favour to two against, with three abstentions, adopted Resolution 2145 which terminated South Africa's mandate over South-West Africa, affirmed the inhabitants' right of self-determination, and brought the territory under the direct responsibility of the United Nations. Shortly thereafter the UN Council for Namibia was established by the General Assembly to administer the country while preparing it for independence.

South Africa refused to comply with this resolution or recognise and cooperate with the Council for Namibia. In 1969 the UN Security Council called upon South Africa to withdraw from Namibia, and in 1970 passed Resolution 276, declaring that the mandate had been properly terminated so that South Africa's continuing presence in Namibia was illegal. All acts taken by South Africa concerning Namibia were also held to be illegal and invalid and UN members, 'particularly those which have economic or other interests in Namibia', were requested to refrain from any dealings with South Africa that were 'inconsistent' with these conclusions.

This resolution produced no relinquishing of power by the ex-mandatory. The Security Council then returned to the ICJ for an advisory opinion. This was given in 1971 under the title *Legal Consequences for States of the Continued Presence of South Africa in Namibia (South-West Africa) notwithstanding*

Security Council Resolution 276 – in short, *The Legal Consequences Case* (1971).

31. Namibia: the Legal Consequences Case (1971). Between the controversial decision of 1966 and the advisory opinion of 1971 the composition of the ICJ had changed, with the replacement of retiring judges from Australia, Greece and Italy by members from the Philippines, Spain and Sweden and the appointment of a different Polish judge. The effect was that four out of the seven judges in the 1966 majority were no longer members of the court, while a fifth, who had been appointed by South Africa for the earlier cases under the ICJ's procedures for *ad hoc* judges, was not involved in the 1971 advisory opinion. On the key question in the case, therefore, the court held (by a vote of thirteen to two, the latter being the only holdovers from the 1966 majority) that, South Africa's continued presence in Namibia being illegal, she was obligated to withdraw from the territory.

32. Termination of the mandate. Avoiding the 1966 cases' problem of how to derive rights and duties from the League Covenant and the general principles of law, the court chose to interpret Article 80 of the UN Charter in such a way as to have it mean that the mandatory powers had assumed the obligation to preserve the rights of the mandated territories' inhabitants *and* to administer those areas according to the Charter duties 'which member states have undertaken to fulfil in good faith in all their international relations'. The ICJ determined that South Africa's written statements to the court undisputedly proved that the policy applied in Namibia was 'to achieve a complete physical separation of races' which, to the extent that it denied fundamental human rights, was 'a flagrant violation of the purposes and principles of the Charter'.

The right of the United Nations to end the mandate in these circumstances arose from its position as legal successor to the League of Nations. The UN had the same right as the League under generally accepted rules of the law of treaties to terminate the mandate agreement when a 'deliberate and persistent violation of obligations' by the other party (South Africa) 'destroys the very object and purpose' of the mandate relationship. Both the General Assembly and the Security Council, as competent organs of the United Nations, had determined on its behalf that, for these reasons, the mandate should be concluded.

Since the ICJ had already decided as far back as the *Status of South-West Africa Case* (1950) that South Africa's authority in the territory was based only on the mandate, it followed that, once the mandate had been terminated, that state's continued presence there had no legal basis and under the circumstances was consequently illegal.

33. Legal effect of Security Council Resolution 276. The problem on the legal effect on UN members of Security Council Resolution 276 was more difficult. They had been requested to refrain from certain dealings with South Africa regarding Namibia: did this amount to a binding decision by the Council? By eleven votes to four the court held that it did.

The Council was acting in this resolution to carry out its Charter responsibility to maintain international peace and security. To do this the Council in effect had general implied powers commensurate with its responsibilities and limited only by the requirement that they be used in accordance with the fundamental principles and purposes of the UN Charter.

The court went on to conclude that Article 25 of the Charter, binding the UN's members to 'accept and carry out the decisions of the Security Council in accordance with the present Charter', applied to all Council decisions to which the Council intended it to apply and not only (as many had previously thought) to decisions on enforcement against aggressors or breachers of the peace under Articles 41 and 42 of the Charter. Therefore, the members of the United Nations were 'under obligation' not to lend any support or assistance to South Africa with reference to its 'occupation' of Namibia.

The court's use of the term 'occupation' was significant in implying that South Africa's continued presence in the territory, since it had no legal basis, was founded simply on the imposition of authority by military force, an act which would normally be considered aggression if committed without legal justification against a state.

The ICJ also determined that even states that were not members of the United Nations were affected by the illegality of South Africa's presence in Namibia since the termination of the mandate in effect created an objective legal fact which could not be ignored. Therefore, no state which entered into relations with South Africa concerning Namibia could legitimately expect the United Nations to recognise that relationship or its consequences.

34. Legal position and rights of Namibia's inhabitants. However, the court was careful to indicate that the ending of the mandate did not mean that Namibia and its people were in a legal limbo *vis-à-vis* South Africa or the rest of the world. The former mandatory's humanitarian and other duties to the Namibians under international law did not automatically cease upon the mandate's termination, and foreign states should continue to treat as valid South African acts of administration such as the registration of births, deaths, and marriages.

35. Namibia since 1971. The ICJ concluded that the precise implementation of these general legal conclusions was a matter for the 'political organs of the United Nations', with the Security Council having to decide on 'any further measures' against South Africa. The story of Namibia since 1971 has essentially been one of continued South African intransigence and a failure of the Security Council (because of British and American vetoes) to impose economic or other sanctions to force the ex-mandatory to comply with international law. Negotiations aimed at persuading South Africa to withdraw from Namibia have floundered on South Africa's insistence on being paid, through political and strategic concessions, to do what she is already legally bound to do.

In the end, the Namibia situation stands as a remarkably comprehensive case study over a long period of time of several significant elements in modern international law: the role of the major international organisations and their organs, the constitutional nature of fundamental international documents like the UN Charter, the importance of the philosophical basis of international law for questions of human rights, the judicial functions of the ICJ and the significance of its composition, and the influence of international politics.

'Proto-states': colonies and peoples entitled to self-determination

36. The background. The distinction between colonies and non-self-governing peoples on the one hand and mandated territories on the other is that until recent decades the first category were not recognised under international law to have any status separate from the imperial power that ruled over them while the latter category was. There was thus no basis in international law for a colonised territory or people to claim a right to independence.

This left colonies entirely dependent on the operation of the international legal principle of effectiveness, that is, the principle that rights over the territory would be presumed to belong, all else being equal, to whoever exercised effective control over it. This was in keeping with the view (*see* 5) of Max Huber in the *Island of Palmas Case*. The consequence of applying the principle of effectiveness to colonial territories and peoples was that a people's right to control its own country could come into existence only after a successful struggle to supplant the colonial masters. While that fight was going on, no such right existed and the colonial insurgents could be classified as illegal rebels and legitimately punished. The classic example of such a fight for freedom was the American Revolution of 1776–1783.

Weighting of the legal dice so completely in favour of the imperial powers was not surprising in the days when the major European states still regarded the use of military force as the legitimate extension of a colonial policy which was itself imbued with notions of religious, racial and cultural superiority. It is equally unsurprising that the modern era has seen a determined effort to restore the balance by elaborating the meaning and effect of self-determination in international law.

37. Origins of self-determination. The principle of self-determination began to develop in its current form towards the end of World War I in the thinking of President Wilson of the United States. In 1917 he told the American Congress:

> No peace can last, or ought to last, which does not recognise and accept the principle that governments derive all their just powers from the consent of the governed, and that no right anywhere exists to hand people about from sovereignty to sovereignty as if they were property.

Although these precepts were applied in Eastern Europe to create new states out of the domains of the Austrian, German and Russian empires (at the same time, however, raising minorities problems in each of the new countries), the imperial ambitions of the victorious European powers frustrated a full implementation of Wilson's vision outside Europe. The League of Nations mandate system offered at best only partial recognition of the right of subject peoples to any say in their own national future.

38. The UN Charter and self-determination. The critical breakthrough in the process of establishing the principle of self-determination in international law came in 1945 via the Charter of the United Nations. Article 1 states that among the purposes of the organisation is that of developing 'friendly relations among nations based on respect for the principle of equal rights and self-determination of peoples'. Although the language of this provision seems several steps away from proclaiming immediate legal rights and duties, it should be noted that the principle mentioned is spoken of as if it were considered to exist already, presumably as a principle of international law since the Article's reference to 'rights' places the provision squarely in a legal context.

Some indirect light on the meaning and application of Article 1 is shed by reading it within the larger framework of the Charter's provisions on the administration of colonial and trust territories and on the use of force in international affairs.

Though not explicitly using the expression 'self-determination', Article 73, which sets limits to the activities of colonial powers, declares that UN members which have, or will take on, responsibility for 'territories whose people have not yet attained a full measure of self-government' recognise the principle that the interests of the inhabitants are paramount. The Article also declares that they 'accept as a sacred trust' the duty to promote the inhabitants' well-being, within the Charter's 'system of international peace and security', and to that end to develop self-government, taking 'due account' of the people's political aspirations.

Article 76 on the trusteeship system, while similarly not directly referring to self-determination, lists as among the basic objectives of that system 'the progressive development towards self-government or independence as may be appropriate'.

It is a rule of interpretation of legal documents like the UN Charter that, unless there is a clear statement to the contrary, provisions must be interpreted so as to avoid making a document internally self-contradicting. Thus, although neither of these articles mentions the principle of self-determination, they must both be regarded as consistent with the Charter's statement of purposes in Article 1 where the observance of that principle is emphasised. They therefore may not legitimately be interpreted as offering alternatives to self-determination but rather should be understood as suggesting how it may be implemented in certain circumstances (e.g. by independence or, alternatively, self-government (not necessarily the same things)).

The consistency of these articles with other provisions of the Charter is reinforced by the requirement that certain activities under Article 73 be kept within the UN's 'system of international peace and security'.

The basis of that system is set out in Article 2(4) of the Charter as one of the United Nations' fundamental principles:

> All members shall refrain in their international relations from the threat or use of force against the territorial integrity or political independence of any state, *or in any other manner inconsistent with the purposes of the United Nations.* [emphasis supplied]

The italicised portion of this paragraph effectively outlaws the use or threat of force in such a way as to inhibit friendly relations based on the principle of self-determination and implicitly channels the activities required under Article 73 away from such displays of force.

Also integral to the Charter system mentioned are Article 2(2)'s requirement that UN members fulfil their obligations 'in good faith' and Article 2(3)'s obliging members to settle their international disputes 'by peaceful means in such a manner that international peace and security, and justice, are not endangered'. The good faith rule may reasonably be taken to prohibit interpreting and implementing the Charter provisions on colonial administration in such a way as to frustrate their underlying purposes, of which the promotion of self-determination would appear to be one. The duty to settle disputes peacefully so as not to endanger justice also seems to restrict the colonial power's room for manoeuvre in any situation which threatens to generate an international dispute about self-determination.

Finally, one notes that in the sphere of economic and social questions, Article 56 of the Charter obliges members to take individual and joint action in cooperation with the UN to create the conditions of stability and well-being which are necessary for peaceful and friendly relations among nations based on respect for the principle of equal rights and self-determination.

Reading all these Charter provisions so as to be consistent with each other, a fair interpretation would seem to be that they recognise a legal principle of self-determination and strongly imply a corresponding right, insofar at least as they establish a system whose principles and purposes are incompatible with the forcible denial of self-determination.

39. Argument about the meaning and effect of the Charter provisions. Some scholars have, however, rejected both these conclusions, while others argue that the Charter at best enunciates only the principle of self-determination, leaving the precise legal ramifications in terms of rights and duties to be worked out according to the particular circumstances of each individual case.

The fear of many of these writers is that to proclaim a right automatically applying in all situations would risk opening a Pandora's box of irresistible claims to independent statehood by minority national groups within existing states. This could destabilize the international community, it is argued, and might, if the United Nations became directly involved, embroil the organisation in a violation of Article 2(7) of the Charter; this says that nothing in that document authorises the UN to intervene in the internal affairs of member states (except in regard to the maintenance of international peace under Articles 39–51).

The counter-arguments are that stability for its own sake is not necessarily a goal of international law, particularly if it can be achieved only at the price of denying justice and right; and that in any case Article 2(7) applies only to dictatorial or forcible UN intervention and does not prohibit the organisation from considering internal questions relevant to the concerns of the Charter and making appropriate recommendations. And to the extent that an internal denial of self-determination may endanger international peace (as has been judged to be the case with apartheid in South Africa) Article 2(7), on its own language, does not apply.

Another objection to self-determination is that it is to blame for introducing into international law the idea that the only proper expression of nationhood is in the form of an independent state, thereby promoting nationalism, with all its dangerous implications for peace and international relations. A justified concern with the negative effects of nationalism cannot be lightly dismissed; but, specifically with regard to self-determination, the situation actually appears to be that the objectors simply resent the application of the national principle more widely than most of the existing nation-states (whose own ethos clings firmly to nationalism) would have liked. In the modern world it is difficult to justify the implication that not every national group is entitled to determine its own destiny because, in some Orwellian way connected with the accidents of history and power politics, all national groups are equal but some are more equal than others.

A better solution to the problem might be to move beyond the confines of nationalism altogether.

It is apparent from the foregoing discussion that a number of questions remained after the UN Charter came into force about the nature, meaning and implementation of self-determination and about the situations where it applied. In the course of time answers to many of them were developed in United Nations practice, particularly in resolutions of the General Assembly that were understood to derive their legal effect from being authoritative interpretations of the Charter's provisions on the matter.

40. Early General Assembly action. In 1952, in Resolution 637A, the Assembly stated that 'the right of peoples and nations to self-determination is a prerequisite to the full enjoyment of all fundamental human rights' and it recommended that the UN's members 'shall uphold the principle of self-determination of all peoples and nations' while promoting 'realisation of the right of self-determination' for the peoples of colonial territories. The document's references to both a principle and a right of self-determination suggest that the drafters were not able to overcome all the objections indicated above (*see* **37, 38**) and preferred to concentrate on getting at least a general recognition of the right in colonial situations. The underlying problem remained to be resolved, however, as did the question of the precise relationship between self-determination and general human rights law.

41. Resolution 1514 (XV). The key General Assembly resolution on self-determination in the colonial context, Resolution 1514 under the title *Declaration on the Granting of Independence to Colonial Countries and Peoples*, was adopted in December 1960 at a critical point in the Algerian war of independence against France. In it the Assembly declared that:

1. The subjection of peoples to alien subjugation, domination and exploitation constitutes a denial of fundamental human rights [and] is contrary to the Charter ...
2. All peoples have the right to self-determination; by virtue of that right they freely determine their political status and freely pursue their economic, social and cultural development.
3. Inadequacy of political, economic, social or education preparedness should never serve as a pretext for delaying independence.
4. All armed action or repressive measures of all kinds against dependent peoples shall cease in order to enable them to exercise peacefully and freely their right to complete independence, and the integrity of their national territory shall be respected.
5. [Requires 'immediate steps' to transfer power 'without any conditions or reservations' to the inhabitants of trust and colonial territories 'in accordance with their freely expressed will and desire, without any distinction as to race, creed or colour, in order to enable them to enjoy complete independence and freedom'.]
6. Any attempt aimed at the partial or total disruption of the national unity and the territorial integrity of a country is incompatible with the Purposes and Principles of the Charter of the United Nations.
7. All States shall observe faithfully and strictly the provisions of the Charter

of the United Nations, the Universal Declaration of Human Rights and the present Declaration on the basis of equality, non-interference in the internal affairs of all States, and respect for the sovereign rights of all peoples and their territorial integrity.

42. Implications of Resolution 1514. This important document can be seen to have clarified the legal position on several aspects of self-determination by:

(*a*) linking it more directly than before to human rights law;

(*b*) indicating clearly that it is a right belonging to all peoples and that its implementation is required by the UN Charter in the case of alien subjugation or foreign domination; and

(*c*) specifying that what outsiders may choose to judge 'backwardness' is no justification for retarding fulfilment of self-determination in the form of independence.

By saying that political unpreparedness is no obstacle to independent statehood, this last provision may run counter to the Montevideo Convention's criterion of 'government' as a necessary element in the establishment of a state. An entitlement to self-determination would then effectively be an initial substitute for some of the traditional attributes of statehood, which would presumably be expected to appear only after independence.

A people which had the right to self-determination would therefore be a new kind of entity in international law, neither a state in the traditional sense of that term nor simply an object of international law, but rather a different sort of international legal person with rights peculiar to itself, a 'proto-state' or 'state-to-be' – a state in the process of appearing.

Paragraph 4 of Resolution 1514 (*see* **40**) spells out the implications of the connection discussed above between the Charter's provisions on self-determination and those on the use of force, namely that forcible denial of that right should stop. This should be followed, according to paragraph 5, by immediate steps towards independence, although the provision does not in the meantime make the existing colonial administrations illegitimate.

Paragraphs 6 and 7, with their emphasis on maintaining the territorial integrity and national unity of all countries, are an attempt to assuage the doubts of those who, as indicated above, feared that self-determination would lead to the break-up of existing entities. Paragraph 6 is understood to apply this even to the colonial territories themselves, so that in general they should have become independent within their colonial boundaries without any revision of them along ethnic, religious, linguistic or other lines.

These provisions have been criticised as being in principle unfair to minorities in new or existing states, by denying them an equal right to self-determination, and in practice dangerous insofar as they lead to the establishment of states that lack homogeneity and promote territorial and border disputes. This has been a particular problem in Africa where, for example, Somalia has wanted to redraw her boundaries so as to include Somalis living in territory forming part of Ethiopia and Kenya. President Qaddhafi of Libya (which also has territorial disputes with its neighbours) has proposed an African Court of Justice to resolve such claims, but the Organisation of African Unity (OAU) has always adhered firmly to the view set out in Resolution 1514 (XV).

Resolution 1514 (XV) thus left open the question how self-determination could apply universally and skirted the often related problem of cases in which it can be achieved only by the use of force against an existing state.

43. Later developments on the use of force in self-determination. Paragraph 4 of the Resolution (*see* **40**) was the starting point for subsequent efforts to elaborate a broader doctrine of self-determination. Its prohibition of armed action or repressive measures against a people entitled to self-determination was taken

(*a*) to invalidate the use of force by the dominant power in a territory claiming independence; and

(*b*) to legitimise both forcible resistance by the subject people and also the giving and receiving of military and other support for the independence struggle from outside.

These conclusions may be based on considering forcible resistance as in effect self-defence under Article 51 of the UN Charter or on treating it as advancing the Charter's purposes on self-determination while not in reality violating the imperial power's metropolitan territorial integrity or political independence in the sense of Article 2(4). The Charter's aim of minimising resort to force makes self-defence seem the better basis.

Although disputed, such applications of the Charter's provisions were reinforced by General Assembly Resolution 2625(XXV), the *Declaration on Principles of International Law* of 1970. This stated directly that peoples resisting forcible suppression of their claim to self-determination 'are entitled to seek and receive support in accordance with the purposes and principles of the Charter.' In 1974, the *Resolution on the Definition of Aggression* [Res. 3314(XXIX)], in paragraph 7, carried this further by effectively excluding from the category of aggression (i.e. use of armed force in violation of the Charter) forcible acts that furthered a struggle for self-determination.

In conjunction with this approval of the use of force to achieve self-determination, the 1970 Declaration may be interpreted as considerably increasing the sorts of cases in which such use would be legitimate. The resolution disclaims any intention of authorising or encouraging the dismemberment of existing states 'conducting themselves in compliance with the principle of equal rights and self determination ... and thus possessed of a government representing the whole people belonging to the territory without distinction as to race, creed or colour'. The clear implication is that states not so conducting themselves or not possessed of such a government may be dismembered by force in the name of self-determination.

The 1974 Resolution implicitly expands the operation of this provision by seeming not to limit itself simply to traditional colonial circumstances. Article 7 of the Definition of Aggression speaks of 'peoples forcibly deprived [of the right of self-determination] ... *particularly* peoples under colonial *and racist regimes or other forms of alien domination*' [emphasis supplied]. The word 'particularly' may be understood to mean that the list following it is not meant to be exclusive; in any event colonial situations are only one of three types of cases to which self-determination may apply. The term 'racist regimes' was presumably intended to cover the white minority governments in Rhodesia and South Africa, while 'other forms of alien domination' would appear broad enough to encompass the Israeli military occupation of Palestinian areas on the West Bank and Gaza after 1967.

Taken together, these two documents have considerably eroded the protection of existing states afforded by Resolution 1514(XV). How far that erosion may go depends on what may constitute alien, racist or unrepresentative government in individual cases (*see* also 16:22-3).

44. Human rights and the expansion of self-determination. The two UN Human Rights Covenants (*see* Chap. 13) which have the binding effect of treaty law for the states that are parties to them, each say in their first articles that all peoples have the right of self-determination. There is no limitation of this right to colonial or similar situations and the mention of it in documents asserting individual human rights would appear to suggest that it may be claimed as widely as those personal rights, that is, universally.

45. The Western Sahara Case (1975). This was the stage of development which self-determination had reached by a combination of treaty law and UN resolutions up to the mid-1970s. A useful opportunity for the ICJ to pull the various strands together and to offer considered conclusions about the status of the doctrine was presented when a complicated dispute arose in the wake of Spain's decision to withdraw from its large colony on the north-west coast of Africa, the territory now known as the Western Sahara.

The area had been under Spanish rule since 1884, but both Morocco and Mauritania claimed title to it based on each one's historic ties to the territory. To resolve the dispute peacefully the UN General Assembly asked the ICJ for an advisory opinion on the various issues that had been raised by the contending parties.

The court chose, however, to broaden its analysis to examine 'the basic principles governing the decolonisation policy of the General Assembly'. The court considered the UN Charter articles already discussed above, along with the various Assembly resolutions on the matter, and drew some significant comments from the ICJ's previous opinion in *The Legal Consequences Case* (1970) relating to Namibia. The court concluded that the Assembly's policy was to emphasise that self-determination required a free and genuine expression of the will of the inhabitants of any territory claiming independence and that the integration of such a territory into an existing state (as Morocco and Mauritania were each demanding) could only properly come about by taking account of the wishes of the people.

In an important separate opinion, the American judge, Hardy Dillard, summarised the court's conclusion as indicating that 'a norm of international law has emerged' applying self-determination as a matter of right to territories 'under the aegis of the United Nations'. The key feature of that right was that 'It is for the people to determine the destiny of the territory and not the territory the destiny of the people'.

Application of self-determination: some problem areas

46. National liberation movements. The development of the concept of self-determination has been accompanied by UN General Assembly efforts to give practical effect to it in two important cases through recognition of liberation movements which were considered to represent peoples struggling for their national rights.

The first group recognised was the Palestine Liberation Organisation (PLO), which in 1974 was accorded observer status at the United Nations, a position previously reserved solely for the representatives of sovereign states (e.g. West Germany) that were not at the time members of the UN. The Chairman of the PLO was furthermore invited to address the Assembly, and in subsequent years the PLO's representatives were allowed to attend various UN conferences and meetings. The British representative on the Security Council commented at one point that the PLO was 'being treated like a member state except for the right to vote'.

The precise significance of this treatment for the legal situation of the PLO and of the Palestinian people has been much debated, but a new status for a liberation movement acting on behalf of a nation that has not yet become a state seems a logical and even necessary outcome of the idea that a people entitled to self-determination has some international legal personality to which it may rightfully give effect on the international scene. In the absence of a government and state this could happen only through something like a liberation movement.

The difficulty with all this is that, while the rights and duties of states, and even governments-in-exile, are fairly well defined in international law, the same cannot be said for liberation movements, a fact which may give rise to considerable legal confusion and argument. Thus, in *Tel-Oren* v. *Libyan Arab Republic* (1984) a United States Court of Appeal declined to accept a case against the Palestine Liberation Organisation in part on the ground that the PLO's obligations under international law were unclear.

When the General Assembly recognised the second movement under consideration, the South-West Africa People's Organisation (SWAPO), as the sole representative of the people of Namibia, this legal problem was highlighted, since on the one hand the UN had already vested full authority for the administration of the territory in the Council for Namibia, while on the other hand South Africa refused to recognise either the Council or SWAPO. The impression that SWAPO was in a legal limbo was at times very strong.

When the United Nations itself is paralysed by political influences or legal hesitations, the standing of liberation movements may be even more dubious. For example, in the case of Eritrea, a linguistically and religiously distinct region on the Red Sea coast of Africa which was incorporated against the wishes of its inhabitants into Ethiopia in 1962, international organisations have been reluctant to recognise any Eritrean liberation movement, partly from a fear of seeming to support the dismemberment of one of Africa's oldest independent states.

47. Non-colonial situations. Another area of difficulty which has yet to be resolved is the application of self-determination in those clearly non-colonial situations which it now appears to govern under the UN Human Rights Covenants. Are Scottish Nationalists, for example, entitled to claim self-determination for their country, or Basques demand it from Spain?

The answers are not at all clear, especially in light of the contention of some states and writers that, even if the right of self-determination may go beyond traditional colonial situations, it nevertheless can only operate in 'non-metropolitan' or overseas territories and not in what is geographically the home territory of an existing state.

48. The Scottish case. It must be said, however, that, in British practice at least, there has been a strong emphasis in recent years on the broad application of self-determination.

Britain is a party to the International Covenant on Civil and Political Rights, which endorses self-determination in Article 1.

Britain was a participating state in the Helsinki Final Act produced by the Conference on Security and Cooperation in Europe in 1975. Principle VIII in that paper says in part:

> By virtue of the principle of equal rights and self-determination of peoples, all peoples always have the right, in full freedom, to determine, when and as they wish, their internal and external political status, without external interference ...

Although the Final Act was considered not to have the rank of a binding treaty, the principles it enunciated, including that just quoted, are often thought to be declaratory of existing customary law as of 1975. In the context of a document dealing only with Europe, an area composed entirely of independent sovereign states, Principle VIII must be read as applying self-determination, probably as a matter of law, to such states and not simply to overseas colonies. Indeed, the principle reaffirms 'the universal significance' of respect for self-determination, although also stressing the need to act in conformity with international norms regarding territorial integrity.

However, it may not be intended to apply to all national minorities, as these are mentioned separately in Principle VII dealing with human rights and fundamental freedoms, but only to peoples which have a constitutionally recognised status, as in a multinational state. Whether even in these circumstances Principle VIII would extend so far as to allow dismemberment of an existing state is not clear, but its reference to territorial integrity leads some writers to argue that it envisages fulfilment of the rights stated only within the framework of states as they currently exist.

On these readings of the principle, it would appear that a limited self-determination for Scotland would be available under the Helsinki Final Act, assuming that Scotland has a constitutionally recognised separate identity within the United Kingdom, as evidenced, for example, by its distinct legal system.

More generally with reference to Argentina's invasion of the Falkland Islands the British Prime Minister stressed both that the islanders were British and that, as she told Parliament on 29 April 1982, 'The right of self-determination for the inhabitants of any territory is fundamental in the UN Charter'. It is presumably on this basis also that the British government has repeatedly affirmed a right of self-determination for the Palestinians following the EEC's Venice Declaration of June 1980.

British practice therefore seems sufficiently sweeping and unqualified by reservations or limitations to allow the inference that self-determination for the people of Scotland would be consistent with Britain's official views on the matter.

49. Objections to Scottish self-determination. In the Scottish case, however, it might be argued that the people of Scotland (or at least their country's Parliament) had already exercised their right as long ago as 1707 by agreeing to the Treaty of Union whereby England and Scotland joined to form Great Britain. But, assuming this was in fact an act of self-determination (a debatable assertion), is a clearly distinct people entitled to only one exercise of the right in its whole history? Or can changing times and circumstances justify further recourse to the will of the people? The answer may partly depend on how one applies the international legal doctrine of *intertemporal law*, whereby, according to a resolution adopted in 1975 by the Institut de Droit International, 'any fact, action or situation must be assessed in the light of the rules of law that are contemporaneous with it'.

But the correct response may also depend on part on whether one adopts a natural law or positivist perspective on international law in general (*see* **1:7–23**). Natural law advocates would see individual and group human rights law having revived in modern times the natural law concept that certain fundamental rights are inalienable, i.e. incapable of being taken, or given, away. If the right of self-determination is, as some suggest, a part of *jus cogens* (*see* **2:20**), then it could well be inalienable.

This conclusion accords with the use of the word 'always' in Principle VIII of the Helsinki Final Act and with the common sense observation that a people can hardly be deemed to have eternally forsworn its rights simply by virtue of the political expediency of a by-gone age, particularly where the circumstances were such that democratic principles were neither widely acknowledged nor implemented.

On the other hand, positivists might argue that the Helsinki accord is not a binding treaty and that *jus cogens* is simply a particularly powerful form of customary law which can, like all customary law, be limited by other norms of equal weight, such as respect for the territorial integrity of existing states.

Even the 1970 Declaration on Principles of International Law (*see* **42**) allows self-determination to break up an existing state only when that is necessary to protect basic political rights. Otherwise the Declaration accepts that the right can be exercised in ways that fall short of independence, for example, 'free association or integration with an independent state or the emergence into any other political status freely determined by a people'.

In the case of Scotland, positivists might on this basis maintain that the rights of the Scottish people were not being so severely violated as to require independence but that the position was sufficiently unsatisfactory to warrant self-determination leading, say, to devolution within the United Kingdom.

If this argument were accepted, it would limit the actual degree of freedom of choice available to the people whose self-determination was at issue and would by implication also diminish that people's potential international legal personality by concluding that it could not form a state. At first blush to call this self-determination might appear a contradiction in terms, but it must be remembered that the choice offered under self-determination is one free of the political or other interference of outside forces and not a choice which is free of the limitations imposed by international law as part of the legal principle itself.

At present neither positivists nor natural law advocates can be said to have converted their opponents or established an undisputed interpretation of self-determination, so the debate continues.

Public international organisations **50. Non-state international legal persons.** With the previous categories of international legal persons we were considering entities that fundamentally fitted within the traditional notion that only states could be the subjects of international law, since those entities either were already states or were aiming to be so.

Non-state international legal persons, however, are a clear departure from traditional law and their existence has consequently been recognised to a greater or lesser extent only as each case has arisen and been resolved. The result is that states retain their position as the primary subjects of international law, although additional ones have appeared from time to time, usually as a result of the actions of the states themselves.

The chief of these new international legal persons are public international organisations, that is, organisations of which states, rather than private individuals or institutions, are the members. The first and greatest of these is the United Nations.

51. The United Nations. In a landmark opinion the ICJ determined the legal character of the United Nations in the *Reparation for Injuries suffered in the Service of the United Nations Case* (1949).

During the Palestine war of 1948, the United Nations sought to end the conflict by appointing a mediator, Count Folke Bernadotte of Sweden, to open a channel of communication between the Arab and Israeli sides and to offer proposals for a settlement. In September 1948 he had drawn up a plan that, while confirming the establishment of Israel, would also have allocated to an Arab state large areas of central and southern Palestine, have confirmed the international status of Jerusalem, and have emphasised 'the right of the Arab refugees to return to their homes in Jewish-controlled territory at the earliest possible date'. But while driving through the Israeli-controlled sector of Jerusalem, Count Bernadotte was assassinated by a gang of Jewish terrorists.

The United Nations organisation wished to claim, on its own behalf and that of the murdered mediator's family, reparations from the government of Israel. This raised a number of questions which are summarised below along with the court's conclusions:

(*a*)(*i*) Was it possible that the UN could have such international legal personality as to enable it to raise these claims?

(*ii*) Yes. International law could have various categories of subjects which were 'not necessarily identical in their nature or in the extent of their rights'. There could thus be legal persons that were not states and that perhaps had rights different from those of states.

(*b*)(*i*) Did the United Nations in fact have international legal personality?

(*ii*) Yes. The UN Charter created the organisation for particular purposes and according to specific principles. International personality was essential to give effect to those purposes and principles, and could therefore be presumed to have been intended by the authors of the Charter.

Indeed, the organisation had clearly been given in that document an identity and a responsibility separate from those of its member states. Article 104 conferred on it legal capacity in the members' territory and Article 105 gave it certain privileges and immunities there and permitted it to conclude appropriate treaties on such matters with the members. All of this could be explained only on the basis of a large measure of international personality.

However, 'that is not the same thing as saying that it is a state ... or that its legal personality and rights and duties are the same as those of a state ... What it does mean is that it is a subject of international law and capable of possessing international rights and duties, and that it has the capacity to maintain its rights by bringing international claims'.

Such claims would be international claims governed by international law and not the municipal law of the offending state.

(c)(i) Could the UN claim *also* on behalf of its agent or his family?

(ii) Yes. The court then elaborated what has come to be called the doctrine of implied powers. 'Under international law, the Organisation must be deemed to have those powers which, though not expressly provided in the Charter, are conferred upon it by necessary implication as being essential to the performance of its duties.'

The right to claim on behalf of its agent or his family was such an implied power because the UN had to provide its agents with support and protection, or at least the assurance that their families would be cared for, so that they could perform their missions efficiently and independently.

(d)(i) In view of the fact that at the relevant time Israel was not a member of the UN (and hence in theory not bound by any provisions of the treaty which established the organisation and gave it its personality), did the UN have the requisite personality *vis-à-vis* Israel?

(ii) Yes. The UN Charter had conferred 'objective international personality' on the organisation *erga omnes* (i.e. with effect against everybody). This meant in effect that the Charter had not merely created treaty relations between the parties to it, but had actually brought into being an organisation that existed in the wider world and whose existence had to be accepted by all as a fact of international life.

These sweeping conclusions are justified very largely by the United Nations' unique position as an organisation whose work is of universal importance and whose membership at the time encompassed almost all the independent states in the world. The opinion should therefore not be taken without reservation as a precedent for determining the status of more limited organisations, of which there are currently over one hundred. Nevertheless, the court's decision did highlight considerations that are relevant in other cases and made it easier for other organisations to acquire some degree of personality. This has been particularly important for the status of the European Communities.

52. The European Communities. To the extent that the European Coal and Steel Community (ECSC), the European Atomic Energy Community (EURATOM), and particularly the European Economic Community (EEC) may individually or together form the nucleus around which a 'supra-national' entity might evolve in Europe the degree of international legal personality which each may be recognised to have could be a significant factor in that development. The position is complicated, however, by the fact that, although the three communities have been merged to some extent by agreements in 1957 and 1967 whereby they came to share a common Court of Justice and Parliamentary Assembly as well as a single Commission and single Council, they nevertheless retain distinct juridical identities deriving from the three treaties which created them.

53. Legal capacity of the Communities. Each community's establishing treaty contains a provision similar to Article 210 of the first Treaty of Rome (the EEC

Treaty) which reads: 'The Community shall have legal personality.' Such provisions must be understood to cover in the first instance the community's legal position within each member state and *vis-à-vis* each member state. But the fact that even on that level the community has a legal identity separate from that of its members provides the basis on which a distinct international legal capacity and personality may be established if the founding treaty otherwise permits the community to act internationally.

The ECSC Treaty of 1951 in Article 6 accords that community 'in international relations ... the legal capacity it requires to perform its functions and attain its objectives'. The EURATOM Treaty (the second Treaty of Rome of March 1957) in Article 101 provides that EURATOM 'may, within the limits of its powers and jurisdiction, enter into obligations by concluding agreements or contracts with a third state, an international organisation or a national of a third state'. Under Article 113(3) of the Treaty of Rome the EEC is similarly empowered to make trade and tariff agreements with third countries to implement the Community's commercial policy; under Article 238 it may conclude association agreements with 'a third state, a union of states or an international organisation'.

The capacity to conclude treaties with states must be taken to confer considerable international legal personality by elevating the communities to a level of equality in this respect with the international system's primary legal persons. The EEC in particular has exercised this treaty-making capacity on a number of occasions by making association agreements with neighbouring states (Greece, Turkey, Cyprus, Malta, Morocco and Tunisia) and on a multilateral basis with Third World countries under, for example, the Lomé Convention of 1975 and its replacements (the Lomé Conventions of 1979 and 1984), to which over sixty states are parties. The EEC has also concluded external trade agreements with Switzerland, India, Pakistan, Israel, Spain and Yugoslavia.

Another important indication of international legal personality is the capacity to maintain diplomatic relations. The EEC has such relations with over one hundred states and receives ambassadors from many of them while itself maintaining a delegation at the United Nations. The Communities engage in discussions and information-sharing with other international bodies such as the International Labour Office and the Council of Europe. The President of the EEC Commission has represented the EEC at several economic summit conferences.

During the United Nations Law of the Sea Conference from 1973 to 1982, the EEC was represented by its own delegation and adopted a Community policy on the question of deep seabed mining. The Community signed the Final Act of the Conference on its own behalf.

The legal power of the EEC to act in this way was confirmed by the Community Court of Justice in *Commission* v. *Council* (1971) when it was held that the Community's treaty making power extended beyond those cases specifically authorised by the Treaty of Rome to embrace any subject within the Community's purview. In *Officier van Justitie* v. *Kramer* (1976) the court went further and indicated that as the Community developed a common policy in some area (here, fisheries control) it also acquired the capacity to implement the policy by concluding international agreements on the matter. So the Community's legal capacity and hence its personality were capable of expanding from within as the organisation developed.

54. Enlarged political role for the EEC. A trend in recent years within the EEC has been to attempt closer cooperation on matters that are, strictly speaking, beyond the realm of economics. In 1976 the Belgian Prime Minister, Leo Tindemans, published a report which recommended that coordinated defence and foreign policies be developed as a means of promoting European union.

In the past, as when the members of the Community agreed in 1972 to recognise Bangladesh but attempted to avoid implying that recognition was in fact a Community affair, there had been a reluctance to engage the EEC in general foreign policy issues. But by 1980 the EEC summit meeting was prepared to adopt the Venice Declaration on the Middle East, with the heads of state or government acting in effect as a 'European Council' to decide a foreign policy question on behalf of the Community. That the Declaration did not embody simply the common policy of the members but that of the Community itself may be inferred from the fact that the Irish Foreign Minister was delegated to address the United Nations later about the matter on behalf of the EEC. This trend was confirmed in Article 30 of the Single European Act 1986 in which the members of the communities agreed to attempt the formulation of 'a European foreign policy'.

Taken together these various moves leave little doubt that the EEC at least has a still developing international legal personality of the 'functional' kind first outlined by the ICJ in the *Reparation Case* (*see* **50**): that is, the degree of personality necessary to the organisation to carry out its functions on the international level.

55. Legal responsibility of international organisations. If international organisations with international legal personality can make international claims and enter into treaties, it follows that they must also have corresponding contractual and delictual (tortious) obligations and legal responsibility. In general, such organisations accept tort liability for the acts of their agents and officials and financial obligations arising out of their own contracts.

Semi-public intergovernmental organisations

56. General note. The period since 1945 has seen the development of a new type of international entity in the form of corporate bodies that are private in their legal structure but public and intergovernmental in their establishment and purpose. For example, the European Company for Financing Railway Equipment (Eurofima) was established under the terms of a treaty signed in 1955 between sixteen European states to coordinate the construction of railway rolling stock, but it was set up as a Swiss company to be governed by Swiss law except when that might conflict with the company's international statute. Although on the very edge of being a public international organisation, such a company would appear in the end more private than public and hence lacking in international legal personality.

An even less structured entity which has appeared in recent decades is the intergovernmental producers association, of which the leading example is the Organisation of Petroleum Exporting Countries (OPEC). The purpose of this organisation is to coordinate the production and pricing of oil exports by the member countries, but OPEC as such appears to exercise no supranational powers, its members do not delegate decision-making to it, and agreements reached through its mechanism are voluntary and to a large degree unenforceable. It does not itself act on the international level but operates through the activities of its member governments. It would therefore also seem to lack international legal personality.

Private international organisations

57. The International Committee of the Red Cross (ICRC). Although in general private organisations whose membership or activities extend beyond national boundaries do not have the status of international legal persons, the position of the ICRC has the potential for being an exception. Based in Switzerland and organised according to the requirements of Swiss law, the Committee enjoys the unique distinction of being directly named in the four Geneva Conventions of 1949 as empowered to intervene with governments on behalf of victims of war. The ICRC has also been active in organising international conferences of states with the aim of promoting further improvements in the law of war. The Committee may not have international legal personality yet, but its standing is clearly more than that of a Swiss charity and is continuing to develop.

58. Multinational enterprises and transnational corporations. Multinational enterprises (MNEs), or, as they are sometimes called, transnational corporations to emphasise their cross-border impact and influence, are companies headquartered in one state but operating in several other states as well. The question of their status on the international scene arises from the enormous resources and economic power which they can bring to bear, often with major social and political consequences for the countries affected. As these are often developing Third World states, while the MNEs are usually from the industrialised West, and particularly the United States, attempts to establish international controls on these companies have become entangled with East-West and North-South antagonisms and little progress towards world regulation has been made. *eg Tax holidays, exemption of labour rights*

This failure has left a number of issues unresolved. There is, first of all, the relationship between the parent company and its overseas affiliates. The MNE's world-wide business strategy or interests may envisage a restricted role for a particular affiliate, while the Third World 'host' state in which the affiliate operates may see its expansion as the key to the country's economic development. For the MNE it may be advantageous to exploit host state raw materials or cheap labour for the benefit of the international corporation, regardless of the debilitating effect this may have on the host's situation. The host state may be interested in seeing the affiliate equipped with the latest technology (the question of 'transfer of technology'), while the MNE wishes to maintain its core operation's business lead by keeping technological advantages firmly in the hands of the parent company. Even the techniques of accounting used between the parent and the affiliates can cause difficulties if the parent adopts so-called 'transfer pricing' whereby the affiliate sells its products to the parent at less than market prices, giving the parent an instant profit but denying the host state's economy badly needed foreign earnings. *eg due to tax*

Another problem area centres on the tendency of MNEs to operate in a way that minimises their overall world-wide compliance with the highest norms for production safety, environmental protection and product quality. When the world's worst industrial accident occurred at a chemical plant in Bhopal, India, in December 1984, international concern with these questions was sharpened by

[handwritten margin note:] Sri Lanka - workers rights are suspended

[handwritten margin note:] Schmithoff - 2 basic ques. of fundamental importance to Third World

revelations that the standards of design, construction and operation of the plant were inferior to what was legally permissible for the parent company in its American installations. The Bhopal disaster also highlighted the related issue of the sharing of information on hazardous products between the parent and its affiliates and between the MNE and host governments.

A third area of concern is the investment policy of multinationals towards the Third World and the terms on which the MNEs agree to operate there. Developing countries need the financial and managerial contribution which the MNE can offer but they have often been made to pay for it with concessions that leave key sectors of the national economy beyond the control of government.

In 1984 a UN Commission produced a revised Draft UN Code of Conduct on Transnational Corporations that attempted to deal with some of these questions, but it was apparent that fundamental disagreements between western and Third World countries remained unresolved.

Thus MNEs continue to be in a position where they can exercise power and influence on an international scale, sometimes beyond the control of states. Are MNEs therefore international legal persons in their own right? The fact that MNEs are often able to deal with some states more or less as equals leads some observers to conclude that they are indeed international legal persons. But it must be said that since the international rights and duties which that status would entail have never been spelt out in treaty or custom, MNEs must for the present continue to be regarded simply as the creatures of national legal systems and consequently as largely beyond the control of the international community as a whole.

An interesting exception, however, is the supranational regulation of national and multinational companies by the European Economic Community, not only in the areas of competition and marketing but latterly in such matters as environmental protection and pollution control.

Individuals

59. Introduction. As with other potential legal persons, some indication of the status of individuals can be gleaned from an examination of whether they have rights and duties under international law.

60. Rights of individuals. Traditionally in international law individuals were considered to be merely objects of the law and not its subjects. This meant that, strictly speaking, individuals did not derive any rights directly from international law. Only states had international legal rights; if an individual was adversely affected by the action of some foreign state, he had to resort to his own state and persuade it that what had been done to him was also a violation of its international rights which it should pursue on the international level.

The Permanent Court of International Justice, in the *Mavrommatis Palestine Concessions (Jurisdiction) Case* (1924), gave the classic formulation of this view:

> it is true that the dispute was at first between a private person and a state ... [then] the Greek Government took up the case. The dispute then entered upon a new phase; it entered the domain of international law and became a dispute between two states ... By taking up the case of one of its subjects ... a state is in reality asserting its own rights - its right to ensure, in the person of its subjects, respect for the rules of international law.

This view has been criticised, particularly because it seems to link the status of individuals under international law to the question of who is capable of enforcing rights on the international level. Sir Hersch Lauterpacht pointed out that there is no necessary connection between being a direct beneficiary of rights and being able to enforce them directly. Under-age children, for example, have a wide variety of legal rights, but must in general depend on a parent, guardian or social services agency to enforce them.

In any event, international law in this century has gone some way towards endowing individuals with the capacity to enforce rights given to them directly from international law. The turning point came with the decision of the PCIJ in the *Jurisdiction of the Courts of Danzig (Danzig Railway Officials) Case* (1928). The Free City of Danzig and Poland had concluded an agreement to regulate the conditions of employment of Danzigers working in the Polish railways. Poland argued that the courts of Danzig had no jurisdiction to hear claims raised against the Polish state by certain Danzig employees because the agreement was between two international entities and could not confer directly on individuals rights which they could ask a municipal court to enforce. The PCIJ held, however, that the agreement in question was specifically intended to establish 'definite rules creating individual rights and obligations and enforceable in national courts'.

The effect of this landmark decision was to make clear that, whatever theoretical objections there may have been, in practice states could by treaty give individuals the status of direct subjects of international law.

The application of this conclusion may be seen in a wide variety of international agreements. The Fourth Geneva Convention of 1949, for example, accords civilians who fall into the hands of the enemy during war or military occupation a broad range of individual and collective rights which they are entitled to enforce directly. The European Convention on Human Rights (1950), Article 25, and the American Convention on Human Rights (1969), Article 44, each allow individuals to petition internationally constituted Commissions established under the Conventions to protect human rights in the participating states, and cases may also proceed to each system's Court of Human Rights.

Thus, the individual is increasingly being endowed with international legal rights and the capacity to pursue them. The fact that these may differ from those of a state should not prevent recognition of the individual's international legal personality, having mind the ICJ's acknowledgement in the *Reparation Case* that different types of international personality may exist according to the circumstances appropriate to each category.

61. Duties of individuals. It is interesting that while individual rights under international law (which imply duties imposed on states) have been late in coming, duties on individuals have been recognised for centuries. It has long been a violation of international law for an individual to commit 'piracy *jure gentium*' (i.e. piracy according to the law of nations). Article 1, s. 8 of the United States Constitution (adopted in 1787) empowered the Congress to 'define and punish ... Offences against the Law of Nations'. Given that it would not have been within the competence of one country to create international law by legislation, this provision must be understood to mean that Congress was the body authorised to determine for the purposes of American statute law which acts the law of nations had made criminal offences.

In modern times the range of international criminal offences for which individuals may be held liable has been expanded. The International Military Tribunal at Nuremberg, set up by the victorious allies at the end of World War II to try German war criminals, operated on the basis that there were crimes against peace, war crimes, and crimes against humanity which the defendants could be personally guilty of. The four Geneva Conventions of 1949 envisage criminal prosecutions before national courts of persons accused of violating their provisions. Similarly, the *Convention on the Prevention and Punishment of the Crime of Genocide* (1948) provides that persons committing offences under it 'shall be punished, whether they are constitutionally responsible rulers, public officials or private individuals'.

In 1974 the UN General Assembly adopted Resolution 3314 on the Definition of Aggression which provides in Article 5(2): 'A war of aggression is a crime against international peace. Aggression gives rise to international responsibility.'

The trend in contemporary international law thus seems clearly to be towards increasing the direct obligations imposed on individuals under international law, although prosecution of international criminals continues to be the responsibility of states in the absence of an international criminal court.

62. The international legal personality of individuals. Having both rights and duties under international law, the individual does seem to have international legal personality derived at least in part from agreements between states but capable in certain circumstances of being exercised against states. It is not personality of the functional kind, since it is not granted in order to allow the individual to perform tasks assigned by states, but seems rather to originate in the needs of human beings and their social obligations to each other.

Progress test 4

1. What is the difference between a 'subject' and an 'object' of international law? **(1)**

2. List the traditional criteria for statehood. **(3)**

3. Is sovereignty an important concept in international law? **(5)**

4. Is independence of government necessary for statehood? **(8)**

5. Do treaty limitations on a state's exercise of sovereignty necessarily entail loss of statehood? **(10)**

6. Does the 'capacity to enter into relations with other states' imply the need for recognition? **(12–14)**

7. Differentiate between the constitutive and the declaratory views of recognition of statehood. **(13)**

8. Describe the structure of the League of Nations mandate system. **(26)**

9. Is South Africa's continued presence in Namibia legal? **(31)**

10. Summarise the contents of General Assembly Resolution 1514(XV). **(41)**

11. May self-determination justify the disruption of any existing state? **(43)**

12. What is the key feature of the right of self-determination according to Judge Dillard? **(45)**

13. Is the Scottish nation entitled at the present time to self-determination? **(48–9)**

14. Analyse the judgment of the ICJ in the *Reparation Case* (1949). **(51)**

15.. Do individuals have international legal personality? **(59–62)**

Bibliography

On Palestine

Cattan, *Palestine and International Law*, 1st ed. (London, 1973)

Sohn, *Cases on United Nations Law*, pp. 416–474, 2nd ed. (Brooklyn, 1967)

On the Bernadotte Mission

Persson, *Mediation and Assassination: Count Bernadotte's Mission to Palestine 1948* (London, 1979)

On Bhopal

Ott, 'Bhopal and the law: the shape of a new international legal regime', *Third World Quarterly*, vol. 7, No. 3, pp. 648–660 (1985)

5 Recognition

1. **Scope of chapter.** Recognition of states has already been covered (*see* 4:13) and we are primarily concerned here with the recognition of governments.

Recognition of governments: the traditional search for criteria

2. **The nature of the problem.** Typically the recognition of governments causes difficulties when a new regime has taken power
   (*a*) unconstitutionally; or
   (*b*) by violent means; or
   (*c*) with foreign help,
in a state whose previous and legitimate government was recognised by the state which now must consider recognition of the new government.

Recognition in such circumstances may appear an endorsement of the new regime's aims or methods of attaining power, and the government considering recognition may wish for political or legal reasons to discourage such aims or methods by refusing to recognise and bestow approval. On the other hand it may be politically or economically disadvantageous not to recognise, and a state may in that case wish to accord recognition but to play down any implication of approval by emphasising that the process of recognising a new régime operates automatically once certain facts are present.

The effect of these contradictory approaches to recognition has been to complicate the law on the question by confounding two different sets of criteria for recognition. The first focusses on an *objective test*: the new régime should be recognised if in fact it exercises the powers of government and has the obedience of the majority of the population. The second set of criteria vary but centre on a *subjective test*: is the new regime going to do what it should internally and externally (e.g. by observing democracy, obeying international law or fulfilling the state's previous treaty obligations)?

3. **The British view: the Morrison doctrine.** Britain has tended to favour the objective test. In 1951 the British Foreign Secretary, Herbert Morrison, indicated to the House of Commons the criteria which the United Kingdom for long regarded, at least in principle, as relevant to recognition of new regimes:

> recognition of a ... government should be distinguished from ... diplomatic relations with it, which [are] entirely discretionary ... it is international law which defines the conditions under which a government should be recognised *de jure* or *de facto* ... a new regime [recognised] as the *de facto* government ... [must have] in fact effective control over most of the state's territory and ... this control [must seem] likely to continue, recognition ... as the *de jure* government ... [requires] that the new regime should not merely have effective control ... but that it should, in fact, be firmly established.

The distinction between *de facto* and *de jure* government is traditional in international law.

(*a*) *De facto* government covers regimes that exercise control in at least part of the state's territory but whose legitimacy is still contested, so that the *de facto* government does not enjoy the full legal status which an undisputed state authority would have.

(*b*) A *de jure* government, on the other hand, would have the full legal legitimacy and status of the state's rightful government.

In dealing with the problem of recognition in the way he did, Morrison is understood to have meant that recognition of governments was a duty whose execution depended entirely on whether the facts on the ground fit the categories established by international law.

By implying the obligatory nature of recognition and flatly denying that it reflected British approval of the regime in question, this approach preserved Britain's moral and legal positions while not slighting the UK's practical interests.

The doctrine also tended to minimise a problem which recognition presented for international law. The law often depends for its effectiveness on the refusal of the international community to facilitate illegal acts by bestowing any sort of legitimacy on the violators. By ruling that out, the British doctrine did something to help uphold the law.

But having a policy and applying it are not the same thing, and the giving or withholding of recognition by Britain was not always done consistently with the Morrison doctrine. The German Democratic Republic in East Germany, for example, was not recognised until 1973, and the United Kingdom does not accept as *de jure* the Soviet government of Latvia, Lithuania, and Estonia, although these Baltic republics have been under Moscow's control since World War II.

Thus the existence of the Morrison formulation did not prevent a subjective element from creeping into British recognition policy.

4. United States views. From the early days of the republic, the United States has veered several times from the subjective to the objective test and back again according to whether the US government at any particular time saw its role as maintaining international morality or as simply dealing with whatever foreign regimes came to power.

At the time of the French Revolution, the Secretary of State, Thomas Jefferson, seemed to imply that recognition was appropriate only in the case of new regimes that were democratically established: 'It accords with our principles to acknowledge any government which is formed by the will of the nation substantially declared.'

By 1852, however, the Secretary of State, Daniel Webster, had abandoned this approach for one closer to the Morrison doctrine: 'it has been a principle, always acknowledged by the United States, that every nation possesses a right to govern itself according to its own will, to change its institutions at discretion, and to transact its business through whatever agents it may think proper to employ.' In practice this meant that the United States would look simply for the acquiescence of the people in whatever changes were made and would not require a positive expression of their will.

During the presidency of Woodrow Wilson (1913–1921), who held strong moral and ethical views about foreign policy, the United States once more veered towards legitimacy as a criterion for recognition: it would not have normal diplomatic relations with a regime attaining power in violation of the constitution of its own state. This policy proved difficult to apply and was eventually abandoned.

But a revival of something like it occurred again in 1949 in the wake of the communist victory in the Chinese civil war and the establishment of Mao Tse Tung's government over the whole of mainland China and its islands (with the significant exception of the island of Formosa/Taiwan, which was held by pro-Western forces under Chiang Kai Shek). A State Department spokesman later described the American view on recognition as follows:

> there is a serious question whether the Chinese Communist regime can in any way be considered to reflect the will of the nation; and there is no doubt, in view of flagrant past treaty violations and violations of the United Nations Charter and violations of international law and in view of statements made by the Chinese Communist regime about disregarding pre-existing treaties, that the Chinese Communist regime is not prepared to honor its international obligations. Thus ... the Chinese Communists are not entitled to recognition.

As the East-West confrontation was joined by Third World antagonism towards the United States in the 1950s and 1960s, additional criteria appear to have been applied to the question of recognition in particular cases:

(a) the degree of foreign intervention in the establishment of the new regime;

(b) the new government's political orientation and its attitude towards foreign economic investment and free enterprise economics; and

(c) the new regime's commitment to democracy.

In one case (which must be regarded as something of an aberration) the State Department even indicated that America's attitude would be formed 'in light of our dedication to the principle of self-determination'.

The ideological and political basis for some of these criteria is apparent and was criticised for preventing the United States from pursuing diplomatic relations with certain governments in its own interests. Some commentators suggested that the view of Winston Churchill was the correct one: 'The reason for having diplomatic relations is not to confer a compliment but to secure a convenience'.

5. The United Nations. The question of China also represented a major difficulty for the United Nations: China was a permanent member of the Security Council and a founder member of the UN. In 1950 the UN Secretary General produced a memorandum on the matter which suggested that the choice of which Chinese government should represent the country at the UN should be made by analogy with Article 4 of the Charter, where admission of a new member of the organisation depended on whether the applicant state was 'able and willing' to carry out the obligations imposed by the Charter. But treating an existing member as if it were a non-member was a dubious proposition, and perhaps for that reason the memorandum formulated its conclusions in a slightly evasive way, namely that the UN should decide 'which of these two governments in fact *is in a position* to employ the resources and direct the people of the state in fulfilment of the obligations of membership'.

The words whose emphasis has been supplied here evidently require something less than a *willingness* to implement the Charter and allow, as the memorandum concludes, simply an inquiry into the new regime's effective control. The UN General Assembly, whose membership at the time was predominantly pro-American, did not accept that. It rejected what the United Kingdom representative called 'the objective test' (based on effective control of the territory and the obedience of the population) and in Resolution 396(V) proposed instead that 'the question should be considered in the light of the purposes and principles of the Charter and the circumstances of each case'.

Avoiding the problem: the Estrada doctrine

6. **The Estrada doctrine.** In 1930, the Mexican Foreign Minister, Señor Estrada, rejected the whole doctrine of recognition on the ground that it 'allows foreign governments to pass upon the legitimacy or illegitimacy of the regime existing in another country, with the result that situations arise in which the legal qualifications or national status of governments or authorities are apparently made subject to the opinion of foreigners'. Henceforward, therefore, the Mexican government would issue 'no declarations in the sense of grants of recognition'.

This Estrada doctrine, as it is called, is understood to deny the need for explicit and formal acts of recognition of governments coming to power in states that are already recognised. The effect is that the new regime will be dealt with as if it is the proper authority just as the old regime was dealt with previously, but without any gesture of approval. All that requires to be determined is whether the new regime has in fact established itself as the effective government of the country.

The implication of all this is that recognition in such circumstances is unnecessary for the continuance of diplomatic relations with the new regime.

If international relations were simply a matter of day-to-day dealings with the authorities controlling a particular territory, the Estrada doctrine could be considered to have pushed aside most of the difficult problems associated with the traditional view of recognition.

But one notes that in practice politics continues to intrude: even Mexico itself refused for thirty years to 'recognise' the fascist regime of Francisco Franco in Spain. And the doctrine offers little help in a situation where there are two rival regimes claiming to be the government: a foreign state may still be forced to choose to acknowledge one and disregard the other – in effect a gesture of recognition.

Some governments in fact still insist on being formally recognised, as did the People's Republic of China in 1979 when discussing 'normalisation of relations' with the United States. This suggests that although the Estrada doctrine may be a convenient way out for the state trying to avoid according recognition, the new government in question may find it unacceptable for political reasons of its own.

Nevertheless, the doctrine has gained ground: a US State Department study in 1969 found that thirty-one states had adopted it, and since then others have explicitly or implicitly followed suit, including the United States and Britain themselves.

7. **The new United States position.** In 1977 the American State Department issued an announcement according to which 'In recent years, US practice has

been to de-emphasise and avoid the use of recognition in cases of change of governments and to concern ourselves with the question of whether we wish to have diplomatic relations with the new governments.'

In 1978, when a revolutionary government came to power in Afghanistan, an American statement indicated that 'the question of recognition ... doesn't arise *per se* ... The important question is not recognition. The question is whether diplomatic relations continue.' The US decided to 'maintain diplomatic relations' with the new government on the express assumption that the new Afghan regime 'will continue to honor and support the existing treaties and agreements in force between our two states'.

8. The new British position. In April 1980 the British Foreign Secretary, Lord Carrington, announced in the House of Lords that the United Kingdom's policy from then on was that 'we shall no longer accord recognition to governments'. He went on:

> we shall ... decide the nature of our dealings with regimes that come to power unconstitutionally in the light of our assessment of whether they are able of themselves to exercise effective control of the territory of the state concerned, and seem likely to continue to do so.

Apart from its adoption of the Estrada approach to the problem of recognition, this statement differs from the Morrison doctrine also in two other respects.

(*a*) It does not make a distinction between *de jure* and *de facto* governments. The reason is that British policy in recent years had been not to recognise any *de facto* regime at all while the struggle between competing 'governments' in a country went on, but rather to wait until one had clearly established itself and then to recognise it as the *de jure* government. Although this doubtless simplified matters for the Foreign Office in some respects, it did not really explain the basis on which British interests in a country split by civil war between rival governments would be protected. Would the British government have no contact at all with the authorities controlling territory in which such interests were situated?

The answer would appear to be that the United Kingdom would have what traditional law calls *relations officieuses* or 'dealings' with those authorities while making clear that no intent to recognise should be inferred.

(*b*) The Carrington statement also used the words 'able of themselves to exercise effective control'. 'Of themselves' was meant to indicate that the British government would look very closely at situations where a new regime appeared to be utterly dependent on external support. For some time before Lord Carrington's announcement Britain had been facing difficulties in Cambodia where the previously recognised government of Pol Pot had been thrust aside by the regime of Heng Samrin, who had the support of Vietnam. In December 1979, the British view was stated in the House of Commons to be that Pol Pot was no longer leading an effective government while 'the dependence of the so-called Heng Samrin regime on the Vietnamese occupation army is complete'. Consequently, 'we emphatically do not recognise any claim by Heng Samrin and our position is that there is no government in Cambodia whom we can recognise'.

9. Problems with the Estrada doctrine. Although the Estrada doctrine has the advantage of allowing a state faced with the problem of whether to recognise a new regime to avoid giving a public seal of approval to a disreputable government, it does not really do away with the problem of criteria for deciding on diplomatic relations with that regime. These criteria may come to resemble those formerly applied to the question of recognition, and the decision on diplomatic relations may come in time to be regarded as just as much a sign of approval or disapproval as that on recognition used to be.

The Estrada doctrine also has the not always desirable effect of shifting from a Foreign Office on to someone else the burden of determining officially what the relationship with a new regime is for legal purposes. In practice, this means that the courts will have to draw conclusions about who is considered the *de jure* government in a foreign country on the basis of each court's own evaluation of the available evidence relating to diplomatic relations. This could cause confusion and uncertainty for potential litigants and raise problems of proof in cases where the foreign ministry's dealings with a regime are not conducted entirely in public. In such circumstances, the courts might be tempted to set and apply their own criteria for 'recognition' of foreign governments.

Finally, one must note that the adoption of the Estrada doctrine by some states, but not all, still leaves the question of recognition and its effects as a real issue in international law which must be studied in the light of state practice before the Estrada doctrine attained its present prominence.

Effect in international law of non-recognition of *de facto* governments

10. Impact. Although non-recognition of a new regime may have significant effects in the municipal law of other states (*see* 15, 16), the impact of non-recognition on the international level may be less important.

11. The Tinoco Claims Arbitration (1923). In January 1917 the constitutional government of Costa Rica was ousted in a coup led by Federico Tinoco. In keeping with President Wilson's policy against acknowledging governments that attained power unconstitutionally, the United States refused to recognise the Tinoco government, and other countries, including the United Kingdom, likewise declined to do so. Nevertheless, Tinoco ruled Costa Rica until 1919 and conducted government business, including the granting of an oil concession to a British company. After Tinoco's overthrow, the restored constitutional government nullified a number of his acts, among them the oil concession. Britain objected to this, but Costa Rica argued that the Tinoco regime was not the legitimate government of the country (as demonstrated by the British and American refusal to recognise it) and so could not be held to have bound the subsequent legitimate government to honour the concession.

The case was referred for arbitration to the Chief Justice of the United States Supreme Court (and former American President), William Howard Taft. Considering the weight to be placed on non-recognition of the Tinoco regime as evidence that it was not in fact a government which by acts like the oil concession could have bound Costa Rica internationally, Taft concluded that non-recognition was of little evidentiary value when based on criteria such as legitimacy of origin rather than criteria of '*de facto* sovereignty and complete governmental control'. He continued: 'Such non-recognition ... cannot outweigh ... the *de facto* character of Tinoco's government, according to the standard set by international law.'

Taft therefore emphasised effectiveness rather than legitimacy and went on implicitly to reject the Wilson test for recognition:

> To hold that a government which establishes itself and maintains a peaceful administration, with the acquiescence of the people for a substantial period of time, does not become a *de facto* government unless it conforms to a previous constitution would be to hold that within the rules of international law a revolution contrary to the fundamental law of the existing government cannot establish a new government. This cannot be, and is not, true.

Thus, non-recognition *per se* does not prevent the acts of an unrecognised regime being treated as binding in international law.

12. Other situations. If, however, the *de facto* regime is not acting as the government of the entire country but only of a subdivision of it, then a subsequent legitimate government of the state may not be liable for that regime's acts. In *Socony Vacuum Oil Co. Case* (1954), the US-Italian Claims Commission held that Yugoslavia should not be accounted liable for the acts of the Nazi-controlled provincial government of Croatia during World War II.

13. Non-recognition and treaty-making. State practice has occasionally allowed what in theory ought to be impossible: the participation of unrecognised governments and even insurgent regimes in agreements with the state or states that do not recognise them. This appears to be treated as a matter of the discretion of the non-recognising state to have whatever level of dealings it chooses with the unrecognised regime. Thus, in June 1970 Greece concluded a trade agreement with Albania, although Greece had never recognised the Albanian communist government. The 1954 Geneva Agreement on Indo-China was signed by insurgent authorities controlling territory in Laos and Cambodia although they were not recognised as *de facto* governments.

14. International legal requirement of non-recognition. International law may approve of, and even require, non-recognition of a *de facto* regime as the *de jure* government in situations where the existing *de jure* government is continuing to resist the insurgents with some reasonable hope of success. Recognition then would be considered premature and an act of intervention in the affected state's internal affairs contrary to international law.

Recognition and municipal law

15. Importance of recognition for municipal legal purposes. Recognition has traditionally been an important, and often decisive, factor when a court has had to decide, for purposes of its own municipal legal system, the notice to be taken of a foreign regime's existence. Judges often felt reluctant to go their own way in such situations because they did not believe their courts were the best forums for evaluating political events in foreign countries, and they thought their national institutions should, for reasons of governmental foreign policy responsibility and the dangers of disturbing international relations, speak with 'one voice' on such matters (the voice of the foreign ministry).

The solution usually preferred by British and American courts was to request an official letter or certificate from their country's foreign ministry as to whether a particular regime had been recognised. The certificate would then be given effect by the court as conclusive and irrefutable evidence on the question of the foreign government's existence.

The adoption of the Estrada doctrine by many countries now leaves their courts without the option of seeking such certificates when the existence of a foreign government is at issue. Explaining the British position in 1980, Lord Carrington, the Foreign Secretary, said:

'our attitude on the question whether it qualifies to be treated as a government, will be left to be inferred from the nature of the dealings, if any, which we may have with it'.

It should be noted, however, that, since the Estrada doctrine does not apply to recognition of states, when the existence of a foreign state is at issue, a certificate would still be sought and given.

In Estrada doctrine countries, cases of recognition of governments will have to be resolved either:

(a) by the courts applying their own criteria (based, perhaps, on an effectiveness test) for whether a foreign regime is a government; or

(b) by the courts scrutinising their own state's dealings with the regime to determine whether they are the equivalent of recognition.

Lord Carrington's statement implies that the British government prefers the second of these approaches, although in recent years some British judges, influenced by American precedent, have been edging towards the first approach, at least in cases involving purely private law rights (see **22–3**).

Another question which often arises is *retroactivity*. Should recognition be considered to have made the newly-recognised government's existence a legal fact for the court's purposes right back to the beginning of the regime?

This problem of how to deal with the time element in the progression of the new government from being powerless rebels to being the legitimate authorities will remain even in states applying the Estrada doctrine, and indeed may be even more difficult for the courts in view of the fact that they will not have precisely dated foreign ministry certificates to rely on.

Typically, recognition becomes an issue for a court in one of two situations:

(a) when the court must consider whether to give effect to a foreign regime's acts (see **16–29**); or

(b) when that regime is directly involved in a case before the court (see **30–35**).

Validity of a foreign government's acts

16. Historical background to the major cases. Many of the major cases in this area arose out of four events:

(a) the 1917 Revolution in Russia, whose new communist regime was for long unrecognised by Britain and the United States;

(b) the 1935 Italian invasion and occupation of Ethiopia;

(c) the Spanish Civil War of 1936–1939 between Nationalist rebels (under the fascist leader Francisco Franco) and the legitimate Republican government; and

(d) the 1949 Communist victory in China over the Nationalist forces of the Chiang Kai Shek government.

British cases

17. Luther v. Sagor. The leading case is *A. M. Luther* v. *James Sagor & Co.* (1921), usually referred to as *Luther* v. *Sagor*. Luthers were a company incorporated in Russia in 1898. In June 1918 a Soviet confiscation decree laid the basis for seizure in January 1919 of a factory owned by Luthers at which was stocked a large supply of wooden boards. In August 1920 a Soviet trade delegate in London sold this wood to Sagors, who imported it into England. Luthers immediately sought an injunction to restrain Sagors from selling the boards on the grounds that title could not have passed to Sagors in view of the fact that an English court could not hold the Soviet confiscation decree enforceable when Britain had not recognised the Bolshevik regime.

The trial court judge found that a letter from the Foreign Office dated 20 November 1920 was conclusive. It said in part: 'His Majesty's Government has never officially recognised the Soviet Government in any way.' The judge held that this left him unable to recognise the Soviet regime or its sovereignty or its capacity to seize the plaintiff's property.

Sagors appealed and before the appeal was heard the Foreign Office issued another letter dated 20 April 1921 stating: 'His Majesty's Government recognise the Soviet Government as the *de facto* Government of Russia.' On the basis of this statement, the Court of Appeal reversed the lower court ruling and held that, since Britain now regarded the Soviet regime as 'the government really in possession of the powers of sovereignty in Russia', the acts of that government must be treated 'with all the respect due to the acts of a duly recognised foreign sovereign state'.

But the problem of the timeframe within which these various stages were passed remained. The Court of Appeal noted from yet another Foreign Office letter that Britain considered that the Constituent Assembly of the Provisional Government had remained in session until 13 December 1917, when it was dispersed by the Soviet authorities. This was accepted as evidence that at some time near that date the Soviet regime became the Government of Russia. Therefore, 'this court must treat the Soviet Government ... as having commenced its existence at a date anterior to any date material to the dispute.'

Strictly speaking, then, this opinion did not hold that recognition was 'retroactive' but rather that it was in effect a key that opened a door (which would otherwise have remained shut) through which the court could look back to determine when the new regime in fact became the government. For practical purposes, however, the decision may be read as confirming that recognition of a *de facto* government can have retroactive consequences, at least in a case where there was no significant rival claimant and the relevant governmental acts were in territory over which the regime exercised control.

18. Extraterritorial effect. The situation in *Luther* v. *Sagor* should not be confused with that where a court is asked to acknowledge some extraterritorial effect of a confiscation decree which purports to seize the property of the confiscating state's citizens who are living outside the country. In *Luther* v. *Sagor* the decree was treated as operating within Russia on property located there at the time.

The *Civil Air Transport Case* (*see* **21**) may be read to support the conclusion that a foreign regime would have to be recognised as the *de jure* government in order for its decrees to have extraterritorial effect over property which it did not control at the time of the decree. The rationale appears to be that only the *de jure* government can exercise those rights of a state which involve governing citizens and property beyond its physical control.

Thus the acts of a *de facto* government may not always deserve the wide respect which the court thought appropriate in the circumstances of *Luther* v. *Sagor*.

19. Haile Selassie *v.* **Cable and Wireless Ltd (No. 2) (1939).** The plaintiff claimed, as Emperor of Ethiopia and the country's head of state, certain sums owed Ethiopia by the defendant. At the time the Emperor was in exile after the invasion and occupation of his country by Italy. Britain had recognised the Italian administration as the *de facto* government in the territory but continued to acknowledge the Emperor as the *de jure* sovereign.

The trial court judge interpreted several recent decisions as indicating only that a British court could not give effect to the acts of a recognised *de jure* government which related to an area of territory actually controlled by a rival authority which Britain recognised as the *de facto* government. The present case, however, 'is not concerned with the validity of acts in relation to persons or property in Ethiopia' but 'with the title to ... a debt, recoverable in England'. The judge went on: 'I ask myself why should the fact that the Italian army has conquered Ethiopia and that the Italian Government now rules Ethiopia divest the plaintiff of his right to sue.' Finding no convincing reason, he gave judgment in favour of the Emperor.

Nevertheless, while an appeal was pending, Britain went so far as to recognise the Italian king as *de jure* Emperor of Ethiopia. The Court of Appeal then held that the effect of this was to entitle the new emperor to have his rights to the public property of Ethiopia upheld in British courts while Haile Selassie's 'title thereto is no longer recognised as existent'. The rights of the Italian emperor 'dated back at any rate to the date when the *de facto* recognition ... took place ... in December 1936'. As this was before the issue of the writ in the present case, 'the title of the plaintiff to sue is necessarily displaced'.

This result is dubious. Given that the conditions which justified *de jure* recognition of the Italian regime in 1938 were presumably not in existence at the time of *de facto* recognition in 1936, the appeal court ought not to have been quite so ready to dispose of Haile Selassie's rights as if those conditions had existed in 1936.

20. Gdynia Ameryka Linie Zeglugowe Spolka Akcyjna *v.* **Boguslawski (1953).** Although involving the acts of the World War II Polish Government-in-exile (*see* **36–39**), the case was treated by the House of Lords as essentially like any other situation in which the validity of a previously recognised *de jure* government's acts is called in question by recognition of the *de facto* regime's *de jure* status.

The Polish exile government had been recognised by Britain throughout the war as the *de jure* government of Poland and it exercised control outside Poland over Polish seamen such as Bogulawski and Polish shipping lines such as the appellant. On 28 June 1945 a *de facto* communist government was established in Polish territory; as of 6 July 1945 Britain extended recognition to the communist regime as the *de jure* government and withdrew recognition from the government-in-exile. In the interim, on 3 July the exile government had made certain promises to Boguslawski which Gdynia Ameryka Linie later refused to honour on the ground that British recognition of the communist regime on 6 July was in effect retroactive to 28 June, so that no act of the exile government after that date was valid.

Lord Reid in his judgment held that recognition does no more than 'enable and require the courts ... to regard as valid ... acts done by [the new government] ... before its recognition in so far as those acts related to matters under its control at the time.' The courts are not required, however, to give such recognition retroactive effect for all purposes, particularly where the action of the old government did not involve matters under the control of the new one, but rather ships and persons which the old government controlled at the time.

21. Civil Air Transport Inc. *v.* Central Air Transport Corporation (1953). In this appeal from Hong Kong to the Privy Council, the central issue was whether British recognition of the communist regime in China as the *de jure* government in January 1950 required the court to give effect to a prior Communist decree about certain airplanes which the previously recognised Nationalist government of China had removed to Hong Kong before the issuing of the decree and had sold to an American company after the decree was issued.

Lord Simon, giving the opinion of the Judicial Committee of the Privy Council, noted that prior to January 1950, Britain had not recognised the Communist regime even as the *de facto* government of China but had recognised the Nationalist administration as the *de jure* government. He was nevertheless apparently prepared to accept that the communist regime had been the *de facto* government before British recognition, but he evidently considered that that made no difference to the outcome of this case. 'Primarily', he said, 'retroactivity of recognition operates to validate acts of a *de facto* government which has subsequently become the new *de jure* government, and not to invalidate acts of the previous *de jure* government.'

He went on to indicate that where the previous and the present *de jure* governments dispute the disposition of some governmental property, recognition would in general, though possibly not always, have retroactive effect only with regard to acts done in the territory of the government so recognised. In the present case, the property in question was in Hong Kong at the relevant times and could be supposed to have continued to belong to the Nationalist government, unless the Communist regime could be shown to have gained possession of it. Although agents of the Communist regime had in fact attempted to do this, their actions were illegal in Hong Kong. These actions therefore could not be deemed to have given the Communist regime possession such as to make recognition retroactive in relation to the decree on the airplanes.

22. Carl Zeiss Stiftung *v.* Rayner and Keeler Ltd (No. 2) (1967). The Stiftung was an East German foundation administering the manufacture of Zeiss optical instruments. It was run by a Special Board established according to the law of the German Democratic Republic (East Germany). Britain did not recognise the GDR as a state, nor its government as the government of a state, but rather regarded East Germany as under the authority of the Russian occupation regime set up there at the end of World War II.

It was argued before the House of Lords that an entity such as the Special Board, whose legal existence depended on the law of a regime which Britain did not recognise, could not be accepted by a British court as entitled to take part in a law suit before it.

Lord Reid, in his opinion in the House of Lords, focussed on Britain's exclusive recognition of the USSR as the only *de jure* authority in eastern Germany. British courts, he said, 'are no more entitled to hold that a sovereign, still recognised by our government, has ceased in fact to be sovereign *de jure*, than they are entitled to hold that a government not yet recognised has acquired sovereign status.' However, it was clear as a matter of fact that the government of something called the German Democratic Republic was exercising authority in East Germany with the approval of the USSR. Since lack of British recognition prevented a British court from considering this regime an independent sovereign, the only alternative was to regard it as a 'dependent or subordinate organisation through which the USSR is entitled to exercise indirect rule'. The GDR's acts had to be regarded as done with the consent of the Soviet Union, whose *de jure* authority Britain recognised. Therefore, British courts could recognise those acts.

Lord Reid considered that this conclusion was reinforced by the fact that far-reaching disruption of business and personal relations would result if British courts were not prepared to recognise the laws of the GDR. East German companies, which had commercial dealings with British citizens, could not sue or be sued in British courts, East German marriages and divorces would be held invalid in Britain, and problems of inheritance would arise.

Lord Wilberforce was prepared to go further and, basing himself on American precedent, to suggest that such cases might in future be decided in a way not tied too strictly to recognition. He favoured the idea that:

non-recognition cannot be pressed to its ultimate logical limit, and that where private rights, or acts of everyday occurrence, or perfunctory acts of administration are concerned ... the courts may, in the interests of justice and common sense, where no consideration of public policy to the contrary has to prevail, give recognition to the actual facts or realities found to exist in the territory in question.

23. Hesperides Hotels *v*. Aegean Holidays Ltd (1978). The tendency of some British judges to consider exercising their own discretion in giving effect to certain acts of unrecognised regimes was evident in remarks made by Lord Denning when *Hesperides Hotels* was before the Court of Appeal. Although the facts of the case (arising from the Turkish military occupation of northern Cyprus) did not require a holding on the matter, Lord Denning indicated in *obiter dicta* that British courts could recognise the laws or acts of regimes which Britain did not recognise as *de facto* or *de jure* governments, 'at any rate, in regard to the laws which regulate the day to day affairs of the people'. He also stated that the courts could receive 'evidence of the state of affairs' in the country to decide whether a regime is in control there.

Such judicial willingness to look beyond the position of the British government on these questions will undoubtedly be increasingly important now that certificates of recognition of governments are no longer issued (*see* **8**).

24. Cases involving statutory interpretation. In cases raising the question whether a particular unrecognised entity is a 'state' or 'government' within the meaning of an applicable piece of legislation, British courts have already established firm precedent allowing them to go beyond the problem of recognition by the British government.

In *Re Al-Fin Corporation's Patent* (1970), a Chancery judge held that the question whether North Korea was a 'foreign state' within the meaning of the Patents Act 1949, s. 24(1), depended not on British recognition but on effective control by a foreign regime over a sufficiently defined area of territory – in other words on the court's application of the Montevideo criteria for statehood to the facts in the case.

Validity: American cases

25. Development of the more liberal American view. As indicated above (*see* 22), American courts have generally been readier to give effect to the acts of unrecognised governments than have British courts, although recognition has been held essential in some cases, particularly where the extraterritorial effect of a foreign regime's law is at issue.

This greater flexibility stems from the difficulties faced by American courts in trying to sort out the legal consequences of the American Civil War (1861–1865). The government of the United States had not recognised the rebel government of the Confederacy or the governments of the rebel states. Yet these governments had been in control of their own territory for several years and had exercised legislative and administrative power. In *United States* v. *The Insurance Companies* (1875), the United States Supreme Court had to determine the validity of rebel state legislation on the organisation of business corporations. The court examined the facts for itself and concluded that even if the state legislative bodies were not *de jure* legislatures from the point of view of the United States government, they were *de facto* ones, and the court could proceed on that basis. The court held that

> All the enactments of the *de facto* legislatures in the insurrectionary states during the war, which were not hostile to the Union or to the authority of the General Government and which were not in conflict with the Constitution of the United States, or of the states, have the same validity as if they had been enactments of legitimate legislatures.

Following this precedent, American courts have been prepared to find on an examination of the facts that certain foreign regimes amounted to *de facto* governments.

26. Salimoff & Co. v. **Standard Oil of New York (1933).** In this case, another involving the purchase of property confiscated by the Soviet government of Russia after the 1917 Revolution, the New York Court of Appeals had before it a letter from the State Department. This said that the United States had not recognised any government in Russia since the pre-Communist Provisional Government of March 1917, that the United States was 'cognizant' of the fact that 'the Soviet regime is exercising control and power' in Russian territory and the US had 'no disposition to ignore that fact', and that American refusal to recognise the Soviet regime was based on other grounds than its actual authority.

The court held that the Soviet regime was the *de facto* government of Russia and its internal acts were entitled to be considered valid by the court, even though 'they do not emanate from a lawfully established authority recognised by the government of the United States'.

Some language in this opinion may be read to mean that the court considered that the evidence provided in the State Department letter justified an inference that the United States tacitly recognised the Soviet regime as the *de facto* government. But the general tenor of the court's judgment suggests that that was not believed to be necessary for its holding.

27. Upright *v.* Mercury Business Machines Co. (1961). The New York Supreme Court developed this line of thinking further in this case. The defendant had bought typewriters from a corporation organised under the laws of the German Democratic Republic (i.e. East Germany) and then refused to pay for them. The defendant argued in part that the New York court could not enforce obligations under an agreement made with a company incorporated according to the laws of a government which the United States did not recognise. The plaintiff was not the East German company itself but a person to whom the company had assigned the defendant's debt.

While noting in passing that the United States still considered the Soviet Union to be the responsible authority in East Germany, the court did not build its judgment on that fact as the House of Lords was to do in *Carl Zeiss Stiftung* (*see* **22**). Rather the court minimised the importance of recognition in deciding the case. 'Realistically,' it said, 'the courts apprehend that political non-recognition may serve only narrow purposes.' The courts would follow the 'suggestions of the political arm in effecting such narrow purposes' but would not be bound by non-recognition in cases going beyond those purposes.

The court quoted with approval a previous New York decision, in *Russian Reinsurance Co.* v. *Stoddard,* that lack of recognition might prevent a court from passing on the legitimacy of a foreign regime or from giving its laws *full* effect as those of a legitimate sovereign. But something less than that was possible:

> A foreign government, although not recognized by the political arm of the United States Government, may nevertheless have *de facto* existence which is juridically cognizable. The acts of such a *de facto* government may affect private rights and obligations arising either as a result of activity in, or with persons or corporations within, the territory controlled by such *de facto* government.

Thus, although 'non-recognition is a material fact', 'the proper conclusion will depend upon factors in addition to that of nonrecognition'. These factors were 'the realities of life' in the *de facto* government's territory and principally whether that government's laws were in fact operative there and actually affecting legal rights and duties. Except when such laws are 'inimical to the aims and purposes of our public or national policy', they may in proper circumstances be deemed valid and effective in altering private rights.

28. De jure recognition needed for extraterritorial effect. American courts have emphasised, however, the importance of recognition where a foreign decree is argued to have an extraterritorial effect over property actually within the jurisdiction of the American court – hence the emphasis in *Russian Reinsurance Co.* (*see* **27**) on the necessity of recognition for according such a decree or law *full* effect: only the legitimate *de jure* sovereign may exercise authority beyond the area of his actual physical control.

Thus, in *Petrogradsky Mejdunarodny Kommerchesky Bank* v. *National City Bank* (1930) the New York court ruled that a Russian bank's assets which had been deposited in the New York defendant bank before the Revolution remained under the control of the pre-revolutionary board of directors regardless of a decree by the unrecognised Soviet regime purporting to nationalise the bank and all its assets.

Validity: a Civil law view

29. The Russian Revolution and the subsequent activities of the Soviet regime confronted courts in various continental civil law countries with the problem of what validity to attach to the laws of the unrecognised government. A French court went so far as to give no effect even to Soviet legislation on the grounds for divorce. But a Swiss court was prepared to 'take cognisance of the Russian rules of law' so long as they did not 'offend against the canons of public policy'.

Recognition and the foreign regime before the courts

30. How foreign regimes may come before the courts. A foreign government may come before the courts of another country in either of two ways: as plaintiff or as defendant.

In both cases the question whether the court is entitled to treat that government as existing and enjoying the rights accorded to a legitimate government will depend to some extent at least on recognition.

The foreign regime as plaintiff

31. De jure recognition required. In general, courts have refused to allow regimes which lack recognition as *de jure* governments to become plaintiffs.

The United States Supreme Court, in *Guaranty Trust Co. of New York* v. *the United States* (1938), explained this by indicating that the question of what government should be regarded as the representative abroad of a foreign state is not a judicial matter but one to be decided solely by the political department, whose recognition of a foreign regime must be regarded by the courts as conclusive.

British decisions are in accord.

The foreign regime as defendant or impleaded party

32. Reluctance to exercise jurisdiction. In theory an unrecognised government is not a government for purposes of being sued in a foreign court and does not have any of the immunities against suit which a legitimate government might claim. Courts are, however, evidently on occasion reluctant to exercise jurisdiction over regimes that may in fact be foreign governments.

33. The Arantzazu Mendi (1939). In this case before the House of Lords, the ship *Arantzazu Mendi* had been the object of conflicting decrees issued by the Republican government of Spain and the Nationalist administration of General Franco during the Spanish civil war. With the ship in England following Nationalist orders, the Republican government asked an English court to grant it possession, but Nationalist representatives objected that the writ, by in effect impleading the Nationalist regime (i.e. bringing them in as defendants), would violate international law, which forbids one state's courts to exercise jurisdiction over another state's sovereign. The question was thus whether the Franco regime was the government of a foreign sovereign state.

A letter from the British Foreign Office stated that Britain recognised the Republican government as the only *de jure* government of Spain or any part of it, and recognised 'the Nationalist government as a government which at present exercises de facto administrative control over the larger portion of Spain' and as 'not /.. subordinate to any other government in Spain'.

Lord Atkin, delivering judgment for the House of Lords, interpreted this to mean that the United Kingdom had recognised the Nationalist government as 'exercising all the functions of a sovereign government' and 'for the purposes of international law as a foreign sovereign state'. As such a state, the 'Nationalist Government of Spain' was entitled to immunity in British courts in the same way that Britain would want immunity in Nationalists courts.

This result has been much criticised. All of the parties involved in the dispute claimed that there was only one Spanish sovereign state, and the Nationalists did not claim to be the government of any state but Spain. The Foreign Office letter made clear that Britain recognised only the Republican government as the government of that particular state, and the British Prime Minister had stated explicitly that no decision had been taken to recognise the Nationalists as either the *de facto* or *de jure* government of Spain. Britain certainly does not seem to have considered the Nationalist-held areas as a secessionist state but perhaps merely a belligerent community.

On these facts, and confining themselves solely to recognition of *de facto* or *de jure* government in a previously recognised state, some writers favour the approach of the Norwegian Supreme Court in the case of *The Spanish Government* v. *Felipe Campuzano* (1938). Campuzano, the Spanish chargé d'affaires in Norway before the Civil War, joined the Nationalists and refused to hand over the archives of the Spanish Legation in Oslo to a representative of the Republican government. The Republican representative sued in a Norwegian court, but Campuzano argued that the Nationalist regime, as the government of Spain, was immune from the court's jurisdiction. The Supreme Court held, however, that since Norway recognised only the Republican government as the government of Spain and of the Spanish state, the Nationalist representative could not claim immunity and the Republican government was entitled to take possession of all Spanish public property in Norway.

34. Wulfsohn v. **Russian Socialist Federated Soviet Republic (1923).** The New York Court of Appeals in this case involving the immunity of the unrecognised Russian regime embraced the doctrine that immunity depended on the factual question whether a regime was a government and not on recognition by the United States.

Although this is consistent with the American cases discussed above regarding validity of a *de facto* government's acts, it seems at first sight harder to reconcile with the view that who represents a foreign government as plaintiff is a matter solely for political determination.

35. R.S.F.S.R. *v.* Cibrario (1923) In this case the same New York court argued, however, that *Wulfsohn* was consistent with its refusal in the present case to allow the unrecognised Soviet regime to sue. That refusal was said to be based on *comity*, the friendly political relations between two states, which might prompt the United States to allow a recognised foreign sovereign to sue in an American court. Where there was no recognition, comity would obviously not operate.

This argument implies that the questions whether a foreign government may be a plaintiff or a defendant are not really opposite sides of the same coin, as one might think, but are based on quite different criteria:

(*a*) the right to sue, on the friendliness of the forum court's government;

(*b*) immunity from suit, on the actual governmental authority of the foreign regime.

The first would then be political, the second wholly factual.

While this may reconcile the cases before the New York courts, it does not help with *The Arantzazu Mendi* decision where Lord Atkin insisted on making the issue hinge not on fact but on what the court chose to regard as British recognition.

Governments-in-exile

36. Anomalous situation of governments in exile. The position of a recognised government-in-exile is something of an anomaly in international law. While the law is usually concerned in the sort of cases already discussed (*see* **15–35**) with reconciling recognition and the *de facto* authority of a regime within a foreign state's territory, governments-in-exile are ones which the law must treat as *de jure* even though they do not exercise effective control within their own states. Such situations generally come about because of a (usually illegal) foreign invasion of the state from which the exiled government has fled.

The justification for recognition is both legal and political: the recognising state wishes to demonstrate that it is not according any *de jure* legitimacy to the illegal occupation authorities and that it supports the speedy ending of the illegal situation. Thus Britain and the United States recognised governments-in-exile from the countries conquered by Germany during World War II. Britain's failure to give such recognition also to Emperor Haile Selassie after the consolidation of Italy's aggression against Ethiopia is criticised as evincing a double standard in such matters when a Third World country was the victim of a European colonialist attack.

37. Effects of de jure recognition. Recognition as the *de jure* government-in-exile brings certain consequences in the municipal law of the recognising state. The exile government is deemed entitled to control its state's assets which are located in the recognising state. The exile government may sue in the courts of the recognising state.

38. Powers over property in occupied territory. A more difficult problem, however, is what effect to give to decrees of the government-in-exile purporting to affect legal rights within the occupied territory or purporting to affect citizens of the occupied state elsewhere.

On the first point, an American Federal Court of Appeal held in *State of the Netherlands* v. *Federal Reserve Bank of New York* (1953) that a decree of the Netherlands government-in-exile during the Second World War aiming to protect securities illegally confiscated by the Nazi authorities could be upheld in the United States. The court indicated that 'absentee legislation intended to interfere with the occupant's *legitimate* rule should not be given effect' but legislation intended to prevent an illegal seizure of property should be regarded as valid. Thus, questions of legitimate and illegitimate authority bulk larger in this sort of situation than do ones of effectiveness.

As regards the exile government's authority over its state's citizens abroad, treating that government as the *de jure* one involves recognising the rights which any *de jure* government has with regard to such citizens.

39. International activity of exile governments. On the international level, one notes that the war-time governments-in-exile participated in international conferences and signed international agreements on behalf of their states.

Effect of non-recognition of a de facto state

40. Non-recognition of a state usually decisive. Although we have primarily been concerned with recognition of governments, a word on states is in order. Generally, when non-recognition of a foreign state is considered by a court to be decisive, it produces in municipal law effects similar to those of non-recognition of a government. This is apparent from some of the discussion in *Carl Zeiss Stiftung* v. *Rayner and Keeler Ltd* (*see* 22).

In *Attorney General* v. *Solomon Toledano* (1963), for example, the Moroccan Court of Appeal refused to give effect to a notarial document issued under the authority of the State of Israeli on the ground that, since Morocco did not recognise Israel as a state, Israeli legislation and all official acts 'are deemed to be non-existent' by Morocco.

When non-recognition of a state is not considered decisive, courts may, as in *United States* v. *The Insurance Companies* (*see* 25), give effect to certain of that state's laws.

Effect of withdrawal of recognition

41. Limitation on withdrawal. Although the granting of recognition to a foreign state or government is widely thought to be discretionary and political, withdrawal of recognition may not be.

In cases where the foreign state or government continues to maintain the conditions of statehood or the exercise of government authority, international law holds that withdrawal of recognition is not permissible. Only where the state as such ceases to exist or the government is displaced by a new regime may recognition legitimately be withdrawn.

42. Effect of severing diplomatic relations. Severance of diplomatic relations with a foreign government does not in and of itself count as withdrawal of recognition according to the United States Supreme Court in *Banco Nacional de Cuba* v. *Sabbatino* (1964). Thus a foreign government with whom diplomatic relations have been broken off may still be treated by the courts as existing and being entitled to participate in suits before them.

43. Disappearance of foreign state. However, it appears that a permissible withdrawal of recognition associated with the disappearance of a foreign state or government will prevent access to the courts or even cause the courts to dismiss actions already begun. In *Republic of Vietnam* v. *Pfizer* (1977), a US Federal Court of Appeal held that following absorption of the territory of the Republic of Vietnam (South Vietnam) into the Socialist Republic of Vietnam (North Vietnam), the refusal of the United States to recognise any government as the sovereign authority in South Vietnam allowed (but perhaps did not require) an American court to dismiss a suit begun by the Republic of Vietnam in 1970.

44. The Taiwan problem. A curious case seemingly involving withdrawal of recognition of a government occurred in 1979 when the United States announced that it 'recognizes the People's Republic of China as the sole legal government of China' and 'is terminating diplomatic relations' with 'Taiwan'. Previously the United States had recognised the government of Taiwan as the sole *de jure* government of what was called the Republic of China (understood to be the *de jure* authority for the whole of China). The effect of this American breaking of relations and the recognition of the People's Republic ought then to have been that the United States recognised the People's Republic as the government of Taiwan. In fact, however, the language of the American announcement as to 'terminating diplomatic relations' seems to have been designed to allow the inference as a matter of American law that recognition had not been withdrawn from the government of Taiwan as such.

This interpretation was confirmed by the Taiwan Relations Act 1979 which ruled out any change in Taiwan's position *vis-à-vis* American law and courts from that existing before 1979 and which maintained in force treaties and agreements previously entered into between the United States and the Republic of China. The Act also provided that relations between the United States and Taiwan would continue by means of the newly-created 'American Institute in Taiwan', described as 'a non-profit corporation incorporated under the laws of the District of Columbia'.

Progress test 5

1. Distinguish the objective and the subjective tests for recognition. **(2)**

2. What were the advantages of the Morrison doctrine on recognition? **(3)**

3. In the past, did the United States adopt a subjective or objective test for recognition? **(4)**

4. Explain the Estrada doctrine. **(6)**

5. What is the present British policy on recognition of governments? **(8)**

6. Does non-recognition of a government outweigh its *de facto* existence as far as international law is concerned? **(11)**

7. Discuss the municipal law problems associated with recognition. **(15)**

8. Analyse the decision in *Luther* v. *Sagor*. **(17)**

9. Is recognition 'retroactive' in every case? **(20, 21)**

10. What ways were outlined in *Carl Zeiss Stiftung* v. *Rayner and Keeler Ltd (No. 2)* for avoiding the negative effects of non-recognition? **(22)**

11. Will American courts acknowledge the effectiveness of the laws of unrecognised governments in the territory controlled by those governments? **(25, 27)**

12. Compare the judgments in *The Arantzazu Mendi* and *The Spanish Government* v. *Campuzano*. **(33)**

13. Should effect be given to the acts of a recognised government-in-exile with regard to situations in that government's national territory during foreign occupation? (38)

14. Does severance of diplomatic relations necessarily amount to a withdrawal of recognition? (42)

6 Acquisition of territory

The traditional view: 'modes of acquisition'

1. **Modes of acquisition versus modern criteria.** Writers on international law have traditionally examined the methods by which existing states acquire additional territory in terms of fairly rigid categories purporting to detail the 'modes of acquisition'. There were said to be five such 'modes' (or methods): occupation, prescription, accretion, cession and conquest (*see* **2–6**). The rigidity of these modes, however, has led modern writers to criticise them as not corresponding to the broader and more flexible criteria which actually operate in the settlement of territorial disputes.

This disagreement faces the student with a problem: he or she must be familiar with the traditional law and at the same time be able to analyse current disputes in a way that makes it possible to predict with some reasonable accuracy how they should be resolved. To meet both these needs, this chapter will outline the traditional and modern views and then examine the cases to determine what rules about territorial acquisition they actually apply.

The modes of acquisition

2. **Occupation.** The key to acquisition by peaceful occupation was that the land in question should have been *terra nullius*, that is, 'land belonging to no one', land to which no other international legal person had valid title. Desert islands are the typical example of such territory, although in the age of European imperialism the imperial powers seem to have been ready in practice to consider territories inhabited by non-Europeans who were not organised on the lines of European states as also being in effect *terrae nullius*. Thus the Privy Council, in *Cooper* v. *Stuart* (1889), held that the British colonisation of New South Wales was a 'peaceful' annexation of 'practically unoccupied' territory, thereby permitting English real property law to be enforced in Australia to the detriment of Aboriginal land rights.

In the early period of European overseas expansion in the sixteenth century, mere discovery of a *terra nullius* by a state's explorers coupled with a symbolic taking of possession was thought legally sufficient to give the discovering state title. As the areas of undiscovered and unoccupied territory decreased over the years, however, and the claims of various European states began to collide in the same territories, discovery came to be considered inadequate to support a claim unless it was substantiated by an actual exercise of effective authority. This was one of the problems dealt with in the *Island of Palmas Case* (*see* **23**).

3. **Prescription.** In contrast to occupation, prescription was a means of

acquiring territory which may originally have belonged to another sovereign whose rights had been extinguished for some reason by the passage of time.

Two types of prescription were identified:

(a) *immemorial possession*, where the acquiring state's ownership had gone on for so long that the possible competing claims of some earlier sovereign had been 'forgotten' by the law in a way similar to English judicial recognition of title in cases where 'the memory of man runneth not to the contrary'; and

(b) *adverse possession*, where the previous sovereign was known but where the acquiring state had exercised control of the territory for so long in despite of that sovereign that he was deemed to have lost his title to the acquiring state. This was the more frequent type of prescriptive acquisition and it raised awkward problems about estoppel, protest and acquiescence, as several of the cases discussed below demonstrate.

4. Accretion. Accretion is the addition of new land to a state's territory by the action of natural forces, such as the silting of river banks or the formation of islands within the state's territorial waters. Changes in the course of a boundary river between two states might also allow one state to acquire additional territory, depending on the slowness or suddenness of the change and on whether the river is navigable. If the change is sudden (producing what is called *avulsion*), the boundary remains along the original river bed. In the case of slow changes, if the river is non-navigable, the boundary will follow the middle line of the river's new course; if the river is navigable, the boundary will run along the middle of the river's principal channel (called the *thalweg*).

5. Cession. Cession is the transfer of territory by one state to another. It is done by agreement between the two states, usually in the form of a treaty. The transferring state must in fact be the legitimate sovereign itself, with title to the affected territory, or the transfer is invalid. The reasoning behind this is expressed in the maxim *nemo dat quod non habet*: No one can give what he does not have.

6. Conquest. In traditional international law, as in international affairs generally, the use of military force to accomplish territorial changes was generally recognised. Acquisition of territory by conquest (as distinct from cession by a peace treaty at the end of a war) came about in one of two ways:

(a) *subjugation* or *debellatio* – the destruction of the enemy armed forces and government, which effectively annihilated the enemy state and left its territory open to annexation by the victor;

(b) *implied 'abandonment'* – withdrawal of the enemy armed forces from part of the state's territory following military defeat, leaving the territory withdrawn from open to seizure by the conqueror.

As will be seen (*see* **16–22**), modern international law no longer admits the possibility of acquisition of territory by conquest.

7. Problems with the traditional modes. Apart from conquest (on which the law has simply changed), these rigidly distinct modes of acquisition have been gradually replaced in practice by composite principles of acquisition which combine features of the various modes emphasised, developed or downplayed according to the facts of each case.

There are basically two reasons for this change.

(*a*) First, the traditional modes were themselves too much based on theoretical ideas drawn from Roman law and applied first to state sovereigns and then to states in a way which sometimes made territorial acquisition appear analogous to private real estate dealings, whereas in fact the activities of states in this regard were quite different and more complex.

(*b*) Secondly, questions of acquisition did not arise on an abstract plane of absolute theoretical rights but rather in the context of definite territorial disputes between particular states. This meant that the decision in each case was most often reached on the basis of which of the contending states had the stronger claim *vis-à-vis* the other, regardless of how good or bad that claim might appear if viewed abstractly. This led to territorial disputes being treated as questions of *relative title* rather than absolute title. Relative title was less a matter of fitting clearly into a specific mode of acquisition (which ought theoretically to have given absolute title as against everybody else) than of being in accord with those legal principles which were applicable to the facts in the situation of the two parties actually in dispute.

Principles of the modern approach: peaceful acquisition

8. Basic principles. In an important analysis of territorial and boundary dispute settlement by adjudication, Athene Munkman, writing in the *British Yearbook of International Law* (vol. 46), isolated the basic principles or rules that seemed to be taken into account by tribinals in reaching their decisions in such cases. Although not all of them were equally firmly lodged in international law, they all had some claim to be considered legal principles. They are discussed below.

9. Recognition, acquiescence and preclusion (estoppel). In searching for the better relative title in a dispute between two states, a tribunal would naturally wish first of all to see whether either of the parties had actually admitted the title or claim of the other.

(*a*) *Recognition* would be an actual open acknowledgement by one party of the other's rights in the territory.

(*b*) *Acquiescence* would be a tacit acknowledgement that might be inferred from a failure of one party to protest at the other's exercise of sovereignty in the disputed territory.

(*c*) *Preclusion or estoppel* is the principle that a party may be deemed to have waived his claim by virtue of a previous act or omission that was inconsistent with the maintenance of that claim, particularly if that act was reasonably relied on by the other party as indicating a relinquishment of any claim.

These three principles, which are obviously very closely related and may jointly apply in a particular case, are undoubtedly fully accepted in international legal practice. Munkman argued, however, that they should not be overemphasised since they may produce unjust results in some cases and may not take account of the relationships of power politics which could discourage or prevent a weak state protesting against the acts of a strong one. In addition, states operate in a much longer timespan than that of individuals and state actions are the product of many different individuals' decisions and activities, so that state acts or omissions over a period of decades or centuries do not fit easily into a conceptual framework based on human inconsistency or bad faith.

These are important reservations and they highlight the danger of carrying over into modern international law ideas about the acts of 'sovereigns' that were more appropriate to the age of individual absolute monarchs in Europe. On the other hand, if it were said that states could never be treated like individuals who have precluded themselves from raising a claim, the way would be open for claims that disrupt settled state boundaries and disturb inter-state relations.

This suggests that in addition to these three principles there must be others that allow a tribunal to weigh the merits of competing claims according to the relevant facts on the ground. Munkman identified several, of varying standing in international law.

10. Possession and administration. The actual exercise of sovereignty over a period of time, which is implied in the principles of possession and administration, has for long been considered by international law as an important element in title to territory, and indeed even a prerequisite. Recognition, acquiescence and estoppel, for example, can operate only in a situation where the state whose title is at issue has already established itself in the territory by exercising sovereignty.

Munkman pointed out, however, that possession and administration could not automatically by themselves give title in cases where a rival claimant or the international community at large deliberately withheld recognition or acquiescence to demonstrate rejection of the possessing state's claim. Thus, possession and administration resulting from the use of force would not give valid title in the face of international condemnation of territorial acquisition by military means (*see* **37–9**).

11. Affiliations of the territory's inhabitants. In cases where the disputed territory is inhabited the connections of the inhabitants with the states claiming title must be an important practical consideration in deciding to whom the territory belongs. This is especially relevant in modern international law, which has rejected the attitudes of European imperialism whereby non-European 'natives' were considered an irrelevance when European powers sought sovereignty overseas, and which has emphasised self-determination and the right of peoples to a say in their own destiny. Such considerations appear clearly in the *Western Sahara Case* (*see* **32**).

12. Geographical factors. In relation to claims of sovereignty over sea areas international law has for some time recognised the importance of geographical considerations in drawing maritime boundaries. Thus, the *Anglo-Norwegian Fisheries Case* and the 1958 Convention on the Territorial Sea and Contiguous Zone, Article 4, allowed a coastal state to incorporate as its own territorial waters areas beyond those normally permitted when the state's coastline is deeply indented – as with Norwegian and Scottish fjords – or there is a fringe of offshore islands in the immediate vicinity of the coast, as with Norway's Skjaergaard and Scotland's Hebrides (*see* **12:18**).

But Munkman doubted that geographical factors were as firmly entrenched in the law on acquisition of land territory, except possibly with regard to uninhabited areas. The reasoning behind a distinction between land and sea territory in this respect is not hard to see. Whereas geographical factors like coastal islands or fjords are by and large clear cut and in some sense 'naturally' allocated to one country or another, 'natural' divisions of land territory are less easy to determine and are usually outweighed by other factors. For example, the fact that the Danube runs *through* Austria (rather than dividing it into two states) but *between* Bulgaria and Rumania is not basically a result of geography but of political, linguistic, ethnic and national considerations.

13. Economic factors. Like geographical factors, economic ones are more important in allocating authority over maritime territory than over land territory. In the *Fisheries Jurisdiction Case (Merits)* (1974), for example, the International Court of Justice was prepared to recognise Iceland's 'preferential rights' with regard to zones beyond its territorial sea on the basis of the 'exceptional dependence' of Iceland's economy on the fisheries areas involved.

14. Historical factors. Historical factors are in one sense clearly recognised as important in the allocation of territory, in that the strength of a state's title to a particular territory will often depend in part on the length of time the state has exercised sovereignty there and on the events, and particularly the favourable or unfavourable reactions of other states, that have taken place during that period. 'Ancient title' and similar concepts are, however, less significant when they purport to base a claim on some distant historic connection with the territory which has in fact long been superseded by the effects of later historical developments. This emerges clearly in the *Island of Palmas (see 24)*, *Western Sahara (see 32)* and *Minquiers and Ecrehos (see 31)* cases.

Historical considerations are specifically taken into account when applying the rule of *uti possidetis*. Derived from Roman private law, this rule was applied by the Latin American states to resolve territorial disputes between them on the basis that their boundaries with each other were to be those possessed by their predecessor Spanish colonial territories at the time of independence from Spain, regardless of any other countervailing factors. Similarly, the Organisation of African Unity has agreed that colonial boundaries in Africa are to be accepted as permanent, even though they have the effect of dividing the same tribal, ethnic or linguistic groups between different states. Considering *uti possidetis* in relation to a frontier dispute in Africa, a chamber of the ICJ in *Burkina Faso* v. *Mali* (1986) noted that, in order to maintain stability by preserving the status quo at independence, the principle would favour abstract legal title in preference to effective possession or even the right of self-determination.

More objectionably, attempts have been made to apply *uti possidetis* to territories held by the victor at the end of a war, without regard to whether the victor's acquisition of territory by force would be legal.   Finally, *uti possidetis* may signify simply that when two states conclude a treaty to settle a territorial dispute, territory not disposed of by the treaty is deemed to remain validly in the possession of the state that held it at the time of the agreement.

15. Other means of acquisition. In addition to these principles, writers have suggested certain rarer bases for territorial claims.

Papal grants, for example, particularly that of Pope Alexander VI in 1493, have sometimes been taken as the basis of claims by Spain, Portugal or their successors, as most recently in a dispute between Venezuela and Guyana.

Novation, whereby a state granted limited territorial rights by the legitimate sovereign comes in time to develop its interests into full title to the territory, may be another distinct basis for acquisition. It must be said, however, that novation appears very like the more generally accepted doctrine of prescription.

As will be seen below, in certain special types of territory, such as the Arctic and Antarctic, unique means of acquiring territory are sometimes suggested, but these have little relevance outside the situations for which they were developed.

Principles of the modern approach: the problem of conquest

16. Development of law undermines traditional view on conquest. In traditional international law (*see* **6**), acquisition of territory by conquest had two aspects: it could result either from destruction of the legitimate sovereign or from his abandonment of some territory following defeat in the war.

The first aspect of conquest could be justified with the argument that the annihilation of the defeated state left no sovereign in existence, so that the former state's territory was no longer subject to the rights of an international legal person and so became in effect *terra nullius*. The second type of conquest was based on the assumption that the rights of a still-existing state could be lost as a result of the victor's successful use of force. Both these justifications need to be re-examined in the light of modern international law.

Furthermore, neither of these types of acquisition by conquest took into account the possibility of another interest's being at stake, namely, that of the international community as a whole in maintaining international law and restricting the use of military force. Since 1920 the developing role of the international community, as reflected in the League of Nations and then the United Nations, in promoting the advancement and observance of international law has brought this possibility to the fore.

Thus, apart from the rights of individual states in a war, there is now also the question of the international community's interest in preserving the international legal order. Aggressive war, for example, appears to be prohibited as a matter of *jus cogens* and to have become an international crime which the international community, through the United Nations, is entitled to suppress.

In that light it appears highly unlikely that even complete subjugation of the enemy could nowadays free the victor from all legal restraints on acquisition of territory by force. Even less, of course, could partial conquest escape those limitations.

An additional factor to be borne in mind is the growing concern of international law with individual and group rights, which may continue to exist (as in the case of the law of war applicable in military occupation) regardless of the position of the defeated state.

To relate these general observations to acquisition of territory by conquest, one must consider the effects of two related but distinct areas of law:

(*a*) that restricting the right of a state to resort to military force (the *jus ad bellum*) (*see* **17–19**); and

(*b*) that dealing with the law applicable in war (the *jus in bello*), particularly with regard to military occupation (*see* **20–21**).

Restrictions on the resort to military force

17. The United Nations Charter. The League of Nations Covenant (1919) and the General Treaty for the Renunciation of War (1928) laid the basis for prohibiting acquisition of territory by force, as the United States indicated in the *Stimson doctrine* (1932), whereby that country would not recognise as legal any situation, treaty or agreement procured by a use of force that violated those treaties. The UN Charter (1945) developed the law further in grouping the use of force under three headings: illegal; permissible in self-defence; and authorised by the Security Council.

Illegal use of force is essentially anything not included in the other two categories. This is clear from Article 2(4) of the Charter which prohibits 'the threat or use of force against the territorial integrity or political independence of any state, or in any other manner inconsistent with the purposes of the United Nations'.

The prohibition of force to disrupt another state's territorial integrity means that a use of force aimed at seizing that state's territory is now illegal under the Charter.

18. Authoritative elaborations of the Charter. Later United Nations resolutions suggest that acquisition of territory by force is itself illegal, regardless of whether the use of force was initially legal.

Thus, Security Council Resolution 242 (22 November 1967), dealing with the situation following Israel's conquest of Sinai, Gaza, the West Bank and the Golan Heights in the Arab-Israeli war of June 1967, emphasises 'the inadmissibility of the acquisition of territory by war'.

The General Assembly Declaration on Principles of International Law of 1970 (Res. 2625[XXV]), without distinguishing between legal and illegal uses of force, says:

> The territory of a state shall not be the object of acquisition by another state resulting from the threat or use of force. No territorial acquisition resulting from the threat or use of force shall be recognized as legal.

The General Assembly's 1974 Resolution on the Definition of Aggression (Res. 3314[XXIX]), in Article 3(a), categorises as an act of aggression (a use of force in violation of the Charter) 'any annexation by the use of force of the territory of another State or part thereof'. Article 5(3) emphasises that 'No territorial acquisition or special advantage resulting from aggression is or shall be recognised as lawful'. Article 5(1) adds that no political or military considerations may serve as a justification for aggression and so by extension none justifies acquisition of territory by force.

Taken together, these and similar pronouncements by the international community in the United Nations constitute an authoritative interpretation of the Charter to the effect that any acquisition of territory by force is legally invalid and cannot properly be recognised as lawful by other states. Indeed, this principle of non-recognition has been found by Prof. Ian Brownlie, in his *International Law and the Use of Force by States*, to impose a duty on states not to recognise such acquisition, with failure to fulfil that duty being itself illegal and placing the recognising state in the position of an accomplice of the conquering state.

But some advocates nevertheless maintain that none of this precludes legitimate acquisition of territory by force used in self-defence. Is this correct?

19. Self-defence. To evaluate the effect of self-defence in this regard two points must be considered:

(a) the general scope of self-defence under international law; and

(b) the limitations which under the UN Charter may be imposed on a particular act of self-defence.

Under Article 51 of the Charter self-defence is allowed only 'if an armed attack occurs' against the defender. There can be no legitimate self-defence without such an attack. Self-defence is therefore a responsive act which is permitted by the Charter as a necessary reaction to the danger posed by the attack. An act by the defender which is not a response to the attack but is motivated by other political or military considerations would appear therefore to be beyond the scope of self-defence.

This interpretation accords with traditional international law, as stated by United States Secretary of State, Daniel Webster, in *The Caroline Case* (1841). A state claiming to justify a use of force as self-defence, he wrote, had to show 'a necessity of self-defence, instant, overwhelming, leaving no choice of means, and no moment for deliberation'. Furthermore, the state acting in self-defence must do 'nothing unreasonable or excessive; since the act, justified by the necessity of self-defence, must be limited by that necessity, and kept clearly within it'.

Self-defence has therefore to meet two criteria:

(*a*) it must be a necessary response to attack; and

(*b*) it must be proportionate to the actual challenge posed by the attack.

Self-defence thus does not give *carte blanche* to the defending state to solve by force all its foreign relations problems with another state. With the application of the two tests mentioned self-defence becomes only a means of neutralising the danger posed by the attack and not a means for the defender to improve his overall position. The defender is entitled merely to return the situation to what it was before the attack occurred, in other words, to restore the *status quo*.

Clearly by definition restoring the *status quo* cannot mean the defender's annexing territory which before the attack belonged to the attacking state.

Self-defence therefore does not justify acquisition of territory by conquest. An attempt to stretch an act of self-defence beyond restoration of the *status quo* would take it into the realm of prohibited use of force against the attacking state's territorial integrity, in violation of Article 2(4) of the UN Charter. Nor is there any place in the United Nations system for the defender to take upon itself the job of 'punishing' the attacker or 'teaching him a lesson' by seizing his territory.

There may be certain situations where the defender finds it necessary, however, to place the attacker's territory under military rule, or to use the technical term, *belligerent occupation*. This may be justified as an act of self-defence as part of military measures to restore the *status quo*. An occupation prolonged beyond that immediate military necessity in order to achieve the defender's larger political or strategic goals would cease to be self-defence.

But might a legitimate belligerent occupation provide the legal basis for acquisition of conquered territory?

Belligerent occupation

20. Rights of the respective states involved. To answer that question international law has traditionally focussed on the position of the two international legal persons who might claim title over the occupied territory: the original legitimate sovereign and the occupying state.

The relevant law on this is part of the *jus in bello* (the law of war) and derives from the Hague Regulations of 1907 which were annexed to the Fourth Hague Convention on the Laws and Customs of War on Land. These are now considered to have become international customary law, binding on all states (and as such enforceable within the municipal legal systems of states adopting the incorporation approach: *see* 3:7).

Articles 42 and 43 of the Hague Regulations make clear that belligerent occupation achieves only the substitution of the occupier's authority for that of the legitimate sovereign. The extent of the occupier's authority is restricted: he may not in general abrogate the laws already in force in the territory (Article 43), nor demand the allegiance of the inhabitants (Article 45), nor confiscate private property (Article 46), nor act as more than the administrator of the legitimate sovereign's public property (Article 55). (*See* also 3:28.)

It is clear from such restrictions that the occupier does not become the sovereign of the occupied territory but is at most only permitted to administer the area in a capacity somewhat like that of a trustee. The 1958 British Manual of Military Law, Part III (The Law of War on Land), section 510, puts the point clearly:

> The occupation of enemy territory during a way creates a condition entirely different from subjugation through annexation of the territory … the sovereignty of the legitimate Government of the territory is temporarily latent and is not exercised, but it continues to exist and in no way passes to the Occupant. His powers are of a provisional nature …

Section 512 draws the logical conclusion from this:

> It is unlawful [for the occupier] … to annex the occupied territory so long as the war continues. The Occupant, therefore, must not treat the country as part of his own territory …

Thus the occupier could achieve title over the territory at the end of the war only in one of the ways which international law recognises as validly transferring sovereignty. The most obvious of these is by a treaty of cession, although even this may in certain cases be qualified by Article 52 of the Vienna Convention on the Law of Treaties (1969), which provides that 'a treaty is void if its conclusion has been procured by the threat or use of force in violation of the principles of international law embodied in the Charter of the United Nations'. Another method for the occupier to acquire the territory at the end of the war might be by 'prescription' (i.e. acquiescence or estoppel by the legitimate sovereign), although this would presumably not operate where that sovereign maintained his claim and protested at the occupier's attempts at annexation.

If the state of war is not ended (although actual fighting may have ceased), the state of occupation may continue indefinitely (subject to the limitations on the continued use of force after self-defence has been accomplished: *see* 19). This is clear from Article 6 of the Fourth Geneva Convention of 1949 for the Protection of Civilian Persons in Time of War. It says that the occupier remains bound by certain of the Convention's fundamental provisions even after military operations have been ended for more than a year.

21. Rights of the occupied territory's inhabitants. Among these provisions is Article 47 which protects the rights and benefits given by the Convention to the occupied territory's inhabitants against the changes which would be brought about by the occupier's annexation of the territory. This effectively makes annexation illegal.

The reason is that among the protections and benefits specifically preserved and supplemented by the Convention (according to Article 154) are those contained in the Hague Regulations. This means that the two documents may be read together as one coherent legal regime whose application the Convention is intended to facilitate. Thus one of the major implicit benefits of the Convention is that it upholds and strengthens the application of the Hague Regulations.

This is important because Article 43 of those Regulations forbids the sort of major changes in the law of the occupied territory which annexation would necessarily entail. Examples of such changes would be the introduction of different legislative, judicial or administrative rules or machinery, application of new immigration rules which might allow entry into the occupied territory to foreigners (i.e. the annexing state's citizens) to the detriment of the area's indigenous inhabitants, alterations of citizenship law, and changes in the relationship of the indigenous inhabitants to the state or government exercising authority over their territory.

Belligerent occupation therefore cannot provide an independent basis for acquisition of territory by conquest.

One should note in this regard that while the Hague Regulations focus on the rights of the ousted legitimate sovereign, Article 47 of the Fourth Geneva Convention follows the more recent tendency in international law to elevate the rights of individuals to the level where they counterbalance the claims of the conqueror. This could be of critical importance in situations where the occupier argues that he has no obligations under the Hague Regulations to the ousted state because it was not the legitimate sovereign. Even if such an argument were correct in the particular case, the occupier's hands would still be tied by his duties to the territory's inhabitants under the Fourth Geneva Convention.

22. No relative title in situations of conquest. Unlike peaceful acquisition of territory, conquest does not raise issues of relative title. This is because the decisive factor preventing acquisition by force is not the relative standing of the victor and the vanquished vis-à-vis the territory, but rather the absolute prohibition imposed by international law.

Cases on peaceful acquisition

23. The Island of Palmas Case (1928). This leading case was an arbitral decision by the Swiss international lawyer Max Huber in a dispute over colonial territory between the United States and The Netherlands. Both claimed title to Palmas, a small Pacific island about sixty miles southeast of the Philippine island of Mindanao.

Palmas had been 'discovered' by Spanish explorers in the mid-1500s and in 1898 Spain purported to transfer title by a treaty of cession giving the Philippines to the United States. The strength of the American claim therefore depended ultimately on the validity of Spain's title to the territory and the case therefore focussed largely on that question. The dispute over sovereignty arose in 1906 when the United States learned that The Netherlands regarded the island as part of the Dutch East Indies.

The arbitrator had to resolve several questions in order to decide to whom Palmas belonged.

24. Legal significance of discovery. What was the present legal significance of Spain's discovery of Palmas in the first half of the sixteenth century?

The answer to this question was greatly affected in Huber's view by what he called the doctrine of *intertemporal law*. This said that 'a juridical fact must be appreciated in the light of the law contemporary with it'. Therefore, in the first instance Spain's discovery (the first relevant 'juridical fact') would have to be evaluated according to the law in force at the time of discovery. However, a second set of juridical facts, those connected with the rival claimants' actual exercise of authority over Palmas in subsequent centuries, was also affected by the question of intertemporal law. Huber believed that these later activities were legally more important than the first act of discovery, since legal rights were not simply created once for all but had also to be maintained in existence over time by such acts of sovereignty as were required by the law in force during the period when that maintenance was supposed to be taking place. The doctrine of intertemporal law 'demands that the existence of the right, in other words its continued manifestation, shall follow the conditions required by the evolution of law'.

25. Effects of evolution of the law. What conditions had the evolution of the law made decisive in cases like that of Palmas?

Huber determined that from the mid-eighteenth century international law had developed a new principle on acquisition by 'members of the community of nations' (i.e. Western states) of uninhabited regions or those 'inhabited by savages or semi-civilized peoples'. That principle was that 'occupation, to constitute a claim to territorial sovereignty, must be effective, that is, offer certain guarantees to other states and their nationals'. The requirement of effectiveness meant that international law would not recognise abstract territorial claims that were not backed up by a real exercise of authority sufficient under the particular circumstances of each situation to enable the sovereign to ensure that international law was respected in that territory.

And, Huber declared, 'it seems ... natural that an element which is essential for the constitution of sovereignty should not be lacking in its continuation'. Therefore, effectiveness was also a requirement in the maintenance of title to territory.

Thus, in Huber's view, 'the continuous and peaceful display of authority' in a territory by one state 'may prevail even over a prior, definitive title put forward by another state'. This represented an abandonment of any idea of absolute title in favour of relative title determined according to which state's display of authority was the more effective.

This emphasis on effectiveness had both theoretical and practical underpinnings. On the theoretical level, Huber believed that, in the absence – as he saw it – of a supra-national legal order, international law as a system depended completely on operating through the sovereign authority of states in their own territory, so that an area without such authority was more or less beyond the control of international law. International law therefore needed sovereigns and their sovereignty. On the practical level, in a system without a supra-national authority to impose abstract rights, one state's exercise of sovereignty in a territory was the only decisive evidence that another state was not sovereign there (*see* 4:5).

By emphasising relative title based on the comparative effectiveness of Dutch and Spanish authority, Huber completely removed from consideration the possibility that a third, but absent, party might have a claim to Palmas, namely the people who lived there, the 'natives' as he called them. In an arbitration case, where the contending states set up the tribunal and determined what questions it should answer and what law it should apply, this result is perhaps not surprising. But it contrasts markedly with the attitude of the International Court of Justice in the *Western Sahara Case* (*see* **32**).

26. Effective display of sovereignty. Had The Netherlands or Spain more clearly displayed the required effective sovereignty over Palmas?

Huber found on the evidence before him that 'no act of occupation nor ... any exercise of sovereignty at Palmas by Spain has been alleged'. In contrast, The Netherlands since 1677 had, directly and indirectly (through the Dutch East Indian Company) on the basis of treaties (or 'contracts') with local rulers, exercised suzerainty (overlordship) over two native states which had successively held Palmas as part of their territory.

Although Dutch display of authority had not been proven for the whole period of 221 years up to 1898, it did appear established for the immediate period leading up to that date. This was important since the year of Spain's purported transfer of Palmas to the United States (1898) was the *critical date* in this case, that is, the date at which one of the contending parties had to be considered sovereign in order to resolve the issues raised by the dispute. Proof of sovereignty in 1898 and immediately before could therefore be considered decisive on the question of title over Palmas.

Although Huber began his search for criteria of title with a discussion of effectiveness in the context of 'occupation', his emphasis on the relative positions of Spain and The Netherlands in the aftermath of Spanish discovery suggests an intention to establish that any title Spain may once have possessed had in the course of time disappeared, at least as compared with Dutch claims. In making this shift, which seems a logical corollary of the idea of relative title, Huber was necessarily moving into the area of what would traditionally have been regarded as 'prescription'.

He indicated that open, continuous and peaceful display of Dutch sovereignty met the criteria of 'so-called prescription' (presumably by establishing adverse possession) and he seemed to hint also at acquiescence or estoppel arising from the complete absence of Spanish protests against two centuries of Dutch suzerainty over the island.

Professor D. J. Harris has suggested that Huber meant by this analysis that the act of peaceful and continuous display of authority gave title either by occupation if the territory was previously a *terra nullius* or by prescription if it was not. In line with Munkman's views (*see* **8–15**), one might also understand Huber to be implying that such a display is itself the core method of acquisition in this area, rather than 'occupation' or 'prescription', since that display establishes the key point where relative title is concerned: namely, that one of the contending parties has put himself in a better position than the other.

27. The problem of intertemporal law. Huber's application of the doctrine of intertemporal law has been criticised for seeming to imply that a sovereign must be constantly re-establishing his title to territory on a basis approved by international law at the time. If, for example, title can no longer be acquired by conquest, all titles previously based on that would have to be renewed by some presently accepted method of peaceful acquisition. As this may not always be possible, particularly where a rival claimant by his protests or refusal to acquiesce inhibits acquisition by 'prescription', Huber's doctrine could be highly disruptive to many established titles.

A case in point is the United Kingdom's sovereignty over Gibraltar, which was acquired from Spain by cession in the Treaty of Utrecht (1713) following seizure by British forces in 1704 and the eventual defeat of Spain in the War of the Spanish Succession. Such forcible acquisition would no longer be valid in current international law, but should Britain's long-standing and once-legal title therefore be held invalid because Spanish protests now prevent the UK from renewing that title by peaceful means? That would appear unreasonable.

28. The Clipperton Island Case (1931). On the facts in the *Palmas Case*, effectiveness required actual exercise of governmental authority over the island. But could something less than that suffice in different circumstances? This was the problem in the Clipperton Island arbitration case between France and Mexico.

Clipperton Island was an uninhabited small coral reef 670 miles to the southwest of Mexico. Mexico, as the legal successor to Spain in the area, claimed it on the basis of Spanish discovery.

The arbitrator, however, found no evidence of Spanish discovery, but held that even if there had been, such discovery would have had to be followed by effective annexation by Spain. No such effective taking of possession had been proved.

The island was therefore a *terra nullius* when in 1858 a French naval officer, on instructions from his government, sailed along the coast of the island and proclaimed French sovereignty over it. The French consulate in Honolulu then notified the government of Hawaii of the French proclamation and a notice about it was published in a Hawaiian newspaper.

No further assertions of any state's sovereignty occurred until 1897 when France and Mexico on separate occasions each purported to exercise sovereignty by asserting its authority over three Americans who were found to be collecting guano there.

The year 1897 was therefore the critical date by which France's title to Clipperton had to have been established. As France's only previous act in this regard was the proclamation of 1858, the key question was whether that proclamation by itself was enough to give France sovereignty.

The arbitrator held that it was. Actual taking of possession was necessary for acquisition of territory by occupation, and in ordinary cases that would involve setting up 'in the territory an organisation capable of making ... [the acquiring state's] laws respected there'. But here, since Clipperton Island was completely uninhabited, there was no need for a French administration. The mere proclamation of sovereignty was therefore sufficient to place the island effectively under France's authority. This result is often regarded as a classic example of acquisition of a *terra nullius* by occupation.

29. Limitations on the Clipperton principle. The view that no act of administration is needed to make occupation of uninhabited territory effective may be uncontestably applicable only to a situation like that in the Clipperton case: a small, isolated, uninhabited island.

Thus, Norway met some opposition when it declared in the early 1920s that it intended to take possession of all lands discovered in Antarctica by the Norwegian explorer Roald Amundsen. The American Secretary of State, Charles Evans Hughes, protested in 1924 that an act of 'so-called discovery' coupled with a merely formal taking of possession without actual settlement and administration would 'afford frail support for a reasonable claim of sovereignty', even where settlement was impossible for climatic or other reasons. In practice this would mean that, in contrast to small islands, certain large but desolate territories over which the exercise of control would be practically impossible could not be acquired by any state. Hence the United States recognises no such claims in Antarctica nor has it made any of its own there.

This amounts to a rejection of the notion of relative title in such cases: the mere fact that one state had slightly more contact with such territory than other states would not give it title in the American view. Norway, however, was not prepared to accept this position and in effect reasserted the possibility of relative title by claiming that, although discovery alone was not a basis for sovereignty, it would give Norway a right of 'priority' in acquiring title later by settlement or 'by other procedure sanctioned by international law'.

30. The Legal Status of Eastern Greenland Case (1933). The importance attached to relative title can be seen also in the decision of the Permanent Court of International Justice in the dispute between Denmark and Norway over Eastern Greenland.

The critical date in this case was 1931 when, following a few expeditions to the area and the establishment of a wireless station there, Norway proclaimed sovereignty over Eastern Greenland on the basis that it was a *terra nullius*. Although Denmark had never actually established colonies there (as she had elsewhere in Greenland), she had for a long period up to 1931 claimed sovereign rights over the area. This claim had been accompanied from 1814 by activities such as the mention of the territory in treaties Denmark made with other states, Danish grants of trading concessions there, application of certain Danish legislative and administrative provisions to Eastern Greenland, and attempts by Denmark to get international recognition of its claim.

The court found that Denmark's actions had demonstrated the two elements necessary for acquisition of title by effective control: 'the intention and will to act as sovereign, and some actual exercise or display of such authority'. The court noted that very little actual exercise of sovereign rights was required in the case of thinly populated or empty territory, 'provided that the other State could not make out a superior claim'.

The court, having in mind that the unsettled parts of Eastern Greenland were *contiguous* to those other parts of the island which Denmark had settled, held that Denmark's acts of sovereignty, coupled with the absence of effective rival claims and Danish protests at Norwegian incursions, had all established Danish title by a continuous and peaceful display of authority that was sufficient for a territory such as Eastern Greenland. As with the *Palmas* decision, the reasoning here can be seen not to rely on strict distinctions between 'occupation' and 'prescription'.

31. The Minquiers and Ecrehos Case (1953). In this dispute between the United Kingdom and France over certain islands in the English Channel, the International Court of Justice began by rejecting French claims of ancient feudal title going back to William the Conqueror. The doctrine of interemporal law required that such a title (which would have no legal effect in modern international law) would have had to have been replaced by 'another title valid according to the law of the time of replacement'. Rather than ancient title, it was 'evidence which relates directly to the possession' of the islands which was of 'decisive importance'.

To know what evidence was relevant in this connection the court had to determine the appropriate 'critical date', before which the sovereignty of one or the other of the parties would have had to have been established. Britain proposed 1950, France 1839 (the point being that the earlier the date chosen, the fewer of Britain's recent acts of sovereignty the court could take into account). The court decided, however, that the actual dispute over sovereignty did not arise before 1886 and so took that as the critical date.

Examining the evidence of British activities in the nineteenth century, the court emphasised the 'probative value' of British acts of jurisdiction and local administration as well as relevant UK legislation. This demonstrated that Britain had maintained in the nineteenth and twentieth centuries its medieval connections with the islands by exercising 'state functions' over them. France had demonstrated no similar display of sovereignty and, since the court's task was to 'appraise the relative strength of the opposing claims', it held in favour of the United Kingdom.

32. The Western Sahara Case (1975). The International Court of Justice, in rendering an advisory opinion to the UN General Assembly on the status of this North American territory over which Spain was relinquishing its colonial authority, emphasised the importance of the inhabitants' right of self-determination (*see* 4:44).

But the General Assembly's request for the opinion also required the court to examine whether, when Spain acquired the Western Sahara in 1884, the territory had been a *terra nullius*, and, if it had not, whether 'legal ties' had existed between it and either the neighbouring state of Morocco or the less politically defined area known as 'the Mauritanian entity' (the forerunner of the present-day state of Mauritania).

On the first question, the court held that the Western Sahara had not been a *terra nullius* in 1884 because 'the state practice of the relevant period indicates that territories inhabited by tribes or peoples having a social and political organization were not regarded as *terrae nullius*'. Such territories came under colonial control by 'cession' through agreements with the local rulers rather than by 'occupation'.

Turning to the second question, the court considered that the notion of 'legal ties' between Western Sahara and neighbouring countries had to be understood as involving not merely their possible connection with its territory but their relations with its people, since the court assumed that the General Assembly's interest in the decolonisation of the territory reflected a concern for the future of its people rather than the disposition of its land.

Morocco argued that its claim rested on 'immemorial possession' dating back to the Arab conquest of the seventh century and maintained by a continuous display of authority which, though spasmodic, was sufficient (given the desert nature of the territory and its geographical contiguity to Morocco) to create a title for Morocco on the same bases as that of Denmark's in the *Eastern Greenland Case.*

The court concluded, however, that this analogy was not appropriate, since the Western Sahara was inhabited by people over whom Morocco would have had to exercise some unambiguous display of authority beyond that which sufficed for Denmark in Eastern Greenland and since the territory was not in fact as geographically contiguous to Morocco as Eastern Greenland was to the rest of the island.

Morocco's display of authority appeared to extend no further than the allegiance of some tribes or tribal leaders (although even the location of these tribes and the extent of their power in the territory was disputed) and occasional Moroccan military expeditions which did not appear to have penetrated into any substantial area of the Western Sahara.

The refusal of the court to accept tribal allegiance to the Sultan as a sign of Moroccan sovereignty was apparently based on the view that international law, operating in a state system, required, in the court's words, evidence of 'effective and exclusive *state* activity' (emphasis supplied) rather than of semi-feudal personal relations between the Moroccan Sultan and individuals or groups in the Western Sahara.

When the court turned to the relations of the 'Mauritanian entity' with the territory, a good deal was found to depend on the legal nature of that entity. The key question, from an international law perspective, was whether that entity had any sort of international legal personality. The essential test, based on the *Reparation Case's* finding on the legal personality of the United Nations, was whether the entity 'possesses, in regard to its members, rights which it is entitled to ask them to respect'. Although the emirates and tribes of the area had many racial, linguistic, religious, cultural and economic ties with each other, they were each quite independent of the others and had no 'common institutions or organs, even of a quite minimal character'. The Mauritanian entity therefore enjoyed no international legal personality which would have supported a claim of sovereignty over the Western Sahara.

However, the court considered that the General Assembly had not limited it to considering only 'legal ties which imply territorial sovereignty' (which pertained primarily to state-like entities), since by combining the notions of 'legal ties' and the 'Mauritanian entity', the Assembly had implicitly recognised the possibility of legal ties of a non-state character.

There had been a common body of inter-tribal custom which regulated both the tribes in the Mauritanian entity and those in the Western Sahara and recognised tribal rights relating to lands through which these nomadic tribes migrated. This link of customary law between the two areas did constitute legal ties 'which knew no frontier between the territories and were vital for the very maintenance of life in the region'. But they were not such links as would establish any tie of territorial sovereignty capable of defeating the right of the people of the Western Sahara to self-determination.

33. Unique features of the Western Sahara Case. In contrast to the other cases in this section, the *Western Sahara Case* was not in form a dispute between two states over a territorial question, but simply a non-binding advisory opinion by the ICJ on the application of international law to a given set of facts. Consequently, the element of relative title which looms so large in most territorial cases was practically absent here. The court could therefore consider the position of a third party (the people of the Western Sahara) and apply a comparatively abstract legal principle (self-determination) to produce the result international law required, regardless of the relative positions of Morocco and Mauritania *vis-à-vis* each other.

34. The Temple of Preah Vihear Case (1962). This dispute before the International Court of Justice between Cambodia and Thailand (Siam) is considered the classic case of 'prescription' operating to give title to territory.

In 1904 the French rulers of Indo-China (of which Cambodia was a part) concluded a treaty with Siam to determine the border between the two territories in the area where the temple was situated. According to the treaty, the borderline was to run along the watershed of a certain mountain range, unless a joint French-Siamese commission decided otherwise.

The commission met and in due course instructed two French officers to draw the appropriate maps. The map for the area of the temple did not follow the watershed line, with the consequence that the temple was included in Cambodia, although a map prepared on the agreed basis would have put it in Siam.

When copies of the whole set of maps were presented to the Siamese government, however, it offered no protest over the incorrect one and indeed even seemed to approve the maps by requesting additional copies. In fact many years passed before Siam complained that the temple had erroneously been given to Cambodia. In the court's view, this failure to object to the map in time had an effect like estoppel: 'Thailand is now precluded by her conduct from asserting that she did not accept it'.

35. The Chamizal Arbitration (1911). In the *Temple Case* Thailand lost because it had done nothing to assert its rights and had even seemed to approve the defective map. But when the aggrieved state does protest, how far must it go to maintain its rights? This was a central question in the Chamizal Arbitration between the United States and Mexico.

Changes in the Rio Grande along the border between the two countries resulted in the Chamizal Tract, which had previously been on the Mexican side of the river, being on the American side. American settlers moved into the area and American officials exercised authority there. The United States claimed, as one of several bases for title, that this exercise of control over a period of time gave it a prescriptive title.

The arbitration commission held that for prescription to operate in such circumstances, American possession would have had to be 'undisturbed, uninterrupted, and unchallenged' as well as 'peaceable'.

The evidence was that Mexico had repeatedly protested over many years, so that American activities in the Chamizal did not go unchallenged. Furthermore, any attempt by Mexico to go further and assert its rights by retaking the territory would have been met by violence, suggesting perhaps that America's possession depended on the threat or use of force and was therefore not peaceable. Under these circumstances, Mexico could not be blamed for relying on diplomatic protests only, and these had to be accepted as sufficient to prevent American acquisition by prescription.

36. The problem of protest. In spite of the Chamizal decision on this point, some writers still maintain that, without active efforts at recovery by military force (in traditional international law) or appeals to the United Nations or the ICJ (in current law), mere protest will fail to preserve title against acquisition by prescription. This view may be justified on the ground that the prolongation of a dispute and the uncertainty flowing from it are detrimental to international relations and should not be encouraged by allowing the claimant state to avoid a decisive test of its rights.

On the other hand, if the purpose of protest is to signal that the aggrieved state does not acquiesce in the loss of its territory, it would appear that any action which makes that position clear should suffice, particularly when more vigorous action might disrupt international relations generally. International law should not confront the aggrieved state with the choice of either raising the international temperature to a critical degree or risking the loss of its rights.

Cases on acquisition by force

37. The Middle East. During the Arab-Israeli War of June 1967, Israel occupied large areas of territory which had until then not been part of the territory of the State of Israel but had been under the administration of Egypt (the Sinai Peninsula and the Gaza Strip), Jordan (the West Bank with its capital of East Jerusalem) and Syria (the Golan Heights).

On 22 November 1967, the UN Security Council adopted Resolution 242 which emphasised 'the inadmissibility of the acquisition of territory by war' and proposed that a 'just and lasting peace in the Middle East' would have to be based in part on 'withdrawal of Israeli armed forces from territories occupied' in the war. Although a few writers have questioned the precise effect of this latter provision (did it mean all of the occupied lands or only some parts of them?), the main thrust of the resolution cannot be doubted: the Security Council had determined that war, even if in self-defence as Israel claimed, could not produce legitimate Israeli acquisition of the occupied territories.

Consequently, the Security Council, in Resolution 478 (1980) and elsewhere, declared Israeli measures to change the status of Jerusalem invalid, and in Resolution 497 (1981) declared that Israeli annexation of the Golan Heights was 'null and void and without international legal effect'.

38. The Falkland Islands. Since seizing them by force in 1833, the United Kingdom has regarded the Falkland Islands as being under British sovereignty. Argentina has, however, in the meantime protested against British rule there and claimed the islands for itself. On 2 April 1982 Argentina invaded the Falklands and gained complete control over them.

In justifying the seizure, the Argentine representative in the Security Council spoke of his country's 'recovery of its national sovereignty over the territories . . . in an act which responds to a just Argentine claim'. This may be interpreted as a recognition that Britain had acquired sovereignty in 1833 but in a way that Argentina believed could not validate the continuation of that sovereignty in modern times. This seems an implicit appeal to the doctrine of intertemporal law which, as analysed in the *Palmas Case* (*see* **24**), could be argued to require Britain to relinquish a title based on the now-illegal mode of conquest and to re-establish it on a peaceful basis acceptable under current law.

Thus, the Argentine Foreign Minister told the Council that the UN Charter's prohibitions on the use of force did not render Argentina's invasion illegal. 'No provision of the Charter', he said, 'can be taken to mean the legitimization of situations which have their origin in wrongful acts, in acts carried out before the Charter was adopted and which subsisted during its prevailing force'. He continued: 'Today, in 1982, the purposes of the Organization cannot be invoked to justify acts carried out in the last century in flagrant violation of principles that are today embodied in international law'.

This argument seems, however, to miss the point: the Charter prohibitions on the use of force do not operate to legitimise previous wrongful acts but simply mean that such acts must be reversed by peaceful means rather than by force.

The Security Council was therefore legally correct in demanding, in Resolution 502, 'an immediate cessation of hostilities ... [and] an immediate withdrawal of all Argentine forces from the Falkland Islands (Islas Malvinas)'. This was in no way a statement about the merits of British or Argentine territorial claims, but simply a reaffirmation of the international legal principle that the use of force cannot produce valid changes in the status of territory.

Interestingly, in the light of the arguments against Britain based on intertemporal law, one notes that during the war of 1982 British statements frequently emphasised the right of the Falkland Islanders to self-determination free of Argentine coercion. This may have been intended in part to provide a currently legitimate justification for Britain's position.

39. The Status of Goa. In December 1961 India invaded and conquered Goa, Danao and Diu, which were Portuguese colonies on the Indian subcontinent. Arguing that decolonisation was 'the new dictum of international law', an Indian representative told the UN Security Council that his country was entitled to use force to liberate the Indians of Goa from illegal Portuguese occupation of their land. He argued that this should really be considered an act of self-defence under the Charter, apparently because India regarded Portugal's presence in Goa as maintained by a continuing Portuguese use of force that amounted to an armed attack on India. Furthermore, 'so far as the achievement of freedom is concerned, when nothing else is available, I am afraid that it is a very debatable proposition to say that force cannot be used at all'.

Although the justification for these arguments under the UN Charter cannot be taken for granted, they correspond to a political conviction that the national destiny of the Indians in Goa should not have been determined irrevocably by the fact that centuries ago one Euopean colonial power rather than another happened to seize that part of the subcontinent. Many Third World countries and liberation movements have found the Indian case appealing, and the Security Council failed to condemn India's action after the Soviet Union vetoed a critical resolution.

Special situations   **The Arctic**

40. General position. The North Polar region is essentially an enormous frozen ocean enclosed within the continental landmasses of Europe, Asia and North America and fringed with islands of various sizes.

The close relationship between the polar ice cap and the continental territories around it has led the Soviet Union to assert a claim to sovereignty over vast areas of the Arctic. As early as 1916 the Russian Government declared that certain Arctic islands constituted 'an extension northward of the continental tableland of Siberia'. This early claim to rights based on the geography of the continental shelf (*see* also Chap. 12) is seen as arising from the *contiguity* of the state's home territory with the area being claimed.

Soviet writers have also pointed out the economic importance of the area to the inhabitants of the Soviet Union's coastal regions. This argument implies a title based on the theory of *continuity*, which allows the state holding a certain territory to extend its authority further to protect the security or development potential of that territory.

41. The Sector Theory. Since 1926 the Soviet Union has generalised these specific arguments by advocating application of the 'sector theory' to the delimitation of the Arctic. According to this, the contiguous polar regions lying between an Arctic state's continental territory and the North Pole belong to that state. The area involved is determined simply by drawing lines of longitude from the eastern and western extremities of the state to converge at the Pole, thus forming a roughly triangular shaped slice of the earth's surface which is designated a sector.

The sector theory, which would give the Soviet Union control over the Arctic between approximately longitudes 30°E and 169°E, has not been adopted by other Arctic states such as Norway and the United States.

Canada, however, has applied a modified sector demarcation in order, according to the Canadian Minister for Northern Affairs in 1956, 'to show the lands and the territorial waters around those lands which were claimed by Canada'. He rejected the 'general sector theory' as involving claims of sovereignty over sea areas beyond Canada's territorial waters. But in the Arctic Waters Pollution Prevention Act 1970 Canada extended its anti-pollution measures well beyond the territorial sea to a distance of 100 nautical miles. This was justified in part by the consideration that there was 'an intimate relationship between the sea, the ice and the land'. Although this explanation is similar to some of those put forward by the Soviet Union to support its claims, Canada has not as yet withdrawn its objections to the general sector theory. The United States denies Canada's right to exercise pollution control over Arctic waters.

42. Exception to the sector theory: Spitsbergen. The islands of the Spitsbergen (or Svalbard) Archipelago lie to the north of Norway, with the easternmost of them extending to longitude 35°E – well within the Soviet sector. In the nineteenth and early twentieth centuries Norway, Russia and several other countries disputed sovereignty over the islands, but the Spitsbergen Treaty of 1920 (to which the Soviet Union later adhered) recognised Norwegian sovereignty over the archipelago under a special regime whereby the other parties to the treaty were allowed to carry on peaceful economic exploitation there. The delimitation of continental shelf areas around Spitsbergen is, however, still disputed between Norway and the Soviet Union.

Antarctica

43. Disagreement over territorial claims. In contrast to the Arctic, the southern polar region is an area of mainland and islands covered and joined together by a vast ice sheet up to 6,500 feet thick. Although it is therefore an actual territory, the problem of whether, and how, any state might acquire sovereignty remains unsettled.

The United States has adopted the view (*see* **29**) that acquisition of a large but desolate and inhospitable territory by discovery alone without effective occupation is legally impossible. Other countries (notably the United Kingdom) have said that title can be established and maintained by discovery coupled with an exercise of administrative and governmental powers no greater than that which the court found sufficient to support Denmark's sovereignty in Eastern Greenland. Some states argue that sovereignty over the interior regions of Antarctica may be obtained by application of the sector theory, although, interestingly, the Soviet Union refuses to accept that it applies there.

Besides Britain, the other claimants are Australia, Argentina, Chile, France, New Zealand and Norway. Argentine, Chilean and British sectors overlap, but under Article 15 of the Treaty of Peace and Friendship (29 November 1984) between Chile and Argentina, the two countries have agreed that certain dispute settlement mechanisms may be used to resolve their disagreement over Antarctica.

44. The Antarctica Treaty (1959). Following successful scientific cooperation in Antarctica during the International Geophysical Year of 1957–1958, the interested governments negotiated 'in the interest of all mankind' an agreement that would enable such work to continue without provoking further discord over sovereignty or undermining the use of Antarctica 'exclusively for peaceful purposes'.

The Antarctic Treaty (in which the seven claimant states were joined by Belgium, Japan, South Africa, the Soviet Union and the United States to form a controlling group of 'consultative parties' under the agreement) imposed a moratorium on territorial claims. Under Article 4(1) no such claims are to be considered either recognised or renounced, while according to Article 4(2) no activities undertaken during the life of the treaty will affect the pre-existing situation regarding sovereignty. Article 1 forbids military activity in Antarctica and Article 5 prohibits nuclear explosions or disposal of radioactive waste there. The Treaty entered into force on 23 June 1961, and by virtue of Article 12(2) will come up for renegotiation thirty years from that date.

45. The Antarctic Treaty's effect on sovereignty. Considered from the point of view of the international community as a whole, Article 4 of the treaty is rather peculiar. In it the treaty parties refuse to recognise each other's claims to sovereignty and yet they purport to exercise a right to exclude any new claims. As between the parties this right might arise from their contractual obligations under the treaty. But states not party to the treaty would have no such obligations. And yet under Article 10 the contracting states undertake to 'exert appropriate efforts' to see that *no one* acts contrary to the principles or purposes of the agreement. Without the backing of treaty law, such efforts could be justified only on the basis of that very sovereignty which the parties refuse to recognise.

Therefore, unless the Antarctic Treaty is considered to have created an 'objective legal regime' (one existing in fact, like the United Nations in the *Reparation Case* for example, rather than simply representing contractual relationships), there are no legal grounds arising from that treaty to prevent non-parties acquiring sovereignty in Antarctica.

46. Gaps in the Antarctic Treaty. A problem of little relevance in 1959 that has become increasingly important in recent years is that of the exploitation of Antarctica's natural resources. The right of exploitation is in normal circumstances one of the attributes of sovereignty and attempts at regulating it raise questions of sovereign rights.

Nevertheless, the interested states were able to agree on a Convention on the Conservation of Antarctic Marine Living Resources (1980) to control fishing and other activities in an enormous zone around Antarctica running generally up to 60° South latitude and beyond that in some areas to the edge of the Antarctic Convergence, the major boundary zone separating Antarctic and sub-Antarctic waters, on the Antarctic side of which are many almost unique species of plants and animals.

But a treaty on the more difficult problem of mineral resource exploitation has proved more elusive, although the Antarctic Treaty parties have been spurred to attempt drafting such an agreement by the efforts of Third World countries in the United Nations to have Antarctica and its resources (which are potentially very great) declared 'the common heritage of mankind'.

47. The 'common heritage of mankind'. This concept, which first became prominent in the 1970s in relation to the resources of the deep seabed, originated in the long-familiar legal notion of *res communis*, a thing which is naturally common property and is incapable of being appropriated by any person.

In traditional international law, *res communis* implied that every state had equal rights of use in the thing concerned, unregulated by other states (e.g. in fishing and navigation on the high seas). The 'common heritage of mankind' takes the idea one step further: what may be used by all should be regulated by all. Whatever is the common heritage of mankind must be subject to the wishes of the international community as a whole through the United Nations or some regulatory body established specially for the purpose.

This approach runs directly counter to the position of most of the Antarctic Treaty parties, and the clash of views is unlikely to soften as the time approaches when oil drilling and mining in Antarctica will become technologically feasible and economically viable.

The whole problem is exacerbated by the need to consider renegotiating the Antarctic Treaty itself at the end of its first thirty years in 1991, when basic issues that were set aside in 1959 may be reopened.

Air Space and Outer Space

48. The problem of boundaries. According to Article 1 of the Chicago Convention on International Civil Aviation (1944) 'every state has complete and exclusive sovereignty over the air space above its territory'. On the other hand, Article 2 of the Outer Space Treaty (1967) says: 'Outer space, including the moon and other celestial bodies, is not subject to national appropriation ...' National regulation of aeronautical activity arises from sovereignty, so that determining the boundary between these two legally distinct areas is vital.

Some writers suggest the boundary should be at the lowest point at which satellites can orbit the earth or the highest point at which airplanes can fly. The difficulty with these proposals is that a limit set in this way could vary with the progress of space and aeronautical technology.

To get around this problem, others have advocated a 'functional approach' applying national air flight regulations or international outer space law (and hence implicitly delimiting the area of territorially-based sovereignty above the earth) according to the nature of each particular activity at issue. This might work in the case of clearly distinct activities (e.g. domestic passenger flights as against the Voyager space probe), but how would it apply, for example, to the American space shuttle, which, after launching into orbit by rocket, glides back to earth to land like a plane? The problem is yet to be resolved.

49. The Moon. The Moon Treaty (1979) supplements the 1967 Outer Space Treaty and provides in Article 11 that the Moon and its natural resources are 'the common heritage of mankind' and may not become the property of any state or entity but will be subject to an international regime which remains to be negotiated.

Progress test 6

1. List the traditional modes of acquisition of territory and briefly describe them. (**2–6**)

2. Explain the implications of the idea of 'relative title'. (**7**)

3. Munkman had objections to complete reliance on acquiescence or estoppel in settling a question of relative title: what were they? (**9**)

4. Are possession and administration always decisive considerations in resolving territorial disputes? (**10**)

5. How much weight should be given to the affiliations of a territory's inhabitants? (**11**)

6. Discuss the rule of *uti possidetis*. (**14**)

7. Is annexation of territory by force legal in modern international law? (**17–18**)

8. Does self-defence permit annexation by force? (**19**)

9. How did Huber apply the principle of effectiveness in the *Island of Palmas Case*? (**23**)

10. Does the measure of effectiveness change according to the circumstances of each territory in dispute? (**28**)

11. Does the *Clipperton Island* principle apply to a territory like Antarctica? (**29**)

12. Does the presence of an indigenous population in a disputed territory increase the degree of effective authority needed to establish title? (**32**)

13. Did the decision in the *Western Sahara Case* to some extent set up self-determination as a countervailing factor to effectiveness in the assessment of title to territory? (**32**)

14. Why did Thailand lose the *Temple of Preah Vihear Case?* (**34**)

15. What must a state do to demonstrate its refusal to accept foreign sovereignty over territory claimed by it? (**35–36**)

16. Did considerations of intertemporal law justify Argentine invasion of the Falkland Islands in 1982? (**38**)

17. Explain the sector theory. (**41**)

18. Did the Antarctic Treaty of 1959 definitively settle the question of sovereignty over Antarctica? (**44, 45**)

19. What effect would application of the 'common heritage of mankind' concept have on the administration of Antarctica? (**46, 47**)

20. Is outer space subject to national appropriation? (**48**)

7 Rights in foreign territory

1. Introduction. Applied rigorously, the concept of absolute, exclusive and unfettered territorial sovereignty would make life difficult, if not impossible, for many states which depend in some way on access to, or partial control over, the territory of others. This chapter looks at situations where a sovereign's exercise of its territorial authority is limited by subjection to the rights of other states.

Servitudes

2. Nature of legal servitudes. In private law, the term servitude denotes the situation where land belonging to one person is burdened by the rights of another in that land, as for example by a right to use a path crossing that land to gain access to a public road. Rights of servitude are said to be *in rem* (against the property itself) rather than *in personam* (against the owner personally), so that they do not depend on contractual ties between individuals (as many private legal rights do) and may run with the land to obligate other owners and give rights to other beneficiaries.

There is disagreement about whether servitudes of this sort can exist in international law. On the one hand, the particular obligations of any state (as distinct from duties imposed generally on all states by international law) are considered, especially by positivists, to arise from its explicit consent in treaties or implicit consent by way of state practice. These duties are therefore *in personam* and do not relate *in rem* to the state's territory. Furthermore, the fact that states generally exist over a very long period of time with only changes in government rather than changes of statehood makes it difficult to establish that such obligations really are transferred from one legal person to another in the way the duties associated with servitudes can be seen to devolve upon the successors of the original owner.

On the other hand it is clear that burdens on territory do exist which are for practical purposes (if not in theory) almost indistinguishable from servitudes. The leading cases reveal how different tribunals have dealt with the problem.

3. The North Atlantic Fisheries Arbitation (1910). In 1818 the United States and the United Kingdom agreed by treaty that American citizens would have 'forever' and 'in common' with British subjects the 'liberty' to fish off the south coast of Newfoundland, a British territory.

When a dispute arose almost a century later over British attempts to regulate American fishing in the area, the United States objected on the basis that the 'liberty' in question amounted to a servitude. The implication was that the treaty of 1818 had burdened the territory with an American right which could not be affected by later British action.

The tribunal rejected the American claim. The rationale for this result is unfortunately not coherently reasoned in the judgment. But it appears to be grounded on the view that, since neither general international law nor the law applied internationally by Britain or the United States acknowledged the existence of international servitudes, a servitude could not have been created tacitly in this case but only by an express British grant of a real property 'sovereign right' in the territory to the United States. In fact, however, Britain had given the US only an 'economic right' which was, in any case, subject to such British regulation as was not contrary to America's right but was rather aimed at securing and preserving the fishery for the common benefit of both countries.

4. The Aaland Islands Case (1920). In 1856 Britain, France and Russia agreed by treaty to the permanent demilitarisation of the Aaland Islands, then a part of Russia's Finnish province and lying strategically at the entrace to the Gulf of Bothnia between Sweden and Finland. Following the Bolshevik Revolution of 1917, Finland achieved independence from Russia and then claimed that it was not bound to maintain the demilitarisation of the islands, as it had not been a party to the 1856 treaty. Sweden, which also was not a party to that agreement, objected to the Finnish position and appealed to the League of Nations. Because the Permanent Court of International Justice was not yet in operation, the League appointed an International Commission of Jurists to consider the case.

The Commission cast some doubt on whether there were true international servitudes, but it did accept that the European powers had on many occasions 'tried to create true objective law, a real political status the effects of which are felt outside the immediate circle of contracting parties'. This appears to mean that so-called objective legal regimes may produce the same legal effects as servitudes, although the basis is not a right *in rem* but rather a far-reaching contractual scheme.

The Commission held that the 1856 treaty's provisions on demilitarisation, having been 'laid down in European interests', created a 'special international status' for the Aaland Islands which, until it was duly replaced, every interested state had the right to insist upon.

5. The Right of Passage Case (1960). In this dispute between India and Portugal about Portuguese access from Portugal's coastal colony of Daman across Indian territory to Portuguese colonial enclaves in the interior, the International Court of Justice held that Portugal had certain rights of passage across Indian territory based upon long-continued, constant and uniform practice which gave rise to local custom accepted as law by the parties.

However, Portugal's rights were still subject to India's exercise of its sovereignty over its territory by controlling the movement of Portuguese persons and goods to and from the enclaves.

6. General treaty provisions on passage. Given that rights of passage in particular situations appear, as in the case above, to rest only on local custom or understandings, a general right of passage in international law can probably come about only by means of multilateral treaties, although a school of thought dating back to Grotius argues that such a right already exists as a matter of customary international law in light of the needs of the international community's commerce and trade.

An example of the treaty approach is Article 3 of the 1958 Geneva Convention on the High Seas which provides that coastal states 'shall by common agreement' with landlocked states allow the latter 'free transit through their territory' on a basis of reciprocity. The 1982 Law of the Sea Convention, in Articles 124–132, elaborates this and makes clear that, although the right of transit exists by virtue of the Convention, the precise terms of its exercise must be agreed with the coastal state so as in no way to infringe that state's 'legitimate interests'.

The fact that transit is subject to an understanding on its detailed terms does not mean, however, that the coastal state has the right to prevent transit by refusing to conclude an agreement. In the *Lake Lanoux Case* (1957) between France and Spain on the question of allocating the lake's outflow between the two countries, the arbitral tribunal noted that an obligation to negotiate an agreement involves dealing in good faith and striving to reach an understanding, the refusal to do so making the offending state liable to sanctions under international law.

International rivers

7. Types of international river. The term international river covers two types of river: one that runs through the territory of more than one state (a successive river), or one that forms the border between states (a contiguous river). A state which lies on an international river is called a *riparian* state. International law, through custom or treaty, often imposes limitations on the scope of a riparian state's unilateral action when that may affect use of the river by other states.

8. Navigation. In the international law of the eighteenth and nineteenth centuries the obligations of riparian states centred almost exclusively on navigation. The Congress of Vienna (1815) developed a regime for international rivers which emphasised freedom of navigation along their whole course and encouraged the establishment of international commissions to supervise and regulate shipping on them. In the course of the next century such commissions were set up for the Rhine (1831), the Danube (1856), and the Oder (1919).

The agreement of 1856 for the Danube stated that the Congress of Vienna's principles on navigation were 'part of the public law of Europe', but the further development of the law on rivers was apparently still considered to depend on treaty rather than custom.

In 1921 forty states signed the *Barcelona Convention and Statute on the Regime of Navigable Waterways of International Rivers*. The Statute provided for freedom of navigation for the merchant ships of the parties in each other's international waterways (Article 3) on a basis of equality (Article 4), with the exception that the riparian state may reserve for its own ships transport between that state's own ports on the river (Article 5). It also imposed duties on each riparian state to keep its portion of an international river navigable, unless that would adversely affect other interests of the riparians such as the maintenance of the normal water conditions, or the use of the water for irrigation or power (Article 10). The Statute did not, however, guarantee freedom of navigation to public war, police or administrative vessels (Article 17).

The precise effect of these international regimes on the territorial sovereignty of the riparians was considered by the Permanent Court of International Justice in the *European Commission of the Danube Case* (1927). The court held, as regards ports on the river, that the territorial sovereigns did not lose their sovereign rights of regulation and jurisdiction, but the exercise of those rights was subject to the supervision of the Danube Commission to ensure freedom of navigation and equality of treatment.

But is there any foundation, apart from treaty law, for freedom of navigation? In the *Jurisdiction of the International Commission of the River Oder Case* (1929), the PCIJ, while dealing with a different question under a treaty, observed that 'the existence of a navigable river separating or traversing several states' gives rise to a 'community of interest' among the riparians which 'becomes the basis of a common legal right'. On that basis, rights of navigation might arguably stem from non-treaty sources such as general principles required by the circumstances of international intercourse.

In 1966 the International Law Association (a private body of lawyers) drew up the *Helsinki Rules on the Uses of the Waters of International Rivers* in an attempt to codify and develop the law in this area; Articles 12–20 deal with navigation.

9. Regulation of other uses. As Article 10 of the Barcelona Statute (*see* **8**) suggests, riparian states have interests in the uses of rivers beyond mere navigation, and in recent decades these uses have become more important as the pressures of population growth and economic development make the effective use of resources more critical.

The accompanying move away from concentrating on navigable rivers and lakes has brought into consideration streams and smaller tributaries which may have been irrelevant for shipping but are significant when viewed as part of what is called an *international river system*.

A further development has been the concept of the *international drainage basin*, defined in Article 2 of the Helsinki Rules as an area encompassing two or more states which is delineated by the watershed limits of a single system of waters flowing into a common terminus. Geologically, this would include all water within the watershed area, including underground sources. The water resources which this concept would bring under international regulation are considerable. Many states object to such sweeping limitations on their sovereign rights and in 1984 ILC draft articles for a convention on the topic dropped the concept of a system and spoke of 'international watercourses', excluding parts of the watercourses that do not affect uses in other riparian states.

10. General principles governing other cases. It cannot be said that a single body of treaty or customary law exists on the matter, but certain general principles seem to be firmly established.

The first and most important is that upper riparians are not entitled to divert or pollute the waters of international rivers without regard to the interests of lower riparian states. The rejected idea that the upper riparian had no obligations to the lower is known as the Harmon doctrine, after the US Attorney-General who proposed it to Mexico in 1895 with regard to the Rio Grande.

Another principle is that each state's use of river waters should be reasonable and equitable with a view to permitting *equitable apportionment* between riparian states of what is considered to be a shared rather than an exclusive resource. Article 5 of the Helsinki Rules lists a number of geographical and human factors which might be relevant in determining on balance what is equitable in a given situation. These include the economic and social needs of each basin state and the comparative costs of alternatives to particular uses, availability of other resources, avoidance of unnecessary waste, and the degree to which one state's proposed use of the water could be undertaken without causing substantial injury to other basin states. (*See* also 15:**12, 13**.)

In the *Lake Lanoux Case* (1957) France and Spain, which were parties to a treaty safeguarding for Spain the outflow of waters from the French lake, disagreed about the consequences of a French hydroelectric generating station at the mouth of the lake. The arbitration tribunal held that an upper riparian state was not obliged to do precisely what the lower state demanded in such situations, but, as a matter of 'international common law', the upper riparian could only implement its own scheme 'provided it takes into consideration in a reasonable manner the interests of a downstream state'.

In 1977 India and Bangladesh agreed that India would limit to some extent its use of certain waters of the Ganges so as not to deprive Bangladesh of a useful share of the river's flow. In 1960 India and Pakistan had signed the Indus Waters Treaty dividing up the use of the Indus system between the two countries and controlling for Pakistan's benefit India's use of certain streams. Both of these agreements represent a shift on India's part away from something resembling the Harmon doctrine towards a concept of equitable apportionment.

Interoceanic canals

11. The three major canals. The three major canals connecting international seas are the Suez, the Panama and the Kiel Canals. Each is entirely within the national territory of a single state but all have nevertheless been subject to international legal restrictions for the benefit of other states.

Although some writers argue that the similarity of the legal regimes applied to these canals has created an international law of canals based either on general principles or custom, it seems more correct to regard the law merely as treaty provisions which were imposed on the territorial sovereigns by powerful maritime states with special interests to protect.

12. The Suez Canal. The Suez Canal, built by the predominantly French-funded Suez Canal Company across Egyptian territory and opened in 1869, is governed by the Constantinople Convention of 1888, whose operative provisions were reaffirmed by Egypt after President Nasser's nationalisation of the Canal in 1956.

The Convention stated in Article 1 that the Canal was to be 'free and open, in time of war as in time of peace, to every vessel of commerce or of war, without distinction of flag'. This sweeping provision has not always been fully observed: Britain took measures to prevent the passage of German ships through the Canal in both World Wars, Israel refused to let the Suez be opened while it occupied the Canal's east bank after 1967, and Egypt kept out Israeli ships between 1948 and 1979.

13. The Panama Canal. The Panama Canal was built across Panamanian territory over which the Hay-Bunau-Varilla Treaty of 1903 granted the United States, as if it were sovereign, rights of use, occupation and control, with only residual sovereignty remaining to Panama. Previously, Britain had insisted that the proposed canal be open to free navigation by ships of all nations and an Anglo-American understanding to this effect was embodied in the Hay-

Pauncefote Treaty of 1901.

In 1977 Panama and the United States signed the Panama Canal Treaty whereby Panama, 'as territorial sovereign', granted the US 'the rights necessary to regulate ... manage ... and defend the Canal' until the year 2000, when Panama will assume total responsibility for its operation and defence.

A separate Neutrality Treaty between the two states provided that the Canal would be permanently neutral and open to peaceful transit by the ships of all nations.

14. The Kiel Canal. In contrast to the two previous cases, the Kiel Canal was built by a major European power (Germany) entirely for its own purposes (navigation of German vessels between the Baltic and the North Sea) and for many years no question of its being regulated by international law was allowed to arise. This would probably have remained the situation had not Germany lost World War I and been forced to accept the Treaty of Versailles (1919), of which Article 380 stated that the Canal 'shall be maintained free and open to the vessels of commerce and of war of all nations at peace with Germany.'

By excluding the ships of states that might be at war with Germany, this provision was not as great an infringement of German sovereignty (*see* 4:**10**) as the agreements relating to the other canals. Germany nevertheless objected, in *The Wimbledon Case* (1923), that Article 380 effectively imposed an international servitude on the canal and should, as a severe derogation of German sovereignty, have been interpreted restrictively rather than in a liberal way that made yet further inroads on German rights. In particular, it should not be applied so as to interfere with Germany's rights and obligations of neutrality in the war then raging between Poland and Russia. The question arose because France wished to send the British ship S.S. Wimbledon through the canal with a cargo of military supplies destined for Poland. The Permanent Court of International Justice declined to decide whether the Versailles Treaty imposed a servitude or merely a contractual obligation but held nevertheless that Germany was clearly bound in one way or another to allow the *Wimbledon* through.

In 1936 Germany unilaterally repudiated the Versailles Treaty without provoking more than *pro forma* protests from other states, although since the end of World War II freedom of navigation on the Kiel Canal has once again been respected.

Progress test 7

1. Are there servitudes in international law? (**2**)
2. What was the basis for third-party rights in the *Aaland Islands Case*? (**4**)
3. Are there treaty provisions on the right of passage? (**6**)
4. What rights of navigation exist on international rivers? (**8**)
5. On what basis should the use of the waters of international rivers be allocated to the riparian states? (**10**)
6. Is there an international regime for interoceanic canals? (**11–14**)

8 State jurisdiction

Read to get a general background.

Introduction to jurisdiction

1. **Definition and basis of jurisdiction.** Jurisdiction is the authority of a state to affect legal interests. International law defines the jurisdiction a state may exercise over persons or property with connections that go beyond that state's own territory. The extent to which international rules on jurisdiction actually operate within municipal legal systems will depend on the relationship of international and municipal law (*see* Chap. 3). On the international level, however, states and other international legal persons (e.g. the European Communities) will be bound in this regard by their obligations to each other under international law.

At the most fundamental level, the common sense basis for a state's exercise of jurisdiction is that the state has some relationship to, or interest in, the person or property concerned. The difficulty comes when more than one state may claim such connections.

Such a situation can arise with respect to the two general categories of jurisdiction:

(*a*) *prescriptive jurisdiction,* the power to legislate or otherwise prescribe legal rules; and

(*b*) *enforcement jurisdiction,* the power to apply such rules through judicial or executive action.

2. **An example of jurisdictional difficulties in practice.** In order to protect its historic cultural property from the depredations of antiquities smugglers, New Zealand in 1962 adopted the Historic Articles Act, whereby any historic article removed from the country without government permission 'shall be forfeited to Her Majesty'. The effect of applying this provision would be to make New Zealand's law operate beyond the state's borders to alter rights in property which may be situated in other countries. In *Atttorney-General of New Zealand* v. *Ortiz* (1982) the English Court of Appeal refused a New Zealand government request to give effect to this Act in England, where an illegally exported Maori wood carving had been found. The Master of the Rolls, Lord Denning, held that to do so would be contrary to the 'rule of international law which says that no country can legislate so as to affect the rights of property when that property is situated beyond the limits of its own territory'.

Clearly, in the absence of an over-arching international legal regime, jurisdictional problems can make it very difficult for a state in New Zealand's position to protect its legitimate interests. But promoting a state's jurisdiction outside its territory also has obvious dangers for the authority of other states and the rights of their inhabitants.

International law has had to struggle with balancing these two countervailing concerns, as will be evident in the material that follows.

Traditional bases of jurisdiction

3. Five traditional bases. Five general principles on which jurisdiction, and particularly criminal jurisdiction, may be based have been put forward:

> (*a*) the territorial principle (*see* **4–7**);
> (*b*) the nationality principle (*see* **8–11**);
> (*c*) the passive personality principle (*see* **12**);
> (*d*) the protective principle (*see* **13**); and
> (*e*) the universality principle (*see* **14–17**).

The first two principles apply equally to civil and criminal jurisdiction, the last three to criminal jurisdiction.

States and legal writers dispute the extent and validity of some of these principles and each must be examined separately to determine its standing in international law and the scope of its application.

The territorial principle

4. Basis of the territorial principle. This principle arises from the view that a state has absolute and exclusive authority over people, things and events within its own territory and therefore may exercise jurisdiction over them in all cases, unless there is immunity from jurisdiction (e.g. for diplomats).

But the question of what may properly be considered 'within a state's territory' for purposes of jurisdiction is not always straightforward.

5. The extent of American anti-trust jurisdiction. American courts have exercised jurisdiction over foreign companies which are present in the United States and then have issued orders to them with respect to property or activities located elsewhere in the world (and sometimes even in their home states).

In *United States* v. *Imperial Chemical Industries Ltd* (1952), ICI, a United Kingdom company whose British subsidiary held in Britain exclusive rights in certain patents under an agreement in restraint of trade entered into between ICI and the American chemical giant DuPont, was ordered by a US Federal District Court to permit in Britain the exercise of rights which the court, in an anti-trust case, had just assured for American companies with regard to these same patents. The subsidiary then sued its parent in an English court to enjoin ICI from following the US order. In *British Nylon Spinners Ltd* v. *ICI* (1952), Lord Evershed MR in the Court of Appeal, held that BNS were in law an independent company from ICI and could therefore not be considered to have been subject to the jurisdiction of the American court without being directly a party to the action before it.

Lord Evershed indicated, however, in *obiter dicta* that 'there is no doubt that it is competent for the court of a particular country, in a suit between persons . . . subject to its jurisdiction, to make orders *in personam* against one such party – directing it, for example, to do something or to refrain from doing something in another country affecting the other party to the action'.

6. Criminal events in more than one country. Another area of difficulty is where a crime occurs in more than one country. Suppose, for example, that a man standing in Ruritania fires a gun across the border into the neighbouring state of Bloggovia, killing a person there. From the perspective of international law, which state may properly exercise jurisdiction for murder in this case?

To deal with such situations the territorial principle has been developed to have 'subjective' and 'objective' applications.

The *subjective territorial principle* is that a crime may be considered to occur in a state's territory when it is begun there but completed abroad. On this basis, Ruritania could exercise jurisdiction in the example above.

The *objective territorial principle* would operate in the reverse situation (that of Bloggovia) to give jurisdiction to the state where the crime, begun abroad, is completed.

7. **Applications of the objective territorial principle.** The scope of the objective territorial principle has gradually expanded over the years. The Permanent Court of International Justice, in *The Lotus Case* (1927), said: 'it is certain that the courts of many countries ... interpret criminal law in the sense that offences, the authors of which at the moment of commission are in the territory of another state, are nevertheless to be regarded as having been committed in the national territory, if one of the constituent elements of the offence, and more especially its effects, have taken place there'.

This statement signalled the development of the objective territorial principle (which initially required an actual element of the crime to occur within the territory of the state) into its variation, the *effects principle* (whereby the crime itself takes place completely outside the state's territory but has some consequences within it). Some writers argue that, to the extent that the effects principle goes beyond the realm of direct physical injury in the affected state, it opens the door objectionably to an almost limitless exercise of jurisdiction if any effect, however remote, can be found.

Nevertheless, the United States has used this application to extend the operation of American anti-trust laws to cover alien individuals and companies whose activities, perfectly legal in the foreign countries where they occur, have some effect on the economy of the United States.

The US Supreme Court, in *Continental Ore Co* v. *Union Carbide & Carbon Corp.* (1962), held that the Sherman Anti-Trust Act applied detrimentally to a Canadian company, appointed by the Canadian government to be the exclusive agent during World War II for purchasing and allocating vanadium for Canadian industries, which had refused to purchase supplies from an American company.

The long-running disagreement between the United States and other countries over this type of jurisdiction has provoked counter-action. Britain, for example, has enacted the Protection of Trading Interests Act 1980, which makes it a criminal offence in Britain for anyone to violate a British government prohibition on complying with foreign legal measures aimed at regulating or controlling international trade.

The European Court of Justice has applied the effects doctrine in a cross-border environmental pollution case. In *Handelswerkerij G.J. Bier and Stichting Reinwater* v. *Mines de Potasse d'Alsace S. A.* (1976), the court held that, where the European Conventionn on Jurisdiction and Enforcement of Judgments (1968) assigned jurisdiction to 'the place where the harmful event occurred', it should be understood to have meant to cover both the place where the act was committed and the place where the damage occurred.

The nationality principle

8. Fundamental connection of individual with his state. The connection between a state and its citizens is a fundamental one in international law, providing, among other things, the basis for exercise of civil and criminal jurisdiction over them even when they are not in the state's territory. This is the meaning of jurisdiction based on the nationality principle.

9. British application of the principle. Under English law, British nationals were liable to punishment for treason, murder, bigamy and perjury, even if the crimes were committed abroad. In *Joyce* v. *Director of Public Prosecutions* (1946), the House of Lords held that possession of a British passport by the appellant, after he had gone over to the German side in World War II and was making pro-Nazi propaganda broadcasts as 'Lord Haw Haw', was sufficient proof of his British nationality and duty of 'allegiance' to Britain to permit his being hanged for treason.

10. American application of the principle. In the United States both federal and state governments have exercised criminal jurisdiction over acts of citizens taking place outside the territory of the state. In *Skiriotes* v. *Florida* (1941), the US Supreme Court allowed the conviction of Skiriotes for illegally taking sponges beyond the state's territorial sea on the ground that Florida could regulate the conduct of its citizens upon the high seas with regard to matters in which the state had a legitimate interest.

In *Blackmer* v. *United States* (1932), the Supreme Court upheld the appellant's conviction for contempt of court in not appearing as a witness at a trial in the United States after a subpoena had been served upon him at his place of residence: Paris, France.

A more controversial exercise of US nationality jurisdiction came during the Iran hostages crisis of 1979–1980. American regulations aimed at freezing Iranian assets purported to control dollar deposits not only in banks in the United States but also in branches or subsidiaries of US banks operating abroad under the laws of other states.

11. The problem of determining nationality. A major difficulty with the nationality principle, in the context of international law, is that the way nationality is determined can be disputed and can have effects outside the national state's own territory. In *Joyce* v. *Director of Public Prosecutions* (*see* **9**), for example, the appellant was also (and indeed perhaps primarily) an American citizen, born in the United States of naturalised Irish immigrant parents. Should this fact have been more determinative of his nationality for the purposes of his 'allegiance' than the fact that he held a British passport? Should each state involved in such a situation be entitled to make its own decision on the matter for its own purposes or should international law somehow intervene in this area of vital concern to the domestic affairs of states?

The general position on nationality in international law is that, although the detailed bases on which a state may grant or withhold its citizenship are not a matter for international regulation, the right of a state to use its discretion is restricted by the state's obligations towards other states. In such circumstances, according to the Permanent Court of International Justice in the *Nationality Decrees in Tunis and Morocco Case* (1923), 'jurisdiction which, in principle, belongs solely to the state, is limited by rules of international law'. Unfortunately, what the resulting limitations may be is not clear.

The International Court of Justice has, however, set out one (highly controversial) theory in a leading case not involving criminal jurisdiction but rather the right of a state to confer its nationality. In the *Nottebohm Case* (1955) the ICJ held that, when faced with conflicting assertions from different states about the nationality of a particular individual, the court should look for a 'genuine connection' which would show that the individual is 'more closely connected with the population of the state conferring nationality than with that of any other state'. This is the principle of *effective nationality* or *dominant nationality*. (*See* also 10:23, 12:52–4.)

The passive personality principle

Fe–lons ?

12. A disputed principle. This must-criticised principle asserts the jurisdiction of a state to punish 'crimes' committed abroad by foreigners when the victim is a citizen of that state.

This basis of jurisdiction is considered by some to be jurisprudentially unsound because it subjects the accused to a legal system with which he has no contact and whose rules he has no necessary reason to know or understand. An act which may be legal in the individual's own country (e.g. inviting an acquaintance to have a drink in a pub) may be illegal in some other state (where consumption of alcoholic beverages may be banned). If it is a crime in Fanatica to invite a citizen of that country to have a drink in public, and Bloggs in another state extends such an invitation to a Fanatican citizen there, the passive personality principle would in theory give Fanatica jurisdiction over Bloggs if he was ever unlucky enough to enter its territory.

Some writers suggest that such jurisdiction should be exercised only with regard to acts which are generally recognised in the law of most states as crimes: e.g. murder or theft. It may be, however, that in such cases the state on whose territory the crime was committed has a stronger claim to jurisdiction which the passive personality principle does not override.

In October 1985 Egyptian authorities received the surrender of several Palestinians who had seized the Italian cruise ship *Achille Lauro*. United States Navy planes then illegally diverted to a NATO base in Sicily an Egyptian state aircraft upon which the Palestinians were being flown across the Mediterranean. Italian and American military personnel at the base almost fired upon each other in a disagreement over American attempts to take the Palestinians into American custody. The United States later requested their extradition from Italy on the ground that American law gave passive personality jurisdiction to the United States because passengers on the ship were American citizens. Italy, however, asserted its primary jurisdiction based on the fact that the ship was registered there.

The protective principle

13. Jurisdiction in the interests of state security. Many national legal systems provide that criminal jurisdiction may be exercised with regard to conduct by foreigners outside the country that threatens the state's security or the operation of its governmental functions, *provided* that, in the words of the authoritative American Restatement of Foreign Relations Law (2nd version), 'the conduct is generally recognised as a crime under the law of states that have reasonably developed legal systems'. States have not always strictly adhered to this proviso.

In *United States* v. *Archer* (1943) a Federal District Court justified by the protective principle an American statute making it a crime for an alien to commit perjury before a US diplomatic or consular official outside the territory of the United States, although presumably that specific misdeed is not a crime under any other country's law.

Israel was criticised in 1972 for enacting penal legislation giving Israeli courts jurisdiction over

> a person who has committed abroad an act which would be an offence if it had been committed in Israel and which harmed or was intended to harm the state of Israel, its security, property or economy or its transport or communication links with other countries.

The Judicial Committee of the Privy Council, in *Naim Molvan* v. *Attorney-General for Palestine* (1948), allowed the criminal convictions of an alien for acts committed on the high seas to abet illegal Jewish immigration into British-controlled Palestine.

It will be clear from these examples that the notion of what constitutes the security of a state for the purposes of the protective principle can become flexibly broad when the state's political organs take an interest in the matter – an important reason for insisting on strict adherence to the Restatement's proviso.

A unique case in this area was *Attorney-General of Israel* v. *Eichmann* (1961), where it was held by an Israeli court that Israel, although it had not existed during World War II, could exercise jurisdiction over a Nazi war criminal on the basis of the protective principle. The court indicated that international law required a 'linking point' between the punisher and the punished which existed here in the defendant's 'crime against the Jewish people', since the 'connection between the state of Israel and the Jewish people needs no explanation' and in any case it was in the 'vital interests' of Israel's 'honour and authority' not to allow the Jewish people to appear to be murdered with impunity.

The universality principle

14. State enforcement of external law. In contrast to the principles discussed above, which must all be strictly limited to a direct connection between the crime alleged and the state claiming jurisdiction, the universality principle does not require such a connection. It is based instead on the fact that the state exercising jurisdiction actually has custody of a person who is accused either of crimes under the national law of another state or of crimes under international law.

In the first of these situations, the state holding an individual alleged to have committed a crime under the law of another state may prosecute that person if the other state declines to do so. This exercise of jurisdiction has traditionally not been much favoured in Anglo-American jurisprudence, presumably because of the difficulties inherent in one state's courts attempting to determine the meaning and effect of another state's criminal law.

Universal jurisdiction over crimes under international law is more widely accepted. It arises from the view that certain crimes under international law constitute a threat to the whole international community any member of which is therefore competent to exercise jurisdiction over the perpetrators. Piracy and several other categories of crime fall under this jurisdiction.

15. Piracy jure gentium. In traditional customary international law, the chief crime over which universality jurisdiction could be exercised was piracy *jure gentium* (i.e. piracy according to the law of nations rather than simply as defined variously by different national legal systems). Thus, a state that has apprehended an individual who has committed piracy against the ships of any nation may try him for that crime, even if the state's own shipping has been unaffected by the pirate's activities.

16. War crimes. Strictly speaking, war crimes are violations of the laws of war and in particular of the Hague Regulations of 1907 and the Geneva Conventions of 1949. To the extent that these have developed into customary international law (as the Hague Regulations at least are generally held to have done), jurisdiction over crimes under them is also a matter of custom. The Geneva Conventions also provide explicitly for the universal jurisdiction of the parties over certain 'grave breaches' of the Conventions.

17. War-related crimes. At the end of World War II, it was asserted by the victorious Allies that universal jurisdiction could also be exercised by them over certain other acts in addition to war crimes. The International Military Tribunal, established at Nuremberg to try captured Nazi leaders, was given jurisdiction over what were called 'crimes against peace' and 'crimes against humanity'.

(*a*) *Crimes against peace* were defined to include the planning or waging of aggressive war or war in violation of international agreements.

(*b*) *Crimes against humanity* were said to encompass extermination, enslavement, deportation, 'and other inhumane acts', and political, racial or religious persecution in connection with any crimes within the jurisdiction of the tribunal.

It is interesting to note that the Allies did not consider racial or other persecution an international crime in and of itself. More recently, however, the *International Convention on the Suppression and Punishment of the Crime of Apartheid* (which entered into force in 1976) declares apartheid to be a crime against humanity. As of 1984, none of the war-time Western Allies were parties to this Convention and the United States in particular had strongly criticised it.

In the *Eichmann Case* (*see* 13), the universality principle was held to provide another basis for Israel's exercise of jurisdiction.

Effect of means used to acquire jurisdiction

18. Are means used irrelevant? It appears from a number of Anglo-American decisions and from the *Eichmann Case*, that the means whereby a person is brought physically within a state's control is irrelevant to the validity or invalidity of that state's exercise of jurisdiction over him on one of the traditional bases. In *Eichmann*, the defendant was kidnapped in Argentina by Israeli agents and transported to Israel. The Israeli court held that as a matter of law only the sovereign rights of Argentina may have been violated by the Israeli action, but not those of the accused.

Similarly, after Palestinians accused of seizing the Italian cruise ship *Achille Lauro* in October 1985 had been brought illegally into Italian territory by American military action, Italy felt able to exercise jurisdiction over them in the normal way.

This position is considered by some to be justified on the ground that an illegal means of acquiring jurisdiction does not affect the fundamental question at issue in a case, namely, whether or not the accused is guilty of the crime charged. The United States has increasingly adopted this attitude in carrying out illicit capture of drug smugglers and others outside American territory with the connivance of foreign police forces.

On the other hand illegally obtaining custody of the accused has the taint of violating his rights of procedural due process: he would in a normal case in which extradition is being sought (*see* 24), be entitled to have his objections to that considered by a court of the state on whose territory he is. Unless it is assumed that no state anywhere ever seeks custody over a person unless it is entitled to have that custody (a scarcely credible idea), these procedural rights of the accused must be seen as a necessary protection and certainly a human right of any innocent person who is being victimised by a foreign state.

Furthermore, the spectacle of a state violating law in the name of law can only bring the international legal system into disrepute and encourage violations by others whom the state by its example has taught to reject the rule of law.

On a narrower legal ground, some writers argue that, since the jurisdiction of a state's courts arises from the jurisdiction of the state itself, if the state has no valid jurisdiction because the seizure of the accused was illegal under international law, then the courts can have none either. In the case of *In re Jolis* (1933) a French court on this basis released a person illegally arrested by French agents abroad. John Westlake, a leading British international lawyer of the late nineteenth century, believed that at least in England a person brought illegally into the jurisdiction should be able to plead his unlawful arrest as a bar to prosecution before English courts.

On occasion in recent years English courts did in fact exercise judicial discretion to prohibit criminal proceedings when the accused had been brought illegally into the jurisdiction, as in the *Mackeson Case* (1981), but in *R.* v. *Plymouth Justices, ex p. Driver* (1985) the court reaffirmed the earlier precedents that such illegality was irrelevant to the exercise of jurisdiction.

Jurisdiction arising from treaties

19. Provision for special situations. States may have an interest in exercising jurisdiction in situations where the traditional principles are difficult to apply or, if applied, would not permit the desired jurisdiction. In such circumstances, they may attempt to provide for special jurisdictional arrangements by treaty, either to establish new bases for jurisdiction or to facilitate application of the traditional ones.

Jurisdiction in the territory of other states

20. Need for agreement. One state may exercise jurisdiction in the territory of another only with the agreement of the territorial sovereign. Some examples follow.

21. Capitulations. This is the name applied to certain agreements negotiated by European powers with non-European governments whereby the European state was given exclusive *extraterritorial jurisdiction* over its own nationals who were in the non-European state. The term 'extraterritorial' as used here means that those nationals were treated for purposes of jurisdiction as if they were outside the non-European state's territory and hence not subject to its law.

This system began in the Ottoman Empire and was initially seen by both sides as a convenient way of providing a legal framework for the activities of foreigners in the Empire. In time, however, it became a device for giving Europeans a privileged position there and for promoting European interference in Ottoman internal affairs.

Similarly disadvantageous arrangements were imposed in the heyday of European imperialism on Egypt, Japan, Siam, China and Morocco. The capitulations were ended as each country reasserted its independence from European domination.

22. Status of forces agreements. A state would normally maintain nationality jurisdiction over the members of its armed forces serving outside the country. Traditionally, such a situation would arise primarily in regard to the military personnel in the state's own colonial territory, to cases of belligerent occupation, and to war-time military activities in foreign territory – in none of which would the permission of a foreign government be an issue.

Since World War II, however, both the United States and the Soviet Union have maintained large forces on a more or less permanent basis in Western and Eastern Europe, respectively, and United States military personnel have also been stationed in Japan, Australia and elsewhere. Jurisdiction over such forces is regulated by treaty, in the case of Western Europe by the *NATO Status of Forces Agreement* (1951). This treaty provides in Article 1 that the 'sending' state's military authorities will exercise 'all criminal and disciplinary jurisdiction' conferred on them by that state's military law over the state's personnel, but that the 'receiving' state shall exercise jurisdiction over such personnel with respect to 'offences committed within the territory of the receiving state and punishable' by its law. Where concurrent jurisdiction arises from this arrangement, the sending state is to have a primary right over offences against its military law or against other members of its forces, while the receiving state will have the primary right over any other offences (Article 3).

The *United Nations* has also concluded status of forces agreements regarding the stationing of UN peacekeeping forces in the Congo, Egypt and Cyprus, providing for legal jurisdiction over UN personnel to remain exclusively with each person's national state.

Asylum and extradition

23. Territorial asylum. An attribute of a state's sovereign authority over its own territory is that the state in general has exclusive and complete discretion to decide who may be in its territory and who may not.

One aspect of this rule was that under traditional international law a state could refuse entry to any alien whom it might choose not to admit into its territory. (*See* also 13:**36**.)

In recent decades, however, the world-wide problem of refugees (about 10 million by UN estimates) has prompted efforts to develop a right of individuals to be granted asylum. This right is embodied in the UN General Assembly's *Declaration on Territorial Asylum* (Resolution 2312 of 14 December 1967) and will be incorporated in the Convention on Territorial Asylum which the United Nations has been attempting to draft in recent years. It is arguable whether repeated United Nations resolutions and practice (particularly by the UN High Commissioner for Refugees) have established this right as a matter of customary law, but a stronger case may be made that a related principle has become law: the right of an individual who has been admitted to a country as a refugee not to be sent back to the place from whence he came (the right of *non-refoulement*).

Another aspect of the traditional rule granting a state exclusive authority over the admission of aliens was that, if a person was admitted and given territorial asylum, no other state could legitimately object to the admitting state's decision. Thus, every state had what was traditionally called in international law a 'right of asylum', i.e. a right to grant asylum, subject only to the duty to prevent its territory being used by the person admitted as a base for hostile military activity against the state from which he came.

Inevitably, however, the problem arises of a person who gains admission to a country as a refugee or simply a normal traveller or immigrant, and who is later accused by another state either of having committed a crime within the latter's jurisdiction or of having fled following conviction for a crime. If the accusing state had an automatic right to have the alleged criminal turned over to it, the accused's asylum would be worthless and the admitting state's sovereign right to grant and maintain asylum would be infringed. On the other hand, the accusing state might have legitimate grounds for wishing to try or punish the individual concerned and international law does not seek to be a barrier to allowing justice to be done. Resolution of this dilemma is by the process of extradition.

24. Extradition. International law gives no general right to a state to demand from another the handing over of a wanted person. Extradition may, however, be provided for by treaty on the basis of reciprocity. The treaty will generally specify the crimes for which extradition may be granted (usually 'grave offences') and will often provide for *double criminality*, i.e. that the act for which extradition is sought must be criminal in the law of both states, and not merely in that of the demanding state. The treaty may also adopt the *rule of speciality* whereby the extraditing state has the right to insist that the person extradited be tried in the receiving state only for the crime for which he was extradited, thus preventing prosecution on other grounds such as political activities or opinions.

In the past, such treaties have usually not required a state to surrender its own citizens for extradition nor to extradite persons accused of 'political offences'.

25. The political offence exception to extradition. The problem of how to classify political offences remains at the heart of the international legal debate over extradition. The *European Convention on Extradition* (1957), for example, excluded extradition for an offence which the requested state regarded as 'a political offence, or as an offence connected with a political offence', but did not define either of these concepts.

Treason, sedition and espionage fall within the category of purely political offences on the ground that they represent acts against a state arising from political convictions and do not *per se* involve 'common' crimes.

26. Relative political offences. In the area of connected or 'relative' political offences, in which the political act is accompanied by the commission of a 'common' crime, lawyers and statesmen encounter considerably more difficulty. Would murder by a band of revolutionaries, for example, count as a relative political offence or be simply a common crime for which extradition would be granted?

Three general approaches have been suggested as a way of resolving such questions:

(*a*) *The incidence test*, traditionally favoured in Anglo-American law, requires, if extradition is to be blocked, that the crime be incidental to, or part of, a political uprising or disturbance.

(*b*) *The political objective test*, applied in French law, requires that the associated crime be against the political organisation or structure of the state.

(*c*) *The political motivation test*, in Swiss law, examines the crime in the context of the predominant circumstances surrounding it, with particular emphasis on the accused's motivations. This approach would give the asylum state wide latitude for distinguishing one crime from another in a discriminating way, but for that very reason may suffer from a certain subjectivity and lack of precision. To clarify matters Professor C. Bassiouni has proposed evaluating the relevant surrounding circumstances in the light of whether the political motivation involves defence of violated rights, rather than simply the realisation of political ambitions. This would require considering:

(*i*) the nature of the rights presumed violated by the state against which the offence was committed;

(*ii*) the factors which bore on the state's conduct in this regard; and

(*iii*) the factors which bore on the conduct of the offender.

An alternative to these attempts at classifying the offence in relation to legal considerations of one sort or another is the weighing of an act's effects against the purpose the offender aims to achieve. One scholar has written that the '*needless* use' of cruelty and atrocity should be 'decisive in determining whether crimes against humanity are to be considered political'.

But this may be a two-edged sword depending on the moral stance of the observer. If one sees the infliction of extreme human suffering as an unpardonable and ultimately counterproductive evil, then all extreme cruelty is needless. On the other hand, if one adopts the balancing attitude of many states when waging war, as with the justifying of the American nuclear bombing of Hiroshima and Nagasaki in 1945 as a means of ending the war without losing more *Allied* lives, then the 'needless use' test may simply enshrine in international law a relativistic disregard for human life and suffering.

27. Terrorism. These problems of definition have in recent years become particularly acute in relation to what political scientists call 'international terrorism'. It is suggested that terrorist acts must be punished in the interests of mankind as a whole, but attempts to develop a legal category of 'terrorism' in international law have so far failed. The reason is not hard to discover: any definition of terrorism that makes a claim to completeness and fairness must include all acts of violence or force aimed at the intimidation or coercion of others for political purposes, whether committed by states or non-states. But many states wish to avoid having their hands tied in this way and in effect claim exemption from the controls they wish to impose on other people's violence.

The problem of special treatment for state terrorism was highlighted in July 1985 when French secret agents sank the Greenpeace environmentalists' ship *Rainbow Warrior* in Auckland, New Zealand, causing the death of a crew member. The suggestion was made in some quarters that, once the French government had acknowledged its responsibility for the sinking, the French agents arrested in New Zealand should not be tried there, as they had simply been following orders to carry out an act of state. No high ranking French officials were either tried in France or extradited for their parts in ordering or planning the attack on the *Rainbow Warrior*.

Against such a background, the problems of defining and controlling international terrorism *as such* become almost insuperable, since if states make an exception in favour of their own violence, it becomes very difficult to formulate a convincing legal regime that impartially lays down one law for all similar acts.

The result is that international agreements 'against terrorism' generally do not create a legal offence of terrorism under international law but operate only as extradition treaties listing those acts which are agreed (by the parties) not to fall within the political offence exception.

Thus, the *European Convention on the Suppression of Terrorism* (1976) indicates in Article 1 that the following acts shall not be considered as political offences or relative political offences: airplane hijacking and sabotage; attacks against the 'life, physical integrity or liberty of internationally protected persons' including diplomats; kidnapping, hostage taking and unlawful detention; offences involving the use of bombs, grenades, rockets, automatic firearms and letter bombs, 'if this use endangers persons'; attempts to commit any of these crimes or acting as an accomplice in such attempts or commissions. Article 2 allows the parties, if they wish, to exclude other acts of violence against persons from the category of political offence.

The difficulty with this approach is that, in the absence of a general definition of terrorism under international law, an act which is not specifically listed in a treaty or covered by customary law may not be an international crime. Thus, when Palestinians seized the Italian cruise ship *Achille Lauro* in October 1985, their act did not amount to piracy according to the law of nations and therefore no universal jurisdiction was exercisable over them for the seizure itself, although their crimes under Italian municipal law were of course subject to Italian jurisdiction.

The solution to such problems lies in an international treaty defining terrorism and providing jurisdiction over it, possibly in conjunction with the establishment of an International Criminal Court for the most internationally significant cases.

28. Related problems. Some treaties have been adopted which apply this approach to particular aspects of terrorism, defining the crimes covered and making jurisdictional arrangements to deal with them specifically. Airplane hijacking and the taking of hostages have been singled out in this way.

29. Airplane hijacking. Plane hijacking has created particular jurisdictional problems since the crime does not necessarily take place within the territory of any state, while the *Chicago Convention on International Civil Aviation* (1944) provided only for territorial jurisdiction over all planes within a state's airspace and nationality jurisdiction over planes beyond state borders.

The jurisdictional difficulty was only partially remedied by Article 15 of the 1958 Geneva Convention on the High Seas which made the seizure of an aircraft by persons on board another aircraft or a ship an act of piracy over which all states could exercise jurisdiction outside territorial waters.

The *Tokyo Convention on Offences on Board Aircraft* (1963), Article 4, allowed criminal jurisdiction also over offences against penal law or the safety of aircraft or passengers in the case of non-national aircraft 'in flight' on the bases of the objective territorial principle (the crime has an 'effect' in the state), the passive personality principle (the offence has been against a national of the state), the protective principle (the offence is against the state's security), and on the basis of enforcing national flight regulations or international obligations.

The *Hague Convention for the Suppression of Unlawful Seizure of Aircraft* (1970) requires that hijacking itself be made an offence in the municipal law of the parties, clarifies (and perhaps expands) the meaning of 'in flight', and allows state jurisdiction if the plane lands in the state's territory with the offender still on board (even if the state would otherwise not have jurisdiction on the bases listed in the Tokyo Convention). Article 4(2) of the Hague Convention establishes a state's 'universality' jurisdiction over an offender who happens to be in its territory, although the state may otherwise have no connection with the offence. The offender may be extradited (subject to the usual rules, including the political offence exception) to another state which has jurisdiction under this Convention. But if he is not extradited, the state holding him must 'without exception whatsoever and whether or not the offence was committed in its territory ... submit the case to its competent authorities for the purpose of prosecution' (Article 7). This is the so-called 'extradite or prosecute' rule which has been much emphasised in recent discussions of terrorism and hijacking.

The *Montreal Convention for the Suppression of Unlawful Acts against the Safety of Civil Aviation* (1971) expands the category of aerial crimes to include sabotage of aircraft and related acts, and extends state jurisdiction over such crimes on bases similar to those in the Hague Convention.

30. Hostage taking. In 1979 the United Nations General Assembly adopted the *International Convention against the Taking of Hostages*, which came into force in June 1983. The Convention defines the crime of 'hostage-taking' as seizing and threatening a person in order to put pressure on a third party (primarily, a government) to act in a certain way. Any state party may detain an alleged offender who is on its territory, regardless of where the hostage-taking occurred, and prosecute or extradite him.

31. Disguised extradition. In all the situations discussed above in which the question of handing a person over from one state to another arises, there is a danger of disguised extradition by means of ordinary deportation. In the days when asylum and extradition were considered mainly from the perspective of the rights of the states involved, the position of the individual concerned was not of great importance. The modern awareness of human rights issues, however, has brought the individual closer to centre-stage, particularly when there are questions of non-refoulement (the right of a refugee not to be sent back to the country from whose political or other persecution he has fled).

In the *Amekrane Case*, Mohamed Amekrane, a Moroccan who had participated in a failed plot to overthrow the government of his country, had in August 1972 sought refuge in the British colony of Gibraltar. After his arrival there, he was declared a prohibited immigrant by the Gibraltar authorities, was turned over to Moroccan officials, and removed to Morocco, where he was tried, convicted and shot. His family raised a case against the United Kingdom under Article 3 of the European Convention on Human Rights, alleging that Amekrane had suffered 'inhuman treatment' at the United Kingdom's hands when, knowing he was sought for a political offence, Britain nevertheless returned him to Morocco under the guise of deportation. The case was settled 'out-of-court' by British payment of the relatively large sum of £37,500 to the Amekrane family. Although this payment was said to be *ex gratia* and not to imply a British admission of guilt, one is not obliged to accept such statements at face value.

The future of jurisdiction

32. National assertiveness versus international solutions. The problems of jurisdiction discussed in this chapter, and particularly the attempts of some states to extend their jurisdiction, signal a significant development in international life – the increasing interconnection and even interdependence of the members of the international community at a time when the mechanisms for international control of the world's affairs have lagged behind. The attempt by individual states to broaden their own external jurisdiction, either to compensate for the absence of effective international machinery or to forestall its creation, is an inherently anarchic and unsatisfactory solution to this problem. In this area of international law, as in others, the international community is moving dangerously close to the point where either the international legal system will collapse or a new international legal order will perforce be established.

Progress test 8

1. List the traditional bases of jurisdiction. **(3)**
2. Distinguish the subjective and objective territorial principles. **(6)**
3. Why did the United Kingdom adopt the Protection of Trading Interests Act 1980? **(7)**
4. Does the nationality principle embroil international law in the problem of how states confer their nationality on aliens? **(11)**
5. Is the passive personality principle sound? **(12)**
6. Explain the protective principle. **(13)**
7. What sorts of crimes are generally covered by the universality principle? **(14-17)**
8. Do the means by which jurisdiction is acquired affect the validity of that jurisdiction's exercise? **(18)**
9. Is there a 'right of asylum' in international law? **(23)**
10. Is extradition a matter of customary international law? **(24)**
11. How can it be determined whether a particular crime is a relative political

offence?   (**26**)

     12. How do treaties 'against terrorism' usually operate?   (**27**)

     13. What attempts have been made to deal with the problem of airplane hijacking?   (**29**)

     14. Is it legally permissible to accomplish the objective of extradition without formal extradition proceedings?   (**31**)

Bibliography

On terrorism and extradition
See the discussion in Weston, Falk, D'Amato, *International Law and World Order*, Chapter 6.

9 Immunity from jurisdiction

1. The effect of sovereign status on jurisdiction. As has been seen (Chap. 8), sovereignty and jurisdiction are closely linked: the exercise of jurisdiction is an act of sovereign authority. It follows therefore that on the international level, where sovereign states are all considered legally equal and none is subject to another's sovereignty, international law holds that no sovereign may be subject to the jurisdiction of another. This is an application of the principle *par in parem non habet imperium*, 'an equal does not have authority over an equal'.

This has practical significance: it implies that one sovereign when within the territory of another will enjoy certain immunities from the operation of the second's municipal law. The precise nature, degree and application of these immunities from jurisdiction become particularly important in actions before the courts when a plaintiff is attempting to sue or implead a foreign state or its representatives or official organs.

Absolute sovereign immunity

2. The traditional view. In the *Schooner Exchange* v. *McFaddon* (1812), Chief Justice John Marshall of the United States Supreme Court set out the classic statement of absolute sovereign immunity:

> One sovereign being in no respect amenable to another; and being bound by obligations of the highest character not to degrade the dignity of his nation, by placing himself or its sovereign rights within the jurisdiction of another, can be supposed to enter a foreign territory only under an express license, or in the confidence that the immunities belonging to his independent sovereign station, though not expressly stipulated, are reserved by implication, and will be extended to him.

This immunity would attach to the foreign sovereign himself as the head of a foreign state, his diplomatic representatives, and his public property (as in this case, where the *Schooner Exchange* was owned by the French government).

It is important to note, however, that Marshall also said that such immunity might not attach to the *private* property of a foreign sovereign situated in another state, nor would it apply to 'private individuals' from the foreign sovereign's state who are in another country for business or other private reasons, nor to 'merchant vessels' which have entered another state for the purposes of trade. This distinction between public and non-public activities and persons provided a basis for significant legal development later on.

3. Problems with the traditional view. The assumption behind Marshall's conception of sovereign immunity is that state governmental activities can be clearly distinguished from private business or personal activities, since the two categories do not overlap.

This may have been a good basis on which to work in Marshall's day; indeed his view was very influential throughout the nineteenth and early twentieth centuries. But more recently states have certainly extended the scope of their operations into many areas of economic and commercial activity, and in doing so have blurred the sharp lines Marshall tried to lay down.

The response of states to this development has depended on a variable blending of municipal and international law, often coloured by strong ideological preconceptions.

4. The view of the Soviet Union. Under Article 73 of the Soviet Union's 1977 Constitution, foreign trade is a state monopoly. Under the 1982 Statute on Trade Representations of the USSR Abroad, trade activities are carried on through trade delegations which are part of the Soviet embassies in foreign countries.

Soviet international lawyers have always maintained that absolute sovereign immunity applies to the USSR and all its activities abroad. In theory, this ought to cover the work of the trade delegations, but Soviet practice is somewhat different. The USSR has entered into a number of bilateral treaties with other states in which these delegations operate. These treaties usually reaffirm the general immunity to which the Soviet Union claims entitlement but then list as exceptions to that immunity such things as disputes about commercial contracts and the enforcement of judgments in such disputes by means of the levying of execution on goods and claims owed to the trade delegation itself by others.

Soviet writers do not see these treaties as establishing any limitation in principle on the USSR's absolute immunity, since the treaties are considered merely to be a waiver of an existing right in particular cases rather than a general renunciation. Western observers argue, however, that the uniformity and generality of such agreements between the USSR and other states reflects the Soviet Union's recognition that commercial activities cannot in practice be treated as immune from foreign jurisdiction if they are to develop at all.

5. The Western view. Where capitalist free-market economics are favoured, rejection of absolute immunity for state commercial activity has been more readily accepted. A leading case which reviewed the history of the controversy over immunity and concluded that there had been a movement away from immunity for commercial activities was *Dralle* v. *Republic of Czechoslovakia* (Austrian Supreme Court, 1950). The Austrian court noted that the 'classic doctrine of immunity arose at a time when all the commercial activities of states in foreign countries were connected with their political activities ... [whereas today] states engage in commercial activities and ... enter into competition with their own nationals and with foreigners'. Consequently, 'the classic doctrine ... has lost its meaning' and should be replaced by a doctrine restricting the immunity of states.

Such thinking gave rise to the *restrictive theory of sovereign immunity*, which narrows the scope of state immunity by focussing on state activities and classifying them into immune and non-immune categories.

Restrictive theory of **6. Purpose of the theory.** In *Victory Transport Inc.* v. *Comisaria General de* **sovereign immunity** *Abastecimientos y Transportes* (1964), a US Federal Court of Appeal said:

The purpose of the restrictive theory of sovereign immunity is to try to accommodate the interest of individuals doing business with foreign governments in having their legal rights determined by the courts, with the interest of foreign governments in being free to perform certain political acts without undergoing the embarrassment or hindrance of defending the propriety of such acts before foreign courts.

Struggling with the problem in judicial decisions

7. Defining immune categories of activity. In attempting to apply the restrictive theory, it becomes necessary to distinguish immune activities from non-immune ones. The starting point for this can be two alternative views of the distinction Marshall suggested between public and non-public activities.

One may think in terms of *public* v. *private* activities. Inevitably this requires possibly controversial assumptions about what is the proper sphere of governmental activity.

The alternative is to adopt the distinction of *public* v. *commercial* activities. However, this distinction fails to allow for acts which are not commercial but which should nevertheless not attract immunity (as in the *Letelier Case* (*see* 15)).

Since neither of these categories is completely satisfactory, the tendency has been to combine them loosely, and sometimes unwittingly, into a formula distinguishing acts *jure imperii* ('by right of government') from acts *jure gestionis* (roughly, 'by the private law of transactions'). Acts *jure imperii* are said to be immune; acts *jure gestionis* are not.

This distinction is not free of difficulties and seems often to conceal problems behind Latin phrases whose meaning is sufficiently vague to allow flexible interpretations. The test also clearly by-passes the Soviet claim that, since government has broad economic responsibilities, governmental business activities are also in effect *jure imperii*. One Soviet writer has even gone so far as to charge that the restrictive theory was a 'weapon of the imperialist reaction' against Soviet communism and newly independent states aiming to build up the public sector of their national economies.

Western courts have been more preoccupied with the more mundane burden, imposed by the *jure imperii/jure gestionis* test, of defining which acts are which. Having in the past had to determine this for themselves, the courts have been troubled by the problem national courts always face when developing municipal law rules which affect the application of international law.

In the *Claim against the Empire of Iran Case* (1963) the West German Constitutional Court concluded that national law was limited in this respect by the requirement that it could not exclude from immunity 'such state dealings as belong to the field of state authority in the narrow and proper sense, according to the predominantly-held view of states', such as foreign affairs, military authority, legislation, policing and the administration of justice. Beyond such acts whose status was determined definitively by international law, the courts of other states were free to make their own determinations. The American Restatement of Foreign Relations Law (2nd version) suggests that the state exercising jurisdiction may apply its own test but not in an 'unreasonable manner'.

Two bases on which a state court might apply the *jure imperii/jure gestionis* distinction are the 'purpose of the act' test (*see* **8**) and the 'nature of the act' test (*see* **9**).

8. The purpose of the act test. This test suggests that an act which is done for governmental purposes should be classified as *jure imperii*. The result might well be to make most state trading and commercial activities immune, and so the test has generally been rejected in the West.

In the *I Congreso del Partido Case* (1981), Lord Wilberforce in the British House of Lords said: 'If immunity were to be granted the moment that any decision taken by the trading state were shown not to be commercially, but politically, inspired, the "restrictive theory" would almost cease to have any content.'

9. The 'nature of the act' test. In 1932 a group of American international lawyers proposed, in the Harvard Research on International Law, a test for whether the act was by nature *jure imperii* or *jure gestionis*. If a foreign government's act in another state was an industrial, commercial, financial or other business activity in which private persons may engage in that other state, then the act is *jure gestionis*. A note by the authors implies that acts in which only governments generally engage (e.g. running a postal system) are *jure imperii*.

Although a sweeping categorisation of commercial acts, this test has the merit of clarity and fairness: since what may be carried on as a private business activity in a particular country is likely to be well known, a foreign state choosing to carry on such an activity there may reasonably be deemed to know what it is getting involved in and to understand the consequences in terms of losing its immunity.

However, in the *Victory Transport* case (*see* **6**), the American court, although rejecting the purpose test, found the nature of the act test as generally applied to be also unsatisfactory. It produced 'rather astonishing results' in some European cases (e.g. holding the erection of fortifications for state defence to be a private act). Furthermore, there was a danger of oversimplified categorising:

> Any individual may be able to purchase a boat, but only a sovereign may be able to purchase a battleship. Should the purchase of a yacht be equated with the purchase of a battleship?

10. The American judicial solution. Having painted itself into a corner on the question, the court in *Victory Transport* was able to escape only by emphasising the role of the US State Department in evaluating claims to sovereign immunity. The Supreme Court in *Republic of Mexico* v. *Hoffman* (1945) had emphasised deference to the State Department's judgment in matters 'intimately associated with our foreign policy'. In other words, the courts should not strike out on their own when to do so might affect the Executive branch's conduct of foreign relations.

On the question of sovereign immunity the State Department had spoken in a general way in the *Tate Letter* of May 1952 in which the Department's acting legal adviser said that it would apply the restrictive theory in particular cases as they came up and that it expected that the courts would take note of the Department's determination.

In *Victory Transport*, therefore, the court held that, 'since the State

Department's failure or refusal to suggest immunity is significant', where no such suggestion has been made, the court will not grant immunity unless the act in question 'falls within one of the categories of strictly political or public acts about which sovereigns have traditionally been quite sensitive'.

These categories, according to the court, were:

(*a*) internal administrative acts, e.g. expulsion of an alien;

(*b*) legislative acts, e.g. nationalisation;

(*c*) acts concerning the armed forces;

(*d*) acts concerning diplomatic activity;

(*e*) public loans.

The court's solution is objectionable, however, because:

(*a*) it does nothing to settle the definitional question but merely makes up an essentially arbitrary list; and

(*b*) it simply transfers responsibility for making decisions to somebody else.

That the State Department should be left to decide allowed the suspicion that the problems of immunity were not susceptible of a legal solution but were in fact political and would be resolved on that basis.

British judicial solutions

11. The Trendtex Case. In *Trendtex Trading Corporation* v. *Central Bank of Nigeria* (1977), the English Court of Appeal had to consider a suit against the Central Bank of Nigeria for refusing to honour a letter of credit previously issued by it in connection with the sale of cement by the plaintiffs to the Nigerian government. The bank claimed sovereign immunity as the organ of a foreign state.

In reviewing the *jure imperii/jure gestionis* problem, Lord Denning MR rejected the purpose test in relation to the original purchase of cement and indicated that when a government 'goes into the market place of the world and buys ... cement ... as a commercial transaction ... [it] should be subject to all the rules of the market place'. This seems to rely on a notion of implied waiver of immunity with perhaps some element of reciprocity and fairness as between the parties.

In any case, the letter of credit itself was a separate transaction, the document having been issued in London through a London bank 'in the ordinary course of commercial dealings'. It was therefore 'completely within the territorial jurisdiction of our courts'.

Even if absolute immunity applied, it did so in Lord Denning's view only with regard to actual organs and departments of the foreign state. Was the Central Bank such an organ? This was difficult to answer because the internal law of states varies in classifying the same sort of entity in different ways. But 'it cannot be right' that international law should determine questions of sovereign immunity according to such internal law: there must be an international legal test.

For Lord Denning there was 'no satisfactory test except that of looking to the functions and control of the organisation', and particularly 'whether the organisation was under government control and exercised governmental functions'. In spite of the considerable evidence which he listed to the contrary, Lord Denning decided that the bank was a separate legal entity and should not be treated in international law as a department of the Nigerian government.

Lord Justice Shaw, concurring, raised the question of fairness with regard to the reliance of the plaintiffs on the seemingly non-governmental character of the Central Bank: 'How can they know that such a risk lurks in dealing with a body which assumes a guise and bears a title appropriate to a commercial or financial institution?' In these circumstances, without positive evidence that the bank was intended to be a governmental organ, the balance should be tipped in favour of the plaintiffs.

Lord Justice Shaw's approach has much to be said for it, since it allows each case to be considered on its merits in relation to the facts and offers a means of drawing legal conclusions from the acts or omissions of the parties themselves, without regard to the awkward theoretical questions surrounding sovereign immunity. If the foreign entity fails to declare its position clearly during the course of its business dealings, and the other party reasonably relies on appearances, then in effect that entity should be estopped from claiming immunity later on.

It should be noted that insofar as the Court of Appeal applied elements of the restrictive theory of sovereign immunity in reaching its decision, it did so by relying on the trend in favour of that doctrine in international law to outweigh English precedents to the contrary. The *Trendtex Case* is in that respect an interesting example of the incorporation doctrine (*see* 3:7) at work.

12. I Congreso del Partido Case. In 1981 the House of Lords delivered judgment in this case on the basis of the law applying in 1973 when the relevant events occurred.

The judges had to unravel a complicated problem arising from the Cuban government's decision, in protest at the American-backed coup against the elected Chilean government headed by Salvador Allende, to divert away from Chile two merchant ships, one owned by, and the other chartered by, the Cuban state trading organisation, Mambisa. The owners of the cargoes on the two ships brought suit for breach of contract and tortious conversion against the Cuban government based on *in rem* jurisdiction arising from the arrest in British waters of another Cuban ship, the *I Congreso del Partido*.

Lord Wilberforce decided that the restrictive theory of sovereign immunity applied. This required evaluating the nature of the relevant acts at issue to determine whether they were within the realm of trading or commercial activities or outside it. However, Lord Wilberforce distinguished between the nature of the specific act complained of and the nature of the overall transactions within which the specific act took place.

With regard to the Cuban-owned ship (the *Playa Larga*), the relevant specific act was the diversion of the ship for political purposes by the Cuban government acting as the owner of the ship. The private commercial nature of this act might be inferred from the fact that the act of diversion was one which a private ship owner might also take, being as a result liable in contract or otherwise to the cargo owners with whom the ship owner had entered into legal relationships. The Cuban government's diversion of the *Playa Larga* therefore seemed to have been done 'in the context of the trading relationship'.

With regard to the Cuban-chartered ship (the *Marble Islands*), however, Lord Wilberforce noted that the Cuban government had not been involved in the overall commercial transaction with the cargo owners but had simply taken certain actions in pursuit of its political determination to break off trading relations with Chile. The Cuban government's action in issuing a decree for the diversion of the *Marble Islands* was taken in a governmental capacity as a sovereign state and not in the capacity of a shipowner. It was therefore an act *jure imperii* and attracted immunity. If the *Marble Islands* cargo owners wanted a remedy, they would have to seek it from Mambisa and not from the Cuban government.

Lord Diplock, however, disagreed with Lord Wilberforce's conclusions on the *Marble Islands*. He argued against immunity on the ground that everything the Cuban government was able to have done in relation to that ship and its cargo relied on the private law dealings of Mambisa and no immunity could attach to these. Two other Law Lords agreed with Lord Diplock, so that the decision of the House of Lords was to reject immunity with regard to both ships.

A different method of solution: legislation and treaties

13. Major effort in the 1970s. The difficulties experienced by courts in sorting out the problems of categorising acts in a coherent and generally accepted way prompted efforts in the 1970s to deal with the matter by treaty and statute.

US legislation

14. The Foreign Sovereign Immunities Act 1976. With the aim of limiting the reliance of courts on possibly suspect recommendations from the State Department, Congress in 1976 passed the Foreign Sovereign Immunities Act (FSIA).

The statute endorses the restrictive theory of sovereign immunity by claiming in s. 1602 that international law does not give states immunity for their commercial activities, and it provides that the commercial character of an activity should be determined by the nature of the act and not its purpose.

The FSIA gives legal expression to this position in the context of setting out in s. 1604 the general rule recognising state immunity but then qualifying that rule with a list of exceptions to it in s. 1605. These exceptions, where immunity does *not* attach, are:

(*a*) when the foreign state has waived its right explicitly or implicitly (s. 1605(a)(1));

(*b*) when the foreign state has carried on a commercial activity in the US, or has acted there in relation to a commercial activity, or when the foreign state's commercial activity elsewhere has a 'direct effect' in the US (s. 1605(a)(2));

(*c*) when rights of property taken by the foreign state in violation of international law are at issue and the property, or the foreign state commercial agency or organ which owns it, is present in the US (s. 1605(a)(3));

(*d*) when property rights in the US are at issue following acquisition by the foreign state through succession or gift or when the case concerns rights in immovable property in the US (s. 1605(a)(4));

(*e*) when the case involves personal injury or death, or property loss, caused in the US by the tortious act or omission of the foreign state, except when that state's action was in exercise of a discretionary function or when the claim is for such actions as libel, slander, deceit or interference with contractual rights (s. 1605(a)(5)); and

(*f*) when the case involves admiralty jurisdiction against a foreign vessel to enforce a maritime lien arising from the foreign state's commercial activity (s. 1605(b)).

15. Letelier *v*. Republic of Chile (1980). Apart from cases involving commercial activity, an interesting application of this Act came in the *Letelier Case*. In a claim based on s. 1605(a)(5), Chile was sued for damages for the tort of wrongful death by the family of exiled Chilean diplomat Orlando Letelier who had been assassinated in the United States by Chilean agents. The government of Chile argued that it was entitled to immunity since the provision that was relied upon applied only to tortious acts and not political assassination, which was an act of public and governmental character.

The Federal District Court for the District of Columbia held, however, that the statute was not limited to private tortious acts but covered all tortious acts. Nor could Chile claim that the assassination was an immune discretionary act under the statute since, according to the court, 'there is no discretion to commit ... an illegal act ... [or an] action that is clearly contrary to the precepts of humanity as recognised in both national and international law'.

The later progress of the case highlights some of the problems of application and definition that remain under the FSIA. When the Letelier family attempted to have the first judgment for monetary damages executed against the property of the government-owned Chilean national airlines (whose facilities had been used by the assassins), a lower court held in the family's favour on the basis of 'equitable principles'. But a Federal Court of Appeal in 1984 reversed that decision on the ground that the airline was legally a separate entity from the Chilean government and its property therefore was not that of the Chilean state for purposes of the FSIA. Furthermore the airline's (unwitting) participation in the assassins' plan was not a 'commercial activity' under the FSIA, since prior cases had established (in accordance with pre-statute definitions) that a commercial activity was one which a private person may *lawfully* undertake.

The appeal court observed that in these circumstances Congress appeared to have created 'a right without a remedy'. This highlights the critical point that state immunity from execution of judgment is more generally upheld than immunity from jurisdiction, since seizing the property of a foreign state is thought to create a greater risk of endangering the seizing state's international relations.

16. Verlinden B. V. *v*. Central Bank of Nigeria (1983). In this case, the US Supreme Court upheld the constitutionality of the FSIA and allowed under it a foreign plaintiff to sue a foreign state in a US court. By allowing litigation under the Act of foreign claims (e.g. by the foreign subsidiaries of American companies), this decision could considerably increase the importance of the FSIA in the international arena.

British developments

17. The State Immunity Act 1978. In 1972 Britain, along with several other

European countries, signed the *European Convention on State Immunity*. This adopted the restrictive theory of sovereign immunity in relation to listed types of cases. As British courts refuse to implement Britain's international treaty obligations without an Act of Parliament, however, the restrictive theory was only absorbed piecemeal into British law (as in the *Trendtex Case*) until the passing of the State Immunity Act 1978.

Under this Act a foreign state is not immune as regards proceedings relating to 'a commercial transaction entered into by the state' or to a contractual obligation to be performed wholly or partly in the United Kingdom.

Section 3(3) defines a commercial transaction as:

(*a*) – a contract for the supply of goods;

(*b*) – a loan or other transaction for the provision of finance and any connected guarantees or indemnities; or

(*c*) – any other commercial, industrial, financial, professional or similar transaction or activity which is not an exercise of sovereign authority.

Thus, under the Act the most important business dealings are clearly placed by s. 3(3)(*a*) and (*b*) in the non-immune category of 'commercial transactions'. This implicitly rejects the purpose of the act test in such cases and applies the nature of the act test instead.

Section 3(3)(*c*) is interesting in refusing immunity for an 'activity' which the state has entered into other than 'in the exercise of sovereign authority'. This still leaves it to the courts to determine what is the appropriate sphere of sovereign authority in such cases.

Specifically excluded from immunity are cases relating to death or injury caused by the state in Britain, questions of immovable property in the United Kingdom, patent and trademark cases, state disputes arising from membership in an organisation incorporated under UK law, *in rem* actions against commercial ships and various other situations.

Immunity does not pertain to any 'separate entity' distinct from the foreign government's executive organs and capable of suing or being sued, unless that entity is acting in the exercise of sovereign authority and 'the circumstances are such that a state ... would have been so immune'.

A potentially important provision is contained in s. 6(4) whereby the courts may exercise jurisdiction in cases against third parties even if a foreign state has an interest in, or possession or control of, the property at issue in the suit, provided that the state would not have been immune if the case had been brought against it directly. This section therefore allows *impleading*, the joining in the action of a party which is not initially a named defendant.

The problem of getting execution of a judgment against a foreign state is highlighted by s. 13(2)(*b*) which prohibits execution against that state's property unless, under s. 13(4), the property is 'for the time being in use or intended for use for commercial purposes'. In *Alcom Ltd* v. *Republic of Columbia* (1984), the House of Lords held that an embassy bank account used for paying routine expenses would have immunity unless it was earmarked 'solely' for paying debts from commercial transactions. This has been interpreted as giving immunity to all embassy bank accounts used even in part for diplomatic expenses.

The 'act of state' doctrine

18. **Definitions of an act of state.** The term 'act of state' is used somewhat differently in the context of international law than it is in British municipal law. In British constitutional law 'act of state' refers to unreviewable acts of the Royal

prerogative in the exercise of sovereign power (particularly in the field of Britain's international relations). In international law, 'act of state' refers to any public act of a foreign state, whatever its status in that state's municipal law.

The act of state doctrine is that the courts of one country will not sit in judgment on the validity of another country's sovereign public acts. It thus has the same effect as an immunity from jurisdiction but with the result that the foreign public act is allowed to continue to operate without outside judicial interference. In some circumstances this may be equivalent to giving effect to the acts of a foreign state (e.g. where the transfer of ownership of property may be at issue). The act of state doctrine is therefore occasionally controversial, particularly where it seems to favour state acts that violate fundamental principles of national or international law.

19. The doctrine in the United States. The classic formulation of the doctrine in American law came from the US Supreme Court in *Underhill* v. *Hernandez* (1897) where Chief Justice Fuller held that 'every sovereign state is bound to respect the independence of every other sovereign state, and the courts of one country will not sit in judgment on the acts of the government of another, done within its own territory'.

Applying this doctrine in the case of *Bernstein* v. *Van Heyghen Frères* (1947), a New York Federal District Court held it could not adjudicate the act of the Nazi government of Germany whereby property extorted from the plaintiff was eventually transferred to the defendant. The judge indicated that the act of state doctrine in such a case even took precedence over 'the well-settled exception to the usual doctrine', namely, that the act of the foreign state may be adjudicated where it is 'abhorrent to the moral notions' of the adjudicating court's state – in effect, an exception to the act of state doctrine based on the 'public policy' of the forum state. The plaintiff persisted, however, and eventually won a related case after the court agreed to follow a letter from the State Department which said that the Department did not expect the courts to apply the act of state doctrine in relation to acts of the Nazi regime. This came to be known in American law as 'the Bernstein exception' to the act of state doctrine.

Thus, although the Supreme Court's opinion in *Underhill* v. *Hernandez* seemed to base the act of state doctrine on the sovereign equality of states (and hence on the rule *par in parem non habet imperium* which Marshall implied in *The Schooner Exchange*), the acceptance of the Bernstein exception suggested that the doctrine actually had to do with the reluctance of the courts to get involved in questions about foreign state acts if that would interfere with the State Department's conduct of foreign relations.

This was the state of play when the Supreme Court gave judgment in *Banco Nacional de Cuba* v. *Sabbatino* in 1964. This case involved Cuban nationalisation measures and it was argued against the Banco Nacional that the act of state doctrine should not apply since the nationalisation was alleged to be in violation of the rules of international law on expropriation of foreign-owned property. This argument in effect was claiming an 'international law exception' to the act of state doctrine.

The Supreme Court reviewed the whole question of the doctrine. It rejected the view that it arose from 'the inherent nature of sovereign authority' or from some other principle of international law. Rather, the doctrine was really an expression of judicial restraint in that the judicial branch of government ought not to disturb the executive branch's conduct of foreign relations by arousing ill feeling in another state through adjudicating cases involving that state's public acts. The court therefore rejected jurisdiction in the *Sabbatino Case*.

This decision was severely criticised and the US Congress enacted the 'Second Hickenlooper Amendment', which required federal courts to hear cases arising out of foreign state acts which were alleged to violate international law.

In the later case of *Banco Nacional de Cuba* v. *Farr, Whitlock & Co.* (1967) a federal court followed the Hickenlooper amendment, once it had determined that the case at bar fell within it, and then proceeded to apply rules of customary international law on the basis that they were part of the law of the United States.

In *First National City Bank* v. *Banco Nacional de Cuba* (1972) a divided Supreme Court allowed the case to be heard after the State Department had indicated in a letter that it did not require the act of state doctrine to be applied. Three judges out of five in the majority explained this as an acceptance of the Bernstein exception. One of the five, however, based his support for the decision on the need to uphold and apply international law. Mr Justice Powell indicated that to reject jurisdiction on the basis of internal or international political considerations would be:

> to assume that there is no such thing as international law but only international political disputes that can be resolved only by the exercise of power ... I am not prepared to say that international law may never be determined and applied by the judiciary where there has been an 'act of state'. Until international tribunals command a wider constituency, the courts of various countries afford the best means for the development of a respected body of international law. There is less hope for progress in this long neglected area if the resolution of all disputes involving 'an act of state' is relegated to political rather than judicial processes.

Apart from these fundamental problems, the act of state doctrine raises the usual difficulty of defining what constitutes such an act. In *Alfred Dunhill of London Inc.* v. *Republic of Cuba* (1976) the US Supreme Court held that the mere refusal of a commercial agency of a foreign government to repay money paid to it by mistake was not an unreviewable act of state any more than it was entitled to sovereign immunity.

20. The British position on the doctrine. In *Anglo-Iranian Oil Co. Ltd* v. *Jaffrate* (*The Rose Mary*) (1953), the Supreme Court of Aden, applying English law, held that the legislation of the Iranian government which nationalised the plaintiff's property in Iran was not excluded from the court's jurisdiction by reason of the act of state doctrine. The court 'must refuse validity to the Iranian laws' because they were 'invalid by international law' and hence invalid by the law of Aden also, since customary international law was incorporated into the law of Aden according to established doctrine in English law.

Professor Greig has criticised the reasoning in this decision: the idea that national legislation is 'invalid' by international law is difficult to support in such a case. But he argues that a nationally valid law may be *illegal* under international law and suggests that in that situation there are English precedents for the proposition that an English court will not give effect to a foreign act of state when that act is in breach of the state's obligations under international law.

Combining this stance with the British attitude in favour of the restrictive theory of sovereign immunity (*see* **17**), one might have expected that the British courts would have been more inclined than the American courts were to hear cases involving the acts of foreign states, especially where the litigants on both sides were private parties and it was material to the case to determine whether a foreign decree or statute was to be treated as law in an English court.

Many observers were surprised therefore when the House of Lords seemed dramatically to expand the act of state doctrine in *Buttes Gas & Oil Co.* v. *Hammer* (1981). This complicated case involved the competing claims of the Buttes Company and Hammer's Occidental Petroleum to an oil concession in sea areas near the Gulf island of Abu Musa, sovereignty over which was in dispute between several countries in the region. To resolve the issues raised the court would have had to consider the territorial claims of the rival states, the motivations of the actions of the various governments, and the relationships between those governments and the litigants. It declined to do so.

On the underlying territorial question, Lord Wilberforce for the House of Lords decided that British courts could not adjudicate 'the validity, meaning and effect of transactions of sovereign states'.

He then rejected Hammer's contention that the courts could consider foreign acts which were contrary to public policy or international law. Lord Wilberforce indicated that, while a court may refuse to enforce internationally illegal foreign municipal law, that court may not 'examine the validity, under international law ... of ... acts in the area of transactions between states'.

But as to the general principle that courts will not adjudicate upon the transactions of foreign states, Lord Wilberforce considered it 'desirable' to regard the principle 'if existing' as one of 'judicial restraint' rather than 'act of state'. He went on: this principle 'is not one of discretion but is inherent in the very nature of the judicial process'. This rationale is different from that of the US Supreme Court in *Sabbatino*: it is not a question of embarrassing the conduct of foreign relations but rather a matter simply of what a court can actually do. A court, he said, had 'no judicial or manageable standards' by which to judge issues of territory, boundaries, sovereignty and the actions of foreign governments.

This reasoning seems basically flawed. If the act of state doctrine is based on notions of sovereign equality, it ought to apply only to acts done in that area reserved by international law exclusively to each state's sovereign authority. Transactions *between* states would appear almost by definition to be outside that area as a matter of international law.

If, however, the House of Lords was not concerned with the act of state doctrine but with what a court can do with the standards available to it, then customary international law could have been referred to as part of the law of England and applied as appropriate. There seems no obvious legal reason why a court should refrain when a case between private litigants who had accepted the court's jurisdiction requires the resolution of the international legal questions.

Diplomatic immunity

21. Background. Diplomatic agents have for centuries been considered exempt from the municipal law jurisdiction of any country where their diplomatic status has been recognised. The theoretical basis on which that immunity rests has, however, never been universally agreed. Three theories have been suggested:

(a) *the extraterritoriality theory*, which regarded diplomatic premises as a kind of extension of the sovereign territory of the sending state;

(*b*) *the representative character theory*, whereby diplomats were considered to personify the immune foreign sovereign whom they represented; and

(*c*) *the functional necessity theory*, according to which diplomatic privileges and immunities are justified as necessary to enable the diplomatic mission to perform its functions.

None of these theories completely escapes criticism: extraterritoriality does not explain why diplomats are immune even outside their own premises; representative character may be questioned when absolute sovereign immunity is under attack; and the functional necessity theory entails problems of application if its logical corollary is assumed to be that the activities of a diplomat beyond his official functions should not be immune.

The problem of diplomatic immunity has considerably increased since 1945, with the growth of the international community having produced very large diplomatic corps in most states. In the United States, for example, diplomatic status was accorded very liberally before 1978 and applied at one time to over 30,000 people.

22. Vienna Convention on Diplomatic Relations (1961). To help regularise the situation the International Law Commission drew up the Vienna Convention on Diplomatic Relations. In its preamble this treaty implicitly adopted the functional necessity theory. It provided for:

(*a*) – immunity of the diplomatic premises (Article 22);

(*b*) – inviolability of the diplomatic mission's archives and documents (Article 24);

(*c*) – inviolability of the mission's correspondence and diplomatic bag (which may contain diplomatic documents or articles intended for official use) (Article 27);

(*d*) – the inviolability of the diplomat's person and his freedom from arrest or detention (Article 29);

(*e*) – immunity of the diplomatic agent from all criminal jurisdiction and from civil and administrative jurisdiction except in cases relating to private real property, succession, or professional or commercial activity by the diplomat outside his official functions (Article 31).

The Convention makes clear, however, that not all members of a diplomatic mission are entitled to full immunity. Under Article 37 a hierarchy of immunity is set out, starting with full immunity for the family of the diplomatic agent, slightly less for administrative and technical staff, less again for the service staff of the mission, and immunity for private servants only if that is allowed by the receiving state.

Article 41(1) provides that all persons enjoying diplomatic immunity have a duty to respect the laws of the receiving state, and Article 41(3) indicates that diplomatic premises must not be used in a way incompatible with their diplomatic functions.

In Britain, Articles 1, 22–24, and 27–40 are enacted into municipal law by the Diplomatic Privileges Act 1964.

Despite the Convention's comprehensive treatment of the subject, a number of difficulties continue to trouble international law.

23. Inviolability of the premises. At Vienna a proposal requiring the head of the diplomatic mission to 'co-operate with the local authorities in case of fire, epidemic or other extreme emergency' was defeated. The position under the Convention is thus that under no circumstances may the authorities of the receiving state force their way into an embassy or other diplomatic building.

But in 1896, in the *Sun Yat Sen Incident,* a Chinese national was held prisoner in the Chinese Embassy in London. The British government condemned this as an abuse of diplomatic privilege and said that such detention 'would justify the use of whatever measures might be necessary for the liberation of the captive', although no forcible action against the Embassy was taken. In 1973, however, Pakistani police did raid the Iraqi embassy in Pakistan where they suspected, and indeed found, a large cache of arms.

State practice thus seemed to be that although the inviolability of diplomatic premises was in theory absolute, states did in fact reserve a right in the most extreme cases to enter those premises – at least where embassy personnel or others in the building are violating their duties under Article 41 of the 1961 Convention.

In the *Iran Hostages Case* (1980), however, these questions were implicitly at issue and the International Court of Justice delivered a categorical answer. The case arose out of events at the American Embassy in Tehran and other American diplomatic and consular premises in Iran in 1979-1980. Iranian students and demonstrators with the initial acquiescence and later support of the Iranian Revolutionary Government seized the Embassy and held American diplomatic and consular staff prisoner in protest at American gestures of friendship to the deposed former Shah of Iran. The students then discovered documents which the Iranian government later published to support its allegation that the embassy had for many years been a 'centre of espionage and conspiracy' by 'people who hatched plots against our Islamic movement' and who therefore 'do not enjoy international diplomatic respect'.

The United States brought suit against Iran in the ICJ in the case officially titled the *US Diplomatic and Consular Staff in Tehran Case.* Iran rejected the court's jurisdiction but the ICJ agreed to hear the case on the merits despite that.

This jurisdictional problem meant that the question of the effect of improper activities by the diplomatic mission on immunity and inviolability was not fully aired. Nevertheless a large majority of the court held that the initial failure of the Iranian government to take action against the embassy seizure was itself a violation of the 1961 Convention and that this was later compounded by the government's endorsement of the students' action, which had the effect of turning the detention of the hostages and the occupation of the premises into acts of the Iranian state.

The court went on:

> even if the alleged criminal activities of the United States in Iran could be considered as having been established, ... [the] court ... is unable to accept that they can [be regarded as a justification of Iran's conduct] ... This is because diplomatic law itself provides the necessary means of defence against ... illicit activities by members of diplomatic or consular missions [through expulsion of such persons or the breaking off of diplomatic relations with their state].

The problems caused by this categorical conclusion were highlighted in acute form in April 1984 when persons inside the Libyan Peoples Bureau (Embassy) in London shot at a demonstration in the street outside, killing a woman police constable. Some legal experts suggested that the British police might have been entitled under international law to enter the Bureau at once to prevent further crimes being committed. But in the event the British government instead laid siege to the building in order to contain the situation and then demanded the removal of all the Bureau's personnel. Diplomatic relations with Libya were broken off. In light of the ICJ's opinion in the *Iran Hostages Case* it would appear that the British government did all that was permitted to it within the tight restrictions of international law.

24. Diplomatic asylum. The relationship of the proper functions of a diplomatic mission and the right of the receiving state to enter diplomatic premises arises also with regard to diplomatic asylum. This is the granting of refuge in diplomatic premises to someone who is fleeing from danger in the country in which the premises are situated. General international law does not appear to recognise the giving of asylum as one of the proper duties or functions of a diplomatic mission, and the granting of such asylum may indeed appear an unfriendly act. The way therefore appears open to the host state to claim a right in extreme cases to enter the premises and seize the wanted person.

On the other hand, states have from time to time given asylum in their embassies at least to persons who are in imminent danger of what the British Foreign Secretary, Sir Edward Grey, described in 1913 as 'summary treatment' at the hands of their pursuers. In Latin America diplomatic asylum is particularly common, and even the United States allowed the Hungarian religious leader Cardinal Mindszenty, to shelter in its embassy in Budapest from 1956 to 1970 after the crushing of the Hungarian uprising.

In October 1984 six Black and Indian campaigners against apartheid in South Africa took refuge in the British consulate in Durban. Although the immunities of a consular mission are less sweeping than those of diplomatic premises, the British government refused to evict the fugitives, who were eventually persuaded to leave the building of their own accord. Five were then arrested and charged with treason by the South African authorities.

Although Grey in 1913 suggested Britain would grant temporary diplomatic asylum only until guarantees had been given that the fugitive would receive 'proper treatment and a fair deal', the determination of what is appropriate in a particular situation seems to be a matter of case-by-case decision. There is probably no specific rule of international law permitting the granting of diplomatic asylum but simply a practice, which states are content not to be too precise about, based on the general immunity of diplomatic premises.

25. Protection of diplomats. In addition to their special immunities from jurisdiction, diplomatic personnel enjoy special protections in the countries where they work. The 1973 Convention on the Prevention and Punishment of Crimes against Internationally Protected Persons including Diplomatic Agents makes the obligations of states in regard to such crimes a matter of international law, provides for jurisdiction and extradition, and makes disputes about the operation of the Convention referable to the International Court of Justice.

Other international immunities

26. General note. The growth of international organisations, and particularly the United Nations, has necessitated a great expansion of immunities.

Article 105 of the UN Charter obliges the organisation's members to respect 'such privileges and immunities as are necessary for the fulfilment of [the United

Nations'] purposes' and to grant immunity to UN officials and the representatives of members. Under the Convention on the Privileges and Immunities of the United Nations (1946), representatives of members are entitled to immunity in connection with attendance at UN meetings, and the United Nations itself and its assets and property are immune from jurisdiction and its premises inviolable. United Nations officials have functional immunity from legal proceedings in respect of statements made or acts performed by them in their official capacity.

The application of these immunities with regard to the United Nations in New York is governed by the 1947 'Headquarters Agreement' between the UN and the United States.

Interestingly, under Article 103 of the UN Charter, in the event of a discrepancy between one of these subsidiary agreements and the provisions of the Charter itself, the Charter would prevail.

Progress test 9

1. What in general terms are the jurisdictional implications of the maxim *par in parem non habet imperium*? (**1**)

2. What view of immunity is Chief Justice Marshall considered to have adopted in the *The Schooner Exchange Case*? (**2**)

3. Describe the Soviet view on state immunity. (**4**)

4. What is the purpose of the restrictive theory of sovereign immunity? (**6**)

5. Distinguish between acts *jure imperii* and acts *jure gestionis*. (**7**)

6. Which is preferable: the 'purpose of the act' test or the 'nature of the act' test? (**8, 9**)

7. Analyse the decision in *Trendtex Trading Corporation* v. *Central Bank of Nigeria*. (**11**)

8. Outline the main provisions of the United States Foreign Sovereign Immunities Act 1976. (**14**)

9. Outline the main provisions of the UK State Immunity Act 1978. (**17**)

10. What is the 'act of state' doctrine in international law? (**18**)

11. Should there be an international law exception to the act of state doctrine? (**19**)

12. Explain the *ratio decidendi* of Lord Wilberforce's speech in *Buttes Gas & Oil Co* v. *Hammer* (**20**)

13. What are the three traditional theories supporting diplomatic immunity? (**21**)

14. Outline the provisions of the Vienna Convention on Diplomatic Relations. (**22**)

15. Are diplomatic premises absolutely inviolable? (**23**)

16. Is the practice of diplomatic asylum founded on a rule of international law? (**24**)

17. What is the legal basis for the privileges and immunities of the United Nations? (**26**)

10   State responsibility

General principles of state responsibility

1. Basis of state responsibility. A state is responsible under international law when an act or omission imputable to it produces a breach of an international obligation arising from a treaty or from any other source of international law.

Thus the substantive grounds for international obligations (and hence for state responsibility) are as broad as international law itself. It is usual, however, to consider such topics as the Law of the Sea, Human Rights, and the Use of Force separately in this regard, and to concentrate under the heading of State Responsibility on the treatment of aliens.

There are, however, some general features of the law on state responsibility which must be examined first.

Is damage to another state necessary for breach of an international obligation to create state responsibility?

2. Damage may no longer be necessary. In classical international law some writers considered that damage or loss to another state was necessary to create state liability for an act or omission. This was said to be in effect a question of standing: no one could maintain an action against the offending state unless he had a direct legal interest arising from the fact that he had been injured by that state's activities.

In 1973, however, the UN International Law Commission determined that actual injury to another state was not necessary to invoke state responsibility in every case. This was particularly evident in relation to the violation of international human rights law, which would clearly be an internationally wrongful act even if not damaging to another state. Thus, the European Convention on Human Rights, in Article 24 allows any state party to raise a complaint against another party, without the complainant state being a victim of the accused state's human rights violations.

Some writers argue that even if one insists on the necessity of damage to another state, the damage (at least in the situation of human rights violations) is the disruption of the international legal order itself, a matter affecting all states and individuals world-wide.

The ILC's draft for a convention on state responsibility in Article 3 omits any requirement of damage from its definition of an internationally wrongful act.

The problem of fault

3. **Development of conflicting views.** Whether fault should always be necessary to create legal liability has in this century been a key issue in national and international law. Should a state be held liable for the harmful consequences of its acts even without the intention to cause such results and in the absence of fault or negligence on its part? The writers disagree. Sir Hersch Lauterpacht believed that fault is required. Professors Brownlie, Starke and Greig hold that fault is not always necessary for international state liability. Some cases have applied liability without fault by following the objective responsibility doctrine.

The *objective responsibility doctrine* holds that, once it is established that a certain state act or omission in violation of the state's obligations under international law has caused the damage complained of, the state is liable simply by virtue of having committed the act or omission. This may be an important point in cases where the act in question was done by an underling unbeknownst to state decision-makers.

The arbitrator in the *Caire Claim* (1929) between France and Mexico supported the objective responsibility doctrine on the ground that international relations would become too complicated and too insecure if a state could avoid liability by arguing that it did not authorise or intend an underling's offending act or that act's consequences. The arbitrator saw the doctrine as a kind of guarantee by the state that it would be responsible for all acts of persons to whom it has given official power, whether or not such persons were in fact doing what the state intended them to do.

But, as the *Caire Claim* decision shows, the difficulty with the consideration of the fault question in many of the cases is that it gets mixed up with the problem of imputability, that is, whether the acts of an underling can actually be attributed to the state so as to make it internationally liable. This tends to cloud the issue of fault, as can be seen in the following case, which is usually interpreted to require fault to be proved.

In the *Home Missionary Society Claim* (1920) the arbitrator held that Britain was not liable to the United States for damage done to American religious missions in Sierra Leone by rebellious 'natives', since it was 'a well-established principle of international law that no government can be held responsible for the act of [rebels] ... committed in violation of its authority' where the government was not guilty of bad faith or negligence.

The International Court of Justice in the *Corfu Channel Case* (1949) between Britain and Albania stated that the mere fact of Albania's control over its own territory did not mean that Albania 'necessarily knew, or ought to have known, of any unlawful act perpetrated therein, nor yet that it necessarily knew, or should have known, the authors'. This control therefore did not involve '*prima facie* responsibility'. The court found on an examination of the facts, however, that the acts complained of (laying mines in the Corfu Channel) 'could not have been accomplished without the knowledge of the Albanian Government'. This being so, Albania's failure to warn British naval vessels of the danger of mines constituted a grave omission giving rise to international responsibility.

Sir Hersch Lauterpacht interpreted this to mean that there is no liability without fault but that circumstantial evidence may be considered to infer fault. It is interesting, however, that the Russian judge on the court understood the decision to be an application of the objective responsibility doctrine and dissented from it on that ground. He argued that responsibility could arise only on the basis of *culpa*, which appears a more exacting standard than mere fault since it requires, according to Judge Krylov, a 'wilful and malicious' act or a 'culpably negligent' omission, in other words 'guilt' rather than mere inadvertence or carelessness.

It does not appear, however, that international law favours such a standard of gross fault, and the reason is not hard to see. A requirement of wilful malice or culpable negligence would impose a heavy burden of proof on the plaintiff, who might not know all the circumstances attendant on the injury to him by the foreign state defendant nor the identity of those responsible, let alone be in a position to prove their intentions.

The choice therefore seems to be between:

(*a*) objective responsibility, which rejects fault as a basis for liability; and

(*b*) what might be called simple fault, which allows liability to arise from an act or omission whose potential for harm might reasonably have been foreseen and avoided. If the reason for failing to avoid the resulting harm is malice or gross negligence, that simply compounds the fault and makes it more evident.

4. The doctrine of created risk. An application of the objective responsibility theory which may become increasingly important is the doctrine of *created risk*. This is a principle of strict liability whereby a state is responsible for the harmful effects of ultra-hazardous but lawful activities it undertakes, even if no fault is imputable to the state.

Such strict liability is imposed in the *Convention on International Liability for Damage caused by Space Objects* (1972), Article II of which makes a launching state 'absolutely liable to pay compensation for damage caused by its space object on the surface of the earth or to aircraft in flight'.

Imputability

5. State liability for imputable acts. Because a state can act only through individuals, and individuals may act for reasons of their own distinct from the intentions of their state, it becomes necessary to know which actions of which persons may be attributed, or imputed, to the state. A state may only be held liable for acts imputable to it.

According to the International Law Commission in its 1973 report on state responsibility, as a general rule the state has imputed to it 'the acts of members of its "organisation", in other words, the acts of its "organs" or "agents" '. 'Organ' in this context must be understood to refer to an individual official as well as to governmental departments and agencies.

This general rule has been elaborated, and exceptional cases provided for, in the ILC's *Draft Articles on State Responsibility* (1979).

6. General provisions of the Draft Articles. Article 5 makes imputable to the state the conduct of any state organ acting in its official capacity. Article 7 does the same for acts of a territorial entity within the state and for acts of 'an entity which is not part of the formal structure' of national or territorial government but which is legally empowered to exercise elements of governmental authority.

Article 6 makes clear that these general provisions apply to all officials and organs, no matter how minor. Thus, when in July 1985 French secret agents sank the *Rainbow Warrior*, a ship belonging to the Greenpeace environmental movement, killing one of the crew, France became internationally liable regardless of whether this act of state terrorism was ordered at a high level in the government or a lower one.

One of the effects of these provisions is that separation of powers among executive, legislative and judicial branches of a state's government does not diminish the state's international responsibility, even though one or more of those branches may have no direct dealings on the level of international law. Similarly, doctrines of parliamentary supremacy do not lessen state responsibility for acts done in accordance with statute. In the *Polish Upper Silesia Case* (1926), the Permanent Court of International Justice noted that 'municipal laws are merely facts which express the will of and constitute the activities of states in the same manner as do legal decisions or administrative measures'. Therefore an international court need not treat municipal laws as legally binding on it by way of an excuse when a state organ under colour of national legislation has committed an internationally wrongful act: the state legislation may indeed itself be evidence of the state's illegal position.

Also imputable to the state (under Article 8) is the conduct of a person or group which was acting on behalf of the state or in fact exercising elements of governmental authority in the absence of the official authorities and in circumstances which justified that activity.

7. Ultra vires acts. One of the major problems of imputability has always been whether a state should be held liable for the acts of a state organ which are *ultra vires*, i.e. go beyond its authorised powers.

Article 10 of the ILC Draft imputes *ultra vires* conduct to the state when the state organ has been acting in its official governmental capacity. Part of the rationale for this position is that a state ought to be responsible for what people to whom it gives the means to act do with that power. The ILC's commentary on this article says: 'The state cannot take refuge behind the notion that, according to the provisions of its legal system, those actions or omissions ought not to have occurred or ought to have taken a different form'.

A tricky aspect of the *ultra vires* acts problem is whether *any* such act is imputable to the state, even if manifestly not within the organ's authorised powers, or whether only acts apparently within those powers are imputable. In its commentary, the ILC explains the difficulty thus: theoretically, if the act was manifestly *ultra vires*, then 'the injured party ... should have been aware of it ... and able to prevent the illicit act from taking place'; on the other hand, actual experience in the majority of cases demonstrates that knowledge that the act was *ultra vires* does not 'enable the victim ... to escape its harmful consequences'.

In these circumstances, relieving the state of responsibility for manifestly *ultra vires* acts would risk providing it with 'an easy loophole' in particularly serious cases where in fact the injured person was powerless to protect himself. Article 10 therefore covers all *ultra vires* acts by state organs acting in their official capacity.

The Draft's general position on *ultra vires* acts accords with most of the cases.

In the *Union Bridge Company Claim* (1924) the arbitral tribunal imputed to Britain the actions of an official of the British-run Cape Province railway during the Boer War in South Africa who improperly diverted the plaintiff company's bridge building materials to the wrong location in the mistaken belief that this was required by his instructions from the British authorities.

The *Youmans Claim* (1926) between Mexico and the United States arose from the killing of several Americans in a Mexican town by a rioting mob. Before the killings, the mayor of the town had attempted to protect the Americans by ordering the local chief of public security and his troops to quell the riot, but on arriving at the scene they had joined the mob and participated in the killings. Mexico argued that it should not be held liable for acts of soldiers who had disobeyed the mayor's instructions. But according to the arbitral tribunal, to accept this argument would mean that no wrongful act by an official would ever entail his government's responsibility (assuming that wrongful acts are always contrary to instructions). Nor could Mexico escape liability by claiming that the killings were done in the soldiers' private capacity. The troops were at the time 'on duty and under the immediate supervision ... of a commanding officer'.

The arbitral award in the *Zafiro Claim* (1925) has been criticised for carrying state liability for *ultra vires* acts even further. The facts were that the *Zafiro* was a private merchant ship which was being used by the United States Navy in the Spanish-American War, the civilian captain and crew having been placed under the command of a US Navy officer. When the ship docked at a Philippine port recently abandoned by the Spanish authorities, the non-American crew were allowed shore leave and soon joined roving bands which were looting the property of British civilians living in the town. The arbitral tribunal held that in the light of the unsettled conditions in the port there had been a failure to exercise 'diligence on the part of those in charge ... to see to it that [the crew] were under control when they went ashore'. Strictly speaking, therefore, US liability was based on the failure of the American naval officer to exercise proper control over the crew and not on the crew's acts *per se*.

8. **Acts of insurrectionaries.** Article 11 of the ILC Draft Articles says that the conduct of persons not acting in behalf of the state shall not be considered an act of the state. Logically, therefore, Article 14 indicates that the conduct of insurrectionaries, who could hardly be considered to be acting on behalf of the state they are trying to overthrow, is not an act of the state. If injury is done to an alien by insurrectionaries, the state may not be responsible.

This result is sometimes justified by the doctrine of acceptance or assumption of the risk (*volenti non fit injuria* ('no injury is done to a willing person'). In the *Gelbtrunk Claim* (1902) the arbitrator held that a person living in another country for business purposes may be considered to have 'cast in his lot with the subjects ... of the state in which he resides and carries on business' and to become 'liable to the political vicissitudes of the country'.

However, a different attitude is taken if the insurrection is ultimately successful and the revolutionaries take over the government of the state. In the *Bolivar Railway Company Claim* (1903), the arbitral tribunal held Venezuela liable for the acts of successful revolutionaries committed *before* they had taken power. This conclusion was justified on the grounds that:

> Nations do not die when there is a change of their rulers or in their forms of government ... The nation is responsible for the obligations of a successful revolution from its beginning, because in theory, it represented ab initio a changing national will, crystallizing in the finally successful result ... success

demonstrates that from the beginning it was registering the national will.

Accordingly, the ILC draft in Article 15(1) makes the act of an insurrectional movement which becomes a state's new government the act of that state itself.

Abuse of rights

9. Exceeding permissible limits. When a state act is not wrongful under international law and is done as a matter of right but produces harmful consequences, the situation is sometimes described as an *abuse of rights,* for which a state is liable under international law. The key concept here is the arbitrary and extreme implementation of a right to the degree that damage is caused to another state. Underlying this is the duty of states to act in good faith in all their dealings and conduct.

The standing of the idea of abuse of rights in international law is sometimes disputed on the ground that what is actually happening in these situations is that state conduct is pushed so far that it goes *beyond* the rights of the state, so that the state is doing something which it has no right to do, rather than abusing a right which it has. The critics point to the use of the 'abuse of rights' concept in cases of cross-border pollution and note that this might also be dealt with as a violation of the positive duty on states under customary international law to use their own territory so as not to harm another, as expressed in the maxim *sic utere tuo ut alienum non laedas.*

The proponents of the abuse of rights concept respond, however, that it imports more than simply the avoidance of wrongful acts and extends to a wider notion of 'neighbourliness' whereby states are obliged to adjust their behaviour so as to balance the international effects of what they do against the positive gains to be achieved. The debate continues.

International crimes

10. State crimes distinct from individual crimes. In one of its more controversial provisions the ILC draft on state responsibility incorporated the concept of an international crime.

> An *international crime* is defined in Article 19(2) as: an internationally wrongful act which results from the breach by a state of an international obligation so essential for the protection of fundamental interests of the international community that its breach is recognized as a crime by that community as a whole.

Article 19(3) lists specific international crimes:
(*a*) serious breaches of the law on peace and security (e.g. aggression);
(*b*) serious breaches of the right of self-determination;
(*c*) serious breaches of international duties on safeguarding the human being (e.g. slavery, genocide, apartheid); and
(*d*) serious breaches of obligations to protect the environment (e.g. massive pollution of the atmosphere or the sea).
In its commentary on this article, the ILC observed that

> The international community as a whole, and not merely one or other of its members, now considers that such acts violate principles formally embodied

in the Charter [of the United Nations] and, even outside the scope of the Charter, principles which are now so deeply rooted in the conscience of mankind that they have become particularly essential rules of general international law.

At least some of these acts are generally regarded as among the more serious international wrongs which 'should entail more severe legal consequences'. The commentary makes clear, however, that an international crime is not the same thing as a 'crime under international law', 'war crime', and so on. These expressions 'designate certain heinous individual crimes' for which guilty individuals should be punished. The term 'international crime' on the other hand indicates the criminal responsibility of the state itself apart from the criminal liability of individuals. It will be apparent from this that the question of what the 'more severe legal consequences' which a state should suffer actually are is a very difficult one, since it is not simply a matter of punishing individuals. Not surprisingly, the ILC left the matter of the punishment entailed in international criminal liability to later consideration.

This difficulty highlights one of the criticisms levelled at the concept of international crime by Western writers, namely that it misconceives the analogy between domestic and international criminal law: states as institutions lack, it is said, the direct connection that domestic criminal law relies on between criminal intent and criminal act, so that while domestic law can locate and punish criminal intent international law in this context cannot.

But it seems clear from the ILC's commentary that the use of the word 'crime' in Article 19 is really quite different from the ordinary sense of the term. It is not really used to define a category of acts for which punishment can be meted out but rather is intended to emphasise the interest of the international community as a whole in maintaining international law and order by classifying certain acts as particularly objectionable. In doing this, the concept of 'international crime' serves to take certain acts out of the context of one-on-one legal relationships (e.g. perpetrator and victim) and put them instead into the context of one-versus-all. Thus each and every member of the international community would have an interest and a right to invoke the criminal responsibility of a state and demand the cessation of the crime and the making of amends.

The International Court of Justice seemed to endorse this idea of state obligations towards the international community as a whole (i.e. *erga omnes*) in the *Barcelona Traction Case* (1970), paragraph 34, with regard to aggression, genocide, slavery and basic human rights.

It will be noted that in its emphasis on 'principles which are now so deeply rooted in the conscience of mankind that they have become particularly essential rules of general international law' the ILC commentary comes close to linking the concept of international crime with that of *jus cogens*, although the two are not identical.

Defences and justifications

11. **International Law Commission's proposals.** As Professor Starke has pointed out, the justification a state may offer for a wrongful act and the defences it may make in a case are not usually considered very carefully. But they are obviously vital in delineating the effective scope of state responsibility and the

International Law Commission felt compelled in 1979 and 1980 to adopt draft articles on the matter.

These allow the following *defences* against a claim:

(*a*) the defendant state was coerced into committing the wrongful act by another state;

(*b*) the defendant had acted with the consent of the harmed state;

(*c*) the defendant was merely taking permissible countermeasures (but actions involving the use of armed forced are excluded from this category of defence);

(*d*) the defendant state's officials acted under *force majeure* or extreme distress and were not wilfully seeking the harm caused.

The *justifications* allowed are of two kinds: (*a*) necessity and (*b*) self-defence.

(*a*) *Necessity* will not serve as a justification for a state's violation of an international obligation unless:

(*i*) the act was the only means of safeguarding an essential state interest against a grave and imminent peril; *and*

(*ii*) the act did not seriously impair an essential interest of the state towards which the obligation existed.

In any case, however, necessity will not justify a violation of a peremptory (*jus cogens*) norm of general international law, nor justify violating a treaty which itself excludes the justification of necessity, nor justify a violation when the violating state has contributed to the occurrence of the state of necessity.

(*b*) *Self-defence* justifies an otherwise wrongful act if the act 'constitutes a lawful measure of self-defence taken in conformity with the Charter of the United Nations'. This does not mean that all acts done in the course of self-defence are lawful, but rather indicates that acts of self-defence which conform to the Charter are legitimate even though the same acts, if not in self-defence, would be wrong.

Reparations

12. Duty to make amends. Once a breach of an international obligations has been committed the 'guilty' state must make amends by restitution, compensation, or satisfaction.

13. Restitution. In the *Chorzow Factory Case* (1928), the Permanent Court of International Justice enunciated the fundamental principle that 'reparation must, as far as possible, wipe out all the consequences of the illegal act and re-establish the situation which would, in all probability, have existed if that act had not been committed'.

This appears to mean that the prime consideration must be restoration of the status quo that existed before the wrongful act was committed. This is known as *restitutio in integrum* (restitution-in-kind, restoration of the original position).

But it is sometimes argued (particularly in cases involving nationalisation of private companies) that the offending state in certain circumstances should from the outset be allowed to choose between restitution and monetary compensation in view of the fact that the state may have policy considerations which make restitution unacceptable.

In the *Texaco* v. *Libya Arbitration* (1977), Libya had indicated that, in line with its general economic policy, it would not restore the position of Texaco under a concession agreement after nationalisation of the company's property and interests but would pay compensation. Texaco sought from the tribunal a ruling that Libya had to offer restitution first. The arbitrator agreed: *restitutio in integrum* had to be made unless this proved an 'absolute impossibility' or unless 'an irreversible situation' which was 'beyond the will of the parties' had been created.

In *BP* v. *Libya* (1974), however, the arbitrator had adopted a different view on similar facts. He wrote:

> when by the exercise of sovereign power a state has committed a fundamental breach of a concession agreement by repudiating it through a nationalisation of the enterprise ... in a manner which implies finality, the concessionaire is not entitled to call for specific performance [of the original contract, which would imply *restitutio in integrum*] ... but his sole remedy is an action for damages.

Some points considered by this arbitrator were that state practice and the decisions of tribunals rarely insisted in fact on restitution, with even the *Chorzow Factory Case* considering the question merely as a preliminary to assessing monetary compensation, and that where restitution was awarded it was usually in the context of only a partial seizure of private property, not a complete extinction of the plaintiff's concession as had occurred to BP here.

The underlying rationale here seems to be that restitution is the preferred remedy only where it is physically or politically possible. Thus, in the *Iran Hostages Case* (1980), the International Court of Justice voted unanimously for restitution by Iran of US diplomatic and consular premises and property, presumably because these still were in existence and could be returned, and voted by twelve votes to three for mandatory reparations for additional injury.

This common sense approach is criticised, however, as being more a matter of expediency than of law, since it may make the legal rules merely a function of the parties' conduct. It is also said to give a state the incentive to make sure that restitution is not possible, so that a state could in effect buy its way out of its legal obligations. Nevertheless compensation instead of restitution seems to be a widespread practice.

14. Compensation. Once it is determined that compensation is to be paid, the measure of it becomes an issue. If, as the PCIJ held in the *Chorzow Factory Case*, the aim is to 'wipe out all the consequences of the illegal act', compensation must cover all the damage which has resulted from that act or is certain to result from it, but not remote or 'speculative' damage. Loss of profits, goodwill, lost earnings may all be compensable damages by this test, if they can be proven.

15. Satisfaction. In some cases the harm suffered by the injured individual or state is of a kind that cannot be appropriately repaired by monetary compensation, as for example injury to a state's, or an individual's, dignity. Reparation in such cases may best be made by satisfaction, which may involve apologising, formally acknowledging guilt, or accepting the award of a declaratory judgment by an international tribunal reaffirming the victim's rights. For example: as part of its response to the sinking of the Greenpeace environmentalists' ship *Rainbow Warrior* by French secret agents in 1985, the French government publicly, though very belatedly, apologised to the victims.

Gaps in the system

16. Is there a duty to regulate? As noted above, states are responsible only for acts or omissions imputable to them, not for all acts occurring in their territory.

But this does not preclude the possibility of a state's bearing responsibility at second-hand as it were in situations where the state has a specific international obligation to oversee certain activities on its soil. For example, a state is expected to make a reasonable effort to prevent its territory being used for hostile military activities by private persons against another country, and the state may be internationally liable for failing to take the appropriate measures when it could have done so.

Although in general a state may be liable under the 'abuse of rights' theory for failing to prevent private acts, like transfrontier pollution from a factory, which are known to be harmful but which follow from a legitimate activity, the outer limits of international law in this area are unclear.

Does a state, for example, have any duty to oversee acts in its territory which are both legal and harmless there but which, given the right conjunction of circumstances, may cause harm in another country? The Bhopal incident in 1984 raised this issue: after a toxic gas leak from the American-owned chemical plant in India, it was alleged that the accident was made possible (but was not necessarily directly caused) by certain managerial acts or omissions at the parent company's headquarters in the United States. Was the United States liable under international law for having failed so to regulate the parent company that such acts or omissions would not have happened? It does not appear that international law would impose such responsibility at present. This gap in international law has the effect of leaving the activities of multinational companies in this area beyond the reach of an international legal regime.

Aliens: introduction

17. Maltreatment violating an international obligation. The area of state responsibility that has generated the largest number of cases and claims relates to the treatment of aliens in a state's territory. Such treatment may become the subject of an international claim when the host state is alleged to have violated by that treatment some international obligation. Thus not every aspect of a state's treatment of aliens is covered by this topic but only those aspects where international legal rules require or forbid state conduct. Where a breach of these rules occurs, an international claim may arise.

Aliens: Whose claim is it?

18. State primacy. As was made clear in the decision of the Permanent Court of International Justice in the *Mavrommattis Palestine Concessions Case (Jurisdiction)* (1924), a claim on the international level is considered to be that of the state whose citizen has been mistreated by the defendant state. The Court said: 'a state is in reality asserting its own rights – its right to ensure, in the person of its subjects, respect for the rules of international law'. This assertion by a state of its own right to take up its citizen's case is called *diplomatic protection*.

The court pointed out an important consequence of the state's role in diplomatic protection: 'once a state has taken up a case on behalf of one of its subjects ... the state is the sole claimant'. This can be a mixed blessing for the aggrieved citizen. Although he may benefit from having the power of his state brought to bear, he loses the ability to control his own case. If the claim is solely that of the state, the state may settle or abandon it as seems best to it for political or any other reasons, regardless of whether the citizen wishes to pursue the case.

The state may not even be under any obligation to pay the original claimant reparations money it receives in settlement from the guilty state. In *Rustomjee* v. *The Queen* (1876) an English judge remarked with what now looks like remarkable condescension that the distribution of monies received by the claimant state in this way 'would be, not the act of an agent accounting to a principal, but the act of the sovereign in dispensing justice to her subjects. For any omission of that duty the sovereign cannot be held responsible.' Yet this is, astonishingly, still regarded as good law.

Despite this, however, when international tribunals assess compensation in these cases, they generally do so on the basis of the damage done to the individual and not that suffered (perhaps only notionally) by the state.

Aliens: What basic legal principles govern claims?

19. International minimum standard versus national treatment standard. Particular types of cases inevitably have their own bodies of law focussing on the problems associated with them, and these will be discussed below. But a preliminary and fundamental question of principle must first be resolved: should these cases be determined according to international law rules or rules of national law?

Although this question is itself one of international law, since it asks in effect which rules that law should favour, the result, depending on the answer given, may be to exclude the case from the international law realm altogether.

Many older arbitral decisions generally follow the position adopted by the arbitrator in the *Neer Claim* (1926) that 'the propriety of governmental acts should be put to the test of international standards'. Since it implies that international law sets at least the basic requirements for proper governmental acts towards aliens, this view is said to encapsulate an *international minimum standard*. Its theoretical justification is that an alien should not be treated barbarously or outrageously merely because he happens to be in a country where barbarism or outrage are the rule.

Western developed countries have been particularly vigorous in upholding this standard, but other states have objected that, since those countries by and large also exercised their power to determine what the content of the minimum standard was, the effect was essentially that the West dictated to its own advantage how it was to be treated by everybody else. The international minimum standard was seen as a device for promoting Western political and economic control of Third World and less developed countries.

The alternative, advocated initially by Latin American states, was the *national treatment standard*, by which a state was only bound to treat aliens in the same way as it treated its own citizens. This dealt effectively with the problem of the more powerful Western states attempting to use international law for their own purposes, but it exposed aliens to fundamentally objectionable treatment in states which also mistreated their own citizens.

In 1957 a proposal was put to the International Law Commission that might have resolved the problem and advanced the rule of law internationally. The proposed draft would have required every state:

to ensure to aliens the enjoyment of the same civil rights ... and the same individual guarantees as are enjoyed by its nationals. These rights and guarantees shall not, however, in any case be less than the 'fundamental human rights' recognized and defined in contemporary international instruments.

Unfortunately, this attempt to join the international minimum standard and the national treatment standard under the umbrella of international human rights law was not adopted. Consequently the debate continues, especially in connection with economic questions like the regulation of multinational companies and expropriation and nationalisation, as discussed below.

Aliens: Procedural questions

20. Obstacles in pursuing a claim. As noted above, on the international level a claim involving a foreign country's responsibility regarding its treatment of an alien is said to be that of the alien's state. International law nevertheless attaches important consequences to the alien's own position or actions in the case, to the extent that certain procedural issues may pose a bar to the claimant state's proceeding further with the case.

Waiver by the alien

21. The Calvo clause. In the first instance, most claims are raised by the alien directly with the foreign state. If at that stage the alien chooses of his own free will and not under duress to settle his claim or waive his rights, that decision is dispositive and the case ends.

A more complicated situation arises when the alien has agreed to limit his possible remedies in advance of any injury. Latin American countries adopted in their foreign policy and often in their municipal law what came to be called the *Calvo doctrine*. Named after Carlos Calvo (1824–1906), an Argentinian diplomat and international lawyer, this stated that the use of diplomatic pressure or military intervention against one state by another in support of a claim by a citizen of the intervening state was illegal. To give effect to this doctrine in individual cases, the Latin American states insisted as a matter of municipal law that contracts with foreigners include a *Calvo clause* whereby the alien agrees not to seek the diplomatic protection of his own country and to submit any dispute arising from the contract to local adjudication.

The difficulty is that if the alien who has signed such a clause later feels aggrieved at the treatment he has received, his state may wish to take up his case. Would the Calvo clause in the contract bar diplomatic protection?

In the *North American Dredging Company Case* (1926), involving a claim by the United States against Mexico on behalf of an American citizen, the arbitrator concluded:

(*a*) that a Calvo clause merely committed the alien to using the available Mexican procedures to settle questions arising from the contract but did not prevent his resorting to his own government for diplomatic protection if a different legal question arose, namely, that of an internationally illegal injury done him through the delay or denial of justice by the Mexican legal machinery in dealing with his claims under the contract; and

(*b*) that since an international claim by a state in any case belongs as a matter of international law to it, an individual could not by his private contract under the offending country's municipal law deprive his own state of its international legal right to pursue the matter.

If, however, the individual, as in this case, did not respect Mexican law and act towards it in good faith, then the question of denial of justice as a matter of international law would not arise and an international claim would not be well-founded.

On this interpretation, a Calvo clause could legitimately limit the alien to local legal or administrative remedies where they are in principle adequate and in practice fairly applied (even if he does not in fact win his case), but could not foreclose diplomatic protection where international law would allow it. The difficulty remains, however, that what is adequate and fair may itself be arguable.

Notice that this merely qualified approval of the Calvo *clause* does not necessarily invalidate the Calvo *doctrine* insofar as that doctrine aims to limit resort to armed force in these cases. The validity of that limitation depends on the international law controlling the use of force. In modern international law under the United Nations Charter such a use of force would in fact be illegal.

Exhaustion of local remedies

22. Justice must be sought if it is available. Even where a Calvo clause is not at issue, it is clear that in general an international claim regarding harm to an individual alien may properly be brought only after a state has failed to deal with an alien's case justly, as required by international law.

Some writers explain this as follows: until the state has failed in this international duty, no international wrong (and hence no basis for an international claim) has occurred. Others suggest that as a matter of convenience and friendly relations a state should be allowed the opportunity to resolve the alien's problem (which may after all have been caused by an underling and not been intended by the state) through its own internal mechanisms before the alien raises the case to the international level by invoking his own country's diplomatic protection.

Whatever the explanation, international law has clearly adopted the rule of *exhaustion of local remedies* (sometimes also referred to as 'the local remedies rule'). In the *Interhandel Case* (1959), the International Court of Justice stated the rule as follows:

> Before resort may be had to an international court ... the state where the violation occurred should have an opportunity to redress it by its own means, within the framework of its own domestic legal system.

In the *Lawless Case* (1961) the European Court of Human Rights indicated, however, that the remedies alleged to have been available must have been an 'effective and sufficient means of redress'.

Therefore, where resort to the local machinery would be obviously futile, the alien would not be obliged to waste his time and money going through the motions of exhausting local remedies. According to the British Foreign Office Rules regarding International Claims (1971), Rule VII, 'A claimant ... is not required to exhaust justice ... where there is no justice to exhaust'. Nor is he obliged to lodge legal appeals when the appellate procedure or rules in the offending state would ensure no reversal of a lower court's decision.

The European Commission of Human Rights, in implementing the local remedies provision in Article 26 of the European Convention on Human Rights, has restricted the rule in a way that significantly benefits plaintiffs (even when they are not aliens but are nationals of the offending state). In *Donnelly* v. *United Kingdom* (1973) the Commission held that the plaintiff need not exhaust local remedies where he is the victim of an 'administrative practice' whose existence has made local remedies ineffective. The basis for this view was set out by the Commission in the *Greek Case* (1969):

> Where ... there is a practice of non-observance of certain Convention provisions, the remedies prescribed will of necessity be side-stepped or rendered inadequate. Thus, if there was an administrative practice of torture or ill-treatment, judicial remedies prescribed would tend to be rendered ineffective by the difficulty of securing probative evidence, and administrative enquiries would either be not instituted or, if they were, would be likely to be half-hearted and incomplete.

Nationality of claims

23. The bond of citizenship. As already noted (*see* 8:8), nationality is a fundamental connection between the individual and the state for purposes of jurisdiction. International law focusses on nationality in cases of diplomatic protection also. The aggrieved alien's having the nationality of a certain state is what justifies that state in extending its protection under traditional international law.

In the majority of cases nationality is clear and thus causes no problems, but difficulties arise when it appears that a state claiming a right to exercise protection of an alien has conferred its nationality on him or her without sufficient justification for doing so. The fear is that by improperly granting nationality a state may lay the basis for unwarranted interference in the affairs of another state.

In the *Nottebohm Case* (1955) the International Court of Justice determined that 'nationality is a legal bond having as its basis a social fact of attachment, a genuine connection of existence, interests, and sentiments, together with reciprocal rights and duties'. The conferring of nationality by a state entitles that state to exercise diplomatic or other protection only if the naturalisation 'constitutes a translation into juridical terms of the individual's connection with the state'. Consequently, on the level of international law, nationality which is not based on a 'genuine connection' may be insufficient to support such protection.

If by this reasoning a person were left (as Nottebohm was) without any nationality on which protection could be based, his position, at least in traditional international law, would be gravely weakened. According to the arbitrator in the *Dickson Car Wheel Company Case* (1931) a state 'does not commit an international delinquency in inflicting an injury upon an individual lacking nationality, and, consequently, no State is empowered to intervene or complain on his behalf either before or after the injury'.

This situation is particularly objectionable in relation to the protection of individuals against human rights violations, and it emphasises the importance of treating human rights as an issue which the entire international community is interested in and entitled to take action on collectively or singly.

As to the general problem of stateless aliens, the *Convention Relating to the Status of Stateless Persons* (1954) attempts to provide a basis in international law for preserving certain fundamental rights for stateless persons in the states in which they may find themselves. It fails, however, to create any mechanism for the international exercise of protection, except insofar as Article 34 (on compulsory referral to the International Court of Justice of unsettled disputes about interpretation or application of the Convention) might be construed to allow it. In any event, by 1985 only thirty-four states had become parties to this Convention.

24. Barcelona Traction Case. In the *Barcelona Traction, Light and Power Company Case* (1970) (the 'Barcelona Traction Case'), Belgium, acting on behalf of Belgian shareholders in the company (which was incorporated in Canada), brought suit before the International Court of Justice against Spain, which had through various measures brought about the effective collapse of the company's business in Barcelona.

The court held that Belgium was not entitled in the first instance to exercise protection in this way. Barcelona Traction itself, as a limited liability company, was a legal person in its own right, had a nationality of its own distinct from that of its shareholders, and could as a matter of law suffer injuries itself and be entitled to seek redress for them through the state of its nationality.

Barcelona Traction's nationality was Canadian, according to what the court called 'the traditional rule', since the company was incorporated in Canada and had its registered office there. The court did not explicitly look for a 'genuine connection' other than that because, it said, 'there can be no analogy' between the Barcelona Traction situation and the *Nottebohm Case*. Although this may be thought to imply that nationalities of convenience are permissible for companies but not for individuals, it must be said in favour of the court's view that a linkage based exclusively on incorporation may be justified by the fact that the act of incorporation actually creates the legal identity and existence of the company.

The court indicated that it might consider 'lifting the corporate veil' to examine the position of the shareholders only in two special situations:

(*a*) when the company had legally ceased to exist; or

(*b*) when the company's national state lacked the capacity to take action.

Neither situation was found here.

In its Rules regarding International Claims, the British Foreign Office indicated that it would 'normally' take up the case of shareholders only 'in concert with the state in which the company is incorporated', unless the company is 'defunct'. The Rules, more dubiously, also allow Britain to take up the case of British shareholders when the company is incorporated in the very state which is taking detrimental action against it, the theory being that in such a situation the state of incorporation is incapable of adequately protecting the company or its shareholders.

Procedural injustice

25. Denial of justice. It is generally accepted that a state is responsible for a 'denial of justice' to an alien, though the meaning of this phrase has been disputed. 'Denial of justice' should probably be confined to the failure by a state to apply proper standards in the arrest and detention of accused persons and the conduct of civil or criminal proceedings, and to the failure to provide procedural protection for an alien in the administration of justice. The term would therefore not relate directly to the question of the ultimate justness or unjustness of a court's judgment in a case, but would be limited to the procedures leading up to and influencing that judgment.

26. Human rights as a guide. A good guide to what the international community might reasonably demand of a state in this regard can be found in the *International Covenant on Civil and Political Rights* (1966), (the ICCPR) which is the key United Nations treaty on human rights. Over seventy-five countries representing a wide range of political and social systems have become parties.

Article 6 of the ICCPR forbids arbitrary deprivation of life, restricts imposition of the death sentence and requires it to be carried out only pursuant to a final judgment by a competent court.

Article 9 prohibits arbitrary arrest or detention and requires that a detained person be informed of the charges against him, be promptly brought before a judge, be allowed to initiate *habeas corpus*-like proceedings, and be tried within a reasonable time or released. Unlawful arrest or detention gives rise to a claim for compensation.

Article 10 requires that all persons in detention 'shall be treated with humanity and with respect for the inherent dignity of the human person', accused persons being segregated from convicted prisoners and being entitled to special treatment appropriate to their status as unconvicted persons.

Article 14 details the individual's rights before courts and tribunals. All persons must be treated as equal before them and be entitled to a fair and public hearing both in criminal and civil cases, although press and public may be excluded in some cases 'for reasons of morals, public order or national security in a democratic society' or if the interests of the parties or the interests of justice so require. A person charged with crimes is to be presumed innocent until proven guilty and is entitled to prompt information on the charge against him, adequate time and facilities to prepare his defence and communicate with counsel of his own choosing, trial without undue delay and in his own presence with his own legal defender, to examine the witnesses against him and summon those in his favour, and not to be forced to confess. Convicted persons are entitled to appeal, and no one should be tried twice for the same crime.

According to Article 13, aliens may be deported only in accordance with lawful procedures and after having been given the opportunity to argue against deportation before the competent authorities.

Finally, under Article 26 all persons are to be treated as equal before the law and to be given the equal protection of the law without discrimination based on race, colour, sex, language, religion, political or other opinion, national or social origin, property, birth or other status. It must be noted, however, that equality in this sense is usually not considered necessarily to exclude differentiating aliens from citizens where there may be a reasonable basis for that (e.g. in protecting national security).

27. Mexican – United States arbitration cases. A number of arbitral decisions in cases between the United States and Mexico support application of such standards.

In the *Roberts Claim* (1926) the tribunal held that overlong detention of Roberts without trial by Mexican authorities was wrongful. Furthermore, detaining him in an airless, crowded and unsanitary cell without facilities to wash or exercise, and providing unclean and coarse food, amounted to cruel and inhumane imprisonment. This was not excused by the fact that all the prisoners were treated the same, since 'equality is not the ultimate test ... in the light of international law'. Rather, the 'test is, broadly speaking, whether aliens are treated in accordance with ordinary standards of civilization', in other words, according to an international minimum standard (*see* **19**).

In the *Chattin Claim* (1927) the tribunal held Mexico liable for 'irregularity of court proceedings' arising from 'absence of proper investigations, insufficiency of confrontations, withholding from the accused the opportunity to know all of the charges brought against him, undue delay of the proceedings, making the hearings in open court a mere formality, and a continued absence of seriousness on the part of the court'. The tribunal emphasised, however, that holding a state liable for the acts of its judiciary was appropriate only when judicial action amounted to 'an outrage, bad faith, wilful neglect of duty, or insufficiency of action apparent to any unbiased man'. The tribunal's reluctance to go further than this appears to have been based on a desire not to undermine the state judiciary's general autonomy and independence of judgment, so that even erroneous court decisions, if made in good faith, would not generate state liability.

In the *Quintanilla Claim* (1926) the United States was held liable after a Mexican citizen, who had last been seen alive in the custody of a Texas deputy sheriff, was found lying murdered by the roadside. The tribunal said that the US government would be liable if it treated a prisoner cruelly, harshly or unlawfully: 'so much the more is it liable if it can say only that it took him into custody ... and that it ignored what happened to him'.

A broader conception of 'denial of justice' is reflected in another of the Mexican-US arbitration decisions, the *Janes Claim* (1926). Here the Mexican authorities had failed to apprehend and punish the murderer of Byron E. Janes, an American citizen, although the identity of the criminal was well known and there were many witnesses to the murder. The United States was claiming for resulting damage to Janes' wife and children. The tribunal considered that if Mexico had not failed in its duty, the Janes family 'would have been spared indignant neglect and would have had an opportunity of subjecting the murderer to a civil suit'. Mexico was therefore liable to them, even though there was no Mexican government complicity in the murder itself.

Damage to an alien's property

28. Legitimate public purpose may justify damage. In principle, wrongful damage to an alien's property is no less the state's responsibility than any other kind of harm caused by the state. But one must distinguish carefully what is wrongful from what is legitimate. In the interests of public safety or health it may be necessary to demolish an alien's house or otherwise damage his property, and this would be legitimate so long as not done in bad faith or in a discriminatory way or without such due process as may be appropriate under the circumstances.

Failure to protect an alien

29. Due diligence required. Although a state is not automatically responsible under international law for all criminal acts against aliens in its territory, it may be responsible for its own failure to prevent such acts through lack of due diligence in policing its own territory and apprehending and punishing criminals. Note, however, that the state owes the alien merely due diligence, not absolute security, since it is recognised that no state can reasonably be expected to prevent all crime.

Thus, in the *Noyes Claim* (1933), Panama was held not liable to an American citizen who had been attacked by a mob, since Panamanian police, at some risk to themselves, had done everything possible to protect him. The arbitral tribunal set out the classic formulation of the appropriate rule:

> The mere fact that an alien has suffered at the hands of private persons . . . does not make a government liable for damages under international law. There must be shown special circumstances from which the responsibility of the authorities arises: either their behaviour in connection with the particular occurrence, or a general failure to comply with their duty to maintain order, to prevent crimes or to prosecute and punish criminals.

These rules found their way into international law through imposition by the stronger Western countries on other states whose conduct was considered not to measure up to the exalted standards of the West. But there is no reason why the failure of a Western country in this regard should be immune from international liability. This could prove an important point in relation to the protection of Algerian immigrants in France or Asian immigrants in Britain from racist assaults and murders.

States may have particularly stringent obligations to protect certain classes of persons, notably diplomats. In the *Mallen Case* (1927) the arbitral tribunal held the United States under a duty of special vigilance to ensure the safety and security of a Mexican consul in Texas. The 1973 *Convention on the Prevention and Punishment of Crimes against Internationally Protected Persons, including Diplomatic Agents* reaffirms in Article 2(3) the duty of states to 'take all appropriate measures to prevent' attacks on those covered by the treaty.

Breach of contract

30. Abusive breach incurs responsibility. Contractual arrangements between states and aliens (often multinational companies) continue to be common despite basic legal problems that remain unresolved.

A state breach of such a contract may reasonably be considered illegal under international law when the state action complained of is simply an unprincipled attempt to evade state obligations. In the *Jalapa Railroad and Power Co. Claim* (1948) a United States Commission, appointed by Act of Congress to distribute money received from Mexico in a lump-sum settlement of American claims, had to decide whether the plaintiff was entitled to any of that money on account of a breach of contract by Mexico. The breach occurred when a Mexican state's legislature decreed that a provision in the plaintiff's contract with the state was nullified. The Commission concluded that the decree was simply an abusive exercise of governmental power to escape contractual obligations and as such was confiscatory and a 'denial of justice'.

31. Legal position and effect of state contracts with aliens. A more fundamental question is whether, given that the state's exercise of sovereignty over its territory and what goes on in it is a matter of international law, a state can be considered to limit its sovereignty by signing a private contract with an alien in the same way that that sovereignty might be limited by an international agreement or treaty. This issue typically arises when a state, in exercise of its exclusive territorial sovereignty under international law, adopts internal economic policies which conflict with its previous undertakings in a contract with an alien.

Does the resulting breach of contract expose the state to international legal liability (with the implication that the existence of such a contract can alter a state's international rights and duties by inhibiting its freedom of action in the internal economic sphere), or does the state have no such liability (with the implication that international law permits a state to destroy an alien's contract rights at will in the legitimate exercise of state sovereignty)?

If it is assumed that a contract derives its legal status only from having been concluded under the contract law of some legal system, the answers to these questions will usually depend initially on what is called 'the law of the contract'. But what might this be, when a state, governed only by international law and its own municipal law, signs an agreement with an alien whose legal position presumably derives from some other state's municipal law?

The parties may attempt to deal with this problem by indicating in their contract what the relevant law is. The tribunal must then determine what the effect of such a 'choice of law' clause actually is.

32. 'Transnational law' and 'internationalized contracts'. In the *Sapphire-N.I.O.C. Arbitration* (1963) the arbitrator found that references in a contract to the parties' undertaking to fulfil their obligations according to the principles of good faith and good will and the absence of any reference to a governing national law may be taken by a tribunal as indicating the intention of the parties to rely on general principles of law based upon reason and upon the common practice of civilised countries. These could be deduced from international law by applying Article 38 of the ICJ Statute. Therefore, according to the arbitrator, this contract between an Iranian government agency and a foreign company had 'a quasi-international character which releases it from the sovereignty of a particular legal system and it differs fundamentally from an ordinary commercial contract'.

The idea of a 'quasi-international' relationship between these two parties implies the existence of a body of law hitherto unknown, neither international nor municipal but rather what has been called *transnational law*.

In *Texaco* v. *Libya* (1977), where Texaco assets were nationalised pursuant to a Libyan breach of an oil concession contract with Texaco, the arbitrator went even further and held that the provision in the contract for international arbitration of any disputes that might arise was 'sufficient to internationalize a contract, in other words, to situate it within a specific legal order – the order of the international law of contracts', where the principle of *pacta sunt servanda* operated.

Therefore, although Libyan nationalisation of Texaco's assets might not of itself necessarily have been illegal under international law, the right to nationalise was counterbalanced by the equal right to undertake international contractual obligations with the related duty to fulfil them. In effect, it is one of the rights of a sovereign that he may by a sovereign act commit himself to limiting his exercise of sovereignty, and that is what Libya had done in its contract with Texaco, as a matter not merely of transnational law but of international law.

This would not be the result in every case, however, since, if general principles based on state practice are to be taken into account, transnational law would have to recognise (as a report of the American Bar Association did in 1963) that even the law of such countries as the United States, France and the United Kingdom held government contracts subject to what the ABA Report called the 'overriding power of the state to terminate or alter them in the public interest, provided proper indemnity is given'.

When Britain initiated the *Anglo-Iranian Oil Company Case* before the International Court of Justice in 1951 following Iranian abrogation of the company's irrevocable concession, the British representatives attempted to get round this problem by arguing that internal law (even of Britain) would not excuse an international legal violation. This is a correct statement of the international rule, but its use here evaded the question of what would be an international legal violation in the circumstances. Did the municipal law and practice of Britain and other Western countries point towards international customary law or general principles of law which would allow breach of contract where the public interest demanded it?

Many developing countries would answer in the affirmative and would deny any international status for such contracts. They would allow abrogation according to municipal law, but with a duty to pay 'appropriate' compensation.

Some Third World writers argue, however, for another approach: acceptance by both parties of an obligation to renegotiate contracts as needed to maintain an understanding between them as their situations and relationship evolves, particularly in the light of the state's economic and development policies. This has certainly not been accepted as a rule of international law but it has the attraction of allowing the contractual relationship of the parties to develop over time without the antagonistic attitudes produced by unilateral abrogation or recourse to arbitration.

Expropriation and nationalisation

33. Problems of definition. In modern international law the expropriation (compulsory taking) of an alien's property by the state has become a complicated question.

There is first of all the problem of what constitutes a *taking*. Action by a state to deprive an alien of the full use of benefit of his assets may amount to *de facto* expropriation and be in practice as much of a taking as would be the actual forcible transfer of title.

Then one must consider what constitutes *property*. The term is capable of referring to tangible or intangible movable or immovable possessions (and this includes not only real estate, fixtures, furniture and machinery, but also goodwill and intellectual property like copyrights and patents). Some argue that contractual rights are also property, but this is disputed.

More generally, expropriation has tended to raise many of the same issues as breach of contract, since expropriation in modern times has usually not been any longer an isolated act but an expression of the seizing state's governmental planning and strategy.

34. Nationalisation. In this context, expropriation of an alien business enterprise as a going concern is usually referred to as *nationalisation* (i.e. bringing the business under national or governmental ownership and control for the purpose of implementing state economic policy). Thus, strictly speaking, the two terms are not identical, since nationalisation denotes one type of expropriation. But because nationalisation is now probably the most important form of expropriation, the terms are often confused.

Some acts of expropriation may be *per se* illegal under international law and theoretically entail restitution as a remedy, as with the seizure in violation of a treaty in the *Chorzow Factory Case* (*see* **13**). Nationalisation, however, appears to be legal unless it fails to meet certain conditions, particularly with regard to compensation. What precisely these conditions are remains a matter of fierce argument centring on whether the international minimum standard or the national treatment standard applies.

35. The two standards on nationalisation. According to a formulation by Professors Baxter and Sohn of Harvard Law School, the 'Harvard Draft Convention of 1961', the international minimum standard would require that nationalisation be:

(*a*) for a public purpose and implemented by a law of general application; and

(*b*) accompanied by payment of prompt, adequate, and effective compensation.

The United Nations General Assembly's *Charter of Economic Rights and Duties of States* (1974) sets out the national treatment standard in Article 2. As an expression of their full permanent sovereignty, states are entitled to nationalise or expropriate foreign property as they see fit, but they 'should' pay 'appropriate compensation' as determined by the nationalising state in light of its own laws and what it considers pertinent circumstances. Disputes are to be settled 'under the domestic law of the nationalising state and by its tribunals'.

Intermediate between these two standards is the General Assembly's 1962 *Resolution on Permanent Sovereignty over Natural Resources*. This says in paragraph 4:

Nationalization ... shall be based on grounds or reasons of public utility, security or the national interest which are recognized as overriding purely individual or private interests, both domestic and foreign ... the owner shall be paid appropriate compensation in accordance [with the nationalizing state's rules] ... and in accordance with international law.

Local remedies must be exhausted in resolving disputes on compensation but resort to an international claim is not excluded.

36. The public purpose requirement. The public purpose requirement, as Baxter and Sohn accepted in their commentary on the Harvard Draft, does not represent much of an obstacle to the nationalising state, since the existence of such a purpose is often presumed by tribunals that are unwilling (in the words of that commentary) to examine 'what the public needs of a nation are and how these may best be satisfied'.

Nevertheless, the question has arisen in two cases involving Libyan oil nationalisations.

In the *BP Case* (1974) the arbitrator agreed with the British argument that Libyan seizure of British Petroleum assets in retaliation against British policy in the Gulf was illegal in being made 'for purely extraneous political reasons'.

But in the *LIAMCO Case* (1977), where the nationalisation was alleged to have been 'in political retaliation against those nations ... whose politics were contrary' to Libya's, the arbitrator held that there is 'no international authority' requiring application of the public purpose test, although he found as a matter of fact that in any case Libya's prime motive for the nationalisation was to preserve the ownership of its oil, other political motives being secondary.

37. Non-discrimination requirement. The requirement in the Harvard Draft that expropriation be according to a law of general application is understood to imply that expropriation should not be directed in a discriminatory way only against certain aliens. In the *LIAMCO Case*, the arbitrator was quite categoric that 'a purely discriminatory nationalisation is illegal and wrongful'. But the 1974 Charter does not mention the point and the 1962 Resolution at best only hints at it by requiring that nationalisation be based on grounds that override not only foreign interests but domestic ones as well.

One difficulty with requiring non-discrimination in every case is that in some situations a state may serve a legitimate public purpose by terminating the activities of a particular foreign company which is in effect the instrument of a foreign government. The International Telephone and Telegraph Company (ITT) was alleged, for example, to have interfered in the early 1970s in the internal affairs of Chile on behalf of the American Central Intelligence Agency; the Anglo-Iranian Oil Company was said to have been deeply involved in the internal politics of Iran. It would appear quite appropriate for a state to discriminate against a foreign company in such circumstances.

Another problem arises when a foreign company dominates the economy of a state. In the *Anglo-Iranian Oil Co. Case* the United Kingdom argued that, when Iran in 1951 nationalised 'the oil industry throughout all parts of the country, without exception', this action was discriminatory because that industry consisted of only one company: Anglo-Iranian. The International Court of Justice did not pronounce on that argument, but it could hardly have been accepted, since it implies that the more comprehensively a foreign monopoly grips the economy of a state, the less that state is entitled to bring the company under state control. A monopoly would then be protected simply by virtue of being a monopoly – a position that would not be tolerated in many Western countries or in the European Economic Community, whose competition law is strict and severe. Such hostility to monopolies suggests that it may now be a general principle of law, derivable from the municipal law of states, that a monopoly cannot benefit in law from its monopolistic position by, for example, pleading that position as a bar to nationalisation.

38. Prompt, adequate and effective compensation. The argument over compensation is at the heart of the dispute over the legal standard to be applied in cases of nationalisation.

Where nationalisation is aimed at taking *control* of a foreign business, compensation may not in principle present much of a problem to the nationalising state. But where nationalisation aims at putting the company's *economic resources* at the disposal of the state, compensation may in practice be impossible. For example, where the foreign company is the largest economic unit in the country, the state may be unable to find elsewhere in the economy the money needed to pay compensation. The situation may be aggravated by the fact that the company, if it has been operating in the country for some time, may already have effectively removed many of the state's assets in the course of exploiting raw material resources such as oil.

In such circumstances, what the state considers 'appropriate compensation' under the UN Resolutions may not be the same thing as the prompt, adequate and effective compensation demanded by the alien whose business has been nationalised.

The resulting disputes usually focus in the first instance on whether the national treatment standard applies as a matter of international law.

In the *Texaco Case* (1977), the arbitrator considered whether the national treatment standard had become customary international law by virtue of having been proclaimed in the 1974 Charter of Economic Rights and Duties of States. He held that the Charter, as a UN General Assembly resolution, could not have been binding in any legislative way. Nor did it simply restate or develop existing customary law. Rather, it proposed rules of law which the states voting for the resolution considered ought to become law, so that its content on this point was merely *de lege ferenda* and not *lex lata*.

If the national treatment standard is held not to be part of international law, the final problem to be sorted out is the precise significance of the international minimum standard's requirement of prompt, adequate and effective compensation.

(*a*) *Prompt* is understood to imply the payment of compensation should not be so long delayed that the alien is unreasonably deprived of it. Determining what is reasonable in the circumstances may involve balancing the needs of the alien with the difficulties of the state in gathering the money to make the payment.

(*b*) *Adequate* requires, according to the judgment in the *Chorzow Factory Case*, payment equal to 'the value of the undertaking at the moment of dispossession, plus interest.' Thus, the alien should not be made to suffer any diminution of value which occurs after dispossession because of a fall in value caused by the expropriation itself. The value at dispossession may also include such items as goodwill and the present value of lost future profit, although claims in this area that are merely for 'speculative' losses will not be allowed.

(c) *Effective* compensation is that which the dispossessed alien can make full use of for his own legitimate purposes. According to Professor Brownlie, this requirement is in practice considered the most important of the three by those seeking compensation. Under it, for example, a nationalisation which completely ends an alien's business and interests in the nationalising state would not be effectively compensated if payment is rendered useless by being given in the form of state bonds that cannot be sold abroad for foreign currency, or if payment in the state's currency is counterbalanced by exchange controls that prevent the money being taken out of the country. A more doubtful case is when payment in the state's currency is not hampered by exchange controls but is paid according to an inflated estimate of that currency's value on international financial markets, with the effect that the alien immediately suffers large losses when he exchanges the money into foreign currency. On balance, however, it would appear that this would not amount to effective compensation.

Progress test 10

1. Is damage required to invoke state responsibility? **(2)**
2. Is fault required for state responsibility? **(3)**
3. What place does the doctrine of created risk have in international law? **(4)**
4. Whose acts may be imputed to the state? **(6)**
5. Is a state responsible for the *ultra vires* acts of its organs? **(7)**
6. Who is responsible for the acts of eventually successful insurrectionaries? **(8)**
7. Explain and discuss the concept of abuse of rights. **(9)**
8. Is there such a thing as an international crime? **(10)**
9. What is the preferred means of reparation under international law? **(13)**
10. When diplomatic protection is invoked, whose claim is made on the international level? **(18)**
11. Distinguish the international minimum standard from the national treatment standard. **(19)**
12. What is a Calvo clause? **(21)**
13. Explain the effect of the local remedies rule. **(22)**
14. Why is nationality important in situations where state responsibility may be invoked on the international level? **(23)**
15. Discuss the holding in the *Barcelona Traction Case*. **(24)**
16. To what circumstances might the term 'denial of justice' apply? **(25)**
17. What is the extent of a state's obligation to protect an alien in its territory? **(29)**
18. Explain what is meant by 'transnational law' and 'internationalised contracts'. **(32)**
19. Discuss the two standards suggested to deal with questions of nationalisation. **(35)**
20. How significant is the 'public purpose requirement'? **(36)**
21. Should the non-discrimination requirement always bar nationalisation? **(37)**
22. What is the international minimum standard on compensation for nationalisation? **(38)**

11   The law of treaties

1. Introduction. Treaties have been a key element in the relations of states for many centuries and a large body of customary law developed over time dealing with the procedures for concluding treaties, their interpretation, their termination and so on. Much of this has now been superseded by the *Vienna Convention on the Law of Treaties* (1969), which to a considerable extent (though not entirely) is declaratory of the previously existing law. The Vienna Convention will therefore be taken as the framework for our examination of the topic, although it should be borne in mind that, under Article 4 of the Convention, it technically applies only to treaties concluded after its entry into force, which occurred on 27 January 1980.

2. Definition of a treaty. Article 2 of the Vienna Convention defines a treaty as:

> an international agreement concluded between States in written form and governed by international law, whether embodied in a single instrument or in two or more related instruments and whatever its particular designation ...

3. Parties to a treaty. As the above definition suggests, treaties are primarily made by states, and it is only such treaties that are covered by the Vienna Convention. Article 3 of the Convention makes clear, however, that there may be legally binding agreements to which other subjects of international law may be parties, notably international organisations. In 1986 a United Nations conference adopted the *Vienna Convention on the Law of Treaties between States and International Organisations or between International Organisations.* Neither Convention recognises any capacity of private individuals or companies to enter into treaties as defined in the Conventions. Private individuals and companies are not recognised to have the capacity to enter into treaties under international law.

4. The effects of Article 2's formal requirement. The requirements that a treaty must be in written form and governed by international law are significant. Although binding oral agreements are possible in international law, they are always subject to the danger that their content and the precise legal significance they have for the parties are open to dispute. An agreement which is in writing and clearly within the domain of international law will more certainly establish the precise intent of the parties to create binding legal relations between themselves. The requirements of Article 2 also have the effect of excluding from the category of treaties such documents as joint policy statements or understandings by which the parties do not intend to be legally bound.

These requirements may also help to avoid the problem of arguably binding international obligations being created more or less informally. Two World Court cases illustrate this problem.

In the *Legal Status of Eastern Greenland Case* (1933), the Permanent Court of International Justice had to consider whether Norway was legally bound by a declaration of its Foreign Minister to the effect that 'the Norwegian Government would not make any difficulty' over Denmark's claim to Eastern Greenland. The court considered 'it beyond all dispute that a reply of this nature given by the minister ... on behalf of his government in response to a request by the diplomatic representative of a foreign power, in regard to a question falling within his province, is binding ...' It is not clear whether the court considered that an oral treaty had been created here (with Norway's undertaking on Greenland being matched by a Danish one in favour of Norway's position in Spitsbergen), or whether the court believed that Norway was estopped after Denmark had relied on the Foreign Minister's statement. The language quoted from the decision above favours the latter explanation.

In the *Nuclear Test Cases* (1974) Australia and New Zealand brought suit against France in an effort to stop French nuclear weapons tests in the South Pacific. France rejected the court's jurisdiction in the case, but French ministers eventually made public statements of one sort or another indicating that France would not hold further atmospheric tests after the series then in progress had been concluded. The court chose to regard these statements as giving the plaintiffs the assurance they sought that no more French tests in the atmosphere would take place. Since Australia and New Zealand refused to accept these statements, it would appear that no treaty or agreement had been entered into between themselves and France. But the court held that a state may be bound *vis-à-vis* other states by its own unilateral act done with the intention of being bound. It must be said, however, that the possible vagueness and imprecision of an undertaking which has not been the product of careful discussions with the other interested states makes this a dubious ground on which to base state obligations.

Treaty making

5. **Negotiation and conclusion of the treaty.** The next section of the Vienna Convention deals with the mechanics of making and becoming bound by a treaty.

Article 7 sets out who may be regarded as a matter of international law as representing a state in the process of concluding a treaty. The head of state, diplomatic envoys, and special representatives authorised to do so may all fulfil this function.

Article 8 provides that a treaty concluded by a person who cannot be considered authorised under Article 7 is without legal effect unless afterwards accepted by the state concerned.

Articles 11 to 18 deal with the means whereby the consent of a state to be bound by a treaty may be expressed. These means include signature at the negotiating conference, exchange of instruments constituting the treaty, ratification, acceptance, approval or accession, or by any other means if so agreed. The key point here is that the means used should be understood by all concerned to be expressing the state's consent to be bound.

In particular, *signature* binds the state when done by its representative with the intention of binding his principal. *Ratification* is a technical term referring to the state's later approval of its authorised representative's earlier signature or agreement to the treaty. *Accession* refers to the process whereby a state which did not participate in the original negotiation and signing of the treaty later becomes a party.

6. The problem of reservations. At the point when a state is indicating its consent to be bound it may wish to qualify its consent by indicating that, although it accepts the treaty in general, it will not consent to certain specified provisions in the treaty. Such a withholding of complete consent to the treaty is called a *reservation*. Reservations have proved a considerable problem in international law.

The legal difficulty is clear if one thinks of the basic question as 'What is the effect of a unilateral attempt to modify an agreement?'

With a bilateral treaty an attempt to do this by a reservation would destroy the parties' original understanding of the agreement and would amount to a counter-offer and a reopening of negotiations. The other party could then accept or reject the reservation as, in effect, part of a new agreement. If the reservation were not acceptable, the treaty would fail.

In the case of a multilateral treaty the situation is more complicated. If one state makes a reservation, some of the existing parties may accept it and consider that the reserving state is a party to the treaty, while other existing parties may reject the reservation and consider that the reserving state is not a party.

The result would be that the applicability of the treaty's provisions would be in doubt and there would be disagreement about which states were parties and which were not. This could present a particular problem with regard to the treaty's coming into force. Most treaties require the adherence of a specified number of states before that can happen. If the adherence of some reserving states were in doubt, it might prove impossible to determine whether or when the treaty had entered into force, with serious consequences for the parties and the international community in general.

The traditional response to this problem was to assume that a multilateral treaty was, in effect, a contract between all the existing parties on one side and the reserving state on the other. The choice for the reserving state would then be to accept without reservation what they had already agreed or alternatively to persuade them *all* to change their agreement in line with the reservation. This response was said to emphasise the *integrity of the convention*, that is, the integrated wholeness of the text, which was not to be undermined by reservations. In this view, unless all the existing parties to a multilateral treaty agreed to a reservation, the attempted adherence of the reserving state would be null and void.

The problem usually came to a head at the time when the reserving state communicated its qualified adherence to the *depositary*, the state or organisation designated in the treaty as responsible for keeping records of the treaty and maintaining the official list of the parties to it. Should the depositary enter the reserving state's name on that list or not?

Consistent practice on this point has come mainly from the two international organisations which have most frequently been designated as depositaries, the League of Nations and its successor, the United Nations.

The League of Nations in this situation strictly applied the integrity of the convention doctrine. After 1945 the United Nations at first was inclined to adopt a similar attitude. This at least had the advantage of making the matter relatively clear and straightforward. But this policy was not very flexible and it could tend to reduce the number of parties to particular conventions – something that seemed undesirable in the case of treaties that were intended to be more or less universally adopted. The matter came to a head in an important case before the International Court of Justice.

7. **Reservations to the Convention on Genocide Case (1951).** In the wake of the mass murder of Gypsies, Jews, and the members of other national or ethnic groups by the Nazi regime during World War II, the United Nations General Assembly in December 1948 unanimously adopted the *Convention on the Prevention and Punishment of the Crime of Genocide*, which is usually, though perhaps unfortunately, referred to as the 'Genocide Convention'. Article 9 of the Convention provided that disputes or cases arising under the Convention should be compulsorily within the jurisdiction of the ICJ. A number of states wished, for reasons of their own, to avoid being subject to the World Court's compulsory jurisdiction, but the Convention had no provision allowing reservations.

The General Assembly therefore requested an advisory opinion from the ICJ on whether reservations were permitted under this Convention and what their effects might be.

In examining the problem, the court acknowledged that the traditional doctrine had been that of the integrity of the convention, 'which is directly inspired by the notion of contract' and which was in general of 'undisputed value as a principle'. Nevertheless in the case of the Genocide Convention a more flexible approach was needed.

The drafters of the Convention intended it to be 'definitely universal in scope', and this was implicit also in the fact that genocide involved 'a denial of the right of existence of entire human groups ... which ... results in great losses to humanity, and which is contrary to the moral law and to the spirit and aims of the United Nations'.

The Convention dealt with the problem according to 'a purely humanitarian and civilizing purpose', so that the parties to it did 'not have any interests of their own' but rather a 'common interest'. In this type of convention, therefore, 'one cannot speak ... of the maintenance of a perfect contractual balance between rights and duties'. By minimising the contractual nature of the Genocide Convention, the court was in effect moving it out of the category of treaties to which the contract-inspired notion of the integrity of the convention applied.

But could states then make reservations to any provisions they disliked and still be parties to the convention? The court emphatically rejected this conclusion as 'so extreme an application of the idea of state sovereignty ... [as to produce] a complete disregard of the object and purpose of the convention'.

The compatibility of a reservation with the object and purpose of the convention thus became the proper test for determining whether a reservation was permissible. If a particular reservation passed this test, the reserving state could be a party to the convention.

But who is to decide the question of compatibility? The court indicated that each existing party to the convention is entitled to appraise individually the validity of a reservation according to this test. But each party is obliged, when doing that, to act in good faith to prevent arbitrary results. Good faith would make the test work.

If, applying the compatibility test in good faith, an existing party still concludes that a particular reservation is objectionable, that party may then consider that the reserving state is not a party to the convention. On the other hand, an existing party which accepts that same reservation may consider that the reserving state is a party.

8. The present position on reservations. This judgment was at first not well received, with four of the court's judges (including the Scottish expert on treaty law, Sir Arnold McNair) dissenting, and with the International Law Commission criticising the compatibility test as too subjective.

Nevertheless the UN General Assembly by 1959 had adopted that test for all multilateral conventions (although the ICJ's opinion was strongly influenced by the uniquely specific issues surrounding the Genocide Convention alone) and the test found its way in 1969 into the Vienna Convention on the Law of Treaties.

Article 19 provides that in general reservations are always permitted except in three instances:

(*a*) when the treaty explicitly forbids reservations;

(*b*) when the treaty does not permit the type of reservation being made;

(*c*) when the reservation is incompatible with the object and purpose of the convention.

The explanation for this complete reversal of the International Law Commission's views on the matter may be found in the ILC's commentary on Article 19, which sets the problem in the context of a rapidly developing international society with widely differing histories, ideologies and attitudes. It says:

> In the present age of change and challenge to traditional concepts the rule calculated to promote the widest possible acceptance of whatever measure of common agreement can be achieved and expressed in a multilateral treaty may be the one most suited to the immediate needs of the international community.

Entry into force of a treaty

9. Treaty provisions govern. Article 24 of the Vienna Convention specifies that a treaty first enters into force as provided for in that treaty (e.g. when a certain number of states have become parties) and comes into effect for a state adhering later to a treaty on the date when the consent of the state to be bound by the treaty is established.

Observance of treaties

10. Pacta sunt servanda. Article 26 of the Vienna Convention incorporates the customary law rule of *pacta sunt servanda*: 'Every treaty in force is binding upon the parties to it and must be perfomed by them in good faith'.

Article 27 prohibits a state from invoking the provisions of its internal law as a justification for failing to perform a treaty.

Application of treaties

11. Non-retroactivity. Article 28 says that a party is not bound by a treaty 'in relation to any act or fact which took place or any situation which ceased to exist' before the treaty entered into force for that state.

This would, however, leave the state bound by a treaty with respect to situations that continued after the treaty came into force, a possibility confirmed by the European Commission of Human Rights in the *De Becker Case* (1958) with regard to the European Convention on Human Rights.

12. Territorial application. Under Article 29 a treaty, unless some other intention is made clear, applies to the whole of each party's territory.

13. Successive treaties on the same subject. The problem of a later treaty inconsistent with an earlier one is complex, but Article 30 of the Vienna Convention sets out general rules that will deal with most cases in a reasonable manner.

It begins by noting that all treaties of United Nations members are subject to the rule in Article 103 of the Charter that the Charter prevails over 'any other international agreement' which conflicts with it. Otherwise, however, the following rules apply:

(*a*) a prior treaty prevails over a later one in any instance of apparent disagreement when the later one specifies that it is subject to, or not incompatible with, the earlier one. A treaty may provide similarly with regard to a later one also;

(*b*) when all the parties to the earlier treaty are also parties to the later treaty, the earlier (if still in effect) applies only to the extent that its provisions are compatible with those of the later treaty:

(*c*) when the parties to the two treaties are not identical, the earlier applies between states that are parties to both only to the extent that the earlier is not incompatible with the later, while as between a state which is party to both treaties and a state which is party to only one of the treaties, the treaty to which both are parties governs their mutual rights and obligations.

Treaty interpretation

14. Three methods of interpretation. Three methods of interpreting treaties have over the years been proposed by writers and tribunals:

(*a*) the *intention of the parties method* aims to give effect to what the parties are shown to have intended at the time of concluding the treaty;

(*b*) the *textual or ordinary meaning of the words method*, which seeks to avoid going beyond the actual treaty itself and to concentrate on analysing the words of the text in the light of the meaning usually given them;

(*c*) the *teleological or aims and objects method*, which considers the purpose of the treaty to be the overriding consideration in interpreting and applying it.

15. The Vienna Convention rule. Article 31(1) of the Convention provides that a 'treaty shall be interpreted in good faith in accordance with the ordinary meaning to be given to the terms of the treaty in their context and in the light of its object and purpose'. This therefore adopts the 'ordinary meaning' approach and allows the treaty's object and purpose, and its terms' context, to be considered only as an aid to discovering that meaning and not as separate bases for interpreting and applying the treaty. The International Law Commission's commentary on Article 31 states that it accords with the approach of the International Court of Justice.

16. The rule of effectiveness and the teleological approach. It is true that in the *Interpretation of Peace Treaties Case* (1950) the ICJ refused to allow the object and purpose of a treaty to override the clear language in it. The court held that it could not apply the rule of effectiveness (expressed in the maxim *ut res magis valeat quam pereat*: 'that the thing may rather have effect than perish') whereby a tribunal may give effect to a treaty on the basis of implementing its purposes even though the treaty's precise language might make it inoperative in the case at hand.

However, the court has accepted the importance of giving effect to the purposes of treaties where their language is not definitive or where it is unclear. The ICJ has also relied on treaty purposes when interpreting and applying the UN Charter, most notably in the *Reparation Case* (which derived the UN's international legal personality from the purposes set out in the Charter) and the *Certain Expenses Case* (where the role of the General Assembly in organising peacekeeping forces was founded on the Charter's aims).

The distinction between the UN Charter and other treaties is that the Charter is a constitutional document in which the parties indicated, in Article 1, a special concern to achieve its purposes within the framework of a long-term and constantly developing legal regime. Judge Jessup in his dissent in the *South West Africa Cases* (1966) emphasised the importance of the teleological approach in interpreting such a treaty.

17. The context of treaty terms as an aid to interpretation. Article 31(2) indicates that the primary context for understanding a term is the text of the treaty itself (including its preamble and annexes) but may also extend to:

(*a*) an agreement between the parties made in connexion with the conclusion of the treaty; and

(*b*) any instrument (e.g. a letter or declaration) made by one or more parties in connexion with the conclusion of the treaty and accepted by the other parties as related to the treaty.

18. Subsequent practice. Under Article 31(3) subsequent agreements between the parties relating to the interpretation of the treaty and subsequent practice of the parties in applying the treaty may also be considered when interpreting the treaty.

Subsequent United Nations practice has been important in modifying the interpretation of Article 27(3) of the UN Charter in such a way that the veto of a permanent member of the Security Council can be exercised only by a negative vote rather than by an abstention (which the language of Article 27(3) might have been thought to favour).

Another example of subsequent practice as an aid to interpretation has appeared under the auspices of the International Maritime Organisation. The IMO has issued Regulations for Prevention of Pollution by Oil which were developed on the basis of state practice in interpreting and applying the 1973 International Convention for the Prevention of Pollution from Ships.

19. A special meaning. A special meaning may be given to a term in a treaty only if it is established that the parties so intended (Article 31(4)).

20. The Vienna Convention's silence on customary law rules and maxims of interpretation. Although customary international law had developed a considerable repertoire of rules of interpretation, the Convention does not refer to them. The reason for this silence was that the various rules or maxims often seemed to conflict and it was difficult to be sure which rules the parties, when drawing up a treaty, may have expected to be applied to their agreement.

Nevertheless, some of these rules and maxims remain in use. A notable example is the maxim *expressio unius est exclusio alterius*, 'the mention of one thing excludes all others', an idea which has been said to be 'a rule of both law and logic'.

21. Preparatory work or 'Travaux préparatoires'. In attempting to discover the meaning of a legal document it is sometimes helpful to examine the process whereby it was drafted. The materials that remain from that process (drafts, discussion papers, minutes of meetings, etc.) are all evidence of the preparatory work or *travaux préparatoires* for the final document.

The usefulness of the *travaux préparatoires* of a treaty has been disputed, since it is argued that statements and drafts produced by some parties during the negotiating process may not reflect even their own final position let alone that of other parties, and that therefore it is best to stick with the treaty itself as the sole embodiment of what all the parties were agreed on.

The Vienna Convention does not exclude the *travaux préparatoires* altogether, but Article 32 makes clear that they can be looked to only as 'supplementary means of interpretation' to 'confirm the meaning resulting from the application of Article 31' or to determine the meaning when application of Article 31 produces an ambiguous or obscure meaning or leads to a result which is 'manifestly absurd or unreasonable'.

22. Interpretation of treaties in two or more languages. When a treaty has equally valid and authentic versions of its text in several languages, the problem may arise of apparent discrepancies between the several versions.

In the *Mavrommatis Palestine Concessions Case* (1924), the Permanent Court of International Justice adopted the view that, where one version has 'a wider bearing than the other', the court should adopt 'the more limited interpretation which can be made to harmonise with both versions' while reflecting so far as it can the 'common intention' of the parties.

Article 33(4) of the Vienna Convention, however, favours adopting the meaning 'which best reconciles the texts, having regard to the object and purpose of the treaty'. This leaves open the possibility of adopting the broader meaning rather than the 'most limited' interpretation required by the *Mavrommatis Case*.

In the *Wemhoff Case* (1968) the European Court of Human Rights also rejected the PCIJ's restrictive approach and adopted a meaning for Article 5(3) of the European Convention on Human Rights which was considered the 'most appropriate in order to realise the aim and achieve the object of the treaty, not that which would restrict to the greatest possible degree the obligations undertaken by the parties'.

In the *Wemhoff Case* the court was presumably influenced in its adoption of a teleological approach by the fact that the European Convention on Human Rights is effectively a constitutional document. Strictly contractual treaties might arguably require a more limited interpretation. Part of the process of determining a treaty's 'object and purpose' under Article 33 of the Vienna Convention could therefore be to decide whether it was part of the purpose that the treaty should establish a constitutional regime or merely a contractual relationship.

Third states

23. **General rule with special exceptions.** Customary international law adopted the position that a treaty can neither impose an obligation on, nor give rights to, a state which is not a party to that treaty, the principle expressed in the maxim *pacta tertiis nec nocent nec prosunt.*

Nevertheless, situations in which the rights and duties of third parties are involved have occasionally been created by treaties which are said to establish objective legal regimes. Professor Hans Kelsen has argued, for example, that Article 2(6) of the UN Charter (whereby the organisation 'shall ensure' that non-member states 'act in accordance' with the principles of the Charter to maintain international peace and security) imposes a duty on third states. The Constantinople Convention of 1888 was for long considered to give a right of passage through the Suez Canal to states that were not parties to the agreement, as did the Treaty of Versailles (1919) with respect to the Kiel Canal. The Aaland Islands, at the entrance to the Gulf of Bothnia between Sweden and Finland, were in 1920 found by a League of Nations Commission to have been demilitarised by a treaty which, like others in Europe since 1815, 'tried to create true objective law, a real political status the effects of which are felt outside the immediate circle of contracting parties'.

Pronouncements by international courts on the matter have been rare. In the *Reparation for Injury Suffered in the Service of the United Nations Case* (1949) the International Court of Justice held that Israel, though not a member of the UN, was obliged to accept the organisation's legal capacity to raise a claim against that state, since the Charter, in creating the United Nations had given it 'objective international personality', which was *erga omnes* (i.e. effective *vis-à-vis* all states). In the *Free Zones of Upper Savoy and the District of Gex Case* (1932) the Permanent Court of International Justice indicated that there was 'nothing to prevent the will of sovereign states' from creating treaty rights in favour of third states, but 'it must be ascertained whether the states which have stipulated in favour of a third state meant to create for that state an actual right which the latter has accepted as such'.

The Vienna Convention on the Law of Treaties in effect adopts the customary law position as seen in the light of the *Free Zones Case*. Article 34 restates the view that a treaty does not bind third states without their consent, and Article 35 indicates that where the treaty creates an obligation consent must be express and in writing, while under Article 36 where the treaty creates a right consent may be presumed.

The International Law Commission's commentary on these provisions indicates that the Commission declined to adopt the notion of treaties creating objective legal regimes.

Amendment of a treaty

24. **Similarity to reservations.** Articles 39 and 40 of the Vienna Convention allow amendment of a treaty by agreement of the parties and set out rules similar to those on reservations to deal with the problem of amendments to multilateral treaties when some parties adopt the amendments and others do not.

General provisions on invalidity, termination and suspension of treaties

25. **Role of the Vienna Convention.** Under Article 42, the validity of a treaty, and a state's consent to it, is to be determined only according to the Vienna Convention, while the treaty's continuance in force may be determined either under the Convention or by the provisions of the treaty itself. It should be noted that logically it would be impossible for the validity of a treaty to be determined

under that treaty itself, since the treaty could have no effect, with regard to that question or any other, until its validity had been otherwise established.

Article 43 says that discontinuance of a treaty does not relieve a state of duties which were embodied in the treaty but which were also imposed independently by international law.

26. Separability of treaty provisions. Sometimes it is in the interest of a state to suspend, withdraw from, or invalidate a treaty as a whole but to claim that certain provisions in it may be separated out and treated as still valid. Article 44 of the Vienna Convention makes clear, however, that in such cases there usually can be no separability, so that all the treaty's provisions must stand or fall together. This is particularly so if the treaty was procured by coercion or violates *jus cogens*, since in such circumstances the treaty in its entirety would have been void *ab initio*.

But if the ground for invalidation or suspension applies only to certain provisions, and not to the treaty as a whole, those provisions alone may be separable (so that the rest of the treaty remains in force) if:

(*a*) the provisions are separable with regard to their application;

(*b*) acceptance of them was not an essential basis for the other party's consent to be bound by the treaty as a whole; and

(*c*) continued performance of the remainder of the treaty would not be unjust.

Under Article 45, if a state knows of a ground for invalidating, terminating, withdrawing from, or suspending, a treaty but agrees to, or acquiesces in, the treaty's continuance, the state loses the right to invoke that ground thereafter.

Specific provisions on invalidity

27. The effect of municipal law. Under Article 46 a state may not invoke as a reason for invalidating its consent to be bound by a treaty the fact that that consent was given in violation of the state's internal law, unless that violation 'was manifest and concerned a rule of its internal law of fundamental importance'.

This can be important in the case of countries like the United States. The American Constitution (obviously a law of 'fundamental importance') provides in Article 2, Section 2 that the president 'shall have Power, by and with the Advice and Consent of the Senate, to make Treaties ...' If the president purported to give other parties to a treaty the United States' consent to be bound without first having secured Senate approval, his act would be invalid under the Constitution. Under Article 46 that failure might also operate to invalidate American consent on the international level, provided the president's violation of the Constitution was considered 'manifest'. But the difficulty is that the president may also enter into 'executive agreements' with other states which do not require Senate approval. What counts as a treaty and what as an executive agreement may not be altogether obvious in certain situations, so that the question of whether the president has manifestly violated the Constitution may be very difficult to answer (*See* also 3:**23**).

It would appear that in such cases the other parties to a treaty would be entitled to consider that there had been no 'manifest' violation by the president, even if the Supreme Court were later to determine that the president's action had in fact been unconstitutional.

28. Error. Article 48 provides that an error may be invoked to invalidate a state's consent to be bound by the treaty only if the error relates to a fact or situation which the state assumed to exist when the treaty was concluded and which 'formed an essential basis' of the state's consent to be bound by the treaty. But if that state contributed to the error or had notice of it, its consent would not be invalidated.

29. Fraud. A state may, under Article 49, invoke fraudulent conduct by another party to the negotiation of a treaty as a ground for invalidating the state's consent.

30. Corruption. Similarly, a state's consent may be invalidated if procured through the corruption of its representative directly or indirectly by another party (Article 50).

31. Coercion. According to Article 51, a state's consent is 'without any legal effect' if procured through coercion of the state's representative by means of threats or acts against him.

The treaty itself is void, under Article 52, 'if its conclusion has been procured by the threat or use of force in violation of the principles of international law embodied in the Charter of the United Nations'. This provision was considered necessary by the ILC in light of modern international law's prohibition of aggressive war and the importance attached by the UN Charter to preventing war and maintaining international peace. The Commission decided that a treaty brought about in this way should be 'void' (i.e. a nullity from the beginning) rather than merely 'voidable' (capable of being declared invalid by the victim if it wishes to do so) so that the victim, once it has been 'liberated from the threat or use of force', may be enabled to consider what to do next from 'a position of full legal equality with the other state'.

It should be noted that, since the Vienna Convention under Article 4 is not retroactive, Article 52 would not invalidate treaties procured by the threat or use of force before the Convention entered into force in 1980. Nevertheless, Communist writers argue that such treaties are now illegal, as for example in the case of the 'unequal treaties' in the nineteenth century between China and Britain with regard to Hong Kong, and China and Russia with respect to the Sino-Russian border in Siberia. If 'unequal treaties' are now illegal, they must be so by virtue of the doctrine of intertemporal law, whereby the continuance in force of a treaty would have to be determined according to the law in effect at the time continuance becomes an issue. But this is not directly provided for in the Vienna Convention, save in Article 64 with regard to emerging *jus cogens*.

Article 52 also does not invalidate treaties procured by threats or pressure of a non-military kind, nor, under Article 75, would it invalidate the treaty obligations of an aggressor resulting from measures taken in conformity with the UN Carter in regard to the aggression.

32. Jus cogens. In the International Law Commission's preparation of the Vienna Convention considerable discussion took place about whether there were in international law certain rules so fundamental and of such universal importance that a state would not be entitled to derogate from them even by agreement with another state in a treaty. The Commission concluded that such rules did exist, e.g. the prohibition on the unlawful use of force.

Article 53 of the Convention applies this conclusion to the question of treaty validity: 'A treaty is void if, at the time of its conclusion, it conflicts with a peremptory norm of general international law.' A peremptory norm (i.e. a rule of *jus cogens*) is defined as one 'accepted and recognized by the international community of states as a whole as a norm from which no derogation is permitted and which can be modified only by a subsequent norm of general international law having the same character'. Article 64 provides that, if a new jus cogens norm emerges, any existing treaty in conflict with it becomes void and terminates.

Terminating, suspending or withdrawing from a treaty

33. Cessation by agreement. Articles 54-59 of the Vienna Convention provide for those situations where, in relation to some or all of the parties, a treaty may by virtue of provisions in it or by agreement between the parties cease operating through termination, suspension or withdrawal of parties. Under Article 56 a treaty may be presumed to allow such a cessation if it is established that the parties intended that or if it may be considered implied by the nature of the treaty. Some parties may agree to suspend the operation of the treaty as between themselves provided that does not affect the rights of the remaining parties and is not incompatible with the treaty's object and purpose (Article 58). According to Article 59 a later treaty may have the effect of terminating an earlier one if the parties intended the later one alone to govern the matters covered by the two agreements or if the later is so incompatible with the earlier that the two cannot be applied at the same time.

A treaty may, however, cease to be operative for reasons other than the agreement or intention of the parties and these situations are covered in Articles 60 to 64.

34. Termination or suspension because of a material breach. Article 60(1) provides that a material breach of a bilateral treaty by one party is a legitimate ground for the other party to terminate or suspend the treaty in whole or in part. Article 60(2) elaborates this basic rule for the more complicated case of multilateral treaties.

A material breach is defined in Article 60(3) as either a repudiation of the treaty not sanctioned by the Vienna Convention or 'the violation of a provision essential to the accomplishment of the object or purpose of the treaty'. The ILC commentary emphasises that the term 'material breach' is used to indicate that not all breaches justify termination or suspension but only those that touch the central purposes of the treaty or provisions essential to effective execution of the treaty.

Article 60(5) indicates that a material breach does not justify termination or suspension in the case of 'provisions relating to the protection of the human person contained in treaties of a humanitarian character, in particular to provisions prohibiting any form of reprisals against persons protected by such treaties'. Most relevant in this context are the Geneva Conventions of 1949, which prohibit reprisals against protected persons in reaction to illegal acts by the state to which those persons belong. It would appear, however, that Article 60(5) also prevents termination or suspension of any human rights treaty on the ground of material breach by a party, even if the question of reprisals is not covered by the treaty.

The International Court of Justice considered the problem of termination of a treaty because of breach by one party in *The Legal Consequences Case* (1971) relating to South Africa's mandate in South-West Africa (Namibia). Technically, the original mandate was in the form of a treaty between the League of Nations and South Africa. In 1966, the United Nations (as legal successor to the League) decided that the mandate was terminated by reason of South Africa's material breaches of the agreement's basic provisions. In its advisory opinion in the 1971 case the ICJ upheld this decision as 'the application of the general principle of law that a right of termination on account of breach must be presumed to exist in respect of all treaties', except as regards provisions on protecting the human person. Although the court's precise categorisation of the mandate is not clear, the judges' approach implies that it was a bilateral treaty, with the League of Nations (and later the United Nations) on one side and South Africa on the other.

In the *Appeal Relating to the Jurisdiction of the ICAO Council* (1972), the ICJ had to consider the effect of India's suspension, *vis-à-vis* Pakistan, of the multilateral conventions on air transport which laid the basis for the International Civil Aviation Organisation's jurisdiction over the treaty parties. India argued that, having suspended the treaties in the way described on account of a breach by Pakistan, she was not subject to ICAO jurisdiction in a case later raised by Pakistan. The ICJ, however, took the view that unilateral suspension does not automatically render jurisdictional clauses inoperative, since one of their purposes was to enable questions as to the validity of a unilateral suspension to be determined by the ICAO.

35. Termination or suspension because of supervening impossibility of performance. Under Article 61(1) of the Vienna Convention a state may terminate a treaty or withdraw from it if it becomes impossible to perform because of 'the permanent disappearance or destruction of an object indispensable for the execution of the treaty'. A temporary impossibility is a ground only for suspension of the treaty's operation. But a party may not invoke impossibility of performance for these purposes if the impossibility results from that party's own breach of the treaty or of some other international obligation towards the other parties to the treaty.

36. Termination or withdrawal because of fundamental change of circumstances. The Vienna Convention in Article 62 gives a limited right to a state to terminate or withdraw from a treaty because the circumstances under which it became a party no longer exist. The fundamental change of circumstances must, however, be one 'not foreseen by the parties' and:

(*a*) the existence of those circumstances must have been an essential basis of the parties' consent to be bound by the treaty; and

(*b*) the effect of the change must be radically to transform the extent of obligations still to be performed under the treaty.

But termination or withdrawal is not permitted in this situation if the treaty establishes a boundary or if the fundamental change is the result of a breach by the party invoking it as reason for termination or withdrawal.

Suspension of the treaty's operation is also permitted on the same terms as termination or withdrawal.

Behind Article 62 lies a long history in customary international law of what is called the doctrine of *rebus sic stantibus* ('things staying as they are'). The doctrine supposed that it was an implicit provision in many treaties (a *clausula rebus sic stantibus*) that the parties would consider themselves bound by the treaty only so long as the fundamental circumstances that prompted it remained in existence.

In the *Fisheries Jurisdiction Case (Merits)* (1974) the International Court of Justice indicated that Article 62 is 'in many respects' a codification of customary law on this question (although the International Law Commission, in drawing up the provision, emphasised that it was more restricted than the broadest interpretations of the customary rule). The court went on to recall the traditional view that 'fundamental' changes were ones 'which imperil the existence or vital development of one of the parties'. Furthermore, 'the change must have increased the burden of the obligations to be executed to the extent of rendering the performance something essentially different from that originally undertaken'.

37. Severance of diplomatic or consular relations. Severance of official relations between the parties does not affect the legal relationships which the treaty established between them except in so far as the existence of such relations is indispensable for the application of the treaty (Article 63).

38. The effect of war on the operation of a treaty. The International Law Commission declined to provide in the Vienna Convention for the effect of war on termination or suspension of a treaty, on the ground that war under current international law must be regarded as abnormal and not something that should be treated as part of the normal relations between states.

As Professor Brownlie points out, treaties intended to govern war and peace (e.g. the UN Charter and the Geneva Conventions of 1949) are certainly not suspended or terminated by war. War may have that effect, however, where it produces a fundamental change of circumstances or leads to impossibility of performance.

In a leading American case, *Techt* v. *Hughes* (1920), the New York State Court of Appeals, in dealing with the question whether a treaty between the United States and Austria-Hungary remained in effect when the two countries were at war in 1917–1918, suggested what seems a sensible rule: 'provisions compatible with a state of hostilities, unless expressly terminated, will be enforced, and those incompatible rejected'. It was therefore up to the court to 'determine whether, alone or by force of connection with an inseparable scheme, the provision is inconsistent with the policy or safety of the nation in the emergency of war, and hence presumably intended to be limited to times of peace'. In *Clark* v. *Allen* (1947) the United States Supreme Court adopted this approach and upheld the application of a treaty in circumstances similar to those in *Techt* v. *Hughes* (where treaty provisions on inheritance in each country by citizens of the other were at issue).

Some writers suggest that multilateral treaties in particular are generally not terminated by war but at most only suspended, although there is doubt whether this would apply in the case of political treaties or treaties of alliance.

Effects of invalidity, termination and suspension

39. Cause of cessation important. Articles 69 to 72 deal with the effects on the legal position and relationships of the parties once a treaty has ceased to operate because of invalidity, termination or suspension. When invalidity is shown,

Article 69 implements the International Law Commission's view that, where neither party is a wrongdoer in relation to the cause of the treaty's nullity, the legal position should be determined on the basis of taking into account both the invalidity of the treaty *ab initio* and the good faith of the parties. However, under Article 71, invalidity arising from a violation of a rule of *jus cogens* produces a situation where, if the treaty *was void from the beginning* under Article 53, the parties must as far as possible eliminate the consequences of illegal acts done under the treaty and conform their conduct to the rule concerned. If the treaty *becomes void* under Article 64, the parties may continue rights, obligations or situations which have arisen under the treaty provided their maintenance is not itself in conflict with the new rule of *jus cogens* involved.

Dispute settlement

40. Use of United Nations techniques. Under Article 65, a party intending to suspend, terminate, or withdraw from a treaty must notify the other parties, with three months being allowed for them to respond or object. If an objection is raised, the parties must apply the dispute settlement procedures listed in Article 33 of the UN Charter (negotiation, enquiry, mediation, conciliation, arbitration, judicial settlement, resort to regional mechanisms, or other peaceful means of their own choice). In the event of failure to reach a solution in this way within twelve months, under Article 66 cases relating to *jus cogens* grounds for termination may be referred to the International Court of Justice, while those relating to other grounds for termination or suspension are to be submitted for conciliation under the auspices of the UN Secretary-General.

State succession to treaties

41. The 'clean slate' doctrine. A thorny problem in international law is whether a state that did not exist at the time a certain rule of law or an international obligation came into being should be held bound by it by virtue of being the successor to a previous state that did exist at that time and was bound. The *Vienna Convention on Succession of States in respect of Treaties* (1978) attempts to deal with this question as regards treaty law.

In Articles 8 to 10 this Convention adopts the basic position that, when one state succeeds another as the internationally responsible authority in a territory, the treaty obligations of the previous state do not automatically devolve on the successor. However, treaty obligations are passed on in cases of treaties establishing boundaries and boundary regimes or otherwise establishing territorial rights and benefits, except in the case of a treaty which allowed the establishment of foreign military bases in the successor state's territory (Articles 11 and 12). The effect of the Convention's provisions overall is that the successor state starts with a 'clean slate' and is in general entitled to decide for itself whether it wishes to become a party to a particular treaty.

Progress test 11

1. What is a treaty? (2)
2. Are oral agreements binding in international law? (4)
3. Are reservations permissible? (8)
4. What is the basic rule on the observance of treaties? (10)
5. What are the three methods of interpreting a treaty text? (14)
6. In what circumstances might a teleological approach be followed? (16)
7. Has subsequent practice ever had a significant effect on the interpretation of a treaty? (18)

8. What use may be made of *travaux préparatoires* in interpreting a treaty? (**21**)

9. May a treaty bind third states? (**23**)

10. Explain the Vienna Convention's provisions on separability. (**26**)

11. What is effect of coercion in procuring a treaty? (**31**)

12. What is the Vienna Convention's position on the concept of *rebus sic stantibus*? (**36**)

13. Does war automatically terminate or suspend a treaty between the hostile parties? (**38**)

14. Does a new state automatically continue to be bound by treaties entered into by the previous sovereign? (**41**)

12   The law of the sea

Development of the law of the sea

1. Interplay of technology and politics. In the early days of international law the law of the sea was one of the major areas of concern since many of the contacts of one state with another occurred in the context of navigation, fishing, and commerce on the high seas, in territorial waters, and in national ports and harbours. These activities have, if anything, increased in significance in modern times and have been joined by interest in deep-sea mining, environmental protection, and the military uses of the oceans.

From its beginnings the law of the sea has been strongly influenced by the interplay of technology and politics, or, to put it another way, by the ability (or lack of ability) to exercise physical control over the oceans coupled with the political determination to pursue national interests there. The law of the sea has therefore often reflected the limits which technology has placed on the exercise of state power, and, as one might expect, technological progress has confronted the law with the problem of state authority continually expanding into areas that were once thought beyond national control.

2. The three-mile limit. A classic example illustrates the point. It used to be the general (though not universal) rule that a state was entitled to exercise territorial jurisdiction over a band of the sea extending up to three miles from the shore. In past centuries this was sometimes said to be based on the distance a cannon on shore could fire out to sea (hence its name: 'the cannon-shot rule'). According to the Dutch jurist Cornelis van Bynkershoek (1673–1743) territorial control could go no further because 'the dominion of the land ends where the power of weapons ends'. But clearly the later development of longer-range guns, and even aircraft and missiles, made nonsense of van Bynkershoek's justification for the three-mile rule. In modern times the range of missiles is such that no rule on the width of the territorial sea can any longer be sensibly based on 'the power of weapons'. Nor does three miles as a limit seem nowadays anything other than arbitrary. Thus, technology overtook the law and confronted it with some awkward problems of determining, and justifying, a new rule on the matter.

3. Freedom of the seas: mare liberum versus mare clausum. A second and even more important example of the interrelationship of technology and politics in the development of the law of the sea had to do with the question of sovereignty and rights of navigation on the high seas. A great debate on this point occurred in the seventeenth century and the results of it, strongly influenced by certain conclusions based on the technology of that time, determined what the law in this area was right up to the 1970s, when technological developments suddenly threw open the whole issue again.

The debate arose out of the attempt by Dutch commercial interests, beginning at the time when Holland obtained *de facto* independence from Spain in 1609, to pry open the sea routes to the Indies. These routes were at the time subject to Spanish and Portuguese claims of exclusive rights over them. Dutch trade was also inhibited by similar British claims over parts of the North Sea and the North Atlantic. The problem was made even more important for the Dutch as the century moved on by their development of an improved ocean-going cargo ship which made it easier for them to contemplate taking over a good part of international maritime trade. Politics and technology were moving forward hand-in-hand.

Indeed, advances in naval architecture and navigational instruments and techniques, by expanding the possibilities for travel and commerce on the seas, tended in general to make the law of the sea a more and more urgent topic in the mid-seventeenth century.

4. Hugo Grotius. In 1609 the great Dutch international lawyer Hugo Grotius published his study *Mare Liberum* ('The Free Sea') in which he put the Dutch case for freedom of the seas. His argument was based on the inability of any nation to exercise physical control over the ocean. A property right in the sea could exist only if the sea and the objects in it could be seized or enclosed. Since this was generally impossible (except in the catching of fish, where the property right was presumably in the fish once they were caught and not in the sea itself), no part of the high seas could belong to the territory of any state. The sea was therefore under the dominion of none but God, and it and its resources were therefore necessarily common to all mankind (*res communis*).

Passing from an argument based on technological factors to one with environmental implications, Grotius maintained that the sea was like the air, inexhaustibly vast. Therefore, since nothing in the sea could ever be significantly diminished by human use, no state could legitimately claim a proprietary right to control such use by others in order to prevent its own interests being adversely affected.

5. John Selden. The counter-argument to Grotius came in 1635 from the English Parliamentarian John Selden in his book *Mare Clausum* ('The Closed Sea'). Selden rejected the claim that the sea could not be appropriated because of its physical properties. The sea may be enclosed, he argued, insofar as its limits are fixed by the position of its shores: if they fall under the control of a particular nation, that nation may be considered able to enclose the sea. Furthermore, boundaries in the sea may be established on the basis of islands, rocks or promontories belonging to a particular state.

Selden also denied that the sea was inexhaustible. On the contrary, he said, the sea may be made worse for him that owns it by reason of other men's fishing, navigation and commerce. The abundance of the sea could be diminished by 'promiscuous' use just as readily as in the case of mining and similar activities on land, particularly as regards fishing.

6. Freedom of the seas. The debate on these questions was eventually won by the Dutch argument in favour of freedom of the seas. This happened in considerable measure because Britain itself later adopted Grotius's arguments when British maritime power attained world supremacy in the eighteenth century: it then became in Britain's interest also not to have a superior maritime position weakened by other states' claims to own part or all of the sea.

The effect was to establish the principle that the sea was common to all (the principle of *commonage*), with limitations on the freedom of the seas being seen as derogations from the general rule.

The victory of freedom of the seas had profound implications for the law of the sea, since that doctrine was grounded in certain assumptions which the progress of technology would later call in question:

(*a*) that the resources of the sea are inexhaustible;

(*b*) that there can be no serious danger of adverse changes over extensive areas of the sea as a result of the activities of man;

(*c*) that high seas navigation does not require close regulation;

(*d*) that the ocean is so vast and its uses so limited that the danger of serious conflict of use in most areas is almost non-existent.

Overfishing, pollution, deep-sea mining, problems of navigation and the great expansion of the international community in the last three hundred years have undermined all these assumptions, and in doing so have undermined the law which was based on them.

The problem in recent years has been whether the collapse of the Grotian concept inevitably means a return to Selden's notions of national control and exploitation based on the ability to dominate the sea and its resources.

The conflict between these different approaches runs through much of the debate on the law of the sea over the past forty years and it is worth bearing in mind while studying the particular topics examined below.

7. Codifying the law of the sea. The pressing need to update the law of the sea produced a comprehensive attempt at codification at the Geneva Conference of 1958, which adopted four conventions that had been drafted by the International Law Commission. These were:

(*a*) the Geneva Convention on the Territorial Sea and the Contiguous Zone;

(*b*) the Geneva Convention on the High Seas;

(*c*) the Geneva Convention on the Continental Shelf;

(*d*) the Geneva Convention on Fishing and Conservation of the Living Resources of the High Seas.

Parts of these conventions were declaratory of existing customary international law, some provisions have developed into new customary law since 1958, and overall the conventions are still binding on the parties to them as treaties. But the conventions had a number of imperfections or gaps and they were in some areas overtaken by events within a decade.

These problems led to the convening of what has come to be called The Third United Nations Conference on the Law of the Sea ('UNCLOS III'). This conference laboured from 1973 to 1982 to produce a comprehensive revamping of the law in a new Law of the Sea Convention, the LOS Convention. Although it is not yet in force and has been strongly opposed by certain powerful states and vested interests, the LOS Convention looks set to have an increasingly formative influence on the law in the years ahead.

There is already considerable debate over whether the Convention should be treated as belonging to that class of treaties about which Judge Sorensen spoke in the *North Sea Continental Shelf Cases*: those 'adopted as part of the combined process of codification and progressive development of international law' which 'may well constitute, or come to constitute the decisive evidence of generally accepted new rules of international law', regardless of their role in the formation of treaty law. As will be evident in the following discussion, the LOS Convention is already coming, again in Sorensen's description, to serve 'as an authoritative guide for the practice of states' and 'the nucleus around which a new set of generally recognised legal rules may crystallise'.

In order to understand the modern law of the sea, therefore, one has to consider not only traditional customary rules but also the Geneva Treaties of 1958, the LOS Convention, developing new customary law, regional practice and other bilateral or multilateral agreements.

Internal waters

8. Ports and harbours. Strictly speaking, internal waters such as lakes, rivers, canals and other landlocked bodies of water are not a matter of concern for the international law of the sea since they are entirely within the territory and sovereignty of one state. But the term internal waters also applies to ports and harbours. Although an extension of the sea, these are considered to be completely under the coastal state's territorial sovereignty while nevertheless being partly governed by the law of the sea with respect to that state's jurisdiction over foreign ships. This question of jurisdiction is usually analysed in terms of the type of foreign ship involved.

9. Foreign merchant vessels. The customary legal rule is that, by voluntarily entering the internal waters of a coastal state, a foreign merchant ship places itself within that state's territorial jurisdiction and is therefore subject to the operation of that state's laws and courts. But alongside this legal rule, a rule of comity (i.e., international convenience and friendly relations) has developed whereby the coastal state will often refrain from exercising its authority and will leave jurisdiction over many matters to the state whose flag the ship flies (the *flag state*).

Exceptions to this rule of comity are:

(*a*) intervention by the coastal state when requested by those in charge of the ship or by official representatives of the flag state; and

(*b*) action by the coastal state when the peace or good order of the port is likely to be affected by events on the ship.

10. Wildenhus' Case. The United States Supreme Court had to grapple with this second type of situation in *Wildenhus' Case* (1887). An American court had exercised jurisdiction over Wildenhus, a Belgian sailor, on a charge of having murdered another Belgian sailor on board the Belgian merchant vessel in whose crew both men served. The murder took place while the ship was in a US port, but below decks and out of sight or sound of the shore, so that it could not have disturbed the physical tranquillity of the port. Wildenhus applied for habeas corpus on the ground that the murder was entirely an internal affair of the ship and therefore could not properly have given rise to American jurisdiction. The Supreme Court denied habeas corpus.

Before examining the 'peace of the port' problem, the court rejected Wildenhus' suggestion that no jurisdiction could be exercised over him because he personally had not entered the United States voluntarily. What mattered, in the opinion of Chief Justice Waite, was that the owner of the ship had voluntarily taken it into American waters so as to subject it to American law and the American courts. The implication is that an individual's freedom from jurisdiction in such situations derives entirely from the status of his ship.

As to whether the peace of the port had been disturbed, the Supreme Court held that, although it was impossible for people on shore to observe what had happened, murder was in fact one of those 'crimes which from their gravity awaken a public interest as soon as they become known'. The 'very nature of such an act is to disturb the quiet of a peaceful community' in such a way as to justify the intervention of the local authorities to punish the offender. Therefore, jurisdiction over Wildenhus was properly taken.

The court admitted, however, that 'it may not be easy at all times' to decide when a case should be left to the jurisdiction of the flag state and when not, and 'much will depend on the attending circumstances of the particular case'. The result is that resolution of the jurisdictional question tends to be done on an *ad hoc* basis, with courts feeling free to decide as seems best in each case. Indeed, since freedom from jurisdiction here is matter of comity and not law, a government which is insensitive to the demands of friendly relations could quite legitimately assert its legal right to exercise full jurisdiction even where there is no question of the peace of the port being disturbed.

11. The Eisler Case. In the *Eisler Case*, for example, British police in Southampton boarded the Polish ship on which Eisler had stowed away when the vessel was in an American port, apprehended him, and took him before a British magistrate for extradition to the United States where he was alleged to have jumped bail during an appeal of two criminal convictions. Poland protested on the ground that a state's jurisdiction over territorial and national waters does not entitle it to arrest persons on board a foreign vessel for the purpose of extradition to a third state (in which case, presumably, the peace of the port would not have been disturbed). The British government, however, replied that it was 'a universally recognised principle of international law that a merchant ship in the ports or roadsteads of another country falls under the jurisdiction of the coastal state', so that Eisler could have no right of 'asylum' on a Polish merchant ship in Southampton.

12. Force majeure. The result in both these cases was influenced at least indirectly by the fact that the ship in each instance had entered the coastal state's internal waters voluntarily. Involuntary entry would have produced a different outcome, since an exception to the general rule which allows jurisdiction arises where a ship is forced into those waters by distress or other compelling circumstances (*force majeure*) beyond its control. In such cases jurisdiction remains with the flag state. The classic example is the *Creole Case* (1855), where the *Creole*, an American slave ship, was compelled by a mutiny of the crew to put in to the British-controlled port of Nassau in the Bahamas. The British authorities attempted to intervene on behalf of the ship's cargo of slaves, but when the case went to arbitration, the arbitrator held that in a situation of *force majeure* of this sort the coastal state was not entitled to exercise jurisdiction.

13. Foreign public ships. The rules applying to foreign public, or government ships (and particularly foreign warships) are quite different from those on private vessels.

Public ships are legally immune from the coastal state's jurisdiction in internal waters when they are lawfully in those waters. This follows from the general principles of state immunity from foreign jurisdiction (*see* Chap. 9). Some writers suggest that these ships enjoy extraterritoriality, i.e. the right to be treated as part of the territory of the flag state, but in *Chung Chi Cheung* v. *The King* (1939) the British Privy Council rejected this view. In this case, a British subject employed aboard a Chinese customs vessel murdered the captain while the ship was in the internal waters of Hong Kong. At the request of the ship's first mate, the British authorities arrested the murderer and he was later tried by a Hong Kong court. On appeal he argued that the ship should have been regarded as Chinese territory in which British jurisdiction could never legitimately be exercised. The Privy Council held, however, that the Chinese vessel did not enjoy 'objective extraterritoriality' but only 'certain immunities' which could be waived by qualified representatives of the foreign state.

14. Internal waters and innocent passage. In certain circumstances (*see* **25–26**) international law recognises a right of innocent passage for foreign ships through the waters of a coastal state when those ships are moving peacefully to and from areas of the high seas.

But with regard to those waters which customary international law recognises as internal, there is no right of innocent passage. It should be noted, however, that under Article 5(2) of the 1958 Geneva Convention on the Territorial Sea and the Contiguous Zone and Article 35 of the 1982 Law of the Sea Convention a right of innocent passage does exist when, by virtue of certain provisions of these treaties, waters which had previously been territorial seas or high seas become internal waters.

Thus, with regard to innocent passage, one must distinguish between customary law internal waters and treaty law internal waters.

Territorial sea

15. What is the territorial sea? From Article 1 of the 1958 Territorial Sea Convention and Article 2 of the 1982 LOS Convention, the territorial sea may be defined as that belt of sea adjacent to the state's coast over which the state exercises sovereignty. The difficulty with this definition is the meaning of the word 'adjacent', which raises the problem of the width of the territorial sea.

As noted earlier (*see* **2**), the traditional international law rule recognised a three-mile limit, but this had never been universally accepted and by the time of the 1958 Law of the Sea Conference technology and politics combined to make many states support a more extended territorial sea. No agreement was reached then and so the 1958 Territorial Sea Convention is silent on the point. This failure to settle the matter led many states to strike out on their own to declare each in its own case a width that seemed suitable to it. Claims ranged all the way from 3 miles to 200 miles, and it was argued by some that the whole question had been effectively taken out of the realm of international law and become merely a matter of the arbitrary decisions of the individual states.

If this were true it would mean that some states could carve up the whole ocean for themselves without regard to the rights of other states. But, as Professor Ian Brownlie has argued, the correct view is rather that of the International Court of Justice in the *Anglo-Norwegian Fisheries Case* (1951): although only the coastal state is competent to set its own maritime boundaries, the validity of the result with regard to the rights of other states must remain a matter of international law. Thus, international law would still have a role to play in deciding whether a certain state's claim was internationally legitimate, even though there was no set limit under that law.

Some progress has been made towards resolving this problem insofar as the 1982 LOS Convention, in Article 3, has provided for a limit 'not exceeding twelve nautical miles', a nautical mile being equal to approximately 1.15 land miles. Given, however, that the 1982 Convention is not yet in force, and that several major countries have not yet become parties to it, the general argument on the role of international law in the matter may continue for some time.

The ultimate resolution of the whole issue is important for states both on account of the advantages obtained for the coastal state from the right to control and exploit the territorial sea and on account of the responsibility resting on the coastal state to police and administer the territorial sea in peace and war.

16. Delimitation of the territorial sea. Determining the width of the territorial sea does not end the problem of deciding where the limits of territorial waters should be drawn, since there are various ways of drawing them depending on the general shape of the coastline. The difficulty is that the starting point (the *baseline*) from which the width is measured out to sea may follow the natural contours of the coast or be drawn more artificially from considerations of convenience.

17. The normal baseline. This is the line which follows the coast's contours. Article 3 of the 1958 Territorial Sea Convention and Article 5 of the 1982 Convention provide that the normal baseline is 'the low-water line along the coast as marked on large-scale charts officially recognized by the coastal state'. Drawing the outer limit of the territorial sea from such a normal baseline produces a *tracé parallèle*, a line exactly corresponding to the shape of the coast.

18. Straight baselines. An alternative method in certain situations is that of *straight baselines*. These were first developed by Norway to deal with the problem of the country's irregular coastline, deeply cut into by fjords and fringed by a line of islands and rocks. The method involved drawing baselines from one prominent coastal feature to another so as to by-pass the irregularities in between. The effect was in some instances to set the baseline (and hence the outer limit of the territorial sea) much further out than it would otherwise have been and thereby to give Norway sovereignty over a larger area of the sea than it would have had according to the normal baseline method of delimitation. For that reason the United Kingdom objected to the Norwegian system and brought suit in the International Court of Justice.

In the *Anglo-Norwegian Fisheries Case* (1951) the ICJ held that the straight baseline method was permissible under international law for countries whose coasts were deeply indented or fringed with islands. Geographical features such as capes and promontories could be taken as the starting points for the straight baselines provided that each line followed the general direction of the coast. The court also required that there should be sufficiently close links between the sea areas enclosed by the lines and the adjacent coast as to make it reasonable to subject those sea areas to the legal regime of internal waters (as all waters to the landward side of any baseline would be). Furthermore, economic factors such as the interests of the coastal region affected might be considered to militate in favour of a special regime not established according to the normal baseline method.

Although thus initially a special method of delimitation applied by Norway, straight baselines soon found their way into general international law via Articles 4 and 5 of the 1958 Territorial Sea Convention and have been confirmed in Article 7 of the 1982 Convention. Interestingly, in 1964 the United Kingdom, in the Territorial Waters Order in Council, applied the straight baseline method to the west coast of Scotland, with the result that the sea areas between the Inner and Outer Hebrides which had been high seas became internal waters with a right of innocent passage.

19. The water-closing line. Where a river flows directly into the sea, the baseline of the territorial sea may be the *water-closing line* drawn across the mouth of the river between points on the low-tide line on its banks. This is provided for in Article 13 of the 1958 Territorial Sea Convention and Article 9 of the 1982 Convention.

20. Bays. A special method for determining the baseline in respect to *bays* that are entirely within the territory of one state is contained in Article 7 of the 1958 treaty and Article 10 of the new convention. This method operates in two stages:

(*a*) The bay has to meet a geometrical criterion: if a line is drawn across the mouth of the bay and that line is then taken as the diameter of a semi-circle on the landward side of the line, the area within the semi-circle must not be greater than the area of water within the bay;

(*b*) If this geometrical requirement is met, then a baseline may be drawn between the low-water marks at the natural entrance points on either side of the bay provided, however, that this baseline does not exceed twenty-four nautical miles in length.

If this line is longer than twenty-four nautical miles, the baseline may not be drawn at the entrance to the bay but must be drawn at appropriate points in the bay that are no more than the required distance apart.

An exception to this general rule exists for *historic bays*, that is, bays whose mouth is wider than twenty-four nautical miles but which have for long been regarded as part of the coastal state's internal waters. Canada, for example, claims that Hudson Bay (whose entrance is fifty miles wide and which embraces about 580,000 square miles of sea and islands) is an historic bay. Although Canadian writers assert that this claim has been tacitly accepted by other states, not all claims to historic bays are uncontested.

21. The coastal state's rights in the territorial sea. Under Articles 1 and 2 of the 1958 Territorial Sea Convention and Article 2 of the 1982 LOS Convention, the coastal state's sovereignty extends to its territorial sea and to the air space above it and the seabed and subsoil below it, subject only to the limitations imposed by international law. This gives the coastal state the exclusive right to exploit the resources of the territorial sea and to enact health, immigration, customs, navigation and overflight regulations for the area which foreign vessels and aircraft must obey. The coastal state may also exclude foreign vessels from *cabotage*, that is, navigating and trading along the coast between ports of the coastal state.

22. Coastal state jurisdiction in the territorial sea. The coastal state may sometimes exercise civil and criminal jurisdiction over foreign private and commercial vessels, as outlined in Articles 19 and 20 of the 1958 Territorial Sea Convention and Article 27 and 28 of the 1982 Convention.

As regards *criminal jurisdiction*, the coastal state is entitled to exercise it if the ship concerned is moving from internal waters into the territorial sea and the crime occurred while the ship was in internal waters. The coastal state should not exercise jurisdiction if the ship on which a crime has occurred is merely passing through the territorial sea without entering internal waters unless:

(*a*) the consequences of the crime extend to the coastal state; or

(*b*) the crime is of a kind likely to disturb the peace of the country or the good order of the territorial sea; or

(*c*) the assistance of the local authorities has been requested by the ship's captain or the flag state's consul; or

(*d*) if the exercise of jurisdiction is necessary for the suppression of illicit trafficking in narcotic drugs or psychotropic substances (substances which affect mental states).

If the crime was committed outside territorial waters and the ship is only passing through the territorial sea, the coastal state has no right to arrest any person on the ship or conduct any investigation on it.

Civil jurisdiction should generally not be exercised over foreign ships passing through the territorial sea (though this is not prohibited in the conventions), although civil jurisdiction is allowed if the ship has sailed from internal waters or has failed to discharge liabilities it has incurred in the state's waters for such things as pilotage or towing.

NOTE: These rules apply only to non-public ships. Warships and similar public vessels are immune from the coastal state's jurisdiction (Articles 29–32 of the 1982 Convention).

23. The duties of the coastal state. As might be expected when dealing with an area of the sea considered to be the sovereign territory of the coastal state, that state's duties are more precisely restricted than its rights. The state has a duty to give appropriate publicity to dangers to navigation within its territorial sea and it has a duty to allow innocent passage without discrimination against the ships or cargoes of any foreign state.

24. Innocent passage in the territorial sea. Under Article 18 of the 1982 Convention (restating and amplifying Article 14 of the 1958 Territorial Sea Convention), the definition of innocent passage is implicitly the result of answering two questions: 'What is passage?' and 'What is innocent?'

25. 'Passage'. This means navigation through the territorial sea *for the purpose of* crossing that sea without going into internal waters or a port or roadstead, or *for the purpose of* proceeding to or from internal waters or calling at a port or roadstead. Passage must be continuous and expeditious, although stopping and anchoring are permissible if required for ordinary navigation or rendered necessary by *force majeure* or distress or the need to help others in peril on the sea.

The importance of the purpose for which navigation is made appears clearly in the decision of the International Court of Justice in the *Corfu Channel Case*

(1949). The court accepted that a British minesweeping operation in areas of the Corfu Channel that were part of Albanian territorial waters was not innocent passage, apparently on the basis that the voyage was not 'passage' since it was not aimed simply at crossing Albanian waters but was intended to collect samples of the mines to use as evidence against Albania in a British claim against that country.

26. 'Innocence'. As regards the *innocence* of passage, the 1958 Convention, in Article 14(4), required simply that it should not be 'prejudicial to the peace, good order, or security of the coastal state'. In the 1982 Convention it was thought necessary to amplify this provision considerably by appending a list of activities whose commission would render passage non-innocent. The list, in Article 19, includes:

(*a*) the threat or use of force against the sovereignty, territorial integrity, or political independence of the coastal state, or in any other manner in violation of the principles of international law embodied in the UN Charter;

(*b*) exercise or practice with weapons of any kind;

(*c*) collecting information prejudicial to the defence or security of the coastal state;

(*d*) acts of propaganda;

(*e*) launching, landing or taking on board any aircraft or military device;

(*f*) illegal embarking or disembarking of commodities, currencies or persons;

(*g*) wilful and serious pollution;

(*h*) any fishing activities;

(*i*) carrying out of research or survey activities;

(*j*) interfering with the coastal state's communications;

(*k*) any other activity not having a direct bearing on passage.

Under Article 16 of the 1958 Territorial Sea Convention and Article 25 of the 1982 Convention, the coastal state may take the 'necessary steps' to prevent passage which is not innocent.

All of the above provisions are in sections of the relevant conventions labelled 'Rules applicable to all ships', and it is therefore usually assumed that the right of innocent passage exists for foreign *warships* as well as for non-military vessels. This conclusion seems supported by the mention in this section of 'submarines' which are almost universally military in character. Nevertheless, some writers object that this may be incorrect because the matter was a very controversial point in the negotiations for both conventions and it is likely that, if the drafters had agreed that their draft was to deal with the question, they would have said so directly rather than leave it to a debatable inference.

The difficulty centres on the fact that a state is entitled to prevent non-innocent passage and the movements of a warship may be thought to be *prima facie* non-innocent until proven otherwise. With this in mind, many states have required prior authorisation for the passage of warships through their territorial seas. This might still be permissible, given that the coastal state's duty is to allow *innocent* passage – a point which the state must be presumed entitled to determine beforehand in the case of ships whose passage is *prima facie* non-innocent.

Thus, the granting of a right of innocent passage to warships need not, under the 1958 and 1982 conventions, imply *carte blanche* for foreign military vessels or a limitation on the right of the coastal state to protect its interests in its territorial waters.

27. Rights of the coastal state with regard to innocent passage. In general, the coastal state may suspend innocent passage temporarily in specified areas of its territorial sea if that is essential for its security. Under Article 21 of the 1982 Convention it may also promulgate and enforce regulations relating to navigation and ship traffic, protection of navigational aids and facilities, protection of cables and pipelines, conservation, fisheries regulation, environmental protection and pollution control, scientific research, and customs, fiscal and immigration controls.

The contiguous zone

28. Police powers. States for long claimed a right to exercise limited authority over a maritime zone immediately adjacent to their territorial sea for the purposes of policing and defence. The 1958 Territorial Sea Convention codified these rights under the heading of the 'contiguous zone'. The contiguous zone was considered to be part of the high seas, not territorial sea, but the coastal state was allowed to exercise there the control necessary to prevent or punish infringement of its customs, fiscal, immigration, or sanitary regulations within its territorial sea or internal waters. Under the 1958 Convention the contiguous zone was set at twelve miles wide, while under Article 33 of the 1982 Convention it is allowed to extend up to twenty-four nautical miles from the baselines from which the territorial sea is measured.

International straits

29. Under the 1958 Territorial Sea and Contiguous Zone Convention. Article 16(4) of the 1958 Convention provided that:

> There shall be no suspension of the innocent passage of foreign ships through straits which are used for international navigation between one part of the high seas and another part of the high seas or the territorial sea of a foreign state.

Although this provision was claimed by its proponents to accord with existing customary international law, a number of states opposed it at the negotiating conference and it was just barely adopted. The difficulty was that the rule stated, though perhaps useful in general, was argued by many states not to apply to situations in which they were particularly concerned.

The Arab states, for example, opposed it on the ground that it did not take sufficient account of the special situation of the Straits of Tiran which lead from the Red Sea into the Gulf of Aqaba. They argued that, as the Gulf was an enclosed body of water largely comprised (in their view) of the territorial seas of three Arab states, these three were entitled to adopt whatever regime of passage in the Straits seemed appropriate to them. Had this view been adopted in the Convention it would have allowed the three Arab states to prevent passage through the Straits by ships sailing to and from the Israeli port of Eilat at the northern end of the Gulf of Aqaba, since at that time none of them recognised Israel's existence as a state. Even apart from the question of the extent of the Arab states' territorial sea, the Arab claim also raised comparisons between the Gulf of Aqaba and other land-locked seas (e.g. the Baltic and the Black Seas) which, in the opinion of some writers, have become open seas only with the acquiescence of the coastal states or by special agreements.

The *Corfu Channel Case* (1949) revealed other problems with the customary law rule on straits. Albania argued that the channel which was the subject of its dispute with Britain was not in fact an international strait since it was not essential for international passage but only secondary, with the principal international shipping route lying further out to sea. The court determined, however, that the channel was an international strait in which there was a right of innocent passage, since 'the decisive criterion is ... its geographical situation as connecting two parts of the high seas and the fact of its being used for international navigation', even though it was 'not a necessary route' but only a 'useful' one.

With questions such as these capable of being raised about international straits it is not surprising that efforts were made to regularise certain situations by treaty. In 1881, for example, Argentina and Chile agreed to the perpetual neutralisation of the Straits of Magellan and to the guranteeing of free navigation in them. But perhaps the most important sea passage regulated by international agreement is that from the Mediterranean to the Black Sea through the Dardanelles and the Bosphorus. Although these straits are entirely within Turkish waters, they were placed under the supervision of an international commission empowered to ensure free navigation under the terms of the Lausanne Convention (1923). The Montreux Convention of 1936 returned sovereign control to Turkey but maintained unlimited navigation for merchant vessels and restricted navigation for warships.

On the other hand, a bilateral agreement between concerned coastal states may attempt to withdraw an international sea passage from the category of an international strait. In 1971, for example, Indonesia and Malaysia announced that the Malacca and Singapore Straits were not international, although they recognised that international shipping should have free use of these waterways according to 'the principle of innocent passage'.

30. International straits under the 1982 Convention. The somewhat unsatisfactory state of the law as indicated above threatened in the 1970s to become even more difficult once large numbers of states began claiming wider territorial seas. The twelve-mile limit adopted in the 1982 Convention will make territorial sea out of every strait which is less than twenty-four miles wide and there are said to be over a hundred of these in the world. The United States and some other leading maritime nations therefore insisted at the UNCLOS III negotiations that special provision should be made for navigation in international straits beyond what was provided for in the 1958 Convention, particularly having in mind that the old regime of innocent passage was argued not to apply to warships, submarines had been required to navigate through territorial waters on the surface rather than submerged, and coastal states had a right to prevent non-innocent passage (a categorisation which they were, in the first instance at least, entitled to determine themselves).

The result was that the 1982 Convention provides for a new right of *transit passage* in straits 'which are used for international navigation between one part of the high seas or an exclusive economic zone and another part of the high seas and an exclusive economic zone' (Article 37), except that the right does not apply to straits already regulated by 'long-standing international conventions' or to those through which there is an alternative route of similar convenience through high seas or an exclusive economic zone.

Under Articles 38 and 39 of the new Convention transit passage, which covers both navigation and overflight solely for the purpose of continuous and expeditious transit of the strait, is a right of all ships and aircraft (including by implication military ones) and may not be impeded or suspended. Transit passage must therefore be regarded as more favourable to foreign vessels (and aircraft) than innocent passage for ships was under the previous law of straits.

Where a strait runs between an island and the mainland and an alternative convenient route lies seaward of the island in the high seas or an exclusive economic zone, and where the strait connects the territorial waters of one state with international waters, the regime of transit passage does not apply and instead a strengthened (i.e. non-suspendable) right of innocent passage like that in Article 16(4) of the 1958 Convention applies.

Although the new Convention's provisions on straits passage restrict the coastal state's rights to limit transit, they apparently do not otherwise narrow its rights, as Article 34 states that:

> the regime of passage through straits ... shall not in other respects affect the exercise by the states bordering the straits of their sovereignty or jurisdiction over such waters and their air space, bed and subsoil.

Continental shelf

31. Encroachment on commonage. As noted at the beginning of this chapter, the victory of the principle of freedom of the seas in the classical period of international law meant that in general the sea was considered common to all and exercises of state authority were seen as exceptions to the fundamental principle of commonage. For nearly three centuries the principal exception was that of the territorial sea but, as was also indicated above, in recent decades additional exceptions have been carved out of the old common domain as technology and politics encourage states to claim more and more for their individual benefit. This process began in earnest with the development of a new legal regime for the continental shelf after World War II.

32. The developing concept of the continental shelf. Initially the notion of 'continental shelf' was essentially a geological one: it meant the relatively shallow and gently sloping continuation of the land out under the sea along a state's coastline. Very often at a depth of about 200 metres below sea-level the underwater terrain becomes noticeably more sloping and it is at that point that the geological continental shelf ends.

But for the lawyer the difficulty is that continental shelves are not all like this and some states from the geological point of view have little or no continental shelf. It was probably inevitable therefore that governments and their lawyers should try to develop definitions of the continental shelf that would apply uniformly to a wide variety of geological circumstances. The result has been the development of what some writers call the 'legal continental shelf' that has become continuously more and more abstracted from the real, geological continental shelf. It is necessary to trace this development through its various stages since the law on the matter is a composite of elements from all of them and is continuing to metamorphose into new and sometimes surprising shapes as time passes.

33. The original concept. In 1945 the president of the United States issued the *Truman Proclamation* in which he defined the continental shelf as 'an extension of the land mass of the coastal nation and thus naturally appurtenant to it'. This physical contiguity entitled the United States to regard 'the natural resources of the subsoil and seabed of the continental shelf beneath the high seas but contiguous to the coasts of the United States as appertaining to the United States, subject to its jurisdiction and control'.

The proclamation makes clear that behind this justification lay a variety of reasons for declaring a continental shelf regime:

(a) to promote development of natural resources;

(b) to encourage conservation and prudent utilization of them; and

(c) to enable the coastal state to protect itself by keeping 'close watch over activities off its shores which are of the nature necessary for utilization'.

The Truman Proclamation can thus be seen to reflect considerations in favour of an extension of state control over the sea that are remarkably similar to those advanced for the same purpose by John Selden in his debate with Grotius, and it is not surprising that once the first claim was made other states would recognise that they too had interests that could be served by declaring continental shelves of their own. But although a number of such proclamations had been made by 1951, the arbitrator in at least one case (the *Abu Dhabi Arbitration*) was not yet prepared to accept that the notion of the continental shelf had become a rule of customary international law since there were still, he said, 'so many ragged ends and unfilled blanks, so much that is merely tentative and exploratory'.

34. The 1958 Geneva Convention on the Continental Shelf. In an attempt to regularise the law on the matter, the Geneva Conference on the Law of the Sea adopted a treaty on the continental shelf that aimed to define the concept, establish its legal effects, and indicate how the boundaries of neighbouring continental shelves should be determined.

Article 1 of the Convention began the process of creating a legal continental shelf distinct from the geological one by defining the continental shelf as 'the seabed and subsoil of the submarine areas adjacent to the coast but outside the area of the territorial sea' *either* to a depth of 200 metres *or*, beyond that limit, 'to where the depth of the superjacent waters admits of the exploitation of the natural resources' (the *exploitability test*). Islands may also have a continental shelf of their own.

Article 2 outlined the nature of the coastal state's rights in the continental shelf, and in doing so developed some themes that were implicit in the original notion of the shelf as the prolongation of land territory under the high seas. The coastal state is said to have *sovereign rights* to explore and exploit the continental shelf (rather than 'sovereignty', which might be thought to entail more extensive rights); these sovereign rights are *exclusive* in the sense that no other state is entitled to explore or exploit the shelf without the coastal state's express consent. Arising (as they were thought to do) from the natural relationship of the land with the undersea terrain, the coastal state's rights existed without the need for an official proclamation of them by that state or for occupation by it. Finally, Article 2 emphasised that the rights in question apply only to the resources of the continental shelf seabed and subsoil but it included amongst those resources (for the first time in the law of the continental shelf) living organisms, provided they are sedentary species (i.e. those which, at the harvestable stage, do not swim off the seabed).

Article 3 made clear that the rights of the coastal state in the continental shelf do not affect the legal status of the waters above the shelf as high seas or the status of the air space above them.

Articles 4 and 5 indicated that the coastal state's rights do not entitle it to prevent the laying or maintenance of submarine cables or pipelines on the shelf or unjustifiably to interfere with navigation, fishing or conservation in the sea above the shelf, but that state may construct and operate installations for exploring or exploiting the shelf's resources and establish *safety zones* around them.

Article 6 provided for the delimitation of the continental shelf between neighbouring states. The Truman Proclamation had indicated that this should be done 'in accordance with equitable principles', but Article 6 merely said that, in the absence of agreement between the coastal states and unless special circumstances justify another boundary, then:

(*a*) states that stand opposite to each other across a body of water should draw a *median line*, i.e. one that runs roughly horizontally between their coasts in such a way that each point on it is an equal distance from the nearest points on the two states' territorial sea baselines;

(*b*) states that stand adjacent to each other should draw up what is sometimes called a *lateral equidistance line*, i.e. one that runs out in a roughly vertical direction from the point on the coast where the common land border of the two states reaches the sea in such a way that every point on it is equidistant from suitably chosen points on their territorial sea baselines.

35. Developments from the 1958 Convention. The 1958 Convention in many ways set the agenda for the future development of the continental shelf concept, either by providing the nucleus around which new law could crystallise or by serving as the backdrop against which the need for radical changes became more apparent. The two main areas which had to be dealt in the following twenty-five years were:

(*a*) the definition of the continental shelf (*see* **36**); and
(*b*) the delimitation of the continental shelf (*see* **37**).

Although these two facets of the subject are closely connected, both in theory and in the cases, since the definition of the shelf will obviously bear heavily on where the boundaries of it may be drawn, for simplicity's sake they are best considered separately.

36. The definition of the continental shelf. Although the 1958 Convention's 200-metre depth test accorded reasonably well with the geological nature of most continental shelf areas, the alternative test of exploitability could have led to an extension of continental shelf claims far beyond what the geology would warrant as technological advances made oil drilling and other extraction possible at ever greater depths.

The only obstacle to stretching continental shelves far out into the ocean was Article 1's requirement that the shelf be 'adjacent to the coast', although the failure to define 'adjacent' left the precise effect of this requirement in doubt. The International Court of Justice attempted in the *North Sea Continental Shelf Cases* (1969) to clarify the point by emphasising that what gives the coastal state its rights in the continental shelf is the fact that the submarine areas concerned may be deemed to be actually part of the territory over which the coastal State already has dominion – in the sense that, although covered with water, they are a prolongation or continuation of that territory, an extension of it under the sea.

While this reference to the original justification for the Truman Proclamation made eminent sense, the later development of the continental shelf concept tended, in fact if not in theory, to minimise its importance.

This happened partly because, as will be seen below, the World Court itself avoided emphasising its practical decisiveness in delimitation cases, and partly because strict adherence to it would have meant that states whose natural prolongation was cut off by deep ocean troughs near their coasts (as occurs along the western seaboard of North and South America) would have been deprived of significant continental shelf benefits.

The need was felt for a new definition of the legal continental shelf that would guarantee every coastal state a substantial minimum shelf (regardless of its natural endowments) and yet avoid the problems inherent in the exploitability test.

The result was that Article 76(1) of the 1982 Convention defined the legal continental shelf as the seabed and subsoil of the submarine areas that extend beyond the coastal state's territorial sea throughout the natural prolongation of its land territory to

(a) the outer edge of the continental margin; or

(b) a distance of 200 nautical miles from its territorial sea baselines where the outer edge of the continental margin does not extend up to that distance.

Article 76(5) indicates that in most cases the continental shelf may not extend beyond 350 nautical miles from the territorial sea baselines.

The effect of this definition is to detach the legal continental shelf quite decisively from the geological one, since the legal shelf is equated with the continental margin. The *continental margin* includes the geological continental shelf plus the more steeply inclined *continental slope* and the *continental rise* that drop from the edge of the shelf to the ocean floor. Furthermore, the distances incorporated in the definition mean that the minimum continental shelf for every coastal state will be 200 nautical miles, regardless of geological configuration. Geological factors will become relevant only for determining the outer edge of the continental margin if it extends beyond 200 nautical miles from the baselines. Article 76(4) and (5) provide complicated mathematical formulae for reckoning this.

37. Delimitation of the continental shelf. With the definition of the continental shelf having become increasingly detached from the natural configuration, it was probably inevitable that, in delimiting the contiguous continental shelves of neighbouring states, international law would also tend to move away from reliance on specific rules derived either from the supposed importance of certain natural features or from overly simplistic and arbitrary criteria.

Thus, while the 1958 Convention in Article 6 dealt with delimitation in terms of agreement, special circumstances and median or lateral equidistance lines, the 1982 Convention is much less restricted and precise. In Article 83(1) it foresees delimitation being 'by agreement on the basis of international law, as referred to in Article 38 of the Statute of the International Court of Justice, in order to achieve an equitable solution'. This is a very broad and rather amorphous standard that introduces into the treaty law on the matter such factors as international custom, general principles of law, and even judicial decisions and the writings of publicists.

The situation has been further complicated by the appearance of a new feature in the law of the sea. This is the *single maritime boundary*, which is intended, for good reasons of practical convenience and order, to combine continental shelf limits with the limits of a state's other maritime zones (such as the exclusive economic zone, as discussed below) so as to produce one coherent area of sea and seabed that is clearly subject to the sovereign rights of the coastal state. The theoretical difficulty is that the various maritime zones did not all originate from identical legal principles and the principles underlying one zone might seem to require its limits to be set differently from those of another type of zone based on other legal principles. Producing a single maritime boundary in these circumstances requires the combined skills of a juggler and a contortionist. The resulting awkwardness is a great encouragement to simplifying the whole business by eliding the rules for delimiting the continental shelf with those for delimitation of the other zones, particularly when the 200-nautical-mile limit is now available for all the zones.

These developments can be traced in a series of important and influential decisions by international tribunals over the past two decades.

38. The North Sea Continental Shelf Cases (1969). Although The Netherlands and Denmark had become parties to the 1958 Convention, West Germany had not. When the three countries brought their inevitable dispute about the delimitation of the continental shelf in the North Sea to the International Court of Justice, the ICJ had to consider the extent to which the 1958 Convention reflected customary law (which would be binding on Germany), particularly with respect to the Convention's provisions on delimitation of the continental shelves of adjacent states.

As noted above (*see* **36**), the court accepted that the basic concept of the continental shelf as the natural prolongation of the land territory had entered international law and it held that Article 2 of the Convention did reflect customary international law on the rights of the coastal state in its own continental shelf. Article 6, however, did not appear to the court a suitable provision around which a rule of customary law could form nor was it declaratory of pre-existing custom. As a matter of customary law, therefore, delimitation had to be done, not according to the equidistance rules of Article 6, but according to 'certain basic legal notions' that were supported by *opinio juris*. These were that delimitation had to be arrived at by agreement between the parties and in accordance with 'equitable principles'.

The apportionment should, in the words of the court, be made:

> in such a way as to leave as much as possible to each party all those parts of the continental shelf that constitute a natural prolongation of its land territory ... without encroachment on the natural prolongation of the land territory of the other.

Factors to be taken into account when doing this were:

(*a*) the general configuration of the coasts as well as the presence of any special or unusual features;

(*b*) physical and geological structure and the natural resources of the continental shelf;

(*c*) a 'reasonable degree of proportionality' between the extent of each state's continental shelf area and the length of its coast, since 'equity does not necessarily imply equality' nor does it involve 'completely refashioning nature' so as to give equal shelf areas to states with unequal lengths of coastline.

39. The English Channel Arbitration (1977–1978). In this arbitration decision to settle the continental shelf line between England and France in the English Channel the tribunal also wrestled with the applicability of Article 6 of the 1958 Convention, to which both states were parties. Here also rigid use of a median line equidistant between the two states was avoided on the ground that Article 6's reference to 'special circumstances' justifying another boundary line created 'a combined equidistance-special circumstances rule'. The effect of this rule was that the obligation to apply the equidistance principle was always qualified by the need to take account of relevant special circumstances. The role of the 'special circumstances' condition in Article 6 was to ensure an equitable delimitation.

Consequently, 'the appropriateness of the equidistance method or any other method for the purpose of effecting an equitable delimitation is a function or reflection of the geographical and other relevant circumstances of each particular case'.

In the circumstances of the English Channel the median line had to be modified to take some account of the Scilly Islands (which were held to justify pushing the dividing line somewhat further towards France, so enlarging Britain's continental shelf) and of the Channel Islands (which were given a twelve-mile shelf as an enclave within France's overall continental shelf).

40. Continental Shelf (Tunisia *v*. Libya) Case (1982). The ICJ developed its notion of an equitable solution further when Tunisia and Libya (neither of which were parties to the 1958 Convention) brought their continental shelf dispute to it. The court said that 'each continental shelf case should be considered and judged on its own merits, having regard to its peculiar circumstances', so that even a fundamental principle such as that defining the continental shelf as the natural prolongation of land territory could be disregarded when the shelf area in question was a prolongation of the territory of both parties.

In such circumstances, the court felt:

> bound to apply equitable principles as part of international law, and to balance up the various considerations which it regards as relevant in order to produce an equitable result. While it is clear that no rigid rules exist as to the exact weight to be attached to each element in the case, this is very far from being an exercise of discretion or conciliation; nor is it an operation of distributive justice.

Thus, the court would not, in its words, 'overconceptualise' the principles relating to continental shelf delimitation, nor would it refashion nature to allocate economic or other benefits more 'fairly' than geography had already done.

41. The Gulf of Maine Case (1984). In this dispute about the continental shelf lying between Maine and Nova Scotia, Canada and the United States asked a special five-judge chamber of the ICJ to delimit a single maritime boundary for the two countries' continental shelves and their exclusive fishing zones. The effect of searching for a single boundary was that the court felt free to take notice of the law on the delimitation of the continental shelf but to depart from it where necessary in search of international custom formed as a composite of that law and the law on other maritime zones.

This involved looking 'for a few basic principles, which lay down guidelines to be followed with a view to an essential objective', rather than for 'a set of rules which are not there', having in mind that 'each specific case is, in the final analysis, different from all the others'.

The basic principles sought could be reflected in conventions, international custom or judicial decisions. The relevant evidence for these ranged from the 1958 Convention, through the *North Sea Continental Shelf Case* and the *English Channel Arbitration*, to the 1982 Convention (which, though not in force, was considered to embody, in relevant provisions 'adopted without any objections', a 'consensus' on the continental shelf and exclusive economic zone legal regimes).

The underlying principles in these sources made it inappropriate to insist exclusively on rules of 'equidistance', 'natural prolongation', 'median lines', 'lateral equidistance lines' or even a 'combined equidistance-special circumstances rule'. Given that 'in this particular field ideas age very quickly', one can state as a matter of the obligatory principles of international law only that the 'fundamental norm' is:

(*a*) No maritime boundary in these cases can be laid down unilaterally but only by agreement, failing which recourse should be had to delimitation by a third party; and

(*b*) delimitation in either case is to be by application of 'equitable criteria' and by the use of practical methods capable of ensuring, with regard to the geographic configuration of the area and other relevant circumstances, an equitable result.

There has been 'no systematic definition of the equitable criteria' involved, a thing that would be difficult in any event 'because of their highly variable adaptability to different concrete situations'. The court therefore considered the various criteria proposed by the two parties, but found that none by itself provided a complete solution of the problem since each, if applied throughout, would have slighted some significant consideration that had to be taken into account.

This was a particular problem when a single maritime boundary was requested since in such a case 'it is necessary ... to rule out the application of any criterion found to be typically and exclusively bound up with one alone of the two natural entities that have to be delimited in conjunction'. That was likely to be a consideration of growing importance as states sought single maritime boundaries more frequently, so that 'preference will henceforth inevitably be given to criteria that, because of their neutral character, are best suited for use in a multi-purpose delimitation'.

Bearing all this in mind, the court felt 'bound' to turn to 'criteria more especially derived from geography'. Consequently:

it is inevitable that the ... [court's] basic choice should favour a criterion long held to be as equitable as it is simple, namely that in principle, while having regard to the special circumstances of the case, one should aim at an equal division of areas where the maritime projections of the coasts [of the states concerned] ... converge and overlap.

This basic criterion must be applied flexibly, however, with corrections made, as necessary, in light of three *auxiliary criteria*:

(*a*) 'a fair measure of weight' should be given to any significant difference within the delimitation area between the lengths of the parties' respective coastlines;

(*b*) it is equitable partially to correct any application of the basic criterion that would result in cutting off one coastline, or part of it, from its appropriate projection across the maritime expanses to be divided;

(*c*) there may be a necessity of granting partial effect to the presence of a geographical feature such as an island or group of islands lying off a coast, when strict application of the basic criterion might entail giving them full effect or, alternatively, no effect.

42. Continental Shelf (Libya *v*. Malta) Case (1985). The full ICJ was asked in this case to delimit only the continental shelf between Libya and Malta and did not feel inclined to pursue the broad hint by the judges in the *Gulf of Maine Case* that future demarcation of such shelves would best be done in the context of a single maritime boundary.

The decision therefore concentrated on the criteria appropriate to continental shelf delimitation. Libya argued that these were:

(*a*) the effect of the shelf's being a prolongation of the land terrain; and

(*b*) proportionality between lengths of coastline and areas of continental shelf allotted to each state.

Malta, in contrast, requested that a median line be drawn.

The court began its examination of the problem by rejecting the idea that equity allowed it simply to aim at 'abstract justice'. Rather, the ICJ should achieve 'justice according to the rule of law', which required its judgments to display 'consistency and a degree of predictability' while reconciling the peculiar circumstances of a particular case with 'equitable principles ... having a more general validity'. The court emphasised the 'normative character' of equitable principles and listed a number which had been stated in previous cases. In discussing equitable principles in this way the court seemed to be trying to draw back from the implication in the *Gulf of Maine Case* that the only general rule of international law in these cases was that delimitation should be equitable.

But, as might have been expected, the court refused to accept any single criterion as decisive. In particular, it rejected the natural prolongation and related arguments about geophysical formations on the seabed. This conclusion was reached on the novel ground that the law on the matter now arose from the 1982 Law of the Sea Convention, even though this was not yet in force. The court said that 'the development of the law' enabled a state to claim continental shelf up to 200 miles from its coast (whatever the geological characteristics of the seabed), so that when opposite states like Libya and Malta are less than 400 miles apart, their legal continental shelves inevitably overlap. Basically, therefore, delimitation should begin by applying 'a criterion of distance from the coast' to divide up the space between the two states equitably.

This emphasis on distance naturally led to drawing a line equidistant from both coasts – a median line. This had to be tested and perhaps modified, however, in the light of other relevant circumstances. In this case, these included:

(a) the considerable disparity between the length of Libya's coastline (192 miles) and that of Malta's (24 miles);

(b) the placing of basepoints for drawing the line (a small island off Malta's coast was discounted in this connection); and

(c) the 'general geographical context'.

The result was that the final delimitation line was moved northward from the median line to achieve a result equitable to Libya as well as to Malta.

43. Islands and the Rockall problem. A once-obscure aspect of continental shelf law that has grown in importance in recent years is the situation of islands.

In principle, under Article 1 of the 1958 Continental Shelf Convention 'islands' may have shelves to the same extent as mainland areas. Unfortunately, no definition of an 'island' was given in the Convention, although the meaning of the word for continental shelf purposes was usually inferred to be the same as that in the 1958 Territorial Sea Convention, Article 10: 'An island is a naturally-formed area of land, surrounded by water, which is above water at high tide.'

The 1982 Convention sets out a general legal regime for islands in Article 121. Article 121(2) indicates that the continental shelf of an island is to be determined in accordance with the Convention's provisions for other land territory, with the exception, however, that:

Rocks which cannot sustain human habitation or economic life of their own shall have no exclusive economic zone or continental shelf (Article 121(3)).

Thus, the new law of the sea is less generous with respect to the generation of continental shelf rights by islands than was the previous legal regime.

The difference could be critical in resolving the competing claims of Britain, Ireland, Denmark and Iceland over continental shelf areas around Rockall, a granite crag rising some sixty feet above normal sea level at a spot about 240 miles west of the Hebrides.

Initially a *terra nullius*, Rockall was formally annexed by the United Kingdom in 1955 for security reasons. In 1974 an Order in Council under the Continental Shelf Act 1964 claimed as UK continental shelf an area of some 52,000 square miles around Rockall on what is known as the Rockall Plateau, an undersea shelf that is physically separate from, and not a natural prolongation of, the continental shelves of any of the contending states.

Thus an important issue in the dispute is whether Rockall may legally have a continental shelf of its own under the current law of the sea. Both Ireland and Denmark argue that it may not, since it cannot sustain human habitation or economic life of its own.

But what constitutes 'sustaining' in this context is itself unclear. Modern technology may make almost anything possible, as Scottish adventurer Tom McClean demonstrated in the summer of 1985 by living on Rockall for nearly forty days in a plywood box fitted out with special equipment and rations.

It seems likely that the ultimate resolution of the dispute will have to transcend such definitional issues and be based on equitable principles.

44. Interests of disadvantaged states. The 1982 Convention's recognition of extensive continental shelf rights beyond 200 nautical miles from the coastline was a significant inroad into the 'commonage' of the high seas and many affected states sought in the Convention a *quid pro quo* for agreeing to an arrangement so advantageous to certain coastal states. This appears in Article 82, which provides that states exploiting continental shelf resources beyond the 200 mile line should make percentage payments or contributions in kind from their annual production to an International Sea-Bed Authority established under the Convention. The Authority will distribute them to the parties to the treaty 'on the basis of equitable sharing criteria, taking into account the interests and needs of developing States, particularly the least developed and the land-locked among them' (*see* also **65**).

Exclusive fishing zone: exclusive economic zone

45. Exclusive fishing zones. While states were developing the idea of continental shelf rights over the resources of the seabed and subsoil a parallel development was taking place with regard to state rights over the waters beyond their territorial seas. Concern about conservation of fisheries and the maintenance of national fishing industries led a number of Latin American states to proclaim in the late 1940s their exclusive right to regulate fishing up to 200 miles from their coasts. But the idea of such *exclusive fishing zones* was not generally adopted or accepted as law for many years.

Nevertheless a number of states, and in particular Iceland, continued to assert their right to fishing zones. The Icelandic claim to a twelve-mile zone aroused British opposition in the late 1950s, although it was not until Iceland extended its zone to fifty miles in 1971 that the dispute threatened the two countries' relations to such an extent that it was referred to the International Court of Justice. In 1974 the court delivered its judgment in the *Fisheries Jurisdiction Case (Merits)*.

Although the ICJ did not feel called upon to determine whether 50-mile or 200-mile zones were legal, the court did agree that twelve-mile exclusive fishing zones had been accepted in customary international law. Furthermore, the court indicated that coastal states which were 'in a situation of special dependence' on coastal fisheries had what it called 'preferential rights' of fishing in waters adjacent to their own fisheries zones. This validation of coastal state rights arising from a need to protect economic interests and resources was reminiscent of Selden's arguments for state control of the sea and gave a good indication of the direction in which the law on this subject was heading.

46. Exclusive economic zones. The next step forward was naturally and inevitably to expand state regulation from jurisdiction over fishing to control of all economic activity in the areas concerned, leading to the creation of *exclusive economic zones* (EEZs). The legal standing of claims to EEZs was much disputed even as recently as the early 1980s, but events moved rapidly after the adoption of the Law of the Sea Convention in 1982. Some twenty articles in the Convention deal with the EEZ.

Article 56 recognises the coastal state's 'sovereign rights' in the EEZ for 'exploring and exploiting, conserving and managing the natural resources, whether living or non-living' of the zone's waters and for exploiting the zone's waters for such things as producing energy from wave power. Article 57 provides that the EEZ may not be more than 200 nautical miles wide. Article 58 maintains the rights of other states to navigation and overflight in the EEZ, subject to the legitimate regulations applied by the coastal state. Under Article 60 the coastal state is entitled to control the building of artificial islands, drilling platforms and other installations in the EEZ, and by Articles 61 and 62 the coastal state may enforce conservation measures and fishing quotas. Delimitation of the EEZs of neighbouring states is, according to Article 74, to be 'by agreement on the basis of international law', as referred to in Article 38 of the ICJ Statute, 'in order to achieve an equitable solution'. Failing that, complicated dispute settlement procedures, laid down elsewhere in the Convention, are to be followed.

These provisions, combined with the Convention's treatment of the continental shelf, have the effect of making the EEZ and the shelf overlap up to a distance of 200 miles from the coast, thus giving the coastal state exclusive sovereign rights over all the resources of the sea up to that limit. That overlapping is one of the most powerful arguments for the adoption of *single maritime boundaries,* as discussed above (*see* 37).

Pending the 1982 Convention's entry into force the question arose whether this EEZ regime could be considered legally operative. In the *Continental Shelf (Tunisia* v. *Libya) Case* (1982) the World Court indicated that the EEZ 'may be regarded as part of modern international law'. In March 1983 the president of the United States proclaimed an American EEZ of 200 miles, justifying this as 'consistent' with those 'fair and balanced' Convention provisions 'with respect to traditional uses of the oceans which generally confirm existing maritime law and practice'. Both of these statements reflect what appears to be a general international consensus that the regime of the 200 mile EEZ has become an element of customary international law.

47. The position of the European Community. Upon signing the new Convention on 7 December 1984, the EEC issued a declaration relating to the organisation's competence in matters covered by that treaty. This competence was said to extend to 'conservation and management of sea fishing resources' and 'protection and preservation of the marine environment'. The implication of this statement would appear to be that certain aspects of the exclusive economic zone allowed by the Convention would fall within the existing powers of the EEC, while others (e.g. those relating to energy from wave power) remain to be developed. Since 1977 the EEC has maintained a 200 mile fishing zone, with responsibility over the zone's 'biological resources'.

The high seas

48. The definition. Under Article 1 of the 1958 Geneva Convention on the High Seas, the term 'high seas' is defined to mean 'all parts of the sea that are not included in the territorial seas or in the internal waters of a state'. The 1982 Convention, however, considerably reduces the extent of high seas by stating in Article 86 that the high seas legal regime does not operate in

(*a*) the exclusive economic zone;

(*b*) the territorial sea or internal waters;

(*c*) the waters of an archipelagic state (for which the Convention establishes a special regime).

Thus, waters up to 200 miles from the coast are excluded from the category of high seas. This represents a significant diminution in the 'commonage' traditionally protected by the law of the sea (*see* 6).

Nevertheless, within what is left of the high seas international law has generally maintained the traditional rights and duties of states, which may conveniently be examined under the headings of freedom of the seas (*see* **49-51**), nationality of ships (*see* **52-54**), jurisdiction (*see* **55-58**) and hot pursuit (*see* **59**).

Freedom of the seas

49. No state sovereignty. Article 87 of the 1982 Convention, which expands Article 2 of the 1958 Convention, emphasises that the high seas are open to all states and indicates that freedom of the seas comprises freedom of navigation and overflight, freedom to lay submarine cables and pipelines and to construct artificial islands and other permitted installations, and freedom of fishing and of scientific research. These freedoms are to be exercised 'with due regard' for the interests of other states which are exercising their own rights to freedom of the seas. Article 89 of the new Convention sets out the logical corollary of these freedoms, namely that no state 'may validly purport to subject any part of the high seas to its sovereignty'.

50. Freedom of the seas and military uses. In the past, some naval powers have claimed certain rights over the high seas with respect to military activities of one kind or another. These were initially limited to a claimed right to conduct naval exercises and to carry on gunnery and bombing practice. This claim was extended to include weapons testing, surveillance and spying activities, the right to make a naval 'demonstration' to intimidate coastal states, and the right to declare large areas of the high seas closed in connection with the testing of nuclear weapons.

These 'rights' were said to be enshrined in customary international law, and, to the extent that they may have been, would appear to come within a reference in Article 87 of the new Convention to exercise of freedom of the seas 'under the conditions laid down ... by other rules of international law'. It must be noted, however, that several of these 'rights' could no longer be exercised without falling foul of modern international law. The naval demonstration or show of force, for example, could constitute a violation of Article 2(4) of the UN Charter, which prohibits the threat of force in any manner inconsistent with the purposes of the United Nations.

51. Freedom of the seas and nuclear weapons. The claimed 'right' of states to use the sea for nuclear weapons tests has also come under considerable pressure in recent decades. In the *Nuclear Test Cases* (1974) Australia argued before the International Court of Justice that France had violated the freedom of the seas by conducting nuclear tests in the Pacific that required closing off a large area of the ocean. Some writers argue that in general nuclear tests above ground (and hence in territorial waters and high seas) have themselves become illegal under customary international law that developed out of the Nuclear Test Ban Treaty of 1963. Relevant also in this connection is Article 88 of the new Law of the Sea Convention, which states flatly: 'The high seas shall be reserved for peaceful purposes'.

Two interesting attempts have been made by groups of states to establish *nuclear free zones* in which nuclear testing would be banned.

(a) The *Treaty for the Prohibition of Nuclear Weapons in Latin America* (1967), the 'Tlatelolco Treaty', commits the parties to preventing tests of 'any nuclear weapons' in their territorial sea, air space 'and any other space over which the state exercises sovereignty in accordance with its own legislation ' – an apparent reference to fishing zones and EEZs.

(b) In 1985 the nations of the South Pacific Forum (including Australia and New Zealand) adopted the *South Pacific Nuclear Free Zone Treaty*, the 'Rarotonga Treaty'. Under Article 6 of this agreement each party undertakes to prevent the testing of any nuclear explosive device in its territory and not to assist or encourage nuclear testing by any other state. The South Pacific Nuclear Free Zone is defined as stretching from the western shores of Australia to a line in the eastern Pacific where it meets the zone of application of the Tlatelolco Treaty, although Article 2 makes clear that nothing in the treaty shall prejudice or affect the rights of any state *under international law* with regard to freedom of the seas.

Nationality of ships

52. Control of shipping. In the as yet decentralised international system of modern times, implementation of international law with respect to ships depends heavily on the connection between any ship and the particular state with which it is most closely associated. This association is usually known as the 'nationality' of the ship.

Article 8 of the 1958 Convention and Article 91 of the 1982 Convention both provide that every state

> shall fix the conditions for the grant of its nationality to ships, for the registration of ships in its territory, and for the right to fly its flag. Ships have the nationality of the state whose flag they are entitled to fly. There must be a genuine link between the state and the ship.

53. Flags of convenience. The 'genuine link' requirement, which recalls that held by the ICJ in the *Nottebohm Case* (*see* 10:23) to apply to the nationality of individuals, is intended to deal with the problem of 'flags of convenience' whereby states (notably Panama and Liberia) grant their nationality to many foreign-owned ships with which those states have little connection and over which they exercise at best minimum control.

But, given the difficulties of applying and enforcing the genuine link test, this practice seems unlikely to be much inhibited by these provisions.

54. Stateless ships. A ship without a flag or flying the flags of more than one state is in a position similar to that of a stateless person, unable to seek the protection of any state.

This point was critical in the Privy Council judgment in *Molvan* v. *Attorney-General for Palestine* (1948). In 1946, the ship *Asya*, owned by Molvan, was seized by the British Royal Navy in international waters off the coast of Palestine on suspicion of transporting illegal Jewish immigrants into that British mandate territory. During the encounter, the ship at first flew no flag, then a Turkish banner, and finally what was described as the 'Zionist flag', although there was no Zionist state at the time. The Privy Council held that, having in effect no legitimate flag, the *Asya* could not claim the protection of any state nor could any state claim that any principle of international law was broken by her seizure.

Jurisdiction over ships

55. The general rule. Since the high seas are not under the sovereignty of any state and are open to the ships of all states by virtue of the freedom of the seas, in theory no state should be entitled to exercise jurisdiction on the high seas over the ships of any other state. Put positively, the general rule, as stated in Article 92 of the new Convention, is that ships, 'save in exceptional cases expressly provided for in international treaties or in this Convention, shall be subject to … [the flag state's] exclusive jurisdiction on the high seas'.

56. Exceptional cases: the right of visit and flag verification. The most important of the exceptions to the general rule centre around the rights of visit and flag verification.

Article 22 of the 1958 High Seas Convention, as supplemented by Article 100 of the new Convention, provides that a warship may board a foreign private or commercial ship on the high seas to check whether it has a right to show the flag it is flying if there is 'reasonable ground for suspecting' that the foreign vessel is engaged in piracy, the slave trade, or unauthorised broadcasting, or that it has no nationality, or that, though not revealing its true nationality, the ship is in reality of the same nationality as the warship.

Interestingly, the right of visit is not stated to apply against ships suspected of illicit drug trafficking, although Article 108 of the 1982 Convention requires states to 'co-operate' in the suppression of this traffic.

If the right of visit turns out to have been exercised without proper justification, the boarded ship 'shall be compensated for any loss or damage that may have been sustained'.

Dealing as they do with the law of the sea in peacetime, neither convention provides for any right of a state at war to interfere with neutral shipping suspected of carrying war materiel to the enemy. This practice has nevertheless been evident on a number of occasions over the past century. Britain, against much international opposition, asserted such a right in both World Wars and as recently as January 1986, Iranian naval vessels stopped and searched British and American commercial ships in the Gulf on suspicion of their carrying weapons to Iraq.

57. Piracy. If a stopped ship is found to be a pirate vessel, i.e. one engaged in piracy *jure gentium* ('according to the law of nations', rather than national law), it is subject to seizure and its crew liable to arrest and prosecution in the seizing state's national courts, under Article 19 of the 1958 Convention and Article 105 of the 1982 Convention.

Piracy is defined in Article 101 of the new Convention as consisting of any illegal acts of violence or detention, or any act of depredation, committed for private ends by the crew or passengers of a private ship or aircraft and directed, on the high seas or outside the jurisdiction of any state, against another ship or aircraft or persons or property on it.

58. Jurisdictional duties of a flag state. Article 94 of the new Convention, expanding Article 10 of the 1958 Convention, requires the flag state to maintain a register of ships under its flag and to assume jurisdiction over administrative, technical and social matters concerning the ship. The flag state must also take the necessary measures to ensure safety at sea with regard to the construction and manning of ships and their use of signals and communications.

Hot pursuit

59. For policing purposes. A traditional right of coastal states that has been incorporated into both the 1958 and the 1982 conventions is that of *hot pursuit*.

Under Article 23 of the earlier treaty a foreign ship reasonably suspected of breaking the coastal state's law within its internal waters, territorial sea or contiguous zone may be immediately pursued onto the high seas and halted there and arrested. Article 111 of the new Convention extends the right of hot pursuit to cover ships in the exclusive economic zone or continental shelf area which commit violations of laws applying to those zones.

Certain conditions must be met;

(*a*) the coastal state's authorities must have good reason to believe that the ship has violated the laws or regulations of that state;

(*b*) the suspect ship must be warned by visual or auditory signal to stop, a radio message being impermissible as it might be sent from some distance by a vessel incapable of undertaking the pursuit, and only after this direct order has been disobeyed may the pursuit commence;

(*c*) the pursuit must be begun while the foreign ship is still within one of the coastal state's maritime zones and the pursuit must continue uninterruptedly onto the high seas;

(*d*) the pursuing craft must be a government ship or airplane and not a private one.

The right of hot pursuit terminates if the escaping ship reaches the territorial sea of its own state or that of a third state.

In the *I'm Alone Case* (1935), the American Coast Guard, after a long pursuit beginning in what was in effect the contiguous zone of the United States and ending on the high seas, sank a British schooner suspected of 'bootlegging' liquor into the United States during prohibition. An international commission, acting on the assumption that the United States had a right of hot pursuit in these circumstances (although this was disputed), determined that the American authorities had been entitled to 'use necessary and reasonable force for the purpose ... of boarding, searching, seizing and bringing into port the suspected vessel'. But the admittedly intentional sinking of the *I'm Alone* was held not justified by hot pursuit.

The deep sea-bed

60. New commercial opportunities. Perhaps in no other area of the law of the sea has the clash of technology, law and politics been so marked as on the legal regime of the deep sea-bed and its exploitation.

The technological achievements of the industrially developed countries have made possible the mining of mineral deposits in the form of 'manganese nodules' lying on the deep sea-bed. These countries would like, in the spirit of John Selden, to control and profit from this possibility themselves, while states that lack the technology but claim an interest in the commonage of the sea want deep sea-bed resources exploited under international control for the benefit of all.

61. The basic principle. In 1970 the United Nations General Assembly, by a vote of 104 in favour, none against and 14 abstentions, adopted in Resolution 2749(XXV) a *Declaration of Principles Governing the Sea-Bed and the Ocean Floor* beyond national jurisdiction. Proclaiming the sea-bed and its resources the 'common heritage of mankind' and not subject to appropriation by any state or person or to any claim of sovereignty or sovereign rights, the declaration called for regulation of all activities there by an international regime 'for the benefit of mankind as a whole, irrespective of the geographical location of states, whether land-locked or coastal, and taking into particular consideration the interests and needs of the developing countries'.

Some writers argue that this resolution, adopted without opposition by a large majority of the United Nations members at the time, laid the basis for the development in customary international law of the principle that deep sea-bed mining must be subject to international regulation, a principle that was strengthened by the emergence of a consensus in its favour during the negotiations on the new Convention.

The principle of an international regime was seen by many to present an opportunity of moving international law much further along the road to a supra-national system in which the interests of individual states would be subordinated to the will of the international community, in the process promoting a fairer international economic order.

62. Negotiations at UNCLOS III. The negotiations on the new treaty began in 1973 and deep-sea mining proved a major point of contention throughout. Although the principle of international regulation was generally accepted, the questions remained whether (and how) international and national mining operations could be coordinated under international supervision.

Eventually, a compromise was reached on the basis of a *parallel system*: national companies and an international body would work in parallel in separate sections of each deep-sea mining zone.

When it came to working out the details of this mechanism, the negotiations were prolonged and difficult but by 1980 it appeared that general agreement had been achieved on most points. The arrival of the Reagan Administration in the United States introduced a new factor into the proceedings, however, as America first delayed discussion of the final details and then announced that, if American demands for significant changes in the already delicately balanced draft text were not accepted, the United States would not become a party to the Convention. Some observers interpreted these tactics as a deliberate attempt to sabotage the Convention, whose foreshadowing of a strong international legal order was thought to be ideologically objectionable to the American government.

The result was that the Convention was adopted by the conference without full American support and opened for signature in 1982. In the meantime, the United States and a number of other technologically developed countries put in place an alternative 'temporary' legal regime of interlocking national legislation. Thus, both the law of the Convention and of the national regimes must be examined.

Deep sea-bed mining in the 1982 Convention

63. Basic principles and structure of the Convention regime. Reaffirming the principles of the 'common heritage of mankind' (Article 136), the prohibition of national sovereignty or sovereign rights in the deep sea-bed (Article 137), and the exploitation of the area's resources for the benefit of mankind (Article 140), the Convention adopts the goal of ensuring 'orderly, safe and rational management' of sea-bed exploitation (Article 150). It enshrines the parallel system in Article 153 but makes clear that activities under it 'shall be organized, carried out and controlled' by an *International Sea-Bed Authority* set up under Articles 156–188.

[margin note: Principles are elaborated in detail in Art 133–91 & Annex's III & IV]

64. The Authority. The Authority will have:

(*a*) an Assembly (in which every party will have a seat) to decide policy questions by a two-thirds majority vote;

(*b*) a Council (of thirty-six states elected by a system designed to ensure the representation of the various international political and economic groupings) to take executive decisions by two-thirds or three-quarters majority vote or by consensus, depending in essence upon the sensitivity and importance of the matter at issue;

(*c*) an Economic Planning Commission and a Legal and Technical Commission to carry out Council decisions;

(*d*) an Enterprise which will actually carry out the resources exploitation to be undertaken by the Authority.

65. Funding. Funds to pay for the Authority's work will come initially from assessments levied on the Convention's parties and then from the income of the Enterprise and a tax on the revenues of the national mining companies working under the parallel system. In time, the Authority might be expected to become the first supra-national body to pay for itself (and so be freed from political manipulation or pressure by state contributors). It will also be the first to distribute the benefits of self-generated income to needy states (Article 160).

66. Technology transfer. The Enterprise, as an international organ, will to begin with have no resources of equipment or expertise at its disposal. Article 144 therefore provides for what is called 'the transfer of technology', 'under fair and reasonable terms and conditions', from the technologically advanced countries to the Enterprise for its use. In time, the Enterprise could be expected to develop into a technological power in its own right.

67. Protectionism. One of the thorniest problems in the negotiations on deep sea-bed mining was whether the Authority's operations should take place in what might be called a 'free enterprise' context or in the context of production quotas and other arrangements designed to control the world market in the minerals produced. Some developing states whose economies rely on the export of minerals feared that deep-sea mining could flood the market and depress raw material prices, giving an advantage to the industrial importers while ruining the raw material exporters.

Article 150 attempts to deal with the question 'in such a manner as to foster healthy development of the world economy and balanced growth of world trade' through the promotion of 'just and stable prices remunerative to producers and fair to consumers' and the promotion of 'long-term equilibrium between supply and demand'. The provision goes on to specify as one of the Convention's aims 'the protection of developing countries from adverse effects on their economies or on their export earnings' caused by deep sea-bed mining.

Interlocking national legal regimes

68. American model. Beginning with the US Deep Seabed Hard Mineral Resources Act 1980, a number of developed countries moved to set up alternative national legal arrangements regulating their own citizens' deep sea-bed activities. The West German Act on Interim Regulation of Deep Seabed Mining 1980 was followed by the UK Deep Sea Mining (Temporary Provisions) Act 1981 and similar statutes in the Soviet Union, France and Japan.

69. The legal importance of similarity. The US, UK and West German statutes (*see* **68**) are particularly comparable in many respects and this is evidently not by accident. General uniformity in the practice of different states makes cooperation easier. It also helps lay the basis for the generation of customary international law which the states concerned may point to, along with treaties, as legitimising their activities outside the regime of the new Convention.

70. 'Reciprocating state' status. The key element in this interlocking pattern of national legislation was imposed from the beginning by the American statute: each state will recognise and honour the deep-sea mining licenses or permits issued by *reciprocating states*. These are states which have adopted similar laws and which in turn will recognise the licenses and permits of other reciprocating states. The designation of another country as a reciprocating state is not automatic but is to be decided upon by the appropriate government minister after assessing the deep-sea mining laws of the other country to determine whether they are substantially like the law of the state making the designation.

The effect of this approach is to make reciprocating state status a benefit to be earned by aligning one's own laws with those of the designating state. Failure to do this could expose a non-reciprocating state's deep-sea mining operations to challenge by the reciprocating states. Interested countries are therefore more or less obliged to fall into line with the American system or risk being squeezed out, despite the fact that the reciprocating system initially had no basis in international law.

71. Dispute settlement. A major difficulty with a system of national laws without the sort of supra-national Authority which the Convention sets up is that it cannot provide more than diplomacy and pressure as a means for settling deep-sea mining disputes. Each country must simply hope to be recognised by the others as a reciprocating state and then to 'stake out' claims in desirable areas before anybody else does. The United States statute makes clear that this is the situation envisaged. Section 102 says the US will settle disputes by peaceful means in the event of 'interference' by foreigners in the activities of American deep-sea mining companies.

72. Licensing. The three national statutes being compared provide for a two-stage system of licenses or permits for mining activities, giving authorisation in the first instance only for exploratory work with approval for actual mining being given at a later stage. Applicants are required to show that they have the capacity to carry on safe and proper mining operations and are able to submit and execute acceptable plans of exploration and exploitation.

73. Exploration and exploitation. Exploration has been allowed under the statutes as from 1981 but exploitation may not begin until 1 January 1988.

74. Effect of national licensing on the Convention regime. Each of the three statutes provides that no person subject to them may explore or exploit without a license. A hidden effect of this prohibition is that no mining company or individual expert would be allowed to work with the Convention's Enterprise on deep-sea mining without the permission of the home state. Since the Enterprise must depend on national personnel and expertise to begin its operations, the effect of this requirement could be to handicap severely mining under the Convention.

75. Special taxes or levies. Another similarity of the three laws is that each provides for some kind of special tax or levy on the earnings of deep-sea mining companies, with the money collected being paid into a special fund. If the Law of the Sea Convention comes into force for the state concerned, monies from the fund are to be paid to the International Sea-Bed Authority for disbursement according to the Convention's provisions.

The American and British statutes have the fund remaining in existence for ten years from the date of the Act. If at the end of that period the Convention is not yet in force for the state concerned (i.e. that state has refused to become a party), then the monies in the fund may be used for other purposes.

The German Act is closer to the spirit of the Convention on this point in that it imposes no time limit on the life of the fund and provides that monies in it are to be used for 'development aid purposes'.

76. The legality of national regimes. Two legal objections may be raised against these statutes:

(*a*) that they may amount to an assertion of sovereignty or sovereign rights over the sea-bed under the high seas, something that is forbidden implicitly in Article 2 of the 1958 Geneva High Seas Convention and explicitly in Article 137 of the new Convention; and

(*b*) that they run counter to the legal principle that deep-sea mining activities are to be governed by an international regime.

To get round these criticisms each statute directly or indirectly indicates that the state is claiming merely to exercise jurisdiction over its own nationals, residents or companies. The United States law, however, in keeping with general American policy in this area, extends the range of that jurisdiction quite far by applying the act even to the activities of foreign companies in which American shareholders have a 'controlling interest'.

77. Later developments. Following the laying of national bases for the control of deep-sea mining, each country has supplemented its legislation with detailed administrative regulations. In addition a number of western countries have joined in the *Agreement Concerning Interim Arrangements relating to Polymetallic Nodules of the Deep Sea Bed* (1982) and the *Provisional Understanding Regarding Deep Seabed Matters* (1984).

Progress test 12

1. Explain the significance of the debate between Grotius and Selden. **(3)**
2. What was the principle of commonage? **(4, 6)**
3. List the major international codifications of the law of the sea. **(7)**
4. Under what circumstances may a state exercise jurisdiction over foreign merchant ships in its internal waters? **(9–11)**
5. Is there a right of innocent passage in any internal waters? **(14)**
6. What is the international law rule on the width of the territorial sea? **(15)**
7. Explain and discuss the holding in the *Anglo-Norwegian Fisheries Case.* **(18)**
8. Explain the right of innocent passage in the territorial sea. **(24–7)**
9. What is transit passage? **(30)**
10. Why has 'the legal continental shelf' departed further and further from the geological one? **(32)**
11. What is the problem with the exploitability test? **(34, 36)**
12. What is the minimum width of the continental shelf under the 1982 Law of the Sea Convention? **(36)**
13. What are the attractions and difficulties of the single maritime boundary? **(37)**
14. Is the 'combined equidistance-special circumstances rule' the mandatory method of delimiting the continental shelf? **(39, 41)**
15. May Rockall have a continental shelf of its own? **(43)**
16. Has international law adopted the concept of the Exclusive Economic Zone (EEZ)? **(46)**
17. What is freedom of the seas? **(49)**
18. What might be the implications of Article 88 of the 1982 Law of the Sea Convention? **(51)**
19. Whose nationality does a ship have? **(52)**
20. Explain the right of visit and flag verification. **(56)**
21. Are there any limits on the use of force permitted in a situation of legitimate hot pursuit? **(59)**
22. What is the basic international law principle regarding deep sea-bed mining? **(61)**
23. How does the concept of 'the common heritage of mankind' affect the law on deep sea-bed mining? **(63)**
24. How will the Enterprise acquire the expertise and technology needed for its operations? **(66)**
25. What is the legal effect of a regime of interlocking national legislation on deep sea-bed mining? **(69)**
26. What is a 'reciprocating state'? **(70)**

Bibliography

On the Grotius/Selden controversy
Fulton, *The Sovereignty of the Sea*, Blackwood & Sons (Edinburgh, 1911)
General
Times Atlas of the Oceans, ed. A. Couper, Times Books, London (1983).

13 International human rights

Introduction

1. **The legal implications of human rights.** In an international legal system oriented towards states the position of the individual and his or her rights must inevitably be awkward, and as has been noted from time to time in the preceding chapters the existence of human rights poses particular problems for the international lawyer.

The debate over natural law and positivism is relevant insofar as human rights might be thought to have a Natural Law basis, as Judge Tanaka argued in the *South West Africa Cases* (*see* 1:**22**). The question whether individuals have international legal personality affects their capacity to claim rights directly under international law (*see* 4:**58**). The relationship of international and municipal law is an issue in human rights law: how and to what extent do international customary or treaty rules on human rights become applicable in municipal courts? (*see* 3:**2, 17, 19, 21, 28, 29**). There is also the problem of international law interfering with the internal jurisdiction of sovereign states (*see* Chap. 8). And issues of state responsibility under international law cannot be ignored (*see* 10:**2, 10, 22, 25, 26**).

Yet in spite of all these potential difficulties, human rights law has continued to grow in importance. The explanation may be that suggested by Dr Andrei Sakharov: that the ideology of human rights is the only one that can be combined with such diverse ideas as communism, social democracy, religion and nationalism. Human rights may also in his view establish a foothold for those 'who have tired of the abundance of ideologies, none of which has brought ... simple human happiness'. For Sakharov, 'the defence of human rights is a clear path toward the unification of people in our turbulent world, and a path toward the relief of suffering'.

In examining human rights law here we will first look at how it has developed and then consider some of the more important human rights regimes now in operation.

Development of human rights

2. **A conceptual framework for analysis: 'three generations' of rights.** Professor Karel Vasak has suggested that the development of human rights law can usefully be considered under three headings provided by the French revolutionary slogan 'Liberty, Equality, Brotherhood' ('Liberté, Égalité, Fraternité'). Each of these goals corresponds to one of what Prof. Vasak has called the 'three generations' of human rights. The history of human rights may be thought of as the gradual appearance of each of these generations in turn, each interpenetrating the others and balancing their particular concerns. Although this analysis cannot be applied too rigorously, it will be helpful in understanding the formation of human rights law.

The first generation: Liberty

3. The French and American Revolutions. Classical libertarian rights in the eighteenth century were based on natural law ideas, as is evident from the emphasis of the American Declaration of Independence (1776) and the French Declaration of the Rights of Man and of the Citizen (1789) on natural rights.

The American Declaration claimed that it is 'self-evident' that:

all men are created equal, that they are endowed by their Creator with certain unalienable Rights, that among these are Life, Liberty, and the pursuit of Happiness.

The French Declaration stated in Article 1 that:

Les hommes naissent et demeurent libres et égaux en droits [Men are born and remain free and equal in rights],

while Article 2 indicated that political life had one goal:

la conservation des droits naturels et impréscriptibles de l'homme (the preservation of the natural and inalienable rights of man).

Among these were the rights of liberty, property ownership, security, and resistance to oppression.

4. 'Negative rights'. These rights of 'freedom from' state interference are sometimes considered 'negative', civil-liberties, rights and are thought to reflect classical eighteenth and nineteenth century liberal individualism. Civil liberties, as the oldest generation of human rights, are reflected in the constitutions and fundamental laws of many states (if not always in their practice) and provide the backbone of such important international law documents as the Universal Declaration of Human Rights (1948), the European Convention on Human Rights (1950), the International Covenant on Civil and Political Rights (1966) and the American Convention on Human Rights (1969).

5. Jurisprudential primacy of civil liberties. Some writers, for example, Sir Norman Anderson, have argued that these civil liberties are the only sort of right that can reasonably be considered universally binding and automatically applicable regardless of differences between social or political systems. This is said to come about because such rights do not require the adoption of a certain political programme nor the resolution of contested economic or social questions in order to be implemented. All that is necessary is that the government and its agents commit themselves to treat individuals in certain approved ways (e.g. by ceasing to torture or illegally imprison them).

This analysis carries the implication that only these civil liberties can be considered 'natural' and inalienable rights in the strict sense. It is argued that other rights, about which there may be legitimate political or ideological disagreement leading to legitimate alternative solutions, cannot occupy such a position. This argument is vigorously disputed.

6. Internationalisation of first generation rights. Apart from helping to outline the nature of these first generation rights, the philosophers and politicians of the French Revolution also unwittingly helped to make them a matter of international legal interest. This came about in two ways.

First, the logic of natural rights was that all persons were entitled to them. The leaders of the Revolution soon came to see that this meant that the rights originally proclaimed only for Frenchman could be exported (by French armies) to the oppressed populations of the conservative European countries with which the Revolution soon found itself at war. The awareness of human rights was being internationalised.

Secondly, the French revolutionary notion that men were born equal (in the civil liberties sense) raised the problem of how to deal with distinctive racial, ethnic or linguistic groups within large states, since it seemed to suggest that all should be treated equally in the political and legal spheres in spite of evident differences. The practical effects of this development were at first felt less in western Europe than in other countries in whose minorities the western European states took a special interest. This helped make minority rights an international concern.

7. The political and legal rights of minorities. The mid-nineteenth century witnessed some significant developments in the situation of minorities in several western countries. In the United States the end of the Civil War in 1865 saw the adoption of three constitutional amendments that raised the position of former black slaves to legal (if not actual) equality with whites. In the Austrian Empire growing nationalism among subject peoples led to a restructuring of political arrangements in 1867 and the enacting of a new constitution whereby 'all nationalities in the state enjoy equal rights, and each one has an inalienable right to the preservation and cultivation of its nationality and language'. The language and focus of this provision were significant in foreshadowing later international law concern with the civil and social rights of minorities as groups as well as simply collections of individuals.

But the main international law developments in this area were taking place on the periphery of Europe as expanding European colonial powers established their rights to 'protect' the various Christian (and sometimes non-Christian) minorities in the Ottoman Empire. This began when the most unlikely protector of human rights in Europe, Tsarist Russia, imposed the Treaty of Kuchuk Kainarji (1774) on the Ottoman government and so obtained an international legal basis for Russian interference in Ottoman internal affairs on behalf of the Sultan's Orthodox Christian subjects.

The improvement of the situation of national, ethnic and religious minorities in the Ottoman Empire became a major theme of the European wrangles in the nineteenth century over the 'Eastern Question', with France and Britain eventually establishing themselves as protectors of Latin Christians, Lebanese Maronites, Lebanese Druze, and Arab Protestant Christians.

The political cynicism and self-interest of these developments should not, however, be allowed to conceal the fact that these interventions did help to establish the point that individual and group rights could become a matter of international law by treaty and even to some extent by state practice. This became an important consideration when the victors at the end of World War I found themselves committed to establishing independent national states in Eastern Europe out of the debris of the German, Austrian and Russian Empires, and in doing so had to wrestle with the fact that all the proposed states would have large linguistic or ethnic minorities.

8. The Minorities Treaties. In 1919–1920 a series of treaties with the new or enlarged states of Eastern Europe (Poland, Yugoslavia, Czechoslovakia, Rumania and Greece), and provisions in the peace treaties with Austria Bulgaria, Hungary and Turkey gave international legal standing to minority rights.

The basic rights recognised for minorities under these treaties were the civil liberties rights to life, liberty, the free exercise of religion without discrimination, and the right to be equal before the law and have the same political and religious rights as the majority. These civil rights of equality were, however, supplemented by what may be thought of as second generation social and cultural rights of equality. Under the treaty with Poland, for example, minorities were given the right to establish and run charitable, religious and social institutions and various educational establishments, and to use their own language.

The concern with minorities which led to the creation of the German Free City of Danzig as an enclave in Polish territory also helped to introduce into international law the idea, recognised by the World Court in the *Jurisdiction of the Courts of Danzig (Danzig Railway Officials) Case* (1928) and other cases, that individuals could have rights bestowed upon them directly by international law which they could enforce themselves through the courts.

9. Shortcomings of the treaty regime. These treaties were, however, only a partial international law regime insofar as they did not make minority rights a part of general international law applicable to all states. Attempts by Japan and the United States to have a significant minority rights provision included in the League of Nations Covenant were defeated, mainly because of British opposition based on fears about possible claims to equality by subject colonial peoples and about the problem of non-white immigration into countries like Australia which at the time pursued a 'whites only' policy.

This failure of certain western countries to live up to their liberal pretensions created a sense of grievance in those countries upon whom minority rights regimes had been imposed by treaty and in non-western states like Japan whose opposition to the implicit racism of western colonialism had been ignored.

The danger of emphasising minority rights *per se* also became apparent in the 1930s when Germany established contacts with over 300 German minority organisations in eastern Europe and used their claims to undermine the Polish and Czechoslovak states.

Furthermore, it began to be seen that if a state acknowledged the existence of a minority in its territory (and many, contrary to the facts, refused to do so), the problem of the minority's 'national' rights, and in particular the right to self-determination, might arise.

10. Post-1945 minorities law. These difficulties, coupled with a growing sense that integrating minorities rather than ghettoising them was the way of the future (especially for countries that did not want special minority regimes on their territory), encouraged a trend after the establishment of the United Nations towards dealing with minority rights as part of general human rights. Within the broader category there would simply be a special emphasis on the rights of equality and non-discrimination. Thus, minority rights, which had helped promote the idea of human rights under international law, were to a considerable extent (though not completely) absorbed into the new regime.

11. Contribution of the law of war (*jus in bello*). The law of war, particularly as expressed in the Hague Regulations of 1907 and the Fourth Geneva Convention of 1949, is another area of traditional law whose contribution to pushing individual rights into the area of international law should be noted, even though it is often categorised as merely 'humanitarian' law. The law of war clearly deals with certain human rights issues, particularly in regard to belligerent occupation (see 6:**20**). The belligerent occupier is required to respect family life, the right to life, the rights of private property and the exercise of religious convictions and practices and is obliged to ensure equality and fair treatment before the law. (*See* also 16:**24, 33**.)

12. The role of national law in developing and applying human rights. National legal institutions can sometimes also have a role to play in promoting first generation rights, since national court decisions may both clarify international human rights law and, as evidence of state practice, help to create international customary law.

This reflexive and interactive relationship between international and national law may be seen in an interesting US Court of Appeals case, *Filartiga* v. *Pena-Irala* (1980). The court had to consider whether torture was prohibited as a matter of international law. In arriving at the conclusion that it was the tribunal examined all the relevant treaties and United Nations resolutions along with the writings of publicists and other judicial decisions. In particular, the court observed that the Universal Declaration of Human Rights (in form merely a UN General Assembly resolution) 'no longer fits into the dichotomy of "binding treaty" against "non-binding pronouncement" but is rather an authoritative statement of the international community'. By implying that this declaration has a legal effect even though it does not fit into any of the traditional 'sources' of international law the court was actually broadening the bases of international human rights law while seeking to determine what it was and to implement it. (*See* 2:**29, 32** and 3:**19**.)

The second generation: Equality

13. Nature of the second generation rights. To the extent that ideas of equality tended to go beyond first generation civil liberties concerns they took on a social orientation which justifies considering them as a separate category of rights.

They began to appear in the nineteenth century in response to the abuses of individualistic capitalism and colonial exploitation and took on the character of 'rights to' fair social and economic circumstances (social security, decent wages and working conditions, adequate health care, etc.) rather than 'freedoms from' government interference.

They were in this sense 'affirmative' or 'positive' rights that required state intervention for their fulfilment. Second generation rights are therefore often seen as standing in opposition to first generation rights, although the contrast sometimes seems to exist more in the minds of ideological apologists than in actual fact.

Nevertheless it must be accepted that it has proved very difficult to bring the two generations together. Although the Universal Declaration of Human Rights (1948) lists both civil and social rights, when these were transformed into treaty law the second generation rights were dealt with separately. Consequently, the International Covenant on Economic, Social and Cultural Rights (1966) stands beside the International Covenant on Civil and Political Rights rather than forming part of it.

Similarly, the Council of Europe developed the European Social Charter (1961) separately from the European Convention on Human Rights.

14. 'Programmatic' or 'aspirational' rights. Some writers argue that second generation rights must be regarded as in some sense legally inferior to first generation ones, since economic and social rights cannot be automatically applied universally like civil rights but can be realised only by pursuing certain government policies or programmes (about which there may be legitimate disagreement, even in a democracy) and may be limited by the resources available in a particular state.

These rights are therefore said to be merely 'programmatic' or 'aspirational', that is, rights for whose fulfilment governments must strive but for whose incomplete realisation they cannot be held accountable.

This analysis has much to be said for it, but its true implications are sometimes misunderstood. Some writers argue that because, say, the right to full employment is only aspirational, a government would be entitled to adopt any policy it wanted in that regard. In fact the situation is better seen as one in which a government cannot be liable for failure to achieve full employment if it has sincerely exerted its efforts in that direction but been frustrated by circumstances, but is liable for a human rights violation if it deliberately works in the opposite sense to increase unemployment.

Put in more general terms, programmatic or aspirational rights do legally bind a government not to adopt a policy that is contrary to them, even if that government's positive duties have a variable character depending upon political or other circumstances.

15. Role of international organisations in promoting social rights. The entry of second generation rights into international law was initially promoted most effectively by the International Labour Organisation, the ILO. This body was established in 1919 and took as its raison d'etre the idea stated in its Constitution that 'universal and lasting peace can be established only if it is based upon social justice'.

To implement its purposes the ILO has helped draft and bring into operation a large number of international agreements regulating employment practices and related social questions. This has established firmly that social issues are as much a legitimate international concern as civil liberties and may be dealt with as a matter of international law.

The example of the ILO, especially when viewed against the background of post-World War I disruption and the mass unemployment of the depression in the 1930s, encouraged a broader concern with the international dimensions of social problems, and in the inter-war period the League of Nations found itself increasingly involved in this area.

The United Nations took up where the League left off. One of the UN's purposes is stated in the Charter to be achieving international cooperation in solving international economic, social, cultural and humanitarian problems. Article 60 gives responsibility in these areas to the Economic and Social Council (ECOSOC), which acts in conjunction with a variety of specialised agencies including the ILO, the Food and Agriculture Organisation (FAO), the World Health Organisation (WHO), and the United Nations Educational, Scientific and Cultural Organisation (UNESCO).

As an example of the UN process at work, one may note that in 1983 the ECOSOC added an element to second generation rights when it adopted a draft entitled *Declaration on a new international human order: moral aspects of development*, which was noted by the General Assembly in Resolution 38/170 of 1984. The draft called on states and peoples to focus on the economic, social and spiritual needs and aspirations of human beings when promoting development.

Regional organisations may also play a role in developing second generation rights, as evidenced by the Council of Europe's promulgation of the European Social Charter (1961) and the European Code of Social Security (1964).

The third generation: Brotherhood

16. Nature of these rights. A moment's reflection will reveal that first and second generation rights are essentially those of the individual *vis-à-vis* the state and society in which he or she lives. Third generation rights, however, transcend national boundaries and may be thought of as rights against the international community of states as a whole.

One of the early formulations of a third generation right illustrates the point. Article 28 of the Universal Declaration of Human Rights (1948) proclaims: 'Everyone is entitled to a social and international order in which the rights and freedoms set forth in this Declaration can be fully realized'. Clearly, this right requires more than simply appropriate action by the individual's own state. All, or at least most, states must cooperate to create the international order suggested, and this in turn implies that the individual is entitled to make certain claims on the good faith efforts of states to achieve this cooperation.

Third generation rights therefore imply an interdependence of individuals and nations and, by extension, of individuals in all countries. But this interdependence would be essentially negative if it involved only mutual obligations. Its positive aspect is that it also involves mutual interests insofar as every individual shares with every other one the need for a suitable international order. This comprehensive interdependence is what is meant by 'brotherhood' or, to use the alternative term now gaining favour, *solidarity*.

Third generation rights are thus ones to which each person is entitled but which each can ensure only by building on the foundation of shared interests and working with everyone else to achieve.

17. Examples of these rights. Among rights which are said to come within the third generation are the right to peace, the right to a healthy environment, the right to self-determination, the right to economic and social development.

Professor Burns H. Weston has pointed to a difficulty with such a list. Certain of these rights – for example, to peace – imply an international order that goes beyond the interests of nation-states and their traditional chauvinistic concerns. But others, such as self-determination, actually focus on national rights. Thus, while some third generation rights seem to foreshadow the breakdown of the state system, others actually promote that system. These apparent inconsistencies have yet to be resolved.

18. Implementation of these rights. The transfrontier nature of these rights affects how they may be implemented. An international system based on states, and national legal systems with limited jurisdiction, are not the best means of realising rights that go beyond simple one-to-one state relations or questions with which municipal law can deal. There are thus relatively few examples of third generation rights *as such* being given effect to, and this dearth of cases and state practice seems likely to continue.

This does not mean, however, that an individual will necessarily suffer violation of all these rights, since some of them may be implemented by activities arising out of other areas of law. International agreements on environmental protection, for example, may promote the individual's right to a healthy environment even if they do not specifically recognise or refer to that right.

Obligations *erga omnes*

19. The traditional view on the maintenance of human rights. The state-centred character of international law has tended to make the implementation of its rules and principles a matter of one-to-one state relations. The state to whom a duty was owed was generally the only entity that could demand fulfilment of that duty if it had been violated. The result was to prevent a state which had experienced no direct violation of *its* rights from vindicating the violated rights of others.

For example, in the *South-West Africa Cases* (*see* 4:**29**) the International Court of Justice held that Ethiopia and Liberia had no standing to sue South Africa over its racial policy in that mandated territory since neither of those countries had suffered directly from South Africa's activities and neither could sue on behalf of the defunct League of Nations or its members. There was no such thing in international law as an *actio popularis* (an individual suit on behalf of the community in general).

20. The new possibility of obligations erga omnes. The traditional view may be in the process of changing. The International Court of Justice, in a comment in the *Barcelona Traction, Light and Power Co. Case* (1970), recognised the possibility that a state might have obligations *erga omnes* (towards the international community as a whole) which all states have a legal interest in protecting (and hence a standing to sue on). Obligations *erga omnes* derive in part 'from the principles and rules concerning the basic rights of the human person'. (*See* also 10:**10**; 15:**7**.)

This view corresponds to what appears to be a growing concern on the part of individuals and governments with the suppression of human rights violations in which, according to traditional law, they would have been deemed to have no legal interest. (*See* also 10:**2**.)

The United Nations human rights regime

21. The United Nations Charter. The Preamble to the United Nations Charter reaffirms 'faith in fundamental human rights, in the dignity and worth of the human person, [and] in the equal rights of men and women.' Article 1(3) states that it is a purpose of the organisation to 'achieve international cooperation . . . in promoting and encouraging respect for human rights and for fundamental freedoms for all without distinction as to race, sex, language or religion'. Under Article 2, 'in pursuit of the purposes stated in Article 1', the members of the United Nations undertake to 'fulfil in good faith' their obligations under the Charter and to refrain from the threat or use of force in any manner 'inconsistent with the purposes of the United Nations'.

Under the heading 'International Social and Economic Co-operation', Article 55 obliges the United Nations to promote 'universal respect for and observance of, human rights and fundamental freedoms for all without distinction as to race, sex, language or religion', and the members, in Article 56, pledge themselves to take joint and separate action in co-operation with the United Nations to achieve this aim.

22. Legal effect of the Charter's human rights provisions. As a multilateral treaty the Charter in principle entails international legal obligations for the parties to it. But the imprecision of its provisions on human rights makes it difficult to determine the content and character of its obligations in this area – a significant problem for national courts faced with a demand to apply the Charter in municipal law.

Article 1 and Article 55 are, however, noticeably more precise in prohibiting discrimination based on race, sex, language or religion, and this has encouraged suits based on that specific right.

As already noted (*see* 3:**21**), the California Supreme Court in the *Sei Fujii Case* rejected such a claim. But in *Re Drummond Wren* (1945) the Ontario High Court declared a restrictive racial covenant void as against public policy, taking the Charter as an indication of what that policy was. In *Oyama* v. *California* (1948) four concurring judges on the United States Supreme Court, holding a discriminatory law unconstitutional, also noted the statute's inconsistency with the Charter.

More generally, some writers argue that, taking the Charter as a treaty, the imprecision of its language has been to a considerable extent cured by subsequent United Nations practice, which has served to spell out the obligations assumed by UN members when they signed the Charter. Subsequent practice by the parties to a treaty may legitimately be considered when interpreting the document (*see* 11:**18**).

A third possibility is that the Charter and United Nations documents and practice, and the practice of member states based on the Charter, have together generated a customary international law of human rights which can be applied by national courts as part of municipal law. This approach was evident in the *Filartiga Case* (*see* **12**).

23. The Charter's human rights mechanisms. Primary responsibility for human rights questions in the United Nations is given by the Charter to the General Assembly. Article 13(1)(b) requires the Assembly to initiate studies and make recommendations regarding the codification and progressive development of international law and with respect to the realisation of human rights and fundamental freedoms.

The Assembly's remit is very wide-ranging and it may receive assistance in its tasks from the Economic and Social Council (ECOSOC), established by Article 61 of the Charter.

The ECOSOC has in turn entrusted much of its work in this area to the United Nations Commission on Human Rights, which further ramifies into sub-commissions, most notably the Sub-Commission on the Prevention of Discrimination and the Protection of Minorities. In addition to preparing draft documents codifying and developing human rights law, the Commission has since 1970 been empowered to consider complaints by individuals alleging human rights violations. The Commission may also appoint *ad hoc* working groups to investigate specific situations of human rights violations, as in the Israeli military occupation of Palestinian territory after 1967, South Africa's implementation of apartheid, and repression in Chile.

Under the International Covenant on Civil and Political Rights, Article 28, a Human Rights Committee has been established to consider and report on violations of the Covenant alleged by individuals who are subject to the jurisdiction of states that have signed the Covenant's Optional Protocol and thereby acknowledged the competence of the Committee to receive petitions from such individuals.

24. Potential jurisdictional limitation on the UN's role. What at first sight may appear a fundamental obstacle to extensive United Nations involvement in human rights problems on a country-by-country basis is contained in Article 2(7) of the Charter, which states:

> Nothing contained in the present Charter shall authorise the United Nations to intervene in matters which are essentially within the domestic jurisdiction of any state ... but this principle shall not prejudice the application of enforcement measures ... [under the Security Council's powers to maintain international peace and security].

The actual effect of this provision has, however, been minimised by a narrow construction of its meaning. Sir Hersch Lauterpacht, for example, points out that the term intervention applies only to dictatorial interference rather than to the investigative and recommendatory activities of the General Assembly.

Furthermore, since 1945 human rights matters have become less and less 'essentially' within domestic jurisdiction as international law has broadened its scope in this area, as in so many others.

In any event, by implication from Article 2(7)'s exclusion of enforcement measures from its restrictions, the United Nations may intervene when issues of peace and security are raised. The Security Council in Resolution 282 (1970), for example, dealt with the question of apartheid partly on the basis that South Africa's policy was a 'potential threat' to peace.

25. Developing United Nations human rights law. The very broad brush with which the drafters of the Charter painted its human rights provisions left much detail to be added later by the General Assembly and its subsidiary bodies.

The first major effort in this direction was the Universal Declaration of Human Rights (UDHR). Drafted by the UN Commission on Human Rights and approved by the General Assembly in 1948, the UDHR was originally conceived of as a 'standard of achievement' for all states to aim at. Binding law was to come later in the form of an international convention implementing the rights sketched in the UDHR. Two agreements were adopted in 1966 (*see* 13):

    (*a*) the International Covenant on Civil and Political Rights (ICCPR); and

    (*b*) the International Covenant on Economic, Social and Cultural Rights (the ICESCR).

In the meantime the standing of the UDHR itself seemed to have undergone a change. Repeated references to it in later UN resolutions and declarations, in the proceedings of international bodies and conferences (most notably in the Final Act of the Helsinki Conference in 1975), and in the statements and agreements of states outside the context of the United Nations have all, in the view of some writers, revealed the UDHR as the basis on which subsequent state practice has erected an edifice of customary international human rights law. (*See also* 12.)

The UDHR thus provides a useful framework for examing the main elements of United Nations human rights law.

26. Substantive human rights law under the United Nations. The UDHR divides easily into three parts. Articles 1–21 deal with civil and political rights (*see* **27–45**); Articles 22–27 indicate social, economic, and cultural rights (*see* **46–51**); and Article 28 foreshadows rights of brotherhood and solidarity (*see* **52**). Each of these areas may be examined in turn.

Civil and political rights under the UN regime

27. Equality and non-discrimination. According to the UDHR, all human beings are born free and equal (Article 1) and are entitled to their rights and freedoms without discrimination based on race, colour, sex, language, religion, political or other opinion, national or social origin, property, birth or other status (Article 2). The ICCPR, Article 2, reaffirms this non-discrimination requirement and Article 3 emphasises equality between men and women in the enjoyment of civil and political rights.

Equality and non-discrimination have been further elaborated in such documents as:

    (*a*) the International Convention on the Elimination of all Forms of Racial Discrimination (1966); and

    (*b*) the Convention on the Elimination of Discrimination against Women (1979).

An example of these principles in practice occurred in the Human Rights Committee's report in 1981 on the *Mauritian Women Case*. Mauritius was held to have discriminated against Mauritian women whose foreign husbands faced deportation under the country's laws although the foreign wives of Mauritian men could not legally be deported.

28. Life, liberty and security of person. Article 3 of the UDHR states unqualifiedly the right of everyone to 'life, liberty and security of person', while Article 9 prohibits 'arbitrary arrest, detention or exile'. In giving these provisions more precise legal shape, the ICCPR introduces certain limitations.

Article 6 of the ICCPR speaks of the 'inherent right to life', which 'shall be protected by law' so that no one shall be arbitrarily deprived of his life. A lawfully imposed death penalty therefore does not violate the Covenant, although Article 6(6) seems to imply that abolition of capital punishment is more in keeping with the spirit of human rights law.

The ICCPR's Article 9 notes the right to liberty and security of person and prohibits arbitrary arrest and detention or any deprivation of liberty which is not in accordance with the grounds and procedures established by law.

This emphasis on the arbitrary nature of illegal deprivation of life or liberty is questionable. It seems to suggest that systematic and legally-approved deprivations cannot be internationally illegal although experience suggests that some of the most persistent violations of human rights in this area (as witness the Soviet Union and South Africa) are in fact not arbitrary but the result of the established legal system's operation.

29. Slavery. Article 4 of the UDHR and Article 8 of the ICCPR prohibit slavery, servitude and the slave trade. Article 8 also precludes forced or compulsory labour, except where imposed by a court as punishment for a crime.

30. Maltreatment. Article 2 of the UDHR and Article 7 of the ICCPR forbid torture and cruel, inhuman or degrading treatment or punishment. Article 7 further prohibits subjecting anyone to medical or scientific experiments against his will. (*See* also 2:**31**; 13:**12**.)

The difficulty with these provisions is to determine what constitutes the forbidden treatment. The new United Nations Convention against Torture and other Cruel, Inhuman or Degrading Treatment or Punishment (1984) defines torture as:

> any act by which severe pain or suffering, whether physical or mental, is intentionally inflicted on a person for such purposes as obtaining from him or a third person information or a confession, punishing him for an act he or a third person has committed or is suspected of having committed, or intimidating or coercing him or a third person, or for any reason based on discrimination of any kind, when such pain or suffering is inflicted by or at the instigation of or with the consent or acquiescence of a public official or other person acting in an official capacity. It does not include pain or suffering arising only from, inherent in or incidental to lawful sanctions.

Although useful in recognising the element of mental pain and suffering in cases of torture and in giving a broad statement of the impermissible role of public officials in torture (their encouraging or allowing it is a violation, even if they do not actually do it themselves), this definition may be questioned insofar as its purpose requirement risks excluding acts that may be motivated otherwise than by the purposes listed, even though the list is clearly not meant to be exhaustive. This same defect appears in the General Assembly's 1975 Declaration on Torture.

Wider United Nations moves against maltreatment are reflected in a number of documents. The Standard Minimum Rules for the Treatment of Prisoners (1955) in Article 31 forbids cruel, inhuman or degrading punishments and in Article 32 requires medical supervision of anyone undergoing special punishments. The General Assembly's Code of Conduct for Law Enforcement Officials (1979) also prohibits torture and inhuman punishments and specifically rules out superior orders or public emergency as justifications for them.

In 1982 the Assembly, alarmed that some medical professionals and other health personnel engage in activities 'which are difficult to reconcile with medical ethics' while others risk punishment for giving assistance to certain prisoners, adopted the Principles of Medical Ethics. The first principle reaffirms the duty of health personnel, and particularly physicians, to provide prisoners and detainees with the same quality of treatment for disease and protection for their physical and mental health as is afforded to patients in general. Under Principle 2 it is a 'gross contravention of medical ethics' for health personnel to engage in, or be accomplices to, the forbidden maltreatment. Principle 3 requires the professional relationship of health personnel and prisoners to be solely for the purpose of evaluating and protecting their physical and mental health. Principle 4 condemns health personnel using their knowledge and skills to assist interrogation in a way injurious to the prisoner's health or certifying a prisoner's fitness for abusive punishment or participating in it. Principle 5 censures the participation of such personnel in restraining a prisoner for other than medical or safety reasons.

Finally, in the belief that practical steps should be taken to help those who have been tortured, in 1981 the General Assembly established the United Nations Voluntary Fund for Victims of Torture to distribute funds for humanitarian, legal and financial assistance to such people. In the first two years of the Fund's existence the largest contributions came from Sweden, Denmark and Norway. No donations were received in that period from Britain, the United States or the Soviet Union.

31. Legal personality and equal protection. The UDHR focusses on the legal position of the individual by proclaiming in Article 6 the right of everyone to recognition as a person before the law and in Article 7 the right to equality before the law and to the equal protection of the law without discrimination. These rights are reiterated in the ICCPR, Articles 16 and 26.

32. Effective remedies. Article 8 of the UDHR lays down the sweeping requirement that everyone has the right to an effective remedy at law for acts violating 'the fundamental rights granted him by the law and the constitution'. In the ICCPR, however, the right to an effective remedy is restricted, in Article 2(3), to a vindication only of the rights and freedoms recognised by the Covenant itself. The explanation for this divergence is presumably that the UDHR was not originally conceived of as generating rights and remedies in and of itself but only through enactment of its provisions through national legislation, whereas the Covenant may legitimately require direct observance of its provisions without regard to national laws or constitutions.

33. Rights in regard to arrest, detention, trial and imprisonment. The UDHR is relatively brief on the subject of procedural and other safeguards in this area, while the ICCPR, as befits a legally binding document, goes into much greater detail.

Article 10 of the UDHR states that everyone is entitled 'in full equality to a fair and public hearing by an independent and impartial tribunal, in the determination of his rights and obligations and of any criminal charge against him'. The ICCPR reaffirms this in Article 14, but with the proviso that the public may be excluded from a trial for reasons of morals, public order (*ordre public*) or national security in a democratic society, or in the interests of the parties or where publicity would 'prejudice the interests of justice'.

This basic guarantee is augmented in Article 9 of the ICCPR by a requirement that an arrested person 'shall be promptly informed of any charges against him', be brought promptly before a judge or other officer authorised by law to exercise judicial power, and be entitled to trial within a reasonable period of time or release. Furthermore, anyone arrested or detained is entitled to initiate *habeas corpus*-like proceedings so that a court may decide without delay on the lawfulness of his detention and order his release if the detention is not lawful.

Article 14 of the ICCPR sets procedural safeguards for criminal trials. The accused is to be presumed innocent until proved guilty and is entitled at a minimum:

(*a*) to be informed promptly, in detail, and in a language which he understands, of the nature and cause of the charge against him;

(*b*) to have adequate time and facilities to prepare his defence and to communicate with legal counsel of his own choosing;

(*c*) to be tried without undue delay, in his own presence, with legal assistance, and with the right to examine the witnesses against him and to summon those on his behalf;

(*d*) not to be compelled to testify against himself or to confess guilt.

A convicted person must have the right to appeal to a higher tribunal.

In the *Weinberger Case*, reported on by the Human Rights Committee in 1981, the complainant had been held in prison incommunicado for over three months, was not brought before a judge and charged for nearly ten months after his arrest (during which time he had not been allowed legal assistance), and was not finally sentenced until three and a half years after his arrest. Neither he nor his counsel was allowed to be present at his trial and the judgment against him was not made public. The Committee found that this treatment violated Weinberger's rights to be promptly brought before a judge and tried within a reasonable time, to have recourse to *habeas corpus* proceedings, to have a fair and public hearing, and to have access to legal assistance.

Article 15 of the ICCPR forbids retroactive application of national criminal laws, although Article 15(2) is careful to note that this does not prevent trial and punishment of a person for an act or omission which, at the time when it was committed, was 'criminal according to the general principles of law recognized by the community of nations'.

Article 10 of the ICCPR requires that all persons deprived of their liberty be treated with humanity and with respect for the inherent dignity of the human person. In line with this, accused persons must be separated from convicted ones and accused juveniles from adults. An essential aim of imprisonment must be the reformation and social rehabilitation of the prisoner.

34. Freedom of movement. One of the more intriguing provisions in the UDHR is Article 13's proclamation of the 'right to freedom of movement and residence within the borders of each state' and the right of everyone 'to leave any country, including his own, and to return to his country'.

These rights as stated are far-reaching and a number of states might be accused of violating them. The Soviet Union regularly imposes internal exile on dissidents and refuses them and others exit visas. South Africa restricts the movements and residence of Blacks. Under the Prevention of Terrorism Act the British government may prevent certain British citizens from travelling between

Northern Ireland and Britain. The United States has from time to time prevented travel by Americans to certain forbidden countries, and this was upheld as constitutional by the US Supreme Court in *Regan* v. *Wald* (1984) by a vote of five to four. With such a wide range of states implicated in such practices, it is perhaps not surprising that the drafters of the ICCPR considerably watered down its provisions on this question.

Article 12 of the ICCPR restricts the right of movement and residence to persons 'lawfully within the territory of a state'. In addition, it significantly limits all the rights of movement, residence, and travel abroad by legitimising restrictions which are:

(*a*) provided by law;

(*b*) necessary to protect national security, public order (*ordre public*), public health or morals or the rights and freedoms of others; and

(*c*) consistent with the other rights recognised in the Covenant.

35. Right of privacy. The UDHR in Article 12 prohibits arbitrary interference with an individual's privacy, family, home or correspondence and forbids attacks on his honour and reputation. Everyone has the right to legal protection against such actions. Article 17 of the ICCPR is similar.

36. Right of asylum. A much-criticised provision of the UDHR is Article 14's assurance that 'Everyone has the right to seek and to enjoy in other countries asylum from persecution'. The criticism centres on a point noted by Sir Hersch Lauterpacht, namely that this somewhat misleading language does not (and was never intended to) confer a right to be *granted* asylum, and yet that is precisely what a person fleeing from political danger needs.

Efforts in the United Nations to develop a Convention on Territorial Asylum that would generally require the admission of persons genuinely escaping persecution may correct this situation (*see also* 8:**23**).

In the meantime, the 1951 Convention relating to the Status of Refugees does at least provide in Article 33(1) for the right of *non-refoulement*, whereby a refugee, once in a country of asylum, may not be returned 'to the frontiers of territories where his life or freedom would be threatened on account of his race, religion, nationality, membership of a particular social group or political opinion'. Since 1951 *non-refoulement* appears to have become a rule of customary international law.

To their discredit, the drafters of the ICCPR avoided these issues altogether and even to some extent cast doubt on the requirement of *non-refoulement*. Article 13 of the Covenant provides that an alien – by implication, *any* alien – lawfully within the territory of a state may be expelled 'in pursuance of a decision reached in accordance with law', although the alien is entitled to submit an argument against expulsion and to be represented before the competent authority, 'except where compelling reasons of national security otherwise require'.

37. Right to a nationality. According to Article 15 of the UDHR, everyone has the right to a nationality and no one may be arbitrarily deprived of his nationality or be denied the right to change it.

Of particular concern in this regard is the problem of persons who lose, or never acquire, a nationality and so are rendered stateless, with all the attendant difficulties of that status (*see* 10:23).

The trend in international law is to minimise instances of statelessness to the greatest extent possible, with, for example, the Convention on Reduction of Statelessness (1961) obliging the parties to grant nationality to such persons on the basis of birth or long-term residence in the granting state and limiting the deprivation of nationality.

38. Family rights and the rights of children. Under Article 16 of the UDHR men and women of full age are entitled to marry and found a family and are entitled to equal rights to marry and during marriage and at its dissolution. The family is proclaimed as the 'natural and fundamental group unit of society', entitled to protection by society and the state. Article 23 of the ICCPR reaffirms these rights and adds that in the case of dissolution of marriage 'provision shall be made for the necessary protection of any children'.

The ICCPR in addition provides in Article 24 that every child is without discrimination entitled to such measures of protection from family, society and state as are required by his status as a minor.

39. Freedom of religious and philosophical belief. Article 18 of the UDHR proclaims freedom of thought, conscience and religion, including the right to change one's religion and to 'manifest' it or one's beliefs, alone or in community with others, by teaching, practice, worship or observance. The ICCPR, Article 18, adds a prohibition of coercion which would impair religious freedom, but allows manifestation to be subject to 'such limitations as are prescribed by law and are necessary to protect public safety, order, health, or morals or the fundamental rights and freedoms of others'.

The ICCPR also requires states to respect the liberty of parents to have their children educated in conformity with their own convictions.

40. Liberty of opinion and freedom of expression. Freedom of opinion and expression is provided for by Article 19 of the UDHR and is reaffirmed in the ICCPR's Article 19. Both provisions make clear that this freedom includes the right to seek, receive and impart information and ideas through any medium and regardless of frontiers. The ICCPR also emphasises that the exercise of these rights entails 'special duties and responsibilities' which may give rise to such legal restrictions as may be necessary for protecting the rights or reputation of others or national security, public order, etc.

Article 20 of the ICCPR then sets out an international law limitation on freedom of speech by requiring states to prohibit by law propaganda for war and any advocacy of national, racial or religious hatred that constitutes an incitement to discrimination, hostility or violence.

41. Peaceful assembly and association. The UDHR provides in Article 20 for the right of peaceful assembly, which Article 21 of the ICCPR reaffirms, with the usual security and public order restrictions.

Article 20 of the UDHR also posits a right of association, which Article 22 of the ICCPR specifies to include the right to form and join trade unions, but subject to the usual restrictions supplemented by one allowing limitation of this right with respect to members of the armed forces and the police.

42. Participation in political life. An interesting divergence occurs between the Declaration and the Covenant with regard to political activity.

Article 21 of the UDHR provides that everyone has the right to take part in the government of his country, either directly or through freely chosen representatives. The article then enunciates the fundamental principle that the will of the people – expressed in periodic and genuine elections with universal and equal suffrage through free or secret voting – 'shall be the basis of the authority of government'.

This is transformed in Article 25 of the ICCPR into a right of every *citizen*, without 'unreasonable' restrictions, to take part 'in the conduct of public affairs' and to vote and be elected at genuine periodic elections, with universal and equal suffrage and secret ballot 'guaranteeing the free expression of the will of the electors'.

Deriving government authority from the will of the people is quite a different thing from providing free elections, and the ICCPR's emphasis on the latter seems designed to avoid the implications of the former. Free elections may not necessarily satisfy the fundamental principle enunciated in the UDHR. If, for example, a state's system of elections, however free, fails to produce a legislative representation which is proportionate to the actual votes cast for the various contending parties, a government formed with a majority in the legislature may have only minority support in the country. The legitimacy and authority of such a government could properly be called in question under the UDHR but not under the ICCPR.

In another area, both documents also require equal access, either for 'everyone' or for 'every citizen', to public service in his country.

43. Minorities and indigenous peoples. Although not specifically mentioned in the UDHR, the right of members of ethnic, religious or linguistic minorities, in community with other members of their group, to enjoy their own culture, practise their own religion and use their own language is set out in Article 27 of the ICCPR.

The emphasis on equality and non-discrimination in UN practice has largely replaced specific guarantees for minorities as such (*see* **27**). But the concept of a special regime for certain groups has remained and been developed in one area, that of the rights of *indigenous peoples*.

The ILO in 1957 adopted the Convention on the Protection and Integration of Indigenous and other Tribal and Semi-Tribal Populations in Independent Countries, which somewhat paternalistically defined the groups covered as those 'whose social and economic conditions are at a less advanced stage ... and whose status is regulated wholly or partially by their own customs or traditions or by special laws' or as those descended from populations which inhabited a country at the time of 'conquest or colonisation and which ... live more in conformity with the social, economic and cultural institutions of that time than with the institutions of the nation to which they belong'.

The inadequacy of a treaty based on the presuppositions evident in this language has prompted efforts in the United Nations to develop a new legal regime. This has proved very difficult, however, because of problems with defining the identity of indigenous groups (are they peoples waiting to be decolonised, or simply minorities, or something else?) and with deciding the content of their rights (are they entitled to self-determination, autonomy, or merely equality and non-discrimination?).

Control over territory and natural resources is an issue (as in Canada, Australia, and the United States), along with the problem of cultural rights and the nature of existing nation-states: should they be unicultural or multicultural, and what might the implications of the eventual choice be for state educational and social policies?

44. Divergences between the UDHR and the ICCPR. As already noted with regard to various rights and freedoms, the ICCPR may be less generous than the UDHR and may allow restrictions and limitations which the UDHR does not mention. These divergences could be significant if the ICCPR is considered to be the only binding legal expression of the rights involved. On the other hand, if the UDHR states what is now customary international law, these rights may be available to the individual without the ICCPR's qualifications. Where national courts may apply customary international law but not treaty law *per se*, this situation could produce some interesting results.

45. National rights. The UDHR makes no mention of national rights, but both the ICCPR and the ICESCR actually begin with identical declarations on the right of all peoples to self-determination and to the free disposition of their natural wealth and resources (*see also* 4:**35–44**).

Economic, social and cultural rights under the UN regime

46. Fundamental provisions. Article 22 of the UDHR lays the basis for second generation rights as follows:

> Everyone, as a member of society, has the right to social security and is entitled to realization, through national effort and international co-operation and in accordance with the organization and resources of each State, of the economic, social and cultural rights indispensable for his dignity and the free development of his personality.

Part II of the ICESCR commits the parties to taking steps towards 'achieving progressively the full realization of the rights' recognised in it, with only such limitations as are determined by law, are compatible with the nature of these rights, and are for the purpose of promoting the general welfare in a democratic society.

Clearly, the drafters of the ICESCR intended to leave no doubt that they were setting out 'programmatic' and 'aspirational' rights, although the language quoted from the UDHR need not necessarily be construed in that way.

47. Earning a living. Everyone has a right to work (UDHR Article 23, ICESCR Article 6), with a duty resting on the state to achieve full realisation of this right through vocational training programmes and policies aimed at steady economic, social and cultural development and the achievement of full and productive employment (ICESCR Article 6). The ILO's Employment Policy Convention (1964) reaffirms these basic goals, which are central to the ILO's work.

All workers are entitled to just and favourable conditions of work, equal pay for equal work, and sufficient remuneration (UDHR Article 23, ICESCR Article 7). For the UDHR sufficiency means ensuring for the worker and his family 'an existence worthy of human dignity', earnings to be supplemented, if necessary, by 'other means of social protection'. For the ICESCR it is simply a question of a 'decent living' in accordance with the Covenant's other provisions, among which is Article 9 on the right of everyone to social security, including social insurance.

Trade union rights are also upheld (UDHR Article 23, ICESCR Article 8), though with the usual restrictions in the Covenant.

48. Standard of living and health. Article 25 of the UDHR states:

> Everyone has the right to a standard of living adequate for the health and well-being of himself and of his family, including food, clothing, housing and medical care and necessary social services, and the right to security in the event of unemployment, sickness, disability, widowhood, old age or other lack of livelihood in circumstances beyond his control.

The ICESCR covers these points in several sections. Article 11 reaffirms the right to an adequate standard of living, with specific provisions on improving food production and distribution on a world-wide basis to relieve hunger. Article 12 recognises the right of everyone to the 'highest attainable standard of physical and mental health', with the parties being required to develop better child care, improve environmental and industrial hygiene, control disease, and create conditions assuring medical services to all.

49. Protection of the family. The UDHR in Article 25 emphasises that motherhood and childhood are entitled to special care, all children, 'whether born in or out of wedlock', being entitled to the same social protection. Article 10 of the ICESCR adds to this a concern with protecting and assisting the family and protecting children and young persons from economic and social exploitation, particularly child labour.

50. Education. Echoing the UDHR, Article 13(1) of the ICESCR provides:

> The ... Parties ... recognize the right of everyone to education. They agree that education shall be directed to the full development of the human personality and the sense of its dignity, and shall strengthen the respect for human rights and fundamental freedoms. They further agree that education shall enable all persons to participate effectively in a free society, promote understanding, tolerance and friendship among all nations and all racial, ethnic or religious groups, and further the activities of the United Nations for the maintenance of peace.

Both documents require provision of elementary, secondary, and tertiary education which is equally accessible to all.

51. Cultural life and patents and copyright. Everyone has the right to participate in the cultural life of the community and to share in scientific progress and its applications (UDHR Article 27, ICESCR Article 15).

Everyone is also entitled to protection of 'the moral and material interests resulting from any scientific, literary or artistic production of which he is the author'.

Rights of brotherhood and solidarity under the UN regime

52. The sources. The United Nations Charter must be regarded as the fount of third generation rights since its preamble asserts the need for international co-operation in realising peace, justice and human rights, while Article 1 envisages the UN as a centre for harmonising the actions of nations to attain these 'common ends'. Article 28 of the UDHR seems therefore to be accurately reflecting the spirit of the Charter when it speaks of the right to 'a social and international order in which the rights and freedoms set forth in this Declaration can be fully realized'.

Which rights are contained in the third generation is disputed, but the following list would be generally acknowledged:

(*a*) the right to peace;
(*b*) the right to development;
(*c*) the right to a healthy environment;
(*d*) the right to the common heritage of mankind (*see* 6:**47** and 12:**61**);
(*e*) the right to communicate across borders;
(*f*) the right to humanitarian assistance;
(*g*) the right to self-determination (*see* 4:**41**).

As entitlements of *individuals* all of these rights must be regarded as having appeared relatively recently, although some can be accepted as firmly fixed in international law insofar as they pertain to states and national groups. The significance of bringing them down to the human level is that their promotion and advancement may then be taken out of the hands of political leaders and entrusted instead to the ultimate beneficiaries.

The difficulty then becomes how the individual can make his voice heard. Professor Antonio Cassese of the University of Pisa has noted in this connection the growth of 'non-governmental' human rights initiatives by individuals and groups in many countries, and it seems undeniable that such grassroots efforts do bring human rights violations of all sorts to light and raise the consciousness of lawyers and politicians. The breakthrough in the area of third generation rights will come when national courts are persuaded to adopt in relation to them the attitude of the American court in the *Filartiga Case* towards first generation rights. (*See* **12**.)

Regional regimes

53. The European Convention on Human Rights (1950). The oldest of the regional human rights regimes, the European Convention in many respects implemented the civil and political rights provisions of the UDHR, even to the extent of using the same language in some provisions. Chapter 14 examines the Convention's provisions in detail.

54. The American Convention on Human Rights (1969). Although clearly influenced by the UDHR and the European Convention, the American Convention provides the states of Latin America – the United States is not a party – with a human rights charter which in tone and range of concerns seems both more modern and more influenced by the moral teaching of the Catholic Church.

Article 5, for example, which announces a positive 'right to humane treatment' rather than a negative right not to be ill-treated, requires respect for every person's 'physical, mental and moral integrity'. Article 11, on the right to privacy, demands recognition of everyone's honour and dignity. The right to life, under Article 4, is to be protected by law 'in general, from the moment of conception', while the death penalty 'shall not be reestablished in the states that have abolished it' nor be imposed for political crimes or extended 'to crimes to which it does not presently apply'.

Other interesting features of the Convention are:

(*a*) Article 14's 'right of reply' to personally offensive or inaccurate statements disseminated to the public in general by a 'legally regulated medium of communication';

(*b*) Article 20's right to a nationality; and

(*c*) Article 26's undertaking by the parties to work to achieve full realisation of recognised economic, social, educational, scientific and cultural rights.

The Convention established an Inter-American Commission on Human Rights and an Inter-American Court of Human Rights, which are both now in operation. Interestingly, the Commission may receive petitions from any person, group or non-governmental entity *without* the accused state having made a declaration recognising the Commission's competence to do so, although a petition by one state against another can be received only if such a declaration has been made. Cases may be referred to the Court only by states and the Commission, if the accused state has lodged an appropriate declaration recognising the Court's jurisdiction.

An important function of the court is the giving of advisory opinions under Article 64, including opinions on the compatibility of a requesting state's domestic laws with the Convention or with other human rights treaties effective in Latin America. In an advisory opinion in 1982 the court held unanimously that this extended to the human rights provisions of any international treaty applicable in the American states, whatever the principal purpose of such a treaty and regardless of whether it applied only to those states.

It appears that the court will not be averse to using its advisory capacity in effect to comment on the laws of a particular state, even if that state objects. In 1983, following a request from the Commission with respect to 'certain differences of opinion' between it and Guatemala over the meaning of the Convention's provisions on the death penalty, the court did just that. It held unanimously that the Convention imposes an absolute prohibition on extension of the death penalty beyond the crimes for which it was imposed at the time the Convention entered into force for the state concerned.

Progress test 13

1. What are the 'three generations' of human rights?   (**2**)

2. Are civil liberties rights jurisprudentially pre-eminent?   (**5**)

3. Why was the protection of minorities important in the development of human rights law in general?   (**7**)

4. What were the objections to special legal regimes for minorities?   (**9**)

5. Explain the distinction between 'negative' and 'positive' rights.   (**4, 13**)

6. What is meant by 'programmatic' or 'aspirational' rights?   (**14**)

7. Explain the human rights influence of the International Labour Office.   (**15**)

8. Why are third generation rights of a different nature than those of the first two generations?   (**16, 18**)

9. Explain the concept of obligations *erga omnes*.   (**20**)

10. Does Article 2(7) of the UN Charter prevent any UN involvement in human rights situations in individual countries?   (**24**)

11. What is the legal standing of the Universal Declaration of Human

Rights? **(12, 25)**

12. Is an emphasis on the arbitrary deprivation of life or liberty misplaced? **(28)**

13. Outline and discuss the prohibition of torture in UN human rights law. **(30)**

14. List the procedural safeguards with respect to arrest, detention, trial and imprisonment. **(33)**

15. Explain the concept of freedom of movement in UN law. **(34)**

16. Is there a right to be granted asylum? **(36)**

17. For what purpose does international law require states to limit freedom of expression? **(40)**

18. What is 'the basis of the authority of government' under UN human rights law? **(42)**

19. Are indigenous peoples in a class by themselves under UN human rights law? **(43)**

20. Is there a 'right to health'? **(48)**

21. List the rights of solidarity. **(52)**

Bibliography

Anderson, *Liberty, Law and Justice*, Stevens & Sons, London (1978)

Brownlie, *Basic Documents on Human Rights*, 2nd ed., Clarendon Press, Oxford (1981)

Cassese, 'Progressive Transnational Promotion of Human Rights' in Ramcharan, ed., *Human Rights Thirty Years after the Universal Declaration*, Nijhoff, London (1979)

Fawcett, *The International Protection of Minorities*, Minority Rights Group, London (1979)

McKean, *Equality and Discrimination under International Law*, Clarendon Press, Oxford (1983)

Weston, article on 'Human Rights' in *Encyclopedia Britannica* 1985 edition.

14 Human rights in Europe

The European Convention on Human Rights

1. Origin and purpose. Following the gross human rights violations in Europe during the Nazi era the member states of the Council of Europe appreciated the need for a binding reaffirmation of what would be called in United Nations parlance 'civil and political rights'. The result was the adoption of the European Convention for the Protection of Human Rights and Fundamental Freedoms (1950) or, as it is more commonly known, the European Convention on Human Rights. Since then eight supplementary Protocols have augmented the Convention's range of rights, though not all parties to the Convention have accepted all the Protocols.

Initially intended as a device for allowing perversions such as had occurred in Germany to be noticed and forestalled by common European action, the Convention in time came to provide also a means for aggrieved individuals to raise complaints about treatment they had received at the hands of their own or another government. This development has generated a fascinating and important body of case law very like that which arises in national legal systems in relation to constitutional guarantees or a bill of rights.

Activating the European Convention's mechanism

2. Raising a case. The Convention's machinery consists of a European Commission of Human Rights (the Commission) and a European Court of Human Rights (the Court), with the Committee of Ministers of the Council of Europe also playing a part occasionally.

Any party to the Convention may refer another party's breach to the Commission via the channel of the Council's Secretary-General. According to the Commission, in *Austria* v. *Italy* (1961), a state raising a matter in this way is not vindicating its own rights but is rather bringing before the Commission 'an alleged violation of the public law of Europe'.

Under Article 25 of the Convention the Commission may also receive petitions (or, as they have come to be called, applications) from individuals, provided that the state against which the complaint is made has declared that it recognises the competence of the Commission to receive such petitions. Most of the parties have made such a declaration. Britain's came in 1966 and has been renewable every five years thereafter (although since 1981 the Isle of Man has been excluded from its scope). The Irish declaration came into effect in 1953 and is for an indefinite period.

3. Admissibility of applications: exhaustion of local remedies. Before proceeding to the substance of a case, the Commission must decide whether the application should be heard at all, i.e. whether it is *admissible*.

Under Article 26 of the Convention admissibility depends in part on whether or not 'all domestic remedies have been exhausted, according to the generally recognised rules of international law'. These rules in fact require only exhaustion of genuine and effective local remedies, so that where a remedy in form but not in substance is all that is available, an applicant need not waste his time and money going through the motions merely to achieve an inevitably adverse result. (*See* also 10:**22**.)

The Commission has adopted this view of Article 26. In *Donnelly* v. *United Kingdom* (1973) it decided that local remedies need not be exhausted when the petitioner is the victim of an administrative practice vitiating local remedies. The court, in *Ireland* v. *United Kingdom* (1978), defined such a practice as 'an accumulation of identical or analogous breaches which are sufficiently numerous and inter-connected to amount not merely to isolated incidents or exceptions but to a pattern or system'. The maltreatment alleged there was a practice because, though 'never authorised in writing in any official document', the procedures involved were taught to police in a seminar at the 'English Intelligence Centre'.

The court explained the reasoning behind this view in *The Greek Case* (1969). Such an administrative practice was said to cause remedies to be side-stepped or rendered inadequate. 'Thus, if there was an administrative practice of torture or ill-treatment', the court continued, 'judicial remedies prescribed would tend to be rendered ineffective by the difficulty of securing probative evidence, and administrative enquiries would either not be instituted, or if they were, would be likely to be half-hearted and incomplete'.

In the *Ireland* v. *UK* case the court added that where a practice was being complained of by another state in the hope of getting it stopped, rather than with a view to settling the claims of particular victims, exhaustion of local remedies was likewise unnecessary.

4. Admissibility: the six-months rule. Article 26 also requires that a petition must be lodged within six months from the date on which the final national decision in a case was taken.

5. Admissibility: other grounds for rejection. In addition to the exhaustion of local remedies requirement, which all cases may face, individual petitions under Article 25 may also be rejected for other reasons. Article 27 requires rejection if:

(*a*) the application is anonymous; or

(*b*) it is substantially the same as a matter already examined by the Commission or submitted to some other settlement procedure *and* it contains no relevant new information; or

(*c*) it is incompatible with (and hence not within the scope of) the Convention, or is manifestly ill-founded, or is an abuse of the right of petition.

The majority of individual applications are in fact rejected at this stage.

6. The Commission's activities. Having admitted a petition, the Commission, according to Article 28, must examine it and if need be undertake an investigation, for which the state concerned must furnish 'all necessary facilities'.

The Commission should also help the parties to reach a friendly settlement. If such a settlement is achieved, the Commission reports briefly to the Committee of Ministers and the case is closed.

Under Article 31, if no solution is reached, the Commission must prepare a fuller report giving its opinion on the merits and send it to the Committee of Ministers. The Committee may then make a determination of its own on the matter and indicate what corrective measures the state concerned must take (Article 32). However, under Articles 44 and 48, the Commission may within three months of making its report in effect take the case out of the Committee's hands by referring the matter to the court.

7. Reference to the court. In addition to the Commission, Articles 44 and 48 also allow a state party to bring a case before the court. But no case may be heard by the court unless its jurisdiction has been recognised as compulsory in a declaration by the accused state or unless that state consents to jurisdiction in the particular case.

Individuals may not refer a case to the court, although the practice of the court has been to allow the concerned person's lawyer to address it on questions of fact or law. In 1983 the court's rules were altered to allow the individual to plead his own case after it has been referred to the court under Articles 44 and 48.

8. Role of the court. The court's judgment in a case is final (Article 52) and legally binding (Article 53). The court may order the offending state to make reparation or, failing that, may provide for 'just satisfaction' (e.g. monetary compensation) to the injured party (Article 50).

9. The problem of derogations. Although not strictly speaking a procedural question, the problem of derogation by a state may conveniently be dealt with here since it can act like a procedural bar limiting or preventing relief to the petitioner.

A *derogation* is an act that lessens, or detracts from, the effectiveness of the Convention.

Article 15(1) provides that:

> In time of war or public emergency threatening the life of the nation any ... Party may take measures derogating from its obligations under this Convention to the extent strictly required by the exigencies of the situation, provided that such measures are not inconsistent with its other obligations under international law.

Article 15(2) makes clear, however, that certain specified provisions, which will be noted below, may not be derogated from.

A close reading of Article 15(1) indicates that a number of factors – relating both to the nature of the emergency faced and to the permissible extent of the derogation – may influence whether a particular derogation is justified. In the first instance, a state acting in good faith must evaluate these factors for itself when deciding whether to derogate. But since the question of a derogation's validity affects the implementation of other parts of the Convention, the Commission and the court also must face the task of evaluating whether events justified derogation.

The problem of review by these bodies has two aspects:

(*a*) the effect it has on the way they handle the complaint and
(*b*) the nature of the review they are entitled to make.

10. Derogation and the handling of the complaint. In *Ireland* v. *United Kingdom* (1978) Sir Gerald Fitzmaurice, in a separate opinion, raised the question of how Article 15 should affect consideration of a case by the court.

The court's practice, he suggested, was to consider whether there had been a violation of a substantive provision and then to determine whether a legitimate derogation *excused* that violation.

Sir Gerald argued, however, that a valid derogation under Article 15 does not merely excuse violations but actually nullifies them as breaches of the Convention, in which case there are no breaches and the state concerned has committed no contravention. Therefore, in his view, the court should consider the Article 15 question first and, if it finds the derogation justified, stop there and not examine the alleged substantive violations.

If the court were to follow this procedure, the result would be that it would not examine large areas of interpretation and application of the Convention's substantive provisions but would confine itself primarily to considering the validity of derogations. This could inhibit development of the Convention's jurisprudence and might tend to conceal human rights abuses – the very opposite of the drafters' original intentions. Not surprisingly, the court has continued to approach the matter in its own way.

11. Reviewing derogations: the 'margin of appreciation'. Derogations arise in situations where the state is faced with complex problems of national safety, politics and law. The Commission and the Court, when assessing the validity of a derogation after the event, inevitably have a different perspective. Yet both bodies are entitled and required to make such an assessment. They must therefore find a way of doing this without on the one hand unduly restricting their own proper activities or on the other trespassing on the state's legitimate area of decision.

To perform this delicate balancing act the two bodies have had to develop the concept of the *margin of appreciation*, a latitude allowed to the state in deciding on derogation. The Court and the Commission will not make their own independent assessment of what should have been done in a particular emergency, but they will examine whether the state's actions could in the circumstances at the time have in principle been considered to be 'required' within the meaning of Article 15(1).

The margin of appreciation idea may be applied not only to sweeping derogations under Article 15 but also to the limitation of specific rights in accordance with any restrictions allowed in the articles of the Convention that set out those rights. But the court has narrowed the margin of appreciation quite considerably in some non-Article 15 cases.

In *The Sunday Times Case* (1979), for example, at issue was Article 10's provision for freedom of expression subject to permissible restrictions in order to maintain the authority and impartiality of the judiciary. The court indicated that, while it would not 'take the place' of competent national tribunals in determining what restrictions might be imposed, its role was *not* 'limited to ascertaining whether a respondent state exercised its discretion reasonably, carefully, and in good faith'. Rather, the court's function extended to 'control' as regards the compatibility of a state's conduct with its obligations under the Convention as seen in the light of generally accepted European standards.

Implementing rights

12. Beneficiaries. Article 1 requires that the parties 'shall secure to everyone within their jurisdiction' the rights provided for in the Convention. Everyone who is actually under a state's authority is covered by this provision, so that in *Cyprus* v. *Turkey* (1975) the Commission could hold admissible a complaint against Turkey over its treatment of persons subject to its military occupation of northern Cyprus.

13. Failure to 'secure' rights. Another question under Article 1 is whether a state, simply by not legislating on the Convention's provisions in its municipal law, may violate that article's obligation to secure to everyone the rights proclaimed. In *Ireland* v. *United Kingdom* (1978) the court indicated that the:

> absence of a law expressly prohibiting this or that violation does not suffice to establish a breach since such a prohibition does not represent the sole method of securing the enjoyment of the rights.

Nor is it easy to find a state law in the abstract violative of Article 1, unless the law 'is couched in terms sufficiently clear and precise to make the breach immediately apparent'. Where that is not so, the law must be considered in relation to concrete applications of it in particular instances.

Right to life

14. Protection of the right and the problem of capital punishment. Article 2(1) requires everyone's right to life to be protected by law, with capital punishment allowed only pursuant to the sentence of a court following conviction of a crime for which such punishment is permitted by law. In contrast to the ICCPR, which speaks of the inherent right to life and is inclined to favour abolition of capital punishment (*see* 13:**28**), this provision seems noticeably more muted. Protocol No.6 to the European Convention (adopted in May 1983) does, however, provide for abolition of the death penalty in peacetime.

The cases brought under Article 2(1) have generally not been about capital punishment but about laws allowing abortion.

15. Exceptions. Article 2(2) provides that it is not a violation of the Convention if a life is taken by a use of force which is no more than what is absolutely necessary to defend someone from unlawful violence, to effect an arrest or prevent the escape of a person who is lawfully detained, or lawfully to quell a riot or insurrection. In the *Stewart Case* (1984) the Commission found no violation in the killing of a boy by a plastic bullet fired to quell a riot in Belfast.

Maltreatment

16. The prohibition. Under Article 3, no one 'shall be subjected to torture or to inhuman or degrading treatment or punishment'. No derogation is allowed from this provision.

The key questions here are what sort of ill-treatment comes within Article 3 and how to distinguish between torture and the other prohibited acts.

17. Torture. In *Ireland* v. *UK*, a case about the detention and interrogation of suspected IRA men in Northern Ireland, the court indicated that ill-treatment 'must attain a minimum level of severity' to come within Article 3 but that this was a relative matter and depended on all the circumstances of the case, including the duration of the treatment, its physical or mental effects and, in some cases, the victim's sex, age and state of health. Thus, what might not violate

Article 3 in the case of a healthy young man might contravene it if applied to a pregnant woman or an elderly or sick person.

In that same case, the court distinguished between torture and inhuman or degrading treatment on the basis of the 'intensity of the suffering inflicted'. This implies, as one might expect, that the distinction between the two categories of ill-treatment is also relative, since it depends on the victim's suffering, his personal reaction to the treatment.

The drawback here is that the law may find it difficult to apply a subjective test in a way that seems consistent from tribunal to tribunal or case to case. In *Ireland* v. *UK*, for example, the maltreatment alleged consisted of 'interrogation in depth' applying the so-called 'five techniques': wall-standing, hooding, subjection to noise, deprivation of sleep, and deprivation of food and drink. The Commission unanimously found that the combined use of these techniques amounted to torture, whereas the court held that they were only inhuman and degrading treatment in that, though they caused 'intense physical and mental suffering' and aroused in their victims 'feelings of fear, anguish and inferiority capable of humiliating and debasing them and possibly breaking their physical or moral resistance', the techniques were not 'of the particular intensity and cruelty implied by the word torture'.

18. Degrading punishment. In the *Tyrer Case* (1978) the court considered the sentencing of a juvenile offender to birching, a punishment which it held to be degrading. Birching entailed by its very nature that one human being should inflict physical violence on another, the violence here having an objectionable institutionalised character which was compounded by the aura of official procedure involved in the punishment. This all reduced the victim to the position of an object in the power of the authorities. It all amounted to an assault on his dignity and physical integrity, and the anticipation of the violence to be inflicted on him aroused mental anguish.

In the *Campbell and Cosans Case* (1982) the parents of children in Scottish schools objected to the possibility that their children might be subject to corporal punishment there in violation of Article 3 and of Article 2 of the First Protocol to the Convention (*see also* **63**). The court, while acknowledging that the threat of treatment prohibited under Article 3 might itself violate that provision, held that there had been no such violation in this case. The court agreed, however, that under the First Protocol parents were entitled to have state schools respect their right to ensure for their children education and teaching 'in conformity with their own religious and philosophical convictions'. Here the parents' philosophical convictions prompted them to try and raise their children to oppose violence in human affairs and the institution and example of corporal punishment ran counter to that.

19. Degrading racial discrimination. The *East African Asians Cases* revealed the protections of Article 3 in a new light. In these cases, British passport holders of Asian descent who had been expelled from East Africa claimed violations of the Convention arising from the United Kingdom's refusal to allow them to enter Britain or remain there. Although most of these complaints were eventually withdrawn, at the admissibility stage in 1970 the Commission was prepared to accept that 'discrimination based on race could, in certain circumstances, of itself amount to degrading treatment within the meaning of Article 3'.

Slavery

20. The prohibition and exceptions. Article 4(1) prohibits slavery and servitude and may not be derogated from. However, paras. (2) and (3), while forbidding forced labour, exclude from that category work required in the course of lawful detention, military service, service required in an emergency, and service or work which forms part of normal civic obligations.

Liberty, arrest and detention

21. Arrest and detention. Article 5(1) proclaims the right of everyone to 'liberty and security of person'.

According to the court in the *Engel Case* (1976), liberty here means the 'physical liberty of the person' and would thus appear to be concerned essentially with whether the individual is under lock and key. But in the *Guzzardi Case* (1980) the court was prepared to consider as also coming within Article 5 the confinement of a suspect to a restricted area of a small island under constant surveillance, even though he was not locked up; in so far as he thereby suffered an actual 'deprivation of liberty' and not merely a less severe 'restriction of liberty'.

Article 5(1) goes on to list the general rule's six exceptions whereby a person may be deprived of his liberty 'in accordance with a procedure prescribed by law'. The most important of these exceptions will be examined in turn.

22. Conviction. Under Article 5(1)(a) a person may be deprived of his liberty through lawful detention after conviction of a crime by a competent court. In *Monnell and Morris* v. *United Kingdom* (1987) the court held that this permitted detention not only under the trial court's original sentence but also under a statutory procedure whereby convicted criminals could, as a penalty and discouragement for filing hopeless applications for leave to appeal, be made to spend more time in detention than they had originally been sentenced to.

23. Enforcement of legal duties. Article 5(1)(b) allows detention for non-compliance with a lawful court order or to secure the fulfilment of any obligation prescribed by law.

24. Committal and preventive detention. Article 5(1)(c) permits:

> the lawful arrest or detention of a person effected for the purpose of bringing him before the competent legal authority on reasonable suspicion of having committed an offence or when it is reasonably considered necessary to prevent his committing an offence or fleeing after having done so.

In *Lawless* v. *Ireland* (1961), G. R. Lawless had been held in preventive detention for five months without being brought before a judicial authority. Ireland argued that this was permitted under Article 5(1)(c), as that provision meant that a person's detention must be for the purpose of bringing him a competent legal authority *only* when he is suspected of having committed a crime but *not* when detention was considered necessary to prevent his committing an offence. The court rejected this argument as one which, 'with all its implications of arbitrary power', would be repugnant to the fundamental principles of the Convention. The correct meaning of Article 5(1)(c) was that no one could be arrested or detained except for the purpose of bringing him before a competent legal authority in the situations mentioned.

Article 5(3) requires that everyone arrested or detained under Article 5(1)(c) be brought 'promptly before a judge or other officer authorised by law to exercise judicial power' be 'entitled to trial within a reasonable time or to release pending trial'.

In the *Cases of de Jong, Baljet, van den Brink et al.* (1984) the court held that this provision required a person to be brought automatically before a judicial officer without delay (a wait of even seven days being too long). A judicial officer for purposes of Article 5(3) must be 'independent of the executive and of the parties', must personally hear the detainee, must have the power both to review the circumstances militating for or against detention and to decide, by reference to legal criteria, whether there are reasons justifying detention and to order release if there are none, and he must actually exercise that power.

As to the requirement for release pending trial or trial within a reasonable time, the court in the *Wemhoff Case* (1968) noted that this right continues in effect up to the delivery of judgment in a case but not after conviction. During the period when Article 5(3) applies, the reasonableness of an accused person's continued detention depends not simply on the length of time he is detained but also on whether there is a need to continue detaining him. This need may arise from such factors as the likelihood of the accused's absconding or attempting to suppress evidence (e.g. pressurising witnesses). But even the danger of his fleeing does not warrant continued detention if adequate guarantees for his appearance at trial can be obtained. If these were not provided, however, the fact that the detention continued for an exceptionally long period of time might not of itself violate Article 5(3) when the investigation and trial were prolonged because of the exceptional complexity of the case.

In the *Stögmuller Case* (1969) the court held that continued detention might be justified to prevent the accused's escape if there is a 'whole set of circumstances ... which give reason to suppose that the consequences and hazards of flight will seem to him to be a lesser evil than continued imprisonment'.

The court determined in the *Matznetter Case* (1969) that continued detention could also be legitimate where in the special circumstances of the case there was good reason to believe that the accused, if released, would commit further serious crimes.

In the *Neumeister Case* (1968) the court held that the danger of flight had to be evaluated in the light of such factors as the accused's character, morals, home, occupation, assets, family ties and links with the country. Furthermore, the danger of flight decreases as the time in detention increases in countries where time spent on remand may be deducted from the eventual sentence upon conviction. In assessing the financial guarantees which a national court should accept to allow release pending trial, the primary consideration is not (as the Austrian court in *Neumeister* seemed to think) whether the money offered approximates to the reparation which the accused might be ordered to make to his victim but whether the funds pledged are sufficient to ensure appearance at trial.

However, the court made clear in the Guzzardi Case (*see* 21) that the preventive detention aspect of Article 5(1)(c) does not permit 'a policy of general prevention directed against an individual or category of individuals' but only gives the state 'a means of preventing a concrete and specific offence'.

25. Detention of unfortunates. Article 5(1)(e) allows:

the lawful detention of persons for the prevention of the spreading of infectious diseases, of persons of unsound mind, alcoholics or drug addicts or vagrants.

As regards vagrancy, in the *Guzzardi Case* (1980) the court held that Italy could not justify the detention of a suspected Mafia figure simply by classifying him as a 'vagrant' when he clearly did not come within the ordinary meaning of that word and had not otherwise been treated as such by the Italian authorities. The *Vagrancy Cases*, decided by the court in 1971, demonstrate, however, that unlimited detention of genuine vagrants is permissible, provided the detainee is allowed to exercise his rights under Article 5(4) (*see* **28**).

In *Winterwerp* v. *The Netherlands* the Commission in 1977 decided that the detention of a person as being of unsound mind must not be arbitrary and must be based on medical confirmation that his mental condition justifies it. The court in 1981 emphasised that such detention is not permitted simply because a person's views or behaviour deviate from prevailing norms. Objective medical evidence must establish the existence of a real mental disorder of such a kind or degree as to warrant compulsory confinement, such confinement remaining valid only so long as the disorder persists. In *X* v. *United Kingdom* (1981) the court made such detention also subject to the detainee's right periodically to take proceedings under Article 5(4) to test the continued lawfulness of his detention.

26. Immigration. Under Article 5(1)(f) a person may be arrested or detained 'to prevent his effecting an unauthorised entry into the country' or when action is being taken against him 'with a view to deportation or extradition'. In *Zamir* v. *United Kingdom* (1985) the Committee of Ministers decided to take no further action in the case of an illegal immigrant to Britain who was detained pending deportation. The Commission had previously determined that such detention was permissible when the detainee had the opportunity to exercise his rights under Article 5(4) but had criticised the slowness of the proceedings, a defect corrected by a change in the relevant British rules. The issue of the right of a person detained pending deportation to challenge his detention arose also in the *Amekrane Case* (1974), but was not ruled upon by the Commission in view of the 'friendly settlement' reached between the parties. (*See* **8:31**.)

27. Information to accused. Article 5(2) requires that everyone arrested or detained be informed promptly, in a language which he understands, of the reasons for his arrest and of any charge against him, thus allowing him to judge in the first instance whether to pursue his rights under Article 5(4).

28. Right to challenge detention. As already noted, Article 5(4) gives a detainee the right to 'take proceedings by which the lawfulness of his detention shall be decided speedily by a court and his release ordered if the detention is not lawful'.

The adequacy of the proceedings available is not necessarily determined solely by the standards of domestic law, especially if the detainee wishes to challenge not merely the legality of the procedures of his detention but also the substantive grounds for that detention. In *X* v. *United Kingdom* (1981) the Court confirmed the conclusion of the Commission that a person detained as criminally insane under an order of the Home Secretary did not have his rights under Article 5(4) fully protected, since *habeas corpus* review in the Divisional Court was limited to considering whether the Home Secretary had acted within his legal powers and in good faith, while the statutory Mental Health Review Tribunal was only an advisory body and hence incapable of ordering the applicant's release.

Case law under the Convention suggests that to qualify as a 'court' under Article 5(4) a tribunal must be independent, able decisively to determine the lawfulness of detention, and must follow at least quasi-judicial procedures and offer a scope of review appropriate to the seriousness of the deprivation of liberty involved: see, most recently, *Weeks* v. *UK* (1987).

29. Compensation. Article 5(5) grants victims of violations of this article an enforceable right to compensation.

The right to a hearing

30. Fair hearing. Article 6(1) provides in part that:

> In the determination of his civil rights and obligations or of any criminal charge against him, everyone is entitled to a fair and public hearing within a reasonable time by an independent and impartial tribunal established by law.

The judgment of the tribunal in such cases must be pronounced publicly, although the press and public may be excluded from the trial in the interests of morals, public order or national security in a democratic society, to protect juveniles and family life, or 'to the extent strictly necessary in the opinion of the court in special circumstances where publicity would prejudice the interests of justice'.

Like Article 5's pre-trial guarantees these provisions have generated a great deal of litigation.

31. Civil rights and obligations. There is first the question of what types of cases Article 6(1) applies to. In the *Ringeisen Case* (1971) the court held that the phrase 'civil rights and obligations' covers 'all proceedings the result of which is decisive for private rights and obligations'. This includes some disputes between a private individual and the government, and not only when the government is acting in a private law capacity. Thus the operation of administrative tribunals and authorities is covered when their determination of public law questions will decisively affect private law rights, provided that, as the court ruled in the *Le Compte Case* (1981), the relationship of the private law right to the public law proceedings is more than 'a tenuous connection' or a matter of 'remote consequences'.

An example illustrates what this means in practice. In the *König Case* (1978) the applicant had suffered the withdrawal of his state licences to operate a private medical clinic and to practise medicine. Proceedings which he had raised to contest these decisions before administrative tribunals had been running for years without result. The court held that this case was one of private law rights – those of Mr König to run his clinic and to work in his profession – even though the proceedings in the tribunals had to do with public law supervision of the practice of medicine in the interests of public health. Article 6(1) therefore applied to the administrative hearings and he was entitled to a conclusion from them 'within a reasonable time'. The court reaffirmed this approach in the *Benthem Case* (1985) dealing with proceedings related to the applicant's request for a licence to install facilities for selling liquid natural gas as motor vehicle fuel.

In the *Winterwerp Case (see 25)* the court held that the proceedings to commit the applicant to a mental hospital under Article 5(1)(e) raised a 'civil rights' question under Article 6(1) insofar as under Dutch law they operated automatically to deprive him of his civil capacity to deal with his own property without that issue of capacity having been litigated during those proceedings.

However, in the *Kaplan Case* (1980) the Commission made clear that Article 6(1) does not apply to all government actions affecting 'civil rights'. It is concerned only with the acts of a body which is engaged in resolving a *claim* or *dispute* about legal rights and obligations of a 'civil' character. It does not deal with the acts of an administrative body or other government entity that is merely exercising or applying a legal power vested in it but is not settling a legal dispute.

A point to note here is that, as the court indicated in the *König Case*, the status of a matter as one of private law 'civil rights' does not depend entirely on the categorisation applied in domestic law, though that may be one factor to be taken into consideration.

On the definitional question it should be noted that the *Ringeisen* definition of 'civil rights' excludes certain significant alternative intepretations. In particular, under it Article 6(1) does *not* deal with civil rights in the sense of 'civil liberties' or constitutional or human rights. Thus, in the *Klass Case* on wire-tapping *(see 43)*, the Commission in 1977 decided that such secret surveillance and interception of communications were typical acts of state authority in the public interest and did not at all concern private law rights for which Article 6 would have guaranteed the applicants a hearing before anything was done against them.

32. Criminal charge. In the *Engel Case* (1976) soldiers who had been punished under the rules of military discipline complained in part that they had not been accorded a fair hearing under Article 6(1). The court indicated that the distinction between a 'disciplinary charge', to which that article did not apply, and a 'criminal charge', to which it did, depended on such factors as the nature of the offence and the severity of the possible penalty. A risk of significant deprivation of liberty would bring the charge into the criminal sphere.

In the *Campbell and Fell Case* (1984) the court concluded that Article 6(1) applied to British prison disciplinary proceedings. The prisoners were charged with acts that by their nature as grave offences that were parallel to ones dealt with in the general criminal law did not appear to be purely disciplinary matters and the possible penalty of substantial loss of remission seemed also to reach the level of 'criminal' punishment.

33. Access to a court. Once it is clear that a case falls within the guarantees of Article 6(1) the next question is the obligations which the individual's right to a hearing imposes on the state.

The classic case is *Golder* v. *United Kingdom* (1975). A prison guard had accused Golder, an inmate of Parkhurst Prison, of having been in a group of prisoners who had assaulted him. The accusation was later discredited but Golder feared that it had remained on his record and he believed that because of it he had been refused parole. To clear the matter up he wished to sue the guard for libel, but was not allowed by the authorities to contact a solicitor to initiate proceedings. Britain argued that Article 6(1) applied only to a hearing in a pending case and did not imply a right to raise a new case. The court decided, however, that the provision covered any dispute relating to civil rights and obligations, including new proceedings which an applicant might wish to initiate in connection with such a dispute. To reach this conclusion the Court adopted a teleological approach to interpreting the Convention (*see* 2:41 and 11:14–16). Its preamble showed that a purpose of the Convention was to promote the rule of law. 'In civil matters,' the court said, 'one can scarcely conceive of the rule of law without there being a possibility of having access to the courts'. Limiting such access to pending cases would not be in keeping with this purpose, since to do so would allow a government arbitrary power to do away with its courts or restrict their jurisdiction and would undermine the prerequisite for a right of access in pending cases, namely, the right to get to a court in the first place. The right of access, including for new cases, was thus an inherent element in the right to a fair hearing.

In spite of this clear and convincing ruling, in the *Silver Case* (1983) Britain was again discovered by the court to have violated Article 6(1) by not allowing a prisoner to write to a solicitor with a view to civil proceedings against the Home Office.

In the *Airey Case* (1979) the court had to deal with quite a different situation. Mrs Airey claimed that, because of the prohibitive costs of legal proceedings and the absence of legal aid, Ireland, her home state, had effectively prevented her from having access to a court to obtain a judicial separation from her allegedly abusive husband. The court considered that Article 6(1) was meant to embody an effective right and that a practical hindrance to the exercise of that right could be as much a violation of the Convention as a legal impediment. Positive state action may be necessary to remove such a hindrance. Therefore, Article 6(1) may compel the state to provide legal assistance when that is indispensable, as it was for various reasons in Mrs Airey's case.

Waiver by the applicant of his right to a hearing may not always be decisive. In the *De Weer Case* (1980), the applicant, owner of a butcher shop where a government inspector uncovered infractions of the price control regulations, had been officially given the choice of paying an immediate fine to settle the case or facing a financially damaging enforced closure of the shop until criminal proceedings could be begun against him. To avoid the considerable losses involved in closure, he paid the fine and so gave up his opportunity to get a hearing. The court found that this waiver had been made 'under pressure so compelling that it is not surprising that Mr De Weer yielded'. Because this renunciation was not made freely and without constraint Mr De Weer's right to a hearing remained and had not been respected by the authorities.

34. Fair and public hearing. When the individual gains access to a court he has certain procedural entitlements.

According to the Commission in *Pataki and Dunshirn* v. *Austria* (1963), a fair trial requires 'equality of arms', with the accused having the same right as the prosecution to be represented at the hearing. The court confirmed this view in the *Delcourt Case* (1970).

In the *Bönisch Case* (1985) equality of arms under Article 6(1) was held to require also that defence expert witnesses be given equal treatment with expert witnesses called against the accused.

In the *Sutter Case* (1984) the court considered the implications of Article 6(1)'s guarantee of publicity for judicial proceedings. This right was intended to protect litigants against secret trials and to promote public confidence in the administration of justice. But the precise mechanisms for achieving these aims (e.g. reading judgments out aloud in court as against issuing them in an easily accessible written form) might legitimately vary from state to state provided the underlying purpose of the Convention was upheld.

35. Independent and impartial tribunal. In *Bramelid and Malmstrom* v. *Sweden* (1983) the Commission stated that a tribunal's independence was an essential precondition for impartiality. A tribunal had to be – and be seen to be – independent of the executive and of the parties.

The *Sramek Case* (1984) concerned an Austrian provincial tribunal empowered to consider decisions of the provincial government relating to land transactions by foreigners. Three members of the tribunal were in fact also civil servants of the provincial government. The court saw this as a violation of Article 6(1), since where 'a tribunal's members include a person who is in a subordinate position, in terms of his duties and the organisation of his work, *vis-à-vis* one of the parties, litigants may entertain a legitimate doubt about that person's independence'.

Alternative means of determining the impartiality of a judge were set out by the court in the *Piersack Case* (1982). Subjectively, his own state of mind in the particular circumstances might be ascertained, or, objectively, an examination could be made to see whether he offered guarantees of sufficient impartiality as to exclude any legitimate doubt.

In the *De Cubber Case* (1984) the court applied the objective method where a judge on the criminal court that was hearing the applicant's case had also been involved with the matter at an earlier stage as the investigating judge under Belgium's civil law system. The court indicated that the existence of a legitimate reason to fear a judge's lack of impartiality would be justification enough for requiring him to withdraw from a case. In Belgium, the investigating judge was an officer of the criminal investigation police and came under the supervision of the *Procureur Général*. In this role he had wide-ranging powers and could conduct his investigation along inquisitorial lines in secret and without the presence of the parties. He would thus have had a detailed knowledge of the case well before the hearing at which the accused would present his defence. In these circumstances the accused might conclude that the judge would play a crucial role in the trial and perhaps bring a preconceived opinion to bear on the court's deliberations. The accused might well doubt the judge's, and the court's, impartiality, and therefore Article 6(1) would be violated by a system that failed to exclude the investigating judge from serving on the tribunal.

36. Hearing within a reasonable time. The 'reasonable time' guarantee in Article 6(1) has been at issue in a number of cases.

The court stated in the *Wemhoff Case* (1968) (*see* 24) that this right covered the period right up to acquittal or conviction, 'even if this decision is reached on appeal'. No violation of Article 6(1) was found in that case, however, in light of the considerations set out in the court's discussion of Article 5(3).

In the *Neumeister Case* (1968) the court found that the seven years which the applicant had waited after being charged without being acquitted or convicted was 'an exceptionally long period which in most cases should be considered as exceeding the reasonable time laid down in Article 6(1)'. But the court discovered extenuating circumstances in the complexity of the case, the difficulty of gathering evidence, and the problems of the judiciary in handling a case that involved a number of defendants. There was thus no violation in these circumstances. Judge Zekia entered a strong dissent to this judgment:

> In a democratic society to keep a man in suspense and in mental agony for seven years and over, in a state of uncertainty and not knowing what would befall him, with the consequential hardships to him and his family in business and society, in my view, constitutes a clear violation ... [of Article 6(1)].

He suggested that where there was doubt about the legality of a delay the court should rule in favour of the individual.

The court was prepared in the *Buchholz Case* (1981) to confirm that the Convention imposes 'a duty on the ... parties to organise their legal systems so as to allow the courts to comply with the requirements of Article 6(1)', but it has apparently been reluctant to issue sweeping condemnations of long-established procedures and arrangements. It has concentrated instead on the facts of individual instances and leaves general inferences to made by others. Thus, in the *König Case* (*see* **31**), although a violation of Article 6(1) was found in administrative proceedings that lasted for almost eleven years, the court wished 'to emphasise that it is not its function to express an opinion on the German system of procedure before administrative courts ... [whose 'procedural maze' and complexity could be accounted for by] the eminently praiseworthy concern to reinforce the guarantees of individual rights.'

However, an interesting hint of a rather more forthright attitude appears in the *Guincho Case* (1984). The court held that the relevant proceedings before a Portuguese court, which had lasted almost four years, exceeded the length of time permitted under Article 6(1). There had, the court noted, been two periods of nearly complete inactivity by the Portuguese authorities, causing delays which could have been justified only by very exceptional circumstances. Portugal contended that some of the problems in the case had arisen because of the disruption attendant upon Portugal's return to democracy and the ensuing increase in litigation. But the court, while 'not in any way' underestimating the efforts made by Portugal to improve the situation, insisted that Portugal had to carry out the international obligations she had undertaken in the Convention, particularly the 'reasonable time' requirement, which was extremely important for the administration of justice. Presumably, the court will from now on be less inclined to tolerate the delays in judicial systems that have not been affected by upheavals like those in Portugal.

37. Presumption of innocence. Article 6(2) requires that everyone charged with a criminal offence be presumed innocent until proved guilty according to law.

38. Procedural rights in a criminal trial. Specifically in relation to criminal cases, Article 6(3) lists a number of procedural rights of the defendant.

The accused must be informed promptly, in a language he understands, of the nature and cause of the accusation against him (Article 6(3)(a). He must have adequate time and facilities to prepare his defence (Article 6(3)(b)), and it is clear from the Commission's report in the *Can Case*, discussed below, that this implies the right to consult a lawyer in the preparatory stages of a case.

The accused must be allowed to defend himself in person or through legal counsel of his own choosing (Article 6(3)(c)). Relying on this right, the applicant in *Goddi* v. *Italy* (1984) complained of a violation when a criminal appeal judgment was passed against him *in absentia* by a court in Bologna while the authorities were detaining him in Orvieto on another charge. The court held that in the circumstances of the case Mr Goddi's rights had been infringed since he had not had the opportunity to defend himself personally or arrange a practical or effective defence by a lawyer of his own choosing. The appeal court's nomination of a lawyer of its choice to represent Mr Goddi did not cure this defect in view of the way that person undertook his duties: he had requested the appeal court to deal with the case at its discretion.

If the accused does not have the means to pay for legal assistance, it must be provided to him free when the interests of justice require. The *Artico Case* (1980) raised the issue of the quality of legal help that must be assured. The court decided that Article 6(3)(c) aimed to guarantee *effective* assistance, something that was not assured merely by appointing a lawyer. If, as in this case, the appointee is reluctant to carry out his assignment, the authorities must either replace him or get him to fulfil his duties.

In the *Can Case* the Commission held in 1984 that the right to effective legal counsel entailed in general a right to consult one's lawyer in private and not always in the presence of a court official, although some restrictions of this right might occasionally be justified by the special circumstances of a case. In 1985 a friendly settlement was reached on the basis of the Commission's report and was noted by the court.

The accused has the right to examine the witnesses against him and to obtain the attendance and examination of witnesses on his behalf (Article 6(3)(d)).

Finally, the defendant is entitled to the free assistance of an interpreter if he cannot understand or speak the language used in court. In two cases against West Germany (the *Luedicke, Belkacem and Koç Case* (1978) and the *Öztürk Case* (1984) the court held that, for both major criminal cases and minor traffic offence charges, it was a violation of this right to provide an interpreter and then charge the defendant a fee for that service if he lost the case.

Retrospective laws
39. No retroactive offences. Article 7 provides that no one shall be held guilty of a criminal offence when the relevant act or omission was not a crime under national or international law at the time it was committed, nor may a heavier penalty be imposed than the one that was applicable at the time the offence was committed. No derogation from these rights is permitted.

Privacy
40. Respect for personal life. According to Article 8(1) 'Everyone has the right to respect for his private and family life, his home and his correspondence', but Article 8(2) permits interference with this right in accordance with the law when necessary in a democratic society in the interests of national security, public safety, or national economic well-being, or to prevent disorder or crime, to protect health or morals or the rights and freedoms of others. This article has been a source of fruitful developments in a number of areas of law and it is worth considering each in turn.

41. Private and family life. Where questions of the protection of society or its members are not at issue, the Commission has tended to define the sphere of protected private life very widely. In the *Van Oosterwijck Case* (1979), where the applicant, registered at birth as a female, had undergone surgery to give him the physical characteristics of a male but was prevented by Belgian law from changing his civil status accordingly, the Commission said that 'private life' within the meaning of Article 8(1) went beyond simply the right to live, as far as one wishes, protected from publicity. The right to private life also comprised 'the right to establish and develop relationships with other human beings, especially in the emotional field for the development and fulfilment of one's own personality'. In this connection, the Belgian law refused to recognise essential elements in the applicant's personality: his sexual identity, his psychical make-up and his social role, and so violated Article 8. This decision cannot be regarded as a final disposition of the matter, however, as the court in 1980 rejected jurisdiction over the case on the ground that domestic remedies had not been exhausted.

The *Marckx Case* (1979) allowed the court to develop its broad conception of Article 8. The applicant complained that Belgian law interfered with her family in not recognising for her illegitimate daughter the same family rights and relationships as for legitimate children. Adopting the position that the Convention 'must be interpreted in the light of present-day conditions', the court found that there had indeed been violations of Article 8. That provision was held to apply to the family life of the 'illegitimate' family as well as to that of the 'legitimate' one; and it does not entail merely the state's negative duty to refrain from interference but also positive obligations inherent in an effective respect for family life. In dealing with the relationships of an unmarried mother and her child, the state must act in a manner calculated to allow those concerned to lead a normal life, allowing in particular the child's integration into its family. In a vigorous dissent, Sir Gerald Fitzmaurice attacked this whole line of thinking and argued that Article 8 was not about any of these matters at all but was simply a device to prevent police-state intrusions into the life of the citizen.

Ireland was found in the *Airey Case* (1979) (*see* 33) to have infringed Article 8 in that, by not effectively making possible for Mrs Airey a judicial separation from her husband, it had failed to protect her rights of private and family life in a situation where that right required her being relieved from the duty of cohabitation.

Where the wider interest seems to warrant interference, the Court and the Commission must attempt to balance competing claims. This can be seen in the decisions of the two bodies in cases involving control of homosexual activities.

In the *Dudgeon Case* (1981) the court had to consider the effect of laws in Northern Ireland making homosexual acts a criminal offence. In light of these laws the police had seized papers belonging to the applicant which implicated him in such offences and had questioned him in a police station about his sex life, although in the end he was not prosecuted and the material seized was returned to him. For the court, given that in a case concerning the most intimate aspect of private life only 'particularly serious reasons' could justify interference, the key issue was whether the legislation's restriction on the applicant's rights under Article 8(1) was 'necessary in a democratic society ... for the protection of morals' in terms of Article 8(2).

Although the moral climate in Northern Ireland and the opposition there to changing the laws on homosexuality were relevant for the purposes of Article

8(2), they were not decisive when the Convention right under attack 'protects an essentially private manifestation of the human personality'. The court noted that the authorities had not in recent times enforced the law with respect to private homosexual acts between consenting adults, and no evidence had been produced to show that this had been injurious to moral standards or had provoked any public demand for stricter enforcement. Therefore, no pressing social need existed for making such acts criminal offences, 'there being no sufficient justification provided by the risk of harm to vulnerable sections of society requiring protection or by the effects on the public'.

Proportionality between the legitimate aims sought and the harm caused by the laws in question was also an issue. The court considered that such justifications as there were for retaining the law in force unamended were outweighed by the detrimental effects which the very existence of the legislation had on a homosexual's life.

The court was at pains to point out, however, that decriminalisation does not imply approval and 'a fear that some sectors of the population might draw misguided conclusions in this respect from reform of the legislation does not afford a good ground for maintaining it in force with all its unjustifiable features'.

In X v. *United Kingdom* (1978), however, the Commission had found no violation in the conviction of the applicant for homosexual offences with a person under the age of twenty-one, since this interference with private life was necessary for the protection of the rights of others, in particular to prevent young men between the ages of eighteen and twenty-one being subjected to social pressures which could be harmful to their psychological development. In the *Dudgeon Case* the court also accepted that some degree of control of homosexual conduct was legitimate 'to provide safeguards against the exploitation and corruption of those who are specially vulnerable by reason, for example, of their youth'.

In the *Brüggemann and Scheuten Case* (1977), the applicants claimed that a West German law limiting abortion in the early stages of pregnancy violated their rights under Article 8(1) since its effect was to force upon them certain choices in their private lives: renouncing sexual intercourse, using contraceptives, or risking an unwanted child. While recognising the wide sphere of life protected by the article, the Commission considered that an individual reduces his right to respect for his private life when he brings that life into contact with public life or other protected interests. The private life of a pregnant woman became closely connected with the developing foetus, so in principle pregnancy and its termination were not solely a matter of the mother's private life. Dissenting from this decision, the British member of the Commission, Prof. J. E. S. Fawcett, argued that an intervention in private life like that at issue here became a prohibited interference if it was not justified on grounds permitted under Article 8(2). Germany had not established in evidence before the Commission what these might be.

In the case of *Leander* v. *Sweden* (1985) the Commission held that the applicant's rights under Article 8 were not violated by the keeping of data about him in the Secret Police Register which were later used to his detriment in regard to his employment by the government, since the state had left to it by Article 8(2) an area of discretion to defend national security and Swedish data protection legislation provided effective safeguards against misuse of the information on file. The Commission has also indicated, in X v. *Federal Republic of Germany* (No. 6357/73), that Article 8(2) may operate to allow deportation of a foreign husband, even though this would separate him from his wife and children in violation of Article 8(1), when his deportation is necessary in a democratic society for reasons of public safety or to prevent crime or disorder.

42. Private life and correspondence. The Commission and the Court have had to deal with cases under this heading in two main areas:

(a) wire-tapping and secret surveillance (*see* 43); and

(b) limitations on the right of prisoners to correspond with their solicitors (*see* 44).

43. Communications. The first major case on clandestine interference with communications was *Klass* v. *Federal Republic of Germany* (1978) in which a West German judge, a public prosecutor and three lawyers challenged a law which permitted secret monitoring of correspondence and telephone calls. Even though the applicants could not point to concrete measures affecting them, this petition was declared admissible on the ground that under certain conditions an individual could claim to be the victim of a violation because of the 'mere existence of secret measures or of legislation permitting secret measures', especially where even the possibility of wire-tapping might inhibit phone conversations and so interfere with rights of privacy under Article 8.

There was no dispute about the interference such surveillance represented, so that the court was able to concentrate on whether it was permissible under the exceptions allowed in Article 8(2). It said: 'powers of secret surveillance of citizens, characterising as they do the police state, are tolerable under the Convention only in so far as strictly necessary for safeguarding ... democratic institutions'. The legislation at issue aimed at such safeguarding, but one had also to wonder whether the means used were necessary. The court noted that 'democratic societies nowadays find themselves threatened by highly sophisticated forms of espionage and by terrorism, with the result that the state must be able, in order effectively to counter such threats, to undertake the secret surveillance of subversive elements operating within its jurisdiction'. Therefore, 'the existence of some legislation granting powers of secret surveillance over the mail, post and telecommunications is, under exceptional conditions, necessary in a democratic society in the interests of national security and/or for the prevention of disorder or crime'.

However, the state does not have 'unlimited discretion to subject persons within their jurisdiction to secret surveillance', in view of the 'danger such a law poses of undermining or even destroying democracy on the ground of defending it'. There must, therefore, be 'adequate and effective guarantees against abuse'. In Germany, such guarantees existed for restricting the imposition of surveillance, its execution, and the use made of the data produced. Two supervisory bodies had 'sufficient independence to give an objective ruling' on such matters.

In the *Malone Case* (1984) the court discovered quite a different situation with regard to secret surveillance in Britain. Telephone-tapping and related activities were held unanimously in that case to have been carried out in so unregulated and discretionary a way that they did not even meet the requirement in Article 8(2) that the interference be 'in accordance with the law'.

That phrase, in the court's view, 'does not merely refer back to domestic law but also relates to the quality of the law, requiring it to be compatible with the rule of law'. Hence, 'there must be a measure of legal protection in domestic law against arbitrary interference by public authorities with the rights safeguarded by' Article 8. The situation in the United Kingdom was attended by 'obscurity and uncertainty' about 'what elements of the powers to intercept are incorporated in legal rules and what elements remain within the discretion of the executive' and the law 'does not indicate with reasonable clarity the scope and manner of exercise of the relevant discretion'. 'To that extent', the court said, 'the minimum degree of legal protection to which citizens are entitled under the rule of law in democratic society is lacking'.

44. Prisoners' correspondence. Britain also fell foul of Article 8 in relation to the right of a prisoner to communicate with his solicitor. In the *Golder Case* (1975), where the applicant had been prevented by the authorities from writing to a solicitor to initiate legal proceedings (*see* **33**), the court held that 'impeding someone from even initiating correspondence constitutes the most far-reaching form of "interference" ... with the exercise of the "right to respect for correspondence"'. The court rejected the British government's argument that there was an implied limitation upon this right in the case of convicted prisoners: the only permitted limitations were those stated in Article 8(2). The court could see no basis for Britain's alternative contention that the interference was somehow necessary to prevent crime, promote public safety, or protect the rights and freedoms of others.

Belief

45. Freedom of thought. Article 9(1) states the right of everyone to freedom of thought, conscience and religion, including the freedom to change his religion or belief and to manifest it, alone or in community with others in public or in private, in worship, teaching, practice and observance. Article 9(2) permits only necessary limitations for the usual reasons.

46. Manifesting belief. An interesting case raising the application of Article 9 was *Arrowsmith* v. *United Kingdom* (1978), in which the Commission determined that there had been no violation in the conviction and sentencing of the petitioner for incitement to disaffection among British troops being sent to Northern Ireland. Miss Arrowsmith had distributed leaflets to the soldiers which advised them to go absent without leave or refuse to be posted to Ulster. Her defence was in part that Article 9 protected her actions as a manifestation of her pacifist beliefs. While accepting that pacifism as a belief fell within that provision, the Commission concluded that the leaflets did not clearly have the purpose of furthering pacifist ideas, did not express pacifist views, and therefore did not manifest Miss Arrowsmith's beliefs within the meaning of Article 9.

Free speech

47. Freedom of expression. According to Article 10(1):

Everyone has the right to freedom of expression. This right shall include freedom to hold opinions and to receive and impart information and ideas without interference by public authority and regardless of frontiers. This Article shall not prevent states from requiring the licensing of broadcasting, television or cinema enterprises.

Article 10(2) states, however, that:

> The exercise of these freedoms, since it carries with it duties and responsibilities, may be subject to such formalities, conditions, restrictions or penalties as are prescribed by law and are necessary in a democratic society, in the interests of national security, territorial integrity or public safety, for the prevention of disorder or crime, for the protection of health or morals, for the protection of the reputation or rights of others, for preventing the disclosure of information received in confidence, or for maintaining the authority and impartiality of the judiciary.

These provisions have generated a number of significant cases mainly relating to newspaper and book publishing, although it is clear that Article 10(2) has the potential to raise much wider issues, most notably perhaps in the area of protecting territorial integrity from information about minority or separatist movements.

48. Imparting information. The applicants in *De Geillustreerde Pers N.V.* v. *The Netherlands* (1976) complained that Dutch laws preventing their publishing company from printing the weekly radio and television listings (in order to preserve the broadcasting companies' lucrative monopoly of such publication) violated their right to impart information. The Commission concluded that, as regarded information of the kind involved here, the protected freedom to impart was limited to information produced, provided or organised by the publisher as the author, originator or owner of it. The applicants' situation did not come within this description and so they had suffered no violation of Article 10.

49. Obscenity. In the *Handyside Case* (1976) the court had to examine the suppression in Britain of the applicant's *Little Red Schoolbook* on the ground that it tended to deprave and corrupt children in violation of the Obscene Publications Act. With reference to Article 10, the court stated that the 'machinery of protection established by the Convention is subsidiary to the national systems safeguarding human rights', at least in the area of morals, where there was no uniform European conception. Consequently, state authorities are in principle in a better position than the international judge to give an opinion on the requirements of morality in each country and on what is necessary to meet them. The national authorities should make the initial assessment of whether there is a 'pressing social need' for restriction. But this domestic margin of appreciation is subject to the supervision of the court, which is obliged to bear in mind that freedom of expression applies:

> not only to 'information' or 'ideas' that are favourably received or regarded as inoffensive or as a matter of indifference, but also to those that offend, shock or disturb the state or any sector of the population.

Therefore, every restriction imposed in this area 'must be proportionate to the legitimate aim pursued'. However, the actions against the applicant and his book met this test, since the competent English judges were entitled in the exercise of their discretion to think that the book would have had 'pernicious effects' on the morals of children.

50. The public's right to know. The *Sunday Times Case* (1979) confronted the court with an injunction from a British court against that newspaper to prevent its printing an article about the thalidomide problem while litigation involving the manufacturers was still pending. The House of Lords had held the injunction valid to prevent a contempt of court which would have threatened the proper administration of justice.

On the European level both the Commission and the Court found the injunction a violation of Article 10. A preliminary question was whether the contempt of court rules in the judge-made common law of England amounted to restrictions 'prescribed by law' within the meaning of Article 10(2). In holding that they did, the court found that they met the two requirements which it said flowed from that phrase: that the law must be accessible, so that the citizen may know the legal rules applicable in a given situation, and that a norm, in order to be 'law', must be formulated with sufficient precision to enable the citizen to regulate his conduct.

On the main issues, the key question for the court was whether the restriction imposed on the newspaper was necessary to the maintenance of the authority of the judiciary in terms of Article 10(2). In considering this the court noted, very importantly, that it was not faced with a choice between two conflicting principles of freedom of expression and of judicial authority, but with one principle (freedom of expression) which was subject to a number of exceptions that had to be interpreted narrowly. The distinction is crucial since it implies that the judicial process is subservient to the public interest and is not an autonomous activity that takes place apart from that.

With this in mind, the court reviewed its previous jurisprudence and concluded that 'necessary' in Article 10(2) was not restricted to only what was 'indispensable', but was not so loose as to be equivalent to terms like 'useful', 'reasonable', or 'desirable'. Rather it implied the existence of a 'pressing social need'. A national tribunal's margin of appreciation in determining whether there was such a need was subject to the court's own powers of review (*see* 11), particularly where, as here, the idea of upholding the authority of the judiciary was a more objective and uniform concept in European law than the 'protection of morals' had been in the *Handyside Case.*

The court thus felt free to conclude that, contrary to what some of the English judges had thought, the *Sunday Times* article had not amounted to 'trial by newspaper', but was rather a legitimate contribution to public debate. If there was a 'pressing social need' in the case, it was for disclosure rather than secrecy:

Whilst ... [the courts] are the forum for the settlement of disputes, this does not mean that there can be no prior discussion of disputes elsewhere ... Not only do the media have the task of imparting such information and ideas: the public also has a right to receive them ... the families of numerous victims of the tragedy, who were unaware of the legal difficulties involved, had a vital interest in knowing all the underlying facts and the various possible solutions. They could be deprived of this information, which was crucially important for them, only if it appeared absolutely certain that its diffusion would have presented a threat to the 'authority of the judiciary'.

... The thalidomide disaster was a matter of undisputed public concern ... fundamental issues concerning protection against and compensation for injuries resulting from scientific developments were raised and many facets of the existing law on these subjects were called in question ... the facts of the case did not cease to be a matter of public interest merely because they formed the background to pending litigation.

51. Contempt of court. Freedom to impart information and contempt of court also clashed in the case of *Harman* v. *United Kingdom*, declared admissible by the Commission in 1984. Ms Harman had obtained a judicial order for discovery of certain documents by the Home Office for use in a case raised against it by her client, a prisoner in a 'special control unit'. After the material parts of these documents had been read out in open court during the hearing of that case, Ms Harman, considering that the documents were no longer confidential, had allowed a newspaper correspondent to peruse them. He then wrote an article based on the documents to expose the special control units. Ms Harman was convicted of having acted in contempt of court, though in good faith. Before the Commission, she argued that enforcing a contempt of court rule against her was not 'necessary', since the information in the documents had already been made public at the hearing. The British government countered with the contention that confidentiality remained important to encourage litigants to cooperate with discovery orders. A hidden issue here is whether a government department which is accountable to the public for its actions is entitled to the same degree of protection of confidentiality as a private litigant who is not publicly accountable. The case was settled in June 1986, with the British government agreeing to change the law so as to allow journalists to be shown documents read out in open court and undertaking to pay £36,000 of Ms Harman's legal costs.

52. Professional restrictions on free speech. In *Barthold* v. *Federal Republic of Germany* (1985) the applicant, a veterinary surgeon in Hamburg, complained of an injunction forbidding him from repeating publicly statements he had made in a newspaper interview concerning the inadequacy of veterinary care in the city and mentioning his own special services. That newspaper article had aroused his professional colleagues to claim that he had sought an unfair professional advantage by covertly advertising his clinic (contrary to the rules of the profession) while purporting to be commenting on a question of public interest. The court held, however, that the publicity effect of these statements was 'altogether secondary' to the principal thrust of the comments, which was to put a real issue before the public.

Joining with others   **53. Freedom of assembly and association.** Freedom of peaceful assembly and freedom of association, including the right to form and join trade unions, is guaranteed by Article 11(1). Article 11(2) makes the usual exceptions, with particular allowance being made for restrictions on the exercise of these rights by members of the armed forces, the police and state administrative services.

54. Trade unions. In the *Belgian Police Case* (1975), the *Swedish Engine Drivers Union Case* (1976) and the *Schmidt and Dahlström Case* (1976), the court held that Article 11 required in relation to public employees that trade unions should be entitled to work to protect the interests of their members and should be allowed the rights necessary for that. But the article did not impose upon the state employer particular methods of dealing with the unions in that connection. Consultation with unions, collective agreements, and even granting of the right to strike might be among the methods permitted, but they were not necessarily required by Article 11.

In the *Young, James and Webster Cases* (1981), where the applicants complained of having been dismissed by British Rail after their refusal to join a trade union under a closed shop agreement, the court noted that the right to freedom of association implied 'some measure of freedom of choice as to its exercise', even if the drafters of the Convention had deliberately omitted a provision, like that in Article 20 of the Universal Declaration of Human Rights, stating that no one may be compelled to belong to an association. Although the closed shop as such may not be forbidden under the Convention, the compulsion involved for existing employees in risking dismissal for failure to join a union under a closed shop agreement negotiated after their employment 'strikes at the very substance' of Article 11's freedoms. Furthermore, the applicants' options as to which union to join were restricted by the agreement, thus raising questions of effectiveness of rights: 'An individual does not enjoy the right to freedom of association if in reality the freedom of action or choice which remains available to him is either non-existent or so reduced as to be of no practical value'.

Note that the court reached these conclusions even though British Rail was not held by it to be a state enterprise. The responsibility of the United Kingdom was involved not because it was directly or indirectly the applicants' employer but because UK domestic law, for which Britain is answerable under the Convention, allowed the treatment of which the dismissed men complained. How far this reasoning might extend is unclear.

Forming a family

55. Marriage. Under Article 12 men and women of marriageable age have the right to marry and to found a family, according to the relevant national laws. In the *Hamer Case* (1979) and the *Draper Case* (1980), the Commission found a British law preventing prisoners from marrying to be in violation of this provision.

Remedies

56. Right to an effective remedy. Article 13 provides that everyone whose rights under the Convention are violated must have an effective remedy before a national authority even if the violation has been committed by persons acting in an official capacity.

On its face this provision might seem to be applicable to almost any case in which there has been an unremedied violation of the Convention's substantive rights. This may not, however, be a correct reading of Article 13. In the *Young, James and Webster Cases* (*see* 54) the Commission in 1979 rejected the applicants' claim that Article 13 had been breached insofar as the British substantive law made it impossible for them to win a challenge to their dismissal. The Commission indicated that the article was not meant to require that there be a remedy against legislation as such. However, in the *Abdulaziz, Cabales and Balkandali Case* (*see* 61), the court held that 'since the United Kingdom has not incorporated the Convention into its domestic law, there could be no "effective remedy" as required by Article 13', bearing in mind that a complaint through the appropriate British channels would have brought a remedy only if the discrimination alleged had resulted from a misapplication of the rules, whereas the applicants' case was that the rules themselves caused the violation.

Equal treatment

57. The rule of non-discrimination. Article 14 read͏

> The enjoyment of the rights and freedoms set fc͏
> be secured without discrimination on any groun͏
> language, religion, political or other opinion, na͏
> association with a national minority, property, birth͏

This comprehensive provision gives plenty of scope fo͏
relationship to other articles in the Convention, the division b͏
and permitted discrimination, and the categories or groups of p͏
the article applies.

58. Applying the rule. In the *Belgian Linguistic Case* (1968) the cou͏
grapple with some of these issues in relation to the requirement under ͏
law that education in certain districts around Brussels be in Flemish
though that denied French-speaking pupils the possibility of studying in th͏
own language.

The court began by pointing out that Article 14's right 'has no independent
existence' but is related to other Convention rights so as to require them to be
respected without discrimination. The interaction of Article 14 and other
provisions might, however, produce a situation where a state act or measure
which, taken alone, does not violate another article will amount to a violation
when Article 14 is read in conjunction with that other provision.

To clarify this somewhat difficult point the court offered an example:

> Article 6 of the Convention does not compel states to institute a system of
> appeal courts ... However, it would violate that Article, read in conjunction
> with Article 14, were it to debar certain persons from these remedies without
> a legitimate reason while making them available to others in respect of the
> same type of actions.

This explanation of Article 14 is generally considered to have significantly
broadened individual rights under the Convention. It means that, while
discriminatory acts must be related to a right guaranteed elsewhere in the
Convention, they need not be an independent violation of another provision in
order to be prohibited under Article 14.

As to distinguishing prohibited from permitted discrimination, the court
pointed out that Article 14 does not forbid every difference in treatment. Rather,
in line with the 'principles which may be extracted from the legal practice of a
large number of democratic states', it prohibits distinctions that have 'no
objective and reasonable justification'. To determine whether there is such a
justification, the court will look to see if the state has a legitimate aim in making
a distinction and will consider the effects of the measure at issue. In particular,
it will seek a 'reasonable relationship of proportionality between the means
employed and the aim.' Distinctions which this examination shows to be
arbitrary violate the Convention.

59. 'Other status'. The problem of whom the Convention applies to arises
particularly with reference to those discriminated against on the ground of
'other status' under Article 14. In the *Marckx Case* (*see* **41**), the court held that the
distinction between legitimate and illegitimate children lacked an objective and

reasonable justification and so violated Article 14 taken in conjunction with Article 8. Article 14's 'other status' also covers persons treated differently because they are members of public service trade unions, though the court in the *Belgian Police Case* and the related cases discussed above (*see* 54) held that differences of treatment there between public sector and private sector workers were in pursuit of a legitimate aim through measures that were not disproportionate.

60. Security and discrimination. In *Ireland* v. *United Kingdom* (*see* 17) the Irish government argued that the singling out of IRA suspects for detention and interrogation amounted to a violation of Article 14 read in conjunction with Article 5. The court held, however, that Britain did this with legitimate aims in view and used proportionate means in pursuing them, having in mind that the IRA represented a greater danger than the Protestant Loyalist terrorists whom the authorities were not pressing so strongly.

61. Sex discrimination. In *Rasmussen* v. *Denmark*, involving a Danish law that imposed a time limit on a man's right to raise a case contesting the paternity of his former wife's child but allowed her to raise a paternity suit against him at any time, the Commission found a violation of Article 14 in conjunction with Article 8. The court in a 1984 judgment held, however, that although there was a clear difference in treatment, it fell within the state's margin of appreciation and the Danish authorities were entitled to consider this law justified to ensure legal certainty about paternity and protect the interests of the child. The discrimination was not disproportionate to these aims.

The *Abdulaziz, Cabales and Balkandali Case* (1985) was about sex discrimination in British immigration rules. The applicants, born abroad but lawfully settled in the United Kingdom, were refused permission for their foreign husbands to join them in the UK, although men similarly placed would have been allowed to bring their foreign wives into the country. The court held that there had been a violation of Article 14 taken together with Article 8 (although there had been no violation of Article 8 on its own). The court considered that the immigration rules' aim of protecting the domestic labour market was legitimate but was counter-balanced by the fact that equality of the sexes was a major goal in the states of the Council of Europe, which could not be set aside except for very weighty reasons. It did not appear to the court that statistics on employment demonstrated the need to distinguish between the admission of foreign husbands and foreign wives, nor was the 'aim of advancing public tranquillity' served by the distinction.

The First Protocol

62. Right to property. Under Article 1 of the First Protocol to the Convention every natural or legal person is entitled to the peaceful enjoyment of his possessions and may not be deprived of his possessions except 'in the public interest' and subject to the conditions provided for by law and by the general principles of international law. In *James* v. *United Kingdom* (1986) the court held that the Leasehold Reform Act 1967, which gives long-term tenants of certain residential properties the right in some circumstances compulsorily to purchase the landlord's interest in the property upon terms specified, did not violate this right.

63. Education. Article 2 of the First Protocol provides:

No person shall be denied the right to education. In the exercise of any functions which it assumes in relation to education and to teaching, the State shall respect the right of parents to ensure such education and teaching in conformity with their own religious and philosophical convictions.

As already noted (*see* **18**), the court in the *Campbell and Cosans Case* (1982) held corporal punishment in Scottish schools to be violating this right with respect to parents whose philosophical views required their children to be taught a non-violent approach to human relations.

In the *Danish Sex Education Case* (1976), however, the court decided that compulsory sex education in Danish schools did not violate this article. The court said that, while the state 'is forbidden to pursue an aim of indoctrination that might be considered as not respecting parents' religious and philosophical convictions', the state is not prevented from imparting knowledge of a directly or indirectly religious or philosophical kind provided it is conveyed 'in an objective, critical and pluralistic manner'. The aim of the sex education programme in Denmark was to provide the students with knowledge 'more correctly, precisely, objectively and scientifically' than the other means available to them.

64. Elections. Under Article 3 of the First Protocol the parties 'undertake to hold free elections at reasonable intervals by secret ballot, under conditions which will ensure the free expression of the opinion of the people in the choice of the legislature'. Notice that this does not say that the *executive* is to be chosen in this way, nor does it state that the composition of the legislature must correspond to the distribution of votes cast for the various parties at an election.

The Fourth Protocol   **65. Imprisonment for defaulting on a contract.** Article 1 of the Fourth Protocol (1963) states that no one shall be deprived of his liberty merely on the ground of inability to fulfil a contractual obligation. This covers a variety of situations, but is most significant insofar as it prohibits imprisonment for debt.

66. Freedom of movement. Article 2 of the Fourth Protocol grants the right to liberty of movement and residence (Article 2(1)) and the freedom to leave any country, including one's own (Article 2(2)). Article 2(3) lists the usual security and public safety exceptions, while Article 2(4) allows a special exception to the rights of movement and residence 'in particular areas' by means of 'restrictions imposed in accordance with law and justified by the public interest in a democratic society'.

67. The territorial effects of nationality. Under Article 3(1) of this Protocol no one may be expelled from the territory of the state of which he is a national, nor, by Article 3(2) may he be deprived of the right to enter that state's territory.

Britain is not a party to the Fourth Protocol.

The Convention in British law   **68. International and municipal law.** The relationship of the Convention, as a treaty, to British municipal law has already been considered (*see* **3:17**).

69. The Convention as a British 'Bill of Rights.' Many people would like to see the Convention play a different role in British life in the future. They suggest that it should be adopted in British law as a Bill of Rights. Professor Michael Zander, after examining the advantages and disadvantages of such a charter of fundamental rights and freedoms, and finding it desirable, has concluded that using the Convention for that purpose is in practical terms the only serious option available.

Zander accepts that as a bill of rights the Convention has some draw-backs. It lacks a proper due process clause. Its style and content are somewhat out-dated and, writes Zander, it is 'not in every Article as broad and open-textured as might be desirable to achieve potentially the most fruitful results'. Nevertheless, it is in his view the best that is to hand and it would, with the adoption also of the First and Fourth Protocols, provide the basic guarantees now lacking.

The Helsinki Final Act

70. Nature of the Helsinki Final Act. In 1975 the Conference on Security and Co-operation in Europe (CSCE) brought together in Helsinki the representatives of thirty-five states (including the United States and the Soviet Union) to produce what has become known as the Helsinki Final Act, a non-binding statement on a wide range of military, political, economic and human concerns. With regard to human rights perhaps the most significant part of the Final Act was the Declaration on Principles Guiding Relations between Participating States.

Although this declaration does not create binding law, it appears to have been intended to restate and apply existing international law, of which it would therefore be in the strict sense 'declaratory'. It is thus an acknowledgment by the participating states of their duties under international law.

71. Human rights in the Final Act. Among the duties so acknowledged are those under Principle VII relating to respect for human rights and fundamental freedoms (including the freedom of thought, conscience, religion and belief) for all without distinction as to race, sex, language or religion.

The participating states will promote and encourage civil, political, economic, social, cultural and other rights and freedoms, 'all of which derive from the inherent dignity of the human person and are essential for his free and full development'.

Principle VII also acknowledges the freedom of the individual to profess and practice his religion or belief, alone or in community with others, in accordance with the dictates of his own conscience.

The participating states in which there are 'national minorities' will respect the rights of persons belonging to such minorities to equality before the law and afford them full opportunity to enjoy their rights and freedoms 'and will, in this manner, protect their legitimate interests in this sphere'. This language suggests that the rights of minorities are limited to equality and non-discrimination. But one notes that Principle VIII (which must be seen in the context of a document concerned with Europe) provides for the equal rights and self-determination of 'peoples', a term that would appear to cover some 'national minorities' (*see* 4:47).

The participating states 'recognize the universal significance of human rights and fundamental freedoms', which, they say, must be respected so as to ensure friendly relations and co-operation between those states.

The states 'confirm the right of the individual to know and act upon his rights and duties in this field'.

Finally, and most significantly as far as the status of international human rights law within the participating states is concerned, they:

> will act in conformity with the purposes and principles of the Charter of the United Nations and with the Universal Declaration of Human Rights. They will also fulfil their obligations as set forth in the international declarations in this field, including inter alia the International Convenants on Human Rights, by which they may be bound.

These undertakings are thought by some experts to amount at the least to an acceptance of the UDHR as binding customary law and, more generally, as a recognition of the human rights obligations of states as members of the United Nations.

In subsequent review conferences to develop the Helsinki system some countries (and notably the United States under President Carter) reported on their implementation of Principle VII in terms which suggested a sense of obligation.

The Helsinki Final Act stands as the potential nucleus around which a Europe-wide human rights regime could crystallise if there were the political will (particularly in Eastern Europe) to make it happen.

Progress test 14

1. Who may raise a case to the European Commission on Human Rights? (**2**)

2. In what circumstances might the exhaustion of local remedies not be required? (**3**)

3. Who may refer a case to the European Court of Human Rights? (**7**)

4. When might a general derogation be permissible under the Convention? (**9**)

5. What is meant by the 'margin of appreciation'? (**11**)

6. Is the official taking of human life ever justified under the Convention? (**15**)

7. What constitutes torture under Article 3? (**17**)

8. Is corporal punishment in schools 'degrading' treatment? (**18**)

9. For what purpose may a person be arrested and detained under Article 5(1)(c)? (**24**)

10. Explain the effect of Article 5(4). (**28**)

11. What are 'civil rights and obligations' for the purposes of Article 6(1)? (**31**)

12. Does the right to a hearing imply the right to raise a case? (**33**)

13. What are some of the implications of the notion of 'equality of arms'? (**34**)

14. What is the time limit for trial within 'a reasonable time'? (**36**)

15. Is the right to legal counsel in a criminal trial a mere formality? (**38**)

16. Is the protection of private and family life under the Convention to be understood and applied narrowly? (**41**)

17. Under what circumstances might interception of private communications be permitted? (**43**)

18. Does the public have a 'right to know'? (**50**)

19. What might constitute a violation of the right to an effective remedy? (**56**)

20. Explain the relationship of Article 14 to other substantive rights in the Convention. (**58**)

21. Distinguish improper from permitted divergences between public education activities and the wishes of parents in light of the First Protocol. **(63)**

22. Should the Convention be enacted as a 'Bill of Rights' in Britain? **(69)**

23. How has the Helsinki Final Act helped to consolidate international human rights law? **(71)**

Bibliography

Bailey, Harris, Jones, *Civil Liberties Cases and Materials*, 2nd ed., Butterworths, London (1985)

Beddard, *Human Rights and Europe*, 2nd ed., Sweet & Maxwell, London (1980)

Brownlie, *Basic Documents on Human Rights*, 2nd ed., Clarendon Press, Oxford (1981)

Harris, *Cases and Materials on International Law*, 3rd ed., chapter 9, Sweet & Maxwell, London (1983)

Jacobs, *The European Convention on Human Rights*, Clarendon Press, Oxford (1975)

Secretary, European Commission of Human Rights, *Stocktaking on the European Convention on Human Rights* (1982) and *Supplement* (1984), (Council of Europe, Strasbourg)

Zander, *A Bill of Rights?*, 3rd ed., Sweet & Maxwell, London (1985)

15 Environmental law

Introduction

1. The nature of the problem. The relationship of human beings to their environment is about as complex and wide-ranging a topic as life itself and extends far beyond the scope of a book on international law. But there are aspects of that relationship that the law is, or is becoming, concerned with, and this chapter will focus on them.

The environment, and the ecosystems within it, may serve a variety of purposes: economic, aesthetic and recreational, or scientific. Which of these may be compatible with each other and which exclusive, and which should be favoured, are fundamental questions for environmentalists and policy-makers. In trying to answer them, new problems are discovered. The interests of individuals (as in exploiting non-renewable resources for their own personal benefit) may conflict with the broader interests of the community (e.g. in using non-renewable resources for the common good). Narrow and short-term concerns may obscure broad and long-term issues, especially in the political arena, where short-sightedness seems almost a built-in factor. These difficulties are compounded on the international level by the state system, which militates against global answers to global problems (e.g. the use and protection of the sea and the air).

Environmentalists have attempted to clarify these difficulties and highlight the choices mankind faces by, in the first instance, imposing a certain order on the chaos of nature. They point out that resources may be grouped broadly into renewable ones, like plants, animals, solar energy and air, and non-renewable ones like fossil fuels and minerals.

In regard to the management of natural resources – a key element in environmental protection – resources may be grouped into non-living and living resources. Non-living and living resources management involves questions of soil maintenance and the prevention of erosion, water use and pollution, and the exploiting of new sources of water as with desalinisation, and questions of air pollution and climatic changes caused by such things as increases in carbon dioxide leading to the 'greenhouse effect' and the consequent rise in global temperature.

Managing living resources requires fundamentally that living communities of the animal or plant involved be maintained by, for example, the establishment of parks and nature reserves and the institution of wildlife and fisheries control schemes that prevent exhaustion of the species concerned.

Energy generation and consumption pose problems with regard both to the use of non-renewable resources and to reliance on alternatives like nuclear power.

On the international level problems may arise in connection with the exploitation of non-living resources for the purposes of international commerce, and with regard to such living resources as aquatic animals in international waters, migratory animals, and plant commodities in international trade. The practices of multinational enterprises (*see* 4:**56**) may also have environmental effects, as can the administration of international aid and development programmes.

Taking the world as a whole as regards all these aspects of environmental concern, some experts have concluded that the danger areas in recent years have been the tropical, semi-arid and sub-Arctic zones, where environmental degradation in a relatively brief period has been as extensive as that which took place over centuries in the more temperate regions. The speed of these changes is considered particularly disturbing since it means that there is little time to consider how to avoid irreparable damage and the ability of ecosystems to adjust to the change is gravely impaired.

2. The causes of the problem. In a report published in 1969, the UN Secretary-General identified three underlying trends leading to environmental problems:
   (*a*) population growth;
   (*b*) urbanisation; and
   (*c*) the effects of new technology,
with their resulting demands on available food, natural resources, and living space. In poor and developing countries, particularly, as these demands exert increasing pressure on such resources as there are to meet them, ecosystems may collapse under the strain. The room for manoeuvre of governments and individuals is reduced and longer-term environmental considerations are ignored in a desperate attempt to meet immediate needs.

Even where the crisis point has not been reached, conflicting economic and political considerations often militate against environmental protection. Many people in the Third World, in particular, charge that the poor and the powerless are made to bear the main burden of environmental degradation or else to surrender the possibility of future environmental well-being for the sake of present economic or social benefits (*see* 4:**56**).

3. The task of environmental law. To impose an orderly system of rights and duties on these complex and intractable problems involves the law in an attempt to indicate how a proper balance of interests might be achieved and to deal with situations where the balance has been improperly disturbed. But accomplishing this may require a rethinking of some traditional tenets of international law. When a cloud of radioactive material spread over most of Europe in April 1986 after an accident at a nuclear power station in Chernobyl in the Ukraine, the apparent tendency of the Soviet government to treat the matter as essentially its own business was criticised in the West. According to the president of the United States, 'you can hardly call this kind of an accident an internal affair'. The foreign minister of Italy put the same point in more legal terms: 'Issues of national sovereignty do not exist in this area because there are no frontiers which will stop radiation.' On that basis environmental law could pose a serious challenge to the present system of sovereign states (*see* **19**).

4. The Stockholm Declaration (1972). In an effort to formulate basic principles the United Nations summoned a Conference on the Human Environment in Stockholm in 1972. Its concluding statement, the Stockholm Declaration, became a source of inspiration for later developments over a wide range of issues. Principle 21 of the Declaration restated and somewhat elaborated the rule which has traditionally been the basis of the customary law of the environment:

> States have, in accordance with the Charter of the United Nations and the principles of international law, the sovereign right to exploit their own resources pursuant to their own environmental policies, and the responsibility to ensure that activities within their jurisdiction or control do not cause damage to the environment of other states or of areas beyond the limits of national jurisdiction.

The core principle here is that reflected in the classic maxim *sic utere tuo ut alienum non laedas* (so use your own property as not to injure another's: *see also* 10:9), but applied here to cover also areas of common interest not belonging to any state.

5. The Trail Smelter Case (1941 decision). The leading case on this principle concerned transfrontier pollution. The Trail Smelter Arbitration dealt with the emission of sulphur dioxide fumes from a Canadian smelter which were carried by the wind across the border into the United States, where they caused considerable damage. The arbitral tribunal accepted the principle that a state has a duty to protect other states against injurious acts by individuals from within its jurisdiction, but considered that this was not always an absolute prohibition.

The tribunal cited a Swiss case in which one Swiss canton was initially enjoined from operating a shooting range which endangered another canton. The grounds for the injunction were that the operation of the range was not only a 'usurpation and exercise' of the injured canton's sovereign rights but also an 'actual encroachment which might prejudice the natural use of the territory and the free movement of its inhabitants'. But when protective measures were introduced at the range, the Swiss court lifted the injunction, even though all risk had not been eliminated. 'The demand', it said, 'that all endangerment be absolutely abolished goes too far'.

Applying this analysis to the case before it, the *Trail Smelter* tribunal held, in carefully nuanced language, that:

> no state has the right to use or permit the use of its territory in such a manner as to cause injury by fumes in or to the territory of another or the properties or persons therein, when the case is of serious consequence and the injury is established by clear and convincing evidence.

The tribunal described this as an equitable solution, 'just to all the parties concerned', with the result that the Trail Smelter was not closed nor its pollution stopped altogether, but rather its sulphur dioxide emissions reduced to an acceptable level.

This equitable balancing is implicit in Principle 21 of the Stockholm

Declaration, which speaks not only of the 'responsibility' of a state towards others but also of its 'sovereign right' to exploit its resources.

Compensation

6. Principle 22. In addition to abating the pollution or ceasing to damage the environment of another state, the state which is responsible for the damage must also pay compensation for the damage already caused. Principle 22 of the Stockholm Declaration requires that states cooperate to develop further the international law on liability and compensation for the victims of pollution and other environmental damage caused beyond a state's jurisdiction by activities within that jurisdiction.

Obligations *erga omnes*

7. Who is protected? The Stockholm Declaration's formulation of the two principles discussed immediately above raised the question of whom the obligations mentioned flow to. Although the *Trail Smelter* decision confined itself to liability for damage in another state, Principles 21 and 22 speak of harm to areas beyond state jurisdiction. Generally, it may be assumed that most cases concerning damage beyond any state's jurisdiction will nevertheless involve the citizens or interests of the state which eventually raises a claim.

However, the Stockholm formulation does not close the door on the possibility that liability may extend further to encompass also damage to the interest of states at large in having an environmentally safer world. In other words, it would appear that the obligations of international environmental law should be included in those which the International Court of Justice considered in the *Barcelona Traction Case* to be *erga omnes*, owed 'towards all' (*see* 10:**10** and 13:**19-20**).

This possibility is likely to become increasingly important as international environmental law moves away from concern with the one-on-one relationship of perpetrator and victim which pollution cases usually involve towards concern with the interests of the international community as a whole.

An example illustrates the point. Intensive whaling over the past three hundred years has reduced many species of whale almost to extinction. The International Whaling Commission recommended, as from the end of 1985, a moratorium on commercial catches as a last-ditch measure of conservation, but Norway, Japan and the Soviet Union continued whaling beyond that date. Who was entitled to object to the activities of these three states? Apart from questions of treaty obligations which they might have had under the International Whaling Convention (1946), it would appear that, without a concept of *erga omnes* obligations, these countries were liable under customary international law only to those other states whose catches of whales were diminished, or which were otherwise materially injured, by this unrestrained whaling. If it had been recognised, however, that the international community and its members had an interest in maintaining the richness of the environment and that there was a corresponding *erga omnes* obligation on each member not to impoverish it, the range of states entitled to complain about Norwegian, Japanese or Russian activities would have been considerably expanded.

The duty to co-operate

8. General note. As occasionally happens in the law, states, although reluctant to acknowledge fundamental and sweeping obligations of substance, have by their practice over several decades begun to generate subsidiary principles of behaviour in the environmental field that may tend to have substantive implications or effects. Such principles reflect what has come to be recognised as a general duty to cooperate in preventing or solving environmental problems.

The main subsidiary norms are:

(*a*) the duty to conduct *environmental impact studies* before embarking on any significant project that may adversely affect the environment;

(*b*) the duty to *inform* and *consult* other states which may have an interest in the effects of a particular project or activity;

(*c*) the duty to *warn* other states in the event of an accident with environmental implications;

(*d*) the duty to deal on a basis of *non-discrimination* and *equality* with persons, be they nationals or foreigners, who may have an interest in some environmental question either as victims after the event or as people whose views on prevention of environmental damage ought to be taken into account beforehand. Non-discrimination also requires that those who cause transfrontier pollution should be subject to the same penalties as would apply to similar pollution within the country.

These subsidiary principles bring environmental considerations to bear on a wide range of activities and imply openness, flexibility, and accountability on the part of those who initiate activities which affect the environment. In the wake of the Chernobyl nuclear accident (*see* **3**), for example, the International Atomic Energy Agency (IAEA) prepared a draft convention requiring the immediate *international* notification of nuclear accidents that risked sending radiation across national frontiers (*see also* **19**). [IAEA texts in 25 ILM 1369.]

The general standing of these principles as elements of international law depends on a combination of treaty law, state practice, general principles of law, and even judicial decisions and the writings of publicists. That they do not arise from one clear source which is easy to refer to suggests that international cases based on these principles are likely to prove difficult to resolve.

Pollution

9. The place of anti-pollution law in the general scheme. Pollution has always been the most obvious form of environmental degradation and it is not surprising that the leading case in environmental law, the *Trail Smelter Arbitration* (*see* **5**), should be about it. Air and water pollution, pollution of the land, and noise pollution are all examples of the problem. At first glance, they may seem to fit comfortably into a category rather like that of nuisance in English law: an activity harmful to the public at large or to private land or one that is an unreasonable interference with the use and enjoyment by another of his land. On this view the maxim *sic utere tuo ut alienum non laedas* would appear particularly apt in pollution cases. But on closer examination the analogy with nuisance appears not to fit so precisely. The concept of pollution in international law may be broader than nuisance and the modern trend is to be beyond the passive approach of abatement and compensation after damage has occurred and to emphasise international control and prevention. But the extent to which one approach or the other prevails will depend on the concept of pollution which is adopted. This definitional question is still much debated.

10. The nature of pollution. It is often said that pollution must be understood as an 'additive' process, that is, one in which damage is inflicted by the addition of some undesirable factor into the environment. But this leaves room for considerable debate about what should be regarded as undesirable.

Professor A. L. Springer has pointed to several concepts of pollution and, implicitly, of undesirability. These are:

(*a*) pollution as *any* additive alteration of the environment which reduces its purity; e.g. in the Antarctic Treaty's absolute prohibition on dumping radioactive wastes in Antarctica (*see* 6:44);

(*b*) pollution as damage, either to human beings or their property (as in the *Trail Smelter Case*) or to the environment;

(*c*) pollution as interference with the use of the environment;

(*d*) pollution as the overloading of the environment's capacity to break down or assimilate 'additives' and render them harmless by natural processes.

For Springer these different definitions of pollution are evidence of the key problem in this area: the inconsistent views held by various people in different situations about what kinds and degrees of environmental change man should be allowed to make.

To some extent, of course, several of these concepts of pollution may be relevant in a single case, and Springer detects in the recent development of international law a tendency to combine definitions, as in the Stockholm Declaration of 1972.

11. The Stockholm view of pollution. Principle 6 of the Stockholm Declaration states in part that:

> The discharge of toxic substances or of other substances and the release of heat, in such quantities or concentrations as to exceed the capacity of the environment to render them harmless, must be halted in order to ensure that serious or irreversible damage is not inflicted upon ecosystems.

Principle 7 adds that states 'shall take all possible steps to prevent pollution of the seas by substances that are liable to create hazards to human health, to harm living resources and marine life, to damage amenities or to interfere with other legitimate uses of the sea'.

Taken together these provisions appear implicitly to reject the notion that pollution can be any additive alteration of the environment and to adopt the view that pollution must involve damage, interference with use, or overburdening of the environment's assimilative capacity. It must be noted, however, that the concept of harm reflected in both principles goes beyond the *Trail Smelter* concern with injury to human plaintiffs and encompasses a more generalised idea of illegal damage to the environment and its ecosystems apart from the direct impact such harm might have on people.

The difficulty with giving effect to this broader concept in the sphere of law is to find a basis for the legal liability or responsibility of states or individuals. In the absence of agreement on the *erga omnes* nature of environmental obligations (*see* 7) the general environmental duties of states or individuals must be derived from their specific duties to each other, most notably in treaties but also as a matter of custom and general principles.

12. Pollution of rivers and lakes. As noted before (*see* 7:**7–10**), the principle that states sharing a common system of international rivers and waterways have obligations to each other with respect to navigation and other uses and with regard to pollution seems firmly established in customary international law. The International Law Commission observed in its 1979 report that many experts believed it was generally recognised that under international law a state 'does not enjoy complete freedom in determining the use of the waters of international watercourses within its territory'. The fundamental consideration here is that reflected in the reasoning of the Permanent Court of International Justice in the *River Oder Case* (1929): the existence of a river (or lake) linking two or more states gives rise to a 'community of interest' among the riparians which 'becomes the basis of a common legal right'.

Thus, in the *Lake Lanoux Case* (1957), in which the arbitral tribunal reached its conclusions on the basis of what it called 'international common law', it was said that a legitimate ground in international law on which Spain could have challenged French interference with the waters of a river flowing into Spanish territory from the lake was that 'the works would bring about an ultimate pollution of the waters ... or that the returned waters would have a chemical composition or a temperature or some other characteristic which could injure Spanish interests'.

13. The Helsinki Rules. Attempting to restate the customary law in more general terms, the International Law Association's Helsinki Rules on the Uses of the Waters of International Rivers (1966) define pollution as 'any detrimental change resulting from human conduct in the natural composition, content, or quality of the waters'. This fairly wide definition is, however, applied in a use-oriented way that somewhat limits its effect. Article X says that a state must prevent any new form of water pollution or increase in existing pollution 'which would cause substantial injury in the territory of a co-basin state'. If a violation occurs, the responsible state must cease the wrongful conduct and compensate the injured state.

But with regard to existing water pollution, the responsible state 'should take all reasonable measures' to 'abate' it 'to such an extent that no substantial damage' is caused to a co-basin state. Violation of this rule merely obliges the responsible state to negotiate with the injured state with 'a view toward reaching a settlement equitable under the circumstances'.

The difference in treatment of new and existing pollution reflects the emphasis in the Helsinki Rules on achieving an equitable balance between the competing uses of a river by the riparian states, with existing pollution being considered in effect as a 'use' which must be worked into the equation.

The ILA's official comment on these provisions reveals some of the difficulties and implications of a use-oriented approach to pollution:

Pollution ... may be the result of reasonable and otherwise lawful use of the waters of an international basin. For example, the normal process of irrigation for the reclamation of arid or semi-arid land usually causes an increase in the salinity of downstream waters. Modern industrial processes ... may result in the discharge of deleterious wastes that pollute the water. Frequently rivers are the most efficient means of sewage disposal ... Thus ... the rule of international law stated in this Article does not prohibit pollution *per se.*

The comment's definition of 'substantial injury' is also use-oriented:

Not every injury is substantial. Generally, an injury is considered 'substantial' if it materially interferes with or prevents a reasonable use...

But this concept of injury is not competely satisfactory, as the comment goes on to recognise:

an injury in the territory of a state need not be connected with that State's use of the waters. For example, the pollution of water could result in 'substantial injury' ... by the transmission, through the evaporative process, of organisms that cause disease.

The difficulty with balancing competing uses appears most clearly when the comment tackles a particularly serious issue:

If the activity or conduct causes pollution that endangers human life in another state, such activity or conduct would *probably* be deemed inconsistent with the principle of equitable utilization ... [emphasis supplied]

In a situation of danger to human life, the state's duty under Article X to 'take all reasonable measures' to abate the existing pollution '*could* become an absolute duty' [emphasis supplied]. That even human life is not definitely excluded from the trade-off of uses required by equitable utilisation suggests the need for a broader concept of pollution and of environmental protection.

When the Institut de Droit International adopted its Resolution on Pollution of Rivers and Lakes in 1979, it adopted a use-oriented definition of pollution as 'any physical, chemical or biological alteration in the composition or quality of waters' which, by affecting the legitimate uses of such waters, causes injury. However, the Resolution appears to allow the possibility of applying other concepts where appropriate:

In specific cases, the existence of pollution and the characteristics thereof shall, to the extent possible, be determined by referring to environmental norms established through agreements or by the competent international organisations and commissions.

14. Marine pollution: general considerations. In the classical period of international law, when the ideas of Grotius led states to regard the sea as inexhaustibly vast (*see* 12:4), the use of the sea as a kind of dump for waste and sewage from the land was common and aroused little concern. But as such effluents came to cause increasing danger by their quantities and toxicity, and as new technology threatened potentially devastating harm, a major shift occurred, with over thirty-five major international treaties and agreements being adopted since the mid-1950s.

15. General treaty regimes on marine pollution. The only comprehensive treaty regime to deal with the whole range of marine pollution is the 1982 Law of the Sea Convention. Article 192 imposes a general duty on states 'to protect and preserve the marine environment'. The Convention goes on to set out specific obligations with regard to land-based marine pollution, pollution from sea-bed activities, pollution coming from dumping in the sea or coming through the atmosphere, and pollution from ships. Article 237 makes clear, however, that the Convention does not supersede or forestall other present or future anti-pollution treaties, provided their obligations are performed in a way consistent with the Convention's general principles and objectives.

Other general treaties with anti-pollution provisions are the Geneva Conventions of 1958 and numerous regional seas conventions, some of which have been concluded under the auspices of the United Nations Environment Programme (UNEP).

Articles 24 and 25 of the 1958 High Seas Convention require states to act to prevent pollution by oil discharge from ships or pipelines or by exploitation of the seabed and pollution from radioactive materials and 'other harmful agents'. In the 1958 Continental Shelf Convention Article 5(7) requires that the coastal state in the zones around its continental shelf installations protect the living resources of the sea from harmful agents.

Among existing regional seas regimes are those for the Baltic and the Mediterranean. The Helsinki Convention on the Protection of the Baltic Sea Area (1974) seeks to limit hazardous substances in the area, reduce land-based pollution, prevent pollution from ships, regulate dumping, and prevent pollution from activities on the seabed. The Barcelona Convention for the Protection of the Mediterranean against Pollution (1976), with several later protocols, establishes a similar legal regime and also provides for cooperation of the parties in emergencies and for the monitoring of pollution. Similar agreements cover the Gulf (the Kuwait Convention of 1978) and West and Central Africa (the Abidjan Convention of 1981).

Apart from such general treaties, pollution is dealt with in agreements covering only specific types of pollution, of which the most important are oil pollution, radioactivity and dumping.

16. Marine oil pollution. Oil pollution may come from shore installations but the primary source is discharge from ships and massive oil spills from the tanker accidents which occur most often in highly vulnerable coastal areas and crowded sea lanes. A number of treaties on this subject have been negotiated under the auspices of a United Nations specialised agency, the International Maritime Organisation (IMO), which was known until 1982 as the Intergovernmental Maritime Consultative Organisation (IMCO).

The 1973 International Convention for Prevention of Pollution from Ships (the 'MARPOL' treaty), which came into force in 1983 along with its First Protocol, sets limits to oil discharges from ships. The Marine Environment Protection Committee of IMO has adopted a set of 'unified interpretations' of IMO regulations on oil pollution prevention.

The International Convention relating to Intervention on the High Seas in Cases of Oil Pollution Casualties (1969) allows each party to intervene as necessary against major oil pollution threats to its coastline, fishing, health, tourism, or conservation interests in cases of maritime accidents.

The International Convention on Civil Liability for Oil Pollution (1969) sets out rules and procedures to settle issues of liability in particular cases and to ensure proper compensation for the victims. The Convention imposes *strict liability* in such cases on the owner of the ship (*see* 10:4), so that fault or negligence need not be proved, but allows the owner to limit his liability according to the ship's tonnage, with a maximum financial obligation of \$16.8

million. This treaty is supplemented by the International Convention on the Establishment of an International Fund for Compensation for Oil Pollution Damage (1971), whose monies would be disbursed in situations where the funds available under the 1969 Convention's provisions would not be sufficient.

17. Radioactive marine pollution. The advent of the atomic age in 1945 brought the threat of massive and persistent pollution from radioactive materials released by nuclear tests, coastal nuclear installations and the dumping of nuclear waste in the sea. Thus such pollution may come from military and civilian activities.

In the military field, Article 1 of the Treaty Banning Nuclear Weapon Tests in the Atmosphere, in Outer Space and Underwater (1963), the 'Partial Test Ban Treaty', forbids nuclear tests in the areas stated and also any other test which 'causes radioactive debris to be present outside the territorial limits of the state' proposing to conduct the test. This applies equally to pollution of the air, land or sea by such debris.

Unfortunately, the effectiveness of this treaty has been reduced by the refusal of some states, notably France, to adhere to it. The harmful effects of French explosions in the Pacific were at issue in the *Nuclear Test Cases* (1974), in which Australia and New Zealand sought from the International Court of Justice an order (which was not given) to ban French tests there.

On the civil side, various international agreements provide for liability for nuclear damage and the payment of compensation. Some deal specifically with radioactive pollution, as, for example, the 1971 Convention relating to Civil Liability in the Field of Maritime Carriage of Nuclear Material, which ensures the liability of the operator of a nuclear installation if damage occurs during the carriage by sea of nuclear materials. Other treaties, like the Convention for the Prevention of Marine Pollution by Dumping of Wastes and other Matter (1972) (the 'London Dumping Convention'), in Article 4, and the Convention for the Prevention of Marine Pollution from Land-based Sources (1974), Article 5, encompass radioactive pollution within their more general provisions.

18. Dumping. In Article 1 of the London Dumping Convention, mentioned immediately above, the parties pledge themselves to 'take all practicable steps to prevent the pollution of the sea by the dumping of waste and other matter that is liable to create hazards to human health, to harm living resources and marine life, to damage amenities or to interfere with other legitimate uses of the sea'. Dumping is defined in part as 'any deliberate disposal at sea of wastes or other matter from [i.e. by means of] vessels, aircraft, platforms or other man-made structures at sea'.

19. Air pollution. Apart from bilateral treaties dealing with problems of local interest to the parties, a major international agreement is the 1979 Convention on Long-range Transboundary Air Pollution, which entered into force in 1983. It commits all the major European countries along with the United States and Canada to undertake exchanges of information, consultation, research and monitoring in order to develop 'without undue delay' policies and strategies to combat the discharge of air pollutants. Under Article 6 each party individually, in the light of what is produced within the Convention's programme, undertakes to develop such responses as air quality management systems and control measures which are 'compatible with balanced development'. Article 9 provides for monitoring of long-range air pollutants subject to the review of an Executive Body established in Article 10. Funding for this work was arranged under a 1984 Protocol to the Convention.

Unfortunately, there is no provision in this Convention for liability in cases of long-range air pollution. It would appear, however, that customary international law, as reflected in the *Trail Smelter Case* could give a sufficient basis for liability once the monitoring activities under the Convention had revealed an incident of such pollution. This could produce significant developments with such problems as 'acid rain', from which major environmental damage to the forests of several European countries is feared.

Air pollution from radioactive materials is a particularly serious aspect of the general problem.

As already seen (*see* **17**), the Partial Test Ban Treaty of 1963 attempted to curtail pollution from nuclear explosions. The incident at the Chernobyl nuclear power station (*see* **3**) demonstrated that other causes of radioactive pollution continue to present dangers. In May 1986 the Soviet leader, Mr Mikhail Gorbachev, proposed several improvements in the international machinery for preventing or dealing with such incidents:

(*a*) 'creating an international system for the safe development of nuclear power based on the close co-operation of all nations dealing with nuclear power engineering', with a 'system of prompt warning and supply of information in the event of accidents' and an 'international mechanism ... for the speediest rendering of mutual assistance when dangerous situations emerge';

(*b*) enhancing the role and capabilities of the International Atomic Energy Agency (IAEA) beyond what was deemed necessary when it was founded in 1967;

(*c*) more active involvement in this area of the United Nations and its specialised agencies, in particular the World Health Organisation (WHO) and the United Nations Environment Programme (UNEP).

A draft treaty has been prepared by the IAEA (*see* **8**).

Conservation

20. The changing goals of conservation. In the early part of the twentieth century conservation focussed on preserving enclaves of protected forest and wild lands in which animal and plant species were permitted to live in their natural habitat undisturbed by the world outside. The legal implications of this approach were generally limited to the municipal law of the states where these reserves were established, although treaties were negotiated on this topic covering European colonies in Africa (the London Convention of 1933) and the Western Hemisphere (the Washington Convention of 1940). Migratory species were sometimes also the subject of international agreements.

But with the passage of time it began to be clear that conservation or reserves was not enough and that protection programmes had to operate throughout each country and indeed on the international level, if massive environmental degradation was to be prevented.

21. International law aspects of conservation. International lawyers are inclined in the context of the regime of the environment to speak in terms of 'soft law', which expresses norms of a legal character, and 'hard law', which entails legal rights and duties. In the area of conservation this distinction is apt insofar as, while many treaties establish hard law for certain regions or groups of states in relation to specific problems, general international law retains an element of soft law.

22. The United Nations Environment Programme (*UNEP*). Much of the current soft law arises from the work of United Nations agencies, and in particular the UNEP, which was given the major responsibility in the UN for overseeing implementation of the Stockholm plans of 1972, as discussed further below. Under UNEP's auspices a World Conservation Strategy was developed in the early 1980s to outline a three-pronged attack on environmental degradation. This called for:

(*a*) the maintenance of essential ecological processes and life-support systems like the natural recycling of oxygen and nutrients, the cleansing of air and water, and the propagation of plants;

(*b*) the preservation of genetic diversity so as to keep alive plant and animal species whose unique features may provide scientific, medical, agricultural or other benefits;

(*c*) the sustainable utilisation of resources, species and ecosystems so as to allow them to renew themselves by natural processes and to avoid exhaustion.

It is suggested that these aims, and particularly the final one, correspond to a legal principle of *eco-management*, whereby states must pursue a balanced exploitation of the environment and careful forward planning in order to achieve sustainable development.

23. Binding conservation law. Conservation hard law focusses on particular problems or areas. Among a wide variety of treaties some of the more noteworthy are:

(*a*) the International Convention for the Protection of Plants and Plant Products (1951), which seeks to control the spread of plant diseases and pests;

(*b*) the Convention on Wetlands of International Importance especially Waterfowl Habitat (1971), for preserving wetlands of ecological, botanical, zoological or other significance;

(*c*) the Convention for the Protection of the World Cultural and Natural Heritage (1972), a UNESCO treaty to which over seventy states are party which, although primarily concerned with the preservation of cultural monuments, also provides for protective measures to save important natural features;

(*d*) the International Convention on International Trade in Endangered Species of Wild Fauna and Flora (1973), to which over eighty states are party, and which aims at international cooperation to prevent excessive commercial exploitation of such species;

(*e*) the Convention on the Prohibition of Military or Any Other Hostile Use of Environmental Modification Techniques (1976), in which the parties agree not to change the basic systems of earth, air or outer space for military purposes, although modification for peaceful purposes is not prohibited;

(*f*) the Convention on the Conservation of European Wildlife and Natural Habitats (1979), protecting specific endangered species in Western Europe;

(*g*) the Convention on the Conservation of Antarctic Marine Living Resources (1980) (*see* 6:46); and

(*h*) the Convention for the Protection of the Ozone Layer (1985), which provides in the first instance for international cooperation in research and information sharing and offers a framework for later harmonisation of national regulations to protect human health and the environment from the harmful effects of depleting ozone in the stratosphere.

Coordinated environmental protection

24. Measures at the Stockholm Conference. The Stockholm Conference's Declaration in 1972 reaffirmed the need to safeguard natural resources and improve environmental quality through careful planning and management, to allocate resources to preserve and improve the environment, to use science and technology not merely to control environmental risks but to enhance the environment, and to promote international cooperation in this field.

To promote implementation of these goals, the Conference adopted an 'Action Plan', whose main features were:

(*a*) the establishment of an 'Earthwatch' programme to gather information on potential environmental problems of international concern;

(*b*) environmental management recommendations, particularly with regard to mobilising the resources of United Nations agencies and international experts;

(*c*) supporting measures to promote public awareness of, and education in, environmental problems and to finance relevant activities.

25. The role of UNEP. Since the Conference, the work of UNEP has been tailored to meet the needs of the Action Plan. The agency identifies the problems on which Earthwatch should concentrate. It has set in operation two information processing units of Earthwatch: the Global Environmental Monitoring System (GEMS), which checks on the movement of dangerous pollutants and monitors resource use and environmental quality, and the International Referral System for Sources of Environmental Information (INFOTERRA).

Of particular interest in recent years have been the developing possibilities of *remote sensing*, the use of satellite monitoring and imaging systems to provide hitherto unavailable information on a world-wide scale.

UNEP is also involved with the International Register of Potentially Toxic Chemicals, whereby information on such hazardous items is disseminated. Unfortunately United Nations efforts in this area have since 1981 been persistently hampered by the reluctance of the United States, one of the world's largest producers of such products, to co-operate with the international community.

In 1975 UNEP's Governing Council noted the importance of the preventive character of environmental law, thereby opening the way for consideration of further positive actions that need to be taken to maintain and improve the environment. In 1981, UNEP undertook an 'In-depth Review of Environmental Law' in which it surveyed and assessed the relevant activities of all international bodies and organisations dealing with these topics and, under the Montevideo Programme for Development and Periodic Review of Environmental Law (1982), the agency will continue to identify areas for future growth.

26. The Conference on Human Settlements (1976). A major step forward in UNEP's promotion of preventative environmental law was the adoption at a conference in Vancouver in 1976 of the Declaration on Human Settlements. This document, which (as Prof. Starke has pointed out) implicitly links environmental and human rights questions, focussed on the problems of rural

15 Environmental law **301**

backwardness, chaotic urbanisation, and the requirements of many for the basic necessities of life like clean water, food and shelter.

27. The Nairobi Conference (1982). On the tenth anniversary of the Stockholm meeting a conference in Nairobi looked closely at the trends in international environmental law over the previous decade, with mixed conclusions.

In its concluding Declaration the conference, noting the intimate and complex interrelationship between environment, development, population and resources, regretted that the 1972 programme had not yet been fully implemented. It expressed concern about major deterioration brought about by continued deforestation and desertification, the extinction of living species and acid rain. The conference emphasised the need for environmental assessment and management and for harnessing technological innovation to promote resource substitution, recycling and conservation. The Nairobi Declaration also linked the quality of the environment with the fostering of an atmosphere of international peace and security, free from the threat of war, 'especially nuclear war'.

28. Armaments and the environment. The Nairobi Declaration's linking of peace and environmental protection is more than an afterthought. Although Article 11 of the UN Charter recognised that the principles governing disarmament and the regulation of armaments were part and parcel of the Charter's programme for the maintenance of international peace and security, by the 1980s the international arms trade was soaking up more of the resources of developing countries than ever before. The Palme Commission on Disarmament and Security Issues noted in 1982 that increased military expenditure in these countries reduced investment in productive capacity and inhibited agricultural production. Foreign debt increased and standards of living dropped. This inevitably meant fewer resources available for development and for the maintenance and improvement of the environment.

The reasons for this situation are complex: in the industrialised countries there is the need to maintain jobs and high technology through military expenditure and to offset some of the huge costs of military research and development by exporting weapons systems; in the developing countries ruling military circles divert national wealth to their own purposes, often with the encouragement of the arms-exporting states, and even where civilians rule the general climate of insecurity promotes military build-ups.

It is clear, however, that only a major reallocation of resources away from military spending towards development would provide the basis on which sensible and effective environmental programmes could operate.

Apart from the environmental consequences of diverting resources into the economically unproductive area of military spending, the direct environmental effects of the use of modern weapons also cause concern, particularly with regard to the potentially catastrophic consequences of the 'nuclear winter' (*see* 16:37). Protocol I (1977) to the Four Geneva Conventions of 1949 on the laws of war (*see* 16:25) in Article 35(3) prohibits methods of warfare that are intended, or may be expected, to cause long-term, widespread and severe damage to the natural environment.

29. International economic law and the environment. In the background of much thinking about environmental problems in Third World and developing countries lies the question of international economic relations. Anxious to end foreign 'neo-colonialist' domination of their economies, these countries have insisted vehemently on the right of states to manage their own economic affairs and control their own natural resources. This emphasis appeared, for example, in the General Assembly's 1962 Resolution on Permanent Sovereignty over Natural Resources (Res. 1803(XVII)) and, more assertively, in the 1974 Charter of Economic Rights and Duties of States (Res. 3281(XXIX)), which both affirm the developing state's entitlement to use its resources in the interest of its national development and the well-being of its people.

In the Stockholm Declaration of 1972 the link between development economics and environmental protection was made explicitly: 'In the developing countries most of the environmental problems are caused by underdevelopment.' It goes on:

> Millions continue to live far below the minimum levels required for a decent human existence, deprived of adequate food and clothing, shelter and education, health and sanitation. Therefore, the developing countries must direct their efforts to development, bearing in mind their priorities and the need to safeguard and improve the environment. For the same purpose, the industrialized countries should make efforts to reduce the gap between themselves and the developing countries.

This idea that the richer countries must help the poorer ones out of their economic and environmental difficulties is formulated more precisely in Principle 9 of the Declaration:

> Environmental deficiencies generated by the conditions of under-development and natural disasters pose grave problems and can best be remedied by accelerated development through the transfer of substantial quantities of financial and technological assistance as a supplement to the domestic effort of the developing countries.

Principle 12 goes so far as to suggest that such assistance should be increased as needed to defray the additional costs which developing countries may face as a result of environmental protection measures, though some experts thought developing countries would have to protect their environment in any case.

This policy was augmented by the General Assembly's adoption, in Resolutions 3201(S-VI) and 3202(S-VI) of 1974 of a programme for what is called there a New International Economic Order (NIEO). The NIEO epitomised the efforts of Third World countries in the mid-1970s to bring about a redistribution of world financial and technological resources to benefit their national development, though little came of it in the period of world-wide economic recession in the following ten years and the basic issues raised have yet to be properly addressed.

Future environmental problems

30. The application of science. Apart from continuation of the world's present environmental problems, there are already visible on the horizon new questions created by advances of scientific knowledge and technique. They appear to be of a different order from the problems of the past: they are considerably more difficult for the non-scientists who make and apply the law to understand and they have the potential to be more devastating than any previous scientific development except nuclear energy. Although some national legal systems have begun to tackle some of these problems, an international legal regime seems far away. Two examples follow to illustrate the nature of these new challenges.

31. Large-scale water projects. For many years scientists in the Soviet Union have been considering whether to divert the northward-flowing Ob, Yenisey and Lena Rivers towards Russia's agricultural heartland for irrigation. Environmentalists objected to this on the ground that such a large-scale diversion could have world-wide repercussions on climate and sea level in all the continents. More recently, however, scientists have begun to argue that such a diversion would be desirable. Their case is that the world sea level has been advancing steadily since the beginning of the Industrial Revolution because of rising temperatures produced by the burning of industrial fuels and the release of carbon dioxide into the atmosphere to produce the 'greenhouse' effect. Massive diversions of water to inland areas might halt this change in sea level, the alternative being inundation of coastal areas where a large part of the world's increasing population lives.

The international regime of environmental protection is at present unequipped to examine and resolve such a complex problem.

32. Genetic modification. The techniques of gene modification now make it possible for new types of living organisms to be developed as required to perform specific tasks like producing new medicines, counteracting disease, or resisting difficult climatic or other conditions. The possibilities seem limitless, but environmentalists fear that introducing such organisms into the environment could involve risks which cannot yet be accurately assessed.

In the United States considerable development of the law on environmental protection has taken place to guard against some of the anticipated dangers, although in early 1986 the US Department of Agriculture did license the sale of the world's first genetically engineered organism for use in agriculture. This was heavily criticised and sale of the organism was suspended for a time.

From the international perspective what is significant here is that nothing like as complete an international legal regime exists in this area, in spite of the fact that experience proves the ease with which organisms can spread beyond national frontiers.

Progress test 15

1. What are the basic causes of environmental degradation in the modern world? **(2)**
2. Does environmental protection challenge traditional ideas of sovereignty? **(3)**
3. Explain the principle of *sic utere tuo ut alienum non laedas*. **(4–5)**
4. Are there environmental obligations *erga omnes*? **(7)**
5. List the norms associated with the duty to cooperate. **(8)**
6. What are the possible definitions of pollution? **(10)**
7. What view of pollution is adopted in the Stockholm Declaration? **(11)**
8. Outline the law on the pollution of lakes and rivers. **(12, 13)**
9. What is the general duty of states with regard to the marine environment? **(15)**
10. Are there any legal controls on the depositing of radioactive material in the sea? **(17)**

11. What should be the basic goals of a world conservation strategy? **(22)**
12. Discuss the role of UNEP in environmental protection. **(25)**
13. Is there a link between armaments and environmental policy? **(27–28)**
14. Is economic development an environmental problem? **(29)**

Bibliography

Hague Academy Workshop 1984, *The Future of the International Law of the Environment*, Nijhoff, Dordrecht (1985)

Independent Commission on International Humanitarian Issues, *Famine: A man-made disaster?*, Pan Books, London (1985)·

Springer, *The International Law of Pollution*, Quorum Books, London (1983)

Starke, *Introduction to International Law*, 9th ed., Chapter 14, Butterworths, London (1984)

Times Atlas of the Oceans, ed. A. Couper, Times Books, London (1983)

For an interesting case on whaling limitations see Japan Whaling Association et al v. *American Cetacean Society et al*, US Supreme Ct. (1986), 25 ILM 1587

16   War and peace

The use of force

1. War. Under the influence of medieval Christian legists, international law in its early period tended to consider the question of a state's right to resort to war (the *jus ad bellum*) in terms of the criteria for the just war (*bellum justum*). According to Francisco de Vitoria (1486–1546), for example, a war could only be just as a defence against attack or for the purpose of righting a great wrong. Before resorting to war a state must attempt to find a peaceful solution, and in any case it must consider whether the war might produce more harm than good.

In the heyday of positivism, however, classical international law abandoned efforts to distinguish right from wrong in this area and in effect accepted war as a legitimate instrument of state policy. The resort to war was not *per se* prohibited, although the European political system allowed the exaction of 'reparations' from the state deemed by the victor to be responsible for causing a war (i.e. the loser).

International law focussed primarily on mitigating the barbarities of warfare through development of the laws of war, as discussed further below. The abandonment of the just war concept is said by some actually to have facilitated this process by making it possible to ignore the rights and wrongs of a conflict and concentrate on requiring proper treatment for both sides, regardless of which one was responsible for causing the war.

2. The League of Nations era. A change in the position of international law began with the establishment of the League of Nations in 1920. Although not prohibiting war outright, Article 12 of the League Covenant required the members to observe during a crisis a 'cooling off' period of three months before resorting to war in order to allow time for peaceful settlement. Failure to do this was a violation of the Covenant and made the violator liable under Article 16 to concerted use of military force by the other members of the League.

The Covenant was followed in 1928 by the Treaty Providing for the Renunciation of War as an Instrument of National Policy (also known as the 'Kellogg-Briand Pact', after the American and French foreign ministers who negotiated it, and as the 'Pact of Paris'). This treaty is still in force, with over sixty parties. In Article 1 the parties 'condemn recourse to war for the solution of international controversies, and renounce it as an instrument of national policy in their relations with one another'. In Article 2 they agree 'that the settlement or solution of all disputes or conflicts of whatever nature or of whatever origin they may be, which may arise among them, shall never be sought except by pacific means'.

Two problems arose in relation to the 1928 Pact. First, given that in the international law of the period 'war', strictly speaking, applied only to the legal state existing between nations following an official declaration of war, there was some question whether the parties' undertakings applied also to a use of armed force other than declared war and to the threat of war without actual hostilities. In 1934 the International Law Association, a private organisation of lawyers, suggested an answer to both these questions by deciding that a 'signatory state which threatens to resort to armed force for the solution of an international dispute or conflict is guilty of a violation of the Pact', but this interpretation was rejected by some governments.

Secondly, there was the question whether and to what extent the Pact permitted self-defence. Most people thought that it did, at least to some degree.

An attempt to strengthen international law's alternative to war was also made in 1928 with the adoption of the General Act on Pacific Settlement of International Disputes (the 'Geneva General Act'). This provided for conciliation, arbitration or reference of disputes to the Permanent Court of International Justice. It was not widely adhered to, but it did influence thinking at the next stage in the law's development.

3. The United Nations Charter. The drafters of the UN Charter in 1945 were very much motivated in their work by a desire to correct the inadequacies in the law which events after 1920 had revealed.

Consequently, the Charter emphasises in Article 1 that it is a purpose of the United Nations to 'maintain international peace and security', which may involve: collective measures to prevent and remove threats to the peace, the suppression of acts of aggression or other breaches of the peace, and the settlement or adjustment of international disputes, or situations which might lead to a breach of the peace, by peaceful means and 'in conformity with the principles of justice and international law'.

The obligations which the members of the United Nations undertake in Article 2 include the following paragraphs:

Article 2(3): All members shall settle their international disputes by peaceful means in such a manner that international peace and security, and justice, are not endangered.

Article 2(4): All members shall refrain in their international relations from the threat or use of force against the territorial integrity or political independence of any state, or in any other manner inconsistent with the purposes of the United Nations.

Thus, the peaceful settlement of disputes is the Charter's obligatory substitute for resort to armed force, which is entirely prohibited, whether on the level of 'war' or otherwise, when contrary to the Charter.

The Charter scheme makes clear that there are basically only three types of use of force:

(*a*) illegal use under Article 2(4);

(*b*) use authorised by the Security Council in the interests of maintaining peace under Articles 39 and 42; and

(*c*) self-defence under Article 51.

4. Use of force authorised by the Security Council. Article 24 of the Charter confers on the Security Council the 'primary responsibility' for the maintenance of international peace and security, and Article 25 makes 'decisions' of the Council legally binding on the members of the United Nations. Although Article 11 allows the General Assembly also to consider questions of peace and security, that provision makes clear that questions on which 'action' is necessary must be referred to the Security Council.

Chapter VII of the Charter deals with 'action' on threats to the peace, breaches of the peace or acts of aggression. Under Article 39 in that chapter the Council must first 'determine the existence' of such a situation and may then 'make recommendations', or 'decide' on measures under Article 42, to maintain or restore international peace and security. (In the light of Article 25 a 'decision' would be legally binding, while a recommendation would not be.) Article 42 permits the Council to 'take such action by air, sea or land forces as may be necessary'. However, although Article 42 does not specifically say so, it appears that the 'forces' which would be used in this way must be those constituted according to Articles 43–47, which provide for contributions of military assistance from the UN's members to the Security Council in coordination with a Military Staff Committee composed of the chiefs of staff of the Council's permanent members. Because of disagreements between the permanent members nothing ever came of this scheme.

But in 1950, at the beginning of the Korean War, the Security Council, in the absence of the Soviet Union, which was boycotting its meetings, got round this problem by the expedient of *recommending* to members willing to cooperate against the incursion of North Korea into South Korea that they should supply military help to South Korea under a unified command headed by the United States but flying the United Nations flag. The Soviet Union has always contested the legality of these arrangements.

In Resolution 221 the Council determined in 1966 that Southern Rhodesia's unilateral declaration of independence under a white minority regime constituted a 'threat to the peace' and then called upon Britain 'to prevent by the use of force if necessary' the arrival at Beira, the Mozambican port from which supplies were shipped inland to Rhodesia, 'of vessels reasonably believed to be carrying oil destined for Rhodesia'.

5. The position of the Council's permanent members. As noted above, the Security Council, in the absence of the Soviet Union, recommended the use of force in Korea in 1950. The resolutions adopted at that time have been criticised by the Soviet Union as unconstitutional under the Charter on the ground that the absence of the USSR prevented the Council from being competent to take a decision in the manner prescribed by the 'veto' provision in Article 27(3), which requires for approval of such a decision the 'concurring votes of the permanent members' of the Council. The Soviet Union is one of those members. The USSR nevertheless seems to accept that abstention by a permanent member who is present at a meeting does not have the effect of a veto, even though in that case also a resolution would not have the concurring vote of a permanent member.

The reasoning here seems to be that an abstention amounts at least to passive acceptance if not active approval, whereas an absence does not permit any inference about a state's attitude to be drawn and so the state's concurrence cannot be ascertained as required by Article 27.

6. The role of the General Assembly. Such difficulties, along with the problems arising when a veto is cast, have led some UN members to attempt to expand the role of the General Assembly in the area of authorised uses of force.

In the 'Uniting for Peace' Resolution (Res. 377(V) of 1950) the General Assembly noted that 'failure of the Security Council to discharge its responsibilities ... does not relieve ... the United Nations of its responsibility under the Charter to maintain international peace and security', nor does it 'deprive the General Assembly of its rights or relieve it of its responsibilities under the Charter'. The Assembly then resolved that:

> if the Security Council, because of lack of unanimity of the permanent members, fails to exercise its primary responsibility ... in any case where there appears to be a threat to the peace, breach of the peace, or act of aggression, the General Assembly shall consider the matter immediately with a view to making appropriate recommendations to Members for collective measures, including in the case of a breach of the peace or act of aggression the use of armed force when necessary.

The Assembly has met under this resolution to consider dangers to peace in the Middle East, Africa and Asia when Security Council action has been blocked by the veto, but the critical question is whether in such cases the resolution could provide the legal basis for the use of force under United Nations' auspices. The answer is almost certainly 'No', for while it is correct that a Security Council failure to act does not prevent the Assembly from exercising its functions under the Charter, it is equally true that such a failure does not augment the Assembly's powers. Only a revision of the Charter could accomplish that.

7. Peace-keeping forces. In the *Certain Expenses of the United Nations Case* (1962) the International Court of Justice stated flatly: 'It is only the Security Council which can require enforcement by coercive action against an aggressor'. The ICJ was prepared to accept, however, that the Assembly could approve the setting up of United Nations peace-keeping forces, since such forces would not take coercive enforcement action but would only operate with the agreement of the parties concerned in a dispute on the territory of states which permitted a UN military presence.

8. Self-defence. Apart from an authorised use of force by the United Nations, the only legitimate use under the Charter is in self-defence. It will be useful to consider first the meaning of self-defence (*see* **9**) and then to examine the limitations which have been placed on it in the Charter (*see* **10**).

9. The definition of self-defence. The United States Secretary of State, Daniel Webster, gave the classic definition of self-defence in the *Caroline Case* (1841) in response to a British military raid on an American Great Lakes port to seize and destroy a ship, *The Caroline*, which was used to supply anti-British rebels in Canada. The raid took place at night and without warning; *The Caroline* was set on fire and allowed to drift over Niagara Falls, with no attempt by the British forces to rescue those on board.

Webster wrote that such an act could only be justified if there was:

> a necessity of self-defence, instant, overwhelming, leaving no choice of means, and no moment for deliberation.

Even if there was such a necessity, there was a requirement of proportionality. The action taken must not be:

unreasonable or excessive; since the act, justified by the necessity of self-defence, must be limited by that necessity, and kept clearly within it.

To demonstrate that the raid was not unreasonable or excessive the British would have had to show:

that admonition or remonstrance to the persons on board the *Caroline* was impracticable, or would have been unavailing ... that day-light could not be waited for; that there could be no attempt at discrimination between the innocent and the guilty; that it would not have been enough to seize and detain the vessel; but that there was a necessity, present and inevitable, for attacking her in the darkness of the night, while moored to the shore, and while unarmed men were asleep on board, killing some and wounding others, and then drawing her into the current, above the cataract, setting her on fire, and, careless to know whether there might not be in her the innocent with the guilty, or the living with the dead, committing her to a fate which fills the imagination with horror.

Thus, justifiable self-defence is the necessary and unavoidable use of proportionate force as a last resort when there is no alternative available for fending off immediate and present danger.

10. Self-defence in the Charter. Article 51 of the United Nations Charter takes self-defence as thus understood and sets out the circumstances in which a state may resort to it. The provision reads:

Nothing in the present Charter shall impair the inherent right of individual or collective self-defence if an armed attack occurs against a Member of the United Nations, until the Security Council has taken measures necessary to maintain international peace and security. Measures taken by Members in the exercise of this right of self-defence shall be immediately reported to the Security Council and shall not in any way affect the authority and responsibility of the Security Council under the present Charter to take at any time such action as it deems necessary in order to maintain or restore international peace and security.

The first significant point to note about this provision is that it subjects any exercise of self-defence to review by the Security Council. This is in keeping with the decision by the International Military Tribunal at Nuremberg, when considering the question of Nazi aggression during World War II, that 'whether action taken under the claim of self-defence was in fact aggressive or defensive must ultimately be subject to investigation and adjudication if the international law is ever to be enforced'.

State action in self-defence is subject to Council review rather than Council permission when, and because, the necessity for such action is instant and overwhelming, as Webster's statement indicated. However, it would appear that where the necessity is prolonged but continues to require self-defence the Security Council must be consulted. Thus, the United Kingdom referred Argentina's invasion of the Falkland Islands in 1982 to the Council, which adopted Resolution 502 demanding a cessation of hostilities and the withdrawal of all Argentine forces from the islands, although Britain carried on with its military response when Argentine forces continued their activities there. The implication is that the necessity for self-defence remains immediate in such a situation so long as the armed attack continues and cannot be ended by other means. The Argentine attack could have been deemed to continue by virtue of the fact that Argentine forces remained in military occupation of the Falklands, an act of aggression under the Charter (*see also* **19**).

What gives rise to the necessity for self-defence under Article 51 is spelt out clearly. The necessity exists '*if an armed attack occurs*' against a state and it has no alternative but to respond militarily, either alone or with help requested from its allies. One may reasonably infer that the required necessity cannot exist unless such an attack occurs. This interpretation was confirmed by the International Court of Justice in its June 1986 judgment in the *Military and Paramilitary Activities in and against Nicaragua Case* (*Nicaragua* v. *United States*).

Thus Article 51 may be considered to adopt the basic definition of self-defence which was applied in customary international law but to limit its application to the one case of response to an armed attack against the defender. An act which is not such a response is therefore not a permitted act of self-defence under the Charter.

11. Reprisals. In spite of the clarity of the UN Charter's limitation of the use of force to self-defence, it is sometimes suggested that international law still permits reprisals, that is, illegal military measures by one state in retaliation for illegal acts by another state with the aim of stopping such acts or deterring the second state from committing them again.

But even before the law of the Charter, military reprisals were restricted and frowned upon. In the *Naulilaa Case* (1928), the arbitration tribunal indicated that, although reprisals were permitted as a response to an illegal act, they had to be preceded by 'an unsatisfied demand' to the originally offending state for reparation, with force only justified 'if absolutely necessary', and there had to be a proportion between the reprisal and the original offence.

With the advent of the Charter, reprisals must now be regarded as completely prohibited under international law because they do not come within permitted self-defence. The Security Council in 1964 condemned reprisals as 'incompatible with the purposes and principles of the United Nations'.

12. Attempts to undermine the Charter regime of self-defence. Webster's very restrictive definition of self-defence came originally in the context of a legal system which imposed few limitations on the resort to outright war. In some sense states could accept such a narrow definition because their pursuit of political goals through the use of force in war was not inhibited by it.

Furthermore, a narrow concept of self-defence served a useful function at a time when international law was divided into two mutually exclusive categories: the 'Law of Peace', applying between states at peace with each other, and the 'Law of War', which applied between states engaged in official hostilities. Webster's definition of self-defence enabled a very limited use of force to be undertaken when absolutely necessary without moving the states involved from the Law of Peace to the Law of War.

Under the UN Charter, however, self-defence is the only legitimate use of force open to an individual state, and a restrictive definition, coupled with limitations on the circumstances in which resort to it is permitted, has the effect of denying states the right to use force as an instrument of national policy.

This has produced some peculiar semantic and legal contortions: states no longer have Ministries of War but rather ones of 'Defence', and some of the most powerful and aggressive states have only 'defence forces'.

On the legal level some states have felt compelled to find ways of wriggling out of their international duty to settle disputes by peaceful means and not resort to force. They can only do this by reducing the Charter's regime of self-defence to vanishing point. Two ways of accomplishing this have been tried: the reinterpretation of Article 51 so as to allow something euphemistically called 'anticipatory self-defence' (i.e. offensive attack), and the implicit redefinition of self-defence.

13. Anticipatory self-defence. Anticipatory self-defence operates essentially on the theory that, where Article 51 says that it allows defensive force 'if an armed attack occurs', it really means to permit the first use of pre-emptive force 'if an armed attack seems possible'.

Strictly as a matter of construing the language of a treaty according to the recognised rules (*see* 11, **14–15**), this interpretation is dubious in the extreme. But there are also fundamental practical and legal objections based on the difficulties of applying it.

Whereas a state acting in legitimate self-defence can present proof of a hostile attack against it, the state claiming anticipatory self-defence can at best offer only suspicion and supposition. To accept a claim of anticipatory self-defence as legitimate therefore requires far greater reliance on the honesty, judgment and good faith of the state acting on that basis.

In these respects anticipatory self-defence is consequently highly unreliable and, as history has proved, is easily open to abuse by strong states looking for an excuse to attack their weaker neighbours rather than negotiate with them. The result is that anticipatory self-defence not only exceeds the limits of Article 51 but also facilitates violations of Article 2(3) and 2(4) of the Charter.

14. Redefinition of self-defence. Redefining self-defence is a somewhat less open tactic than anticipatory self-defence and for that reason may be an even more insidious danger. A prime example illustrates the problem.

In April 1986, the United States launched night-time air raids against Libya in which the main Libyan cities of Tripoli and Benghazi were bombed along with military camps and airfields. A large number of innocent civilians were killed or injured.

Explaining this attack in a television broadcast, the American president recalled past terrorist attacks against Americans in Europe, which he said were planned by Libya, and indicated that yet more attacks had been foiled (presumably by intelligence and police work) while plans for others had been uncovered. He went on:

It must be the core of Western policy that there be no sanctuary for terror ... for us to ignore by inaction the slaughter of American civilians and American soldiers ... is simply not in the American tradition. When our citizens are abused or attacked, anywhere in world, on the direct orders of a hostile regime, we will respond so long as I am in this office.

This statement indicates quite clearly that the United States attack did not come within self-defence under Article 51. There was no immediate necessity for the raid, as on the president's own evidence the terrorist attacks, having occurred in other countries, were not an armed attack on the United States and were not in any case being immediately responded to in an effort to fend them off. Alternative means of dealing with the danger of terrorism were evidently available, since the president indicated how some plots had been foiled without air raids on Libya while others were known about and presumably could have been guarded against or prevented in their turn in the same way. The raids appeared disproportionate in scope and consequences to the terrorist acts which were claimed to have prompted them. Furthermore, the president's language suggested that the air strikes were designed to display 'the American tradition' of fighting back in retaliation or reprisal for attacks on Americans.

Nevertheless, the president stated categorically that 'Self-defence is ... the purpose behind the mission ... a mission fully consistent with Article 51 of the United Nations Charter.' This statement, if taken seriously, implies a new definition of self-defence. It must now mean the unnecessary and disproportionate use of force, without an armed attack on the 'defender's' territory, for the purposes of reprisal, deterrence, and national assertiveness. It would be difficult to be further away from the spirit and meaning of Article 51.

15. 'Humanitarian' intervention. A grey area between legitimate self-defence and illegal use of force is what classical international law knew as *humanitarian intervention*. This should not be confused with such activities as bringing relief aid and other humane assistance to people suffering in some natural or man-made disaster. The term refers rather to the use of armed force by one state against another for the purpose of saving the lives or property of the intervenor's citizens or others in the second state or rescuing them from an imminent threat of grave injury.

In classical international law such action was seen by some governments as legitimate self-help by a state to protect persons who were not being properly protected by the state in which they were. In the age of European imperialism humanitarian intervention easily became tainted by its use as a means of exerting European influence in Third World countries that reacted in a hostile way to the intrusion of Europeans in their territory. The most famous instance of this was the invasion of China by a joint Western and Japanese military force in 1900 to put down the so-called 'Boxer Rebellion', in which Chinese nationalist bands were murdering Westerners.

In modern international law, Article 2(4) of the Charter appears to prohibit humanitarian intervention involving the threat or use of force. Nevertheless, the United States claimed to be acting on that basis when it invaded the Dominican Republic in 1965 and Grenada in 1983, although both of these attacks were generally seen to have political or security motivations and attempts were also made to justify them as self-defence.

A more genuine act of humanitarian intervention by the United States was President Carter's attempt at the military rescue of Americans held hostage in Iran in 1980, although it was criticised by the International Court of Justice as a resort to force at a time when the *Iran Hostages Case* was still before the court (*see* 9:23).

Another action that seems closer to humanitarian intervention in the classic sense was the raid by Israeli forces on the airport at Entebbe, Uganda in 1976 to rescue Israelis and other foreigners who were held captive there by a group who had hijacked an Air France jet on a flight to Tel Aviv. Israel justified this on two distinct grounds: protection of Israeli nationals suffering injury within the territory of another state, and self-defence. Self-defence, however, does not justify this kind of action unless an armed attack has occurred against the territory of the state taking action. The protection of nationals as a separate justification has some support amongst international lawyers insofar at least as the action is, in the words of Brierly, 'strictly limited to securing the safe removal of the threatened nationals'.

16. Illegal uses of force. As indicated above (*see* 3), any use of force that is neither authorised by the United Nations nor in legitimate self-defence must be illegal under Article 2(4). A definition of illegal use of force is therefore theoretically unnecessary. But in practice the attempts of states that are violating the Charter to bring their actions within Article 51 have demonstrated the need to detail those acts which can never amount to self-defence. Efforts in that direction have focussed on clarifying the meaning of 'aggression'.

17. The definition of aggression. After many years of considering the matter, the General Assembly in 1974 produced Resolution 3314(XXIX), the Resolution on the Definition of Aggression. Given that aggression is a term used in the Charter, this Resolution may be read as providing an authoritative interpretation of the Charter rather than as attempting to create new law.

The Resolution approaches aggression in three steps: a general definition (*see* **18**), followed by a list of forbidden acts (*see* **19**), with finally a statement of general principles (*see* **21**) relevant to the matter and a comment on self-determination (*see* **22**).

18. General definition of aggression. Aggression is defined in Article 1 of the Resolution as:

> the use of armed force by a State against the sovereignty, territorial integrity or political independence of another state, or in any other manner inconsistent with the Charter of the United Nations, as set out in this Definition.

Although this definition is clearly based on Article 2(4) of the Charter, one notes that the mere threat of force is not deemed to be aggression, though it would violate Article 2(4), and that a use of force against a state's sovereignty joins uses against territorial integrity and political independence as illegal acts.

19. List of forbidden uses of force. Article 3 of the Resolution provides that any of the following acts qualify as aggression, unless, under Article 2 of the Resolution, the Security Council determines that in a specific case such an act is not aggression:

(*a*) invasion or armed attack by one state against another or any resulting military occupation, or annexation by the use of force of part or all of another state's territory;

(*b*) one state's bombardment of, or use of any weapons against, another state's territory;

(*c*) one state's naval or other blockade of another state's coasts or ports;

(*d*) the use of one state's armed forces, which are within another's territory with the agreement of the second state, in ways that contravene that agreement or prolong the presence of those forces after the agreement has terminated;

(*e*) the action of a state in allowing its territory to be used by another state for perpetrating an act of aggression against a third state;

(*f*) 'The sending by or on behalf of a state of armed bands, groups, irregulars or mercenaries, which carry out acts of armed force against another state of such gravity as to amount to the acts listed above, or its substantial involvement therein.'

20. The first use of armed force. According to Article 2 of the Resolution the 'first use of armed force by a State in contravention of the Charter' of the United Nations 'shall constitute *prima facie* evidence of an act of aggression', although the Security Council may determine (by approving a resolution to this effect) that a particular first use was not aggression 'in the light of the relevant circumstances, including the fact that the acts concerned or their consequences are not of sufficient gravity'.

The effect of this provision is to create a legal presumption of aggression, which may be rebutted and then removed by a vote of the Security Council. If the presumption is not removed in that way, it remains.

The value of this presumption is that it allows an act of aggression to be recognised as such while avoiding the risk of such recognition being frustrated by a permanent member's veto in the Security Council. This could be important in a case like that of the American attack on Libya (*see* **14**), in which the possible aggressor is a state possessing a power of veto.

So long as this presumption is not taken as a basis for UN use of coercive force without Security Council authorisation, it could support a wide range of actions against the aggressor by UN members individually or collectively or via the General Assembly.

21. General principles. Article 5 of the Resolution lists three principles relating to aggression.

(*a*) 'No consideration of whatever nature, whether political, economic, military or otherwise, may serve as a justification for aggression.' An explanatory note in the drafting committee's report suggests that this provision was meant to reaffirm in particular the legal prohibition of intervention in the internal affairs of other states (*see* **23**). But it would appear to have a more general application in, for example, making clear that although a use of force may appear politically or militarily advantageous, it does not for that reason become legal.

(*b*) 'A war of aggression is a crime against international peace. Aggression gives rise to international responsibility.'

(*c*) 'No territorial acquisition or special advantage resulting from aggression is or shall be recognized as lawful.' This is in effect a reiteration of the long-standing duty of non-recognition (*see* **6:17–18**). The drafting committee's report makes clear that this provision is not meant to imply that acquisition of territory by a use of force other than aggression would be legal. Such acquisition continues to be 'inadmissible'.

22. Self-determination and the use of force. According to Article 7 of the Resolution nothing in this definition:

> could in any way prejudice the right to self-determination, freedom and independence, as derived from the Charter, of peoples forcibly deprived of that right and referred to in the Declaration on Principles of International Law ... particularly peoples under colonial and racist regimes or other forms of alien domination.

Nor does anything in the Resolution prejudice 'the right of these peoples to struggle to that end and to seek and receive support' in accordance with the Charter and the Declaration.

That Declaration on Principles of International Law (General Assembly Resolution 2625(XXV) of 1970) says that peoples with a right to self-determination may not be forcibly deprived of it, and, if they are so deprived, are entitled, in pursuit of self-determination in the face of forcible deprivation, 'to seek and to receive support in accordance with the purposes and principles of the Charter of the United Nations'.

From reading between the lines of this Declaration and the Definition of Aggression taken together, it would appear that a use of force to achieve self-determination is not illegal in the circumstances indicated but amounts to self-defence against an 'attack' on the people concerned by the state which is forcibly denying them self-determination. This in effect raises peoples entitled to self-determination to the level of states with regard to the legal rights and duties associated with the use of force. (*See* also 4:43.)

But a critical question here is whether a people struggling for self-determination may receive outside military help in their fight. If the people is acting in self-defence, such help might arguably also be legal as a kind of collective self-defence under Article 51. The legitimacy of such help is disputed, however, and commentators note that the Definition of Aggression and the 1970 Declaration speak only of 'support' without elaborating.

The issue is important in view of the wide scope which the 1970 Declaration allows for the right to pursue self-determination forcibly. That right is said not to authorise dismemberment –

> of sovereign and independent states conducting themselves in compliance with the principle of equal rights and self-determination of peoples ... and thus possessed of a government representing the whole people belonging to the territory without distinction as to race, creed or colour.

The implication seems to be that a state *not* conducting itself in that way or possessed of such government *may* be dismembered in a fight for self-determination.

If the 'support' mentioned above means outside military help, that dismemberment could take place as a result of foreign interference.

Militating against this conclusion, however, is the general and quite strong sentiment in the United Nations against intervention in the internal affairs of states.

23. Non-intervention. In 1965 the General Assembly adopted Resolution

2131(XX), the Declaration on the Inadmissibility of Intervention in the Domestic Affairs of States and the Protection of their Independence and Sovereignty. This states categorically that:

No state has the right to intervene, directly or indirectly, for any reason whatever, in the internal or external affairs of any other state.

It goes on to condemn armed intervention and all other forms of interference or threats against another state. It then continues:

No state may use or encourage the use of economic, political or any other type of measures to coerce a state in order to obtain from it the subordination of the exercise of its sovereign rights or to secure from it advantages of any kind. Also, no state shall organize, assist, foment, finance, incite or tolerate subversive, terrorist or armed activities directed towards the violent overthrow of the regime of another state, or interfere in civil strife in another state.

The 1970 Declaration, in a section on non-intervention adopted much of this language.

It would appear, then, that intervention, even to help a people resisting the forcible denial of self-determination within an existing independent state, is at the very least not favoured by the law of the United Nations and may actually be prohibited by it.

Basing itself on the accumulation of resolutions and declarations by international organisations in this regard, the International Court of Justice, in *Nicaragua* v. *United States* (1986), determined that there is in customary international law a principle of non-intervention whereby every sovereign state has the right to decide for itself, and without outside interference, such questions as the choice of a political, economic, social or cultural system and the formulation of its foreign policy. The backing of the United States for anti-government *contra* forces in Nicaragua by 'training, arming, equipping, financing and supplying' them and by 'otherwise encouraging, supporting and aiding' their 'military and paramilitary activities' was held to violate this principle. (*See* also 17:**24**.)

The difficulty is that the practice of a wide variety of states indicates that many are prepared when it suits their interests to intervene quite decisively in the internal affairs of weaker countries. In 1968, for example, the Soviet Union forcibly intervened in Czechoslovakia under the so-called 'Brezhnev doctrine' to put down a reformist movement which the USSR said had 'capitalist' backing, while the United States in 1983 invaded Grenada for the purpose of countering communist influence there and installed a government of which America approved. Most international legal experts would agree, however, that such interventions remain illegal regardless of how often they may be perpetrated.

It should be noted in conclusion that the problem of intervention in the internal affairs of countries experiencing civil conflict is intimately connected with the difficulties arising from the international legal status of anti-state forces (*see* 4:**7**). In general, it would appear that intervention ceases to be prohibited when a legally acknowledged international entity such as a belligerent community comes into existence, as the conflict then loses its purely internal character.

The law of war   **24. Scope of the law of war.** The law of war (the *jus in bello*) in classical international law was the legal regime that came into operation when the relations of particular countries with each other were no longer governed by the law of peace because a state of declared war existed between them. The law of war dealt with all aspects of the hostile relationship.

The modern development of legal restrictions on resort to 'war' has caused a shift in attitude on the law of war. With many multilateral treaties (most notably the UN Charter) continuing in operation even between warring states, the law of war is less an alternative to the law of peace and more a device for alleviating the suffering caused by war. Since World War II a concerted attempt has been made, under the leadership of the International Committee of the Red Cross (ICRC), to strengthen that branch of the law of war which is now generally known as International Humanitarian Law, where the law of war and the law of human rights approach each other (*see* 4:55 and 13:11). This humanitarian legal regime will be the main focus of the present discussion.

The relative prominence of this branch of the law of war is emphasised by the reluctance of countries to admit that they are engaged in 'war', having in mind the pejorative connotations of that word and the legal and political inconveniences a state of war entails.

At the time of the Falklands conflict in 1982, for example, the British Prime Minister stated publicly that the United Kingdom was not at war with Argentina and that the laws of war therefore did not apply. She seems to have been concerned that a state of war would raise legal problems in such areas as the neutrality or co-belligerency of other countries (notably the United States), although Britain eventually accepted that the humanitarian laws of war were in operation.

To avoid these sorts of problems some people speak nowadays of the 'law of armed conflict'. This change seems appropriate also in light of the increasing international concern with regulating what are called non-international armed conflicts, i.e. civil wars and hostilities in which not every party is a state.

25. The sources of the law of war. Originally an element of customary international law, the law of war has in the last 125 years been principally developed through treaties. Among the most important of these are:

(*a*) the Hague Conventions of 1899 and 1907, and particularly the Fourth Hague Convention of 1907 with its annexed Hague Regulations on the Laws and Customs of War on Land; and

(*b*) the four Geneva Conventions of 1949 and their two Additional Protocols of 1977.

In addition a large number of treaties deal with specific problems such as the prohibition of objectionable weapons.

26. The key concept of the law of war. Central to the idea that the conduct of hostilities is subject to the rule of law is the principle stated in Article 22 of the Hague Regulations and reaffirmed in Article 35(1) of the 1977 Protocol I:

The right of belligerents to adopt means of injuring the enemy is not unlimited.

This provision has far-reaching implications since it signals a rejection of the doctrine of unlimited military necessity. That doctrine had been advocated by German writers under the name of *Kriegsraison*, the view that whatever was necessary to the prosecution of a war was permitted.

The preamble of the Fourth Hague Convention of 1907 indicated that the annexed Hague Regulations had been drafted so as to provide rules which would apply even after legitimate military necessity had been taken into account. This meant that the Regulations could not properly be disregarded on the excuse of military necessity, as only where specific exceptions were made in favour of such necessity could that factor impinge on the implementation of the Regulations.

27. The 'Martens clause'. The 1907 preamble also clarified another important point. Although the Convention and Regulations did not include provisions on every possible point, that did not mean that such matters were unregulated by international law. According to the Martens clause, inserted into the preamble at the behest of Fyodor F. Martens, the Russian representative and a distinguished international lawyer, those affected by war in any case –

> remain under the protection and the rule of the principles of the law of nations, as they result from the usages established among civilized peoples, from the laws of humanity, and the dictates of the public conscience.

28. Ramifications of the basic principles. The rejection of *Kriegsraison*, the insistence that not everything that might help win a war was legal, and the emphasis on the laws of humanity had important implications for three areas of the laws of war: the treatment of enemy combatants, the treatment of civilians, and the limitation of the use of weapons.

29. The treatment of enemy combatants. Enemy combatants engaged in active hostilities may legitimately be attacked and killed, although the law's limitations on means of injuring the enemy have the effect of ruling out certain methods of accomplishing this. Article 23(b) of the Hague Regulations and Articles 37–39 of the 1977 First Protocol forbid 'treacherously' killing or wounding persons belonging to the hostile nation or army. Article 23(d) of the Regulations and Article 40 of the Protocol forbid a declaration that 'no quarter' will be given, so that the surrender of enemy combatants must be accepted and they may not be killed once having laid down their arms.

Although a combatant may, subject to the limitations mentioned, be killed or injured while he is maintaining resistence, once he is put *hors de combat* (roughly speaking, 'out of action') by injury or surrender he must not be the object of attack.

Consequently, enemy military hospitals and other clearly designated medical facilities, and their staffs and patients, must not be attacked or interfered with and prisoners of war (POWs) are entitled to humane treatment and proper maintenance while in captivity. Under Article 118 of the Third Geneva Convention of 1949 the captivity of POWs is to be terminated 'without delay after the cessation of active hostilities' and sick prisoners should be repatriated even sooner.

30. The problem of combatant and POW status. One of the most difficult and persistent problems in applying the law on protecting combatants and POWs is the refusal of some states to recognise the legal status of hostile forces operating against them. In the past 'partisans' or 'guerrillas' have often been summarily executed, and in 1982 during its invasion of Lebanon Israel refused to give official POW status to Palestinian and Lebanese prisoners while accepting it for captured members of Syrian regular forces.

The basis of classification of combatant status is set out in <u>Article 1 of the 1907 Hague Regulations</u>:

> The laws, rights, and duties of war apply not only to armies, but also to militia and volunteer corps fulfilling the following conditions:
> 1. To be commanded by a person responsible for his subordinates;
> 2. To have a fixed distinctive emblem recognizable at a distance;
> 3. To carry arms openly; and
> 4. To conduct their operations in accordance with the laws and customs of war.

Article 4 of the Third Geneva Convention of 1949 adds to those who qualify as POWs by meeting the conditions stated persons who are members of 'organized' resistance movements' 'belonging' to a party to the conflict and operating 'in or outside their own territory, even if this territory is occupied'.

In the case of a mass uprising (*levée en masse*) of the civilian population, Article 2 of the Hague Regulations provides that:

> The inhabitants of a territory which has not been occupied, who, on the approach of the enemy, spontaneously take up arms to resist the invading troops without having had time to organize themselves in accordance with Article 1, shall be regarded as belligerents if they carry arms openly and if they respect the laws and customs of war.

The extent to which part-time guerrillas or partisans might be entitled to combatant and POW status has always been much debated, although Protocol I of 1977, in Articles 43–45, is understood to extend this status to such fighters provided that they are distinguishable from the civilian population and carry arms openly at the time they are engaged in military operations, though they need not be distinguishable at other times.

It is clear from Article 5 of the Third Geneva Convention of 1949 that a captured fighter is to be given the benefit of the doubt as to his entitlement to POW status until a 'competent tribunal' decides otherwise.

Curiously, although the development of the law has generally been towards widening the scope of combatant and POW status at the behest of Third World countries who support national liberation struggles, with regard to mercenaries the movement has been towards outlawing them, as in Article 47(1) of the 1977 First Protocol. But given that the aim of the law is to promote and increase humane treatment of the enemy in war, this development seems scarcely defensible, however repugnant the idea of hired killers may be, and could well encourage mercenary fighters to even greater brutality (e.g. murdering civilian witnesses to their activities) in order to avoid being caught and treated as outlaws.

31. The problem of individuals in non-international conflicts. Because of the concentration of classical international law on the relations between states, the concern of the classical law of war with armed conflict within states was minimal, the one major exception being the American Civil War from 1861 to

1865 when President Lincoln issued the *Instructions for the Government of Armies of the United States in the Field,* regulations which inspired the later codifications at the Hague Conferences.

Until 1977 the only treaty provisions were contained in Article 3 of each of the four Geneva Conventions of 1949, where an identical common provision on non-international armed conflict requires that –

> Persons taking no active part in the hostilities, including members of armed forces who have laid down their arms and those placed *hors de combat* by sickness, wounds, detention, or any other cause, shall in all circumstances be treated humanely, without any adverse distinction founded on race, colour, religion or faith, sex, birth or wealth, or any similar criteria.

The Article then prohibits:

> (*a*) violence to life and person, in particular murder, mutilation, cruel treatment and torture;
> (*b*) the taking of hostages;
> (*c*) outrages upon personal dignity, in particular humiliating and degrading treatment;
> (*d*) the passing of sentences and the carrying out of executions without previous judgment pronounced by a regularly constituted court, affording all the judicial guarantees which are recognized as indispensable by civilized peoples.

Article 3 also requires that the wounded and sick be 'collected and cared for' and allows for involvement of the ICRC.

To provide a fuller protection for individuals in such conflicts Protocol II of 1977 applies to them some of the basic guarantees elaborated in Protocol I for international armed conflict.

32. The treatment of civilians. Where unlimited military necessity might in some cases have served to excuse the annihilation of the enemy's civilian population, the Hague Regulations' rejection of the *Kriegsraison* approach reaffirmed a vital rule of the law of war: that a clear distinction must be maintained between combatants, who might lawfully be attacked (*see* **30**), and civilians, who could not legitimately be the object of attack.

Thus, Article 25 of the Hague Regulations (which is echoed in Article 57 of Protocol I) prohibits the 'attack or bombardment, by whatever means, of towns, villages, dwellings, or buildings which are undefended' and so retain a civilian character.

In 1923 a commission of jurists appointed by the governments of the United States, Britain, France, Italy, Japan and The Netherlands drew up the *Hague Rules of Aerial Warfare* with the purpose of codifying customary law as it would apply to this new method of attack and in the hope (which was not fulfilled) that the rules would be incorporated in a treaty. Article 22 of the Rules prohibits 'aerial bombardment for the purpose of terrorizing the civilian population, of destroying or damaging private property not of a military character, or of injuring non-combatants'. Article 24 states that an air attack 'is legitimate only when directed at a military objective' and prohibits the bombing of 'cities, towns, villages, dwellings or buildings not in the immediate neighbourhood of the operations of land forces'.

The general rule of customary law on which these earlier prohibitions were based is stated in Protocol I of 1977. Article 48 says that:

the parties to the conflict shall at all times distinguish between the civilian population and combatants and between civilian objects and military objectives and accordingly shall direct their operations only against military objectives.

Under Article 51 the civilian population 'as such' must not be the object of attack and 'Indiscriminate attacks are prohibited'. An indiscriminate attack is one not directed at a specific military objective, or employing 'a method or means of combat which cannot be directed at a specific military objective' or whose effects cannot be limited as required by the Protocol. An attack would be indiscriminate if it caused incidental civilian injury, death, or damage 'which would be excessive in relation to the concrete and direct military advantage anticipated'.

Article 54 of the Protocol prohibits starvation of civilians as a method of warfare and the destruction of objects indispensable to civilian life such as food stores and drinking water installations.

These fundamental customary rules are sometimes criticised, however, for being out of touch with the practice of states. Target area bombing in World War II destroyed large parts of London, Coventry, Berlin, Hamburg and Dresden; nuclear weapons obliterated Hiroshima and Nagasaki; over 17,000 civilians were killed during Israel's invasion of Lebanon and besieging of Beirut in 1982. In the age of 'total war', it is said, everyone is a legitimate target because everyone contributes to the economy on which a state's war effort depends.

But these objections are misconceived for a number of reasons. They are based on the premise that the practice of a handful of powerful governments can be taken to reflect the standards of the whole international community. They ignore the implications of the rule that not everything which may help win a war is legitimate. They disregard the nature of international humanitarian law, which does not derive its legitimacy from the policies of states but from the needs of individuals.

Thus, the correct position seems to be that, just as criminals do not by their crimes make national law cease to exist, so international violators of the laws of war do not destroy the law but simply reveal themselves in a true light. One notes, furthermore, that none of these violators has renounced the protections which the laws of war give it and many of them may be conscious of the fact that if the distinction between combatants and non-combatants is removed, no basis any more exists for showing mercy to captured prisoners or wounded soldiers who are out of action in hospitals and similar installations.

Therefore, although some states and strategists do attempt (without admitting it) to revive the discredited doctrine of *Kriegsraison*, it appears no more legitimate or acceptable now than it did in 1907.

33. Protection of civilians under military occupation. As already indicated (*see* **6:20**), the law of war has an important bearing on belligerent (i.e. military) occupation. The 1907 Hague Regulations and the Fourth Geneva Convention of 1949 are relevant here by virtue of the protections they give to civilians who come under the control of the enemy during hostilities, occupation being one of the ways this may happen.

The underlying principle applicable to military occupation is stated in

Article 43 of the Hague Regulations, which indicates that the occupying power is merely exercising authority in lieu of the displaced legitimate sovereign and must respect, 'unless absolutely prevented', the laws already in force in the country. The occupier is therefore not permitted to treat the territory as if it were part of his own state, although he is entitled to maintain public order and safety for the reasonable protection of his troops who are in the occupied territory and of the civilian population. The occupier is not entitled, however, to abuse this privilege by imposing controls or restrictions designed to further his general strategic or political goals.

Under Article 46 of the Regulations family honour and rights, the lives of persons, religious convictions and practice, and private property must be respected, and such property cannot be confiscated. This is reaffirmed and amplified in Article 27 of the 1949 Convention and is linked with prohibitions in Articles 28–34 against torture, collective punishments, pillage, reprisals and the taking of hostages.

Article 47 of the Convention makes clear that the occupier cannot change the legal status of the occupied territory by annexation or similar measures and thus cannot extinguish the rights of the inhabitants. Article 49 prohibits deportation of the occupied territory's population and also forbids settling citizens of the occupying state in the occupied territory. Article 53 prohibits destruction of the real or personal property of individuals unless that 'is rendered absolutely necessary by military operations', which must be understood as immediate hostilities, rather than large-scale strategic or political arrangements effected by military means after the fighting has ceased.

34. War crimes. To discourage violations of these and related rules international law has developed the concept of war crimes. Although sometimes defined to include 'crimes against peace', such as the planning and waging of aggressive war, and 'crimes against humanity', like genocide, extermination, enslavement and deportation, strictly speaking war crimes are violations of the laws and customs of war.

War crimes include the murder or ill-treatment of prisoners of war or survivors of attacks at sea, wanton destruction of towns and villages, attacks on protected installations such as hospitals, the use of forbidden weapons, and bombardment of civilian targets for the purpose of terrorising the civilian population.

With regard to the protection of civilians under the Fourth Geneva Convention of 1949, Article 147 lists as grave breaches of the Convention, for which individuals should be held criminally liable, the following:

> wilful killing, torture or inhuman treatment, including biological experiments, wilfully causing great suffering or serious injury to body or health, unlawful deportation or transfer or unlawful confinement of a protected person, compelling a protected person to serve in the forces of a hostile power, or wilfully depriving a protected person of the rights of fair and regular trial prescribed in the present Convention, taking of hostages and extensive destruction and appropriation of property, not justified by military necessity and carried out unlawfully and wantonly.

The Convention makes clear that states have a positive duty to try to punish persons committing these crimes who come within a state's jurisdiction (*see* **8:16**).

35. Limitations on weapons. Attempts to limit or prevent the use of particularly cruel or devastating weapons have been a feature of the developing law of war since the St Petersburg Declaration of 1868 forbade the use of exploding bullets. The underlying principle of customary law is expressed in Article 35(2) of Protocol I of 1977, which reiterates and amplifies Article 23(e) of the Hague Regulations. The Protocol prohibits the employment of 'weapons, projectiles and material and methods of warfare of a nature to cause superfluous injury or unnecessary suffering'.

Thus the Hague Regulations prohibit the use of poison or poisoned weapons. The 1925 Geneva Protocol for the Prohibition of the Use in War of Asphyxiating, Poisonous or other Gases, and of Bacteriological Methods of Warfare is understood also to reflect the customary law with regard to use of the weapons mentioned. The progress of science and concern over the accumulation of even more lethal devices promoted the 1972 Convention on the Prohibition of the Development, Production and Stockpiling of Bacteriological (Biological) and Toxin Weapons, although strictly chemical weapons have yet to be covered by a similar treaty.

The United States from 1969 to 1982 observed a moratorium on the production of new chemical weapons but under President Reagan resumed manufacture and deployment of them as a 'deterrent' to use by the Soviet Union of its allegedly large stockpiles of poison gases. Experts foresee a chemical weapons arms race between the superpowers, particularly with regard to binary nerve gas munitions. None of this is *per se* prohibited by the 1925 Geneva Protocol, which was concerned only with use and had no inspection or verification provisions to inhibit preparations for use.

The latest in this line of treaties is the 1981 Convention on Prohibitions or Restrictions on the Use of certain Conventional Weapons which may be deemed to be Excessively Injurious or to have Indiscriminate Effects and its Protocols. These prohibit weapons causing injury by non-detectable fragments, limit the use of mines, booby traps and other devices which cannot be specifically targeted and may thus endanger civilians, and restrict the use of incendiary weapons so as to minimise injury to civilians.

 36. The problem of new weapons. A key question in the limitation of weapons is whether the use of new devices may be illegal by reason of contravening the customary law prohibitions or by analogy with weapons specifically mentioned in existing treaties. Some argue that an existing prohibition must be taken to apply only to weapons which could have been imagined at the time it came into being.

But the correct view seems to be that the law aims at preventing certain consequences rather than simply outlawing specific means of producing them. Thus Article 36 of Protocol I of 1977 can legitimately remind states that:

> In the study, development, acquisition or adoption of a new weapon, means or method of warfare, a ... party is under an obligation to determine whether its employment would, in some or all circumstances, be prohibited by this Protocol or by any other rule of international law applicable to the ... party.

 37. Nuclear weapons. These general observations lead inevitably to the great debate of the present time over the legality of nuclear weapons.

To begin with defenders of these weapons argue, as did the American government volume on *The Law of Naval Warfare* in 1955, that, since there is 'no rule of international law expressly prohibiting ... the use of nuclear weapons ... such use ... against enemy combatants and other military objectives is permitted'. To the extent that this is a version of the 'new weapons' argument (*see* **36**) it would not appear to carry much weight. Its careful limitation of use to enemy military objectives would therefore still be subject to evaluation in the light of the traditional criteria in the law of war regarding the means of injuring the enemy.

No case has dealt with the specific question of nuclear attack solely on military targets, but a Japanese court in the *Shimoda Case* (1963) held that the atomic bombing of Hiroshima and Nagasaki violated the prohibition against inflicting unnecessary suffering and did not discriminate between combatants and civilians but hit undefended targets in which there were protected installations like hospitals and schools. It would appear that at least some of these objections would apply also to attacks on military targets, particularly in the situation of large-scale nuclear war.

In use against both civilian and military targets nuclear weapons might also be considered illegal by analogy with the forbidden use of poisonous and biological weapons.

The counter-argument is that the customary law specifically as it affects nuclear weapons has been changed by the practice of the nuclear weapon states in accepting them as legal. But the general rule on the development of new custom has been stated by the International Court of Justice in the *North Sea Continental Shelf Cases* (see Chapter 2, Section 26) to be that such speedy change cannot take place without the participation of specially affected states. As all states would be affected by a general nuclear war, it would appear that the views on the matter of a handful of nuclear states could not be decisive in changing the law.

The attitude of non-nuclear states may be gauged from General Assembly Resolution 1653(XVI), the Declaration on the Prohibition of the Use of Nuclear and Thermo-nuclear Weapons, adopted in 1961 by a vote of fifty-five in favour, twenty against, and twenty-six abstentions.

This resolution stated that the use of nuclear weapons would be 'a direct negation of the high ideals and objectives' of the United Nations and went on to declare that:

(*a*) the use of such weapons is a direct violation of the Charter; and

(*b*) it would exceed the scope of war and cause indiscriminate suffering and destruction in contravention of international law and the laws of humanity; and

(*c*) it would be 'a war directed not against an enemy or enemies alone but also against mankind in general, since the peoples not involved in such a war will be subjected to all the evils generated by the use of such weapons'; and

(*d*) any state using such weapons would be 'acting contrary to the laws of humanity' and 'committing a crime against mankind and civilization'.

Since the adoption of this resolution, which had in mind the effects of blast and radiation on belligerents and neutrals, scientific research has raised the possibility of another wide-spread consequence of a nuclear war, the 'nuclear winter' caused by the blocking out of the sun's rays by clouds of smoke and debris thrown up by the nuclear blasts.

Confronted with the law of war and the realities of a nuclear holocaust, defenders of nuclear weapons seek to move the argument onto a different point by arguing that even if the use of these devices is prohibited that prohibition does not extend to the possession and deployment of them as part of the psycho-political strategy of deterrence with a view to forestalling use.

But, apart from the question whether it constitutes a threat of force in violation of Article 2(4) of the UN Charter, deterrence is criticised for necessitating, in order to be credible, a readiness to use nuclear weapons. This implies a willingness to unleash mass destruction in order to prevent the enemy's victory, while the Hague Regulations do not permit resort to every possible means of injuring the enemy and thus imply that in some circumstances a state must be prepared to accept defeat rather than use forbidden weapons.

Furthermore, from a military point of view some experts argue that the deterrent may not be credible insofar as the use of nuclear weapons in response to a nuclear attack by the enemy would not be likely to improve the defender's military position and would therefore appear useless. The legal implications of this analysis are:

(a) that there would be no military necessity for use in defence and all the resulting suffering would thus be 'unnecessary' in terms of the law of war; and

(b) that the logic of deterrence, on which its legitimacy is based, would be undermined.

Another sombre conclusion may be drawn from this military argument: that, although defensive use of nuclear weapons in response to a nuclear attack might serve no purpose, the first use of nuclear weapons might seem militarily advantageous, so that the possession of such weapons could encourage their illegal use. Even a war begun with conventional weapons could thus escalate into a nuclear war – a scenario which has been publicly foreseen by the military commanders of the North Atlantic Treaty Organisation (NATO). The possession and willingness to use nuclear weapons might thus make it possible to cross the 'nuclear threshold', an event which deterrence, the only justification for deploying those weapons in the first place, is supposed to prevent.

A hidden element in this debate about military and legal considerations is that autonomous political motives appear to lie behind the acquisition of nuclear weapons by some states: the desire to have the political 'leverage' which such weapons give to those who thereby gain, in the words of a British politician, 'a seat at the top table'. There appears to be no legal support for this motive at all.

Disarmament

38. **Definition.** Strictly speaking, disarmament implies the abolition of all weapons of war. But Article 8 of the League of Nations Covenant shifted the focus of disarmament after 1920 to the coordinated reduction and limitation of armaments through international agreements. Disarmament in effect became arms control.

39. **The United Nations.** Article 26 of the UN Charter gave to the Security Council responsibility for 'formulating ... plans to be submitted to the members of the United Nations for the establishment of a system for the regulation of armaments' and, under Article 47, for 'possible disarmament'. The Council was to do this with the assistance of a UN Military Staff Committee composed of the chiefs of staff of the Council's permanent members, but little was accomplished

in this way.

The General Assembly, however, was empowered by Article 11 of the Charter to consider 'the general principles of co-operation in the maintenance of international peace and security, including the principles governing disarmament and the regulation of armaments', and much of the work of the United Nations in this field has been done by the Assembly.

The Assembly's 1970 Declaration on the Principles of International Law (Res. 2625(XXV)), in explaining the implications of the principle that states must refrain from the threat or use of force, says:

> All states shall pursue in good faith negotiations for the early conclusion of a universal treaty on general and complete disarmament under effective international control.

No such treaty has been produced, however, and world arms expenditure in the decade after 1970 rose some 3 per cent a year in real terms, with a massive increase in weapons sales by the developed countries to the Third World (*see* **15:28**).

Thus, although the UN's forty-nation Committee on Disarmament has continued work in Geneva and the Assembly has remained involved in the problem through two Special Sessions on Disarmament in 1978 and 1982, such steps towards arms control as have been taken have been either in areas where the superpowers feel that it may serve their interests or where other states were prepared to act in defiance of the superpowers. These piecemeal measures may be grouped into the topics of nuclear weapons (*see* **40–43**), strategic arms limitation (*see* **44**) and other measures of restraint (*see* **45**).

40. Nuclear weapons. Though the great powers have refused to abolish their own nuclear arsenals they have been keen to limit the spread of nuclear weapons to other states.

This was attempted in the Treaty on the Non-Proliferation of Nuclear Weapons (1968) whereby the United States, the Soviet Union and the United Kingdom, as 'nuclear-weapon states', undertook not to supply such devices to any of the other, 'non-nuclear-weapon', states that were party to the treaty, nor assist or encourage those other states to develop their own nuclear weapons or nuclear explosive devices. The non-nuclear-weapon states in their turn agreed not to acquire or develop such weapons or devices for themselves. To give some substance to their commitments, the non-nuclear-weapon states agreed in Article III to accept safeguards arrangements negotiated with the International Atomic Energy Agency (IAEA), a body operating under the aegis of the United Nations to promote the peaceful and safe uses of nuclear energy. These agreements would enable compliance with the treaty to be verified and would prevent diversion of nuclear materials or equipment from peaceful to military purposes.

The nuclear powers did not get this concession without paying a price. In Article VI they were required:

> to pursue negotiations in good faith on effective measures relating to cessation of the nuclear arms race at an early date and to nuclear disarmament, and on a treaty on general and complete disarmament under strict and effective international control.

This commitment by the nuclear-weapon states has not yet been fulfilled and that failure has provided a negative example to certain other countries that are glad of the excuse not to sign the treaty and to move openly or secretly towards developing their own nuclear weapons. France, China, Israel, South Africa, Argentina, Brazil, India and Pakistan did not sign the Non-Proliferation Treaty, and the danger to peace which proliferation may bring has been highlighted by regional conflicts in the Middle East and Asia in which some of these countries are involved. In 1981 Israel, generally believed to have developed a nuclear weapons capability itself at nuclear facilities not under IAEA safeguards, bombed an Iraqi nuclear installation which, according to the Iraqi government, was being built under IAEA safeguards for peaceful purposes, although Israel claimed that in secret the facility was being used to develop nuclear weapons. The possibility of a similar clash over nuclear weapons exists between India and Pakistan, as India, which exploded a 'peaceful' nuclear device in 1974, is believed to have resolved to ensure that Pakistan's main nuclear installation not be used for weapons manufacture.

41. Nuclear weapons testing. The nuclear powers' lack of progress in fulfilling their obligations under the Non-Proliferation Treaty is particularly noticeable in the area of nuclear testing, the limitation of which could be important in curtailing experiments to develop new nuclear weapons.

Five years before the signing of the Non-Proliferation Treaty, Britain, the United States and the Soviet Union negotiated the Treaty Banning Nuclear Weapon Tests in the Atmosphere, in Outer Space and Under Water (1963), the 'Partial Test Ban Treaty'. As will be evident from its title, this agreement allowed nuclear tests underground to continue. Hope of restricting tests in that area also were raised by the agreement of the US and the USSR to the Treaty on the Limitation of Underground Nuclear Weapon Tests, the 'Threshold Test Ban Treaty' of 1974, which forbade tests yielding more than 150 kilotons (seven-and-a-half times the power of the bomb dropped on Hiroshima but only one-fourhundredth of that of some thermonuclear devices). Unfortunately, the United States never ratified this treaty and it is not in force. The two parties did for a time agree, however, not in practice to exceed the limits set by the agreement when conducting underground tests. Efforts to negotiate a comprehensive test ban treaty have come to nothing.

Although the nuclear powers seem unworried by their persistent failure to abide by their obligations under the Non-Proliferation Treaty, the matter has remained of concern to most other countries. Following the UN General Assembly's special sessions on disarmament in 1978 and 1982, the Assembly in December 1982 adopted by massive majorities resolutions calling for the cessation of nuclear weapons production, and the ending of their deployment and testing. The Assembly has also urged the outlawry of nuclear tests. The 1978 special session was notable for, among other things, its support of nuclear-weapon free zones, which it encouraged the nuclear powers to commit themselves to.

42. Nuclear-weapon free zones. Such a zone has been established in the Treaty for the Prohibition of Nuclear Weapons in Latin America (1967), the 'Tlatelolco Treaty', which forbids the testing, use, production, acquisition, storage, installation or deployment of nuclear weapons by the nations of Latin America, with safeguards being provided by agreements on application of the IAEA safeguards system. Protocol I of the treaty requires colonial states with possessions in the region to agree to denuclearize these territories. The Netherlands and Britain (with reservations) and the United States are parties to this protocol, while France has signed it. Protocol II commits the nuclear weapon states to respect the denuclearization of Latin America as a whole and not to contribute to violation of the treaty or to employ nuclear weapons against its parties. France, the USSR, Britain and the United States are all, with reservations, parties to Protocol II and China is a party without a reservation.

A difficulty with the operation of this treaty amongst the Latin American states themselves is that under Article 28(1) the treaty enters into force for states that have ratified it only on fulfilment of certain requirements, most notably the ratification of Protocols I and II by the states to whom they are addressed, and the conclusions of IAEA safeguards agreements. However, Article 28(2) allows states to waive this requirement if they so choose and thus bring the treaty into operation more quickly with regard to themselves.

But the most likely states in Latin America to develop nuclear weapons either did not make such declarations (Brazil and Chile) or did not become a party (Argentina).

The South Pacific Nuclear Free Zone Treaty (1985), the 'Rarotonga Treaty', also commits the parties to a comprehensive regime banning the testing and acquisition of nuclear weapons, the sale of nuclear material to other countries (except under IAEA safeguards), and the 'stationing' of such weapons on the soil of the parties, although each state 'in the exercise of its sovereign rights' may allow visits or navigation by foreign ships or aircraft in its territory and seas. Three protocols open to the nuclear-weapon powers outside the region require commitments from those powers not to manufacture, station or test nuclear weapons in the region nor use them against parties to the treaty.

43. Special regimes prohibiting nuclear weapons. The nuclear-weapon states themselves have managed to agree on special regimes for certain areas.

(*a*) The *Antarctic Treaty* (1959) demilitarizes Antarctica and in Article 5 forbids nuclear explosions and the disposal of radioactive waste there.

(*b*) Building on General Assembly resolutions which may reflect customary international law on the peaceful uses of outer space, Article 4 of the *Outer Space Treaty* (1967) obliges the parties:

> not to place in orbit around the Earth any objects carrying nuclear weapons or any other kinds of weapons of mass destruction, install such weapons on celestial bodies, or station such weapons in outer space in any other manner.

The *Moon Treaty* (1979) reaffirms these undertakings with regard to the Moon and other celestial bodies, which it characterises as the common heritage of mankind (Article XI).

In 1983, however, the president of the United States initiated the study of a Strategic Defence Initiative (SDI), the so-called 'Star Wars' programme, which could lead to the stationing of some American nuclear weapons in space as part of an anti-missile defence system. Critics of the plan charged that this was a potential violation of the Outer Space Treaty.

The Soviet Union in 1981 proposed a treaty to ban the stationing of weapons of any kind in outer space, but this has not borne fruit.

(c) The 1971 *Sea-Bed Treaty* prohibits placing on the seabed, ocean floor or the subsoil thereof, any nuclear weapons or other weapons of mass destruction or any installations associated with their testing, storage or use.

44. Strategic arms limitation. In the 1970s the United States and the Soviet Union entered into a series of agreements that came out of two rounds of Strategic Arms Limitation Talks, SALT I and SALT II.

The Salt I package included an Interim Agreement (1972) on freezing for five years the aggregate of fixed land-based intercontinental ballistic missile launchers and launchers on submarines, with 'national technical means of verification' (e.g. spy satellites) permitted to ensure each side's compliance with the agreement. A Memorandum of Understanding in 1972 set up a Standing Consultative Commission on arms limitation.

The SALT II Treaty in 1979 provided for reduction of missile launchers in a complicated package balancing the various types of launch vehicles and their 'throw-weights'. The United States refused to ratify this agreement but did undertake for a time to abide by its limitations in practice.

Of all the SALT agreements the most solidly enduring seemed to be the 1972 *Treaty on the Limitation of Anti-ballistic Missile Systems* (the 'ABM Treaty'), which prohibited the deployment of anti-missile defences for the whole territory of the two parties. The aim was to keep operative the deterrent effect of each side's nuclear aresenal by leaving open the possibility that each side could devastate the other's unprotected cities, thus delivering up the civilian population of each state as hostages for their own government's good behaviour. This was regarded by advocates of the theory of deterrence as a positive development.

The decision of the United States in 1983 to proceed with the SDI-'Star Wars' programme, whereby an anti-missile system would be deployed in space, was criticised as a potential violation of the ABM Treaty and as destabilising the deterrent strategies on which the Superpowers had relied, since the country which could deploy a total defensive shield would then be able to consider the offensive use of nuclear weapons without fear of being devastated in a retaliatory nuclear attack.

45. Other measures of restraint. As already seen (*see* **35**), the 1972 Biological Weapons Convention prohibits the development, production or acquisition of biological and toxin weapons, including, in the view of the 1980 Conference which met to review the Convention's operation, agents produced by genetic engineering.

Progress test 16

1. Did classical international law accept the idea of the just war?   (**1**)
2. What were the basic provisions of the Pact of Paris?   (**2**)
3. Outline the fundamental provisions of the UN Charter on war and peace.   (**3**)
4. In what circumstances may the Security Council decide on the use of force?   (**4**)
5. Under the UN Charter may the General Assembly authorise the coercive use of force?   (**6, 7**)
6. What distinguishes enforcement actions from UN peacekeeping?   (**7**)

7. In what circumstances is self-defence justified according to the Secretary of State, Daniel Webster, in the *The Caroline Case?* (**9**)

8. What is the significance of the phrase 'if an armed attack occurs' in Article 51 of the UN Charter? (**10**)

9. Is 'anticipatory self-defence' permitted under the UN Charter? (**13**)

10. Explain the concept of humanitarian intervention. (**15**)

11. Outline the provisions of the Resolution on the Definition of Aggression. (**17–22**)

12. Is forcible intervention in the affairs of another state ever justified? (**23**)

13. What is the key concept of the law of war? (**26**)

14. Is there a distinction between the rights of combatants and those rendered *hors de combat?* (**29**)

15. Do the laws, rights and duties of war apply only to members of regular armies? (**30**)

16. Does the international law of war apply to non-international armed conflicts? (**31**)

17. Is the distinction between combatants and civilians important? (**32**)

18. Is it permissible to launch indiscriminate attacks against civilian targets? (**32**)

19. May an occupying power treat occupied territory as belonging to it? (**33**)

20. What are war crimes? (**34**)

21. In general, of what sort of weapons does international law prohibit the use? (**35**)

22. May the use of new weapons be prohibited by pre-existing law? (**36**)

23. Are nuclear weapons legal? (**37**)

24. Outline the international controls on nuclear weapons proliferation. (**40**)

25. Discuss some of the attempts to establish nuclear-weapon free zones. (**42**)

26. Have efforts at strategic arms limitation been notably successful? (**44**)

Bibliography

Best, *Humanity in Warfare*, Weidenfeld & Nicholson, London (1980)

Carver, *A Policy for Peace*, Faber & Faber, London (1982)

Howe, *Weapons*, Abacus, London (1980)

International Commission on Disarmament and Security Issues (the Palme Commission), *Common Security: A Programme For Disarmament*, Pan Books, London (1982)

Luard, ed., *The International Regulation of Civil Wars*, Thames & Hudson, London (1972)

W. T. & S. V. Mallison, *The Palestine Problem in International Law and World Order*, Longman, London (1986)

Roberts & Guelff, eds., *Documents on the Laws of War*, Clarendon Press, Oxford (1982)

Starke, *An Introduction to the Science of Peace (Irenology)*, Sijthoff, Leyden (1968)

Stockholm International Peace Research Institute (SIPRI):

   – *The Law of War and Dubious Weapons*, Stockholm (1976)

   – *The Arms Race and Arms Control*, Taylor & Francis, London (1982)

Thompson, ed., *Star Wars*, Penguin Books, Harmondsworth, Middlesex (1985)

Whiteman, *Digest of International Law*, vol. 10, pages 143–150, 420–424, 480–503.

17 Peaceful settlement of disputes

Methods and disputes

1. Methods listed in the UN Charter. Article 33(1) of the Charter lists the following obligatory methods for the peaceful settlement of disputes whose continuance may endanger international peace and security:

(*a*) negotiation;

(*b*) enquiry;

(*c*) mediation;

(*d*) conciliation;

(*e*) arbitration;

(*f*) judicial settlement;

(*g*) resort to regional agencies or arrangements; or

(*h*) other peaceful means of the parties' own choice, among which may be included 'good offices'.

These methods may, of course, be used to resolve other problems as well but resort to them would not necessarily be obligatory.

2. Classification of methods. An examination of this list of methods reveals that it can be divided into two basic classifications: non-adjudicatory methods and adjudicatory methods, that is, methods which rely on dealings and arrangements and ones which involve dispositive determination by a third party.

3. Classification of disputes: justiciability. In relation to the types of disputes which may be submitted to adjudicatory or non-adjudicatory methods of settlement, writers often distinguish between justiciable and non-justiciable disputes.

(*a*) *Justiciable disputes*, strictly speaking, are those which are basically legal in nature in the sense that they raise a question of international law which can be answered by applying that law. Justiciable disputes may therefore be submitted to adjudication based on international law.

(*b*) *Non-justiciable disputes* are those which involve only questions of policy or other extra-legal concerns and therefore cannot be subjected to adjudicatory settlement.

In the heyday of positivism in the nineteenth century the tendency was to consider most disputes non-justiciable, but the development of international law in the twentieth century has considerably expanded the matters on which states are subject to legal duties and rules. In particular, the almost universal adherence to the UN Charter has created a framework of legal obligations and rules relating to the most fundamental questions of international relations, those of war and peace, which must now be considered justiciable despite their political content (*see also* **18**).

In any event, parties to a dispute always have the option to submit even 'non-justiciable' disputes to certain adjudicatory procedures (though perhaps not all), and justiciable disputes may be resolved by political or non-adjudicatory means provided that the requirement of Article 2(3) of the Charter is met, namely that the settlement does not endanger 'international peace and security, and justice'.

Non-adjudicatory procedures

4. Negotiations. Talking with the opposing party as a means of resolving a dispute is probably the oldest method known to international relations. The practice of ancient Rome was to send envoys to present demands for compliance to the enemy before a military attack was launched. The Church in medieval times required negotiations before resort to war could be considered just, and in the period of classical international law war had to be preceded by an ultimatum and a declaration of war.

In modern international law the obligation to talk has been reinforced by the binding commitment of UN members in Article 2(3) of the Charter to pursue the peaceful settlement of disputes.

The Permanent Court of International Justice, in the *Mavrommatis Palestine Concessions Case* (*Jurisdiction*) (1924), indicated that negotiation should be a preliminary to bringing a case before the court in order that the subject matter of a dispute be clearly defined.

An important element in the law on negotiations is suggested in Article 2(2) of the UN Charter, which requires states to fulfil their obligations under the Charter 'in good faith'. Good faith in negotiations means, among other things, a genuine effort to reach agreement, but it does not import an obligation to reach an agreement when that is impossible.

Apart from such general principles, negotiations appear to offer fairly unrestricted flexibility to the parties in achieving a prompt solution of their dispute before it can escalate, and they promote an atmosphere of give-and-take compromise.

Some observers suggest, however, that negotiations may inhibit a lasting solution because an inequality of bargaining power between the parties could prevent problems being fairly dealt with and may lead to pressure and exaggerated demands being made on the weaker party. Negotiations may also be objected to when they are conducted in the manner of a 'zero sum' game in which one side 'wins' and the other 'loses'. Professor Roger Fisher and others have attempted to develop more productive alternatives to this method of negotiation.

Although negotiations can focus on political issues and interests, they do have legal significance insofar as they may generate state practice and rules of state behaviour which could contribute to the development of customary international law.

5. Enquiry. Insofar as a dispute may centre on disagreements over points of fact it may be useful to have an independent determination of those points. Under the Hague Conventions on the Pacific Settlement of Disputes of 1899 and 1907 arrangements were made for instituting commissions of enquiry by agreement of the parties to a dispute.

In the *Dogger Bank Case* (1905), a classic example of this method, such a commission was set up to examine a dispute between Britain and Russia.

During the Russo-Japanese War, in which Britain was known to favour Japan, the Tsar's government despatched Admiral Rozhestvensky's Baltic Squadron to the Far East to reinforce Russian naval strength there. On the way through the North Sea, elements of this fleet, separated from the rest in fog and fearing attack from Japanese torpedo boats, exchanged fire with some unidentified naval ships and shot at several smaller vessels. At the time the Russians were apparently convinced that they were fighting off an enemy attack and they later rejected claims by Britain that the smaller craft had been nothing more than British fishing trawlers, which had been badly hit. Public feeling in both Britain and Russia was aroused and war between the two countries seemed a real possibility. But what had actually happened was that different units of the Russian fleet had fired on each other with the trawlers caught in between, and the commission of enquiry was able to calm the situation by establishing that there had been no torpedo boats and that the action by the Russian squadron had been unjustified.

Although in more recent years the UN General Assembly, in Resolution 2329 (XXII) of 1967, urged members to make better use of fact-finding and enquiry methods in solving disputes, they do not appear to be a favoured technique, perhaps because, in contrast to the Dogger Bank incident, in most disputes the parties (or some of them) already know what really happened.

6. Good offices. The method of good offices involves intercession by a third party, with the consent of the states in dispute, to help them establish direct contacts or take up negotiations.

The good offices of the UN Secretary-General can play an important part in facilitating communication between contending parties, and he may, on behalf of a concerned international community, play an active role in encouraging negotiations and promoting a successful outcome.

7. Mediation. A step beyond good offices, mediation requires the third party to participate officially in the settlement process itself by offering his own advice or proposals on a solution. Such suggestions are not binding, however, and the mediator's work may be brought to an end if any of the parties indicates that it finds his continuing involvement unacceptable.

Since 1948 the Middle East has been an area where mediation has been attempted repeatedly. The United Nations in 1948 appointed Count Folke Bernadotte and then, after his assassination by Jewish terrorists, Dr Ralph Bunche as mediators in the Arab-Israeli dispute, although this effort failed to resolve any aspect of the Palestinian question and led only to armistice agreements between the Arab states and Israel. Following the 1967 Middle East war Dr Gunnar Jarring was named mediator, but it eventually became apparent that some of the parties were determined to see that his mission should fail. A somewhat more successful effort was the mediation of US President Carter in the tough negotiations leading up to the Egyptian-Israeli Peace Treaty of 1979, which ended the thirty-year state of war between the two countries but failed to tackle the Palestinian issue effectively.

8. Conciliation. In contrast to mediation, where the mediator is actively involved in the negotiation of a settlement, conciliation entails a more detached examination of the situation and the official presentation of recommendations which the parties may then adopt or not, as they wish. Conciliation is often undertaken by a commission of conciliation acting as a formal body.

The rationale for establishing conciliation mechanisms was that referral of a dispute to a body able to examine the facts and make recommendations would help defuse the dangers of war by introducing a cooling-off period, clarifying the issues, and offering the disputants a reasonable, though not mandatory, alternative to hostilities.

Since American Secretary of State, William Jennings Bryan, began in 1914 to provide for such enquiry and conciliation in his 'Bryan Treaties' with various countries, conciliation has proved popular with treaty drafters as a method of dispute settlement, but the procedures provided under such agreements have apparently been little used.

9. United Nations involvement. Although, as noted above at various points, the Secretary-General of the United Nations may, on his own initiative or at the behest of UN organs, become involved in various dispute settlement efforts, it must be recognised that the United Nations itself has unique settlement procedures of its own as provided for in Chapter VI of the Charter, on the 'Pacific Settlement of Disputes'.

Under Article 33(1) the parties to a dispute whose continuance is likely to endanger international peace and security must seek a solution by the methods listed there and discussed in this chapter. Article 33(2) permits the Security Council 'when it deems necessary' to call upon the parties to settle such a dispute by these means. Under Article 34, the Council may investigate any dispute, or any situation which might lead to international friction or give rise to a dispute, 'in order to determine whether the continuance of the dispute or situation is likely to endanger the maintenance of international peace and security'.

The effect of such a determination under Article 34 would appear to be that Article 33(1) would become applicable and the parties would be legally obliged to seek a peaceful solution by the methods listed there.

Under Article 36 the Council is allowed when faced with such a dispute or with 'a situation of like nature' to recommend appropriate procedures or methods of adjustment, taking into consideration that 'legal disputes should as a general rule be referred by the parties to the International Court of Justice'.

Article 37 requires parties to such a dispute to refer it to the Council if they fail to settle it by the means indicated in Article 33; the Council, if it deems it likely that peace may be endangered, must decide whether to make a recommendation on settlement procedures under Article 36 or itself to recommend such actual terms of settlement as it may consider appropriate.

According to Article 35, any dispute or situation like that referred to in Article 34 may be brought to the attention of the Security Council or the General Assembly by any UN member (and not just one directly involved in the problem) and any non-member which is a party to a dispute may do likewise if it accepts in advance, for the purposes of the dispute, the Charter's obligations of pacific settlement.

Adjudicatory methods: arbitration

10. Definition of arbitration. Arbitration is the settlement of a dispute on the basis of law by the binding decision of a judicial tribunal whose composition is determined by the parties.

Differences between arbitration and judicial settlement. Arbitration differs from judicial settlement in two respects:

(*a*) as mentioned, in arbitration the parties to a dispute can determine how the tribunal is selected, whereas in judicial settlement the composition of the court is generally beyond the control of the parties; and

(*b*) in arbitration the parties may agree on the law, or the interpretation of the law, which they wish the adjudicator to follow in reaching a decision, and he is bound to abide by that agreement, whereas a court operates according to a whole system of law whose content and interpretation is not immediately under the control of the parties.

The agreement between the parties on these points is called the *compromis d'arbitrage* or simply the *compromis*.

The ability to control the adjudication process in these respects seems to make arbitration a less risky proceeding for the parties than judicial settlement, and arbitration has the additional advantage that the procedures of the tribunal can also be tailored by agreement to suit the requirements of the parties.

11. Development of arbitration. Practised by the ancient Greek city-states amongst themselves as a prime method of dispute settlement and often provided for by treaty, arbitration retained a certain measure of popularity in medieval Europe, where states could submit disputes to adjudication by the Pope.

In private law, arbitration of commercial disputes between merchants was often the favoured method of settlement, as it enabled the parties to avoid the complicated and arcane procedures and rules – often irrelevant to commercial concerns – which characterised the state legal systems of medieval and early modern Europe. Similar motives keep arbitration to the forefront of commercial thinking today, particularly with regard to disputes on transnational contracts between a state and a foreign company or individual. Provisions in such contracts on 'choice of law' and arbitration help overcome the legal difficulties inherent in agreements between entities that operate in different legal systems (*see* 2:47 and 10:31–32). Machinery for this purpose has actually been established by treaties, most notably the Convention for the Settlement of Investment Disputes between States and the Nationals of other States (1965), to which over eighty states are parties. The Convention established the International Centre for the Settlement of Investment Disputes (ICSID) in Washington D.C. In 1985 the United Nations Commission on International Trade Law (UNCITRAL) prepared for enactment by individual states a model law on commercial arbitration.

Yet, in spite of such public and private law examples, states in the early period of international law seem to have been reluctant to resort to arbitration. The modern revival of interstate arbitration really began only in 1794 with the Jay Treaty between Great Britain and the United States, which established three arbitral commissions to settle disputes that had arisen out of the American Revolution.

These same countries in the Treaty of Washington (1871) provided for arbitration of a major dispute centring on Britain's failure, as a supposed neutral at the time of the American Civil War, to prevent the building in Britain of several vessels, most notably the cruiser *Alabama*, for use by the Confederacy for naval purposes and commerce raiding against Northern shipping. In 1872 the arbitral tribunal, having held Britain's actions to be a violation of her duties as a neutral, awarded the United States $15 million in gold as compensation.

The success of the *Alabama Claims Arbitration*, as it was called, gave renewed impetus to arbitration as a means of defusing disputes and achieving fair settlements. Bilateral arrangements between states, usually involving the appointment of 'mixed arbitral tribunals' (with adjudicators appointed in equal numbers by each side and presided over by a neutral umpire) became more common.

But the major advance came in 1899 with the establishment of the so-called Permanent Court of Arbitration under the Hague Convention for the Pacific Settlement of Disputes. The 'Court' is a panel of arbitrators appointed by the parties to the Convention and available for selection by disputing states to arbitrate between them. It is little used, however, at the present time.

One of the difficulties with arbitration was that, as states had voluntarily to submit disputes to this procedure, they could determine what subjects were suitable for settlement in this way. Thus, they could claim to be prepared to allow arbitration of 'legal' differences but not 'political' ones involving 'vital interests', and the classification of a dispute in one category or the other could be decisive.

12. Claims tribunals. In addition to tribunals established to arbitrate directly between states on disputes involving international law, agreements sometimes establish commissions or tribunals whose function is to hear and resolve complaints of private persons against one or both of the governments that have signed the agreement. This amounts to state-private arbitration under an international law umbrella.

Two interesting arrangements of this kind are

(*a*) the Gut Dam Claims Agreement (1965) between Canada and the United States to settle claims by American citizens for compensation for flood damage caused by the Canadian dam; and

(*b*) the Algiers Accords of 1981 between the United States and Iran, under which a 'Claims Settlement Declaration' set up the Iran-United States Claims Tribunal to deal with disputes following the hostages crisis of 1979–1980 (*see* 9:23).

13. Problems with international arbitration. In contrast to a court, which exists and operates independently of the parties to a case, an arbitral tribunal is in large measure the creature of the parties which have set it up. Since they appoint it to do the specific things they ask of it, in the way they choose, and according to the law they select, the tribunal has no power or authority to act otherwise. Consequently, an arbitral 'award' (i.e. decision) may be open to challenge if the tribunal has departed significantly from the instructions given it by the parties.

This is particularly a problem when the parties in their *compromis* frame the question at issue as an 'exclusive disjunction' requiring the arbitrator to choose *either* the view of one party *or* that of the other. Arbitrators occasionally find that this instruction conflicts with their understanding of the law which the *compromis* has instructed them to apply and they opt for a third solution. Arbitral awards in such circumstances have sometimes been rejected by the parties.

But in the *Island of Palmas Case* (1928) (*see* 6:23), Arbitrator Huber argued that the parties should not necessarily be assumed to intend that the arbitrator fail to give an award because of a *non liquet* (*see* 1:22). The implication was that the arbitrator should apply the law he has been given to produce an appropriate result regardless of whether it is one of the alternatives offered in the *compromis*.

Another problem area is error in the arbitral proceedings. When this can be shown to have occurred because of false evidence or fraud by one of the parties, the case can be reopened and the award be revised.

If, however, the error is one of law, the situation is more difficult. There is something to be said for revising an award based on the arbitrator's 'manifest error' as to the law he was instructed to apply where, for example, he has entirely misunderstood the legal questions put to him in the *compromis* or has applied the wrong treaty. In the *Trail Smelter Arbitration* (see 15:5), the tribunal approved of allowing revision on account of manifest error.

But if the 'error' is a more debatable one involving disputed theories or interpretations of law, the justification for revision seems much less sure, since the arbitrator's judgment and knowledge of the law must be considered in some sense what the parties bargained for when they chose him. In any event, allowing a case to be reopened on this ground would introduce a considerable element of uncertainty into arbitration inasmuch as clever and unscrupulous lawyers (or their political masters) will often be able to detect some 'error' of law if they work hard enough at it, so that requests for revision might be made when they are wholly unjustified.

Adjudicatory methods: the World Court

14. Development of the World Court. The term 'World Court' is applied as a convenient designation for two separate courts:

(*a*) the Permanent Court of International Justice (PCIJ), in operation from 1920 to 1946; and

(*b*) the International Court of Justice (ICJ), from 1946 to the present.

The ICJ amounts to a continuation of the PCIJ, so that for practical purposes the two may be regarded as one body and their case law taken as a whole.

The PCIJ was established pursuant to Article XIV of the League of Nations Covenant, which gave the court jurisdiction over 'any matter which the parties recognize as suitable for submission to it for arbitration'. In spite of this apparent limitation, however, the PCIJ developed as a full court of law (though with occasional reversions to the mind-set of arbitral tribunals), and the ICJ has built on that legacy.

The relationship of the two courts to their parent bodies differed. The PCIJ was simply a court attached to the League of Nations system, whereas the ICJ under Article 92 of the UN Charter is the 'principal judicial organ of the United Nations'. As such it is part of the United Nations machinery and has a role to play, as may be required and appropriate, in realising the organisation's purposes. Article 92 emphasises this link by making the Statute (constitution) of the ICJ 'an integral part' of the UN Charter, to which it is annexed.

15. Powers of the ICJ. Under Article 38 of the Statute, the ICJ is given the power to decide contentious cases between states on the basis of international law or *ex aequo et bono* if the parties so agree (*see* 2:51).

Under Article 59, a decision is binding between the parties to a contentious case and is, according to Article 60, 'final and without appeal'.

The United Nations Charter in Article 94 embodies the undertaking of UN members to comply with ICJ decisions in contentious cases to which they are parties. That provision also permits a party to resort to the Security Council for recommendations or measures to give effect to a judgment which the other party is not complying with.

The court may also give advisory opinions, as discussed further below in Section 000.

16. Composition of the ICJ. The International Court of Justice has fifteen judges elected for nine-year periods by the UN Security Council and the General Assembly, acting separately, according to an informal system of distribution that roughly and in a somewhat politicised way allows the court's composition to reflect what Article 9 of the ICJ Statute calls 'the main forms of civilization and ... the principal legal systems of the world'.

In practice, this system has ensured that each permanent member of the Security Council (with the exception of China) has always had one of its nationals on the court, with the remaining places being filled by persons from a variety of countries. In 1985 a Chinese judge was elected to the court for the first time in eighteen years, so that in 1986 the ICJ had judges from the following countries: Algeria, Argentina, Brazil, China, France, India, Italy, Japan, Nigeria, Norway, Poland, Senegal, the United Kingdom, the United States and the USSR.

Article 2 of the Statute requires the judges to be 'independent'. Under Articles 17 and 24 the court may decide that one of its judges should not participate in the hearing of a case 'for some special reason' or because of his previous involvement in some aspect of the case, and a judge may on his own initiative withdraw from the hearing of a case 'for some special reason'.

17. Ad hoc judges. In spite of the care with which the Statute avoids suggesting that the regular members of the court in any way represent their respective governments, Article 31 allows each party to a dispute to have one of its nationals serve as a judge during the hearing of the case, either by continuing to sit if he is currently a regular elected member or by appointment by his state to act as a judge on an *ad hoc* basis if no national of the state is at the time a member of the court.

Ad hoc judges are required to meet the same standards of disinterestedness as a regular member of the court under Articles 17 and 24, but the Statute's provision for them appears to refer to the concepts of arbitration, in which the parties have more of a say in the tribunal's composition than seems proper in the case of court.

The suspicion that, in some sense, *ad hoc* judges 'represent' their countries is hard to overcome, although some argue that this has a positive aspect insofar as it allows the *ad hoc* judge either to supply the court with useful background information about his country's situation or to ensure the fairness of the court's deliberations by seeing to it that his state's case is properly considered.

In recent years, however, there has been a tendency on the part of Third World states in particular not to appoint their own nationals as *ad hoc* judges but to select instead respected international legal figures such as former World Court members. If this practice becomes universal, it could remove some of the objections to the arrangements for *ad hoc* judges.

18. Subject-matter jurisdiction in contentious cases. Article 38 of the ICJ Statute says that the function of the court 'is to decide in accordance with international law such disputes as are submitted to it'. Article 36(2), dealing with compulsory jurisdiction, speaks of 'all legal disputes'. These two provisions appear to imply broad jurisdiction over disputes which, by virtue of their legal character, may be dealt with by application of international law. Disputes with regard to which international law is irrelevant would therefore not come within the court's jurisdiction.

But does the word 'disputes' in this context mean that the entire controversy between the parties must be of a legal nature, or may the court exercise subject-matter jurisdiction over disagreements on questions of law that are part of larger political differences which in themselves might be beyond the court's competence?

This was the problem raised in the *Case concerning Military and Paramilitary Activities in and against Nicaragua (Jurisdiction)* (1984) in which the United States objected to the court's subject-matter jurisdiction over a dispute with Nicaragua arising from American activities against the Sandinista government of that country (*see* also **24, 30**).

Unanimously rejecting this argument, the court noted that it 'has never shied away from a case brought before it merely because it had political implications or because it involved serious elements of the use of force'. The court indicated that the legal aspects of such disputes were properly subject to its jurisdiction, as it had previously decided when asked to do so by the United States itself in the *Iran Hostages Case* (1980) (*see* 9:**23**). The ICJ was emphatic that, contrary to the further submissions of the United States, the Security Council does not have exclusive jurisdiction with regard to questions involving the use of force, as the Council operates in the political sphere only while the court acts in the legal area, with the functions of each body being 'separate but complementary … with respect to the same events'.

19. Jurisdiction over the parties in contentious cases. Under Article 34(1) of the ICJ Statute only states may bring cases before the court, either as parties to the Statute or by special arrangements for states that are not members of the United Nations.

The court's jurisdiction over the parties is dealt with in Article 36, which treats this point as if it were an aspect of subject-matter jurisdiction in the sense that the ICJ does not exercise general jurisdiction over states but only limited jurisdiction to the extent necessary to decide each particular case which the states involved have consented to let the court deal with.

Consent once given remains in effect until properly withdrawn, and where existing consent has allowed jurisdiction over a case to be established subsequent withdrawal of that consent does not destroy jurisdiction.

The difficult question is to decide whether such consent has been given, and in this regard one may look for consent embodied in an agreement of the parties or in overlapping unilateral declarations.

20. Consent by agreements. Article 36(1) of the Statute allows the court jurisdiction over:

> all cases which the parties refer to it and all matters specially provided for in the Charter of the United Nations or in treaties or conventions in force.

Reference of a particular case by the parties involved in it is done by means of a *special agreement* or *compromis* whereby they confer jurisdiction and set out the case they wish the court to decide.

But consent need not always be express: in the *Rights of Minorities in Polish Upper Silesia Case* (1928) the PCIJ allowed it also to be 'inferred from acts conclusively establishing it … [such as] the submission of arguments on the merits, without making reservations in regard to the question of jurisdiction'. Thus a case may be submitted unilaterally (by one party only), jurisdiction being achieved by virtue of the other party's acting later in a way that indicates consent. This type of jurisdiction, perfected after the case has been raised, is known as *forum prorogatum*.

The advantage of *forum prorogatum* as a basis for jurisdiction is that it offers one party a means of manoeuvring the other into court without an agreement in advance. The applicant state can get away with this because the court's rules do not require in an application a statement of the grounds on which jurisdiction is based. The applicant can therefore institute proceedings in the hope that a basis for jurisdiction will eventually appear by reason of the other party's response.

But *forum prorogatum* has the disadvantage that, if it is the only possible basis for jurisdiction and the other state simply makes no response nor gives any grounds for inferring its consent, the court will in the end have to reject the case.

Apart from express or implied consent by agreement in a particular case, Article 36(1) permits general agreement in advance by means of treaties which provide for World Court jurisdiction over the types of questions with which each treaty deals.

A major treaty of this kind is the 1928 Geneva General Act for the Pacific Settlement of International Disputes, which in Article 17 required the parties to submit all disputes involving their respective rights to the PCIJ for decision. Although many states seemed uninterested in settling disputes in this way, and either did not adhere to the General Act or withdrew their adherence when they were sued by another party, the Act seems still to be in force for that score of states that have remained parties, with the ICJ (under Article 37 of its Statute) now fulfilling the role originally assigned to the PCIJ. In the first stage of the *Nuclear Test Cases* (1973) the ICJ found that there was a *prima facie* case for its jurisdiction after Australia and New Zealand had argued, among other things, that the respondent (France) and themselves were bound as parties by the General Act. However, the court has never squarely dealt with the nature and extent of the General Act's continuing effect.

In the *Iran Hostages Case* (1980) the court took jurisdiction (despite Iran's objections) on the basis of provisions for referral of disputes to it in the bilateral Treaty of Amity, Economic Relations and Consular Rights between the two countries and in the protocols to the multilateral *Vienna Conventions* of 1961 on Diplomatic Relations and of 1963 on Consular Relations.

21. Unilateral declarations. Article 36(2) of the ICJ Statute, in what is usually referred to as the 'Optional Clause' (because it is a matter of choice whether a state does as it provides), says that states may:

> at any time declare that they recognize as compulsory *ipso facto* and without special agreement, in relation to any other state accepting the same obligation, the jurisdiction of the court in all legal disputes concerning:
> (*a*) the interpretation of a treaty;

(b) any question of international law;

(c) the existence of any fact which, if established, would constitute a breach of an international obligation;

(d) the nature or extent of the reparation to be made for the breach of an international obligation.

Article 36(3) adds that these declarations may be made unconditionally or on condition of reciprocity.

22. The effect of 'reciprocity'. The first important point to notice about these provisions is that jurisdiction under them is circumscribed by the limits which a state puts on the areas within which it will accept the ICJ's compulsory jurisdiction. Although the language of Article 36(2) might be thought to suggest that all declarations were intended to be more or less identical, states have made a variety of declarations, qualified in some cases by considerable limitations as to the time period within which cases must have arisen (a limitation *ratione temporis*) or as to the subject matter over which jurisdiction is conceded (a limitation *ratione materiae*).

The consequence of such limitations and qualifications is that, since the declarations are operative only 'in relation to any other state accepting the same obligation' and may be made on condition of reciprocity, the court has jurisdiction only over those disputes which fall within the area where the declarations of both parties overlap or where they are reciprocal. It is usual for convenience to speak of both of these possibilities as matters of 'reciprocity', although some writers suggest that the term is not strictly accurate when referring to the possibility of overlapping (or coinciding) declarations, since in that instance it is not a question of reciprocal relationships but simply of a congruence of unilateral statements. For simplicity's sake, the term 'reciprocity' will be used here to refer to both possibilities.

The requirement of reciprocity may prove useful to the respondent if it does not wish the court to proceed with the case. For, where it appears that, although the respondent's declaration did confer jurisdiction over the subject of the dispute, that of the applicant did not, the respondent may claim that the court has no jurisdiction because there is no coincidence or reciprocity between the two declarations. But reciprocity does not require that the declarations be identical in terms. All that is necessary is that, when applied, they are seen to bring the same areas within the court's jurisdiction.

Thus, in the *Interhandel Case* (1959) the United States contested jurisdiction in a suit raised by Switzerland, on the ground that, while the American declaration was effective as from 26 August 1946 with regard to legal disputes 'hereafter arising', the Swiss declaration came into operation only from 28 July 1948, so that there was no coincidence in the two declarations as to disputes arising between those two dates, as the Interhandel dispute had. The court held, however, that, since Switzerland's declaration was not limited to disputes 'hereafter arising' and so could cover disputes arising before the declaration was made, there was an overlap which encompassed disputes arising after the entry into force of the American declaration in 1946.

The effect of this understanding of reciprocity is that a challenge to jurisdiction can come only from the state which has made the wider declaration, on the ground that it has accepted obligations which the party making the narrower declaration has not accepted, whereas in the *Interhandel Case* the objection came from the state that had made the limited declaration while Switzerland's declaration had no limitation *ratione temporis*.

When there is a coincidence or overlapping between the declarations of certain states, there appears to be an implicit contractual or treaty relationship established between them to the effect that, so long as the declarations do coincide, each state will accept the court's jurisdiction in cases involving the other states to the extent of the overlapping.

In the *Right of Passage Case (Preliminary Objections)* (1957) the ICJ held that the 'consensual bond' between two states comes into being the very moment that the second files with the court a declaration which overlaps with that of the first state. So Portugal, on the day when it filed its declaration, was entitled to bring suit immediately against India, even though India was unaware of Portugal's declaration and had not expected to be subject to the court's jurisdiction in disputes involving Portugal (and might have withdrawn or modified its declaration if it had had time to do so before the filing of Portugal's case).

23. Possibly impermissible limitations in a declaration. When states make declarations under the optional clause, they frequently exclude certain subjects or areas of dispute from the court's jurisdiction. One of the most contentious limitations of this kind is the 'self-judging reservation'.

In the *Norwegian Loans Case* (1957), France sued Norway with regard to certain Norwegian government bonds held by French citizens. Norway objected to jurisdiction on the ground that, although its declaration contained no relevant limitation, the French declaration excluded 'matters which are essentially within the national jurisdiction as understood by the Government of the French Republic'. On the basis of reciprocity, Norway argued that it also was entitled to regard as excludable matters which it deemed to be within its national jurisdiction. The court agreed, but in a separate opinion Sir Hersch Lauterpacht went further and argued that such a self-judging reservation as was in the French declaration invalidated that document in its entirety, so that France should be regarded as never having accepted the court's jurisdiction at all. The reasons for the invalidity, in Lauterpacht's view, were

(*a*) that a document according to which a state is entirely free to decide for itself whether it is under an obligation is not a legal instrument at all but merely 'a declaration of a political principle and purpose'; and

(*b*) that such a reservation conflicts with Article 36(6) of the Statute, which gives solely to the court the authority to decide jurisdictional questions.

In the *Interhandel Case* (1959) Judge Lauterpacht expanded his objections to this type of limitation in a case involving a clause in the United States declaration (the 'Connally Amendment', named after the American senator who insisted on its insertion) which excluded 'disputes with regard to matters which are essentially within the domestic jurisdiction of the United States ... as determined by the United States'. But the president of the court, Judge Klaestad, and some other judges concluded that, although the self-judging clause was contrary to Article 36(6), it could be severed from the rest of the declaration, which would then be valid and applicable by the court.

Although the invalidity of such clauses seems pretty clear, some states have made reservations which deal with the domestic jurisdiction question without being self-judging. These, by speaking of matters which 'by international law' are within national jurisdiction, would appear to be valid, though perhaps of little practical significance in view of the fact that the court is in any case competent to decide only cases subject to international law.

24. Absence of coinciding declarations. It is evident from the foregoing discussion that in order for there to be overlapping consent to jurisdiction there must be declarations embodying that consent. In the *Case concerning Military and Paramilitary Activities in and against Nicaragua (Jurisdiction)* (1984) the United States argued that no such declaration by Nicaragua, the applicant, was in force, in that Nicaragua's declaration with respect to the jurisdiction of the PCIJ in 1929 was of uncertain standing and could not be regarded as having been carried over automatically to the ICJ system (as was possible under Article 36(5) of the Statute for declarations in force at the time the ICJ came into being). The court held, however, that there was a valid Nicaraguan declaration. The United States then withdrew from the case, although the court's determination that it had jurisdiction meant that, under Article 53 of the Statute, Nicaragua was entitled to ask the court to proceed to a decision on the merits. In June 1986 the court held that the United States had violated international law by promoting military and paramilitary activites against Nicaragua, and indicated that the United States would be required to pay reparation to Nicaragua. (*See* 16:**23**.)

25. Jurisdiction and interim measures. A difficult conceptual problem is generated by Article 41(1), which says that the court 'shall have the power to indicate ... any provisional measures which ought to be taken to preserve the respective rights of either party'.

One school of thought holds that this article in and of itself confers an independent power to indicate such interim measures (as they are usually called), so that the court may act before it satisfies itself that it has jurisdiction to decide the case on the merits.

The opposite view is that the Article 41 must be taken to operate only after jurisdiction has been established, so that, where no jurisdiction can be shown to exist, interim measures cannot be ordered. Advocates of the first view say that the value of interim measures would often be destroyed if the court had first to spend some considerable time examining the jurisdictional question, and that this could hardly have been the result intended in that provision.

The ICJ in its decisions has tended towards the second view but has not adopted it completely. While not requiring that jurisdiction be conclusively established before interim measures are indicated, it has striven implicitly to link the application of Article 41 with the jurisdiction provisions of Articles 36 and 37 by requiring some basis – either negative or positive – for inferring that it has jurisdiction on the merits.

In the *Anglo-Iranian Oil Company Case (Interim Measures)* (1951), the court indicated such measures in a situation where 'it cannot be accepted *a priori* that a claim based on such a complaint falls completely outside the scope of international jurisdiction'. In the *Fisheries Jurisdiction Cases* (1972) the ICJ said that 'it ought not to act under Article 41 ... if the absence of jurisdiction is manifest'. This appears to mean that the court may order interim measures unless jurisdiction clearly does not exist.

But the court has been concerned in the more doubtful cases to justify interim measures on the tougher test of whether there are positive indications that jurisdiction does exist. In the *Nuclear Test Cases* (1973), and the *Iran Hostages Case* (1979), the court required that the suits appear *prima facie* to come within its jurisdiction before interim measures could be indicated. In other words, there must be some positive basis for believing that jurisdiction does exist and it will not be presumed to exist merely because it is not manifestly absent.

But even this position did not satisfy dissenting judges in the *Nuclear Test Cases*, who argued either that, in Judge Forster's words, 'the court . . . must satisfy itself that it has jurisdiction' or that, as Judge Petren said, the mere possibility of jurisdiction was not enough and only a probability of it would permit the court to indicate interim measures.

26. Types of relief in contentious cases. Generally, an applicant will want the court to determine its rights and to order that the respondent take certain actions to rectify an illegal situation and/or make reparation to the applicant by, for example, monetary compensation.

Questions have arisen, however, as to the circumstances in which an applicant may be entitled to seek only a *declaratory judgment*, that is, one stating the legal rights of the applicant without ordering any actions by the respondent.

In the *Northern Cameroons Case* (1963), the Republic of Cameroon sought a declaratory judgment on alleged illegalities in Britain's administration of the Northern Cameroons some time previously, although by the time of the suit Britain had given up her control of the territory and it had been incorporated into Nigeria. In these circumstances, there was no current legal dispute on the matter between Britain and the Republic of Cameroon, so that a declaratory judgment from the court would have had no effect on existing legal rights. The ICJ, while accepting that a declaratory judgment could be given in an appropriate case, held that the court's function was 'to state the law, but . . . only in connection with concrete cases' where there exists an actual legal controversy between the parties. The court's judgment 'must have some practical consequence in the sense that it can affect existing legal rights or obligations of the parties, thus removing uncertainty from their legal relations'. For the court to give a declaratory judgment in a case where, as with the Northern Cameroons, the legal relations of the parties had been terminated and no ongoing legal rights and obligations would be affected would be 'inconsistent with its judicial function'.

This position has been criticised as unduly restricting the court's capacity to clarify and develop the law by means of declaratory judgments and as perhaps denying some applicants 'satisfaction' in the sense of vindicating their legal position, even if they cannot do anything about it after the event.

27. Advisory opinions. Under Article 65(1) of the ICJ Statute the court may give an advisory opinion on any legal question at the request of any body authorised 'by or in accordance with' the UN Charter to make such a request. Article 96(1) of the Charter directly authorises the General Assembly and the Security Council to do this and Article 96(2) allows General Assembly authorisation 'in accordance with' the Charter for other bodies such as the Economic and Social Council (ECOSOC), the UN specialised agencies, and the International Atomic Energy Agency (IAEA).

As its name implies, an advisory opinion is not binding on the body requesting it but is an authoritative interpretation and application of the law to assist the requesting body in carrying out its assigned duties.

Two problems raised by the advisory opinion arrangements are: the nature of the legal questions which the court may properly be asked to answer, and the propriety of giving an advisory opinion when the matter at issue involves contending states.

28. Suitable subjects for an advisory opinion. In the *Conditions of Admission of a State to Membership in the United Nations Case* (1948) the ICJ indicated that Article 65(1)'s reference to 'any legal question' allowed the court to give an advisory opinion on a question that involved 'an essentially judicial task' like the interpretation of a treaty provision, particularly when that could be done in an abstract legal way rather than with particular cases or broader political issues in mind.

In the *Western Sahara Case* (1975) the court spoke of questions 'by their very nature susceptible of a reply based on law'. These need not necessarily be present-day legal questions but may focus on past legal situations that have some current significance for a problem confronting the requesting body. (For the Western Sahara problem *see* 4:44 and 6:32.)

The relevant context of the questions posed is thus, for the court, not whatever dispute or legal controversy there may be between states involved in a problem but rather the connection of the problem with the work of the requesting body. If legal answers to these questions will assist that body to carry out its functions, then the matter is a suitable subject for an advisory opinion.

29. The propriety of giving an advisory opinion. In the *Eastern Carelia Case* (1923) the PCIJ declined to give an advisory opinion to the League of Nations Council in regard to a dispute between Finland and Russia over the effect of a treaty and its annexed declaration relating to the status of Eastern Carelia, a territory lying between the two states. Russia was not a member of the League and had not consented to have the dispute settled by the PCIJ: 'The court therefore finds it impossible to give its opinion on a dispute of this kind'.

The court went on to suggest 'other cogent reasons which render it very inexpedient' to give such an opinion. The question at issue was essentially one of fact and the absence of Russia would put the court at a very great disadvantage in enquiring into the facts, since there would be neither a statement of facts agreed between the parties nor sufficient 'materials' (i.e. evidence) by which the court could arrive at a judicial conclusion. Furthermore, the question put to the court concerned directly the main point of the controversy between Finland and Russia. 'Answering the question would be substantially equivalent to deciding the dispute', and the PCIJ, 'being a court of justice', could not properly do that by way of an advisory opinion when that would involve departing 'from the essential rules guiding their activity as a court'.

The meaning of this key decision has been subject to varying interpretations by the ICJ. In the *Interpretation of Peace Treaties Case* (1950) the court found that it was not required to deal with the substance of the dispute and so was able to distinguish its situation from that in the *Eastern Carelia Case*, in which the PCIJ had:

declined to give an opinion because it found that the question put to it was directly related to the main point of a dispute actually pending between two states, so that answering the question would be substantially equivalent to deciding the dispute between the parties, and that at the same time it raised a question of fact which could not be elucidated without hearing both parties.

But no mention here of the question of consent, which seemed to be the one which made an opinion 'impossible' in the minds of the PCIJ's judges.

In the *Western Sahara Case* (1975) the court explained the *Eastern Carelia* result as based on:

(*a*) the fact that Russia was not a member of the League of Nations and that that organisation had no competence to deal with disputes involving non-members;

(*b*) the concern of the PCIJ with the 'judicial propriety' of giving an opinion in the absence of a party's consent to judicial settlement; and

(*c*) the lack of information on which to base a conclusion.

These slightly different readings of the *Eastern Carelia Case* seem influenced by the rather different situations which the ICJ faced in each of the later cases and are an example of the Court concentrating on what was relevant to the problem before it at the time.

30. The future of the World Court. A continuing theme in discussions of the role of the World Court in today's international community is the reluctance of states to refer their legal disputes to it.

But an even more serious problem is the refusal of states to abide by the commitments they have already made with regard to the court's jurisdiction.

In particular, all members of the United Nations and all the parties to the ICJ's Statute are bound by Article 36(6) of the Statute, which gives to the court complete and sole authority to settle disputes about jurisdiction. Yet in a number of cases in which the court has exercised this power in recent years some parties have refused to abide by its decision and have declined to participate in the court's hearings.

The United States, for example, in perhaps the most serious incident of this kind, withdrew from the proceedings in the *Case concerning Military and Paramilitary Activities in and against Nicaragua* after the ICJ refused to accept various American arguments against the court's jurisdiction. This move was followed in October 1985 by US termination of the American declaration on compulsory jurisdiction under Article 36(2) of the Statute. When the ICJ's final judgment in June 1986 held that the United States had violated international law in this case, the American State Department dismissed the ruling as 'not self-enforcing'. (*See* also **18, 24**.)

The ability of the World Court to carry out its functions is gravely impaired by the refusal of states to play by the rules which they themselves wrote and accepted. The interests of the world's peoples in promoting the rule of law in international affairs requires something better from their governments.

Progress test 17

1. List the principal methods of peaceful dispute settlement. (**1**)
2. What is the main issue in justiciability? (**3**)
3. Are 'good faith' and the 'zero-sum game' approach compatible in negotiations? (**4**)
4. Is fact-finding a cure-all for disputes? (**5**)

5. What may the Security Council do to promote the peaceful settlement of disputes? **(9)**

6. What distinguishes arbitration from judicial settlement? **(10)**

7. In what circumstances might a state be justified in disregarding an arbitral award? **(13)**

8. What are the powers of the International Court of Justice? **(15, 25, 27)**

9. Should *ad hoc* judges be appointed to the World Court? **(17)**

10. May the ICJ have jurisdiction in cases in which there are political as well as legal disputes between the parties? **(18)**

11. Explain jurisdiction by *forum prorogatum*. **(20)**

12. What is the effect of 'reciprocity' on jurisdiction deriving from Optional Clause declarations? **(22)**

13. Are 'self-judging reservations' permissible under the ICJ Statute? **(23)**

14. Does the ICJ need to establish jurisdiction on the merits before indicating interim measures of protection? **(25)**

15. Are declaratory judgments consistent with the ICJ's judicial functions? **(26)**

16. What matters are suitable for ICJ advisory opinions? **(28)**

17. In what circumstances might the ICJ consider the giving of an advisory opinion improper? **(29)**

Bibliography

Bowett, *The Search for Peace*, Routledge & Kegan Paul, London (1972)

Fisher, *International Conflict for Beginners*, Harper and Row, New York (1969)

Fraser, *The Middle East 1914-1979*, Arnold, London (1979)

Persson, *Mediation and Assassination: Count Bernadotte's Mission to Palestine 1948*, Ithaca Press, London (1979)

18 International institutions

Introduction

1. **Reasons for international institutions.** A striking feature of modern society is the extent to which major problems have been thought to require concerted group action for their solution. Within national legal systems this has led to a growth in the power of central governments and to the setting up of administrative agencies to deal with particular questions by applying relevant expertise in the context of special legal regimes.

On the international level something similar has happened. From time to time states have by treaty established in their common interest various universal or regional public international institutions (or organisations, as Article 34 of the ICJ Statute calls them) with prescribed powers in the specific areas over which each institution may have been given competence.

One should note that these institutions are sometimes also referred to as 'intergovernmental organisations' to distinguish them from private 'non-governmental organisations' (NGOs), although the word 'intergovernmental' might more properly be restricted to institutions that coordinate the transnational activities of only the executive branches of member governments.

Classification of international institutions

2. **The nature of the problem.** Being established on varying constitutional bases and composed of large or small groupings of various states or governments, international institutions may often be classified under more than one heading.

Constitutionally institutions may range from true legal entities to more or less loose groupings of states. If classification is according to membership, an institution may be universal (e.g. the United Nations), regional (the European Communities), or have some unique criterion for membership (as, for example, the geopolitical basis of the North Atlantic Treaty Organisation, NATO). Classification based on purposes or functions may highlight the difference between institutions with broad responsibilities (as, once again, the United Nations) and those with narrower duties (e.g., the Universal Postal Union). Another way of classifying institutions is by the powers they exercise: legislative, regulatory, judicial, enforcement, legal, or political powers may, individually or in combination, be exercised by an institution.

3. **A more general approach.** Categorisation along these lines is helpful when attempting to describe and compare a large number of organisations, although there is a danger that any system of categories may break down when faced with the need to fit a particular organisation into more than one category depending on what aspect of it is being considered at the moment. Furthermore, the founders of an organisation may choose to give it any combination of characteristics they wish, so that in some sense every organisation has the potential to be unique.

With that in mind, this chapter will not attempt to categorise institutions but will highlight legal issues that are generally relevant to most institutions.

Origins of international institutions in the search for world order

4. Early projects for international organisation. The realisation that human beings live in a world community has been traced back to the Greek idea of the *oikoumene* (the civilised world). This developed in the Hellenistic era that followed the conquests of Alexander the Great and it implied, among other things, a universal legal order and a world state. Underpinning these was a notion of natural law first propounded by the Stoic philosophers and then adopted by Roman jurists, most notably Cicero (*see* 1:7).

Medieval Christian Europe thought in terms of the *universitas humana*, the whole community of mankind, and the great Florentine poet, Dante Alighieri, drew the logical inference from the existence of this community: that it should be reflected in a universal government. In *De Monarchia*, written sometime around 1310, Dante argued in effect that only world government (under the Holy Roman Emperor) could bring world peace, the essential precondition in his view for individuals and nations to attain that 'fullness of life' which comes from realising their human potential rather than wasting it in discord and strife.

A few years earlier, in 1306, the French lawyer Pierre Dubois, had given concrete form to the institutional arrangements such a system might require. He proposed a Christian alliance (under French leadership this time) to abolish war and promote cooperation by means of a general council and a permanent court to arbitrate disputes between the allies. Peace, it should be noted, was to be only between the nations of Christendom, the better to enable Europe to maintain a Crusade against the Muslim powers in the Near East.

The implicit assumption that harmony and cooperation can exist only between people who share the same religion (or, in modern terms, ideology) reflects the historical tendency of nations to regard only themselves as 'civilised', in spite of a sense that, as Arnold Toynbee has said, 'our horrifying and humiliating experience of the atrocities that we have committed has taught us that civilization has never yet been an accomplished fact'.

The egocentric approach to international organisation is particularly dangerous when it leads to inflicting the values of the proposer on everybody else rather than deriving the principles of a world government from the shared needs of humanity. Yet later schemes in fact often involved taking Europe and its values as the core of a system into which other states and peoples would be drawn as European influence expanded. They were to that extent reflections of the long process of Europe's rise to world domination in the period after 1500.

Even apart from dubious ideas like Cardinal Alberoni's for partitioning the Ottoman Empire among the princes of Europe in 1736, no positive later scheme – neither William Penn's proposal in 1694 for a European parliament, nor the Abbé Saint-Pierre's project in 1713 for a European union for peace, nor Immanuel Kant's plan in 1795 to establish a permanent congress of nations to maintain international peace – was brought to fruition in its author's lifetime. But it is worth noting that each of these positive schemes foreshadowed elements of the arrangements western European states were forced to make in the aftermath of World War II, when the consequences of ignoring so many good ideas had left them too weak to do anything else.

Thus, until the twentieth century only the loosest sort of international coordination proved possible.

5. The nineteenth century. In the nineteenth century the resolution of political and diplomatic problems affecting several or many states was typically attempted, if at all, only on an *ad hoc* basis by means of conferences or 'congresses' held to arrange agreement on the particular issues causing concern at the time. This fitful approach highlighted the absence of permanent machinery capable of focussing sustained attention on the increasingly complex and dangerous relations of states in the world community.

And yet, the growing economic and geographical interrelationship of states brought about by the nineteenth century's advances in industry, commerce, and communications also demonstrated the need for multilateral institutions of an essentially non-political character to coordinate action on matters which could not be dealt with by individual countries.

6. Private international organisations. Interestingly, many of the new problems were initially handled by non-governmental organisations, or 'private international unions' as they are sometimes called, whose founders could not afford to let things drift until governments had caught up with the times.

A prime example here was the Red Cross, whose originator, Jean-Henri Dunant, recognised the need to provide emergency care for soldiers injured on the battlefield after he had seen the inadequate provision made for such care by the Austrian and French authorities at the Battle of Solferino in 1859. From this personal initiative grew not only the Red Cross's own world-wide programme but also a long series of treaties in which states gradually bound themselves (though with many discreditable reservations) to observe something akin to the humanitarian standards which the highest private morality has accepted for centuries.

7. The first public international organisations. Some private international unions, having alerted states to the problems to be dealt with, eventually found their work paralleled and complemented by public international unions. And governments had already begun to appreciate the value of public international organisations in spheres of particular interest to them, notably communications.

A commission to regulate navigation on the Rhine was established on the basis of principles laid down at the Congress of Vienna in 1815. The Treaty of Paris set up a European Commission for the Danube in 1856 and accorded it legislative and administrative powers, including the right to levy tolls in those parts of the river under its supervision. The Danube River Statute, adopted after World War I, consolidated the Commission's authority over the whole course of the waterway from Ulm to the Black Sea and recognised the Commission's standing as an international institution.

Other notable public organisations from the mid-Victorian period were the International Telegraphic Union (1865) and the Universal Postal Union (1874).

The example of private and public organisations, the increasingly apparent need for international political coordination on a regular basis, and finally the catastrophe of World War I, led in 1919 to the establishment of the world's first nearly-universal political organisation: the League of Nations.

The League of Nations

8. The intended role of the League. Mindful of the collapse of international diplomacy in the 'July Crisis' that preceded the outbreak of hostilities in 1914 and of the absence at that time of any machinery to retard the slide towards war, the drafters of the League of Nations Covenant (the organisation's constitutional document) were concerned primarily with establishing an institution to 'promote international cooperation' and 'achieve international peace and security'. This was to be accomplished by what came to be called the system of collective security whereby the members undertook to cooperate against agressor states (Article XVI of the Covenant) while promoting judicial or arbitral settlement of international disputes (Articles XIII-XV), delaying the resort to war (Article XII), and formulating plans for the 'reduction of armaments' (Article VIII).

9. Structure of the League. The League's organisation consisted of:

(a) an Assembly, with representatives of all the members, and having the general power to make resolutions or recommendations on any matter within the League's competence or affecting world peace (Article III);

(b) a Council, composed of the main Allied powers in the war plus a selection of other members rotated from time to time, and exercising particular responsibility for invoking the Covenant's peace-keeping provisions;

(c) a Secretariat, which was in effect an international civil service headed by a Secretary-General.

Linked with the League but maintaining a certain autonomy from it was the Permanent Court of International Justice.

The voting procedures of the Assembly and the Council in the League's early days required unanimity for the adoption of any substantive measures and neither the decisions of the Council nor the resolutions of the Assembly were binding on the member states. The effect of these limitations was that the League was not always able to deal with the problems confronting it.

Professor Bowett points out that the difficulties of this situation produced a significant constitutional development in the League's procedures. The Assembly, after going over to the adoption of resolutions by a simple majority, gradually expanded its role in the League's work and came to be considered, because of its methods of inquiry and general debate, a more effective body than the Council, which followed the more traditional approach of diplomatic negotiation. This development foreshadowed attempts to promote the authority of the General Assembly of the United Nations after that organisation's Security Council found itself frustrated by the veto power of the permanent members (*see* **16:6–7**).

10. Successes and failures of the League of Nations. Although judged harshly in retrospect, the League had some notable successes to its credit.

Following the territorial and demographic upheavals of the two Balkan Wars of 1912–1913, unresolved antagonisms between Greece and Bulgaria led in 1925 to a border incident and subsequent Greek invasion of Bulgaria that threatened to set off another general war between the two states. At the instigation of the League's Secretary-General, Sir Eric Drummond, the organisation's Council intervened to stop the fighting and separate the hostile forces and it then established a Commission of Inquiry. The Commission eventually concluded that each state should pay the other certain indemnities arising from the border incident and invasion, while more generally the League itself should become involved in efforts to settle the long-standing problems between the two countries.

This League intervention demonstrated how the organisation could bring the concern and authority of the international community to bear when the parties to a conflict were prepared to accept the League's decisions and when the Great Powers on the Council were willing to coordinate their response to the crisis.

In later crises, however, some of the major powers were themselves instigators of efforts to upset the international status quo established at the end of World War I (which the League was meant to maintain), while others were unwilling to act in the League against aggression. In these circumstances the League was unable to maintain international peace and security.

A critical failure of the League, in spite of persistent efforts, was its inability to achieve disarmament or even a permanent reduction of armaments, even though there was a general realisation that the naval arms race between Britain and Germany before 1914 had contributed significantly to the tensions that led to World War I. The collapse of the League's Disarmament Conference in 1934 and the beginning of a new arms race in 1935 helped pave the way for the second great war in Europe in 1939. Japanese expansion in the Far East, the resurgence of German nationalism coupled with France's insistence on keeping Germany weak while remaining strong herself, Russian unwillingness to fall in with western diplomacy on the matter, doubts about Britain's commitment to collective security under the League system, American inability to be fully involved in European affairs after having refused to join the League of Nations, and the boost which arms manufacture seemed to give to Europe's Depression-wracked economies all contributed to this failure and helped demonstrate how critical and intractable a problem disarmament was, even before the advent of nuclear weapons.

The League's establishment and administration of the Mandate system (*see* 4:**26-34**) were also dogged by political difficulties, most disastrously in Palestine and South-West Africa.

These political failures were parelleled to some extent by the League's inability to implement fully Article 24 of the Covenant, which envisaged all existing or future public international unions being placed 'under the direction of the League'. Because of legal obstacles or institutional politics few such organisations in fact came under the League's umbrella and a great opportunity was missed to develop a central coordinating authority for these unions. In this, as in much else, the League provided a negative example, which the founders of the United Nations deliberately rejected when, under Article 57 of the UN Charter they made mandatory the establishment of a 'relationship' between the UN and certain 'specialised agencies'.

One must note, however, that Article 23 of the Covenant, by bringing within the purview of the organisation such problems as workers' rights, white slavery, drug trafficking, native welfare in colonial territories, communications, and disease control, became the springboard from which the League was able, in the words of F. P. Walters, to make 'an immense contribution to human welfare' over a range of economic and social issues that was constantly, though in piecemeal fashion, being broadened as the League developed.

Concern with these responsibilities deepened during the world-wide economic crisis of the 1930s, when many observers concluded that economic and social disruption promoted a political instability that undermined world peace. With all this in mind, a League Committee, presided over by a former Prime Minister of Australia, Stanley Bruce, recommended in August 1939 the regularising of the League's activities by the setting up of a Central Committee for Economic and Social Questions. Although coming too late for implementation under the League of Nations, the Bruce Report laid the basis for the Economic and Social Council of the United Nations.

The United Nations

11. Introduction. The ongoing work of the United Nations in such areas as the use of force (*see* 16:3–6), human rights (13:21–52), and the peaceful settlement of disputes (17:1, 9) has inevitably formed a large part of this book already. The main focus here will therefore be on the general aims and structure of the organisation.

The aims, purposes and principles of the UN

12. The preamble of the UN Charter. In the preamble to the United Nations Charter, the organisation's founders in 1945 expressed their determination 'to save succeeding generations from the scourge of war', 'to reaffirm faith in fundamental human rights, in the dignity and worth of the human person, in the equal rights of men and women and of nations large and small', 'to establish conditions under which justice and respect for the obligations arising from treaties and other sources of international law can be maintained', and 'to promote social progress and better standards of life in larger freedom'. These aims would be furthered, according to the preamble, by the resolve of the founders 'to practise tolerance and live together in peace with one another as good neighbours', 'to unite our strength to maintain international peace and security', 'to ensure, by the acceptance of principles and the institution of methods, that armed force shall not be used, save in the common interest', and 'to employ international machinery for the promotion of the economic and social advancement of all peoples'.

Although this statement of aims and philosophy is often overlooked in discussing the meaning and application of the Charter's substantive provisions, the preamble to a treaty is recognised by the Vienna Convention as part of the context in which the rest of the document is to be understood (*see* 11:17), and reference to a preamble seems particularly appropriate in the case of a constitutional treaty like the Charter (*see* 2:41 and 11:16).

It is thus evident from the preamble that the United Nations must be seen as an organisation with a broad area of responsibility extending far beyond the mere facilitating of inter-state relations.

13. The purposes of the United Nations. Article 1 of the Charter lists the purposes of the organisation as:

(*a*) to maintain international peace and security, and to that end: to take collective measures to prevent or remove threats to the peace and to suppress acts of aggression and other breaches of the peace; and to bring about the peaceful adjustment or settlement of dangerous disputes, 'in conformity with the principles of justice and international law';

(*b*) to develop friendly relations among nations based on respect for the principles of equal rights and self-determination of peoples, and to take other appropriate measures to strengthen universal peace;

(*c*) to achieve international cooperation in solving international economic, social, cultural, or humanitarian problems and in promoting and encouraging respect for human rights and for fundamental freedoms for all without distinction as to race, sex, language, or religion;

(*d*) to be a centre for harmonising the actions of nations in the attainment of these common ends.

This statement of purposes lays out the agenda for the United Nations and accounts for its structure and organisation, with responsibilities and specified powers for achieving these purposes being assigned by the Charter to the organisation's major organs.

The purposes also entail legal obligations at least insofar as the members may not resort to the threat or use of force in any manner inconsistent with these purposes (Article 2(4)).

14. The principles of the UN. Article 2 commits the organisation and its members, in pursuing the purposes stated in Article 1, to acting in accordance with certain fundamental principles. These are:

Article 2(1). The Organization is based on the principle of the sovereign equality of all its Members. (*See* 4:4.)

Article 2(2). All Members, in order to ensure to all of them the rights and benefits resulting from membership, shall fulfil in good faith the obligations assumed by them in accordance with the present Charter. (*See* 4:**37**; 17:4.)

Article 2(3). All Members shall settle their international disputes by peaceful means in such a manner that international peace and security, and justice, are not endangered. (*See* 16:3; 17:**1–10**.)

Article 2(4). All Members shall refrain in their international relations from the threat or use of force against the territorial integrity or political independence of any state, or in any other manner inconsistent with the Purposes of the United Nations. (*See* 4:**37**; 6:**17**; 16:**3, 13, 15, 18**.)

Article 2(5). All Members shall give the United Nations every assistance in any action it takes in accordance with the present Charter, and shall refrain from giving assistance to any state against which the United Nations is taking preventive or enforcement action.

Article 2(6). The Organisation shall ensure that states which are not Members of the United Nations act in accordance with these Principles so far as may be necessary for the maintenance of peace and security. (*See* 2:**40** and 11:**23**.)

Article 2(7). Nothing contained in the present Charter shall authorise the United Nations to intervene in matters which are essentially within the domestic jurisdiction of any state or shall require the Members to submit such matters to settlement under the present Charter; but this principle shall not prejudice the application of enforcement measures under Chapter VII. (*See* 4:**38**; 13:**24**.)

Membership

15. Distinction between original and subsequent members. Under Article 3 of the Charter the UN's 'original Members' are those which signed and ratified the

Charter after having either participated in the negotiating conference at San Francisco or signed the 'United Nations' declaration by the anti-Axis wartime allies in 1942.

Subsequent members, however, must, according to Article 4(1), be 'peace-loving states' which accept the obligations contained in the Charter 'and, in the judgment of the Organization, are able and willing to carry out these obligations'. Under Article 4(2) admission of such a new member is to be 'effected by a decision of the General Assembly upon the recommendation of the Security Council'.

Article 4 was the source of some difficulty as the question of membership became imbroiled in the political antagonisms of the existing members. To begin with, Article 4(2) has been interpreted by the International Court of Justice (in its Advisory Opinion of 30 March, 1950) to require approval of a new member's admission by the Security Council before the General Assembly is entitled to act in the matter. This in effect makes admission subject to the veto of the Council's permanent members.

Secondly, the tests set in Article 4(1) are sometimes thought to require a higher standard from new members than from original ones – how many of the latter qualify as 'peace-loving' for example? – and are criticised for allowing the subjective political judgments of the existing members to influence decisions on admission.

In the *Conditions for Admission of a State to Membership in the United Nations Case* (1948) the International Court of Justice attempted to deal with some of these problems by determining that existing members, when voting on admission, are not entitled to have regard to other considerations than those specified in Article 4(1) and may not link their consent to the admission of one new member to any bargaining for the admission of another new member.

Nevertheless, admission has in fact on occasion been on the basis of 'package deals' providing for entry into the UN of clients or allies of the Superpower blocs in counterbalancing groups.

16. Suspension and loss of membership. Article 5 allows the suspension of a member against whom preventive or enforcement action has been taken by the Security Council, if the General Assembly, upon the recommendation of the Council, so decides. Under Article 6, a member which has persistently violated the principles contained in the Charter may be expelled by the General Assembly upon the Security Council's recommendation.

Organs of the United Nations

17. Principal and subsidiary organs. Article 7 of the Charter provides that the principal organs of the United Nations are to be the General Assembly, the Security Council, the Economic and Social Council, the Trusteeship Council, the Secretariat, and the International Court of Justice. The ICJ is discussed in detail in 17:14–30. Subsidiary organs are also envisaged by Article 7 and may be established as necessary by the General Assembly (under Article 22) or the Security Council (Article 29).

18. No sex discrimination. According to Article 8 men and women are to be eligible, without restrictions and on conditions of equality, to participate in any capacity in the UN's principal and subsidiary organs.

The General Assembly

19. Composition. The General Assembly consists of all the members of the United Nations (Article 9).

20. Functions and powers. Under Article 10 the Assembly may discuss anything within the scope of the Charter and may make recommendations accordingly to the members or to the Security Council, except when the Security Council is exercising its functions with regard to a particular question (Article 12).

The General Assembly may also 'consider the general principles of cooperation in the maintenance of international peace and security, including the principles governing disarmament and the regulation of armaments' (Article 11) and may make appropriate recommendations. It may also discuss and make recommendations on any particular issues relating to peace and security which are brought before it by a member state, the Security Council or a non-member state that accepts in advance the obligations of pacific settlement of disputes as provided for in the Charter. However, 'any such question on which action is necessary shall be referred to the Security Council' (Article 11(2)).

Article 13 requires the General Assembly to initiate studies and make recommendations for the purpose of:

(*a*) promoting international cooperation in the political field and encouraging the codification and progressive development of international law (*see* 2:**55**); and

(*b*) promoting international cooperation in the economic, social, cultural, educational, and health fields, and assisting in the realisation of human rights and fundamental freedoms for all without distinction as to race, sex, language, or religion.

Under Article 14 the Assembly may recommend measures for the peaceful adjustment of any situation held likely to impair the general welfare or friendly relations among nations, including situations arising from violations of the Charter's purposes and principles.

These four articles have together formed the basis of a wide range of General Assembly resolutions. Over the years the Assembly has dealt with such varied specific questions as the rights of the Palestinian refugees (Resolution 194(III) of 11 December 1948), the situation in southern Africa, and the Soviet invasion of Afghanistan in 1979 (which was deplored in Resolution ES-6/2 of 14 January 1980). But the Assembly's contribution to developing the law more generally is perhaps its most notable achievement. Human rights (*see* 13:**25**), the law of the sea (*see* 12:**61**), economic relations (*see* 15:**29**), and the principles of international law concerning friendly relations and cooperation among states (*see* 6:**18**; 16:**39**) are among the areas in which General Assembly resolutions by themselves have affected the growth of international law. The Assembly has also been the channel through which treaties drafted by the International Law Commission and special conferences have found their way into the international legal system. (*See* also 2:**28–33**.)

But the power of the General Assembly to examine and discuss important questions is also of some significance, particularly in regard to subjects of widespread concern like nuclear weapons and disarmament (*see* 16:**37, 39**).

With the admission of nearly a hundred new states into the United Nations in the wake of decolonisation, the ability of the Assembly to reflect general international concerns without the hindrance of big power vetoes has made it the favoured vehicle for promoting Third World causes.

An area of difficulty for the Assembly has been the limits imposed on its activities by the requirement in Article 11(2) that questions of international peace and security on which action is necessary must be referred to the Security Council. Under the Uniting for Peace Resolution of 1950 the Assembly attempted to take certain powers of action for itself although the circumstances in which such an arrogation of authority would be legitimate are debatable (*see* 16:**6**).

However, in the *Certain Expenses of the United Nations Case* (1962), the International Court of Justice did uphold the power of the Assembly to establish peace-keeping forces and incur expenses for the organisation when that did not involve enforcement action and was in accordance with the Assembly's power to approve the UN's budget and apportion its expenses among the members under Article 17. (*See also* 16:**7**.)

The Assembly's budgetary powers have another interesting ramification. Under Article 19 a UN member which is in arrears in the payment of its assessed financial contributions to the organisation 'shall have no vote in the General Assembly if the amount of its arrears equals or exceeds the amount of the contributions due from it for the preceding two full years'. This provision could have serious repercussions for countries in the position of the Soviet Union and France in the 1960s and the United States in the mid-1980s, who refused for political reasons to pay all of their legitimate assessment. Although Article 19 allows the Assembly to excuse a state that is delinquent in its payments by reason of *force majeure,* in general members should be held to their obligations as a matter of the treaty law principle of *pacta sunt servanda* (*see* 11:**10**) – a point emphasised by the European Communities in 1986 when criticising the United States' refusal to pay its full assessment (see the EC's memorandum in 25 ILM 482).

The Security Council

21. Composition. Although under the Charter as adopted in 1945 the Security Council was to consist of eleven members of the organisation, its current membership is fifteen, by virtue of an amendment of the Charter in 1965. China, France, the Soviet Union, the United Kingdom and the United States are the Council's five 'permanent members', while the remaining ten members are elected by the General Assembly for two terms.

22. Voting. Whereas under Article 18 the General Assembly may adopt resolutions on 'important questions' by a two-thirds majority of those present and voting and on other questions by a majority of those present and voting, Article 27 provides that in the Security Council decisions on procedural matters require an affirmative vote of any nine members of the Council while decisions on all other matters 'shall be made by an affirmative vote of nine members including the concurring votes of the permanent members'. This embodies the 'veto' power of the permanent members and is qualified only by the proviso in Article 27(3) that a party to a dispute shall abstain from voting on decisions relating to the peaceful settlement of disputes under Chapter VI of the Charter (Articles 33-38) or relating to the peaceful settlement of disputes under regional arrangements (Article 52(3)). The problems caused by the veto have been considered earlier (*see* 16:5).

23. Functions and powers. Article 24(1) bestows on the Security Council 'the primary responsibility for the maintenance of international peace and security' and the members agree that in carrying out the duties this entails the Council acts on their behalf.

Article 24(2) provides that in discharging these duties the Council 'shall act in accordance with the Purposes and Principles of the United Nations' and it indicates that 'The specific powers granted to the Security Council ... are laid down in Chapters VI, VII, VIII and XII'. These specific powers are very sweeping and seem to exclude almost no diplomatic, political or military option in appropriate situations. The only overriding restriction is that Council action be in accordance with the purposes and principles of the Charter, although even here the Council is presumably entitled to decide to implement one purpose or principle even if doing so may conflict with another purpose or principle. It is also argued by some writers that, to the extent that the Council's specific powers are insufficient to permit it to perform its duties, it must be taken to have implied powers as well.

The Council's specific powers have been treated elsewhere in this book: *see* 17:**9** for Chapter VI powers for the pacific settlements of disputes and 16:4 for Chapter VII powers regarding action on threats to the peace, breaches of the peace and acts of aggression.

The Council's powers under Chapter VIII relate to regional arrangements for dealing with questions of peace and security. Under Article 53 the Council 'shall, where appropriate, utilize such regional arrangements or agencies for enforcement action under its authority'. However, that article makes it unmistakably clear that in every current case 'no enforcement action shall be taken under regional arrangements or by regional agencies without the authorization of the Security Council'. Nevertheless, during the 1962 Cuban Missile Crisis the United States, on the basis of activities in the Organisation of American States (a regional agency for purposes of Chapter VIII), imposed a naval 'quarantine' on Cuba and threatened to intercept Russian ships sailing to that country. To the extent that this was an enforcement action rather than an act of self-defence under Article 51 (and the United States did not claim that it had been the victim of an armed attack by Cuba or the Soviet Union) it would appear to have violated Article 53, since the Security Council gave no authorisation for it.

The United States also appears to have acted contrary to the Charter's provisions on the role of the Security Council under Chapter XII, which deals with the international trusteeship system.

24. The Security Council and strategic trust territories. When the founders of the United Nations established the international trusteeship system to carry on and develop the work of the League of Nations mandate system, they provided for the designation of some trust territories as 'strategic areas' (Article 82). Under Article 83 'All functions of the United Nations relating to strategic areas, including the approval of the terms of the trusteeship agreements and of their alteration or amendment, shall be exercised by the Security Council'.

Only one strategic trust was created, that of the Trust Territory of the Pacific Islands (Micronesia), which was placed under the administration of the United States. Over the years, as all the other trust territories became independent or merged with existing states, pressure built up for settling the future of the Pacific Islands as well. Various schemes were discussed between the islanders and the United States, with the poverty and dependence of the islands on the one hand and the continuing strategic interest of the United States on the other being important considerations for both sides.

Although the United Nations was believed to favour independence for the territory, the United States eventually determined that the trusteeship should be ended on the basis of dividing the Pacific Islands into four entities: the Northern Mariana Islands, the Republic of Palau, the Federated States of Micronesia, and the Republic of the Marshall Islands. The first was to become an American 'commonwealth' while the latter three were to be given 'independence' in conjunction with 'compacts of free association' with the United States. These compacts provided for considerable American economic aid to the islands and for American rights of overflight and navigation for air force and naval craft.

In November 1986 President Reagan unilaterally proclaimed the end of the trusteeship and the independence of the new states. But, as this was done without the approval of the Security Council (where a Russian veto was feared after the Soviet Union indicated that it suspected the United States of permanently tying Micronesia to itself without the burden of UN supervision), it appeared that the American action violated Article 83 of the UN Charter.

The Economic and Social Council

25. Composition. The Economic and Social Council (ECOSOC) consists of fifty-four members elected by the General Assembly for a term of three years (Article 61).

26. Voting. Each member of the ECOSOC has one vote and decisions of the Council are taken by a majority vote.

27. Functions and powers. According to Article 60 of the Charter questions relating to international economic and social cooperation are the responsibility of the General Assembly and, under the Assembly, of the ECOSOC. The nature of the matters that come within this remit is indicated in Article 55:

> With a view to the creation of conditions of stability and well-being which are necessary for peaceful and friendly relations among nations based on respect for the principle of equal rights and self-determination of peoples, the United Nations shall promote:
>
> > a. higher standards of living, full employment, and conditions of economic and social progress and development;
> > b. solutions of international economic, social, health, and related

problems; and international cultural and educational co-operation; and

    c. universal respect for, and observance of, human rights and fundamental freedoms for all without distinction as to race, sex, language, or religion.

The General Assembly and the ECOSOC are to be helped in carrying out their responsibilities by the UN's members, who pledge themselves in Article 56 'to take joint and separate action in cooperation with the Organization for the achievement' of Article 55's purposes, and by the 'specialized agencies'. Under Article 57 these agencies, 'established by intergovernmental agreement and having wide international responsibilities, as defined in their basic instruments, in economic, social, cultural, educational, health, and related fields', are to be 'brought into relationship' with the United Nations by means of agreements between themselves and the ECOSOC (Article 63). The ECOSOC is empowered to coordinate the activities of the specialised agencies and obtain reports from them on their work and on their implementation of ECOSOC and General Assembly recommendations (Articles 63 and 64).

More generally, under Article 62 the ECOSOC may study and report on, and make recommendations about, the matters listed in Article 55(b), may make recommendations to promote human rights, may prepare draft conventions on matters within its competence for submission to the General Assembly, and may summon international conferences on such matters.

The ECOSOC is assisted in its work by functional commissions on economic, social, and human rights matters and regional commissions for Europe, Asia, Latin America and Africa.

28. The specialised agencies. Among the more significant of the specialised agencies, whose work gives a good idea of the ECOSOC's range of interests, are the following:

International Labour Organisation (ILO). Established in 1919 as part of the Versailles treaty arrangements connected with the founding of the League of Nations, the ILO in its first two decades concentrated on promoting international conventions to regulate working conditions. In the Philadelphia Declaration of 1944, however, the aims and purposes of the organisation were broadened to include the more general promotion of economic and social welfare. These aims and purposes are accomplished by means of ILO-drafted conventions which create binding legal obligations on the parties to them and by means of ILO recommendations offering guidelines on labour policy, practice and legislation. Delegates to ILO conferences come not only from member governments but also from national trade union and employers organisations.

International Bank for Reconstruction and Development (IBRD) and the International Monetary Fund (IMF). These two organisations developed out of the Bretton Woods economic conference of 1944 and are intended to complement each other in the promotion of economic growth. The IBRD, or the World Bank, as it is more usually known, is a channel for long-term capital loans for basic development and infrastructure projects involving such things as railways, power generation, pipelines, and telecommunications facilities. Since World Bank loans are offered on a commercial basis, they are generally regarded as 'hard' loans, and countries that might not qualify for such financing must turn to the Bank's 'soft loans' affiliate, the *International Development Association (IDA)*. The IDA depends for its funds on contributions from the better-off countries and its loans are largely interest-free. In contrast to the World Bank and the IDA, the IMF aims at relatively short-term intervention to stabilise international financial relationships by providing funds to countries facing temporary balance of payments difficulties. These funds, pledged by the members of the IMF, are available to needy members according to a system of 'drawing rights' and 'Special Drawing Rights'. The existence of these rights acts in effect like an increase in the world supply of credit and thus helps to promote international financial liquidity. But as a member exhausts its various drawing rights (in staged slices or 'tranches'), it is progressively subjected to closer scrutiny by the IMF with regard to its domestic and international economic policies. Countries in desperate financial straits may find their national economic programmes being dictated by the Fund, usually with the aim of curtailing domestic spending so as to increase the resources available for correcting balance of trade problems and paying off external debt. The internal effects of such policies can often be severe: cut-backs in government services, increased unemployment, social hardship and unrest, and even major political instability. Not surprisingly, help from the IMF is often regarded as a last resort.

International Civil Aviation Organisation (ICAO). Under the Chicago Convention on International Civil Aviation (1944) and its later amendments, the ICAO operates to raise the technical and safety standards of civil air transport, to arbitrate between member states in disputes about the implementation of the Convention, and to promote international agreements relating to civil aviation.

United Nations Educational, Scientific and Cultural Organisation (UNESCO). Inaugurated with the ringing affirmation that it is in the minds of men that the foundations of peace must be built, UNESCO aims to promote international peace through educational, scientific and cultural cooperation and stimulation of the concern for human rights, international justice and the rule of law. It facilitates programmes for teacher training, the improvement of national education systems, and the exchange and communication of scholarly knowledge and information. In recent years UNESCO has been criticised in the West for having become too 'politicised' in its advocacy of Third World causes and its hostility to American policy in the Middle East and elsewhere. These criticisms might have carried more weight if the countries that made them had themselves never used international organisations for their own political purposes. The critics were on firmer ground, however, in objecting to UNESCO's programme for a new international information order designed to limit and control reporting on the Third World by western information media and to undermine the western monopoly on the international dissemination of news. While it is clear that the public in the West is often badly informed about Third World problems and concerns and that this results not only from excusable ignorance but also from arrogant prejudices and deep-seated bias in the media, it can hardly be supposed that the problem will be cured by restricting information and filtering it through the biases and prejudices of censors and bureaucrats in the Third World. What is needed for both sides is the dissemination of the truth.

International Telecommunications Union (ITU). The successor of the International Telegraph Union of 1865, the modern ITU aims to foster international cooperation in the improvement and use of telecommunications and to promote the better operation of technical telecommunications facilities. The ITU allocates and registers radio frequencies, works to eliminate radio interference, attempts to reduce telecommunications charges, encourages the improvement of telecommunications networks and equipment, promotes life-saving measures of cooperation between different telecommunications services, prepares studies and recommendations on matters within its competence and collects and disseminates relevant information.

World Health Organisation (WHO). Under Article 1 of its constitution the World Health Organisation's primary aim is the 'attainment by all peoples of the highest possible level of health'. To accomplish this the WHO directs and coordinates international health efforts, works to eradicate disease, promotes better health education, sets international pharmaceutical and medical diagnostic standards, promotes mental health work, and offers information and technical services, while encouraging cooperation among health care professionals and proposing treaties and regulations dealing with international health matters. In doing this the WHO exercises a legislative competence insofar as, under Article 21 of its Constitution, regulations adopted by its governing body, the World Health Assembly, become binding on all members of the organisation except those who notify the WHO's Director-General that they reject the regulations in question.

Other UN agencies. Other specialised agencies are: the Food and Agriculture Organisation (FAO), the Universal Postal Union (UPU), the World Meteorological Organisation (WMO), the London-based International Maritime Organisation (IMO) (*see also* 15:**16**), the World Intellectual Property Organisation (WIPO), which deals with the international protection of patents and copyrights, and the United Nations Industrial Development Organisation (UNIDO).

In addition the General Agreement on Tariffs and Trade (GATT) and the International Atomic Energy Agency (IAEA) (*see* 15:**8**; 16:**40**) are associated with the UN while not being specialised agencies.

The Trusteeship Council

29. Administering the trusteeship system. Chapter XIII of the UN Charter (Articles 86 to 91) established the Trusteeship Council to run the system of trust territories developed out of the League of Nations mandate system (*see* 4:**26, 28**). At the time of writing all the trust territories save that of the Pacific Islands (*see* **24** above) have gone out of the trusteeship system either by way of independent statehood or through association with an existing state. For practical purposes, therefore, the primary task of the Trusteeship Council has been fulfilled and so its work need not be further considered here.

The Secretariat

30. The structure of the Secretariat. Under Article 97 of the Charter the Secretariat is to comprise a Secretary-General 'and such staff as the Organization may require'. This vague provision has in fact been the basis for the growth of an international civil service of several thousand persons. Although appointment is according to merit, Article 101(3) requires that 'due regard' be paid to the importance of recruiting the staff on as wide a geographical basis as possible. In practice the tendency has been to recruit the largest number of employees from those countries that make the largest contributions to the organisation's budget.

The Secretary-General is assisted by Under Secretaries-General and Directors of departments and offices.

31. The role of the Secretariat. The implications of the idea of an international civil service are spelt out in Article 100. The Secretary-General and his staff are instructed not to seek or receive instructions from any government or authority external to the organisation and not to engage in any action which might reflect on their position 'as international officials responsible only to the Organization'. Correspondingly, members of the United Nations undertake 'to respect the exclusively international character of the responsibilities of the Secretary-General and the staff and not to seek to influence them in the discharge of their responsibilities'.

Nevertheless, accusations have from time to time been made that certain officials do act as agents for their national governments. The most notable case was that of Mr Arkady Shevchenko, a former Soviet diplomat and then UN under Secretary-General for Political and Security Council Affairs, who left his UN post in 1978 and defected to the United States after admitting to having acted on behalf of the Soviet Union during his UN employment.

32. The Secretary-General. Under Article 97 the Secretary-General is to be 'appointed by the General Assembly upon the recommendation of the Security Council' and he is thus in the first instance never likely to be someone of whom any permanent member of the Council disapproves. The Secretary-General's term of office is for five years and he can be re-elected.

Article 97 also provides that the Secretary-General is to be the UN's chief administrative officer. He is, according to Article 98, to act in that capacity at all meetings of the UN's principal organs (other than the International Court of Justice) and 'shall perform such other functions as are entrusted to him by these organs'. In addition, Article 99 authorises the Secretary-General to 'bring to the attention of the Security Council any matter which in his opinion may threaten the maintenance of international peace and security'.

The lack of specificity in these provisions is significant, since in practice they leave a wide latitude to the Secretary-General to determine for himself the character and direction of his term of office, particularly by developing what can reasonably be considered his implied powers under the Charter. For example, the power to alert the Security Council to threatening matters has been taken to imply the power to investigate the situation to try to find out for the Council's benefit exactly what is happening. Furthermore, the power to alert the Council gives the Secretary-General a political role, since his opinion as to whether a matter is threatening is bound to carry some weight and his ability to focus the Council's attention on the question inevitably activates political interests and relationships among the Council's members and within the international community generally.

Secretary-General Dag Hammarskjöld, who served from 1953 until his death in a mysterious plane crash in Northern Rhodesia in 1961, adopted a particularly activist posture and justified it by taking the purposes and principles of the UN Charter as the framework within which he was legally entitled to act. Mr Hammarskjöld's view of his role was implicitly endorsed by the General Assembly with regard to the Lebanon crisis of 1958, when it gave him the very broad mandate of making 'such practical arrangements as would adequately help in upholding the purposes and principles of the Charter in relation to Lebanon and Jordan in the present circumstances'. Similarly, the Security Council in the Congo debacle of 1960 authorised him to 'take the necessary steps, in consultation with the government of the Republic of the Congo, to provide the government with such military assistance as may be necessary ...'

It seems clear that the international community by and large needs, and can benefit from, the presence and activity of a world figure such as the Secretary-General who can mobilise the legal, diplomatic and political resources of the United Nations organisation in situations where individual states are unable or unwilling to act. The difficulty is that by taking the burden of action on himself the Secretary-General risks becoming (or being thought to have become) almost another party in those situations.

Secretary-General Hammarskjöld found himself in that position in the Congo intervention, when he was vociferously attacked by the Soviet Union for claiming the right to operate according to his own interpretation of the Security Council resolution setting up the UN force in the Congo (ONUC) until such time as the Council in another resolution rejected that interpretation. By adopting this stance Hammarskjöld in effect left himself free to act as he saw fit within the limits of the Charter so long as disagreement among the Council's permanent members meant that a veto would prevent any new resolution being passed. In the circumstances of the Congo at that time this meant his continuing to pursue a policy which seemed to some to favour western interests there, particularly in regard to the secessionist province of Katanga, where Belgian soldiers and a Belgian mining company were supporting the break-away government. Against this background the Soviet Union would not accept a constitutional situation in the UN which nullified the ability of the Council's permanent members to control UN action by means of the veto. Russian representatives proposed that Mr Hammarskjöld should resign and be replaced by a 'collective executive organ' formed as a triumvirate (or *troika*, the Russian term for a three-horse sleigh team) which would represent respectively the western, communist and neutralist blocs. But, since Mr Hammarskjöld refused to bow to Soviet pressure and could not be removed in the face of western opposition to the Soviet proposal, the situation remained a stalemate until the Secretary-General's death.

Although succeeding Secretaries-General have not renounced any of their powers and have continued to exercise their discretion and judgment in controversial ways, it seems fair to say that no Secretary-General since 1961 has had quite so high a profile as Mr Hammarskjöld nor has any been publicly so threatened and attacked by a great power.

Regional international organisations

The European Communities

33. **Nature of the Communities.** As explained earlier (*see* 4:51–4), the European Communities are the European Coal and Steel Community (ECSC), the

European Atomic Energy Community (EURATOM), and the European Economic Community (EEC). Since the founding of the EEC by the Treaty of Rome in 1957 there has been a continuing process of assimilating the three communities, although constitutionally they remain distinct as to the division of powers among their organs. Nevertheless, under the provisions of the 1957 treaty and a Merger Treaty that was implemented in 1967 the three communities share a common Commission, Council of Ministers, Court of Justice and Parliament. In the Single European Act of 1986 the member states of the EEC strengthened further the coordination of a common European policy on a number of points. For the purposes of general international law, the EEC is undoubtedly the most interesting of the three communities and perhaps the world's only truly supra-national entity.

34. Objectives and activities of the EEC. The preamble of the Treaty of Rome expressed the intention of establishing 'the foundations of an ever closer union among the European peoples' and Article 2 spoke of promoting harmonious economic development, expansion, stability, a higher standard of living and closer relations among the members. Article 3 envisaged eliminating customs duties between the members, establishing a common external tariff for the community vis-à-vis the rest of the world, achieving freedom of movement within the member states for persons, services and capital, adopting common agricultural and transport policies, ensuring that competition in the common market not be distorted, coordinating the members' economic policies, approximating the laws of the member states to the extent required for the proper functioning of the common market, creating a European Social Fund to improve employment opportunities and European Investment to promote the Community's economic expansion, and associating overseas countries and colonies with the EEC to increase trade and promote development.

35. Structure of the EEC. Article 4 of the Treaty provides for an EEC Assembly, Council, Commission, and Court of Justice.

The Assembly, or as it is now commonly called the European Parliament, has since 1979 been composed of members elected directly by the people of the member countries according to agreed quotas for each state. This is the only public international body in the world to be so constituted, but the symbolism and implications of this remarkable arrangement seem not to be fully appreciated by the citizens of the member states, who, along with their governments and the mass media, persist in thinking in national rather than European terms. The ability of the European Parliament to arouse public interest is hampered somewhat by the fact that within the EEC system most important decisions are taken by the Council and the Commission. In recent years, however, the elected Parliament has felt justified in asserting itself by using one of its few powers, that of withholding its approval of the Community's budget, to persuade the Council and Commission to adopt certain policies. The Parliament may also vote to censure the Commission and thereby force that entire body to resign. Historically, in national constitutional development such 'power of the purse' and power of censure have been important weapons in the struggle of elected legislatures to assert control over the executive. Whether they produce the same effect in the EEC remains to be seen.

The Council is in fact the constitutional seat of power within the EEC. With one member appointed by each EEC country the Council is the legislative and executive body in which the member states determine the Community's basic policies and programmes. The Council is thus the EEC's highest political authority.

The Commission is the EEC's executive body, but exercises considerable legislative power as delegated to it by the Council. 'Legislation' under the EEC system may be by *regulations*, which are directly binding in all member states, or by *directives*, which bind member governments to implement within their territory in a manner each thinks appropriate to its own case the purpose stated in the directive. The EEC authorities may also issue *decisions* in particular cases and these bind only the states or persons to whom they are addressed. Non-binding *recommendations* may also be issued. (On the effect of community legislation in Britain, *see* 3:**17**.)

The Court of Justice, a panel of judges appointed by the unanimous agreement of the EEC members and assisted by advocates-general who, 'with complete impartiality and independence, ... make, in open court, reasoned submissions on cases brought before the Court' (Article 166 of the Rome Treaty), exercises wide powers. Applying in general the provisions of the EEC treaties, subsequently developed 'Community law' and even on occasion the European Convention on Human Rights, the Court may hear appeals for annulment of Council or Commission regulations, directives and decisions, appeals against penalties imposed on states or individuals by the Council or Commission, and petitions to enforce the contractual or non-contractual liabilities of the Community or to force a Community institution to take action which it has improperly failed to take. In regard to such cases, an interesting feature of the Court's jurisdiction is that under Article 173 'any natural or legal person' may institute proceedings against a decision of the Council or Commission addressed to that person 'or against a decision which, although in the form of a regulation or a decision addressed to another person, is of direct and individual concern to the former'. This is in some respects a legal and jurisdictional analogue to the right of individuals to elect the European Parliament and it is a concomitant of the power of the EEC institutions to issue decisions addressed directly to individuals. The Court also has jurisdiction to decide questions arising before the municipal courts of the member states in regard to interpretation of EEC treaties and the validity and effect of acts of the EEC's institutions, thereby reducing the possibilities for conflicting municipal and EEC decisions on the same matter. The Court may hear cases brought by the Commission against member states and those between member states and it may resolve disputes between the different organs of the Community itself.

The Council of Europe

36. Nature and role of the Council. While the European Communities were at first designed to link their members through organisational structures exercising authority in particular areas of national life and have since become the means for developing a closer political union, the Council of Europe, according to Article 1 of its Statute (1949), aims to promote 'greater unity between its Members for the purposes of safeguarding and realising the ideals and principles which are their common heritage and facilitating their economic and social progress'. This will be done 'by discussion of questions of common concern and by agreements and common action in economic, social, cultural, scientific, legal and administrative matters and in the maintenance and further education of human rights and fundamental freedoms'.

Thus, although the Council of Europe may be classed as an organisation of general competence in regard to its wide terms of reference, from the point of view of its powers it is considerably weaker than the European Communities. The Council is essentially consultative and achieves its purposes by discussion and agreement rather than legislation and regulation.

And yet many hoped in the early post-war period that a United States of Europe might be created and it has always been a question whether the Council of Europe could be the nucleus around which such an entity could develop. The answer seems to be that, although the Council continues to play a major role in European life (particularly through the European Convention on Human Rights, as discussed in Chapter 14), the hard political decisions about European union are being taken in the framework of the European Communities. This may in the long-term have significant implications for the kind of Europe that emerges in the next century. For the members of the Communities are all (with the exception of Ireland) also members of the North Atlantic Treaty Organisation (NATO), while the Council of Europe includes Switzerland, Austria, and Sweden – three neutralist countries whose political and cultural contribution to a united Europe could be beneficial.

37. Structure of the Council of Europe. Apart from the European Commission and Court of Human Rights, the Committee of Ministers and the Assembly are the Council's principal organs, assisted by various committees and a Secretariat.

The Committee of Ministers is composed of the foreign ministers (or alternates) of the member states. It has the task of considering what action is required to further the aims of the Council, such as the concluding of treaties and agreements among the members and the adoption of common policies on particular matters, and of recommending action to the members' governments and requesting reports from them on what action they have taken. The Committee of Ministers may also be the final arbiter in cases under the human rights Convention which are not referred to the European Court of Human Rights (*see* 14:**6**).

The Assembly is composed of persons elected by the national parliaments of the members according to a distribution of the seats which is proportionate to the relative populations of the member states. The Assembly does not have legislative powers but is merely a 'deliberative' organ capable of making recommendations to the Committee adopting resolutions or 'opinions' for the Committee's consideration. The Assembly may also direct resolutions to the member governments. According to Prof. Bowett, the Assembly has over the years been much more energetic in attempting to further the Council's goals than has the Committee of Ministers, which he describes as demonstrating 'conservatism and even apathy'.

38. Work of the Council of Europe. Besides the human rights convention and the European Social Charter (*see* 13:**15**), the Council has promulgated more than a hundred other conventions and agreements on subjects ranging from patent protection to the suppression of terrorism (*see* 8:**27**), state immunity (*see* 9:**17**), and the protection and development of Europe's common cultural heritage (in the European Cultural Convention(1954)).

The Council also has under its umbrella European conferences (i.e. deliberative groups) of local and regional authorities, ministers of education, ministers of justice, and for scientific and environmental questions.

The Council by treaty coordinates its work with the United Nations, the International Labour Organisation and other UN specialised agencies as well as various European organisations.

Other regional international organisations

39. General observations. There are over twenty other regional organisations in the world, and space does not permit examining them all. Three of the most important, because of their range of interests or large membership or both, will be briefly examined to give an idea of the diversity of regional organisations at the present time. Of the three, the Organisation of American States is the best developed, but it lacks, as do the other two, any judicial body with the functions of the European Court of Justice. This is an indication of the more political, less justiciable, nature of the relations existing between the members of these organisations and tends to confirm the opinion of many writers that the European Communities are unique in the degree to which they have attained a supra-national character to which the members have legally subordinated a part of their sovereignty (*see* 4:**51** and **33** above).

The Organisation of American States

40. Problems preventing an American organisation. The United States has historically regarded North and South America as its special sphere of influence, and under the Monroe Doctrine of 1823 the United States proclaimed its intention of opposing the intervention of any European power in Latin America. The United States reserved for itself, however, the power to intervene militarily in the affairs of any American nation and did so on many occasions.

The inequality inherent in such a relationship between the United States and its neighbours made it virtually impossible to establish an international organisation in the region until American pretensions had, at least on paper, been curbed. The process of doing that began with the Montevideo Convention on the Rights and Duties of States (1933) (*see* 4:**3, 13**).

The way was opened for the estabishment of the Organisation of American States (OAS), whose Charter is contained in the Bogotá Pact of 1948.

41. Fundamental concerns of the OAS Charter. Against the background of conflict, intervention, and instability that had marked the relations of the American states for so long, it is not surprising that the Charter focussed on problems of international law and order. Article 5 reaffirmed that international law is the standard of conduct for states in their reciprocal relations and that international order 'consists essentially of respect for the personality, sovereignty and independence of States and the faithful fulfilment of obligations derived from treaties and other sources of international law'.

Article 5 went on to emphasise the requirements of good faith and solidarity and condemned wars of aggression. 'Victory', it said, 'does not give rights'. Social justice and social security were declared to be the basis of lasting peace, and the 'education of peoples should be directed toward justice, freedom and peace'.

The Charter went on to provide for mandatory resort to methods of peaceful dispute settlement listed in Article 24, which are similar to those in Article 33 of the UN Charter (*see* 17:1), and it provided also for measures of collective security against aggression. In addition, cooperation for economic and social improvement was agreed upon, as was the promotion of education and free cultural exchange.

Under Article 102, none of the provisions of the OAS Charter are to be construed as impairing the rights and obligations of members under the Charter of the United Nations.

42. Important human rights developments. A particular success of the OAS since 1948 has been the development, through the Inter-American Commission of Human Rights, of the American Convention on Human Rights, an important and increasingly effective contribution to the international legal regime on that subject (*see* 13:**54**).

43. Recent progress: the Cartagena Protocol (1985). Over the years a feeling grew among many of the members that the various problems with which the OAS Charter dealt needed to be more effectively addressed in it. The result of years of effort was the adoption of the Protocol of Cartagena de Indias (1985) in which a number of significant amendments to the Charter were set out.

The Protocol proclaims the purpose of achieving effective limitation of conventional weapons so as to free more resources for economic and social development. It states that the principles of democracy are an essential condition for stability, peace and development. It includes the principles that every state has the right to choose, without external interference, its political, economic, and social system and to organise itself in the way best suited to it, while itself abstaining from intervening in the affairs of any other state. Furthermore, none of the provisions of the Charter are to be understood as authorising the OAS to intervene in matters that are within the internal jurisdiction of each member state.

The resolution of regional disputes is promoted by permitting the Secretary-General of the OAS to bring to the attention of the organisation's General Assembly or its Permanent Council any matter which in his opinion might threaten the peace and security of the hemisphere or the development of the member states. In addition, it will now be possible for the Permanent Council to offer its good offices and recommend procedures for settling disputes between members if only one party to a dispute (rather than all the parties, as required under the 1948 Charter) requests the Council to do so.

The Protocol also attempts to advance the jurisdictional claims of the Latin American countries over foreign companies. It provides that transnational enterprises and foreign private investment will be subject to the legislation and jurisdiction of the host countries and to the international treaties and agreements to which those countries are parties. This is in effect a reaffirmation of the principle of the Calvo clause (*see* 10:21) and may entail the application of the national treatment standard, since the reference to subjection to international treaties tends to exclude customary international law rules on the international minimum standard (*see* 10:19).

44. The League of Arab States. Founded in 1944 as an institution for coordinating cooperation among the Arab states in such areas as foreign policy, defence, communications, economic and cultural relations, and social and health questions, the Arab League ranks as one of the older international institutions. But its concentration on inter-state dealings in a period of troubled relations between its members and long-term crisis in its region has tended to keep it from developing into any sort of supra-state organisation. From the point of view of its members and their peoples this is in many ways unfortunate and even rather difficult to justify, since the Arab states have more in common as regards culture, language and religion than do the members of the Council of Europe and share a common historical experience to as great an extent as the states and peoples of the OAS.

Strikingly, whereas in Europe the movement towards greater union seems to come largely from governments while the peoples of the continent have little conception of what is at stake and even less interest, in the Arab world the consciousness of a shared identity seems largely to exist in the minds of the people, while governments, pushed this way and that by self-interest and foreign pressure and manipulation, fall far short of the ideal. A general realisation that this is the situation may account for the extraordinary popularity of President Nasser of Egypt, who held up to the Arab peoples an image of themselves that corresponded to what they wanted to see and offered them hope rather than politics.

In spite of this fundamental problem, the League has managed on occasion to play a role in regional security questions and has from time to time been the vehicle for formulating joint Arab policies in areas in common interest, notably the Palestine question and the economic boycott of Israel. But even on these issues there has been political discord and practical evasion, the dichotomy between popular sentiment and government actions being revealed most glaringly during Israel's invasion of Lebanon in 1982, when the Arab states were entirely supine and ineffective.

Indeed, since 1979 the League has suffered particularly from what many in the Arab world regarded as the treacherous defection from Arab ranks of President Sadat at the time of the Egyptian-Israeli Peace Treaty (*see* 17:7), an act which led to the transfer of the League's headquarters from Cairo to Tunis.

45. The Organisation of African Unity (OAU). Like the Arab League, the OAU, founded in 1963, appeared in a period of great internal and external pressures on its region and was formed by states that were not in complete control of their own destinies. Nevertheless, the OAU set itself a comprehensive agenda: 'absolute dedication to the total emancipation of the African territories which are still dependent', 'non-alignment with regard to all blocs', and the promotion of cooperation in political, economic, defence, health, and scientific matters.

For the OAU the questions of Namibia and South Africa have proved almost as difficult as the Palestine issue has been for the Arab League. The OAU's problems have been compounded by dissension in its ranks over other disputes, most notably in recent years the continuing struggle in the Western Sahara between Morocco and the Algerian-backed forces of the Polisario liberation movement's government-in-exile, the Saharan Arab Democratic Republic (SADR) (*see* 4:**44** and 6:**32–33**).

Nevertheless, the OAU has over the years been instrumental in dealing with a number of common problems in Africa. It promulgated the African Convention on the Conservation of Natural Resources (1968). In 1981 it adopted the African Charter on Human and Peoples' Rights, which covers both civil and political rights and economic, social and cultural rights, and which sets up the African Commission on Human and Peoples' Rights and provides for a system of petitions in cases of alleged violation of rights.

At its 1985 summit the Organisation concentrated on what was described as Africa's 'unprecedented economic and social crisis' brought on by years of drought and the world recession of the 1970s and 1980s. Speakers at the summit attributed Africa's problems not only to its underdevelopment but to the debilitating political fragmentation which prevents it from organising its resources effectively. The OAU adopted a programme for economic recovery based on five principal steps: action to rehabilitate agriculture and increase food supplies; efforts to stop desertification; creation of an African common market by the year 2000; agreement with the developed countries on measures to ease the problem of Africa's huge external debt; and development of a common programme for inter-African and international cooperation.

General legal problems of international institutions

46. Nature of the problems raised. In his *Law of International Institutions*, Professor Bowett analyses the common legal problems of international institutions under two general headings. The first covers issues arising from the nature and extent of the institution's international legal personality. It touches on questions that have been highlighted elsewhere in this book: the question of personality itself and the related problems of inherent and implied powers and the rights and legal responsibility of the organisation (*see* 4:**50, 54**); the treaty-making power of international institutions (*see* 11:**3**); and the privileges and immunities of such institutions and their personnel (*see*, as regards the UN, 9:**26**).

But Prof. Bowett's second heading is of rather more general interest in a book on international law: the impact of international organisations on the sovereign equality of states (*see* 4:**4**). The key point here is that international organisations, by virtue of the fact that they must generally take action as a result of group decision-making, inevitably pose the question of whether or not a state is going to subordinate to the majority opinion in such an institution its own sovereign powers of decision.

This question may arise in relation to a number of aspects of a state's involvement with an international organisation, and it is worth while looking at each major one in turn.

Membership

47. Distinction between members and non-members. In the broadest perspective the very existence of an international organisation poses problems of state equality, since its members, simply by virtue of being so, necessarily take to themselves the power to decide whether other states should be admitted and on what terms. As noted above (15), even the United Nations, an ostensibly universal organisation, does not recognise an automatic right of membership but instead gives the existing members the power to judge the qualifications of new applicants.

48. Reservations. The members of an organisation may also affect the treaty-making powers of other states that are applying for admission. An applicant may be required to forego the right to make reservations to the organisation's constitutional treaty. Indeed, in the opinion of Prof. Bowett, it must do so for the sake of organisational coherence and collegiality, regardless of the Vienna Convention's rules permitting reservations in some circumstances (Article 20(3) of the Convention).

49. The international status of an applicant entity. The question of membership also allows the existing members an opportunity to make judgments with important legal and political consequences about the applicant's international status. Where membership is confined to states, admission implies a determination that statehood has been legally established. This was a major question, for example, in the case of Israel's admission to the United Nations in 1949. On the other hand, refusal to admit may reflect adversely on statehood, as in the case of Liechtenstein (*see* 4:**18**).

50. Suspension from membership. Where membership rights may be suspended because of failure to fulfil some obligation under the organisation's constitution, as in the United Nations (*see* **15** above), suspension in effect amounts to the subordination of the suspended state's powers of decision to the general will of the other members. While in one sense this may be seen merely as an application of the principle *pacta sunt servanda* and of the rules on material breach of a treaty (*see* 11:**34**), the membership issue adds to those considerations elements of judging and enforcement that are not always present in other situations. Also, membership may involve a wide spectrum of duties and relationships, all of which will be affected by suspension, even though the contravention justifying it may relate to only a part of the organisation's activities.

And yet such a situation seems inherent in the nature of international organisations, whose fundamental principles are usually broadly expressed and whose function is not simply the carrying out of a treaty but the application of it in circumstances not foreseen by the founders. The members must be permitted to make decisions in such matters and the possibility of suspension would appear necessary to give teeth to the power of decision.

51. Withdrawal. If a member wishes to withdraw from an organisation, but no provision is made for that in the organisation's constitution, is it obliged to continue its membership even where that involves continuing and unwanted subjection to the decisions of the other members? Prof. Bowett's conclusion is that the absence of a withdrawal provision cannot be presumed to extinguish the right of a state to terminate its membership.

Nevertheless, the practice of the United Nations, the WHO, and UNESCO (none of which initially had a withdrawal provision in its constitution) has been to treat withdrawal followed by resumption of participation as a temporary step by the member rather than termination of membership. In line with this view, the WHO and UNESCO have assessed financial contributions from returning members for the period of their absence.

52. Expulsion. Expulsion of a member by the organisation raises the problem of sovereign equality in acute form. In terms of treaty law, explusion is analogous to the termination of a multilateral treaty as between a defaulting state and all the other parties when the defaulter has committed a material breach. But one must note that, in the usual multilateral treaty situation under Article 60(2) of the Vienna Convention, termination of a breaching state's participation must be by the unanimous agreement of the other parties. In the case of an international organisation, however, where expulsion is allowed, as in the United Nations (*see* **15** above), it may be decided on merely by a majority vote.

Thus, the treaty relationship between the expelled state and those other members that did not vote for expulsion is ended by the decision of those that did vote for it.

If on the other hand unanimity were required, the majority, who would not wish to continue in a legal relationship with the potential expellee, would be forced to do so by the attitude of the minority.

A particular problem arises when, unlike the UN Charter, an organisation's constitution has no specific provisions for expulsion. A number of western states have argued for non-expulsion in cases where universal organisations without such constitutional provisions voted to expel South Africa. The United States did not make similar arguments, however, when Cuba was expelled from the Organisation of American States in 1962. American writers have distinguished the expulsion of Cuba and the attempted expulsion of South Africa by arguing that the OAS, as a regional organisation with specified political and defence concerns, could not be presumed (as a universal organisation might be) to have been intended by the founders to maintain full regional membership no matter what disagreements arose.

As will be evident from these two examples, the legality of expulsion and its political desirability are often confused. Some writers have attempted therefore to rise above the confusion by concentrating on what might be called the public policy aspects of the question. They argue that amicable settlement of disputes might be facilitated by retaining even undesirable members within the organisation, particularly where such states might represent a greater danger to the organisation when outside it than when in it.

On the other hand, as a matter of principle, should a state be allowed the benefits of continued membership in an organisation whose fundamental aims and purposes it is committed to undermining? And might not a refusal to expel be interpreted by the victims of that state's activities as acquiescence in its illegalities and be seen by other potential wrong-doers as a licence to proceed with their own unlawful plans?

53. The participation of non-state entities. Although public international organisations may confine their membership to states, non-state entities or individuals may in certain respects be placed on the level of member states and allowed a role to play in the activities of the organisation.

Observer status is sometimes given to such entities, as in the case of the PLO at the United Nations (*see* 4:45). The effect may be to enable such an entity to deal on more equal terms with states, to enjoy diplomatic privileges, and so on.

The International Court of Justice is an institution in which individuals who are meant to act on a personal basis rather than as representatives of states (*see* 17:16) are in the position to decide questions of inter-state relations.

Some technical organisations, such as the International Law Commission, rely on the work of experts rather than government representatives in reaching decisions that have important consequences for states. Other organisations may have both state and non-state representatives, as with the ILO (*see* 28).

Accommodating state power

54. **Voting arrangements.** In the League of Nations voting was originally intended to be on the basis of unanimity (*see* 9). This requirement for unanimity was an expression of the idea of the sovereign equality of states: no decision could be imposed by some states on others but all had to agree.

But this was criticised for hampering the work of the League and as not corresponding to the realities of international power politics.

The view that smaller and weaker states could in fact legitimately be imposed on by a majority was enshrined in the UN Charter's provisions on voting in the Security Council, where only the permanent members were exempted from majority rule. This was effectively the death-knell of sovereign equality as the basic principle of voting in international organisations.

However, in institutions where the great powers are not protected by the veto, bare majorities may not be considered sufficient in situations where those powers might find themselves in a minority.

As Roderick Ogley notes, for example, the great powers, when negotiating the voting system of the Council of the International Sea-Bed Authority to be set up under the 1982 Law of the Sea Convention, insisted that the majorities required for decisions should vary according to the importance of the matter under consideration, with particularly sensitive decisions even having to be taken by 'consensus', something that sounds very like informal unanimity (*see* 12:64).

An alternative to requiring large majorities or even consensus as a protection for the great powers is to weight the votes of members according to the interests they have at stake in the organisation. This is sometimes done by adjusting voting power according to each member's financial contribution, evidently on the principle that he who pays the piper should call the tune.

The refusal of the United States in the mid 1980s to pay its full assessment to the United Nations was evidently intended to force the adoption of a weighted voting system in the General Assembly's budgetary decision-making. In December 1986 agreement was in fact reached to change that voting system so as to give major contributors to the UN's funds a greater say in the organisation's expenditures than the poorer countries which make smaller contributions.

55. **Amendment of the organisation's constitution.** If a constitution were regarded as an ordinary multilateral treaty, then amendments to it under Article

40(4) of the Vienna Convention (*see* 11:24) could only bind states which agreed to them.

In fact, however, the United Nations Charter, in Article 108, provides that an amendment approved by a two-thirds vote of the members (including the five permanent members of the Security Council) is binding on all the members. A number of organisations adopt this 'legislative principle', to use Prof. Bowett's term.

But some organisations distinguish between secondary and fundamental amendments. They require only majority votes for the first but unanimous votes, or majority votes plus ratification by each state before it can be bound, in the case of fundamental amendments.

56. Budgets. The principle of majority voting comes into its own in organisations like the United Nations, where it may be used to adopt budgets and take decisions involving expenditure, and to apportion the contributions of members towards the resulting expenses.

In the *Certain Expenses Case* (*see* **20** above) the International Court of Justice held that the expenses of peace-keeping forces established by the General Assembly were legitimate obligations of the United Nations. Consequently the members were bound to pay for these according to the apportionment properly determined by the Assembly. Thus a state might find itself in the position of the Soviet Union in such a case: obligated to pay towards expenses incurred in operations of which the Soviet Union strongly disapproved.

The future of international institutions in the search for world order

57. Lessons from the past? As this chapter has indicated, the trend in the development of international institutions has been from grand designs of world government based on a concern with world order and a conception of shared humanity, through an anarchic period in which powerful states brooked few limits on their powers of action, into the modern period when states and international institutions exist uneasily together in a state of constant tension over the legal relationship between them.

The present situation is a far cry from world government and past experience might seem to demonstrate that little better can be hoped for.

58. A change for the better? Some observers argue, however, that this conclusion should not be acccepted uncritically, for it may rest on a false assumption.

If projects for world government have failed because their designers saw more deeply and perceptively into the meaning and significance of mankind's shared humanity than most people could, this does not necessarily preclude the possibility of similar plans succeeding in the future on the basis of a realisation of common needs and interests.

To put this concretely: although Americans and Russians (to take only the most dangerous case) may yet be incapable of regarding each other as brothers, this might not stop them realising that they have a shared interest in, say, preventing environmental degradation from future Chernobyls or the destruction of mankind in a nuclear war (*see* 15:**3**, **8**; 16:**40**). The establishment and growth of the European Communities and the Council of Europe may be taken to show just such a (belated) awakening among European nations whose relations had traditionally been motivated by the deepest hostility.

59. Need for a more comprehensive approach. The difficulty with relying on such developments is that they are piecemeal rather than comprehensive and may simply multiply international organisations and arrangements rather than producing the basic changes that world order may require. And there is no guarantee that developments based on the self-interest of particular states will serve the wider needs of mankind.

60. A way forward. In their stimulating book *International Law and World Order* Burns Weston, Richard Falk and Anthony D'Amato consider these problems in some depth.

In Falk's view there is a possibility that the menace of catastrophic war and ecological pressure will merely provoke a Darwinian struggle for survival of the fittest in which the powerful will do their best to ensure that they are winners while the weak are losers.

In the 1980s great power assertiveness from Afghanistan and the Middle East to Central America and the Pacific, and the general degradation of international life and conduct which is evidenced in the growing refugee problem, the spread of hunger and poverty, the increase in private and state terrorism, and the continuing violation of fundamental human rights, all tend to confirm Falk's picture of a state system relying on 'threats, force, and cunning'. States place 'stress upon alliances', intervene 'in foreign societies to assist the efforts of sympathetic elites to retain or acquire power in struggles against potentially hostile elites', and offer 'ideological rationalizations that convey to one's own population a higher motive than the maintenance of position in the structure of international power, wealth and prestige'.

The solution in Falk's view requires making a fundamental moral choice between individual and community orientations of law and policy. In implementing this choice one must insist on 'the coherence of the whole'. Although 'no federalist scheme [is] buried' in the community orientation, one must deal with human welfare 'in terms of wholes, the human species, the earth, the overall pattern of linkage between man and earth, as well as between the present and the future'. The ultimate vision is a 'human community in which men live in harmony with each other and in relation to their natural habitat'.

As one way of achieving this Falk presents a model of international relations based not on great power hegemony or world government but on a system of central guidance and local autonomy. This would leave room for separate international institutions, regional arrangements, and even states, and would take account of cultural diversity, but would incorporate numerous checks and balances and would allow scope for broad participation and influence in a set up where coercion and bureaucratic intrusion are minimised.

In the awakening concern with transnational issues like environmental protection, human rights and fairer resource allocation Falk sees some indication of the 'acquisition of a planetary outlook and its embodiment in thought, feeling and action'. This is the first step in the direction of a 'system-transforming' approach that could lead to a new world order.

But both Falk and Weston emphasise that the time period needed for achieving a major transformation may have to be measured in decades or even centuries rather than years and they implicitly concede that this creates grave difficulties for the individual. Faced with enormous problems that are likely to extend beyond one human lifespan, does the individual have any real contribution to make to long-term progress?

Some people might give a religious answer based on the individual moral responsibility of each person and each person's inherent worth as a human being.

Weston's answer is in effect that the general movement of history is composed of the actions of individuals, so that inevitably 'how each person conducts his or her life fundamentally affects our nation and world and consequently makes a difference to the future'.

In the end therefore the international lawyer cannot seek refuge in the illusion that he or she may morally get away with being merely a cog in the legal machine. Even the cogs face moral choices and must decide how their work will help or hinder the progress of humankind.

Progress test 18

1. What role did the concepts of *oikoumene* and *universitas humana* play in the search for world order? **(4)**

2. Was the nineteenth century 'congress' system adequate for the needs of the time? **(5)**

3. In what field were many of the early public international unions active? **(7)**

4. Discuss the successes and failures of the League of Nations. **(10)**

5. Is the concern of the United Nations with maintaining international peace and security solely a matter of stopping conflict or is there also an interest in achieving justice? **(13, 14)**

6. Are 'package deals' on admission of new members to the United Nations legal under the Charter? **(15)**

7. Have the limitations on the General Assembly's powers inhibited its activities? **(20)**

8. Is regional enforcement action subject to the control of the Security Council? **(23)**

9. Was the placing of strategic trust territories under the authority of the Security Council a good idea? **(24)**

10. Outline the scope of the Economic and Social Council's responsibilities. **(27-28)**

11. Is the UN Secretary-General an international bureaucrat or an international statesman? **(30-32)**

12. Does the EEC have legislative powers? **(35)**

13. Is the Council of Europe the nucleus around which a united Europe is likely to be built? **(36)**

14. Discuss the view of international law and international relations which is expressed in the Charter of the Organisation of American States. **(39)**

15. Should expulsion of a delinquent state from an international organisation always be permissible? **(52)**

16. Does the principle of the sovereign equality of states operate in the voting arrangements of all major international organisations at the present time? **(54)**

17. Discuss the views of Falk and Weston on the future world order. **(60)**

Bibliography

Abi-Saab, *The United Nations Operation in the Congo 1960-1964*, Oxford Univ. Press, Oxford (1978)

Bowett, *The Law of International Institutions*, 4th ed., Stevens & Sons, London (1982)

Bowle, article on 'Political Philosophy' in *Encyclopedia Britannica* 1982 edition

Holmes, *Dante*, Oxford Univ. Press (Past Masters series), Oxford (1980)

Kirgis, *International Organizations*, West Publishing Co, St. Paul, Minn. (1977)

Lasok and Bridge, *Introduction to the Law and Institutions of the European Communities*, 3rd ed., Butterworth, London (1982)

Ogley, *Internationalizing the Seabed*, Chapter 9, Gower Publishing, Aldershot (1984)

Sabine and Thorson, *A History of Political Theory*, 4th ed., Dryden Press, Hinsdale, Ill. (1973)

Toynbee, *Mankind and Mother Earth*, Oxford Univ. Press, Oxford (1976)

Ullmann, *Principles of Government and Politics in the Middle Ages*, Methuen, London (1961)

Walters, *A History of the League of Nations*, one volume ed., Oxford Univ. Press, Oxford (1969)

Weston, Falk, D'Amato, *International Law and World Order*, chapters 11 and 12, West Publishing Co., St. Paul, Minn. (1980)

Appendix 1

General Bibliography

American Society of International Law, *International Legal Materials*, 1962 – present.

Bernhardt, ed., *Encyclopedia of Public International Law*, Elsevier Science Publishers, Amsterdam

Brierly, *The Law of Nations*, 6th ed. (Sir H. Waldock, ed.), Oxford (1963)

Brownlie, *Principles of Public International Law*, 3rd ed., Clarendon Press, Oxford (1979)

Greig, *International Law*, 2nd ed., Butterworths, London (1976)

Harris, *Cases and Materials on International Law*, 3rd ed., Sweet and Maxwell, London (1983)

Henkin, Pugh, Schachter, Smit, *International Law Cases and Materials*, West Publishing, St. Paul, Minn. (1980)

Lauterpacht, ed., *Oppenheim's International Law*, Longman, London, vol. I (1955), vol. II (1952)

Schwarzenberger & Brown, *A Manual of International Law*, 6th ed., Professional Books, Oxfordshire (1976)

Sorensen, ed. *Manual of Public International Law*, Macmillan, London (1968)

Starke, *Introduction to International Law*, 9th ed., Butterworths, London (1984)

von Glahn, *Law Among Nations*, 4th ed., Macmillan, London (1981)

Weston, Falk, D'Amato, *International Law and World Order*, West Publishing, St. Paul, Minn. (1980)

Whiteman, ed., *Digest of International Law*, in 15 volumes, Department of State, Washington, D.C., 1963-1973

Appendix 2

Passing your examination

To pass an examination in international law a student must do two things: prepare properly and answer properly.

1. Proper preparation. There is no real substitute for actually studying the subject on which you will be examined by attending lectures and tutorials, taking good and copious notes and doing the required reading. This is particularly important with regard to topics such as human rights or the law of war, which a lecturer may treat differently or more thoroughly than the standard general textbooks do.

Nor should one pass up the opportunity of asking the lecturer about any points that one is not clear on. But to ask intelligent questions one must already understand something about the subject so as to realise what more one needs to know.

It is therefore wise to keep up with the course as it progresses (rather than wait till the last minute to mug it all up) and to do at least one round of comprehensive revision before consulting the lecturer.

If nevertheless you somehow find yourself close to the exam and still feel you don't understand the subject, this book can help, if you use it properly.

The critical thing that you must manage before the exam is to get into your head the overall framework of the course. The system of headings and sub-headings in this book can give you that framework and help you construct around it a detailed understanding of international law. Go through the book a chapter at a time, making a particular point of noticing the headings and discovering how the various points relate to one another and to the overall structure of the chapter.

Studying the subject in this way gives you the inestimable advantage of being able to tell the woods from the trees and not mistaking secondary detail for fundamental principles. Your answer can then reflect this structured knowledge by dealing with the important points raised by the question and avoiding the minor ones.

Once this framework is firmly established you can fit into it as much detail from this book and your lecture notes as you can manage in the time available. In this regard, you should treat this book as providing the basic knowledge you need to pass a general examination in international law, but only you can add those details which reflect the particular emphasis or requirements of your course.

A final point on preparation: the time to think about international law and organise your thoughts on it is *before* the examination, *not during* it. If you have to sit in the exam room trying to divine the difference between Monism and

Dualism or Transformation and Incorporation, you will waste so much time without writing anything that you will be almost certain to fail. When you enter the examination room, you should be ready to answer questions, not puzzle over them.

2. Proper answers. Law examinations generally have two types of questions: 'hypotheticals', which describe an imaginary situation and ask you to analyse its legal implications, and 'essays', which ask a straightforward question of fact or opinion.

(*a*) *Hypothetical questions* are usually constructed so as to raise, in the guise of stating facts, a number of legal points related to a particular topic in the course. For example:

> Ruritania has invaded Slobovia and occupied a large part of Slobovian territory. The Prime Minister of Ruritania has just announced that the occupied territory is being annexed to Ruritania 'so that we may protect ourselves from Slobovian machinations'. Discuss.

The phrases 'acquisition of territory', 'use of force', 'conquest' and 'self-defence' do not appear anywhere in this question, yet its facts clearly point to those topics as the ones the examiner wishes to see discussed, and the student must be sufficiently aware of the implications and application of the law to be able to detect that without being told.

(*b*) *An essay question* on the same subject might simply say:

> Under modern international law, is the acquisition of territory by force ever permissible?

Here you are given the main topic to be discussed but are otherwise left entirely to your own devices.

Thus with both types of question the first thing you must do is determine what the examiner is requiring you to discuss. Having done that, you should spend a few minutes (but no longer) jotting down an outline of the main points in your answer, or at least a list of things you want to say. This will help give your answer some structure and make it clear to the examiner that you know what you're doing and where you're going.

Then start to write. Be prepared for the process of thinking and writing to produce additional points as you go along, but try to control your answer and do not let it wander off course.

In general, the more control you exercise over your material (by structuring your answer carefully and deploying your knowledge effectively) the more impressive your answer will be and the higher your mark.

Study the following examination question and the accompanying answer, both of which are genuine. Although not perfect, this answer is a very good attempt at a difficult question and shows what a student who is well-organised and well-prepared can do in the space of half an hour.

3. A sample Question and Answer.
The Question
For the past 15 years Grand Utopia, along with over 130 other nations, has been participating in an international conference drawing up the new International Convention on the Regulation of Sport. The final text, which

generally reflects principles enunciated over a period of years in a series of United Nations General Assembly resolutions passed by large majorities, has one article (out of 347 articles) which prohibits the playing of tiddlywinks, Grand Utopia's national sport. — *Anglo Norwegian fisheries Case - persistent objector*

Although the Grand Utopian negotiators at the conference tried unsuccessfully to have this article deleted, there was no indication at the time that Grand Utopia believed that the inclusion of the article would render the Convention as a whole unacceptable. Under pressure from the tiddlywinks lobby, however, the government of Grand Utopia has just announced that it will not after all ratify the Convention, although it has been approved by the United Nations General Assembly and ratified by a large majority of the negotiating states.

Regarding the universal regulation of sport as a matter of fundamental international importance, the General Assembly has asked the International Court of Justice for an advisory opinion on the following questions: (1) Is a state in Grand Utopia's position bound by the International Convention on the Regulation of Sport? (2) If so, to what extent?

As a judge on the ICJ, you are asked to write the opinion of the court.

An Answer

(A) Is the International Convention on the Regulation of Sport a treaty binding on Grand Utopia?

The common view on this is seen in Article 34 of the Vienna Convention on the law of treaties which says a 3rd party is not bound by a treaty unless it expressly agrees to it. This is also underlined by Article 38 of the Statute of the ICJ Paragraph (a) which says international conventions are a source of law and it states they are to be expressly agreed to by the contesting states.

However in the Case on the Continental Shelf decided by the ICJ, Judge Sorensen (dissenting) said that he believed that the <u>Geneva Convention on the Continental Shelf was law</u> because it was the <u>product of a particularly powerful process of law creation</u>. According to Article 13 of the UN Charter the General Assembly, which was representative, could request a draft treaty from the ILC which was representative, who would return it back to the General Assembly. This process, which I assume was applied in my own case, was a reliable indication of the existence and development of a rule of law. Note that Sorensen did not say customary law. He went on to say that a convention may well constitute or come to constitute the decisive evidence of a generally accepted new rule of international law. Sorensen is saying that the Convention is some form of legislation.

However the general view which I accept is that if Utopia does not sign the Convention it is not bound by it as a treaty.

(B) Could Utopia be bound by customary law?

This seems to hearken back to the North Sea Continental Shelf Case. The court said that a provision in a treaty could be the basis of customary law if it was followed by practice accompanied by opinio juris and that provision was a norm-creating provision. In that case however the provision was found not to be norm-creating because there were a large number of exceptions to the provision and reservations could be made to it. Could reservations be made to the tiddlywinks provision? It does not say, but if it were possible then that provision is unlikely to be norm-creating.

Duration is another criterion which can be taken into account. The lack of a long time having elapsed since the treaty was signed does not mean that that provision cannot become customary law provided there is a very wide spread of participants in the practice and the states whose interests are particularly affected have agreed to it.

The treaty could become a basis for customary law, but since tiddlywinks is the national sport of Utopia and thus its interests are particularly affected, it seems that it would have to agree to the practice before a short duration would be allowed before conversion into customary law.

Uniformity and consistency.

The practice would have to be widespread, extensive and virtually uniform if the article was to become customary law and what practice there was would have to be accompanied by *opinio juris*. Therefore if most states who followed the practice did so not because of the treaty but because they regarded it as customary law, the article could become customary law. But *see* also Sorensen and Sir Hersch Lauterpacht who claim that simply the following by the state of the practice is enough to demonstrate opinio juris. They say you need not look at subjective motive. I would disagree.

(C) General Assembly resolutions as a source of customary law

Could these lead to customary law? In the Texaco case it was decided that resolutions were only binding if lex lata and not de lege ferenda. But due to the fact that it says 'the final text which generally reflects principles enunciated over a period of years ... passed by large majorities', could these large majorities and repetitions add weight to the resolutions? Yes they could according to a Federal US court who decided that resolutions on torture had by repetition become customary law.

(D) It is also a question that since Utopia made some remark as to its disquiet about the article during the negotiations as I believe it did, so it will have shown itself not to be bound by these resolutions as customary law. See Anglo-Norwegian Fisheries Case. Thus Utopia is perhaps a persistent objector and it might even be a subsequent objector who will be bound unless other states acquiesce.

(E) Reservations

Could Utopia be a party to the treaty if it reserves to the Tiddlywinks provision?

The Vienna Convention Article 19 says reservations can be made to all treaties unless (1) the treaty forbids all reservations or that type of reservation (2) it is contrary to the object and purpose of the treaty.

This is consonant with the 1952 General Assembly position extending the ICJ's opinion on the Genocide Convention to all conventions of which the UN was depositary under Article 102 of the UN Charter.

It is doubtful whether 1 article re Tiddlywinks out of 347 will be contrary to the object and purpose of the Convention, so I will assume that Utopia can reserve. It is doubtful whether Article 20 of the Vienna Convention about a presumption against reservations will apply, as it seems implied that this treaty has more than one purpose and many members. Any state who disagrees with the allowing of the reservation has to apply the object and purpose test in good faith and if it still considers Utopia not to be a member it is legally allowed to do so.

Index

Aaland Islands 24, 49, 130, 198
Aboriginal rights, 45, 105
Abuse of rights, 171
Abyssinia, *see* Ethiopia
Accretion, 106
Achille Lauro, 142, 146
Acid rain, 299
Acquiescence, 16, 107
Act of state, 158–61
Adjudication, 335–7
Admissibility under ECHR, 260–1
Advisory opinions, 345–7
Afghanistan, 89, 357
Africa, 353
Aggression, 111, 171, 314–16
Aid, 303, *see also* Development,
    Humanitarian assistance
Aircraft, 147
Air pollution, 298–9
Airspace, 126–7
Alabama Claims Arbitration, 336
Algeria, 69
Aliens, treatment of, 175–89
Alvarez, Alejandro, 10
American Convention on Human Rights,
    257–8, 370
Ancient title, 109, 119–20
Antarctica, 118, 125–6, 329
Anticipatory self-defence, 312
Anti-trust laws (US), 136
Anzilotti, Dionisio, 8, 53
Apartheid, 62, 68, 171, 247
Aqaba, Gulf of, 216
Arab League, *see* League of Arab States
Arbitration, 29–30, 335–8
Arctic, 123–4
Armaments, 302
Arms control, 326–30
Arrest and detention, 181–2, 250–1, 266–9
Assembly and association, rights of, 253,
    281–2
Asylum, 143–4, 252
Atomic energy, *see* nuclear activities
Australia, 45, 105, 125, 229, 230, 298, 341

Baltic Sea, 297
Bantustans, 51

Baselines, 212–3
Baxter, Judge Richard R., 186
Bays, 213
Beirut, 322
Belligerency, 50–1, 318
Belligerent community, 50, 317
Bellum justum, 306
Bentham, Jeremy, 7
Bernadotte, Count Folke, 76, 334
Bhopal, 80–1, 175
Bhutan, 59
Bill of Rights, 285–6
Biological weapons, 324, 325
Blackstone, Sir William, 4
Bosphorous-Dardanelles, 217
Bowett, D. W., 352
Breach of contract, 183–5
Breach of treaty, 201–2
Brezhnev Doctrine, 14, 18, 317
Brierly, James, L., 5, 13, 314
Brotherhood, 244–5, 256–7
Brownlie, Ian, 111, 189
Bruce, Stanley, 354
Bryan Treaties, 335
Bukhara, 58
Burckhardt, Jacob, 6
Burke, Edmund, 4, 7
Bynkershoek, Cornelis van, 206

Calvo Clause, 177–8
Calvo Doctrine, 177
Cambodia (Kampuchea), 89, 121
Canals (Interoceanic), 133–4
Capitulations, 143
Cassese, Antonio, 257
Cession, 106, 114
Chamizal tract, 121–2
Charter of Economic Rights and Duties of
    States, 186–8
Chernobyl, 290, 293, 299
Children, 253
China, 87–8, 95–103, 143, 200, 313, 339
Churchill, Sir Winston, 87
Civilians, 321–3
Civilised nations, 25
Civil liberties, 239–55
'Clean slate' doctrine, 204

Clipperton Island, 117
Coastal state rights, 209-12, 213-14, 216,
    219-20, 226, 227-8
Codification, 30-1, 208
Coercion in treaty-making, 200
Colonies, 66
Combatants/non combatants, 319-20, 321-2
Comity, 209
Commonage, 208, 218
Common heritage of mankind, 126, 233, 257
Compensation, 174, 188-9, 292
Compromis, 336, 337, 338, 341
Conciliation, 334
Congo, 365
Conquest, 106, 110-14, 315
Conscience juridique, 27
Conservation, 299-301
Constitution of US, 24, 41, 42
Contempt of court, 281
Contiguity, 118, 120
Contiguous zone, 216
Continental Margin, 221
Continental Shelf, 218-27
Continental slope, 221
Contracts, 26, 183-5
Conventions, *see* Treaties
Corporal punishment in schools, 265, 285
Council of Europe, 367-9
Created risk, 168
Crimes in international law, 140-1, 171-2
Cuban Missile Crisis, 359
Custom, 12, 13
Customary Law, 13-20
    elements, 15-16
    evidence of practice, 14
    from treaties, 19-20
    regional 17-18
Cyprus, 57-8, 96
Czechoslovakia, 14, 317

Dante, 350
Danube, 131
Danzig, 82, 241
Darwinism, 7
Death penalty, 248-9, 258, 264
Decolonisation, 69-72
De facto governments, 86, 89, 90-1, 94, 97
De jure governments, 86, 89, 94, 96
De lege ferenda, 22
'Denial of justice', 181-2
Denning, Lord, 37, 39, 96, 154
Depositary, 192
Derogations under ECHR, 262-3
Developing states, 227, 234-5
Development, 244, 257, 302-3
Diplomatic asylum, 17-18, 164
Diplomatic immunity, 161-4
Disarmament, 326-30, 353
Dogger Bank incident, 333-4
Double criminality, 144

Dresden, 322
Drummond, Sir Eric, 352
Dualism, 32
Dubois, Pierre, 350
Dunant, Jean-Henri, 351

Economic, social and cultural rights, 255-6
Education, right to, 256, 285
Egypt, 122, 133, 143, 334
Enquiry, 333-4
Entebbe raid, 314
Environmental law, 289-304
Environmental protection, 301-3
Environment, right to healthy, 257
Equality, 238, 242-4, 248
Equal treatment, 283, 284
Equidistance rule, 220
Equitable apportionment, 132-3
Equity, 27-8, 222-5
Erga omnes obligations, 172, 245, 292
Eritrea, 73
Estoppel, 107
Estrada doctrine, 88-90
Ethiopia (Abyssinia), 73, 94
EURATOM, 77, 78
Eurofima, 79
European Atomic Energy Community
    (EURATOM), 366
European Coal and Steel Community
    (ECSC), 366
European Convention on Human Rights,
    179, 260-86, 367, 368
European Economic Community (EEC),
    77-9, 228, 366-7
Ex aequo et bono, 28
Exclusive Economic Zone (EEZ), 227-8
Exclusive fishing zone, 227
Exhaustion of local remedies, 178-9, 260-1
Exploitability test, 219
Expression, freedom of, 253, 278-81
Expropriation, 185-6
Extradition, 144-6
Extraterritoriality, 143, 161-2

Failure to protect, 183
Falkland Islands, 74, 122-3, 310-11, 318
Falk, Richard, 377-8
Family rights, 253, 282
Fault, 167-8
Finland, 24, 49, 130
Fishing, 227-8
Fitzmaurice, Sir Gerald, 23, 24, 26, 32, 263,
    275
Flag of convenience, 230
Food and Agriculture Organisation (FAO),
    363
Force majeure, 210, 358
Force, use of, 110-12, 307
Forum prorogatum, 341
France, 44, 69, 119, 121, 125, 133, 146, 168-9,

229, 239, 298, 341, 343
Freedom of the seas, 206-8, 229-30
Fundamental change of circumstances,
    202-3

Gaza, 111, 122
General Agreement on Tariffs and Trade
    (GATT), 363
General Assembly resolutions, 20-2
General principles of law, 24-7
Genetic engineering, 304
Geneva Conventions (1949), 44, 82, 113, 141,
    318ff
Geneva General Act (1928), 307
Genocide, 18, 171, 172, 193, 323
Genuine link, 139, 230
German Democratic Republic (East
    Germany), 56, 86, 95-6, 98
Germany, Federal Republic of, (West
    Germany), 19, 43-4, 56, 222, 277, 353
Goa, 123
Golan Heights, 111, 122
Good faith, 67, 177, 193-4, 195, 333
Gorbachev, Mikhail, 299
Governments-in-exile, 101-2
Governments, recognition of, see
    Recognition
Greece, 57, 78, 261, 352
Greenland, 118
Greenpeace, 146, 169, 175
Grenada, 14, 313, 317
Grotius, Hugo, 3, 6, 30, 207

Hague Conventions (1899, 1907), 113, 318
Hague Regulations (1907), 44, 113, 141,
    318ff
Hammarskjöld, Dag, 364-5
Harman, Harriet, 281
Harmon Doctrine, 132, 133
Harris, Prof, D. J., 116
Harvard, 186
Headquarters Agreement (UN-US), 165
Health, right to, 256, 257
Hearing, right to a fair, 250, 269-74
Helsinki Final Act, 74, 75, 248, 286-7
High Seas, 206-8, 228-32
Hijacking, 147
Hiroshima, 145, 322, 325, 328
Historic bays, 213
Holy Roman Empire, 2
Holy See, 58
Hong Kong, 200
Hostage taking, 147
Hot pursuit, 232
Hughes, Charles Evans, 118
Humanitarian assistance, 257
Humanitarian Intervention, 313-14
Human Rights, 9, 82, 113-14, 166, 181-2
    European, 260-88
    international 238-59

ICSID, 336
Immigration, 144, 265
Implied powers doctrine, 77
Imputability, 168-71
Incorporation, 33-4 and ff
Independence, 48, 49-53
Indigenous peoples, 254
Individuals, 81-3, 238, 254
Innocent passage, 211, 214-16
Institutions, international, 75-9, 349-78
Insurgency, 50
Insurrectionaries, acts of, 170-1
Integrity of the convention, 192
Intergovernmental organisations, 349
Interim measures, 344-5
Internal waters, 209-11
International Atomic Energy Agency
    (IAEA), 292, 299, 327-9, 363
International Bank for Reconstruction and
    Development (IBRD), 361-2
International Civil Aviation Organisation
    (ICAO), 202, 362
International Court of Justice (ICJ), 338-47,
    349, 356, 358
International crimes, 171-2
International Development Association
    (IDA), 362
International drainage basin, 132
Internationalised contracts, 26, 184-5
International Labour Organisation (ILO),
    243-4, 361, 369
International Law Commission (ILC), 30-1,
    168ff, 357
International legal personality, 47ff
International Maritime Organisation (IMO),
    297-8, 363
International minimum standard, 176-7,
    186-9
International Monetary Fund (IMF), 361-2
International Telecommunications Union
    (ITU), 362-3
Interpretation of treaty, 195-8
Intertemporal law, 75, 115, 116-17, 122-3
Intervention, see Non-intervention
Intervention by UN, 68, 247
Iran, 163, 187, 231, 341
Ireland, 39, 79, 226, 260, 261, 264, 266
Islands, 219, 226
Israel, 44-5, 56-61, 76, 78, 111, 122, 133,
    140-2, 198, 216, 230-1, 247, 314, 320,
    322, 328, 334
Italy, 44, 92, 94, 142, 146, 339

Japan, 25, 51, 125, 143, 235, 333-4
Jerusalem, 122
Jessup, Judge Philip, 21, 24, 63
Judges (ICJ), 339
Judicial decisions, 28-9
jure gestionis, 152ff
jure imperii, 152ff

Jurisdiction, 135–48, 213–14, 231–2, 238
Jurisdiction (ICJ), 339–45
Jus ad bellum, 110, 306
Jus cogens, 18–19, 200–201
Jus gentium, 3
Jus in bello, 110, 113, 242, 317
Jus naturale, 3
Justiciability, 332–3
Just war, 306

Kant, Immanuel, 350
Kellogg–Briand Pact, 306
Kelsen, Hans, 24, 32, 198
Kiel canal, 51, 134, 198
Khiva, 58
Korean War, 308
Kriegsraison, 318–19, 321, 322

Lauterpacht, Sir Hersch, 30, 247, 343
League of Arab States, 371
League of Nations, 60–1, 62, 63, 192, 306,
    352–4
    Covenant, 352, 353
    intended note, 352
    structure, 352
    successes and failures, 352–4
Lebanon, 51, 240, 320, 322, 365
Lex lata, 22
Liberty, 238, 239–42
Libya, 70, 163–4, 185, 187, 225, 312–13
Liechtenstein, 57
London, 322

McDougal, Myres, 10
Machiavelli, Niccolo, 6
Mandate system, 60–5, 353, 360
Mansfield, Lord, 5, 33–4
Mare Clausum, 207
Mare Liberum, 207
Margin of appreciation, 263
Marine pollution, 296–8
Marshall, Chief Justice John, 24, 150
Martens clause, 319
Material breach, 201–2
Mauritania, 72, 119–21
Maxims of law, 25–6
Mediation, 334
Medical ethics, 250
Mercenaries, 320
Micronesia, 360
Minority rights, 240–2, 254–5
Monism, 32
Moon, 127
More, Sir Thomas, 3
Morocco, 59, 72, 119–21, 143
Morrison doctrine, 85–6
Movement, freedom of, 251–2, 285
Multinational enterprises (MNEs), 80–1
Municipal Law, 32, 199–200

customary law in, 32–8, 40–1
treaty law in, 38–40, 41–3
Munkman, Athene, 107ff.

Nagasaki, 145, 322, 325, 328
Namibia (South-West Africa), 9, 61–5, 73,
    202, 353
Nationalisation, 185–9
Nationality, 138–9, 252–3, 285
Nationality of claims, 179–80
Nationality of ships, 230–1
Nationality principle, 138–9
National liberation movements, 72–3
National treatment standard, 176–7, 186–9
Natural Law, 3–5, 9–10, 27, 238
Natural rights, 4, 239
Navigation
    in the law of the sea, 206, 213, 214–15,
        216–18, 229–30
    on international rivers, 131–2
Negotiation, 333
New International Economic Order (NIEO),
    303
New weapons, 324
New Zealand, 125, 135, 146, 229, 230, 298,
    341
Nicaragua, 311, 317, 344, 347
Non-discrimination, 283
Non-governmental organisations (NGOs),
    349, 351
Non-international armed conflict, 318, 320
Non-intervention, 49–50, 316–17
Non-recognition, duty of, 110–11, 315
Non-refoulement, 144, 252
North Atlantic Treaty Organisation
    (NATO), 349, 368
Nuclear activities
    explosions, 299
    peaceful uses, 289, 290, 298, 299
    tests, 229, 298, 299, 328
    weapons, 229–30, 302, 324–30, 353
Nuclear-weapon free zones, 328–9
Nuremberg trials, 83, 310

Objective international legal regime, 24,
    130, 198
Occupation
    belligerent, 112–14, 322–3
    peaceful, 105
Oder river, 132
oikoumene, 350
Oil pollution, 297–8
Opinio Juris, 15, 17, 21
Opinion, freedom of, 253
Organisation of African Unity (OAU), 371–2
Organisation of American States (OAS),
    369–71
Organisation of Petroleum Exporting
    Countries (OPEC), 79–80
Organs of state, 168

Ottoman Empire, 60-1, 143, 240
Outer space, 126-7

Pacific Islands strategic trust, 360
Pacta sunt servanda, 8, 194, 358, 373
Pact of Paris, 306
Palestine and Palestinian, 61, 71-3, 230, 247, 320, 334, 353, 357
Palestine Liberation Organisation (PLO), 72-3
Palmas, 114-17
Panama Canal, 133-4
Papacy, 2, 58
Parallel system, 233
Passive Personality principle, 139
Peaceful settlement of disputes, 332-47
Peacekeeping (UN), 309
'Peace of the port' problem, 209-10
Penn, William, 350
Permanent Court of International Justice (PCIJ), 338
Personality, *see* International legal personality
Phillimore, Lord Walter, 25
Phillimore, Sir Robert, 39
Piracy, 141, 231
Poisonous weapons, 324, 325
Political offences, 144-6
Pollution, 293-9
Positivism, 5-10, 238
Powell, Enoch, 39
Precedent, 12, 37
Preclusion, 107, 121
Prescription, 105-6, 121
Prisoners of War (POWs), 319-21
Prisoners rights, 270-1, 278
Privacy, 274-8
Programmatic rights, 243
Progressive development, 30
Property and possessions, right to, 239, 284
Protective principle, 140
Protectorates, 58-9
Protest, 107, 121-2

Rainbow Warrior, 146, 169, 175
Reagan, Ronald, 290, 312-13, 324, 329, 360
Rebus sic stantibus, see Fundamental change of circumstances
Reciprocating states, 235
Recognition, 55-6, 107
   effects in municipal law, 91-101
   of governments, 85-104
   of states, 53-5
   withdrawal of, 102-3
Red Cross, 80, 318, 351
Refugees, 144, 252
Regional custom, 17
Relative title, 107
Reparations, 173-5
Reprisals, 311

Res communis, 126, 207
Reservations, 19, 192-4
Restitution, 173-4
Rhine, 131
Rhodesia, 53-4, 55, 308
Rights of passage, 130-1
Right to know, 280-1
Riparian state, 131-3
Rivers, 131-3, 294-6
Rockall, 226
Rousseau, Jean Jacques, 4
Russo-Japanese War, 25, 334

Sacred trust, 60
Saint-Pierre, Abbé, 350
Sakharov, Andrei, 238
SALT Agreements, 330
Satisfaction, 174-5
Schwarzenberger, Georg, 29
Scotland, 73-5
Seabed, 232-7
   demilitarisation, 330
   exploitation, 232-7
Sea, Law of, 206-37
Sector theory, 41
Selden, John, 207
Self-defence, 111-12, 309-13
Self-determination, 65-75, 120, 257, 316
Self-executing treaties, 38, 41-2
Servitudes, 129-31
Sex education, 285
Sic utere tuo ut alienum non laedas, 171, 290-1
Single maritime boundary, 222, 223-5
Slavery, 171, 249, 266
Solidarity, 244, 257
Sorensen, Max, 20, 30, 208-9
Sources of International Law, 12
South-West Africa, *see* Namibia
Sovereign equality of states, 48
Sovereign immunity, 150ff
   absolute, 150-1
   relative, 151-8
Sovereign Rights, 219, 227
Sovereignty, 48, 51-3, 115-16, 125-6
Space objects, 168
Spain, 51, 100
Special circumstances, 223
Speciality, rule of, 144
Spitsbergen, 124
Springer, A.L., 294
Starke, J.G., 172
'Star Wars', 329, 330
State Immunity Act (1978), 157-8
State practice, 14-15
State responsibility, 166-89, 238
States and statehood, 47-8, 53-5, 68
State succession, 204
State system, 2-3, 68
Status of forces agreements, 143

Stimson Doctrine, 111
Stockholm Declaration, 290-1, 292, 294, 301
Straits, 216-18
Strategic area trusts, 360
Strict liability, 167-8, 297
Suarez, Francisco, 3, 20
Subject-matter jurisdiction (ICJ), 339-40
Suez Canal, 133, 198

Taft, William Howard, 90-1
Taiwan, 103
Tanaka, Judge Kotaro, 9, 22, 27, 32, 63, 238
Tate letter, 153
Teachings of publicists, 30
Technology and the environment, 290, 302
Technology, influence of on sea law, 206,
    211, 220, 232
Technology transfer, 234, 303
Teleological interpretation, 24, 195-6, 263
Terra nullius, 105, 119
Territorial principle, 136-7
Territorial sea, 211-16
Territory, acquisition of, 105-27
Terrorism and terrorists, 24, 76, 145-6, 251,
    312-13, 334
Thalweg, 106
Third state and treaties, 198
Third World, 6, 8, 87, 227, 234, 290, 302-3,
    358, 362
Threat of force, 200
Three mile limit, 34-5, 206
Torture, 249-50, 264-5
Toynbee, Arnold, 350
Transformation, 33-4 and ff
Transit passage, 217
Transkei, 51
Transnational Law, 184-5
Travaux préparatoires, 197
Treaties, 22-4, 190-204
Truman Proclamation, 218-19
Tunkin, G.I., 8

Ultra vires acts, 169-70
UNCITRAL, 336
UNEP, 300, 301
Unequal treaties, 200
UNESCO, 362
United Nations, 76-7, 87-8, 192, 335, 349,
    354-65, 369
  aims and purposes, 354-5

Charter 64, 66-8, 110-12, 246-7, 307-13,
    332, 333, 354
Economic and Social Council, 354, 356,
    360-3
expenses, 358
General Assembly, 20-2, 30-1, 63, 69-72,
    308-9, 345, 352, 356, 357-8
immunities, 164-5
Industrial Development Organisation, 363
membership, 355-6
principles, 355
Secretariat, 356, 363-4
Secretary-General, 335, 363-5
Security Council, 63, 64, 307-8, 345, 352,
    356, 357, 358-60
Trusteeship Council, 356, 363
trusteeship system, 61-2, 359-60, 363
Universality principle, 140-1
Universal Postal Union, 349, 351, 363
Universitas humana, 350
Use of force, *see* Force, use of
Uti possidetis, 109

Vagrants under ECHR, 268
Vatican City, 58
Vattel, Emerich de, 6-7, 30
Versailles treaty, 52, 134
Vienna, Congress of, 131, 351
Vitoria, Francisco de, 306
Voluntarism, 7

Waldock, Sir Humphrey, 26
War, 203, 306
War Crimes, 82-3, 141, 323
War, law of, 112-14, 317-26
Weapons, 324-6
Webster, Daniel, 86, 112, 309
West Bank, 44-5, 111, 122
Western Sahara, 72, 119-21
Weston, Burns, 245
Westphalia, Peace of, 3
Whaling, 292
Wilson, Woodrow, 60, 66, 87
Wire tapping, 277-8
World Bank, *see* International Bank for
    Reconstruction and Development
World Health Organisation (WHO), 363
World Intellectual Property Organisation
    (WIPO), 363
World Meteorological Organisation
    (WMO), 363